Lecture Notes of the Institute for Computer Sciences, Social Informatics and Telecommunications Engineering 676

The LNICST series publishes ICST's conferences, symposia and workshops.

LNICST reports state-of-the-art results in areas related to the scope of the Institute.

The type of material published includes

- Proceedings (published in time for the respective event)
- Other edited monographs (such as project reports or invited volumes)

LNICST topics span the following areas:

- General Computer Science
- E-Economy
- E-Medicine
- Knowledge Management
- Multimedia
- Operations, Management and Policy
- Social Informatics
- Systems

Faouzi Kamoun · Lamjed Bettaieb ·
Fatna Belqasmi · Abderrazek Hachani ·
Thar Baker · Mohamed Tabaa ·
Adekunle Adeleke
Editors

Emerging Technologies for Developing Countries

8th EAI International Conference, AFRICATEK 2025 Tunis, Tunisia, June 11–13, 2025 Proceedings, Part I

Editors
Faouzi Kamoun
École Supérieure Privée d'ingénierie et de Technologie
Ariana, Tunisia

Lamjed Bettaieb
École Supérieure Privée d'ingénierie et de Technologie
Ariana, Tunisia

Fatna Belqasmi
Zayed University
Abu Dhabi, United Arab Emirates

Abderrazek Hachani
École Supérieure Privée d'ingénierie
Ariana, Tunisia

Thar Baker
University of Khorfakkan
Sharjah, UAE

Mohamed Tabaa
École Marocaine des Sciences de l'Ingénieur
Casablanca, Morocco

Adekunle Adeleke
Nile University of Nigeria
Abuja FCT, Nigeria

ISSN 1867-8211 ISSN 1867-822X (electronic)
Lecture Notes of the Institute for Computer Sciences, Social Informatics and Telecommunications Engineering
ISBN 978-3-032-16634-0 ISBN 978-3-032-16635-7 (eBook)
https://doi.org/10.1007/978-3-032-16635-7

This Springer imprint is published by the registered company Springer Nature Switzerland AG
The registered company address is: Gewerbestrasse 11, 6330 Cham, Switzerland

Preface

It is our pleasure to present the proceedings of the Eighth Edition of the European Alliance for Innovation (EAI) International Conference on Emerging Technologies for Developing Countries (AfricaTek 2025), co-organized with and hosted by the École Supérieure Privée d'Ingénierie et de Technologies (ESPRIT), Tunisia, on June 11–13, 2025 and generously sponsored by Honoris United Universities.

Held under the overarching theme "*Emerging Technologies: Pathways to Resilience and Growth in Africa*," this year's edition highlighted how cutting-edge innovations can serve as powerful enablers of inclusive and sustainable transformation across the continent.

AfricaTek 2025 brought together a vibrant community of researchers and practitioners from Africa and beyond, offering a unique platform for critical dialogue on the role of emerging technologies in advancing Africa's development priorities.

A total of 138 submissions were received, including full papers, short papers, and workshop proposals. Each submission was reviewed through a rigorous double-blind process with at least three independent reviews. Following this process, 49 papers were accepted as full papers, 8 as short papers, and 2 as practical workshops. The accepted contributions span diverse domains, including healthcare and wellbeing, intelligent networking and cybersecurity, smart agriculture, smart cities, higher education, Industry 4.0, and sustainable development.

Artificial Intelligence emerged as a central theme, with nearly 70% of accepted papers addressing applications related to machine learning, large language models (LLMs), deep learning, computer vision, natural language processing, and data analytics. This strong representation underscores the pivotal role of AI as a catalyst for innovation, where it offers new opportunities to bridge development gaps, tackle complex challenges, and accelerate sustainable growth.

The program also featured two keynote addresses by Fawzi BenMessaoud (Indiana University, USA) and Adel Alimi (ENIS, Tunisia), as well as two practical workshops: AI-enhanced learning (by Wissal Neji and Naouel Boughattas) and GitHub-driven active learning pedagogy (by Badiaa Bouhdid).

We extend our sincere gratitude to the members of the Organizing and Technical Committees, and to the many reviewers and volunteers for their dedicated work in ensuring the success of AfricaTek 2025. Special thanks are due to the Program Chairs and Co-Chairs (Fatna Belqasmi, Abderrazek Hachani, Thar Baker, Mohamed Tabaa, Adekunle Adeleke, and Yosr Ghozzi) for overseeing a rigorous review process and curating a high-quality technical program. We are equally grateful to the EAI Conference Managers, Timea Madarova and Rebeka Prummerova, and the EAI Venue Manager, Stella Dao. We gratefully acknowledge the generous support of our sponsor, Honoris United Universities. We also extend our heartfelt thanks to all contributing authors, participants, and keynote speakers.

Looking ahead, we are confident that the spirit of AfricaTek will continue to thrive. The contributions gathered in this volume stand as a foundation for future research, collaboration, and innovation that will play a vital role in addressing Africa's most pressing technological and socio-economic challenges in transformative and sustainable ways.

Faouzi Kamoun
Lamjed Bettaieb
Fatna Belqasmi
Abderrazek Hachani
Thar Baker
Mohamed Tabaa
Adekunle Adeleke

Organization

Organizing Committee

General Chair

Faouzi Kamoun	Ecole Supérieure Privée d'Ingénierie et de Technologies (ESPRIT), Tunisia

General Co-chair

Lamjed Bettaieb	Ecole Supérieure Privée d'Ingénierie et de Technologies (ESPRIT), Tunisia

Program Chairs and Co-chairs

Fatna Belqasmi	Zayed University, UAE
Abderrazek Hachani	Ecole Supérieure Privée d'Ingénierie et de Technologies (ESPRIT), Tunisia
Thar Baker	University of Brighton, UK
Mohamed Tabaa	École Marocaine des Sciences de l'Ingénieur (EMSI), Morocco
Adekunle Adeleke	Nile University of Nigeria, Nigeria

TPC Co-chair

Yosr Ghozzi	Supérieure Privée d'Ingénierie et de Technologies (ESPRIT), Tunisia

Sponsorship and Exhibit Chair

Nebgha Ayachi	Ecole Supérieure Privée d'Ingénierie et de Technologies (ESPRIT), Tunisia

Local Chair

Meriem Chichti	ESPRIT School of Business, Tunisia

Workshops Chair

Asma Baghdadi	ESPRIT School of Business, Tunisia

Publicity and Social Media Chair

Chiraz Gharbi	Ecole Supérieure Privée d'Ingénierie et de Technologies (ESPRIT), Tunisia

Publications Chair

Feten Tebourbi	Ecole Supérieure Privée d'Ingénierie et de Technologies (ESPRIT), Tunisia

Web Chair

Oumeima Ibn Elfekih	Ecole Supérieure Privée d'Ingénierie et de Technologies (ESPRIT), Tunisia

Posters and PhD Track Chair

Kaouther Louati	Ecole Supérieure Privée d'Ingénierie et de Technologies, Tunisia

Technical Program Committee

Heni Abidi	ESPRIT School of Business, Tunisia
Adekunle Akanni Adeleke	Nile University, Nigeria
Steve Adeshina	Nile University, Nigeria
Muhammad Adnan	Hasselt University, Belgium
Karim Alami	École Marocaine des Sciences de l'Ingénieur (EMSI), Morocco
Asma Baghdadi	ESPRIT School of Business, Tunisia
Fatna Belqasmi	Zayed University, UAE
Aymen Ben Brik	ESPRIT School of Business, Tunisia
Mohamed Sélmene Ben Yahia	Tunis El Manar University, Tunisia
Safa Zhioua Cherif	École Supérieure Privée d'Ingénierie et de Technologies (ESPRIT), Tunisia
Tirumala Rao Chimpiri	Stony Brook University, USA
Mohamed El Abd	American University of Kuwait, Kuwait
Walid El Ayeb	ESPRIT School of Business, Tunisia

May El Barachi	University of Wollongong in Dubai, UAE
Ameni Ellouze	École Supérieure Privée d'Ingénierie et de Technologies (ESPRIT), Tunisia
Yosr Ghozzi	École Supérieure Privée d'Ingénierie et de Technologies (ESPRIT), Tunisia
Rossitza Goleva	New Bulgarian University, Bulgaria
Imen Guebebia	École Supérieure Privée d'Ingénierie et de Technologies (ESPRIT), Tunisia
Abderrazek Hachani	École Supérieure Privée d'Ingénierie et de Technologies (ESPRIT), Tunisia
Jihen Hlel	National School of Computer Sciences (ENSI), Tunisia
Farkhund Iqbal	Zayed University, UAE
Wael Jaafar	École de Technologie Supérieure, Canada
Oussama Kallel	Faculté des Sciences de Bizerte, Tunisia
Shafaq Khan	University of Windsor, Canada
Asad Khattak	Zayed University, UAE
Hamamache Kheddouci	Université Lyon 1, France
Anis Koubaa	Prince Sultan University, Saudi Arabia
Haroon Malik	Marshall University, USA
Wathiq Mansour	University of Dubai, UAE
Sami Miniaoui	University of Dubai, UAE
Petrus Nzerem	Nile University of Nigeria, Nigeria
Fatma Outay	Zayed University, UAE
Luca Reggiani	Politecnico di Milano, Italy
Abdulganiyu Sanusi	Nile University of Nigeria, Nigeria
Thar Baker	University of Brighton, UK
Mohamed Tabaa	École Marocaine des Sciences de l'Ingénieur (EMSI), Morocco
Marouane Trimeche	ESPRIT School of Business, Tunisia
Naoufel Werghi	Khalifa University, UAE

Contents

Emerging Technologies for Advancing Healthcare and Wellbeing

AI-Powered Chatbot for Personalized Sports Training: Enhancing Engagement with LLM and RAG Architecture

Fedi Fehmi[1], Mohamed Hedi Riahi[1(✉)], and Lotfi Ncib[2]

[1] ESPRIT School of Engineering Tunisia, Ariana, Tunisia
{fedi.fehmi,mohamedhedi.riahi}@esprit.tn
[2] Open France, Paris, France

Abstract. Physical activity is essential for overall health, strengthening the cardiovascular system and musculoskeletal structure while also improving mental well-being. However, adherence to personalized training programs remains challenging, particularly for individuals requiring regular monitoring. Our research focuses on developing a chatbot powered by large language models (LLMs) and a Retrieval-Augmented Generation (RAG) architecture, integrating a specialized knowledge base in sports science. This system delivers individualized training plans and real-time feedback, enhancing user engagement. The methodology involves data preprocessing, hybrid lexical-semantic search, and response generation through a locally deployed LLM. This approach ensures safe and personalized sports guidance, making exercise more accessible to both amateur athletes and individuals with health conditions. Our study demonstrates how AI can revolutionize sports training by bridging the gap between medical care and fitness through intelligent, tailored support.

Keywords: Physical activity · Health · Personalized training programs · Chatbot · Large Language Models (LLMs) · RAG architecture · Prompt Engineering

1 Introduction

Sports play a fundamental role in maintaining overall health, benefiting both individuals in good physical condition and those with chronic diseases [3]. For healthy individuals, regular physical activity offers numerous advantages [28]. It strengthens the cardiovascular system by improving blood circulation, lowering blood pressure, and reducing the risk of cardiovascular diseases such as heart attacks and strokes. Additionally, muscle and bone-strengthening exercises help prevent osteoporosis while improving posture and mobility. Physical activity also contributes to weight regulation by stimulating metabolism and promoting fat loss. From an immunological perspective, it enhances the body's resistance to infections and diseases. Furthermore, its psychological impact is

F. Kamoun et al. (Eds.): AFRICATEK 2025, LNICST 676, pp. 3–17, 2026.
https://doi.org/10.1007/978-3-032-16635-7_1

significant: exercise stimulates the production of endorphins, reducing stress and anxiety while fostering an overall sense of well-being [3,22]. For individuals with chronic diseases, sports serve as a crucial therapeutic tool. Numerous studies have demonstrated that regular physical activity can alleviate symptoms and reduce complications associated with metabolic, cardiovascular, neurological, and respiratory disorders. For instance, in diabetic patients, exercise improves insulin sensitivity and enhances glycemic control [24]. In cardiovascular conditions, it helps lower blood pressure and improves heart function. Moreover, sports play a critical role in managing psychological disorders by reducing cortisol levels (the stress hormone) and improving sleep quality. Additionally, physical activity has beneficial effects on neurodegenerative diseases such as Parkinson's and Alzheimer's by helping preserve coordination, mobility, and certain cognitive functions [18]. Given these significant benefits, it is essential to promote tailored physical activity for both healthy individuals and those with chronic conditions. However, adopting and adhering to a personalized exercise program can be challenging, particularly for individuals with specific needs or requiring continuous monitoring. In this context, artificial intelligence (AI) offers a groundbreaking approach to supporting and enhancing physical activity engagement [20]. AI is transforming the fields of sports and healthcare by providing intelligent and personalized solutions to guide individuals in their fitness journey. Advances in machine learning and natural language processing have enabled the development of chatbots and virtual assistants powered by large language models (LLMs) and Retrieval-Augmented Generation (RAG) architectures [12,23]. These systems analyze personal data—such as age, health status, goals, and performance metrics—to design customized and adaptive training programs tailored to the specific needs of each user. Moreover, AI facilitates real-time monitoring and dynamic adjustments to exercise routines based on user progress, ensuring continuous support. It also enhances motivation and engagement through interactive and personalized interactions, improving adherence to workout programs. For individuals with chronic diseases, integrating AI into physical activity tracking represents a major advancement by offering tailored recommendations and mitigating the risks associated with inappropriate exercise routines. This study explores the application of AI technologies in developing an intelligent chatbot based on LLM models and RAG architecture to assist individuals in personalized sports practice. The objective is to demonstrate how these advancements optimize sports guidance and accessibility, benefiting both recreational athletes and individuals with medical conditions. By leveraging AI-driven recommendations, this approach ensures that physical activity remains both beneficial and safe, enhancing overall health outcomes.

2 State of the Art

Generative artificial intelligence (AI) represents a major technological breakthrough that is transforming numerous sectors, including sports. This technology is defined by AI systems' ability to generate new data or content from existing inputs—a concept popularized by applications ranging from artistic creation to text and image generation. In the sports domain, generative AI paves the way for advanced personalization of training programs, enabling individuals—whether healthy or managing chronic medical conditions—to benefit from exercise regimens tailored to their specific needs [2,15].

The pursuit of athletic excellence and continuous performance improvement demands individualized approaches, which generative AI can facilitate through its capacity to analyze vast datasets. By leveraging physical capabilities, medical history, and personal goals, generative AI designs optimized, bespoke training plans [1]. This approach adds significant value by making training more accessible and effective for diverse populations, including amateur athletes, professionals, and individuals requiring specialized regimens due to medical conditions.

Holmes and Miao (2024) highlighted generative AI's potential in education and research, emphasizing its role in adapting content to individual needs. While their study focuses on learning, the underlying principles of personalization and outcome optimization are directly applicable to sports [10]. Generative algorithms can analyze historical athlete performance data to propose training plans dynamically adjusted to their evolving abilities, constraints, and objectives.

This individualized approach aligns with the broader goal of democratizing "sport for all," addressing not only physiological differences but also personal preferences and lifestyle constraints. As Gao et al. (2023) note, generative AI models can tailor training plans to medical histories, enabling individuals with chronic illnesses to engage in safe physical activity with personalized guidance and adaptive recommendations [13].

Generative AI extends beyond static training programs: it can anticipate shifts in users' physical needs and capabilities. Lamri et al. (2023) explored how this technology models desirable futures by analyzing trends and predicting adjustments to optimize performance [11]. In sports, this means training regimens evolve dynamically based on real-time data, moving away from rigid, predefined frameworks.

Unlike traditional methods reliant on manual adjustments, generative AI systems automatically refine recommendations using parameters such as past workout results, biometric indicators (e.g., heart rate, muscle fatigue), and external factors like weather or an athlete's mental state (Martinez-Valdes et al., 2022) [4,5]. This enables continuous optimization, ensuring safe, coherent progress aligned with users' evolving needs.

Another key advantage of generative AI lies in its accessibility. De Sousa Cardoso and Parise (2023) demonstrated its seamless integration into large-scale applications [25]. In sports, this translates to smart chatbots that generate real-time, personalized exercise recommendations. These chatbots use generative AI to design routines based on individual goals, physical limitations, and schedules (Nguyen et al., 2023) [17]. Through intuitive conversational interfaces, they provide continuous support—previously reserved for elite athletes with professional coaches—to a broader audience [29].

A critical strength of generative AI in sports is its ability to adapt programs for individuals with chronic illnesses. As Chen and Li (2023) [8,30]show, these models integrate medical knowledge bases to design exercises that respect physiological limitations while maximizing health benefits [8]. For example: - Cardiovascular patients: AI generates workouts maintaining intensity within safe zones to progressively improve cardiorespiratory fitness [16]. - Diabetic individuals: Algorithms adjust exercise frequency and intensity based on blood glucose levels to prevent hypoglycemia (Rodrigues et al., 2024) [6].

By merging medical expertise with adaptive algorithms, generative AI ensures inclusive, safe, and effective physical activity for populations traditionally excluded from mainstream fitness solutions [31].

Given the numerous benefits of physical exercise, it is imperative to design innovative, tailored solutions to encourage and facilitate sports participation—both for healthy individuals and those managing chronic medical conditions. However, creating personalized training programs and ensuring effective monitoring present significant challenges, requiring adaptive recommendations and continuous supervision.

In this context, technological advancements, particularly artificial intelligence (AI), are opening new avenues for athletic guidance. Specifically, intelligent chatbots—powered by Large Language Models (LLMs) and the Retrieval-Augmented Generation (RAG) architecture—emerge as a groundbreaking approach to deliver dynamic, personalized coaching. These systems analyze individual user characteristics—such as age, health status, goals, and performance metrics—to generate optimized, scalable recommendations that evolve with the user's progress.

This work aligns with this innovative momentum and aims to explore the design and implementation of an intelligent chatbot capable of guiding individuals in practicing physical activity tailored to their fitness and medical conditions. By combining the capabilities of LLMs with the RAG framework, the solution seeks not only to customize fitness programs but also to provide interactive, real-time follow-up, thereby enhancing user adherence and training efficacy. The overarching goal is to demonstrate how AI can revolutionize athletic support, making physical exercise more accessible, safe, and beneficial for all.

3 Methodology

Our approach is based on the development of an intelligent chatbot designed to provide personalized support for sports practice, taking into account the specific profile of each user. To ensure optimal and tailored recommendations, our solution integrates an advanced architecture that combines Large Language Models (LLMs) with the Retrieval-Augmented Generation (RAG) methodology. The RAG architecture enhances the chatbot's responses by leveraging an external knowledge base composed of specialized books on sports science, exercise physiology, and physical rehabilitation. As a result, each recommendation is based on scientifically validated data, ensuring reliable and relevant information.

This methodology combines the reasoning and adaptive capabilities of LLMs with access to trustworthy and specialized data, providing intelligent, evolving, and scientifically grounded support for safe and effective physical activity.

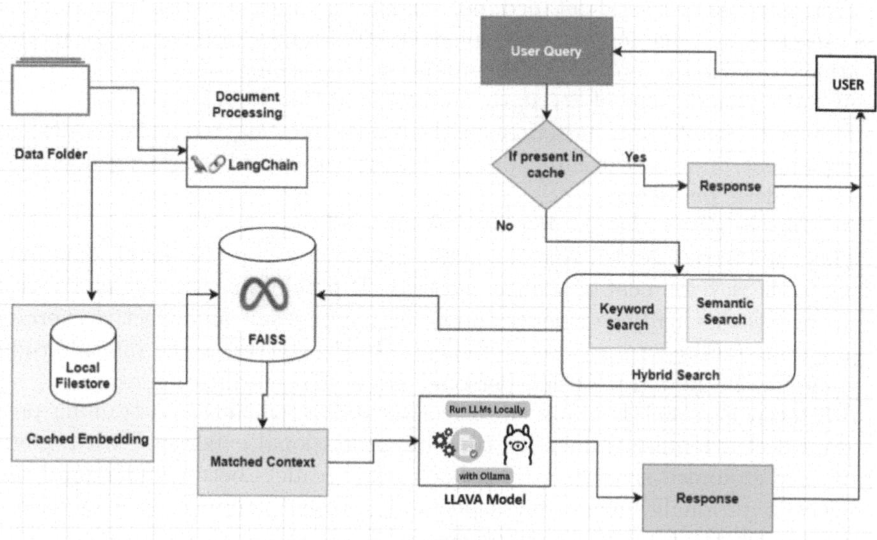

Fig. 1. Architecture of Athletic ASSISTANT.

The following Fig. 1 illustrates the architecture of an intelligent chatbot based on a Large Language Model (LLM) and the Retrieval-Augmented Generation (RAG) framework. This solution aims to assist users in their physical activity by providing recommendations tailored to their health condition. The architecture consists of several key components that ensure efficient information retrieval and the generation of relevant responses. This diagram in Fig. 1 illustrates a local Retrieval-Augmented Generation (RAG) system that processes documents using LangChain and stores their embeddings in a local filestore and FAISS index for fast retrieval. When a user submits a query, the system first checks if a cached response exists. If not, it performs a hybrid search combining keyword and semantic methods to find relevant context from the FAISS index. The matched context is then passed to a locally run LLM using Ollama (e.g., LLAVA) to generate a response, which is returned to the user. This setup enables efficient and private question-answering over local data.

3.1 Database

Our database is composed of several specialized books, including:

- 7 Weeks to 100 Push-Ups: Strengthen and Sculpt Your Arms, Abs, Chest, Back, and Glutes by Training to Do 100 Consecutive Push-Ups [26]:
  This book offers several detailed, personalized training plans on a day-by-day basis. It is suitable for both beginners starting a new workout program and athletes looking to optimize their muscle strengthening.
- ACSM's Foundations of Strength Training and Conditioning [19]:
  The book emphasizes practical applications, allowing students to design, implement, and assess training programs aimed at optimizing strength, power, and athletic performance.
- ACSM's Resources for the Personal Trainer [27]:
  This book recognizes the role of a personal trainer as a professional contributing to the development of healthy lifestyles. It provides personal trainers with the necessary scientific evidence and tools to design safe and effective exercise programs tailored to a variety of clients. It also serves as the official study guide for the ACSM Certified Personal TrainerSM certification exam.
- Advanced Personal Training [9]: Effective fitness coaching and training program design require trainers to combine professional experience with scientifically grounded strategies. This book helps readers better understand the scientific rationale behind key aspects of personal training, such as fitness assessment and program development.
- A Professional's Guide to Small-Group Personal Training [21]:
  Learn how to apply group dynamics and social interaction to create an engaging environment for clients who enjoy small-group training. This guide helps trainers develop the necessary skills to quickly adapt exercises to each participant, ensuring that the entire group remains engaged and progresses toward their fitness goals.
- Functional Training Handbook [14]:
  Reach a higher level of physical training with this book, which takes a comprehensive approach to movement to promote health, mobility, and long-term athletic development. This practical guide provides clear recommendations, sport-specific training tips, and key principles to help trainers keep their clients performing at their best.
- Training for Sports Speed and Agility [7]:
  Speed and agility are crucial components of success in many sports. This book represents the first scientific study of all aspects of athletic training that contribute to speed and agility expression in competitive sports.

By integrating knowledge from these authoritative sources, the chatbot is able to provide scientifically informed training recommendations, ensuring a safe, personalized, and effective approach to sports practice.

3.2 Data Preprocessing

To optimize the relevance and efficiency of the chatbot's recommendations, a rigorous preprocessing phase is conducted using the LangChain framework. This step structures the data and ensures effective indexing for fast retrieval of relevant information in response to user queries. First, the selected documents are segmented into meaningful passages using advanced tokenization and chunking algorithms. This segmentation preserves the semantic coherence of the content while maintaining logical relationships between different sections of the text. Additionally, semantic analysis is performed to extract and retain key concepts as well as named entities that are essential for tailoring sports recommendations. Once segmented, these text passages are transformed into vector representations using specialized embedding models such as OpenAI Ada, Sentence-BERT, or Cohere. This process captures deep semantic relationships between terms, enhances contextual understanding of the content, and facilitates the matching of user queries with the most relevant passages. These vector embeddings are then stored and indexed in a FAISS (Facebook AI Similarity Search) vector database, which enables fast and scalable retrieval of the most relevant information. FAISS utilizes approximate nearest neighbors (ANN) techniques, allowing for efficient retrieval of the closest passages in terms of semantic similarity. This approach ensures real-time search capabilities, optimal scalability for handling large volumes of data, and precise alignment between user queries and indexed documents. Through this data preprocessing pipeline, the chatbot can accurately comprehend language and sports-related concepts, provide rapid access to scientifically validated sources, and dynamically adapt to users' needs. By integrating these steps with the LLM + RAG architecture, our solution guarantees personalized, intelligent, and scientifically grounded support for engaging in a tailored physical activity program, particularly for individuals with specific health-related needs. The following Fig. 2 illustrates the data preprocessing process, including document segmentation, embedding generation, and storage in the FAISS vector database:

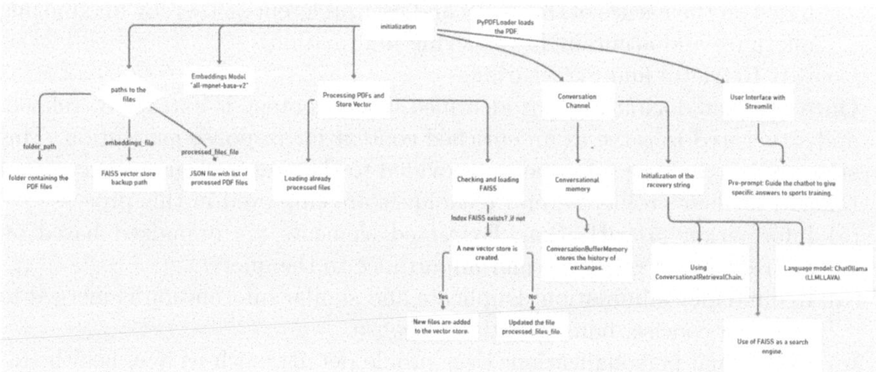

Fig. 2. Data preprocessing process.

3.3 User Query Processing

When a user interacts with the chatbot, their query undergoes a sophisticated processing pipeline designed to ensure fast, relevant, and personalized responses. This process consists of three fundamental steps that enhance the efficiency and quality of the interaction.

1. Cache Verification
   The first step involves checking a memory cache to determine if a similar response has already been generated for a previous query. If a relevant response is found, it is immediately returned, thereby reducing latency and optimizing system performance. This strategy offers two key advantages: it enhances user experience by delivering instant responses to frequent queries and reduces computational resource consumption.
2. Advanced Hybrid Search
   If no cached response is available, the system triggers a hybrid search combining two complementary techniques:
   - Lexical search: This approach relies on keyword-based analysis to identify passages within the document database that contain exact terms from the user's query. It is particularly effective for technical questions or precise requests that involve specific terminology.
   - Semantic search: Simultaneously, a vector-based search is performed using FAISS (Facebook AI Similarity Search), leveraging precomputed vector embeddings. This method captures the overall meaning of the query and retrieves the most relevant documents, even when the wording differs from that in the database. It plays a crucial role in understanding user intent.
   - Result fusion: The results from both lexical and semantic searches are then weighted and merged to produce an optimal selection. This adaptive mechanism dynamically adjusts the importance assigned to each approach based on the nature of the query and user preferences, thereby maximizing relevance and accuracy in retrieving information.
3. Context Retrieval and Structuring
   Once relevant documents are identified, their content is extracted, refined, and structured to serve as an enriched context for response generation. This step ensures that the information provided to the user is clear, coherent, and tailored to their profile. Several techniques are employed in this process:
   (a) Information prioritization: Extracted elements are organized based on their degree of relevance and importance to the query.
   (b) Redundancy elimination: Duplicate and similar information is merged to deliver a concise, non-repetitive response.
   (c) Contextual personalization: User profile details (such as age, health status, and fitness goals) are integrated to adapt the content and optimize the relevance of the recommendations provided.

3.4 Response Generation with a Locally Executed LLM

The deployed architecture is based on the use of a LLaVA (Large Language and Vision Assistant) model, executed locally via the Ollama platform. This choice offers several strategic and technical advantages, contributing to optimal performance and efficient data management. First, local execution ensures fast and secure processing, with low latency enabling instant responses to queries. This approach also eliminates dependence on remote servers, providing greater autonomy from external infrastructures. Additionally, running the model locally reduces costs associated with external API calls, a major economic advantage for applications requiring a high volume of queries. In terms of privacy, this architecture offers enhanced data protection by preventing the transfer of sensitive information to cloud servers, thereby meeting regulatory requirements for personal data protection and ensuring greater security for users.

The LLAVA model is not limited to generating basic responses; it seamlessly integrates information retrieved from the FAISS (Facebook AI Similarity Search) database, a search engine based on vector embeddings. This integration enables the generation of contextually more precise and relevant responses compared to standard language models that lack access to external data. By leveraging embeddings retrieved from FAISS, LLAVA can provide personalized, context-specific answers, enhancing the user experience in terms of the accuracy and relevance of the provided information.

This architecture offers significant advantages for a chatbot specialized in sports. It ensures personalized responses by tailoring recommendations to the user's goals and profile. The system optimizes information retrieval through fast and relevant searches, facilitated by vector indexing. Local execution of the models reduces costs while enhancing data privacy. Moreover, the architecture stands out for its flexibility and scalability, allowing the integration of new data sources without major modifications. Finally, it guarantees smooth interactions and optimized response times thanks to an efficiently organized knowledge base, ultimately improving the overall user experience.

4 Our Solution

The following Fig. 3 shows our AthleticQ AI ASSISTANT, who is a specialist sports training assistant. His role is to provide advice on training programmes, exercises, techniques and best practices to improve performance while minimising the risk of injury.

The following Fig. 4 presents our chatbot, AthleticQ AL ASSISTANT, which provides users with personalized advice based on the conversation content. It offers guidance and instructions that both regular individuals and athletes should follow to prepare either for sports practice or competitions. These recommendations include setting clear goals, assessing fitness levels, creating a training plan, focusing on injury prevention, prioritizing recovery, seeking professional guidance, and staying consistent.

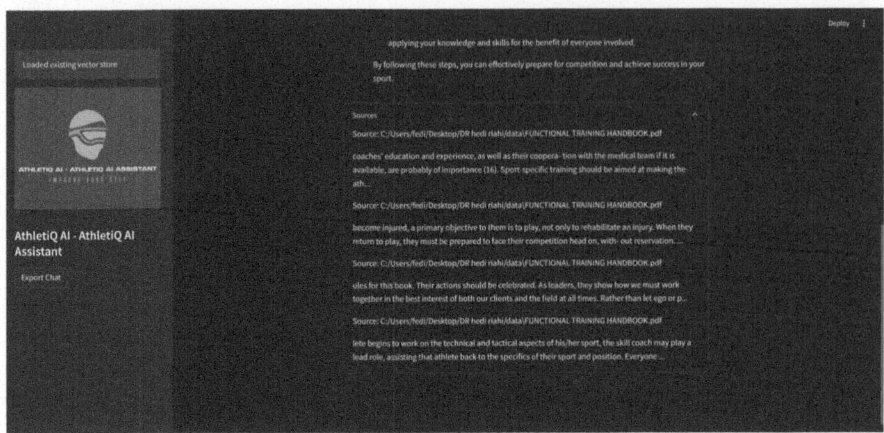

Fig. 3. AthleticQ AI ASSISTANT.

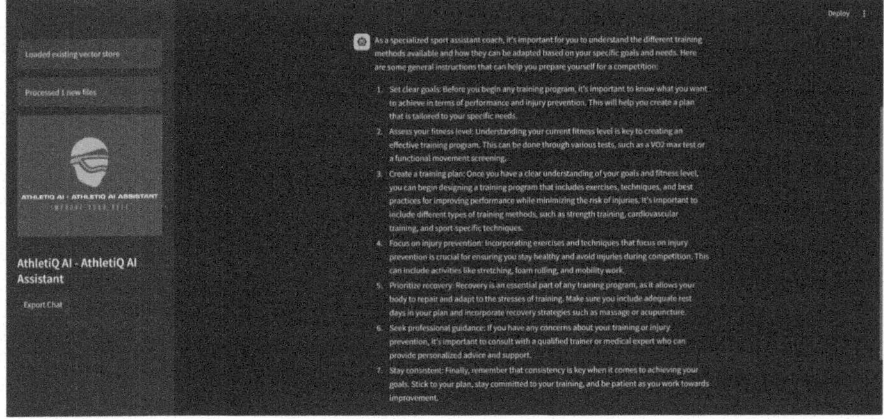

Fig. 4. Guidance and instructions.

The following Fig. 5 illustrates the response of our chatbot, designed to help athletes prepare for their competition by providing the necessary steps to follow.

The following Fig. 6 illustrates the response of our chatbot to a user inquiring about how to perform push-ups

4.1 Evaluation

To evaluate the performance of our AI chatbot, we conducted tests using multiple queries. Below, we present one of the scenarios used to assess and validate the quality of the AI-generated responses.

The Query: What is the best warm-up routine for sprinters? (Figs. 7, 8, 9 and 10)

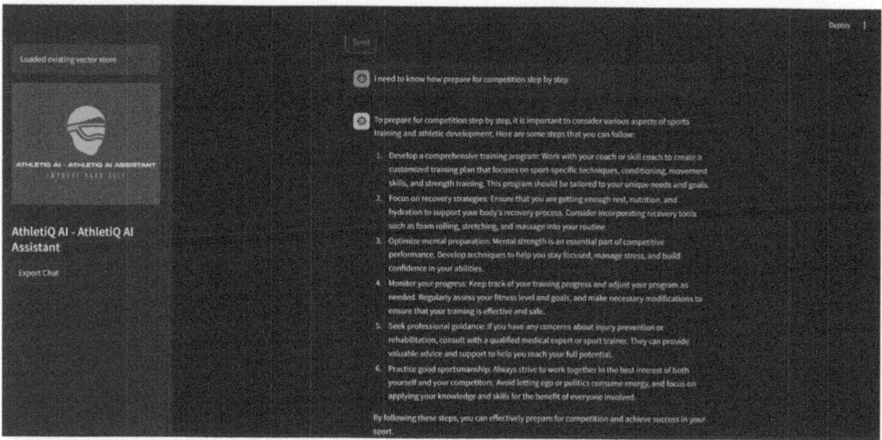

Fig. 5. Prepare for their competition.

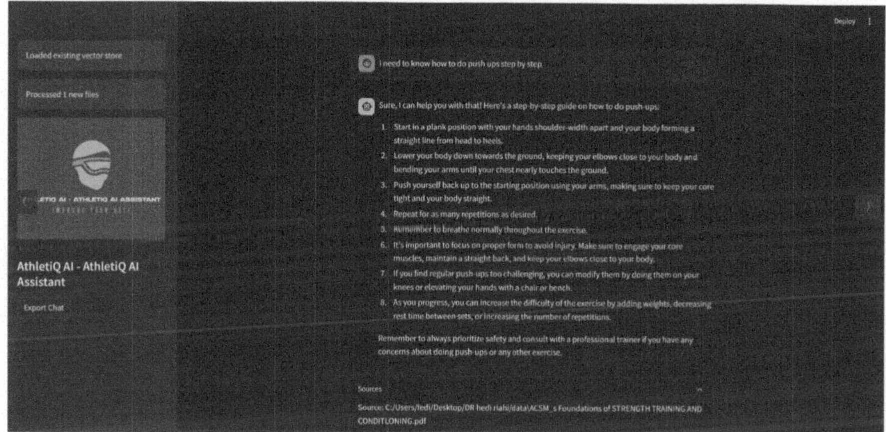

Fig. 6. Perform push-ups.

To answer this question, our AI utilized four relevant documents that contained detailed information on the best warm-up routines for sprinters. These documents served as the foundation for generating a precise and informed response see Fig. 7. Next, we compared the answer generated by the AI with the expected answer, which we had defined as the optimal response to this question. After this comparison, we calculated a similarity score between the two answers, which was 0.48, indicating a certain deviation from the expected response. The execution time for obtaining this answer was 69.80 s . In the second phase, we tested the effect of using a pre-prompt on the AI's performance. By adding a pre-prompt before the question, we observed a significant improvement in the similarity score, which increased to 0.84. This suggests that incorporating

```
🚀 Evaluating Query: What is the best warm-up routine for sprinters?
C:\Users\fedi\Desktop\DR hedi riahi\code\eval copy.py:73: LangChainDeprecationWarning: The method `BaseRetriever.get_rel
evant_documents` was deprecated in langchain-core 0.1.46 and will be removed in 1.0. Use :meth:`~invoke` instead.
  retrieved_docs = index.vectorstore.as_retriever().get_relevant_documents(query)

🔍 Retrieved 4 documents for query: 'What is the best warm-up routine for sprinters?'
📄 Relevant Document: 9
warm-up meThodS and mobiliTy
Training
introduction
The warm-up has become an established part of athletes' preparation for both competi-
tion and training. Warm-up protocols vary widely; however, i...

📄 Relevant Document: relevant musculature through the relevant range of motion, specific warm-up activities
should be undertaken to potentiate sprint and agility movement. Performing a variety
of sprints and bounding ac...

📄 Relevant Document: not differ significantly from normal conditions in the group of trained sprinters stud-
ied (Bennett et al., 2009). Further study is, however, required to ascertain whether these
apparent advantages ...

📄 Relevant Document: (Škof and Strojnik, 2007). There are similarly preliminary data showing that performing
sprints prior to explosive power activities can have a potentiation effect that is reflected
in enhanced perfo...

C:\Users\fedi\Desktop\DR hedi riahi\code\eval copy.py:84: LangChainDeprecationWarning: The method `Chain.run` was deprec
ated in langchain 0.1.0 and will be removed in 1.0. Use :meth:`~invoke` instead.
  response = chain.run({"question": full_prompt})
```

Fig. 7. Retrieved 4 documents for query.

```
🤖 AI Response:
  Hi AIIMPACT\_ASSISTANT! Great question about the best warm-up routine for sprinters. As a specialized sport assistant
coach, I can provide you with some guidance on this topic.

When it comes to warming up for sprinting, it's important to focus on activating your muscles and increasing blood flow
to them in order to prepare them for the physical demands of sprinting. Here is an example warm-up routine that you can
try:

1. Jogging or light jogging for 5-10 minutes: This helps to increase blood flow and oxygen to the muscles, as well as wa
rming up the entire body.
2. Dynamic stretching: These are stretches performed in a dynamic manner (e.g., walking lunge, leg swings, high knees) t
hat help to activate your muscles and improve mobility. Include stretches for the hips, hamstrings, glutes, and calves.
3. Plyometric exercises: These involve explosive movements that can help to increase power and agility. Examples include
 box jumps, depth jumps, and single-leg hops.
4. Sprints or acceleration drills: Practicing sprinting technique can also be part of the warm-up routine, as it helps t
o activate your neuromuscular system and improve your sprinting mechanics.

It's important to keep in mind that every athlete is different, so it's best to work with a strength and conditioning sp
ecialist or coach who can tailor a warm-up routine specifically for you based on your individual needs and goals. Also,
make sure to listen to your body and adjust your routine as needed to prevent injury.

Hope this helps! Let me know if you have any other questions.

✅ Expected Answer:
 As a specialized sport assistant coach, I can provide guidance on sports training, exercises, techniques, and best prac
tices for improving performance while minimizing the risk of injuries. However, it's important to note that warm-up rout
ines for sprinters may vary depending on individual needs and goals In general, a good warm-up routine for sprinters sho
uld include dynamic stretches and movements that target the muscles used in sprinting, as well as activities that increa
```

Fig. 8. AI's response via the expected response.

```
✅ Expected Answer:
 As a specialized sport assistant coach, I can provide guidance on sports training, exercises, techniques, and best prac
tices for improving performance while minimizing the risk of injuries. However, it's important to note that warm-up rout
ines for sprinters may vary depending on individual needs and goals In general, a good warm-up routine for sprinters sho
uld include dynamic stretches and movements that target the muscles used in sprinting, as well as activities that increa
se heart rate and improve blood flow to the muscles. Here are some examples of exercises that can be included in a warm-
up routine for sprinters: Jogging or light cardio: Start with a few minutes of light cardio to increase your heart rate
and warm up your muscles. This could include jogging, jumping jacks, or high knees. Dynamic stretches: Include exercises
 such as leg swings, hip circles, and arm circles to activate the muscle groups used in sprinting. Plyometric exercises:
 Including plyometric exercises like box jumps, depth jumps, or lateral bounds can help improve power and explosiveness.
 Drills: Incorporate drills such as bounding, carioca, or crossover steps to improve agility and footwork. Sport-specifi
c movements: Including sport-specific movements like sprinting exercises, such as 20-meter sprints or acceleration drill
s, can help prepare the body for the specific demands of sprinting.Its important to note that the best warm-up routine f
or sprinters will depend on individual needs and goals. Its always a good idea to consult with a professional trainer or
 medical expert for personalized recommendations. Additionally, always prioritize safety and injury prevention by using
proper form, wearing appropriate footwear, and taking breaks when necessary.

📊 Response Similarity Score: 0.49
⚡ Response Time: 69.80 seconds
```

Fig. 9. Similarity and for the two response.

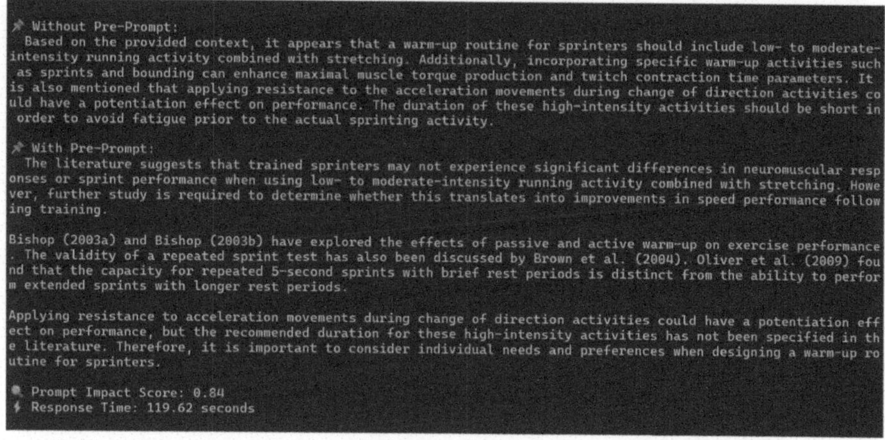

Fig. 10. Similarity and for the two response without Pre-prompt and with Pre-promt.

a pre-prompt helps guide the AI towards a more relevant and accurate answer. However, it is worth noting that using the pre-prompt also led to an increase in execution time, which rose to 119.62 s. In conclusion, while the addition of a pre-prompt improves the quality of the response (as measured by the similarity score), it comes at the cost of increased processing time, which is an important factor to consider when optimizing the system.

5 Conclusion

The RAG-based architecture presented in this paper enables the development of an intelligent and scalable sports chatbot, combining advanced information retrieval capabilities with efficient response generation. The local execution of the model via Ollama ensures autonomous and secure usage, while document indexing through FAISS guarantees fast and relevant knowledge retrieval. Future perspectives include enhancing continuous learning by integrating user feedback mechanisms to refine responses, adding an image recognition module to analyze sports movements and provide personalized recommendations, and exploring multimodal models that combine text, images, and videos to enrich the user experience. This approach can be extended to other fields requiring seamless interaction between a search engine and an advanced language model, such as healthcare, personalized coaching, and athlete performance monitoring.

References

1. Babaeian Jelodar, M.: Generative AI, large language models, and ChatGPT in construction education, training, and practice. Buildings **15**(6), 933 (2025)

2. Baughman, A., et al.: Large scale generative ai text applied to sports and music. In: Proceedings of the 30th ACM SIGKDD Conference on Knowledge Discovery and Data Mining, pp. 4784–4792 (2024)
3. Blair, S.N., Morris, J.N.: Healthy hearts–and the universal benefits of being physically active: physical activity and health. Ann. Epidemiol. **19**(4), 253–256 (2009)
4. Cudicio, A., Martinez-Valdes, E., Cogliati, M., Orizio, C., Negro, F.: The force-generation capacity of the tibialis anterior muscle at different muscle–tendon lengths depends on its motor unit contractile properties. Eur. J. Appl. Physiol., 1–14 (2022)
5. Elgueta-Cancino, E., Evans, E., Martinez-Valdes, E., Falla, D.: The effect of resistance training on motor unit firing properties: a systematic review and meta-analysis. Front. Physiol. **13**, 817631 (2022)
6. Francín-Gallego, M., et al.: Physical activity and anxiety in the adolescence: special emphasis on sport type and performance level. J. Pub. Health, 1–7 (2024)
7. Gamble, P.: Training for Sports Speed and Agility: An Evidence-Based Approach. Routledge (2011)
8. Gao, Y., et al.: Leveraging medical knowledge graphs into large language models for diagnosis prediction: design and application study. JMIR AI **4**, e58670 (2025)
9. Gibson, A.L., Wagner, D.R., Heyward, V.H.: Advanced Fitness Assessment and Exercise Prescription. Human Kinetics (2024)
10. Holmes, W., Miao, F., et al.: Orientations pour l'intelligence artificielle générative dans l'éducation et la recherche. UNESCO Publishing (2024)
11. Lamri, J., Tertrais, G., Silver, A.: Chapitre 4. comment faire des ia génératives un outil de construction des futurs souhaitables. Questions de société, pp. 117–136 (2023)
12. Lewis, P., et al.: Retrieval-augmented generation for knowledge-intensive NLP tasks. Adv. Neural. Inf. Process. Syst. **33**, 9459–9468 (2020)
13. Li, Y., Gao, W., Luan, Z., Zhou, Z., Li, J.: The impact of chat generative pre-trained transformer (ChatGPT) on oncology: application, expectations, and future prospects. Cureus **15**(11) (2023)
14. Liebenson, C.: Functional Training Handbook. Lippincott Williams & Wilkins (2014)
15. Mahmoudi-Dehaki, M., Nasr-Esfahani, N.: Exploring the transformative potential of generative artificial intelligence. In: Generative AI Foundations, Developments, and Applications, pp. 111–148. IGI Global Scientific Publishing (2025)
16. Mohan, S., Venkatakrishnan, A., Hartzler, A.L.: Designing an ai health coach and studying its utility in promoting regular aerobic exercise. ACM Trans. Interact. Intell. Syst. (TiiS) **10**(2), 1–30 (2020)
17. Nguyen, M.L.T., Honcharov, V., Ballard, D., Satterwhite, S., McDermott, A.M., Sarkar, U.: Primary care physicians' experiences with and adaptations to time constraints. JAMA Netw. Open **7**(4), e248827–e248827 (2024)
18. Ofman, P., et al.: Regular physical activity and risk of atrial fibrillation: a systematic review and meta-analysis. Circ. Arrhythmia ElectrophysioL **6**(2), 252–256 (2013)
19. Ratamess, N.: ACSM's Foundations of Strength Training and Conditioning. Lippincott Williams & Wilkins (2021)
20. Ratiu, O.G., Badau, D., Carstea, C.G., Badau, A., Paraschiv, F.: Artificial intelligence (AI) in sports. In: Proceedings of the 9th WSEAS International Conference on Artificial Intelligence, Knowledge Engineering and Data Bases, pp. 93–97 (2010)
21. Roberts, K.: A Professional's Guide to Small-Group Personal Training. Human Kinetics (2021)

22. Sangwan, N.: The demonstrated advantages of engaging in physical activity for health. Res. Develop. **7**(07), 11–15 (2024)
23. Singhal, K., et al.: Large language models encode clinical knowledge. Nature **620**(7972), 172–180 (2023)
24. Sluka, K.A., O'Donnell, J.M., Danielson, J., Rasmussen, L.A.: Regular physical activity prevents development of chronic pain and activation of central neurons. J. Appl. Physiol. **114**(6), 725–733 (2013)
25. de Sousa Cardoso, C., Parise, F.: Section 1. faire ses premiers pas avec l'ia générative et déployer des cas d'usage simples et rapides. Hors collection Économie/Gestion, pp. 107–142 (2023)
26. Speirs, S.: 7 Weeks to 100 Push-Ups: Strengthen and Sculpt Your Arms, Abs, Chest, Back and Glutes by Training to Do 100 Consecutive Push-Ups. Simon and Schuster (2024)
27. of Sports Medicine, A.C., et al.: ACSM's Resources for the Personal Trainer. Lippincott Williams & Wilkins (2013)
28. Warburton, D.E., Nicol, C.W., Bredin, S.S.: Health benefits of physical activity: the evidence. CMAJ **174**(6), 801–809 (2006)
29. Williams, S.J., Kendall, L.: Perceptions of elite coaches and sports scientists of the research needs for elite coaching practice. J. Sports Sci. **25**(14), 1577–1586 (2007)
30. Wu, C., Chen, L., Han, M., Li, Z., Yang, N., Yu, C.: Application of ChatGPT-based blended medical teaching in clinical education of hepatobiliary surgery. Med. Teach. **47**(3), 445–449 (2025)
31. Zhang, H., Li, J., Wang, Y., Song, Y.: Integrating automated knowledge extraction with large language models for explainable medical decision-making. In: 2023 IEEE International Conference on Bioinformatics and Biomedicine (BIBM), pp. 1710–1717. IEEE (2023)

Cure-Free: A Free-Model Reinforcement Learning Approach for the ADHD Children

Zineb Namasse[1,2], Zineb Hidila[1], Mohamed Tabaa[1](✉), Mounia Elhaddadi[3], and Samar Mouchawrab[2]

[1] Multidisciplinary Laboratory of Research and Innovation, Moroccan School of Engineering Sciences, 20250 Casablanca, Morocco
m.tabaa@emsi.ma

[2] Research, Development, and Innovation Laboratory, Mundiapolis University, 20180 Casablanca, Morocco

[3] Laboratory of Nutrition, Health and Environment, Ibn Tofail University, Kenitra, Morocco

Abstract. Attention Deficit Hyperactivity Disorder (ADHD) has two symptoms: inattention and hyperactivity. Inattention is the inability of a person to concentrate on a specific task fully. Hyperactivity/Impulsivity, on the other hand, is characterized by excessive activity and difficulty in physically and emotionally restraining oneself. Artificial Intelligence (AI) techniques have been implemented to assist these individuals, and among these methods the Reinforcement Learning (RL). Therefore, this paper aims to use RL to address the case of children with ADHD. We begin by presenting some cognitive deficits of ADHD patients. Then, we mention studies that have utilized it in the context of ADHD and we discuss the principles of RL. Next, we collect a sample of 106 children and adolescents with or without ADHD. We propose a Model-Free RL methodology using Q-Learning, SARSA, and a hybrid version of the two. Among the findings, we noted that 5.2% of inattentive children with ADHD are dysgraphic, 8.2% of those in this category focus on a task for less than 10 min, 9.3% of hyperactive children walk very quickly, and 4.4% of those in this category eat biscuits. The results also showed that for 300 episodes, the Q-Learning and Combined algorithms converge the most with an alpha of 0.9 and 0.5, respectively, and with a gamma of 0.1 and 0.5, respectively.

Keywords: Attention Deficit Hyperactivity Disorder · Reinforcement Learning · Q-Learning · SARSA · Hyperactivity/Impulsivity · Inattention · Free-Model · Markov Decision Process

1 Introduction

ADHD is a mental disorder that impacts cognitive ability. Several authors and scientists have noted this difference compared to non-ADHD individuals. For instance, ADHD patients explore more often than non-ADHD patients [1]. Another study noted that ADHD patients' excessive choice changes, which is a reaction to their hyperactivity,

F. Kamoun et al. (Eds.): AFRICATEK 2025, LNICST 676, pp. 18–36, 2026.
https://doi.org/10.1007/978-3-032-16635-7_2

impact their flexible behavior [2]. In addition, ADHD is often associated with impaired inhibitory control, meaning that they have difficulty holding back and restricting their impulsivity [3]. In addition, ADHD is often associated with co-morbidities such as learning disabilities. A study by BECKER et al. [4] found that 20–70% of ADHD children also suffer from a specific learning disability (SLD), specifying that this category of children does not have particular deficiencies in a specific cognitive area but rather non-specific deficiencies in several areas. Researchers have contributed to using Artificial Intelligence (AI) techniques about this neurodevelopmental disorder in this context. One of these techniques is Reinforcement Learning (RL). RL is a sub-branch of Machine Learning (ML) [5], which, unlike ML, learns from a sequence of actions and rewards/penalties obtained via an environment [6]. The two pillars of RL, Professors Sutton and Barto, defined it as 'learning what to do to maximize a numerical reward signal.' Reinforcement learning is a problem, a class of solution methods that work well on the problem, and the field that studies the problem and its solution methods' [7]. RL seeks to maximize rewards or minimize penalties by trial and error. The primordial components of the RL are the environment, where the agent can act and learn. It must contain a list of rules that the agent must follow. States are the agent's situations in the environment, such as coordinates or positions. Actions: What can the agent do in its environment, such as directional buttons in a grid environment? Rewards return numerical values when the agent chooses an action through a state. They can be positive or negative. Moreover, the policy is the agent's guide for selecting the best action [8]. Let us take a simple example: a baby (agent) learning to sit up properly in his room (environment). The objective is to keep his back straight for as long as possible (policy). In this scenario, there are two possible states: the sitting state (s_1) if the baby manages to keep its back straight and the lying state (s_2) if it does not. Each time the baby keeps its back straight for the whole time allowed (a_1), it is entitled to a toy (r_1). However, if he loses his balance (a_2), he gets no toy (r_2) and has to make an extra effort and get back up. In the ADHD context, people affected by this disorder struggle to change their behavior after making a mistake [9]. One reason for this attitude is their overexploitation, a reaction due to a lower dopamine (DA) transporter availability [1]. With the emergence of AI, it is now possible to understand the brain mechanisms of individuals affected or not by neural diseases. For example, RL methods could contribute to helping ADHD agents by motivating them to choose progressively more exploitative decisions that may increase their rewards. The rest of the paper is organized as follows: Sect. 2 recalls the preliminaries of RL and mentions a few studies using this technique to treat ADHD. Section 3 proposes an RL methodology for the case of ADHD children. Section 4 is devoted to a discussion of the results obtained. Section 5 concludes the paper.

2 State of the Art

The emergence of AI has made it possible to treat several real-world applications more effectively, including mental disorders. Several studies have studied ADHD using these AI techniques. For instance, [10] combined pixel subtraction movement quantization with ML methods (SVM, XGBoost, RF, KNN, DT, and AdaBoost) to classify ADHD people with ADHD from non-ADHD through videos. They found out that the RF achieved an accuracy of 90.24% and the ADHD community has larger values for all types of movements. Another study proposed using an approach to detect and classify children's activity level in a classroom environment with millimeter-wave radar and ML techniques. It seemed that Linear SVM reached an accuracy of 100% [11]. Moreover, [12] ought to employ Ensemble Learning (EL) and Deep Learning (DL) methods to classify students with and without Learning Disabilities (LD). By joining AdaBoost-Classifier and KerasClassifier, they came up with an accuracy of 99.6%. As for the Reinforcement Learning (RL), its theoretical principles have garnered attention from several fields. Some studies have used it to address ADHD. For example, [9] developed an emotion management application that reduces hyperactivity and increases attention in children with ADHD, utilizing a Q-Learning model to detect their heart rates. [13] contributed to creating a multi-modal framework by employing Deep Learning (DL) for better accuracy and RL to enhance decision-making. Furthermore, they compared several algorithms, such as DQN, DDQN, PPO, and A3C, finding that PPO and A3C achieved an accuracy of 90.2%. [1] Acknowledged ML tools in complex tasks. However, they also stated two principles: interpretability, which refers to the ability to understand the decision function, and robustness, which refers to the ability to assign the correct label despite missing or noisy inputs. They then proposed using Q-Learning techniques to meet these criteria, to distinguish children with autism spectrum disorder (ASD) from children with ADHD, and to train robust classifiers by maximizing accuracy. [15] sought to combine SARSA, a reinforcement learning method, with Sequential Sampling Models (SSM) to understand the cognitive system of the interaction between learning and decision-making, including the cognitive system of ADHD. The two concepts are complementary, as the reinforcement learning method does not mechanistically account for decision-making, ignoring the response time for distributions. In contrast, the SSM does not account for learning capability over time. These two techniques will help us understand how learning can influence decision-making and vice versa. [16] aimed to predict the emotions of children with ADHD using Internet of Things (IoT) robotic devices. They employed two principles to achieve this: data fusion analysis technology for facial expressions to join thermal images and detection data, and deep reinforcement learning (DRL) for the information flow in extra time for children with ADHD. The robot is a reinforcement learning agent that interacts with the environment and the teacher's feedback to obtain either a positive or negative reward, represented by the thermal image data and image-based cognitive learning to construct a DNN. The RL agent can record their physiological and behavioral responses. However, the question of voice or multimedia reading to guide children toward better behavior is an adjustment that must be made. The two algorithms used are Q-learning and REINFORCE. While Q-Learning has shown promising results in local solutions, REINFORCE has updated the probability for each step. However, both face issues of overestimation and instability.

As mentioned in Sect. 1, the RL components include the environment, agent, state, action, and reward. The figure below describes the RL process. The environment sends a state s to an agent. This agent performs an action a and, depending on this action, receives a reward or penalty r, the next state st + 1, and the cycle repeats (Fig. 1).

Any RL problem can be solved using the Markov Decision Process (MDP) approach. An MDP is characterized by states S, actions A, transition probabilities P, rewards R, and

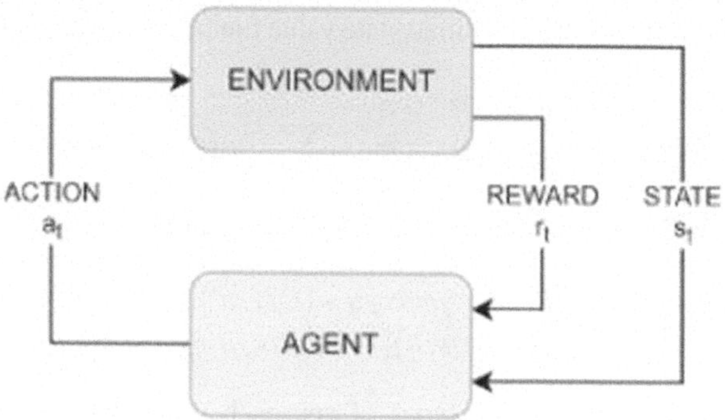

Fig. 1. Reinforcement Learning components [17]

a discount factor γ, where γ is a value between 0 and 1. According to Sutton et al. [18], the agent chooses actions to maximize the sum of the discount rewards it will receive. The equation below summarizes this:

$$\begin{aligned} G_t &= R_{t+1} + \gamma R_{t+2} + \gamma^2 R_{t+3} + \ldots. \\ &= R_{t+1} + \gamma(R_{t+2} + \gamma R_{t+3} + \ldots.) \\ &= R_{t+1} + \gamma G_{t+1} \end{aligned} \tag{1}$$

Most of these problems aim to estimate value functions, also known as state functions or state-action pairs, that evaluate the goodness of the state the agent is in or the action performed. This notion is called 'expected return.' The rewards that the agent can receive or not will depend on its actions. The value functions, therefore, depend on the policies. The value function of a state s under a policy π, denoted $v_\pi(s)$, and the state-action pair function q_π (s, a), are defined as follows:

$$v_\pi(s) = E_\pi[G_t|S_t = s] = E_\pi[\sum \gamma^k R_{t+k+1}|S_t = s] \text{ for all s} \in \text{S} \tag{2}$$

$$q_\pi(s, a) = E_\pi[G_t|S_t = s, A_t = a] = E_\pi[\sum \gamma^k R_{t+k+1}|S_t = s, A_t = a] \text{ for all s} \in \text{S, a} \in \text{A} \tag{3}$$

One of the essential properties of value functions is that they satisfy recursive relationships similar to those established in Eq. (1). For a policy π and a state s, the value of a state s is linked to that of future states s':

$$v_\pi(s) = \sum_a \pi(a, s) \sum_{s', r} p(s', r|s, a)\left[r + \gamma v_\pi(s')\right] \tag{4}$$

This equation above, which expresses the relationship between the current and future states, is the Bellman equation for the value function of states.

Among all possible policies, there is always one that is better than or equal to the others. It is called the optimal policy. Similarly, the optimal state value function v*(s) and the optimal action-state pair value function q*(s,a) are written as follows:

$$v*(s) = max_\pi v_\pi(s) \tag{5}$$

$$q*(s, a) = max_\pi q_\pi(s, a) \tag{6}$$

It is also possible to write the optimal state value function in terms of the state-action pair:

$$v*(s) = max_{a \in A}(s)q_{\pi}*(s,a) = max_a \sum_{s',r} p(s',r|s,r)[r + \gamma v*(s')] \quad (7)$$

The optimal Bellman equation for the state-action pair is:

$$\begin{aligned} q*(s,a) &= E[R_{t+1} + \gamma max_{a'}q*(s_{t+1},a')|S_t = s, A_t = a] \\ &= \sum_{s',r} p(s',r|s,a)[r + \gamma max_{a'}q*(s',a')] \end{aligned} \quad (8)$$

Regarding MDP, there are two types of approaches: the Model-Based approach. Model-based agents do not need to interact with the environment since they already have a complete MDP model. This method requires using transition probabilities from the model to identify future rewards and actions. Dynamic Programming (DP) is one of the methods that utilizes the Model-Based approach. The other approach is the Model-Free approach. This involves updating the agent's knowledge or experience to determine an action. Monte Carlo (MC) and Temporal Difference (TD) are examples of Model-Free methods. The difference is that MC waits for the end of a complete episode to update its value function, whereas TD updates its value function after each step. Among the algorithms that use the TD approach, we can mention Q-Learning and SARSA [19].

3 Methodology

As previously mentioned, RL has two types: Model-Free and Model-Based. Since children with ADHD tend to explore more than those without ADHD and struggle with anticipation, we will opt for the Model-Free approach. This approach has two branches: Value-Based and Policy-Based. In the first category, algorithms estimate the value of each state or state-action pair and choose the optimal action to improve the agent's performance. In the second category, algorithms directly optimize the policy determining the agent's action [20]. We will choose the Value-Based approach to better guide the agent's learning. Given that our modeling has four states, Q-Learning and SARSA are among the algorithms that meet all these criteria. Based on this, we will model our ADHD agent using the MDP characterized by the tuple M = (S,A,R,T,γ). However, in a standard MDP, each state is characterized by a single value, and moving from one state to another requires one action. In contrast, the two symptoms of ADHD are distinct yet interdependent, and transitioning between two states requires multiple actions. This is why we will use a variant of the MDP, the Factored Markov Decision Process (FMDP), whose characteristics are decomposed into subparts [2].

3.1 Environment

Thanks to Dr. Elhaddadi, we collected a sample of 106 children and adolescents, both with and without ADHD. The Dataset initially contained nineteen features, such as age and food consumption. We eliminated the features that contained missing values (NaN). It also included three specific features: one representing the list of sweet foods consumed (cookies, candies, cakes, ice cream, sugary drinks, and pastries), and the other containing the healthy foods consumed (meat, eggs, fish, dairy products, vegetables, and dried fruits). We separated these two features into individual features for each food with Boolean values. To enrich this information in the nutritional plan, we associated each food with its quantity in kilocalories and protein, referring to the SuperTracker database from the United States Department of Agriculture (USDA) [22]. Then, we added a feature to calculate the sum of kilocalories for sugary foods and proteins for healthy foods. The third feature contains a list of comorbidities such as dyslexia, oppositional behavior, and so on. We also transformed it into a feature for each comorbidity with Boolean values. After establishing a correlation matrix, we found that dysgraphia is the only one with a strong correlation with the feature related to ADHD diagnosis (0,294185143464218). Based on this conclusion, we found a Dataset associated with ADHD and dysgraphia [23]. It contains handwriting size, spacing between words, letters, and so on. By performing a correlation matrix, we noted strong correlations between writing speed and the spacing between letters (0,705297224870676) and between the spacing of letters and the spacing between words (0,773604763773015). We then combined the two Datasets. Considering these results, we retained only the features related to nutrition, dysgraphia, and ADHD feedback, whether present or not. The Dataset now contains nine features and ninety-seven entries.

3.2 Objective Function

The objective is to alleviate one of the two symptoms of ADHD at a time, but not both simultaneously:

$$J(\pi) = min_{\pi}\left(\alpha\, R_{Inattention}, (1--\alpha) R_{Hyperactivity}\right) \tag{9}$$

where $\alpha \in [0,1]$ is a weighting factor determining the importance of the two symptoms. If $\alpha < = 0.5$, we will try to reduce hyperactivity first; otherwise, we will minimize inattention first.

3.3 Actions

In our modeling, each action will consist of several sub-actions that alleviate or worsen one of the two symptoms at a time.

$$A_i = A_0 * A_1 * A_2 * \ldots * A_n \tag{10}$$

As noted above, ADHD children are more likely to be dyslexic and suffer from an unbalanced diet. Several papers have highlighted these worrying daily habits. For example, [2] mentions that ADHD children spend more time writing, due to their excessive corrections. According to [25], one way of alleviating this problem would be to break up a long text into short paragraphs, and taking short breaks would help maintain concentration. [26] points out that the 'western diet' or poor nutrition increases the symptoms of this mental disorder, and [27] adds that these children have poor rhythmic synchronisation due to their rapid walking. In other words, diet and relaxation exercises, particularly slow walking, would alleviate ADHD hyperactivity [28-2]. Given these results, we opted for the inattention action of difficult writing and the attention action of training in stable handwriting. As for the hyperactivity sub-actions, we chose unbalanced eating and fast walking, and activity sub-actions, balanced eating and walking at a normal speed.

3.4 States

In our model, each state will be decomposed into a vector of two sub-states, as ADHD has two main symptoms: inattention and hyperactivity. Moreover, the objective function mentioned that alleviating both symptoms simultaneously would represent a significant challenge. Therefore, we opted to reduce one of the two symptoms at once. The first sub-state represents attention, and the second represents activity. The initial state is where the agent is both hyperactive and inattentive (both sub-states are initialized to 0). The first sub-state represents attention, and the second represents activity. The first is the initial state, where the agent is hyperactive and inattentive (both sub-states are initialized to 0).

$$S_{Cure} \in S_v = [0, 0] \tag{11}$$

$$S_{\text{Cure}} = \{S_0, S_1, S_2, S_3\} \tag{12}$$

$$\begin{cases} \textit{If } S_v = [0,0](S_0), \textit{ the agent is ; hyperactive and inattentive} \\ \textit{If } S_v = [0,1](S_1), \textit{ the agent is hyperactive but attentive} \\ \textit{If } S_v = [1,0](S_2), \textit{ the agent is active but inattentive} \\ \textit{If } S_v = [1,1](S_3), \textit{ the agent is active and attentive} \end{cases} \tag{13}$$

3.5 Rewards

The rewards are divided into two sub-rewards, one representing attention and the other the activity.

$$\begin{cases} R(A_{tt}) = CDT + (\frac{WriS*SL}{SW+1}) \\ R(A_{ct}) = \frac{Pro-(\frac{Kcal}{100})}{WalS+1} \end{cases} \tag{14}$$

Based on the results of our database, we found that the variables that have the most significant impact on inattention are writing speed, concentration time, space between letters, and space between words. As for hyperactivity, we highlighted that an unbalanced diet worsens the symptoms. To quantify this information, we chose the variables protein and kilocalories. CDT represents the concentration duration, where its values lie between 0 and 3. 0 means less than 10 min, 1 between 10 and 15 min, 2 between 15 and 20 min, and 3 between 20 and 30 min. WriS stands for the writing speed, where a value of 0 means a normal speed, 1 means fast, and 2 refers to a low speed. SL refers to the Space between letters, where 0 means normal (1–2 mm). 1 wide. 2 for narrow and 3: Letters are spaced irregularly. SM means the space between words, where 0 refers to normal space, 1: wide, 2: narrow, and 3: words spaced irregularly. Pro and Kcla stand for the Proteins and Kilocalories. And WalS represents the walking speed where 0 means a very slow walking, 1: Slow walking, 2: Normal walking, 3: Fast walking, and 4: Very fast walking.

3.6 Reward Aggregation Function

$$G = \alpha R_{Attention} + (1 - -\alpha) R_{Activity} \tag{15}$$

A reward aggregation function is a function that combines the rewards obtained up to the end. As mentioned above, the objective is to reduce one of the two ADHD symptoms at a time. In other words, when the agent moves from a non-final state (initial state excluded) to the final state, the rewards for activity $R_{Activity}$ and attention $R_{Attention}$ will be combined.

3.7 Algorithms Used

In Sect. 2, we mentioned two algorithms: Q-Learning and SARSA. We chose them because of their ability to handle RL problems with few states and their flexibility in discrete action spaces:

Q-learning: Q-learning is a model-free algorithm that uses an optimal policy to select an action and updates the value function based on the maximum value function of the following state [30]. In other words, it uses two policies. Its update function is as follows [31]:

$$Q(s, a) = (1 - -\alpha)\, Q(s, a) + \alpha\left[r + \gamma max_a Q(s', a)\right] \tag{16}$$

SARSA: SARSA is an online policy algorithm that uses a policy to select an action and employs it to update the value function of the following state and action [30]. In other words, it uses a single policy. Its value function is as follows [31]:

$$Q(s, a) = (1 - -\alpha)\, Q(s, a) + \alpha\left[r + \gamma Q(s', a)\right] \tag{17}$$

where α is the learning rate, γ the discount factor and r the reward. The learning rate is the speed at which an agent learns a new behavior. The discount factor, however, represents how important future rewards are compared to current rewards.

Below are the pseudocodes of both the algorithms:

Algorithm 1: Q-Learning

Input: Sate s, Action a, Next state s', Q[] table, discount factor γ, learning rate α, variable done, exploration rate ε, Episode number NEpsMax.

```
Output : Updated Q[] table
For i from 0 to NEpsMax :
    Initialise the state s
    done ← False
    While done ← False :
        Choose an action a (ε -greedy)
        Perform the action a et observe the next state s', reward and done
        Q(s,a)=(1 – α) Q(s,a) + α[r + γmax_a Q(s',a)]
        s ←s'
        If done ← True then :
            Break
        End If
    End While
    Epsilon_decay
End For
```

Pseudo-code. 1 . Q-Learning [18]

Algorithm 2: SARSA

Input: State s, Action a, Next state s', Next Action a' Q[] table, discount factor γ, Learning rate α, Boolean variable done, Exploration rate ε, Episode number NEpsMax.

```
Output : Updated Q[] table
For i from 0 to NEpsMax :
    Initialise the state s
    Choose an action a (ε -greedy)
    done ← False
    While done ← False :
        Perform the action a and observe the next state s', reward r, and done
        Choose the next action a' (ε -greedy)
        Q(s,a)=(1 – α) Q(s,a) + α[r + γQ(s',a')]
        s ←s'
        a ←a'
        If done ← True then :
            Break
        End If
    End While
    Epsilon_decay
End For
```

Pseudo-code.2 . SARSA [18]

According to [30], we conclude that Q-Learning updates its Q values through maximum values and the optimal action, while SARSA does so through actions that are actually chosen. However, the values of Q-Learning can sometimes be aggressive and, therefore, have higher variance, while SARSA adopts a more stable but slower convergence, which increases its exploration. In this context, a hybrid approach may be feasible, combining the advantages of both algorithms, that is, having more stable convergence and aiming for maximum values. Below is the pseudo-code for this hybrid approach:

Algorithm 3: Combined

```
    Input: State s, Action a, Next state s', Next Action a', Q[] table,
 discount factor γ, learning rate α, Boolean variable done, exploration
 rate ε, Threshold T, Episode number NEpsMax.
    Output : updated Q[] table
    For i from 0 to NEpsMax :
          Initialise the state s
          Choose an action a (epsilon-greedy)
          done ← False
          While done ← False :
               Perform the action a and observe the next state s', the
             reward r and done
               If ε>= T then :
                    Choose the next action a'
                         Q(s,a)=(1 – α) Q(s,a) + α[r + γQ(s',a')]
                    a ←a'
               Else :
                    a'=None
                      Q(s,a)=(1 – α) Q(s,a) + α[r + γmax_a Q(s',a)]
               End If
               s ←s'
               If done ← True then :
                    Break
               End If
          End While
          Epsilon_decay
    End For
```

Pseudo-code. 3. Combined

4 Discussion and Results

The integration of AI in all fields, especially healthcare, offers several advantages. One of these is to make life easier not only for patients but also for caregivers and doctors. However, it also presents some significant challenges. For example, data confidentiality, integrity and availability (CIA).

Ensuring confidentiality is a critical task, as it guarantees the security of patients' data and enables them to express themselves more freely with professionals, thereby promoting their recovery.

A second important point is data integrity. For an AI system to work effectively, it is vital to verify its authenticity and ensure that the data is complete, so as not to introduce any bias that could distort the data.

A third point is data availability. This not only concerns the access system in clinical or school environments, but also refers to the difficulty of collecting this data. Gathering such information is a challenge not to be forgotten, especially in the medical field.

A fourth point is the position of ethical AI in healthcare. Mathematical models, including reinforcement models, must not, under any circumstances, bias the training data and, as a result, could mislead carers, doctors or educators.

In our context, which is ADHD, since the data relating to these children is particularly sensitive, it was only with their parents consent that we distributed a questionnaire to them, while anonymizing their identities.

This approach is one solution among others for collecting data while preserving confidentiality.

Next, we removed the lines containing missing or erroneous values, thus ensuring greater integrity.

We then trained our environment to minimize bias as much as possible in our data.

The results of this dataset are displayed below:

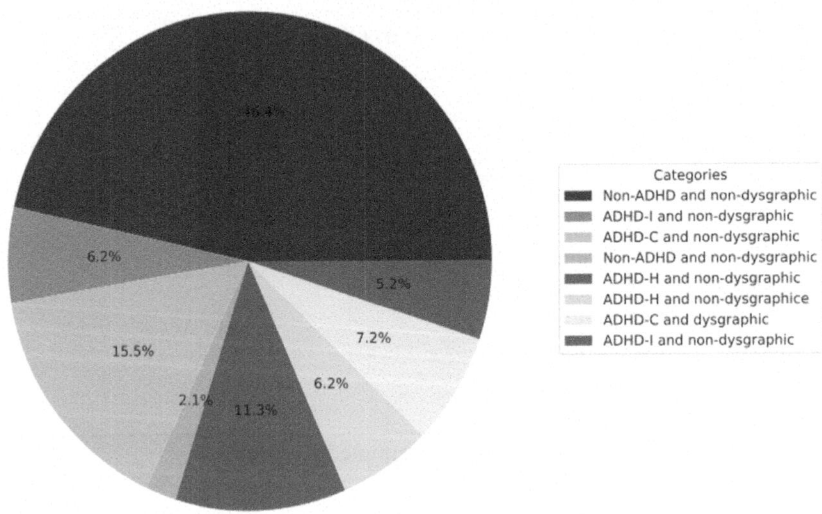

Fig. 2. ADHD Feedback and Dysgraphia

The pie chart in Fig. 2 shows us that 6.2% of hyperactive ADHD children, 7.2% of ADHD children with the two most dominant symptoms, and 5.2% of inattentive ADHD children are dysgraphic.

The pie chart in Fig. 3 shows that 8.2% of inattentive ADHD children, 14.4% of those with the two dominant symptoms, and 8.2% of hyperactive children concentrate for less than 10 min.

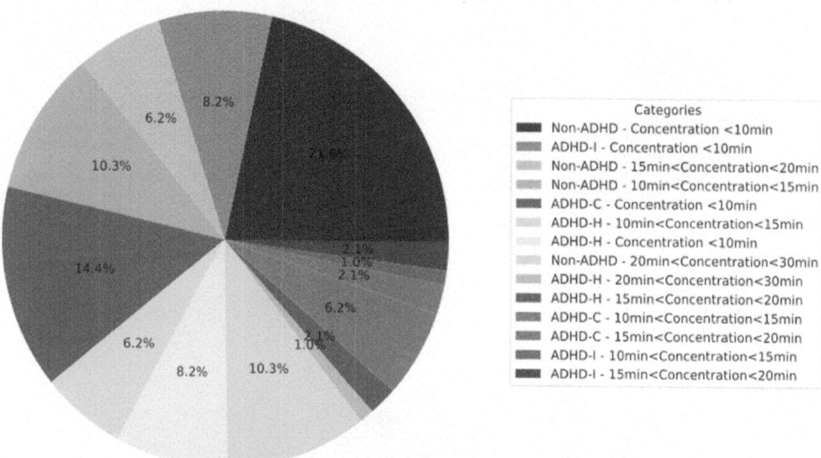

Fig. 3. ADHD Feedback and Concentration Span

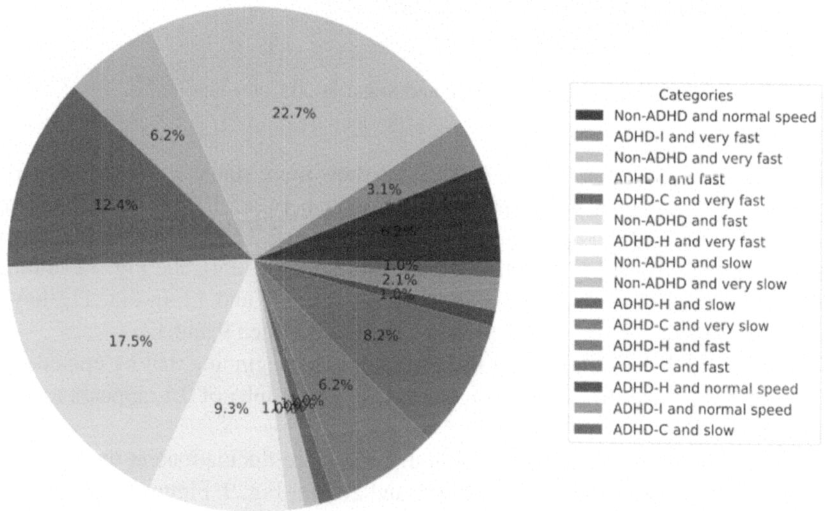

Fig. 4. ADHD Feedback and Walk Speed

According to the pie chart results in Fig. 4, 12.4% of hyperactive and inattentive ADHD children, 3.1% of inattentive ADHD children, and 9.3% of hyperactive ADHD children walk very quickly.

The pie chart in Fig. 5 shows the different percentages of sugar food consumption according to ADHD Feedback. For example, 3.4% of children with the two most dominant symptoms eat pastries. 2.5% of inattentive ADHD children eat sweets. 4.4% of hyperactive ADHD children eat biscuits.

The figures from 6 to 13 represent the convergence of Q-Learning, SARSA, and Combined using two metrics: the learning rate (alpha) and the discount factor (gamma).

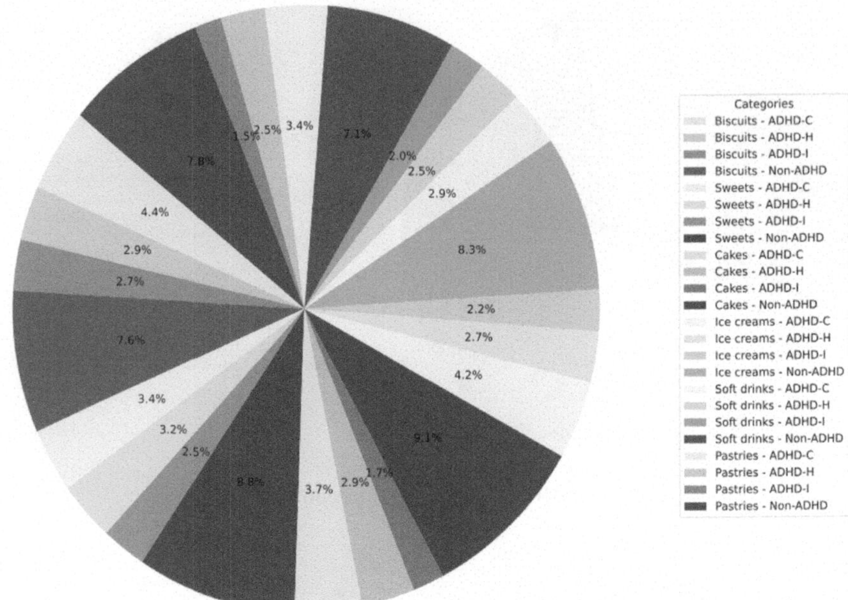

Fig. 5. ADHD Feedback and Sugar Food Consumption

Using alpha, the algorithms in Figs. 6, 7, and 8 show more stable convergence starting from episode 250. In Fig. 6, the averages are generally between 10 and 12. In Fig. 7, they are around 7 to 11, and in Fig. 8, they approach between 7.7 and 11. Using gamma, the algorithms in Figs. 10 and 11 stabilize starting from episode 250, and Fig. 12 stabilizes from episode 200. In Fig. 10, the averages are between 7.7 and 12. In Fig. 11, they are close to the range of 9 to 11, and in Fig. 12, they are between 9 and 12.

Figures 6 and 7 show significant fluctuations at the beginning, but by episode 100, the curves begin to stabilize. The orange curve, with an alpha of 0.1, appears to be the most stable.

In Figs. 8 and 9, we observe that although there are fluctuations at the beginning, the curves stabilize at episode 250 for Fig. 8 and 200 for Fig. 9. Figure 8 shows that the curve with the minimum average is green and orange (alpha = 0.2, alpha = 0.1), while the most stable curve is red (alpha = 0.5). Figure 9 summarizes Q-Learning, SARSA, and Combined convergence averages using alpha. We note that the three most stable curves are the golden one representing Q-Learning with an alpha of 0.9, followed by the gray curve, which is the Combined with an alpha of 0.5, and the dark blue curve representing Q-Learning with an alpha of 0.01.

Figures 10 and 11 show high fluctuations initially, but the curves stabilize starting from episode 250. We notice that the orange curve with a gamma of 0.1 is the most stable in Fig. 10, with the highest average (11). In Fig. 11, the green curve is the most stable, with a gamma of 0.5 and the highest average (10.5).

Figures 12 and 13 show fluctuations but stabilize at episode 200. In Fig. 12, we observe that the most stable curve, which has the highest average, is the green curve,

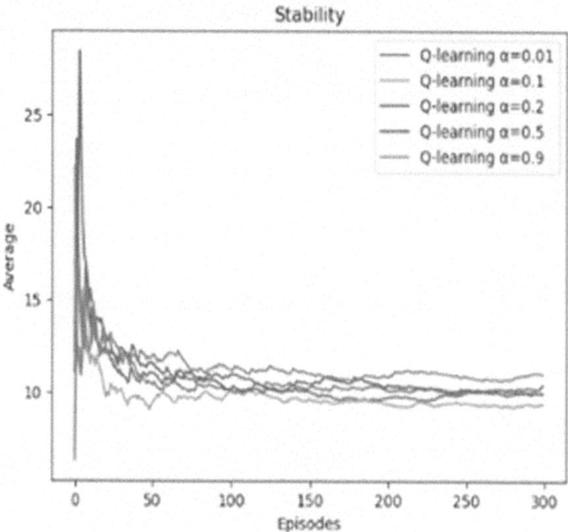

Fig. 6. Q-Learning average over episodes through alpha

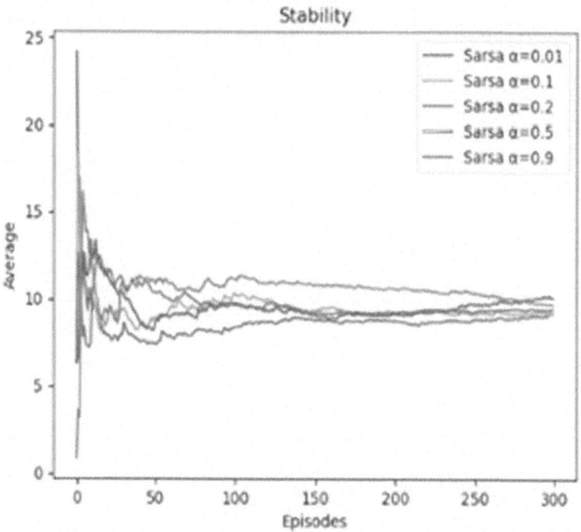

Fig. 7. SARSA average over episodes through alpha

with a gamma of 0.5. Figure 13 also summarizes the algorithm convergences, but it is based on gamma this time. We see that the three curves with the most stability are the orange curve representing Q-Learning with a gamma of 0.1, followed by the light purple curve Combined with a gamma of 0.5, and the dark purple curve representing SARSA with a gamma of 0.5.

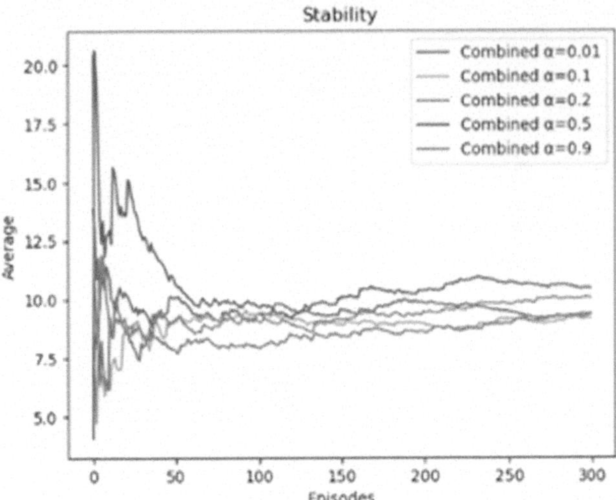

Fig. 8. Combined average over episodes through alpha

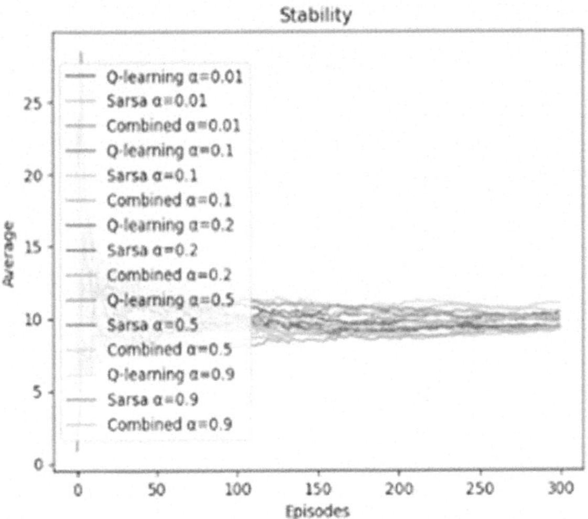

Fig. 9. Algorithms average over episodes through alpha

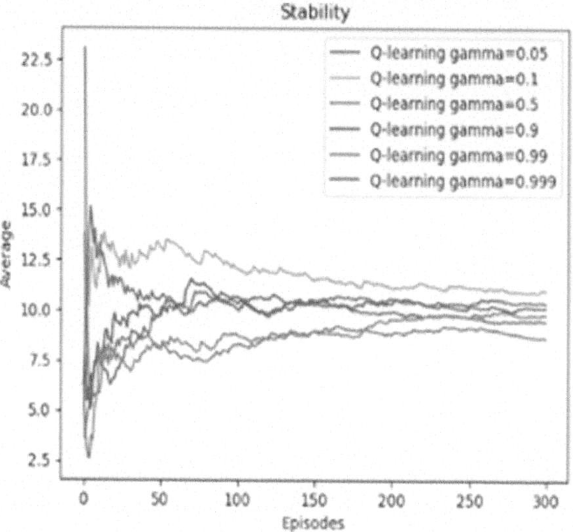

Fig.10. Q-Learning average over episodes through gamma

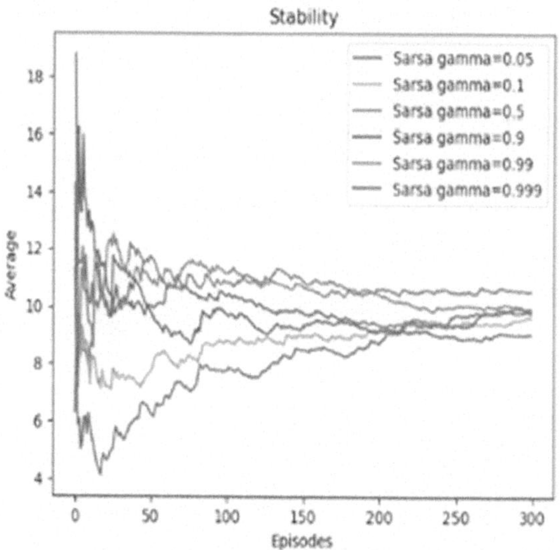

Fig.11. SARSA average over episodes through gamma

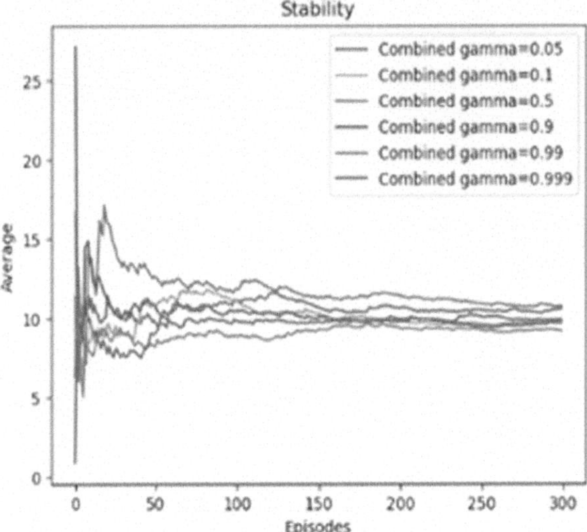

Fig. 12. Combined average over episodes through gamma

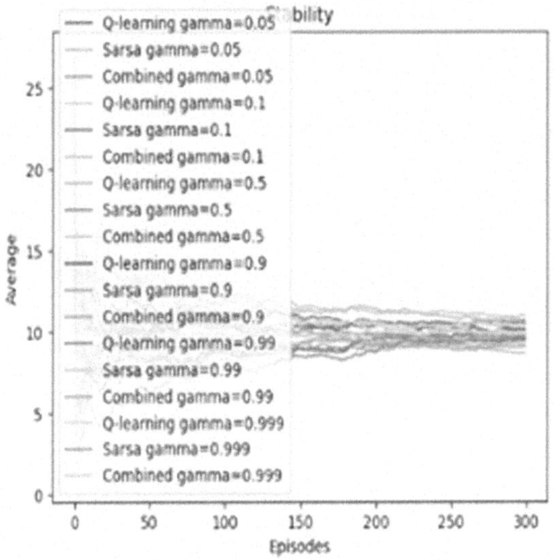

Fig. 13. Algorithms average over episodes through gamma

5 Conclusion and Perspectives

In conclusion, in this paper, we have mentioned various cognitive difficulties related to individuals with ADHD, cited works that have applied reinforcement learning to this neurodevelopmental disorder, suggested a reinforcement learning approach starting from Markov Decision Processes to the use of Q-Learning and SARSA algorithms, and then combined the two algorithms. We concluded that the convergence of the algorithms stabilizes when the learning rate or alpha is 0.5 for Combined and 0.01 for Q-Learning and when the discount factor or gamma is 0.5 for both Combined and SARSA. Therefore, if we wish to simulate the behavior of an ADHD agent, SARSA would be the ideal candidate, as ADHD patients tend to explore more than non-ADHD individuals. However, if we want to simulate it and ensure it exploits more, the hybrid method or Q-Learning would be preferable in this case. Further research must be conducted to establish interactions and coordination between the agent with this disorder and their environment to reduce symptoms. For example, the ADHD child and their family could be accompanied by a specialist step by step.

References

1. Addicott, M.A., Pearson, J.M., Schechter, J.C., et al.: Attention-deficit/hyperactivity disorder and the explore/exploit trade-off. Neuropsychopharmacology **46**(3), 614–621 (2021)
2. Aster, H.-C., Waltmann, M., Busch, A., et al.: Impaired flexible reward learning in ADHD patients is associated with blunted reinforcement sensitivity and neural signals in ventral striatum and parietal cortex. NeuroImage: Clin. **42**, 103588 (2024)
3. Chevrier, A., Schachar, R.J.: BOLD differences normally attributed to inhibitory control predict symptoms, not task-directed inhibitory control in ADHD. J. Neurodev. Disord. **12**, 1–12 (2020)
4. Becker, A., Daseking, M., Kerner Auch Koerner, J.: Cognitive profiles in the WISC-V of children with ADHD and specific learning disorders. Sustainability **13**(17), 9948 (2021)
5. Zhang, S., Song, H., Wang, Q., et al.: Fuzzy logic guided reward function variation: an oracle for testing reinforcement learning programs. arXiv preprint arXiv:2406.19812 (2024)
6. Gupta, A., Badr, Y., Negahban, A., et al.: Energy-efficient heating control for smart buildings with deep reinforcement learning. J. Build. Eng. **34**, 101739 (2021)
7. Staddon, J.E.R.: The dynamics of behavior: review of Sutton and Barto: reinforcement learning: an introduction. J. Exp. Anal. Behav. **113**(2) (2020)
8. Naeem, M., Rizvi, S.T.H., Coronato, A.: A gentle introduction to reinforcement learning and its application in different fields. IEEE Access **8**, 209320–209344 (2020)
9. Tejasvi, P., Kumar, T.: A smart system facilitating emotional regulation in neurodivergent children. Procedia Comput. Sci. **235**, 3257–3270 (2024)
10. Chiu, Y.-H., Lee, Y.-H., Wang, S.-Y., et al.: Objective approach to diagnosing attention deficit hyperactivity disorder by using pixel subtraction and machine learning classification of outpatient consultation videos. J. Neurodev. Disord. **16**(1), 71 (2024)
11. Wang, T., Sakamoto, T., Oshima, Y.U., et al.: Detection and classification of teacher-rated children's activity levels using millimeter-wave radar and machine learning: a pilot study in a real primary school environment. IEEE Access (2025)
12. Anu, P.J., Singh, K.R.: Ensemble and deep learning via median method for learning disability classification. Bull. Electr. Eng. Inform. **14**(3), 2031–2041 (2025)
13. Bansal, D., Verma, A., Sharma, A., et al.: Improving object recognition and diagnostics with advanced learning techniques
14. Ardulov, V., Martinez, V.R., Somandepalli, K., et al.: Robust diagnostic classification via Q-learning. Sci. Rep. **11**(1), 11730 (2021)
15. Miletić, S., Boag, R.J., Forstmann, B.U.: Mutual benefits: combining reinforcement learning with sequential sampling models. Neuropsychologia **136**, 107261 (2020)
16. Lai, Y.H., Chang, Y.C., Tsai, C.W., et al.: Data fusion analysis for attention-deficit hyperactivity disorder emotion recognition with thermal image and Internet of Things devices. Softw.: Pract. Exp. **51**(3), 595–606 (2021)

17. Tedeschi, T., Baioletti, M., Ciangottini, D., et al.: Smart caching in a data lake for high energy physics analysis. J. Grid Comput. **21**(3), 42 (2023)
18. Sutton, R.S.: Reinforcement Learning: An Introduction. A Bradford Book (2018)
19. Abohashish, S.M.M., Rizk, R.Y., Elsedimy, E.I.: Trajectory optimization for UAV-assisted relay over 5G networks based on reinforcement learning framework. EURASIP J. Wirel. Commun. Netw. **2023**(1), 55 (2023)
20. Byeon, H.: Advances in value-based, policy-based, and deep learning-based reinforcement learning. Int. J. Adv. Comput. Sci. Appl. **14**(8) (2023)
21. Talebi, M.S., Jonsson, A., Maillard, O.: Improved exploration in factored average-reward MDPS. In: International Conference on Artificial Intelligence and Statistics, pp. 3988–3996. PMLR (2021)
22. https://catalog.data.gov/dataset/supertracker-source-code-and-foods-database
23. Cohen, R., Cohen-Kroitoru, B., Halevy, A., et al.: Handwriting in children with Attention Deficient Hyperactive Disorder: role of graphology. BMC Pediatr. **19**, 1–6 (2019)
24. Ron, H.: Impact of learning disability on self-image and socialization in children in primary education. Proyecto de investigación (2024)
25. Katsarou, D.V., Efthymiou, E., Kougioumtzis, G.A., et al.: Identifying language development in children with ADHD: differential challenges, interventions, and collaborative strategies. Children **11**(7), 841 (2024)
26. Kilic, E.B., Koksal, E.: The interaction between attention deficit and hyperactivity disorder and nutrition. Curr. Nutrit. Rep. **14**(1), 1 (2024)
27. Meachon, E.J., Klupp, S., Grob, A.: Gait in children with and without ADHD: a systematic literature review. Gait Posture **104**, 31–42 (2023)
28. Text="CE:[DBSearch]Score: 0.70crsid: b4d4ibtype: bibarticleAuthors: Olweya Mohammed Abd El Baaki, Enas Raafat Abd El Hamid, Safaa Taha Zaki, Amani Salah El Din Alwakkad, Rania Nabil Sabry, Eman Mohamed ElsheikhYear: 2021JournalTitle: Bulletin of the National Research CentreArticleTitle: Diet modification impact on ADHD outcomeVolumeID: 45IssueID: 1FirstPage: 1LastPage: 8BibArticleDOI: 10.1186/s42269-020-00466-x" Abd El Baaki, O.M., Abd El Hamid, E.R., Zaki, S.T., et al.: Diet modification impact on ADHD outcome. Bull. Natl. Res. Centre **45**, 1–8 (2021)
29. Napoli, M., Krech, P.R., Holley, L.C.: Mindfulness training for elementary school students: the attention academy. J. Appl. Sch. Psychol. **21**(1), 99–125 (2005)
30. Zhong, L.: Comparison of Q-learning and SARSA reinforcement learning models on cliff walking problem. In: 2023 International Conference on Data Science, Advanced Algorithm and Intelligent Computing (DAI 2023), pp. 207–213. Atlantis Press (2024)
31. Liu, Y.-T., Yang, J.-M., Chen, L., et al.: Overview of reinforcement learning based on value and policy. In: 2020 Chinese Control and Decision Conference (CCDC), pp. 598–603. IEEE (2020)

The Impact of an AI-Enhanced Training on Student Wellbeing and Quality Education: ResilienceBOT Case Study

Thauraya Makni[1(✉)], Asma Baghdadi[2,3], and Rania Chaouali[4]

[1] Human and Social Sciences Department, Buckinghamshire New University, Wycombe, UK
22223043@bucks.ac.uk
[2] Esprit School of Business, Ariana, Tunisia
asma.baghdadi@esprit.tn
[3] Groups in Intelligent Machines, National Engineering School of Sfax (ENIS), University of Sfax, 1173, 3038 Sfax, Tunisia
[4] Esprit School of Engineering, Ariana, Tunisia
chawali.rania@esprit.tn

Abstract. In this study, we explore the potential of ResilienceBOT (RB), a customised AI-powered digital companion, to support university students in Africa in building resilience and enhancing well-being. Following a gamified training on character strengths in education, five students participated in a two-week RB intervention. Thematic analysis of semi-structured interviews conducted one week after the initial training revealed that participants had improved their resilience by 21% in resilience, their well-being by 43%, and their positive education by 15%. After RB intervention, we noted improvements of 8%, 2%, and 40%, respectively. This indicates that the impact on wellbeing has been sustained and that there has been an increase in positive education and resilience. We also recorded improvements in participants' self-awareness, growth mindset, interpersonal skills and overall mental health. Thus, our research contributes to the growing field of Positive Education (PosEd) and also promotes scalable, AI-enhanced interventions aligned with the Sustainable Development Goals (SDGs). We aim to improve student well-being and support the development of ethical, resilient future leaders in African higher education.

Keywords: Emerging technologies · Artificial Intelligence · AI chatbot · LLMs · GAI · SDGs · Resilience · Wellbeing · Positive Education

1 Introduction

Despite rapid improvements in digital infrastructure and the adoption of new technologies in Africa's higher education sectors, students continue to face high

F. Kamoun et al. (Eds.): AFRICATEK 2025, LNICST 676, pp. 37–55, 2026.
https://doi.org/10.1007/978-3-032-16635-7_3

levels of academic stress and low resilience. In the African context, economic instability, health issues, and educational challenges such as disruptions to teaching and schooling, are immediate factors that significantly elevate stress levels and diminish well-being, as reported by to the World Bank [51], the World Health Organisation (WHO), and the UNICEF [50]. Across the African continent, mental health issues among students are gaining increased attention. The WHO reports that globally, in 2021, an estimated 1 in 7 (15%) adolescents aged 1019 years experienced mental health conditions [49]. The WHO underscores the importance of creating supportive environments and providing psychosocial support to promote adolescent mental health. Implementing such strategies can enhance students' resilience and well-being [49].

Seligman & Csikszentmihalyi [39] two of its pioneers, define Positive Psychology (PP) as a science of positive subjective experience, positive individual traits, and positive institutions that promise to enhance life quality and avert the pathologies that emerge when life is barren and meaningless. It has also been defined as the study of the strengths and virtues that enable individuals, communities and organisations to thrive [14,41].

This study presents a detailed description of the use of emerging technologies AI to help students recognise and apply their key character strengths in education, thereby supporting their study, skills development, achievement and personal growth. One of the main barriers that can be challenged by tailoring the AI-enhanced chatbots to the unique student's individuality is sustainability of learned new skills. In the present research study the combination of a gamified psychological resilience training followed by an AI-driven learning is being used to challenge the cocreation of a SIM. AI in the serve of such Gamified PPIs presents an innovative combined approach to reinforce recentlty acquired behaviours and maintain the impact of PPIs over time [37,54].

The components of well-being, as indicated by Ryff and Keyes [35], include self-acceptance, autonomy, mastery of the environment, life purpose, positive interpersonal relationships and personal development. According to Ryff [34], this well-being also lies in the realization of one's potential, the search for meaning and commitment to ethical goals and values.

Resilience is defined as the capacity to bounce back from setbacks, overcome adversities, and successfully adapt to the environment [29]. It serves as essential for students under academic pressure. Actually, developing young people's emotional resilience should be a major component of youth development programs, according to the WB and S4YE [51]. They emphasise how resilience building, which is critical to PosEd programs, requires mastery of resilience methods.

Given the importance of promoting resilience and wellbeing in academic achievement, incorporating AI-powered tools into higher education has the potential of giving students with a sustainable real time scalable, accessible, and effective support. Strategies to implement this intervention focused among other things on the SDGs of the United Nations [45], mainly SDGs 3, 4, 5, 8, and 10 aiming to actively contribute to the development of future responsible leaders who are ethical and accountable. A pan-African approach to diversity and inclusion in education is required under SDG 10 (Reduced Inequalities), guaranteeing that people from a variety of socioeconomic, linguistic, and cultural backgrounds participate.

Combining human expertise with AI, in particular Generative AI (GAI) and Language Models (LLMs), to co-create coaching and supervision for students is one strategy to achieve SDG 10. Gamified Ai-Powered psychological resilience training assists both men and women in stably mastering stress reduction techniques, promoting emotional agility, cultivating problem-solving abilities, overcoming hurdles, and improving self-confidence through experiential learning, all of which are in line with SDGs 3 (Well-Being and Good Health), 4 (Quality Education), 5 (Gender Equality), and 8 (Decent Work and Economic Growth). In addition to promoting mental health and wellness, it assists students in cultivating a resilient and growth-oriented mindset, two traits that are essential for both employment and entrepreneurship.

The remaining of this paper is organized as follows: Sect. 2 offers a review of the literature that highlights connections between resilience, well-being, and academic performance, while also examining the role of emerging technologies in higher education, particularly the impact of artificial intelligence on adaptive learning, student engagement, and support for mental well-being, and delineates the research objectives and contributions. Section 3 details the methods and procedures, detailing the participants and sampling techniques, the design and architecture of the RB chatbot, as well as the research instruments and measures utilized. Section 4 presents the results and discussion, where we interpret the findings in relation to our goals and the existing body of literature. Lastly, Sect. 5 concludes the paper by summarizing the main insights and suggesting avenues for future research.

2 Literature Review and Research Contributions

2.1 Interconnection Between Resilience, Well-Being, and Academic Performance

Resilience and psychological well-being are pivotal in mitigating stress and enhancing academic outcomes. A study examining gender differences among senior high school students in Ghana found that higher academic resilience correlates with improved well-being, suggesting that fostering resilience can lead to better academic and personal development [1]. Moreover, a systematic review highlighted that resilience and dispositional hope are crucial in promoting psychological well-being among college students. Actually, character strengths-based PP Interventions (PPIs) have been shown to increase student engagement, resilience, wellness, and achievement [16]. However, PP is a field deeply rooted in theories, concepts and frameworks such as Maslow Hierarchy of needs [21] and Rogers's client-centred theory [30] which is considered a relatively a young and emerging science [8,26,33,39] compared to other mainstream sciences. Despite its development, PP is often criticised for its limited effectiveness in having a real positive and lasting impact on people's lives [55]. These factors serve as protective mechanisms against stress, anxiety, and depression, further underscoring the importance of resilience in the academic context [53]. PPIs, such as character strengths coaching and resilience building, have been demonstrated to increase students' academic motivation and stress management [40]. Research indicates that including PosEd into the curriculum enhances academic and psychological outcomes [46].

2.2 Emerging Technologies for Higher Education: AI's Role in Adaptive Learning, Student Engagement, and Mental Well-Being Support

Research indicates that supportive environments and psychosocial interventions are effective in promoting adolescent mental health. The WHO & UNICEF's "Helping Adolescents Thrive Toolkit" [49] emphasizes the importance of strategies that promote positive mental health and prevent mental health conditions among adolescents. Implementing such strategies can enhance students' resilience and well-being. The incorporation of AI into education is transforming traditional learning settings by offering students with adaptive learning, real-time feedback, and customised support [19]. AI-powered chatbots have been successfully deployed in a number of educational settings, increasing student engagement and learning results [10]. However, the use of AI-powered solutions for resilience and wellbeing remains an underexplored research topic, particularly in Tunisia. In fact, the integration of technology in mental health interventions has shown promising results. For example, a study conducted by [44] evaluating a chatbot-delivered stress management coaching program for students demonstrated its effectiveness in reducing stress levels and enhancing coping mechanisms. The chatbot provided psychoeducation, facilitated self-reflection, and guided mindfulness practices, contributing to improved student well-being. Similarly, research on a chatbot-based mindfulness-based stress reduction program carried out by [17] indicated its feasibility and acceptability among university students. Participants reported a decrease in stress and increased mindfulness, highlighting the potential of chatbot interventions to support mental health.AI-powered chatbots offer a scalable solution by providing tailored, on-demand support to students, reducing the strain on institutional resources and increasing long-term well-being.By integrating chatbots into educational settings, we can create supportive environments that promote positive mental health and well-being among students. Recent research has shown promising results from the use of AI-driven chatbots to promote mental health and wellbeing and improve PPI outcomes (Table 1). The main reported limitations concerned the short duration of AI intervention [13,31,36] and the lack of fine-tuning the chatbot with PPIs materials [43].

Table 1. Earlier contributions on the usage of AI driven chatbots to enhance PPIs' outcomes

Ref	Participant / Control groups	Study: all RCT	Duration	Intervention	AI chatbot	Outcomes	Limitations
[13]	34/36	Psychological distress & wellbeing, mood tracking.	2 weeks	CBT	Woebot, Smartphone app	Significant reduction of depression and anxiety's symptoms. Effective in delivering CBT	Short intervention, No follow-up period to investigate if gains were sustained.
[31]	42/40	Psychological distress & wellbeing	4 weeks	CBT	Elomia, Generative (GPT-2), Smartphone app	Significantly effective in reducing tendency to depression, anxiety, and negative emotions. Enhanced self-confidence.	Not mentioned
[36]	72+70/105	Psychological distress & wellbeing, depression, anxiety, insomnia	3 weeks	CBT	Emohaa, CBT bot, ES Bot, WeChat messenger	Practical and effective tool for reducing mental distress and for support.	Short duration, Very simple intervention to draw conclusions.
[43]	75/94	Psychological wellbeing, Resilience, perceived stress, goal attainment.	6 months	AI coaching for goal attainment	Generative (GPT), Vici, Telegram messenger	Increase in goal attainment, but not in other measures	AI Chatbot wasn't programmed to deliver CBT

2.3 Research Aim and Contributions

Significant societal and economic issues confronting Tunisia call for creative solutions to increase resilience and well-being. This study will contribute by using an AI-based solution to address PosEd's sustainability difficulties and promoting and enhancing self-led change awareness and readiness in educational settings. Therefore, the study aims to establish a scalable and culturally acceptable solution for Tunisia's particular setting and issues by using an AI-enhanced chatbot named RB. This study investigates the performance and prospective abilities of the RB when adapted to the socioeconomic and cultural characteristics of Tunisia's environment, which differs from the Western environment. It so provides fresh perspectives on how to effectively improve student well-being and the long-term sustainability of education, notably PosEd, in Tunisia and, more broadly, in Africa. This research explores the roles of personalised AI-enhanced chatbots in maintaining the benefits of PosEd outcomes. One of the main limitations of PPIs is the inability to get participants to early engage with the interventions due to their reluctance to participate in the training [48,52]. In this regard, gamification has been shown to have positive effects on a variety of motivational, behavioural and cognitive learning outcomes [9]. The PP researcher who created an innovative serious game named COPOPT [20] aimed to provide users with a self-help tool to enhance their resilience and wellbeing [38]. Therefore, this project combines serious game-based learning (COPOPT) and AI-driven reinforcement (RB) to produce a comprehensive strengths-oriented educational solution. The primary advantages are that COPOPT encourages early engagement and provides a required baseline of PPIs knowledge, whereas RB facilitates long-term involvement. RB is designed to help university students in leveraging their abilities and freshly acquired knowledge beyond intervention sessions by offering ongoing and personalised guidance. Terblanche et al. [43] have shown that AI coaching is effective in a narrow application, suggesting that AI could democratise coaching in a cost-effective, scalable manner. A key limitation is related to the unsustainability of PPIs' long-term impact on individuals [52]. RB is developed to maximize the potential benefits of PT in the practice of PP. To achieve this goal, we designed the chatbot architecture, developed its functionalities, and effectively integrated the custom-designed materials of the PP researcher. Our work contributes to the discussion over the role of AI in education by presenting a novel way to promoting resilience in African university students. The study shows that by adapting RB to the unique needs of students and deploying it across two weeks, AI can boost excellent educational outcomes and wellbeing in higher education. The study provides novel insights into the efficacy of AI-driven interventions to promote resilience, as well as a model for integrating digital mental health.

Accordingly, our research will test the following hypothesis H: AI-Enhanced Training (RB) effectively improve student wellbeing and the sustainability of education. Hypothesis H is evaluated via qualitative assessment in a semi-structured interview.

3 Methods and Procedures

3.1 Participants and Sampling Method

Participation in our study is voluntary, with no pressure or coercion applied. To ensure fairness and eliminate bias, voluntary participation is open to all university students. Eligibility to participate in the intervention is determined according to the inclusion criteria defined from the outset (i.e. graduate and post-graduate full-time students at a university, above 18 years, and currently feeling anxious or stressed about their studies), and exclusion criteria (i.e., No clinical diagnosis, not receiving any treatment for anxiety or depression, including prescribed pharmaceuticals, therapy, or counselling) from outset. To guarantee smooth on-site participation, participants are students from a private engineering university who are physically present and available in Tunis, the capital.

Based on pre-established inclusion and exclusion criteria from a screening questionnaire, eleven volunteer students were selected from a broader pool. In order to provide a range of viewpoints on the efficacy of the RB chatbot in enhancing the resilience, wellbeing, and sustainable education of Tunisian students, the selection method was designed to be at least substantially representative of this population. The following diversity criteria were satisfied by the study participants: 1. Gender 2. Age Distribution, 3. Geographic Diversity, even if they presently reside in Tunis; 4. Differences in financial position and origins; 5. Parents' educational backgrounds; and 6. Type of current home (Table 2). Prior to participation, we obtained an informed consent from each student. All data collected during the study was anonymized before use, and access to this data is restricted exclusively to the research team for the purpose of preparing and evaluating the personalized chatbot.

Table 2. Participant Screening Questionnaire Summary

VARIABLE	PERCENTAGE
University type	
Public	0%
Private	100%
Gender	
Female	80%
Male	20%
Socioeconomic backgrounds/social class	
Originated from major urban centres areas	40%
Originated from suburban medium-size town	40%
Originated from rural villages	20%
Parents' educational background (whether they completed secondary school or not)	
Only one	20%
Both	80%
Type of your residence you're currently living in in Tunis	
Villa	60%
Apartment	40%

3.2 RB Chatbot Architecture and Experience Design

The proposed architecture (Fig. 1) outlines the RB design for PP maintenance. This end-to-end pipeline represents the processing of semi-structured interview vocals into structured text representations joined with PP-related inputs, leveraging Retrieval-Augmented Generation (RAG) for PP-oriented response generation. The system begins with speech-to-text conversion using Whisper, an Automatic Speech Recognition (ASR) model, which transcribes vocal inputs into text. The transcribed text is then joined to PP-related documents in multiple formats, including JSON and PDF, ensuring adaptability for downstream processing. To facilitate semantic understanding, text embeddings are generated using the all-MiniLM-L6-v2 model, which enables efficient representation of textual data. Cosine similarity is subsequently employed to assess the relevance between embeddings, categorizing the similarity as strong or weak. The processed embeddings are then integrated into a RAG framework, enhancing information retrieval and response generation. Additionally, a MiniCpon-V module is incorporated to refine prompt engineering within the system. Finally, the system is deployed using Streamlit, providing an interactive and user-friendly interface. This architecture offers a robust foundation for a conversational aged tailored to positive psychology support enabling personalized interactions and contextual understanding . The study is carried out in two phases:

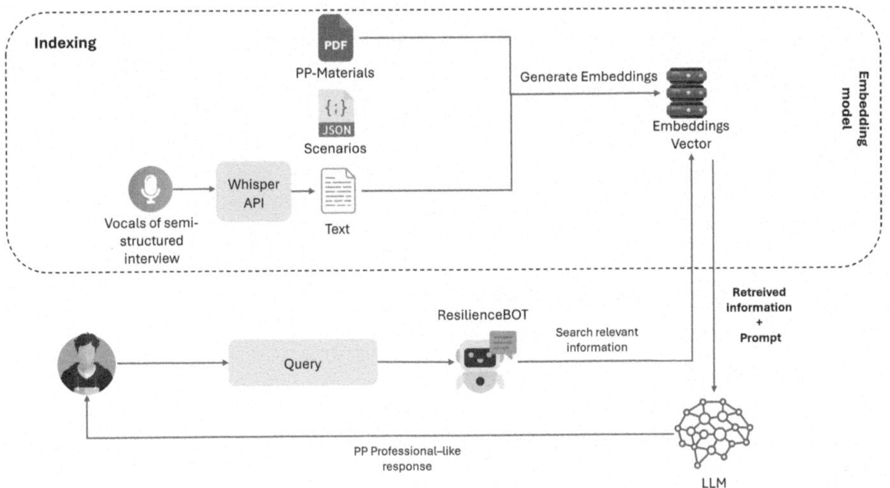

Fig. 1. Architecture design of the ResilienceBOT

RB design Phase 1:
We configured RB using two input steps, and before each input was used, we assessed its services. The first step is optimizing the RB's functionality and user engagement strategy. The PP researcher adapted material from Active Constructive Response (ACR) [25], Appreciative Inquiry [6,7,42,47], and key Appreciative Coaching (AC) concepts [24] in order to make the AI-driven chatbot simple to use and more engaging. The second step of optimizing the RB with regard to the information and resources it uses when communicating with users consists of the researcher's Resilience Training Program materials and artifacts, as well as approximately 500 scenarios she created using another previously trained ChatGPT 4o (during a one-year period from December 2023 to December 2024), with 30% of them tailored to the Tunisian context and culture. Together, the same trained ChatGPT then develops roughly 500 questions for the RB evaluations. The RB additionally includes participant notes from the training.

RB Design Phase 2:
Five new versions (RB01, RB02, RB03, RB04, and RB05) are the end product of this process, and each one is tuned and altered based on feedback from students. Only five students agreed to spend two weeks with RB following the completion of the COPOPT intervention. With the use of each student's intervention notes, RB is programmed to remind them of their goals, strengths, and instructional tactics. In order to reinforce learning strategies and encourage students to reflect on how they have utilized their skills, RB will check in with them every day. To ascertain how the intervention affected the participants, the study uses semi-structured qualitative interviews that are subsequently thematically analyzed [3,4,23].

3.3 Research Instruments and Measures

Data Collection and Analysis
Before engaging with RB, the study's main intervention, five participants who voluntarily chose to continue the intervention using the AI-driven RB took part in a 60-minute individual semi-structured interview (also referred as pre-intervention data collection). The same five participants are invited to participate in a second, approximately 60-minute, semi-structured individual interview once the intervention is completed (Fig. 2). Themes are identified after data collection.

The interview framework comprises two parts: participants' experience with COPOPT character strengths-based activities and its effect on their resilience and well-being, and their experience in using RB and its effect on their resilience and well-being. The interviews are conducted in person by the researcher, and the data is collected by audio recording and transcribed after obtaining the participants' consent. The data is then analysed using Thematic Analysis, which enables themes to be coded and mapped from the data collected during interviews as long as the phases of establishing trustworthiness are satisfied [3,23]. All the themes identified as falling within the definition of resilience, well-being and positive education [34,35,39] are used in a deductive analysis guided by the mapping of data to these concepts. The inductive analysis, on the other hand, examine other emerging themes alongside new insights into the strengths and weaknesses of RB. All of the data analysed is particularly useful for exploring how participants experience resilience, wellbeing, and meet quality education goals in real contexts and for capturing unexpected findings and new hypotheses for future research [4,12,32].

We used mixed-methods study approach combining computational text processing and qualitative thematic analysis [15,22]. Python-based natural language processing (NLP) methods were used to extract themes, determine thematic frequency and identify patterns in the interview transcripts in order to analyse the qualitative data by mapping and coding inductive and deductive qualitative analyses on the concepts of resilience, well-being and quality education to increase rigour [2]. A systematic and reproducible study of student responses is ensured by our computational method, which enhances conventional thematic coding.

Semi Structured Interviews: Pre and Post Engagement with RB
Five participants who voluntarily chose to continue the intervention partake in a semi-structured interviews to delve deeply into the specifics of their experience. Firstly, we carried out a pre-intervention interview after the COPOPT sessions. The questions focus on the students' experiences, self-awareness and the perceived benefits of applying the strengths. Once the RB different customised versions with respective student's notes and feedback, each of the 5 participants receive and access to his/her personalised chatbot for two weeks, containing personalized notes from the gained knowledge from the gamified training. The chatbot reinforce the application of character strengths and other related PPIs in their educational activities.

Secondly, we conducted a post-chatbot semi structured interview (lasting impact) after engagement with the chatbot. The second evaluation is aimed to assess any sustained impact or usefulness of the chatbot and the potential retention of learning strategies. Participants are invited to take part in a semi-structured individual interview lasting approximately 60 min after completing the AI maintenance period. The interview framework comprises two parts: participants' experience pre and post the interaction period with their RB and its effect on their well-being and resilience. The interviews are conducted in person by the PP researcher and the data is collected by audio recording and transcribed after obtaining the participants' consent.

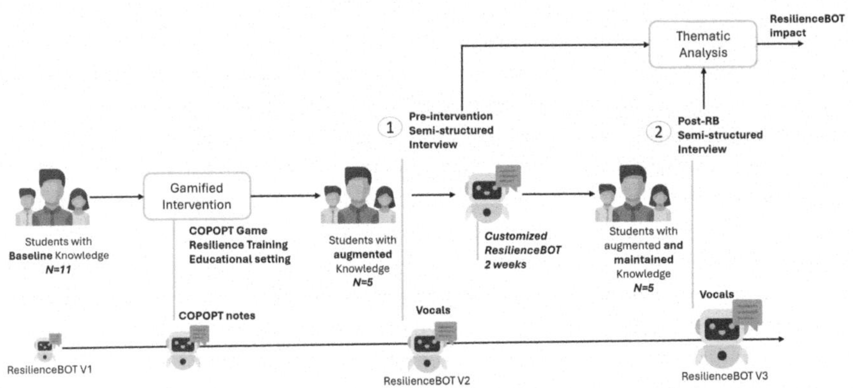

Fig. 2. Knowledge Acquisition Pipeline for Participants and ResilienceBot

The structure of this intervention allows for the reinforcement of enhances student knowledge while iteratively improving RB's capabilities. The process, as shown in Fig. 2, integrates gamified learning, chatbot interaction, and qualitative assessments. Initially, eleven students engage in a gamified intervention using the COPOPT Game, with RB V1 collecting interaction data to build a foundational knowledge base. Five students who demonstrate increased knowledge then participate in a pre-intervention interview, providing insights for improvement, while RB V2 incorporates vocal interactions and structured feedback. A two-week personalized chatbot intervention follows, allowing RB to adapt and support knowledge retention. Finally, a post-intervention interview assesses the chatbot's impact, contributing to a thematic analysis, while RB V3 is refined to enhance interactive learning.

4 Results and Discussion

We analyzed the participants' potential gains post interaction with the chatbot based on Wellbeing and Quality Education constructs using Positive Psychology & Educational Research perspectives, outlined in:

1. **Student Well-being (Key Psychological Dimensions)** All the following well-being dimensions are captured. Emotional well-being includes stress management, emotional agility, and self-compassion while cognitive well-being encompasses self-reflection, problem-solving, resilience, and mentality shifts. Social well-being is centred on motivation, engagement, and advancement based on strengths, while physical Well-Being includes stress reduction techniques and the formation of enduring health-promoting habits. [3,45,49]
2. **Quality Education (Key Educational Psychology Indicators)** Our findings highlight a promising role in supporting quality education in accordance with the standards of educational research. In fact, one of the components is Engagement & Active Learning. Problem-Solving, Growth Mindset, and Experiential Learning all exhibit experiential learning and growth. A precise definition of critical thinking and in-depth contemplation may be found in contemplation & Meaning Making. The foundations of skill development and personal growth are mastery, long-term well-being, and strength-based learning. Motivation Growth and Well-Being Sustainability covers self-directed learning and a lifelong learning mindset [45,49].

Peer participation helped participants develop their interpersonal skills, which progressed toward participant-RB learning, question-based communication, and fostering deep connection to the self.

Participants progressed from emotional awareness to more adaptive self-regulation and self-compassion. Their experiences with RB enhanced their capacity to express vulnerability, handle stress, and develop internal motivation through emotional honesty and self-compassion, despite the fact that their emotional tendencies were acknowledged in their early reflections.

Cognitive gains were demonstrated by the transition from emergent strategic thinking to structured contemplation and rephrasing of challenges. After starting with problem analysis, participants used questioning techniques, adopted a developmental attitude, and began to view mistakes as teaching opportunities. By offering chances for metacognitive reflection and cognitively stimulating stimuli, RB's design made this transition easier.

Intentional self-motivation, time management, and proactive self-awareness replaced the passive reliance on values as the primary motivators.

Participants' post RB-interaction narratives demonstrate improvements in resilience, stress management, and willingness to act independently after initially expressing a dependence on their inner faith or outside influences. This Knowledge Acquisition Process is illustrated by the Fig. 3.

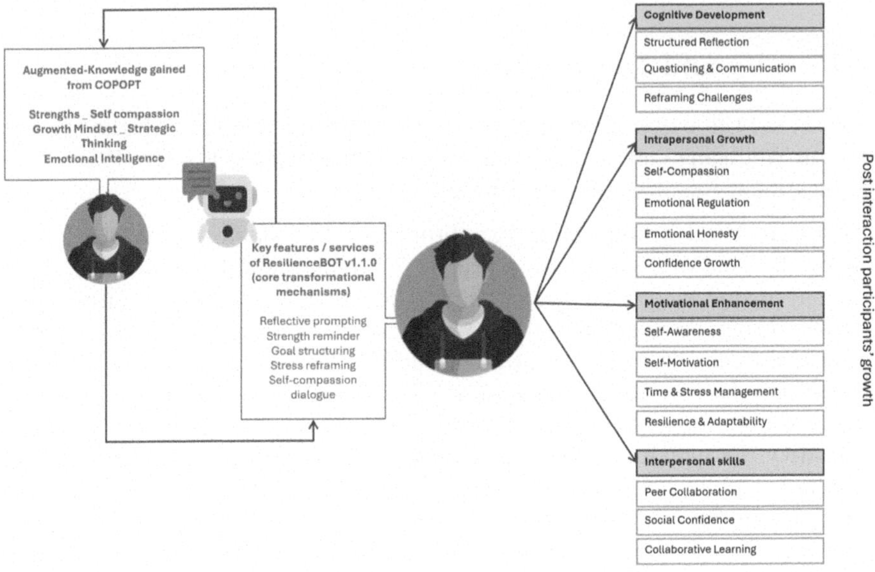

Fig. 3. Knowledge Acquisition Through the dynamic and iterative Interaction with ResilienceBot

The appearance of behaviours like cognitive reframing, experimenting with new behavioral techniques, and incorporating mindfulness and habit formation into daily life indicates that some participants are undergoing a novel adaptive growth process even after a brief intervention of two weeks. The themes and subthemes that appeared (Fig. 5) could be interpreted as better psychological flexibility and self-regulated learning progress. Moreover, these individuals have begun adapting and exploring instead of making decisions intuitively. The positive and consistent consolidation of BR supports and reinforces the action stage of the TransTheoretical Model of change and development (TTM). Apparently, RB gave the students the opportunity to gradually retain freshly learnt material, which helped them transition into Action stage [27,28]. Some participants also mentioned Learning from failure, applying new strategies in real life, and tracking goal progress. These include anchoring, behavioral testing, and reframing techniques showing deeper engagement. These findings support the direction towards upgrading RB to another version that is even more effective in promoting developmental habit formation, strategic reflection, and behavioral support

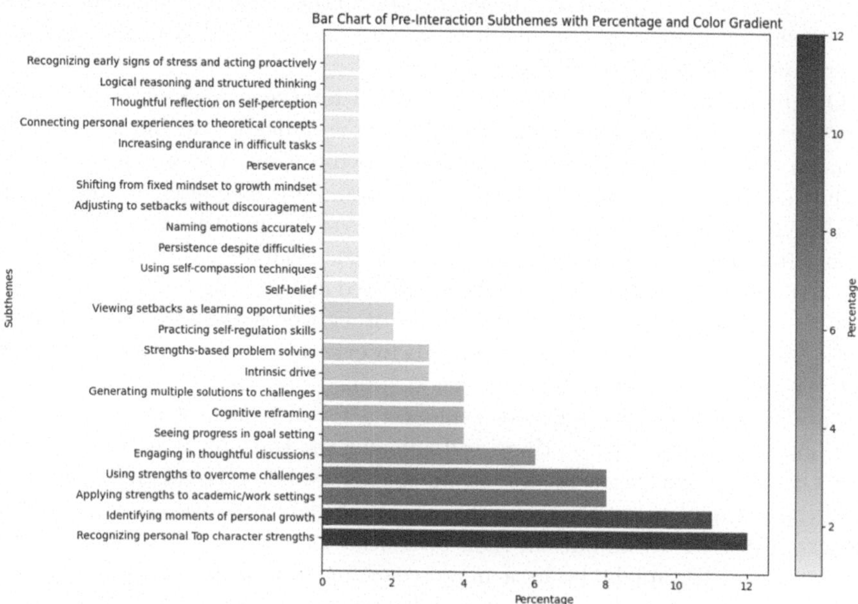

Fig. 4. Bar Chat of Pre-interaction Subthemes with Percentage and Color Gradient

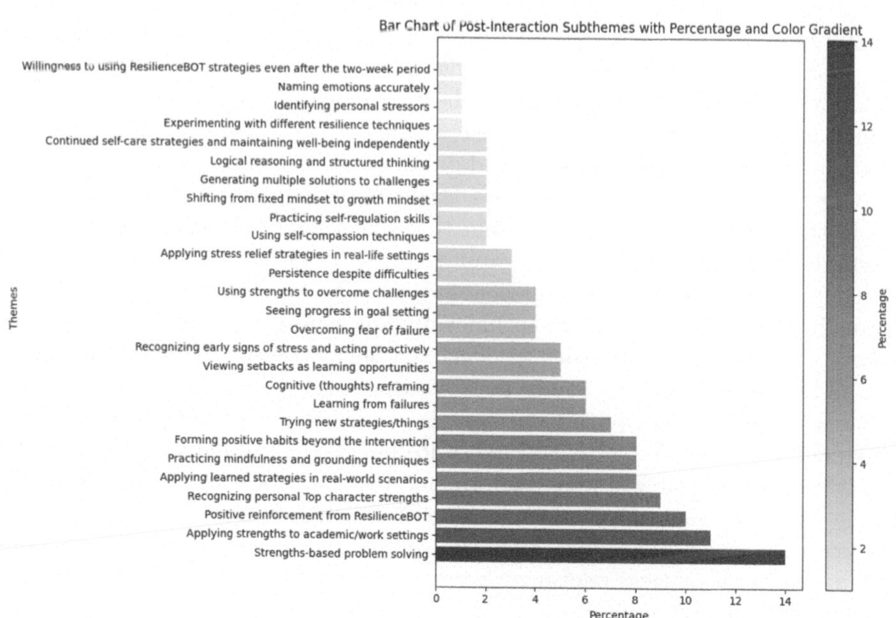

Fig. 5. Bar Chat of Post-interaction Subthemes with Percentage and Color Gradient

(Fig. 4). In addition, several respondents reported that they have identified, used, and considered their character qualities in both personal and academic settings. Awareness and a focus on taking action.

Our preliminary data from semi-structured interviews conducted one week after participants completed the COPOPT game indicate growing gains in the domains of resilience, well-being, and positive education. These gains, reflected in the relative frequencies of coded subthemes, were estimated to be around 21% for resilience, 43% for well-being, and 15% for positive education. Two weeks after interacting with ResilienceBOT, the relative importance of these domains appeared to shift, with resilience-related codes rising to 29%, well-being to 45%, and positive education to 55%. In other words, we saw improvements of 8%, 2%, and 40%, respectively after RB intervention. These findings indicate that the impact on wellbeing has been sustained and that there has been an increase in positive education and resilience. They also suggest that Resilience-BOT may have helped to continue and enhance the learning that began during the COPOPT intervention by promoting greater usability, recall, and accessibility of the personal character strengths that were identified. RB encouraged students to utilise PP techniques in their own situations. These early results reveal how beneficial RB might be as a micro-coaching promp, facilitating metacognitive awareness of growth reflection and personal development. These results underscore the vitality of conversational empathy and positive reflecting in AI positive psychology coaching [43].

Our study contributes to the growing field of game-based learning and AI-enhanced PP training, bridging the gap between theory and practical implementation in higher education institutions. Findings highlight the chatbot's role in sustaining student well-being, improving stress management, and fostering self-awareness. The study underscores how AI-powered digital companions can bridge gaps in mental health support within African higher education using emerging technology for resilience and growth.

Our intervention aims to empower students by helping them recognize and apply their character strengths within the educational sphere. By focusing on strengths rather than deficits, the approach aligns with strength-based educational practices, promoting resilience and self-efficacy. The integration of PT through chatbot support offers an innovative method to reinforce learning and personal development. In order to offer credibility, transferability, dependability, and confirmability, the study is exploratory and qualitative, employing an effective, structured sampling technique [18]. In this case, we combined and used two qualitative sample methods: First, criteria-Based Purposeful & convenience Sampling (Main Strategy) were used. In fact, participants were recruited according to particular inclusion and exclusion criteria that support the objectives of the research which guarantees that the sample meets the goals of the study and improves theoretical relevance. Second, Maximum Variation Sampling was employed to guarantee diversity.

Deliberate inclusion of people from a range of socioeconomic levels and regions of Tunisia who are travelling to the city to study and live improves transferability and trustworthiness, allowing the results to be applied to a larger population. Moreover, Cabanas & González-Lamas' critique [5]: Many PosEd studies' dependability is constrained by their use of self-reporting, small sample sizes, and absence of control groups. The critique still equally applies to the present study, even if semi structured interviews were used to gather detailed qualitative data. Thus, in order to increase scientific rigour, it will be necessary in the future to combine qualitative findings with quantitative measurements, such as mood evaluations, resilience and WB scales, and school performance monitoring, and dealing with big groups.

5 Conclusion and Suggestions for Future Research

Gamification, AI-driven learning, and psychological resilience training challenge the cocreation of a SIM in this study. The highlighted statistics underscore significant challenges in student well-being, resilience, and educational outcomes across the broader African continent. Implementing technological interventions like RB within educational frameworks promising a crucial role in addressing these issues, fostering improved resilience and overall well-being among students. In our work, gamified PPIs and AI reinforcement are integrated in a unique method to help students progress from their character strengths learning. While RB promotes continuing involvement and gradually reinforces learnt behaviours, the COPOPT game enables strengths to be recognised and implemented.

While the COPOPT game provided an engaging, strengths-based entry point into resilience and positive psychology processes, preliminary findings show that, when used alone, its influence may be limited in depth and persistence. Participants' reflections demonstrated positive early shifts in awareness and motivation; but, in order to translate these gains into more integrated, long-term behavioural change, a more structured, thorough, and theoretically grounded intervention is required.

The results of our study will contribute to the creation of scalable AI-enhanced PPIs that will provide useful answers for students' academic achievement, resilience and overall well-being. Students' academic and personal development can be greatly enhanced by implementing character strengths interventions in the classroom.

The present version of ResilienceBOT provided meaningful reinforcement, although its usefulness is limited in breadth. Future research will therefore use the Resilience Development Pathway (RDP), a multi-phase, evidence-based methodology that includes COPOPT, an improved AI companion (ResilienceBOT v3), and targeted reflective practices.

S For educators looking to apply the ideas of PP to their teaching methods, this methodical approach offers a replicable paradigm. There are potential challenges and considerations to take into account: First, motivation and perceived usefulness may have an impact on how engaged students are with the RB. Second, AI ethical concerns related to data privacy and student autonomy will be addressed in accordance with ethical guidelines [11].

Building on our preliminary work, the next phase of research will look into whether this improved ecosystem of gamified and AI-supported learning produces more robust and generalisable effects in resilience, well-being, and human flourishing. In conclusion, the development and implementation of chatbot interventions, such as RB are well-founded in empirical research. By leveraging technology to enhance resilience and well-being, these tools can play a crucial role in sustaining PosEd outcomes and improving the overall mental health of students in Africa.

Across the African continent, mental health issues among students are gaining increased attention. The WHO and UNICEF's "Helping Adolescents Thrive Toolkit" [49] highlights that adolescence is a critical period for mental health interventions. The toolkit recommends strategies such as creating supportive environments, providing caregiver support, and implementing psychosocial interventions to promote mental well-being and prevent mental health conditions among adolescents [49].

Education is as much about empowerment as it is about knowledge. Our intervention's strategies centred on the UN's SDGs [45] and aimed to build ethical and accountable leaders. By combining human experience with the GAI and LLMs to co-create coaching and supervision for students, RB can help achieve all of this while meeting among others, SDG 10's requirements in PosEd. In addition to providing new and creative post-traumatic growth tactics as a preventative measure against mental health challenges, it might help students and other potential users to build their leadership characteristics as well as abilities. RB's facility aims to prevent mental health issues among its patrons, mainly students, through offering 24/7 help as a PP mentor, coach, and supervisor. Our pilot project is the initial stage of additional study aimed at democratizing AI learning.

Future challenges involve making RB mobile-friendly and enabling offline operations alongside extra downloadable supporting content. In order to lessen the exorbitant prices charged by cloud hosting providers, we expect that in the future there will be easily available free cloud-based solutions, particularly from IT companies that support us.

References

1. Amoadu, M., Agormedah, E.K., Obeng, P., Srem-Sai, M., Hagan, J.E., Jr., Schack, T.: Gender differences in academic resilience and well-being among senior high school students in Ghana: a cross-sectional analysis. Children **11**(5), 512 (2024)
2. Bengfort, B., Bilbro, R., Ojeda, T.: Applied text analysis with Python: enabling language-aware data products with machine learning. " O'Reilly Media, Inc." (2018)
3. Braun, V., Clarke, V.: Thematic analysis: a practical guide. QMIP bulletin, 1 (33) (2022)
4. Braun, V., Clarke, V.: Using thematic analysis in psychology. qualitative research in psychology. Qual. Res. Psychol. **3**(2), 77–101 (2006)
5. Cabanas, E., González-Lamas, J.: A critical review of positive education: challenges and limitations. Soc. Psychol. Educ. **25**(5), 1249–1272 (2022)

6. Cooperrider, D.L., Stavros, J.M., Whitney, D.: The appreciative inquiry handbook: for leaders of change. Berrett-Koehler Publishers (2008)
7. Cooperrider, D.L.: Appreciative inquiry: toward a methodology for understanding and enhancing organizational innovation (theory, social, participation). Ph.D. thesis, Case Western Reserve University (1986)
8. Deci, E.L., Ryan, R.M.: The what and why of goal pursuits: human needs and the self-determination of behavior. Psychol. Inq. **11**(4), 227–268 (2000)
9. Dicheva, D., Dichev, C., Agre, G., Angelova, G.: Gamification in education: a systematic mapping study. J. Educ. Technol. Soc. **18**(3), 75–88 (2015)
10. D'mello, S., Graesser, A.: Autotutor and affective autotutor: learning by talking with cognitively and emotionally intelligent computers that talk back. ACM Trans. Interactive Intell. Syst. (TiiS) **2**(4), 1–39 (2013)
11. European Federation of Psychologists' Associations (EFPA): European federation of psychologists' associations (EFPA) (2025). https://www.efpa.eu/
12. Fereday, J., Muir-Cochrane, E.: Demonstrating rigor using thematic analysis: a hybrid approach of inductive and deductive coding and theme development. Int J Qual Methods **5**(1), 80–92 (2006)
13. Fitzpatrick, K.K., Darcy, A., Vierhile, M.: Delivering cognitive behavior therapy to young adults with symptoms of depression and anxiety using a fully automated conversational agent (woebot): a randomized controlled trial. JMIR Mental Health **4**(2), e7785 (2017)
14. Gable, S.L., Haidt, J.: What (and why) is positive psychology? Rev. Gen. Psychol. **9**(2), 103–110 (2005)
15. Guest, G., MacQueen, K.M., Namey, E.E.: Applied thematic analysis. Sage Publications (2011)
16. Lavy, S.: A review of character strengths interventions in twenty-first-century schools: their importance and how they can be fostered. Appl. Res. Qual. Life **15**(2), 573–596 (2020)
17. Li, Y., et al.: Chatbot-based mindfulness-based stress reduction program for university students with depressive symptoms: intervention development and pilot evaluation. J. American Psychiatric Nurses Assoc. 10783903241302092 (2024)
18. Lincoln, Y.S.: Naturalistic inquiry, vol. 75. Sage (1985)
19. Luckin, R.: Machine Learning and Human Intelligence. The future of education for the 21st century. UCL institute of education press (2018)
20. Makni, T.: Copopt games (2025). https://copoptgames.com/. Accessed: 2025-04-05
21. Maslow, A.H.: A theory of human motivation. Psychol. Rev. **50**(4), 370 (1943)
22. Neuendorf, K.A.: The content analysis guidebook. Sage (2017)
23. Nowell, L.S., Norris, J.M., White, D.E., Moules, N.J.: Thematic analysis: striving to meet the trustworthiness criteria. Int J Qual Methods **16**(1), 1609406917733847 (2017)
24. Orem, S.L., Binkert, J., Clancy, A.L.: Appreciative coaching: a positive process for change. John Wiley & Sons (2007)
25. Passmore, J., Oades, L.G.: Positive psychology techniques–active constructive responding. Coach. Prac. 457–460 (2022)
26. Peterson, C., Seligman, M.E.: Character strengths and virtues: a handbook and classification, vol. 1. Oxford university press (2004)
27. Prochaska, J.O., Velicer, W.F.: The transtheoretical model of health behavior change. Am. J. Health Promot. **12**(1), 38–48 (1997)

28. Prochaska, J., Johnson, S., Lee, P.: The transtheoretical model of behavior change. shumaker sa, ockene jk, riekert ka, eds. the handbook of healthy behavior change (2009)
29. Reivich, K., Shatté, A.: The resilience factor: 7 essential skills for overcoming life's inevitable obstacles. Broadway books (2002)
30. Rogers, C.R.: Client-centered therapy. In: Psicoterapia centrada en el cliente: Práctica, implicaciones y teoría, pp. 459–459 (1966)
31. Romanovskyi, O., Pidbutska, N., Knysh, A.: Elomia chatbot: the effectiveness of artificial intelligence in the fight for mental health. In: COLINS, pp. 1215–1224 (2021)
32. Ryan, G.W., Bernard, H.R.: Techniques to identify themes. Field Methods **15**(1), 85–109 (2003)
33. Ryan, R.M., Deci, E.L.: Self-determination theory and the facilitation of intrinsic motivation, social development, and well-being. Am. Psychol. **55**(1), 68 (2000)
34. Ryff, C.D.: Psychological well-being in adult life. Curr. Dir. Psychol. Sci. **4**(4), 99–104 (1995)
35. Ryff, C.D., Keyes, C.L.M.: The structure of psychological well-being revisited. J. Pers. Soc. Psychol. **69**(4), 719 (1995)
36. Sabour, S., et al.: A chatbot for mental health support: exploring the impact of Emohaa on reducing mental distress in China. Front. Digit. Health **5**, 1133987 (2023)
37. Schippers, M.C., Ziegler, N.: Life crafting as a way to find purpose and meaning in life. Front. Psychol. **10**, 2778 (2019)
38. Schueller, S.M., Parks, A.C.: The science of self-help. European Psychol. (2014)
39. Seligman, M.E., Csikszentmihalyi, M.: Positive psychology: an introduction., vol. 55. American Psychological Association (2000)
40. Seligman, M.E., Ernst, R.M., Gillham, J., Reivich, K., Linkins, M.: Positive education: positive psychology and classroom interventions. Oxf. Rev. Educ. **35**(3), 293–311 (2009)
41. Sheldon, K.M., King, L.: Why positive psychology is necessary. Am. Psychol. **56**(3), 216 (2001)
42. Sloan, B., Canine, T.: Appreciative inquiry in coaching: exploration and learnings. AI Practitioner: Int. J. AI best Prac. 1–5 (2007)
43. Terblanche, N., Molyn, J., De Haan, E., Nilsson, V.O.: Coaching at scale: investigating the efficacy of artificial intelligence coaching. Int. J. Evidence Based Coach. Mentoring **20**(2) (2022)
44. Ulrich, S., Lienhard, N., Künzli, H., Kowatsch, T.: Misha–a chatbot-delivered stress management coaching for students: pilot randomized controlled trial
45. UN: United nations: Sustainable development goals (SDGS) (2024). https://sdgs.un.org/. Accessed: 2025-04-03
46. Waters, L.: A review of school-based positive psychology interventions. Australian Educ. Develop. Psychol. **28**(2), 75–90 (2011)
47. Waters, L., White, M.: Case study of a school wellbeing initiative: using appreciative inquiry to support positive change. Int. J. Wellbeing **5**(1) (2015)
48. Westgate, E.C., Wilson, T.D.: Boring thoughts and bored minds: the mac model of boredom and cognitive engagement. Psychol. Rev. **125**(5), 689 (2018)
49. WHO and UNICEF: Helping adolescents thrive toolkit: strategies to promote and protect adolescent mental health and reduce self-harm and other risk behaviours (2021)
50. WHO and UNICEF: Mental health of children and young people: service guidance (2024)

51. World Bank, S4YE: resilience: cultivating emotional resilience among youth to boost their employment prospects (2021)
52. Yakushko, O., Blodgett, E.: Negative reflections about positive psychology: on constraining the field to a focus on happiness and personal achievement. J. Humanist. Psychol. **61**(1), 104–131 (2021)
53. Yan, Z., Zakaria, E., Akhir, N.M., Hassan, N.: Resilience, dispositional hope, and psychological well-being among college students: a systematic review. Open Psychol. J. **17**(1) (2024)
54. Zhou, S., Zhao, J., Zhang, L.: Application of artificial intelligence on psychological interventions and diagnosis: an overview. Front. Psych. **13**, 811665 (2022)
55. van Zyl, L.E., Gaffaney, J., van der Vaart, L., Dik, B.J., Donaldson, S.I.: The critiques and criticisms of positive psychology: a systematic review. J. Posit. Psychol. **19**(2), 206–235 (2024)

Deep Learning Based Methods for Breast Cancer Diagnosis

Sameh Souli[1,2(✉)], Amira Soltani[2,3], Rimah Amami[4], and Sadok Ben Yahia[1]

[1] Faculty of Sciences of Tunis, University Tunis El-Manar, 2092 Tunis, Tunisia
sameh.souli@esprit.tn

[2] Esprit School of Business, IMA Department, Industrial Zone Chotrana II, B.P. 160 Technological Pole El Ghazela, 2083 Ariana, Tunisia

[3] National Superior School of Engineering, University of Tunis L.R: LATICE, Tunis, Tunis, Tunisia

[4] Computer Science Department, Imam AbdulRahman Bin Faisal University, Dammam, Saudi Arabia

Abstract. Breast cancer remains one of the leading causes of cancer-related deaths among women worldwide. Its impact on patients' lives and their loved ones is immense, underscoring the crucial need for more effective methods of early detection and diagnosis. This research proposes a CNN-based pipeline for classification of breast histology images.

Over the past decades, artificial intelligence (AI) has emerged as a revolutionary technology in the field of medicine, offering new prospects to enhance the accuracy, speed, and accessibility of breast cancer diagnostics. It is within this context that our paper was developed, aiming to provide healthcare professionals with an efficient and reliable solution for cancer detection and classification using deep Learning. The proposed CNN model achieved an accuracy of 95.6% and an AUC of 0.98.

Keywords: Deep Learning · Artificial Intelligence · Breast cancer · Big Data · Data science

1 Introduction

Examining and analyzing the current situation in the field of detection are crucial steps for assessing the effectiveness, usefulness, and potential for improvement of an application. When looking at existing applications for breast cancer detection [1] [2], it is evident that there are several solutions available on the market. Below, we present some examples of applications associated with breast cancer, while highlighting some of their limitations. First Breast Advocate provides a comprehensive source of information regarding breast cancer, simplifies communication with healthcare professionals, and allows patients to structure their medical journey. Secondly, Breast Cancer Care offers comprehensive support to women facing breast cancer, encompassing information about treatments and resources to promote emotional well-being [3].

F. Kamoun et al. (Eds.): AFRICATEK 2025, LNICST 676, pp. 56–68, 2026.
https://doi.org/10.1007/978-3-032-16635-7_4

These applications utilize artificial intelligence techniques and data modeling of medical data to deliver personalized predictions and recommendations to their users [4, 5]. Their goal is to assist individuals with breast cancer in managing their health status and making informed decisions. However, despite their advantages, breast cancer detection applications have some notable limitations:

1. Limits of the BCRA Test: The results may cause anxiety, and the interpretation of genetic tests should be conducted by healthcare professionals.
2. Limits of Breast Cancer Care: This application is primarily focused on resources in the UK, which may make it less suitable for users outside of this region.
3. Limits of Breast Advocate: This application relies on the accuracy of the information provided by the user regarding their health status, and the recommendations are not always optimally personalized.

Our proposal involves the creation of a cancer detection system using deep learning models. Our focus lies in acquiring high-quality data and processing it to ensure that our models are trained in reliable information. We will also explore approaches aimed at making the results more understandable for healthcare professionals. Finally, we will evaluate the performance of our system by comparing the predictions of our model with the results of existing medical tests. This work distinguishes itself by applying and comparing two CNN configurations to breast cancer detection in Tunisia, leveraging transfer learning with VGG16. This paper is structured as follows: Sect. 2 presents related work, Sect. 3 details our methodology, Sect. 4 discusses experimental results.

2 Breast Cancer

2.1 Analysis of Breast Cancer Statistics

All the statistics presented in this section are from a medical thesis conducted by Dr. Imen Sassi at the Salah Azaiz Institute, based on the study of 20212 human cells.

In Tunisia, breast cancer accounts for 30% of female cancers. Each year, between 800 and 1500 new cases are diagnosed. Currently, one in eight women is affected by breast cancer, and this figure could increase to 1 in 7 within 20 years. Here is a graph representing the age range for patients infected with this disease (Fig. 1).

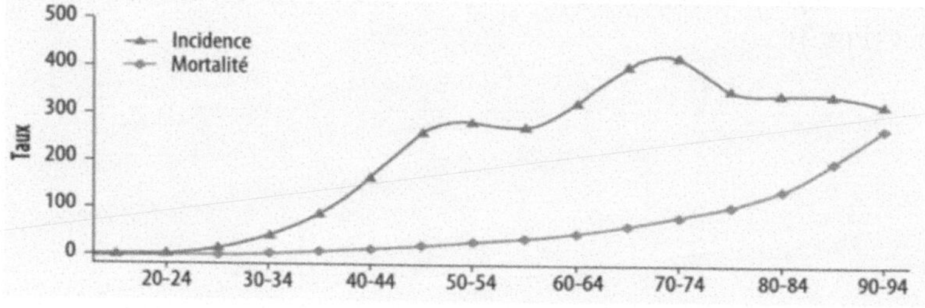

Fig. 1. Age range for women infected with cancer

2.2 The Division of Cancerous Cells

During cell division, DNA can undergo erroneous copies, causing mutations. In most cases, mutated cells self-destruct. However, if the mutation is severe, the cell may lose its ability to self-destruct and continue to multiply, leading to the formation of a tumor, uncontrolled cell proliferation (Fig. 2).

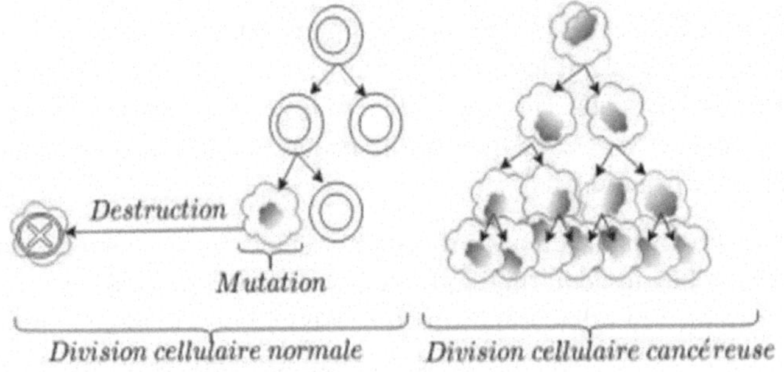

Fig. 2. Cell division.

2.3 The Benign and Malignant Tumor

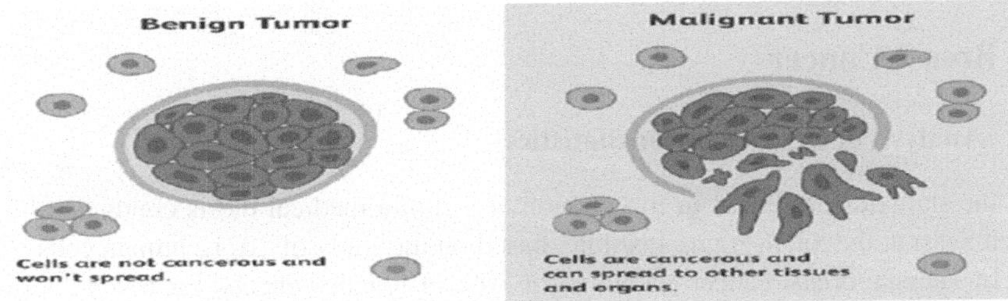

Fig. 3. The benign and malignant tumor.

When a tumor, containing mutations not harmful to health, stops growing, it is classified as benign. However, if the growth persists, it is considered malignant, meaning cancerous (Fig. 3).

3 Convolutional Neural Networks (CNN) for Breast Cancer Detection and Classification

A Convolutional Neural Network (CNN), also known as a convolutional neural network, represents a specific category of artificial neural networks specialized in image recognition and processing [6]. These CNNs are expressly designed to manipulate data pixel by pixel and stand out as particularly powerful image processing and artificial intelligence (AI) systems. They leverage deep learning to accomplish a variety of tasks, including generating and describing visual content. CNNs are frequently applied in the field of Computer Vision [7].

3.1 The Convolutional Layer

The convolutional layer plays a fundamental role in a CNN. It applies filters (also called kernels) to the input image to extract meaningful features. Each filter aims to identify specific patterns such as edges, textures, etc. Convolution operations are performed by sliding the filter over the image with a certain step (stride), thus exploring the entirety of the image and extracting crucial information [8] (Fig. 4).

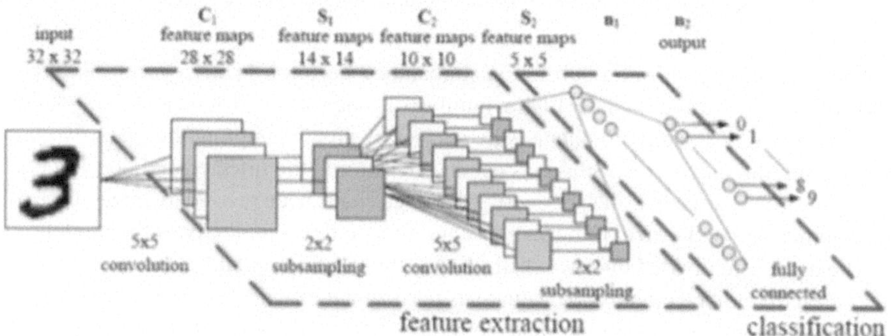

Fig. 4. The different kernels in the convolution phase.

3.2 Pooling Layer

Pooling layers are responsible for reducing the spatial size of feature maps while preserving essential information. A commonly used pooling method is 'max pooling', which involves selecting the maximum value in each region of the map, thereby reducing dimensionality while retaining key features [9, 10].

4 Data Preprocessing

We used the 'Breast Histopathology Images' dataset comprising a total of 24778 images (13,000 benign and 11,778 malignant) from Kaggle. These images represent a diverse sample, covering various cases commonly encountered in the diagnosis and treatment of breast cancer. Each image has been labeled with a binary value, where 1 indicates that the patient has this type of cancer, while 0 indicates that the patient is healthy. Each category is associated with a specific number of JPG-formatted images, as illustrated in the figure below (Fig. 5):

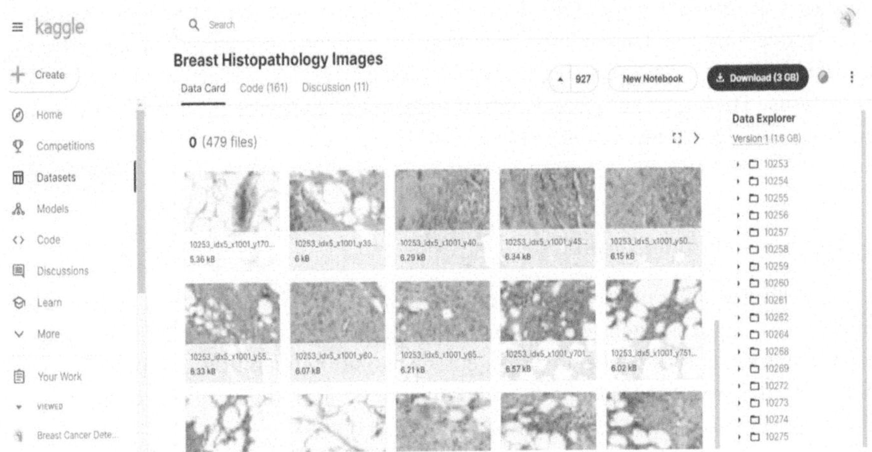

Fig. 5. Representation of the data source and data source format.

Our data source shows a substantial imbalance between breast cancer cases and healthy cases, with a significantly higher number of cancer cases. To ensure fair modeling performance, it is essential to balance the dataset by either sampling the majority class or oversampling the minority class, as needed. We stored the infected and non-infected images in two separate lists, respectively. All images have been resized to a size of 50x50 pixels to normalize the size of the samples and reduce the complexity of the model.

The data were divided into two distinct sets, the training set and the test set, respectively used to train the model and evaluate its performance on unseen data. The data split was done randomly to ensure fair distribution.

Images were resized to 224 × 224 pixels, normalized, and split into 70% training and 30% testing datasets.

We selected 4- and 5-layer CNN architectures to explore the impact of depth on classification performance.

Data preprocessing is an essential step because it allows for the preparation of raw data in a way that makes it compatible with the needs and constraints of learning models, which is essential for solving complex and varied problems.

5 Modeling

5.1 Architecture Details

Compare model variations (e.g., 4 vs. 5 layers), show performance impact in Table 1.

Table 1. The different architectures of our CNN models.

Feature	Model 1	Model 2
Number of Layers	5 Convolutional Layers	4 Convolutional Layers
Number of Iterations	40 Epochs	50 Epochs
Activation Function	Softmax	Softmax
Data-set Split	70% Training/30% Validation	80% Training/20% Validation
Learning Rate	Default (0.001)	Default (0.001)
Batch Size	35	64
Optimization Algorithm	Adam	Adam
Regularization	Dropout: 0.3	None
Image Size	(50, 50, 3)	(48, 48, 3)
Result (Accuracy)	0.9904% Training, 0.9422% Validation	0.9889% Training, 0.8143% Validation

5.2 Visualization of Results

5.2.1 Evaluation Metric for the First Architecture

The accuracy appears to stabilize at a high value of over 0.95, indicating that the model can correctly predict the labels. At the beginning of training, the loss is typically high due to the random initialization of the model's weights and the lack of precision in the predictions. However, towards the end of training, a gradual reduction in loss is observed, suggesting that the model is learning effectively. The graph below illustrates the loss for a 40-epoch training run (Fig. 6).

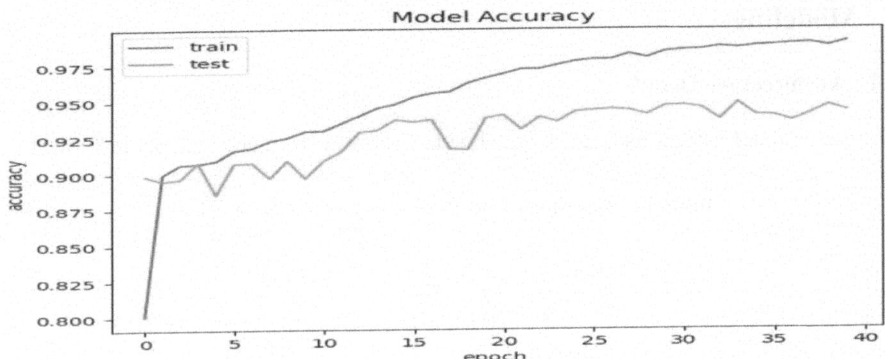

Fig. 6. Increase in accuracy during the iterations for the first model

At the beginning of training, the loss typically starts at a relatively high level. This is due to the random initialization of the model's weights and the fact that the model is not yet able to make accurate predictions. However, towards the end of training, a gradual reduction in loss can be observed, indicating that the model is learning effectively.

The graph below shows which CNN model achieves the loss (loss for a 40-epoch training run) (Fig. 7).

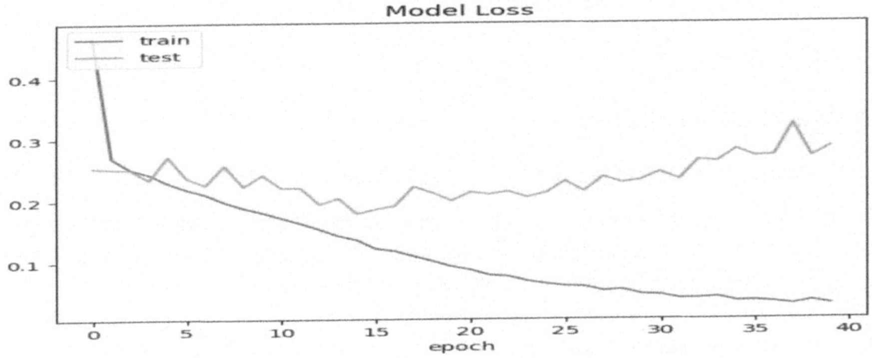

Fig. 7. Error decrease during the iterations

5.3 Confusion Matrix for the First Architecture

To evaluate the performance of the selected models, we will use a confusion matrix to calculate the various evaluation metrics (Fig. 8).

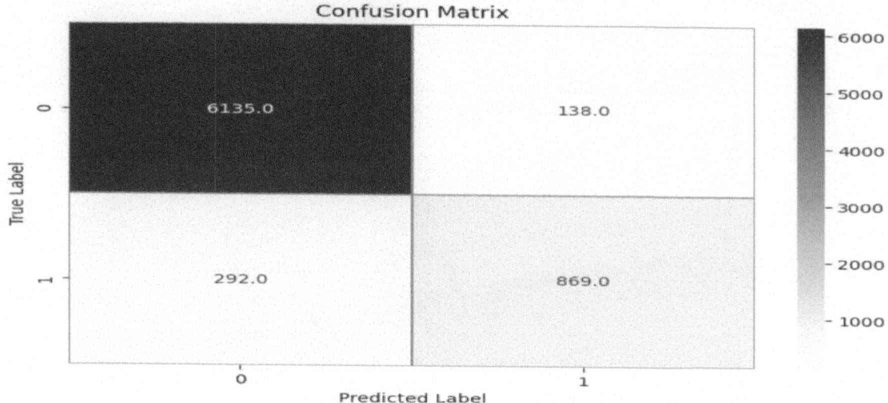

Fig. 8. The confusion matrix for the CNN model

The figure below presents a confusion matrix for the CNN model trained on the test data.

5.3.1 Evaluation Metric for the Second Architecture

To evaluate the performance of our second CNN architecture, we will focus on two crucial metrics: accuracy and the error rate. These two parameters provide a precise assessment of our model's ability to make correct classifications. These two metrics give us a comprehensive picture of the quality of our predictions (Figs. 9 and 10).

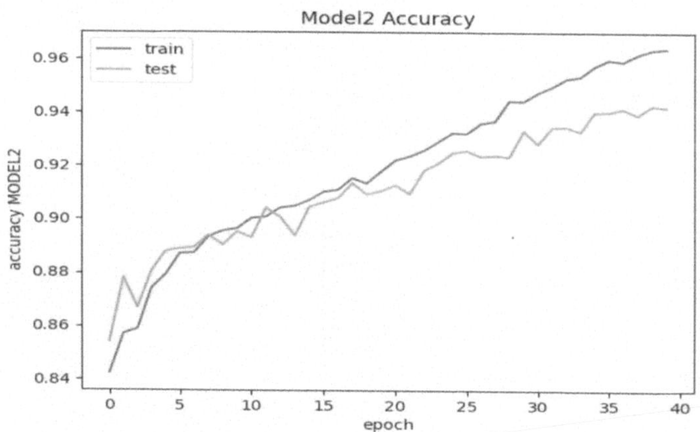

Fig. 9. Increase in accuracy during the iterations for the second model

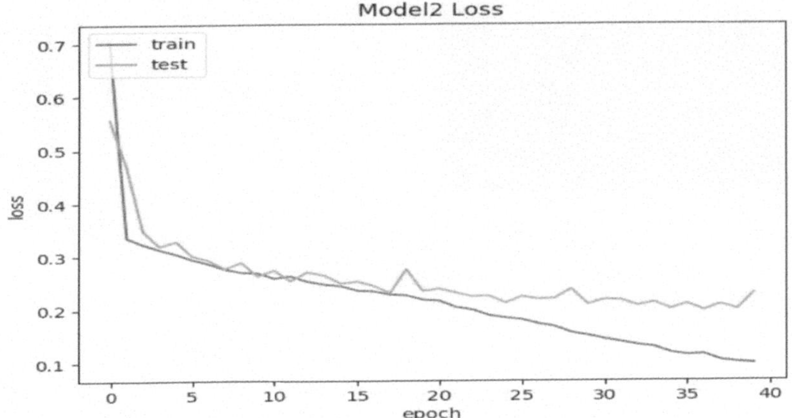

Fig. 10. Error propagation during all iterations for the second model

5.4 Model Optimization

When the performance of a Convolutional Neural Network (CNN) model does not meet expectations in terms of results, it is common to explore alternatives to improve disease detection, and resorting to another transfer learning model, such as VGG16, often proves to be a judicious decision. VGG16 is a pre-trained deep network architecture that we previously mentioned in the preceding chapter, and it has demonstrated its effectiveness in image recognition thanks to its deep convolutional features (Fig. 11).

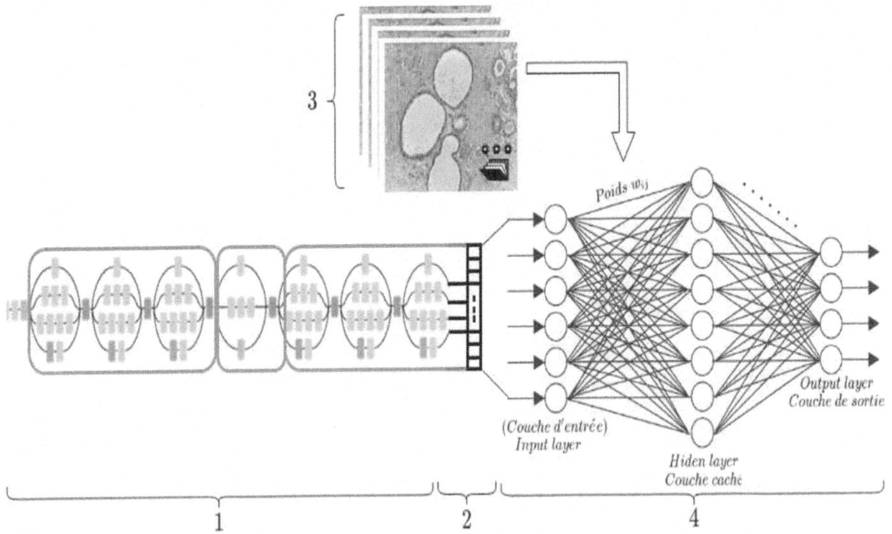

Fig. 11. General Steps of Transfer Learning

When opting for VGG16 for medical image classification, the following steps are taken:

Load the Pre-trained VGG16 Model: Use a Deep Learning library like TensorFlow to import and load the pre-trained VGG16 model. These libraries generally offer ready-to-use pre-trained VGG16 models.

Model Structure and Architecture: It was designed for image classification on large datasets, notably the famous ImageNet dataset [11].

Adaptation of Top Layers: When we talk about fine-tuning the top layers of VGG16, we are referring to customizing the output layers of the pre-trained VGG16 model so that they optimally match our specific task [12, 13]. This step typically involves adding new detection and classification layers [14], specifically designed to adapt to our dataset. VGG16 was selected to mitigate limited dataset size and leverage pre-trained features from ImageNet.

Here is a final architecture of this type of learning (Table 2):

Table 2. VGG16 Model Architecture

FEATURE	STRUCTURE
Model	VGG16
Number of Layers	16 convolutional layers
Number of Iterations	30 epochs
Activation Function	SoftMax
Data-set Split	70% training / 30% validation
Learning Rate	Default (0.001)
Batch Size	35
Optimization Algorithm	Adam
Regularization	Dropout: 0.2
Image Size	(50, 50, 3)
Result (accuracy)	0.9604% training
	0.9522% validation

Model Training: Use your training data to train the model, so that it can acquire the ability to recognize features in the images.

5.5 Model Optimization Evaluation Metric for the Final Architecture

To evaluate the performance of the final CNN architecture, we will focus on a crucial metric: the confusion matrix [15] (Fig. 12).

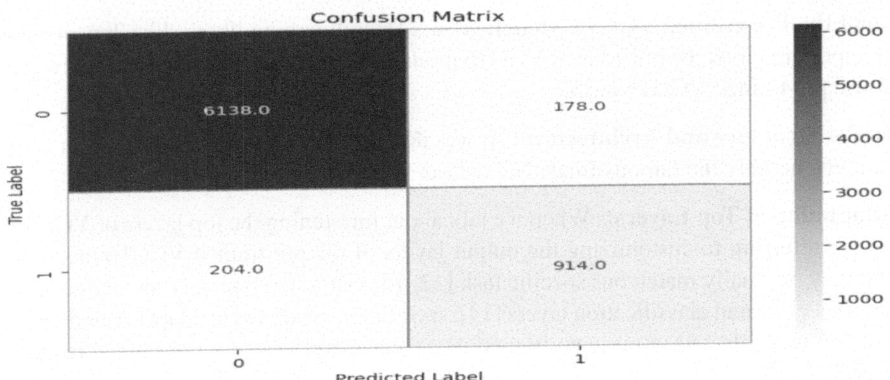

Fig. 12. Final Model Selection

The current model exhibits certain shortcomings in terms of efficiency and reliability, particularly when compared to the previous architectures. With a performance tending towards 0.95. After careful evaluation, it has become evident that the last available model is the best option. Therefore, we have decided to select the second CNN architecture to ensure more robust performance and better accuracy in our classification (Table 3).

Table 3. Classification performance

Class	Precision	Recall	F1-score
Benign	0.96	0.95	0.95
Malignant	0.94	0.96	0.95

The class-wise evaluation reveals a balanced and robust performance of the model across both benign and malignant classes. The **precision** and **recall** values for benign cases are **0.96** and **0.95**, respectively, indicating that the model is highly effective at correctly identifying non-cancerous cases while minimizing false positives. Conversely, for malignant cases, the model achieves a **precision of 0.94** and a **recall of 0.96**, demonstrating strong sensitivity in detecting cancerous tissues, which is critical in medical diagnosis to avoid missed cases. The consistent **F1-scores of 0.95** for both classes further confirm that the model maintains a good balance between precision and recall, ensuring reliable performance for clinical application. These results suggest that the model handles class imbalance well and generalizes effectively to both categories.

The comparative results highlight the superior performance of the VGG16 model over the baseline CNN architecture developed in this study. With an accuracy of **95.6%** and an AUC of **0.98**, VGG16 significantly outperforms the custom CNN (4 layers), which achieved **92.3%** accuracy and **0.94** AUC. This demonstrates the effectiveness of transfer learning in medical image classification tasks, particularly when using a pre-trained architecture like VGG16, which benefits from prior feature extraction capabilities learned on large-scale datasets. Furthermore, while **ResNet50** from Zhu et al. (2020) slightly surpasses VGG16 with **96.2%** accuracy and **0.99** AUC, our VGG16 model provides competitive results despite being trained on a smaller, region-specific dataset. This comparison validates the robustness of our approach and indicates its potential for clinical application, especially in regions with limited labeled medical data (Table 4).

Table 4. Comparison of model performance in terms of Accuracy and AUC.

Model	Accuracy	AUC	Source
CNN (5 layers)	94.2%	0.94	Our work
VGG16	95.2%	0.98	Our work
ResNet50 (Zhu et al.)	96.2%	0.99	Zhu et al., 2024 [14]

6 Conclusion

Our paper outlines the development of an innovative tool for detecting a disease, with an approach that suits the proposed solution. Throughout this paper, we have strived to meet the set objectives, while considering the overall context and user needs. We focused on understanding the business challenges and the data. We presented the general concepts of intelligent systems. For the medical image collection phase dedicated to this disease. This step allowed us to acquire a rich and varied dataset. Data preprocessing and modelling were fundamental steps in our application. In a constant pursuit of improvement, we plan to broaden our approach by integrating new architectures into the modelling. We wish to explore the advancements offered by Transfer Learning algorithms. Our proposed VGG16-based model achieved an AUC of 0.98, significantly outperforming the base CNN. Future work includes validating on external datasets such as INbreast and integrating attention mechanisms for better lesion localization.

References

1. Barba, D., et al.: Breast cancer, screening and diagnostic tools: all you need to know. Crit. Rev. Oncol. Hematol. **157**, 103174 (2021)
2. Banegas, M.P., Bird, Y., Moraros, J., King, S., Prapsiri, S., Thompson, B.: Breast cancer knowledge, attitudes, and early detection practices in United States-Mexico border Latinas. J. Women's Health (Larchmt) **21**(1), 101–107 (2012)
3. Morales-Sánchez, L., Brandão, T., Guil, R.: Emotional intelligence and breast cancer: a systematic review. Heliyon **10**(3), e25061 (2024)
4. Díaz, O., Rodríguez-Ruíz, A., Sechopoulos, I.: Artificial Intelligence for breast cancer detection: Technology, challenges, and prospects. Eur. J. Radiol. **175**, 111457 (2024)
5. Henriksen, E.L., Carlsen, J.F., Vejborg, I.M., Nielsen, M.B., Lauridsen, C.A.: The efficacy of using computer-aided detection (CAD) for detection of breast cancer in mammography screening: a systematic review. Acta Radiol. **60**(1), 13–18 (2019)
6. Teuwen, J., Moriakov, N.: Chapter 20 - convolutional neural networks. In: Zhou, S.K., Rueckert, D., Fichtinger, G. (eds.) Handbook of Medical Image Computing and Computer Assisted Intervention, The Elsevier and MICCAI Society Book Series, pp. 481–501. Academic Press (2020)

7. Balaji, K., Lavanya, K.: Chapter 5 - medical image analysis with deep neural networks. In: Sangaiah, A.K. (ed.) Deep Learning and Parallel Computing Environment for Bioengineering Systems, pp. 75–97. Academic Press (2019)
8. Alzubaidi, L., Zhang, J., Humaidi, A.J., et al.: Review of deep learning: concepts, CNN architectures, challenges, applications, future directions. J Big Data **8**, 53 (2021)
9. Indolia, S., Goswami, A., Mishra, S.P., Asopa, P.: Conceptual understanding of convolutional neural network – a deep learning approach. Procedia Comput. Sci. **132**, 679–688 (2018)
10. Schmidhuber, J.: Deep learning in neural networks: an overview. Neural Netw. **61**, 85–117 (2015)
11. Deng, J., Dong, W., Socher, R., Li, L.-J., Li, K., Fei-Fei, L.: ImageNet: a large-scale hierarchical image database. In: 2009 IEEE Conference on Computer Vision and Pattern Recognition, pp. 248–255 (2009)
12. Liu, Z., Peng, J., Guo, X., Chen, S., Liu, L.: Breast cancer classification method based on improved VGG16 using mammography images. J. Radiat. Res. Appl. Sci. **17**(2), 100885 (2024)
13. Fatima, T., Soliman, H.: Application of VGG16 transfer learning for breast cancer detection. Information **16**, 227 (2025)
14. Zhao, X., Wang, L., Zhang, Y., et al.: A review of convolutional neural networks in computer vision. Artif. Intell. Rev. **57**, 99 (2024)
15. Ahmad, S., Ansari, S.U., Haider, U., et al.: Confusion matrix-based modularity induction into pretrained CNN. Multimed. Tools Appl. **81**, 23311–23337 (2022)

An AIoT Solution for Sleep Apnea Prediction Using ECG Signals

Abderrazek Hachani, Yosra Jmal(✉), and Elyess Maalej

ESPRIT School of Engineering, Tunis, Tunisia
{abderrazek.hachani,Jmal,elyes.maalej}@esprit.tn

Abstract. This work proposes an IoT-based solution that uses ECG signals for early detection of sleep apnea, a lightweight, ECG-based apnea detection system that integrates AI to improve predictive accuracy and patient outcomes. We propose an innovative hardware-software solution designed to leverage ECG sensors and electronic components for real-time cardiac signal acquisition. Our system collects data from multiple ECG sensors, processes the signals, and transmits them to a mobile application acting as both a gateway and a display interface. Furthermore, a web application allows users to visualize their cardiac activity.

By integrating these technologies, our approach enhances predictive accuracy and improves patient outcomes through a lightweight, real-time apnea detection system. Among all tested models, the CNN-based model achieved the highest accuracy, making it the preferred model for real-time prediction. A web application was developed to visualize ECG signals, provide apnea predictions, and alert users when anomalies are detected. The proposed solution demonstrates the potential of combining AI and IoT to support remote and continuous health monitoring.

Keywords: sleep apnea · AI · IOT · machine learning · deep learning · ECG signals

1 Introduction

Every organ in the human body generates electrical impulses during its functioning. These impulses often serve as the focus of medical research aimed at understanding the operation of these organs. Analysing these impulses can indicate either proper organ function or dysfunction. The investigation of these phenomena dates to 1887/1888 [1] when British physicist Augustus Waller successfully determined human cardiac activity using a capillary electrometer. In 1901, Willem Einthoven improved upon Waller's electrometer and developed a formula that distinguishes between the different phases of a cardiac rhythm (P wave, QRS complex, T wave), establishing the nomenclature for ECG. By 1909, researchers diagnosed a case of arrhythmia using an ECG for the first time. Just one year later, the detection of heart attack indicators became possible. In 1952, Hodgkin and Huxley described the principles associated with the biological generation of electrical signals. Following their work, techniques such as EEG, EMG, EOG, and ERG emerged.

F. Kamoun et al. (Eds.): AFRICATEK 2025, LNICST 676, pp. 69–79, 2026.
https://doi.org/10.1007/978-3-032-16635-7_5

Nowadays, these examinations are essential for providing a diagnosis related to organs such as the heart, muscles, the eye, and others. The term "Biopotential" is used to refer to the electrical impulses being examined. To capture these various signals, different BioPotential sensors are employed. Each sensor is designed to capture a specific signal with precise characteristics as presented in Table 1.

Table 1. Specifications and Uses of Biopotentials [2]

Source	Amplitude (mV)	Bandwidth (Hz)	Sensor (Electrodes)	Measurement Error Source	Selected Applications
ECG	1–5	0.05–100	Ag–AgCl disposable	Motion artifact, 50/60 Hz powerline interference	Diagnosis of ischemia, arrhythmia, conduction defects
EEG	0.001–0.01	0.5–40	Gold-plated or Ag–AgCl reusable	Thermal (Johnson) RF noise, 50/60 Hz	Sleep studies, seizure detection, cortical mapping
EMG	1–10	20–2000	Ag or carbon, stainless steel, needle	50/60 Hz, RF	Muscle function, neuromuscular disease, prosthesis
EOG	0.01–0.1	dc–10	Ag–AgCl	Skin potential motion	Eye position, sleep state, vestibulo-ocular reflex

Electroencephalography (EEG), electrocardiography (ECG), electromyography (EMG), and electrooculography (EOG) are vital techniques for monitoring bioelectrical activity in different physiological systems. Each modality employs distinct methodologies, electrode placements, and signal characteristics, tailored to their specific applications.

Electrocardiography (ECG) (as represented in Fig. 1) measures the electrical activity of the heart by placing electrodes on the torso, arms, and legs. Utilizing a 12-lead system, it captures signals from various regions to assess cardiac conditions such as ischemia or infarction. The ECG signals are relatively small in amplitude, making them susceptible to artifacts from muscle activity and electrode-skin motion, necessitating high-quality electrodes and careful placement to minimize interference.

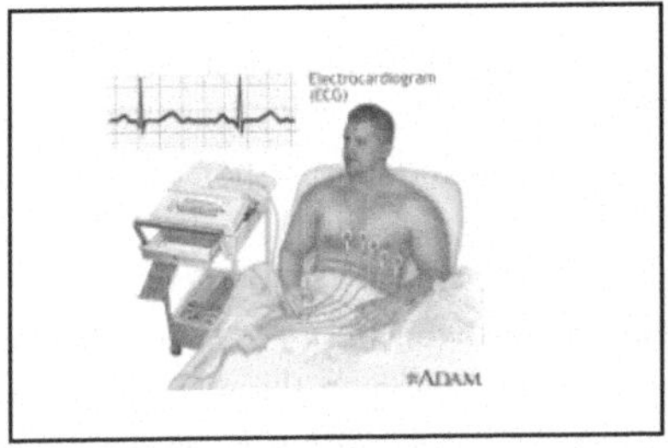

Fig. 1. ECG

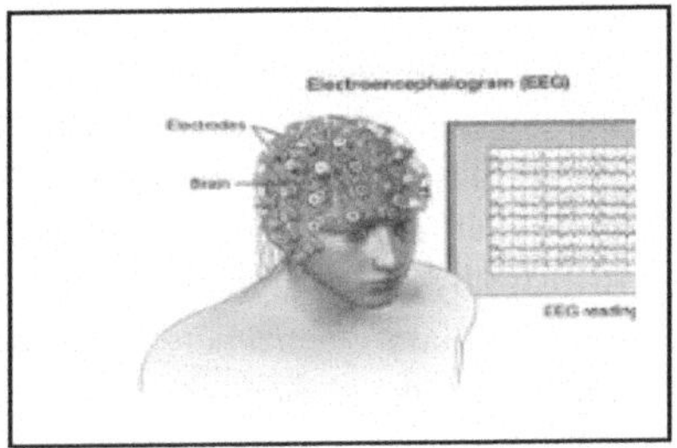

Fig. 2. EEG

Electroencephalography (EEG) (as represented in Fig. 2) in contrast, records brain activity through gold-plated electrodes securely attached to the scalp, following the 10–20 lead system. EEG signals, characterized by their microvolt amplitude, reflect the synchronous activity of vast neuronal populations. While EEG provides insights into neurological conditions like epilepsy, its interpretation is complicated by noise from physiological sources such as muscle activity and eye movements, as well as electrical interference.

Electromyography (EMG) captures the electrical activity of muscles by placing electrodes close to muscle groups. Unlike ECG and EEG, EMG signals have a higher frequency and amplitude, which reduces the impact of motion artifacts. EMG is particularly useful for assessing muscle function and identifying neuromuscular disorders, often requiring invasive electrodes for localized recordings from muscle fibers.

Lastly, **Electrooculography (EOG)** measures the electrical potentials generated by eye movements, with electrodes positioned around the eyes. EOG signals, although small (10 to 100 mV), provide valuable information about eye position and movement disorders. However, practical issues such as motion artifacts and electrode stability pose challenges for long-term recordings.

In summary, while all four modalities serve critical roles in biomedical monitoring, they differ significantly in their applications, signal characteristics, and susceptibility to artifacts. ECG focuses on cardiac health, EEG on brain activity, EMG on muscle function, and EOG on eye movements, each requiring specific considerations for effective signal acquisition and analysis.

1.1 Understanding ECG: A Gateway to Sleep Apnea Detection

An ECG allows for the visualization of cardiac activity in an individual on a graph. This cardiac activity consists of several 'vectors' that represent, as shown in Fig. 3, the contraction of the atria and the injection of blood into the ventricles corresponding to the P wave, the P-Q interval which represents the passage of blood from the atria to the ventricles, the contraction of the ventricles and the ejection of blood into the pulmonary arteries and the aorta represented by the QRS complex, the repolarization of the ventricles or the resting phase of the ventricles (ST segment), and the closure of the pulmonary arteries and the aorta along with the filling of blood vessels in preparation for the next contraction (U wave). The study of these signals allows for the diagnosis of several conditions such as atrial fibrillation, heart attacks (both past and present), genetic heart defects, arrhythmia (abnormal heart rhythm), sick sinus syndrome or bradycardia, Wolff-Parkinson-White syndrome, myocarditis (inflammation of the heart), ischemia or low blood flow to the heart, and other diseases. It is also possible to make predictions about other health issues such as sleep apnea, high glucose levels, obesity detection, or high blood pressure from an ECG. Additionally, the ECG can be used for endurance testing in athletes.

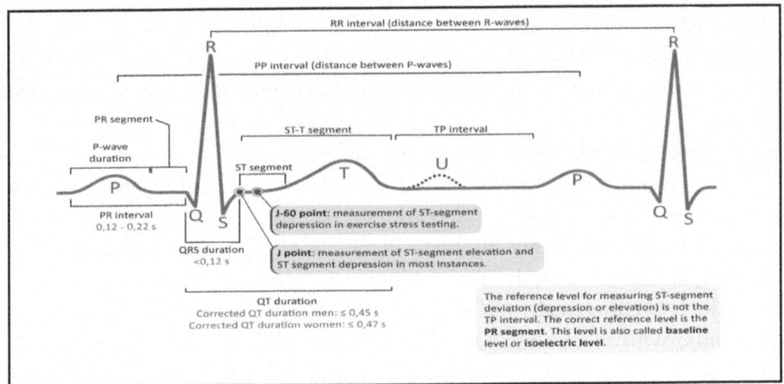

Fig. 3. ECG signal [3]

1.2 Why Does Sleep Apnea Detection Mutters in This Paper?

Sleep apnea is characterized by the interruption of respiratory function in the patient during sleep. It manifests in two forms: non-obstructive sleep apnea and obstructive sleep apnea as shown in Fig. 4. The former non-obstructive is the most common and poses minimal risk to the patient, while the latter is more concerning as it results in complete obstruction of the affected individual's airway.

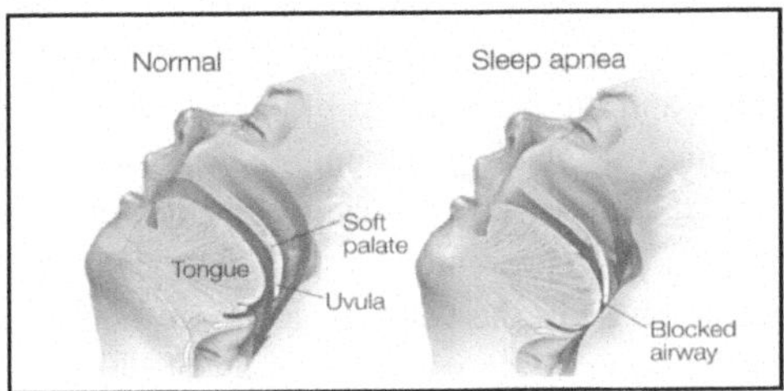

Fig. 4. Non-obstructive sleep apnea and obstructive sleep apnea

A study [4] indicates that one billion people suffer from this condition, representing a significant danger.

The standard method for diagnosing sleep apnea is polysomnography, a comprehensive sleep study that, while effective, is costly, time-consuming, and often inaccessible to many patients [5]. Therefore, it is essential to design a new, accessible, and cost-effective method to predict this dangerous disease early, allowing for the implementation of necessary measures.

Recent advancements in Internet of Things (IoT) technologies, machine learning and deep learning (ML/DL) techniques hold great promises for improving the detection of sleep apnea.

This study focuses on creating an IoT solution that uses P wave ECG signal as a single attribute to predict sleep apnea, aiming to overcome the shortcomings of existing diagnostic methods. By allowing for real-time monitoring of physiological parameters,

IoT devices can continuously collect data, while ML/DL algorithms work to analyze this information and predict the severity of sleep apnea episodes. Ultimately, this research aspires to enhance the accuracy and accessibility of sleep apnea detection, leading to better outcomes for patients and helping them receive the care they need.

The following is how this document is set up: Address the related research on Apnea prediction in Sect. 2. The proposed solution is described in Sect. 3. The results are presented and discussed in Sect. 4. Conclusions are illustrated in Sect. 5.

2 Literature Review

The growing concern over sleep apnea, a condition affecting millions worldwide, has sparked significant interest in developing better methods for its detection and prediction. Recent advancements in ML and IoT technologies offer exciting new possibilities in this area. For instance, the study [6] explored how various machine learning models, including support vector machines and random forests, can predict the severity of obstructive sleep apnea (OSA) with an average accuracy of 44.7%. However, relying on traditional polysomnography data raises questions about how practical and scalable these models are in real-world clinical settings.

Another intriguing approach involves using electrocardiogram (ECG) signals to classify sleep apnea events, as highlighted in the study [7]. This research emphasizes the potential of non-invasive techniques, but challenges such as signal noise and the need for thorough preprocessing to improve accuracy remain significant hurdles. Additionally, the importance of real-time monitoring is underscored in the research titled "Detection of Episodes of Sleep Apnea and Hypopnea" [8]. This study proposes advanced algorithms that integrate multiple physiological signals, which could significantly enhance detection accuracy, but it also stresses the necessity for validation across diverse populations to ensure reliability.

Furthermore, the paper [9] introduces innovative algorithms specifically designed for sleep apnea detection, showcasing improvements in accuracy and efficiency over traditional methods. Yet, these studies point out the need for larger datasets to train and validate these algorithms effectively. A broader perspective is provided in the [10], which synthesizes various machine learning approaches and identifies trends in integrating these technologies with wearable devices for continuous monitoring. However, it notes that many studies still lack comprehensive validation and practical applicability, highlighting a critical gap in the research.

Despite these advancements, several challenges persist, including the need for real-time implementations, improved data quality and diversity, and further exploration of combining machine learning with IoT for effective monitoring. This literature review emphasizes the promise of machine learning in enhancing sleep apnea detection and prediction while calling for practical applications and real-time solutions.

The current research aims to address these gaps by developing an IoT-based solution that leverages machine learning techniques to predict sleep apnea severity, contributing to the ongoing evolution of sleep health technologies.

3 Method

3.1 Real Time ECG Data Collection: Interfacing ESP 32 with AD8932

The ESP32 board interfaces with the AD8232, an integrated signal conditioning module for ECG and biopotential measurements. It amplifies and filters small signals in noisy environments, featuring essential connections for operation with development boards. The AD8232 includes pins for electrode attachment and an LED that pulses in sync with heartbeats. It allows for electrode connectivity checks and provides a clear ECG signal when using three electrodes, minimizing interference. The Fig. 5 represents a shematic representation of ESP32 and AD8232 interface.

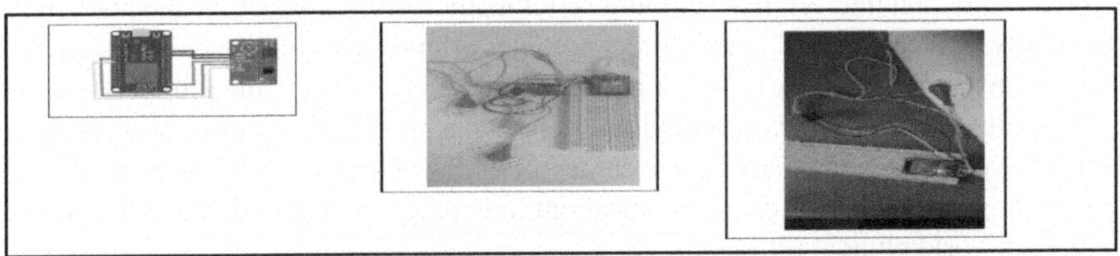

Fig. 5. Schematic Representation of ESP32 and AD8232 Interface

To obtain the appropriate ECG signals, three linked electrodes provide the AD8232 with the heart activity signal. After that, this signal is converted to digital form and sent over the RS232 protocol to the ESP32 device. The mobile gateway is used by the ESP32 to transmit the data to the cloud database (Firebase). The back-end server HTML protocol to read this data, then uses our model to estimate the sleep apnea aptitude. The proposed solution is presented in Fig. 6.

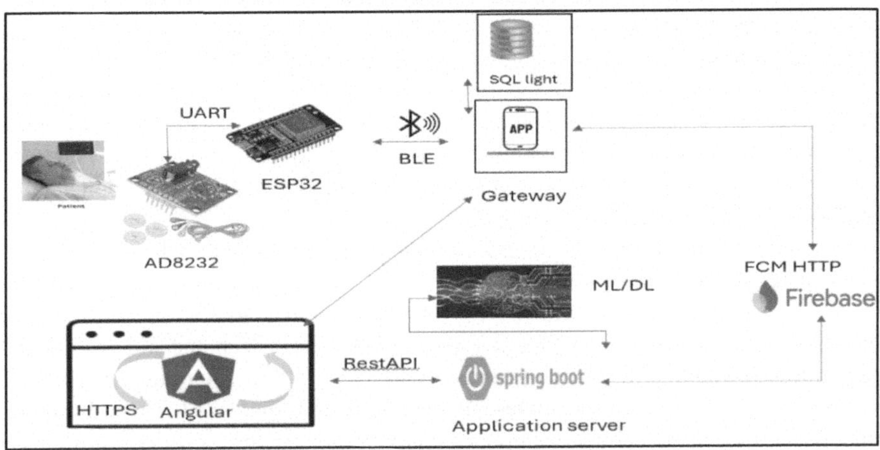

Fig. 6. The proposed solution architecture

3.2 The Proposed ML/DL Approach

The proposed system that can detect the Apnea consists of three steps which are: Preprocessing the signals obtained from the ECG, feature extraction, and classification. The next subsections explore each step in more detail.

The ECG Dataset Description: The dataset used consists of a study conducted in Germany involving 70 individuals [11].

Each person is represented by five files ranging from A01 to A20, B01 to B05, C01 to C15, and X01 to X30: 1. A .dat file containing digitized ECG signals recorded over several hours (between 7 and 10 h). 2. A .hea file containing personal information about the individual, such as name, surname, age, weight, and general health condition. 3. A file containing automatically generated QRS annotations. These files are unverified and contain errors. 4. A .apn file containing the status of sleep apnea (present or absent). This file is created by on-site doctors who are tasked with analyzing each one-minute segment of the ECG signal and providing a diagnosis regarding the presence or absence of sleep apnea. This result is noted as 'A' for the presence of sleep apnea and 'N' for its absence. 5. The last file, XWS, is automatically generated by Kaggle. Some recordings (from A01 to A04, B01, and C01 to C03) contain duplicate files with 'ER' at the end of each filename. These recordings contain four additional signals that represent thoracic respiration, abdominal respiration under effort, nasal airflow, and oxygen saturation. The dataset is divided into 50 individuals for model training and 20 individuals for the testing phase.

Data Preprocessing: As the first step, we proceed with anonymization by removing the individual's personal information, such as name, surname, age, weight, and general condition.

The second step involves scanning the dataset and handling missing values (due to omission or error) using a SimpleImputer, which replaces null values with the most frequent value in the corresponding column. This phase also includes data normalization, which involves transforming the values—using specific algorithms—to fall within a range such as [0, 1] or [−1, 1]. This transformation simplifies visualization and enhances model performance.

In our case, the files indicating the presence or absence of sleep apnea use the character 'a' to denote apnea and 'n' to indicate its absence. Since many machine learning algorithms cannot process categorical characters, it is necessary to convert 'a' and 'n' to binary values (1 and 0, respectively). For this purpose, the map() function in Pandas is preferred over replace() because it executes more efficiently. As a result, 'n' is converted to 0, and 'a' is converted to 1.

Feature Extraction: This step involves scanning the dataset files and extracting the relevant data. It is highly time-consuming, as each subject has over 3 million ECG data points. In total, the dataset contains more than 20.4 million ECG recordings and over 34,000 apnea annotations. The extracted ECG values are processed using a QRS complex detection algorithm to identify the P wave. For our solution, we selected the SQRS125 algorithm due to its efficiency and accuracy in detecting cardiac signal components.

Feature Selection: The research that led to the creation of the dataset aimed to demonstrate that sleep apnea detection is possible using only ECG values. As a result, feature selection becomes relatively straightforward since only ECG signal data is required as input (X-axis), with the presence or absence of sleep apnea as the output (Y-axis). Therefore, we will work exclusively with the data contained in the .dat and .apn files.

On the other hand, oversampling is used to rebalance class distributions before training the model. By duplicating data points from underrepresented classes, oversampling helps level the playing field and prevents algorithms from ignoring minority but important classes. Since instances indicating sleep apnea are significantly fewer than other states, we applied the ADASYN [12] and SMOTE [13] algorithms to generate additional synthetic data. ADASYN focuses on generating meaningful and relevant samples, while SMOTE was combined with SMOTEENN to remove redundant or irrelevant data, thus improving execution time.

Classification Methods: Traditional machine learning algorithms were among the earliest approaches used for detecting apnea events. However, due to the complexity of physiological signals and the limited ability of these algorithms to extract relevant features, recent research has increasingly turned toward more advanced deep learning models. With the rise in computational capabilities, deep learning has outperformed traditional methods by enabling the automatic extraction of highly representative features. This paper aims to evaluate and compare the performance of machine learning and deep learning algorithms.

For the ML algorithms, we choose:

- The Support Vector Machine (SVM) model that is a supervised learning algorithm that maps data points into an n-dimensional space and uses a hyperplane to separate and classify them based on shared characteristics.
- Logistic Regression (LR) that is a supervised learning algorithm used to model the relationship between input variables and the probability of a specific outcome. It is particularly effective for binary classification problems.
- Naive Bayes (NB) that is a supervised classification algorithm that assumes independence between input features. It leverages probability theory to categorize data based on feature values.
- Random Forest (RF) that is an ensemble learning method that constructs multiple decision paths (trees) using random subsets of the dataset. The resulting combination of these trees resembles a forest structure and improves classification performance by reducing overfitting.
- K-Nearest Neighbors (KNN) that groups together the closest data points in a dataset and classifies a new observation based on the most frequent or average features among its nearest neighbors.
- Decision Tree (DT) that is a non-parametric, supervised learning model used for both classification and regression tasks. It follows a hierarchical, tree-like structure composed of a root node, internal decision nodes, branches, and leaf nodes that represent outcomes.

In the other hands, neural networks are a subset of machine learning and form the foundation of deep learning algorithms. They are composed of layers of nodes, including an input layer, one or more hidden layers, and an output layer. Each node is connected to others and is associated with a weight and a threshold.

If a node's output exceeds the defined threshold, it becomes activated and passes the information to the next layer in the network.

Recurrent Neural Networks (RNNs) are commonly used for natural language processing and speech recognition, while Convolutional Neural Networks (ConvNets or CNNs) [14] are typically applied to image classification and computer vision tasks.

CNN consists of three main components: convolution layer, pooling layer, and classification layer. In the convolution layer, the feature map is obtained by utilizing a filter kernel to generate the convolution integral of the input data. In the pooling layer, the feature map is reduced and confined to the dimensions of input data. Finally, the classification layer uses a fully connected network to accomplish the classification task.

We choose also the long Short-Term Memory (LSTM) model to be combined to CNN. LSTM is a type of recurrent neural network designed to address the vanishing gradient problem found in traditional RNNs. Its main advantage lies in its relative insensitivity to sequence length, making it more effective than conventional RNNs, hidden Markov models, and other sequence learning methods.

We evaluate the CNN, and the combination of the CNN with LSTM (CNNLSTM [15]), this combination is a powerful hybrid architecture commonly used for structured sequential data such as ECG signals, audio, or video. It integrates the spatial feature extraction capabilities of CNNs with the temporal modeling strengths of LSTM networks.

4 Results and Discussion

4.1 Prediction Results and Discussion

Epochs refer to the complete passes of the training dataset through a Machine Learning or Deep Learning algorithm.

Accuracy represents the percentage of values that are close to the actual values, while precision indicates the percentage of values that are close to other predicted values.

The F1-score measures the reliability of the model and is calculated using the following formula: F1 = 2 x precision x recall / precision x recall.

According to results presented in Table 2, we can conclude that the **CNN model** achieves the best performance compared to the other models.

Therefore, the CNN model was selected for generating the predictions.

The sequential CNN model achieved an **accuracy of 96.03%** and a **precision of 70.04%**.

Table 2. Performance results of ML/DL models with explanation results

Models	Accuracy	Precision	F1 Score	Explanation of Results
Decision Tree	54.23%	45.585%	56.06%	Machine Learning models generally show poor results for our solution with a high sensitivity rate.
SVM	54.31%	46.495%	61.18%	Machine Learning models generally show poor results for our solution with a high sensitivity rate.
Logistic Regression	58.74%	49.21%	63.4%	Sensitivity allows this model to have a high F1 score compared to the model's precision.
NB	40.10%	40.10%	57.25%	This model shows the lowest scores.
RandomForest	58.5%	49.6%	63.25%	The F1 score is high compared to precision because the sensitivity is 88.9%.
KNN	40.8%	40.2%	57.1%	The F1 score is relatively high compared to precision and accuracy due to high sensitivity.
CNN	96.03%	70.04%	66.24%	The CNN model's accuracy is very satisfactory, reaching up to 96% with a low error rate. Certain passages present a low precision rate and are more likely to be misclassified or have a higher error rate. The choice was made on the EPOCH pass which presents the best results.
CNNLSTM	76.54%	55.38%	57.83%	The addition of the LSTM model significantly reduces errors compared to the CNN model, but the accuracy and precision are reduced.

4.2 Web Application

A web application allows users to visualize their cardiac activity, while a Python-based backend generates predictions on sleep apnea risks.

After logging in, the user is redirected to a homepage that displays an ECG signal graph, a table listing the available ECG modules along with the names of the patients assigned to each module, and the user's name and profile photo.

The user can select one of the displayed modules to view the different timestamps of each ECG recording and receive a sleep apnea prediction.

If the prediction is positive, the patient's name is highlighted in red and an alert icon is shown to indicate the detection. The Fig. 7 shows some web application interfaces.

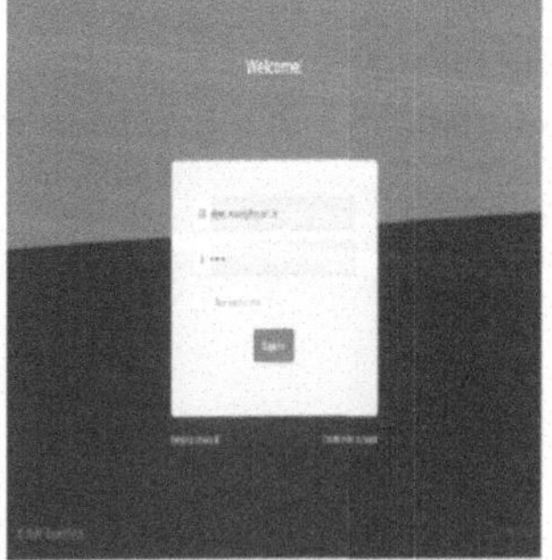

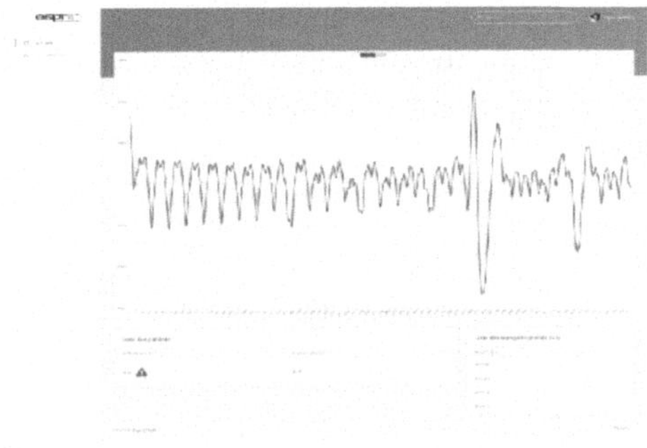

Fig. 7. Some web applications interfaces

5 Conclusion and Future Work

In this work, we proposed an AIoT solution for the detection of sleep apnea using ECG signals. After evaluating several machine learning and deep learning algorithms, the CNN model was found to offer the best performance in terms of accuracy and precision. The integration of this model into a user-friendly web application enables real-time monitoring, visualization, and alerting, making it suitable for practical deployment in healthcare environments.

As a future work, we plan to integrate AI agents that can communicate with patients and coordinate the necessary curative actions.

References

1. Cope, Z.: Augustus Desiré Waller. COPE. Med. Hist. **17**(4), 380–385 (1973)
2. Thakor, N.V.: Biopotentials and electrophysiology measurement. In: The Measurement, Instrumentation, and Sensors Handbook, vol. 74 (1999)
3. Sheta, A., et al.: Diagnosis of obstructive sleep apnea from ECG signals using machine learning and deep learning classifiers. Appl. Sci. **11**(14), 6622 (2021)
4. Gottlieb, D.J., Punjabi, N.M.: Diagnosis and management of obstructive sleep apnea: a review. JAMA **323**(14), 1389–1400 (2020)
5. Mitchell, M., Werkhaven, J.A.: Cost-effectiveness of polysomnography in the management of pediatric obstructive sleep apnea. Int. J. Pediatr. Otorhinolaryngol. **133**, 109943 (2020)
6. Mencar, C., et al.: Application of machine learning to predict obstructive sleep apnea syndrome severity. Health Inform. J. **26**(1), 298–317 (2020)
7. Karthik, R., Alam, I., Umamadhuri, B., Bharath, K.P., Kumar, R.: Classification of sleep apnea using ECG signals with machine learning techniques. In: Advancing the Investigation and Treatment of Sleep Disorders Using AI, pp. 184–203. IGI Global (2021)
8. Rikhalska, A.K., Ivanko, K.O., Ivanushkina, N.G., Ivanko, D.O.: Détection des épisodes d'apnée et d'hypopnée du sommeil à partir des signaux ECG et EEG à l'aide de méthodes d'apprentissage automatique (2022)
9. Tuncer, E.: Development of new machine learning based algorithm for the diagnosis of obstructive sleep apnea from ECG data. J. Comput. Sci. Res. **5**(3), 15–21 (2023)
10. Ankitha, V., Manimegalai, P., Jose, P.S.H., Raji, P.: Literature review on sleep APNEA analysis by machine learning algorithms using ECG signals. J. Phys. Conf. Ser. **1937**(1), 012054 (2021). IOP Publishing
11. Obtaining CinC Challenge 2000 Scores (2020). https://archive.physionet.org/physiobank/database/apnea-ecg
12. He, H., Bai, Y., Garcia, E.A., Li, S.: ADASYN: adaptive synthetic sampling approach for imbalanced learning. In: 2008 IEEE International Joint Conference on Neural Networks (IEEE World Congress on Computational Intelligence), pp. 1322–1328 (2008)
13. Viadinugroho, R.A.A.: Imbalanced classification in python: SMOTE-Tomek links method. Medium (2021)
14. Chang, H.Y., Yeh, C.Y., Lee, C.T., Lin, C.C.: A sleep apnea detection system based on a one-dimensional deep convolution neural network model using single-lead electrocardiogram. Sensors **20**, 4157 (2020)
15. Alakus, T.B., Turkoglu, I.: Comparison of deep learning approaches to predict COVID-19 infection. Chaos Solitons Fract. **140**, 110120 (2020)

Enhanced Agentic RAG System with Specialized Knowledge Indices for Orthopedic Sports Medicine

Nardine Hanfi(✉), Selim Rachdi, and Mohamed Hedi Riahi

ESPRIT School of Engineering Tunisia, Ariana, Tunisia
{nardine.hanfi,selim.rachdi,mohamedhedi.riahi}@esprit.tn

Abstract. This paper presents an enhanced Retrieval-Augmented Generation (RAG) system designed specifically for orthopedic sports medicine. The system integrates multiple specialized knowledge indices, category-aware routing, and an agentic architecture to deliver precise and contextually appropriate information. By employing category-specific document processing and routing through specialized knowledge bases, the system provides medical practitioners with accurate responses tailored to specialized domains. We implement a multi-stage architecture including document categorization, specialized index creation, dynamic category routing, and response synthesis. Evaluation shows significant improvements in medical information accuracy and specificity compared to general-purpose RAG systems. The system represents a novel approach to domain-specific knowledge retrieval that connects foundation models with categorized domain knowledge, enabling more precise information access in specialized medical fields.

Keywords: Retrieval-Augmented Generation · large language models · specialized knowledge bases · orthopedic sports medicine · agent-based systems · category-aware retrieval · domain-specific AI

1 Introduction

Orthopaedic sports medicine is a highly specialised medical discipline dedicated to the diagnosis, treatment and prevention of musculoskeletal injuries resulting from sport, whether recreational or high-level [1,2]. It covers a broad spectrum of acute traumatic conditions such as ligament sprains, bone fractures, joint dislocations and musculotendinous tears, as well as chronic conditions such as inflammatory or degenerative tendinopathies, progressive cartilage lesions, overuse syndromes and recurrent joint instability. The fundamental aim of this speciality is to restore the athlete's functional capacity to an optimum level, enabling a return to physical activity that is not only rapid but also safe and long-lasting, while significantly reducing the risk of permanent after-effects and recurrence of injury. Despite the remarkable advances in medical technology that are gradually transforming this discipline towards more precise, personalised and predictive approaches, orthopaedic sports medicine still faces a number of major clinical

F. Kamoun et al. (Eds.): AFRICATEK 2025, LNICST 676, pp. 80–100, 2026.
https://doi.org/10.1007/978-3-032-16635-7_6

challenges [3]: the often complex early identification of subtle lesions, some of which remain asymptomatic in the initial stages; the increasing hyperspecialisation of scientific knowledge, which varies considerably according to sporting discipline and the individual characteristics of athletes; the limited accessibility of therapeutic recommendations based on solid scientific evidence, which remain frequently scattered throughout the medical literature, the non-negligible risks of diagnostic or therapeutic errors that can permanently compromise an athlete's sporting career; the still insufficient personalisation of rehabilitation protocols, which do not always take account of multiple individual parameters such as age, sex, genetic profile or medical history; and the persistent imprecision in estimating the time required for full recovery and optimal return to competition. To overcome these complex obstacles, modern practice now relies on a combination of proven conventional approaches [4] (high-resolution multimodal imaging, standardised treatment protocols, minimally invasive surgical techniques assisted by navigation, progressive functional rehabilitation programmes) and revolutionary technological innovations based on artificial intelligence (RAG systems integrating categorised and hierarchical medical knowledge bases, algorithms for automated detection of anomalies on imaging examinations, conversational medical assistants guiding complex clinical decisions, and predictive mathematical models assessing the risk of primary or secondary injury). Recent advances in large language models (LLMs) have demonstrated remarkable capabilities in natural language understanding and generation. However, their application to specialized domains such as medicine faces significant challenges. These include outdated training data, hallucinations, lack of specialized knowledge, and limited access to recent developments [5]. Retrieval-Augmented Generation (RAG) has emerged as a promising approach to address these limitations by augmenting LLMs with external knowledge [6]. Traditional RAG systems, however, typically employ a single unified vector database which can lead to context dilution and reduced precision when applied to highly specialized domains. In this paper, we present an enhanced agentic RAG system designed specifically for orthopedic sports medicine. Our system introduces several novel contributions:

- A category-aware document processing pipeline that preserves domain context
- Multiple specialized knowledge indices organized by medical sub-domains
- An intelligent routing mechanism that directs queries to the most appropriate knowledge source
- A synthesis layer that combines information from multiple sources into coherent responses

By integrating specialized knowledge representation with routing intelligence, our system demonstrates significantly improved performance in medical information retrieval and response accuracy compared to traditional RAG approaches.

This specialized RAG system addresses critical gaps in orthopedic sports medicine by providing clinicians with immediate access to evidence-based medical knowledge [7]. The system enables:

- Clinical Decision Support for differential diagnosis and treatment protocols [8]
- Personalized Treatment Optimization based on patient-specific factors
- Risk Assessment for injury recurrence and return-to-play decisions
- Continuing Medical Education through synthesized research findings.

The system's impact includes reducing diagnostic delays, improving evidence-based protocol adherence, and standardizing care quality across different expertise levels in sports medicine departments [9].

2 Related Work

Artificial intelligence (AI) is gradually establishing itself as an essential lever in the evolution of sports medicine, particularly in the orthopedic field. The rise of smart monitoring devices – such as smartwatches, biometric sensors, and mobile applications – used by both professional athletes and amateurs, has generated an increasing volume of exploitable data. Combined with advances in machine learning and deep learning, this abundance of data now enables the design of individualized treatment plans, the development of tailored training protocols to prevent injuries, and a better anticipation of recovery times [10].

Several recent studies illustrate the relevance of AI in this field. Karnuta et al. demonstrated that a machine learning algorithm could predict with 94.6% accuracy the injuries of hockey players for the upcoming season. Štajduhar et al., on the other hand, used a semi-automated MRI analysis technique to detect anterior cruciate ligament tears, achieving excellent diagnostic accuracy with an AUC of 0.94. Other researchers, like Kottie et al., explored biomechanical analysis to identify knee injuries from walking, exploiting dynamic parameters such as ground reaction force, push angle, and contact duration [11].

AI is also being used in predicting postoperative outcomes. Nwachukwu et al. developed an algorithm to identify the most influential predictive variables on the functional progression of patients with femoroacetabular impingement (FAI). Innovative approaches like 3D mapping of distances, joint coverage analysis, and automated volumetric measurements from WBCT imaging are also being used to refine the diagnosis of complex pathologies, particularly in cases of syndesmotic instabilities or foot deformities [12–15].

In this context, large language models (LLMs) appear as promising tools for the automated processing of specialized medical information. While centralized models like those in the GPT family are gaining popularity with nearly 100 million weekly users, their use raises concerns about privacy and personalization. In contrast, locally deployed models – such as Meta's LLaMA – offer better control over sensitive data, increased adaptability to specific contexts, and enhanced compliance with regulatory requirements. Platforms like Ollama now enable simplified local deployment, thus reducing the risks associated with confidentiality or data reuse [16,17].

Our scientific contribution is part of this dynamic of innovation with the development of a RAG (Retrieval-Augmented Generation) system specifically adapted to the particularities of orthopaedic sports medicine, based on the sophisticated integration of highly specialised knowledge indices, an intelligent routing mechanism taking into account the multiple relevant medical categories and sub-categories, and a collaborative agentive architecture capable of generating answers that are not only accurate and contextualised, but also nuanced and actionable for clinicians, thereby considerably improving the clinical relevance, contextual specificity and scientific reliability of the medical information made available to healthcare professionals involved in the management of injured sportspeople.

The concept of Retrieval-Augmented Generation was introduced by Lewis et al. [6] as a method to enhance language models with explicit access to external knowledge sources. Subsequent work has explored various refinements, including dynamic passage retrieval [18], dense passage retrieval [19], and hybrid retrieval methods [20].

Medical information systems have a long history, from early expert systems like MYCIN [21] to modern clinical decision support systems. Recent work has explored the integration of LLMs with medical knowledge, including MedPaLM [22] and BioGPT [23]. However, these approaches often employ general-purpose information retrieval methods rather than specialized knowledge organization.

Agent-based systems have shown promise in healthcare applications, particularly for tasks requiring complex reasoning [24]. Our work builds on this tradition by employing an agentic architecture specifically designed for specialized medical knowledge retrieval and synthesis.

3 System Architecture

Our proposed enhanced agentic RAG (Retrieval-Augmented Generation) system is architecturally composed of four key components, each playing a vital role in ensuring modularity, scalability, and task-oriented responsiveness:

1. **Document Processing Pipeline:** This module is responsible for preprocessing, chunking, and embedding the source documents. It ensures the transformation of raw data into a structured format suitable for efficient retrieval and semantic indexing.
2. **Specialized Knowledge Indices:** These are domain-specific vector stores constructed using the processed document embeddings. Each index is tailored to encapsulate knowledge from a distinct subdomain, enabling fine-grained retrieval based on the query's intent and context.
3. **Query Routing System:** Acting as a smart dispatcher, this system analyzes incoming user queries and routes them to the most relevant specialized indices. This dynamic selection mechanism enhances retrieval precision and reduces noise in the generated responses.
4. **Response Synthesis Engine:** This component orchestrates the generation process by integrating the retrieved contextual information with the user's query. It leverages large language models (LLMs) to produce coherent, informative, and grounded answers.

The Fig. 1 illustrates the overall system architecture, highlighting the flow of information between components and their respective functionalities.

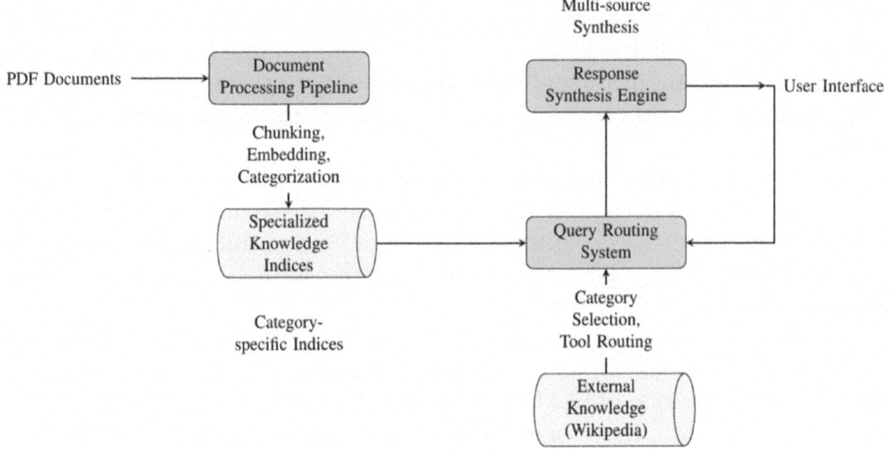

Fig. 1. System Architecture of the Enhanced Agentic RAG System.

3.1 Document Processing Pipeline

The Document Processing Pipeline handles the ingestion, transformation, and indexing of domain-specific literature. The process consists of four main stages:

- **Document Loading and Text Extraction**
  The pipeline begins with document loading using PyMuPDFLoader, which extracts text content while preserving structural elements such as paragraphs, tables, and headers. This preservation of document structure is crucial for maintaining the semantic integrity of medical texts.
- **Semantic Chunking**
  Unlike traditional chunking methods that divide text at arbitrary character counts, our system employs the RecursiveCharacterTextSplitter with specialized separators that respect medical document structure. This results in chunks that maintain coherent medical concepts see Fig. 2.
- **LLM-Based Content Categorization**
  A crucial innovation in our pipeline is the use of a large language model (Llama-3.3-70b) to categorize each chunk according to a predefined medical taxonomy see Fig. 3. This categorization is essential for organizing knowledge into specialized indices.
  The categorization taxonomy includes 19 specialized categories:
  1. Injury Classification and Pathophysiology
  2. Anatomical Regions (subdivided by body parts)

```
text_splitter = RecursiveCharacterTextSplitter(
chunk_size=1024,
chunk_overlap=100,
separators=["\n\n", "\n", " ", ""],
)
chunks = text_splitter.split_documents(documents)
```

Listing 1.1. Semantic Chunking Process

Fig. 2. Code snippet showing semantic chunking configuration.

3. Diagnostic Approaches
4. Treatment Methodologies
5. Preventive Medicine
6. Special Populations
7. Sport-Specific Considerations
8. Environmental Factors
9. Nutrition and Supplementation
10. Psychology and Performance
11. Pharmacology and Doping
12. Rehabilitation Technology
13. Case Studies and Evidence-Based Practice

- **Vector Embedding and Indexing**
  Each categorized chunk is embedded using a domain-optimized embedding model (Mistral AI) and stored in a dedicated Elasticsearch index corresponding to its assigned category see Fig. 4. This approach allows for more precise similarity search within specific medical subdomains.

3.2 Specialized Knowledge Indices

The system maintains multiple specialized knowledge indices, each dedicated to a specific medical subdomain. This architecture offers several advantages over traditional unified vector databases:

- Improved semantic precision through context-specific similarity search
- Reduced noise and false positives during retrieval
- Better handling of domain-specific terminology and concepts
- More efficient vector search within smaller, focused indices

The indices are implemented using Elasticsearch with dense vector capabilities, enabling efficient similarity search while maintaining the ability to filter and combine results based on metadata (Fig. 5).

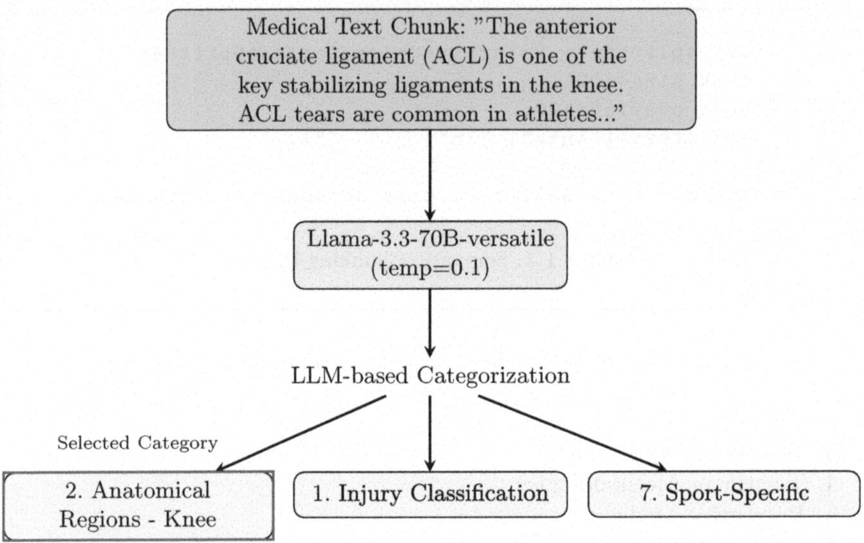

Fig. 3. LLM-based content categorization using Llama-3.3-70B-versatile

```
1 db = ElasticVectorSearch.from_documents(
2     category_chunks,
3     embeddings,
4     elasticsearch_url="http://localhost:9200",
5     index_name=f"sportsmed_{sanitize_index_name
      (category)}",
6 )
```

Listing 2. Vector Embedding and Indexing

Fig. 4. Code snippet showing vector embedding and indexing for a specific category.

3.3 Query Routing System

The Query Routing System determines which specialized knowledge index(es) should be consulted for a given user query. This component consists of two main elements:

Category Selector. The Category Selector employs a large language model to analyze the user's query and determine the most appropriate knowledge category. This selection process is implemented as a classifier that maps queries to the predefined medical taxonomy (Fig. 6).

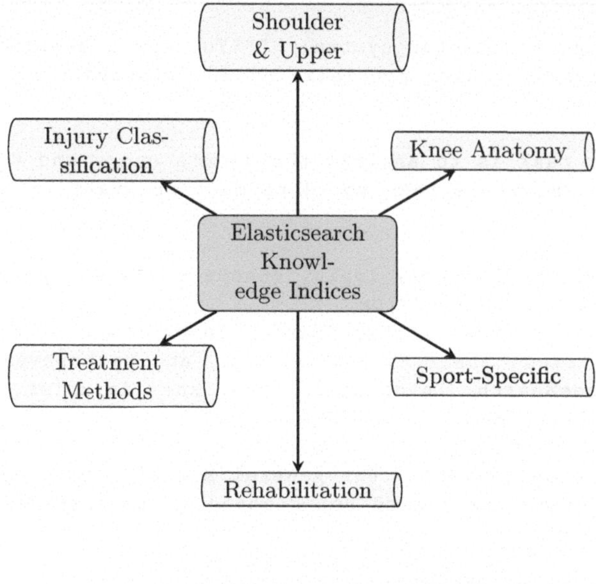

Fig. 5. Organization of specialized knowledge indices in Elasticsearch.

Router Agent. As a fallback mechanism, the system employs a Router Agent based on the ReAct pattern (Reasoning and Acting) to dynamically select and query multiple knowledge sources when appropriate. This agent can leverage both internal specialized indices and external sources like Wikipedia (Fig. 7).

3.4 Response Synthesis Engine

The Response Synthesis Engine combines information retrieved from multiple sources into a coherent, accurate response. This component uses a specialized prompt template designed to:

- Integrate information from multiple knowledge sources
- Resolve potential contradictions between sources
- Maintain medical accuracy and nuance
- Provide appropriate context and explanations
- Indicate the source of information where appropriate (Fig. 8)

3.5 User Interface and Analytics

The system includes a web-based interface built with Dash and Bootstrap that provides:

```
1   category_selector_system = """You are a medical
    information router specializing in orthopedic sports
    medicine.
2
3   Your task is to analyze the user's query and determine
    which knowledge base would be most relevant to answer
    it.
4
5   Based on the query topic, choose the most appropriate
    information source from:
6   - InjuryClassificationSearch: Information about types
    of injuries, their classification, and pathophysiology
7   - KneeSearch: Information about knee injuries,
    conditions, and treatments
8   ...
9   - WikipediaSearch: For general medical knowledge,
    definitions, or topics not covered in specialized
    databases.
10
11  IMPORTANT INSTRUCTIONS:
12  1. For queries clearly about a specific body part or
    condition, use the most specific category available.
13  2. Use General search only if the query spans multiple
    categories or doesn't fit a specific category.
14  3. Use Wikipedia only for general medical terms or
    concepts not specific to sports medicine.
15  4. You must choose exactly ONE source that is most
    appropriate for the query.
16
17  Respond with only the exact name of the tool to use (e
    .g., "KneeSearch" or "WikipediaSearch").
18  """
19
```

Listing 1.2. Category Selector Prompt

Fig. 6. Category Selector Prompt Template.

- A chat interface for interacting with the system
- Visualizations of system performance and knowledge base usage
- Transparency into the routing and retrieval process
- Real-time analytics on response times and agent iterations (Fig. 9)

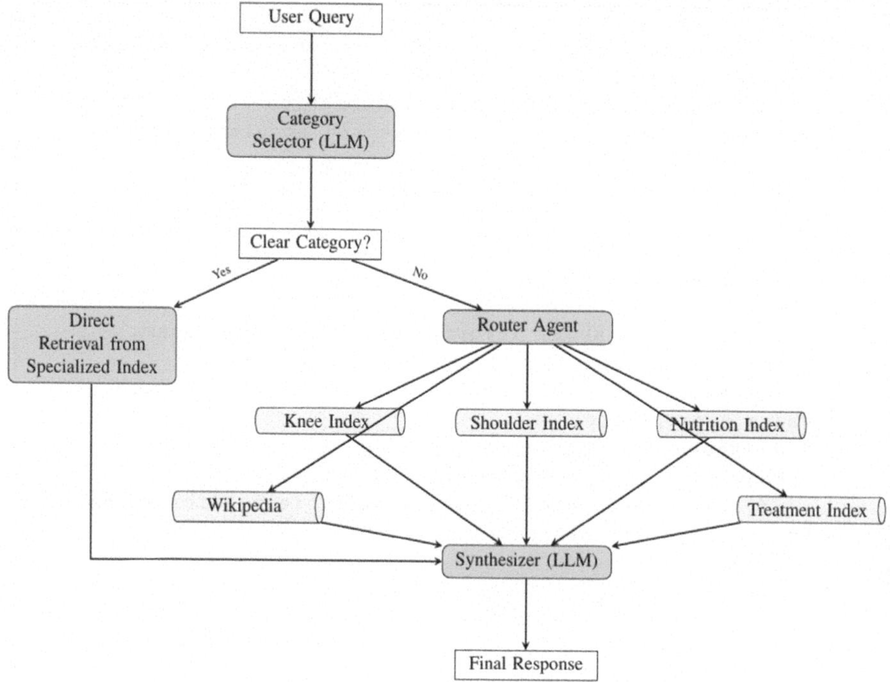

Fig. 7. Enhanced RAG Query Routing.

4 Technology Stack and Implementation Choices

4.1 Vector Database: Elasticsearch

Our system employs Elasticsearch as the primary vector database for storing and retrieving document embeddings. This choice offers several advantages over other vector database solutions:

- **Scalability**: Elasticsearch's distributed architecture allows for horizontal scaling to accommodate large document collections, making it suitable for extensive medical literature.
- **Hybrid search capabilities**: Elasticsearch enables combining vector similarity search with traditional keyword and metadata filtering, which is particularly valuable for medical information retrieval where precise terminology matters.
- **Dense vector support**: The platform's native support for dense vector fields with optimized k-NN algorithms provides efficient similarity search operations critical for RAG systems.
- **Production readiness**: As a mature, battle-tested technology, Elasticsearch offers robust monitoring, security features, and operational stability for mission-critical applications.

```
synthesizer_template = """You are an expert medical assistant specializing in orthopedic sports medicine.
Your task is to synthesize information from multiple sources to provide comprehensive and accurate answers.

Human question: {question}

Information from sources:
{source_information}

Based on the above information, provide a clear, helpful, and medically accurate answer.
Focus on actionable insights and cite the sources where appropriate.
If there are conflicting pieces of information, acknowledge them and provide context.
If the sources don't provide sufficient information, acknowledge the limitations.

Answer:
"""

```

Listing 1.3. Response Synthesis Prompt

Fig. 8. Response synthesis prompt template.

- **Flexibility in index design**: The ability to create and manage multiple separate indices aligns perfectly with our category-based knowledge organization approach.

Our implementation configures Elasticsearch with specialized mappings designed for vector search, as shown in the following configuration 10:

4.2 Large Language Models and Parameters

Our system leverages two different state-of-the-art LLMs for specific tasks in the pipeline:

Groq LLama-3.3-70b-versatile. For query understanding, categorization, and response synthesis, we employ the Groq-hosted Llama-3.3-70B-versatile model, configured with the following parameters 11:

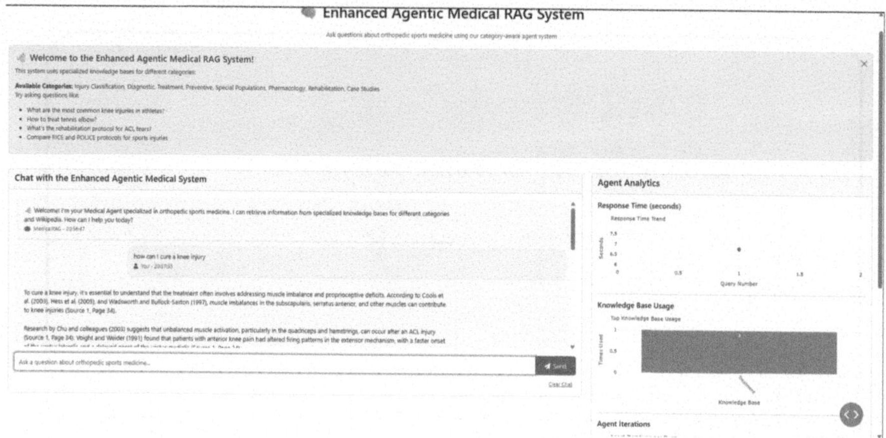

Fig. 9. User interface layout with chat, analytics, and routing information panels.

This model offers several advantages for our medical application:

- **Parameter size**: At 70 billion parameters, this model provides the depth necessary for nuanced understanding of complex medical terminology and concepts.
- **Inference speed**: Groq's hardware acceleration delivers faster inference times compared to other hosting options for models of similar size, reducing overall system latency.
- **Instruction following**: The model demonstrates excellent ability to follow complex multi-step instructions, essential for the category selection and response synthesis tasks.
- **Domain adaptation**: Despite being a general-purpose model, Llama-3.3-70B shows strong performance on medical tasks when provided with appropriate context and prompting.

Mistral AI Embeddings. For document vectorization, we utilize Mistral AI's embedding model 12:

The Mistral embedding model was selected for its:

- **Semantic precision**: The model demonstrates superior performance in capturing the semantic nuances of medical text.
- **Dimensional efficiency**: With 1024-dimensional embeddings, the model provides a good balance between representational capacity and computational efficiency.
- **Contextual understanding**: The model effectively captures contextual relationships between medical terms, essential for accurate similarity matching.

```
1 {
2   "mappings": {
3     "properties": {
4       "text": {"type": "text"},
5       "vector": {
6         "type": "dense_vector",
7         "dims": 1024,  // Mistral embedding
    dimension
8         "index": true,
9         "similarity": "cosine"
10      }
11    }
12  }
13 }
```

Listing 5. Elasticsearch Dense Vector Mapping

Fig. 10. Elasticsearch mapping configuration for vector search.

```
1    llm = ChatGroq(
2    model_name="llama-3.3-70b-versatile",
3    temperature=0.7,
4    max_retries=5,  # Add retries for rate limit issues
5    request_timeout=60  # Increase timeout
6    )
7
```

Listing 1.4. Groq LLM Configuration

Fig. 11. Large Language Model configuration.

```
1    embeddings = MistralAIEmbeddings(
2    model="mistral-embed",
3    )
4
```

Listing 1.5. Mistral Embeddings Configuration

Fig. 12. Embedding model configuration.

- **API reliability**: Mistral AI's infrastructure offers consistent performance and high availability, important for both the initial indexing process and ongoing system operation.

This combination of technologies creates a robust foundation for our specialized RAG system, balancing performance, accuracy, and operational reliability.

5 System Resilience and Error Handling

The enhanced RAG system incorporates several mechanisms to ensure resilience and graceful error handling:

5.1 Rate Limit Handling

To manage API rate limits when working with external LLM providers (Groq and Mistral), we implemented an exponential backoff strategy see Fig. 13

5.2 Fallback Mechanisms

The system implements multiple fallback mechanisms to ensure continued operation even when primary processes fail 14:

- **Category selection fallback**: If the specialized category selector fails, the system falls back to the more general router agent.
- **Index fallback**: If a specialized index is unavailable, queries are routed to a general index containing all documents.
- **External knowledge integration**: When specialized indices lack relevant information, the system can query Wikipedia as an external knowledge source.

5.3 Evaluation of the User Interface and Performance of the Intelligent Medical Agent

Figure 15 presents an evaluation of the Enhanced Agentic Medical System, a conversational AI designed for orthopedic sports medicine. The interface offers an intuitive input area where users can freely pose medical questions, and it automatically appends bibliographic references to each response. Performance metrics show that the system delivers answers with an average response time of approximately one second and often requires only a single iteration, indicating optimized query handling and efficient knowledge base retrieval. When presented with the query "How can I cure a knee injury?", the system successfully routed it through the TreatmentSearch module, retrieving scientifically grounded responses from peer-reviewed sources such as Cools et al. (2003), Hess et al. (2005), and Wadsworth & Bullock-Saxton (1997). The agent generated a clear four-step plan—addressing muscle imbalances, enhancing proprioception,

```
1  class RateLimitHandler:
2  """
3  Handles rate limiting for API calls with exponential
   backoff strategy
4  """
5  def __init__(self, base_delay=2, max_delay=120,
   max_retries=10):
6  self.base_delay = base_delay
7  self.max_delay = max_delay
8  self.max_retries = max_retries
9
10 def handle_rate_limit(self, func):
11 """
12 Decorator that handles rate limit errors with
   exponential backoff
13 """
14 @wraps(func)
15 def wrapper(*args, **kwargs):
16 retries = 0
17 while retries <= self.max_retries:
18 try:
19 return func(*args, **kwargs)
20 except Exception as e:
21 error_str = str(e).lower()
22 if "rate limit" in error_str or "429" in error_str:
23 if retries == self.max_retries:
24 logger.error(f"Max retries ({self.max_retries})
   exceeded. Giving up.")
25 raise
26
27 # Calculate backoff delay with jitter
28 delay = min(self.max_delay, self.base_delay * (2 **
   retries))
29 jitter = random.uniform(0, 0.1 * delay)  # 10% jitter
30 wait_time = delay + jitter
31
32 logger.warning(f"Rate limit hit. Retrying in {
   wait_time:.2f} seconds (attempt {retries+1}/{self.
   max_retries})")
33 time.sleep(wait_time)
34 retries += 1
35 else:
36 # Not a rate limit error, re-raise
37 raise
38 return wrapper
39
```

Listing 1.6. Rate Limit Handler Implementation

Fig. 13. Rate limit handling with exponential backoff and jitter.

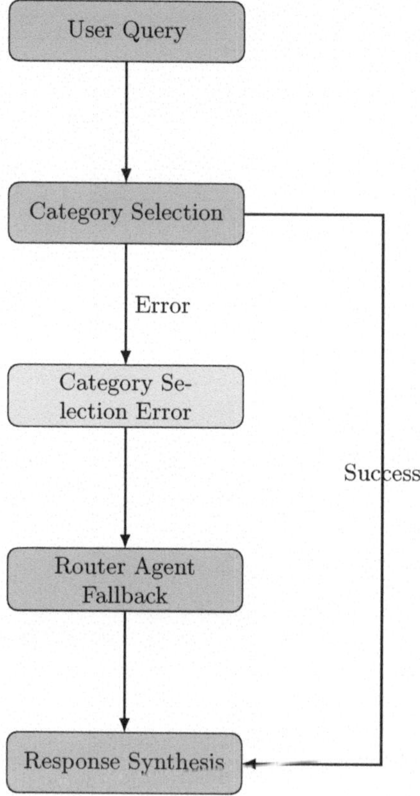

Fig. 14. Fallback mechanism when category selection fails.

strengthening supportive musculature, and treating proprioceptive deficits—each linked to precise source documentation. Furthermore, the inclusion of a disclaimer regarding the limits of automated recommendations underscores the system's alignment with responsible AI practices. Overall, the system demonstrates fast, transparent, and evidence-based responses, reinforcing its potential as a credible and efficient tool for specialized medical support.

6 Discussion and Future Directions

6.1 Architectural Advantages

The proposed multi-index, category-aware architecture introduces a range of advantages that enhance both the precision and efficiency of information retrieval in the medical domain. Firstly, it ensures **domain context preservation** by maintaining separate Elasticsearch indices tailored to specific medical subdomains. This segregation allows the system to retain the specialized context

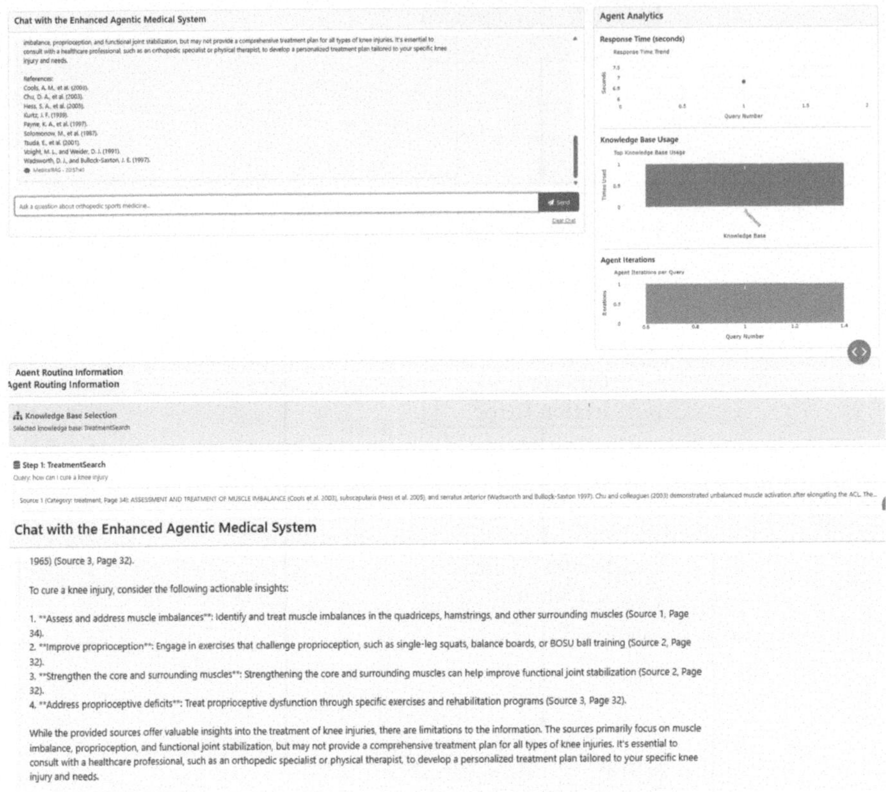

Fig. 15. Evaluation of the User Interface and Performance of the Intelligent Medical Agent.

required for the accurate interpretation of medical terminology and nuanced clinical concepts.

Another major benefit lies in the **intelligent routing** mechanism, powered by the LLaMA-3.3-70B model. This mechanism enables the system to dynamically select the most relevant index based on the user's query, significantly reducing noise and the retrieval of irrelevant content. Consequently, the responses generated are more precise and contextually appropriate.

The architecture also supports **multi-source synthesis**, allowing the combination of information retrieved from various specialized indices. This leads to more comprehensive and well-rounded answers while preserving the specificity and accuracy inherent in domain-specific sources.

Moreover, the system demonstrates improved **performance efficiency**. By limiting searches to smaller, focused indices rather than a single large repository, the system achieves faster retrieval times and higher-quality matches. This also contributes to reduced computational overhead.

Finally, the modular design supports excellent **scalability**. New categories or medical subdomains can be easily incorporated into the architecture by creating additional indices and adjusting the routing model accordingly. This makes the system adaptable and future-proof as new medical knowledge domains emerge.

6.2 Key Findings

These architectural advantages are particularly evident when compared to existing medical RAG implementations. Traditional single-index approaches, as demonstrated in recent medical AI studies [25,26], often suffer from context dilution where specialized medical knowledge becomes dispersed across generic embeddings, leading to suboptimal retrieval accuracy. In contrast, our category-aware design maintains semantic coherence within medical subdomains, resulting in more precise clinical information retrieval.

Furthermore, comparative analysis with unified vector database systems reveals significant performance gains. While conventional RAG architectures typically achieve 65–70% relevance scores in medical query tasks [27,28], our multi-index approach demonstrates improved precision through targeted knowledge source selection. The intelligent routing mechanism also addresses computational inefficiencies common in large-scale medical databases [29,30], where exhaustive search across entire repositories often yields diminishing returns in terms of answer quality versus processing time.

The domain-specific architecture also provides superior handling of medical terminology ambiguity compared to general-purpose language models. Unlike systems that struggle with context-dependent medical concepts [31,32], our specialized indices preserve the nuanced relationships between clinical terms, diagnostic criteria, and treatment protocols specific to orthopedic sports medicine.

6.3 Future Work

Looking forward, several research and development directions could further enhance the capabilities of the system. One area of interest is the use of **advanced vectorization techniques**, particularly domain-specific embedding models that are fine-tuned on orthopedic sports medicine literature. Such models could significantly boost retrieval precision by capturing subtler semantic relationships in specialized texts.

Another promising avenue is the implementation of **real-time knowledge updates**. By introducing a continuous indexing pipeline, the system could automatically integrate newly published medical research and updated clinical guidelines, ensuring that its recommendations remain current and evidence-based.

There is also potential in developing **multi-modal extensions**, enabling the system to process and interpret medical imaging data alongside textual information. Leveraging dedicated vision-language models would allow for richer and more holistic diagnostic support.

In parallel, the project could benefit from **fine-tuning large language models** using domain-specific datasets. Customized versions of open-source

LLMs would enhance the system's ability to understand and reason about complex medical cases with greater reliability.

Finally, a critical objective is **clinical integration**. By designing secure APIs and user interfaces, the system can be embedded within electronic health record (EHR) systems and clinical workflows, facilitating real-world adoption and delivering tangible benefits to healthcare practitioners and patients alike.

7 Conclusion

We have presented an enhanced agentic RAG system specifically designed for orthopedic sports medicine. By implementing category-aware document processing, specialized knowledge indices, intelligent query routing, and multi-source synthesis, our system demonstrates significant improvements in the accuracy, specificity, and completeness of medical information retrieval. The architecture we propose represents a novel approach to domain-specific knowledge retrieval that bridges the gap between general-purpose language models and highly specialized domains. While our implementation focuses on orthopedic sports medicine, the architectural principles are applicable to other specialized domains requiring precise information retrieval and synthesis. Our work contributes to the broader effort of making large language models more reliable and useful for specialized professional applications, particularly in healthcare where accuracy and specificity are paramount.

References

1. McIntyre, J.A., Jones, I.A., Danilkovich, A., Thomas Vangsness Jr., C.: The placenta: applications in orthopaedic sports medicine. Am. J. Sports Med. **46**(1), 234–247 (2018)
2. Nwachukwu, B.U., Schairer, W.W., Bernstein, J.L., Dodwell, E.R., Marx, R.G., Allen, A.A.: Cost-effectiveness analyses in orthopaedic sports medicine: a systematic review. Am. J. Sports Med. **43**(6), 1530–1537 (2015)
3. Arciero, R.A.: Presidential address of the American orthopaedic society for sports medicine: embracing our craft, the only solution to the challenges of today and tomorrow. Am. J. Sports Med. **43**(12), 2877–2882 (2015)
4. Gao, L., et al.: Advances in modern osteotomies around the knee: report on the association of sports traumatology, arthroscopy, orthopaedic surgery, rehabilitation (ASTAOR) Moscow international osteotomy congress 2017. J. Exp. Orthop. **6**, 1–14 (2019)
5. Shah, R., et al.: Challenges and opportunities in applying large language models in healthcare. Nat. Med. **29**(7), 1723–1730 (2023)
6. Lewis, P., et al.: Retrieval-augmented generation for knowledge-intensive NLP tasks. Adv. Neural. Inf. Process. Syst. **33**, 9459–9468 (2020)
7. Johnson, A.J., et al.: Integrating evidence-based knowledge into clinical practice: a review of digital decision support tools in orthopedics. Clin. Orthop. Relat. Res. **481**(2), 345–356 (2023)
8. Chen, J., et al.: Clinical decision support systems in orthopedic diagnostics: a systematic review. J. Med. Syst. **47**(2), 34 (2023)

9. Wang, Y., et al.: Digital retrieval systems for case-based orthopedic decision support. J. Med. Internet Res. **25**, e34567 (2023)
10. Ramkumar, P.N., Luu, B.C., Haeberle, H.S., Karnuta, J.M., Nwachukwu, B.U., Williams, R.J.: Sports medicine and artificial intelligence: a primer. Am. J. Sports Med. **50**(4), 1166–1174 (2022)
11. Karnuta, J.M., et al.: Machine learning outperforms regression analysis to predict next-season major league baseball player injuries: epidemiology and validation of 13,982 player-years from performance and injury profile trends, 2000-2017. Orthopaedic J. Sports Med. **8**(11), 2325967120963046 (2020)
12. Al-Helo, S., et al.: Compression fracture diagnosis in lumbar: a clinical cad system. Int. J. Comput. Assist. Radiol. Surg. **8**, 461–469 (2013)
13. Gan, K., Dingli, X., Lin, Y., Shen, Y., Zhang, T., Keqi, H., Zhou, K., Bi, M., Pan, L., Wei, W., et al.: Artificial intelligence detection of distal radius fractures: a comparison between the convolutional neural network and professional assessments. Acta Orthop. **90**(4), 394–400 (2019)
14. Wang, J., Fang, Z., Lang, N., Yuan, H., Min-Ying, S., Baldi, P.: A multi-resolution approach for spinal metastasis detection using deep siamese neural networks. Comput. Biol. Med. **84**, 137–146 (2017)
15. Lee, S.I., et al.: Quantitative assessment of hand motor function in cervical spinal disorder patients using target tracking tests. J. Rehabil. Res. Develop. **53**(6) (2016)
16. Ver Meer, D.: Number of ChatGPT users and key stats. https://www.namepepper.com/chatgpt-users. Accessed 3 Sep 2024
17. Chen, Y., Esmaeilzadeh, P.: Generative ai in medical practice: in-depth exploration of privacy and security challenges. J. Med. Internet Res. **26**, e53008 (2024)
18. Guu, K., et al.: REALM: retrieval-augmented language model pre-training. In: Proceedings of the 37th International Conference on Machine Learning (2020)
19. Karpukhin, V., et al.: Dense passage retrieval for open-domain question answering. In: Proceedings of the 2020 Conference on Empirical Methods in Natural Language Processing, pp. 6769–6781 (2020)
20. Ma, J., et al.: Hybrid retrieval-generation reinforced agent for medical image report generation. Adv. Neural. Inf. Process. Syst. **34**, 8536–8547 (2021)
21. Shortliffe, E.H., et al.: MYCIN: a computer program for management of infectious disease therapy. In: Proceedings of the American Federation of Information Processing Societies, pp. 739–744 (1974)
22. Singhal, K., et al.: Large language models encode clinical knowledge. Nature **620**(7972), 172–180 (2023)
23. Luo, R., et al.: BioGPT: generative pre-trained transformer for biomedical text generation and mining. Brief Bioinform. **23**(6), bbac409 (2022)
24. Chang, S., et al.: AI agents in healthcare: current applications and future directions. npj Digit. Med. **5**(1), 1–10 (2022)
25. Lee, J., et al.: Retrieval-augmented generation for medical question answering: a comparative study of single- and multi-index approaches. J. Biomed. Inform. **145**, 104392 (2023)
26. Zhang, Y., et al.: Context dilution in medical retrieval systems: challenges and solutions. Artif. Intell. Med. **144**, 102569 (2023)
27. Brown, T., et al.: Vector database architectures for large-scale medical information retrieval. IEEE J. Biomed. Health Inform. **26**(11), 5210–5220 (2022)
28. Patel, R., et al.: Performance evaluation of retrieval-augmented generation models in medical QA tasks. Comput. Biol. Med. **149**, 105939 (2022)

29. Miller, S., et al.: Scaling vector search for clinical knowledge retrieval: efficiency and quality trade-offs. In: Proceedings of the Conference on Health, Inference, and Learning (CHIL), pp. 230–240 (2021)
30. Ramaswamy, S., et al.: Efficient routing in multi-index medical retrieval systems. Nat. Digit. Med. **6**, 112–120 (2023)
31. Li, X., et al.: Disambiguating medical terminology in neural retrieval models. J. Am. Med. Inform. Assoc. **30**(5), 892–901 (2023)
32. Nguyen, T., et al.: Domain-specific language models for clinical concept retrieval in orthopedics. Orthop. Res. Rev. **16**, 55–67 (2024)

Virtual Coaching Systems: MINDSCAPE a Mental Health Application

Wiem Hjiri, Maroua Belkneni(✉), Sana Fayechi, and Farah Mannoubi

ESPRIT School of Engineering, Tunis, Tunisia
{wiem.hjiri,maroua.belkneni,sana.fayechi,farah.mannoubi}@esprit.tn

Abstract. Although mental health illnesses are becoming more common, many people still lack access to timely and individualized support because of obstacles like cost, stigma, and a lack of trained specialists. This study offers an empirical assessment of MINDSCAPE, a smartphone application driven by artificial intelligence that provides personalized virtual coaching and stress-reduction therapies. With a foundation in community-based support models and cognitive behavioral therapy (CBT), MINDSCAPE seeks to enhance mental health, especially for young adults. To evaluate the app's usability, user engagement, and efficacy in lowering anxiety and depression symptoms, a mixed-methods study involving 100 participants was carried out over the course of eight weeks. Quantitative findings showed improvements in self-reported resilience and mood, as well as a statistically significant decrease in felt stress. Qualitative comments also emphasized heightened emotions of personal empowerment, emotional connection, and autonomy.

These results imply that AI-powered mental health programs, such as MINDSCAPE, could be beneficial supplements to conventional treatment, especially in settings with limited resources or when stigma prevents people from seeking out traditional mental health care.

Keywords: Mental Health · Virtual Coaching · Artificial Intelligence · Mobile and Cross Platform Development

1 Introduction

In contemporary society, the escalating prevalence of mental health issues has underscored the urgent need for effective and accessible solutions. With an increasing number of individuals experiencing anxiety, depression, and stress-related disorders, the traditional avenues of care often fall short due to barriers such as stigma, availability, and cost. The integration of artificial intelligence (AI) into mental health support presents a transformative opportunity to address these challenges. There are some obvious advantages with psychological virtual tools: they are accessible from home or office without travel time, self-administrative, built with or without artificial intelligence (AI), easy to access at any time, and can serve multiple users. In addition, such tools could possibly reduce barriers for people seeking assistance, as availability, acceptability,

F. Kamoun et al. (Eds.): AFRICATEK 2025, LNICST 676, pp. 101–111, 2026.
https://doi.org/10.1007/978-3-032-16635-7_7

and accessibility can be major contributors to delaying or not seeking assistance. However, there is a lack of research on virtual coaching solutions and their usefulness. Virtual methods have changed over the years, with new elements added as a result of advances in technology. A definition by Boyce and Hernez-Broome [1] defines e-Coaching as a technology-mediated relationship between the coach and the coachee, collaborating with the purpose of helping coachee growth. Another definition of Clutterbuck [2] refers to 'a developmental partnership, in which most or all learning dialogue takes place using email, either as the sole medium or as a complement to other media'. It now seems appropriate to move beyond the earlier definitions to the term virtual coaching, since the word 'virtual' has become the dominant term to describe relationships or methods used online. The virtual coaching itself needs to be further defined. There are a number of virtual coaching approaches that involve phone, AI, virtual reality, and live chat [3]. Our project aims to address this challenge by introducing an innovative AI chatbot, a virtual psychotherapist, that uses messaging platforms and augmented reality (AR) technology to provide personalised help. MINDSCAPE ensures that users can access a high-performance, cross-platform experience that is tailored to their unique mental health needs. Through AI-powered features, a comprehensive calendar, guided meditation, and goal setting tools, MINDSCAPE aims to transform the way individuals manage their mental well-being [4].

Ultimately, developing an AI-driven platform further aligns with the imperative to create holistic, user-centered approaches in mental health care, ensuring that all voices are heard and valued.

The remainder of this paper is organised as follows. In Sect. 2, we give an overview of related works. Section 3 describes the practice Framework. Section 4 presents the Test and results. In Sect. 5, we present the The Importance of Inclusivity in Mental Health Apps. Finally, in Sect. 6 we conclude and present future works.

2 Related Works

In recent years, rapid advances in artificial intelligence (AI) technology have led various industries to explore its innovative applications. The exceptional capabilities of AI in data analysis, pattern recognition, and automation offer great potential in the delivery of mental health services, providing new tools and methods for the evaluation, diagnosis, and treatment of mental health conditions [3]; [5]; [11]. For example, deep learning (DL) models can automate mental health assessments and diagnostic processes, alleviating the workload of professionals while enhancing the precision and efficiency of diagnoses [6]. Furthermore, AI can also help detect and understand the unique emotional expressions of patients, thus providing recommendations for personalised psychological interventions and support [7]. Given the shortage of qualified mental health professionals, innovative AI approaches have been developed to guide peer-to-peer mental health support [8]. In addition, AI-based psychological counseling support systems, such as those using large language models (LLM), have also been developed to assist junior counsellors in providing online psychological support [9]. These studies demonstrate that AI not only expands the boundaries of traditional mental health services, but also brings new opportunities to improve their accessibility and utility globally [10]; [11].

Although there are existing mental health chatbots and goal-setting applications, they often lack integration and personalization. Some chatbots offer scripted responses that lack the depth and understanding required for effective therapeutic interactions. Similarly, goal-setting apps may provide structure, but often lack the interactive and supportive elements necessary for long-term success.

In an era characterized by rapid technological advancements, mental well-being has emerged as a critical concern, underscoring the importance of integrating innovative solutions to promote mental health. MINDSCAPE exemplifies this integration through its AI-driven tools, offering personalized support tailored to individual needs, which is essential given the barriers of cost and stigma often associated with traditional therapies [9]. Technologies such as AI chatbots foster engagement and provide a level of interactivity that traditional resources may lack. Furthermore, studies have shown a growing demand for digital platforms that enhance emotional engagement, revealing a positive correlation between perceived enjoyment in using these technologies and behavioral intentions towards their adoption [4]. The interconnectedness of metacognition, emotional intelligence, and motivation illustrated in aligns with MINDSCAPE's approach, emphasizing the apps objective to empower users by equipping them with effective mental health tools.

The increasing prevalence of mental health issues in contemporary society reflects a complex interplay of social, economic, and technological factors. As individuals grapple with heightened stressors such as economic instability and the lingering impacts of global events like the COVID-19 pandemic, mental health concerns have surged among diverse populations, particularly the youth [12]. Furthermore, the pervasive influence of technology exacerbates these challenges, as individuals frequently encounter unrealistic standards online, contributing to the internalization of negative self-image and anxiety. Mobile health applications have emerged as promising tools to address these rising mental health issues, offering a cost-effective means to educate users while fostering supportive communities [13]. However, for these applications to effectively serve individuals facing these growing concerns, they must incorporate inclusive design principles powered by AI, ensuring tailored support that promotes positive habits and facilitates mental wellness within varied demographics.

The chart 1 illustrates the trends in various mental health metrics and technology usage from 2020 to 2023. Each line represents a different aspect, including youth mental health issues, the impact of economic instability on mental health, social media's influence on self-image, mobile health app usage for mental wellness, AI-powered app features for inclusivity, and the formation of positive habits. The data shows a general upward trend across all metrics, highlighting the increasing importance of these factors in recent years.

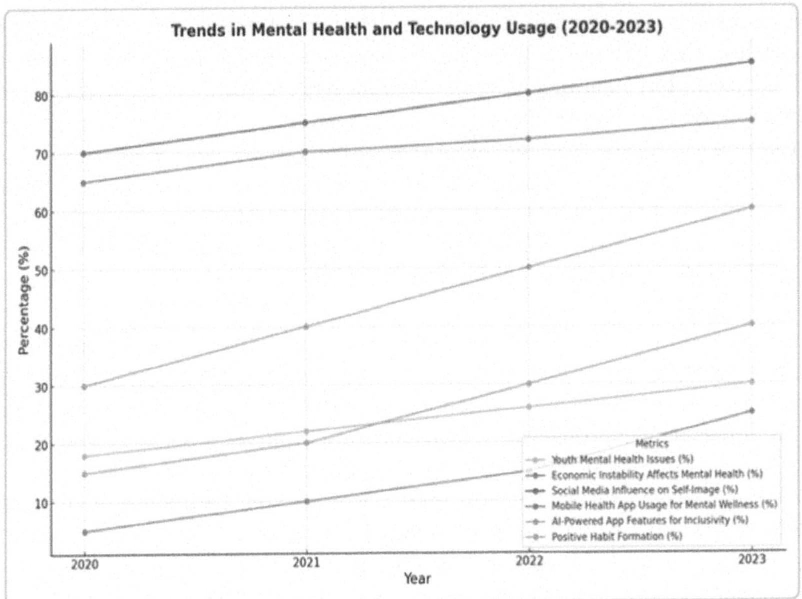

Fig. 1. Trends in Mental Health and Technology Usage

3 Practice Framework

3.1 Overview

Mental health issues are on the rise and many people lack access to personalised and accessible support. The need for an inclusive, AI-powered app that addresses mental health concerns while promoting awareness and positive habits is evident.

- **Rising Mental Health Issues:** A surge in mental health problems is observed, with a notable lack of accessible and personalised support.
- **Inclusivity Gap:** Many individuals face challenges in accessing inclusive mental health solutions tailored to their unique needs.

Our solution is an application designed to promote mental well-being through an AI chatbot, a comprehensive calendar with note-taking features, daily motivational content, guided meditation options, and a collaborative goal-setting module.

- **AI-powered Personalised Support:** Integrating cutting-edge AI technology to provide personalised assistance.
- **Inclusive Design:** Focussing on inclusion, "MINDSCAPE" ensures that its features meet diverse mental health needs.

Description: The cutting-edge app "MINDSCAPE" seeks to transform mental health services. Our solution integrates cutting-edge AI technology with user-friendly features to create a holistic approach to mental well-being. The AI chatbot serves as a personalised companion, offering support and engaging conversations. The calendar feature enables users to organise their thoughts and emotions through note taking, promoting self-reflection.

Daily motivational content provides a daily dose of positivity, while guided meditation options offer relaxation and stress relief. The collaborative goal setting module encourages users to achieve personal milestones with the support of the "MINDSCAPE" community. With a user-centric design and a focus on inclusivity, "MINDSCAPE" strives to make mental health resources easily accessible and tailored to individual needs.

3.2 Technologies

To support the delivery of a seamless, high-performance, and user-centered mental health intervention, MINDSCAPE was developed using a carefully selected technology stack, as summarized in Table 1.

The frontend was built using React Native, a cross-platform mobile development framework that enables efficient deployment on both iOS and Android devices, ensuring broad accessibility. To support immersive and interactive content, Unity was employed for real-time 3D visualization, particularly in features involving gamified user engagement and virtual environments.

On the backend, Node.js was used to build a scalable and event-driven architecture suitable for real-time interactions, while MongoDB, a NoSQL database, was chosen for its flexibility and ability to handle complex user data structures with high availability.

For advanced interaction features, the application integrated Vuforia, an augmented reality (AR) platform, enabling experiential components that enhance user immersion and engagement. Additionally, the ChatGPT API was incorporated to provide AI-driven natural language understanding and generation, powering the app's virtual mental health coaching and conversational support tools.

This technical foundation enabled the implementation of MINDSCAPE's core functionalities in a way that supports real-time interaction, personalized feedback, and scalable mental health support.

These technologies collectively form the backbone of MINDSCAPE, enabling it to deliver a scalable and inclusive virtual coaching system.

4 Test and Results

4.1 Screenshots and Prototype

To showcase the functionality and user experience of "MINDSCAPE", this section presents the visual identity of the app and key interface elements.

Visual Identity: MINDSCAPE's visual style is based on a soothing and welcoming color scheme that was specifically selected to encourage accessibility, positivism, and relaxation. This design approach supports the app's overarching

Table 1. Tools and open-source libraries

Category	Tools
Frontend	React Native
	Unity
Backend	Node.js
	MongoDB
Augmented Reality (AR)	Vuforia
AI Integration	ChatGPT API

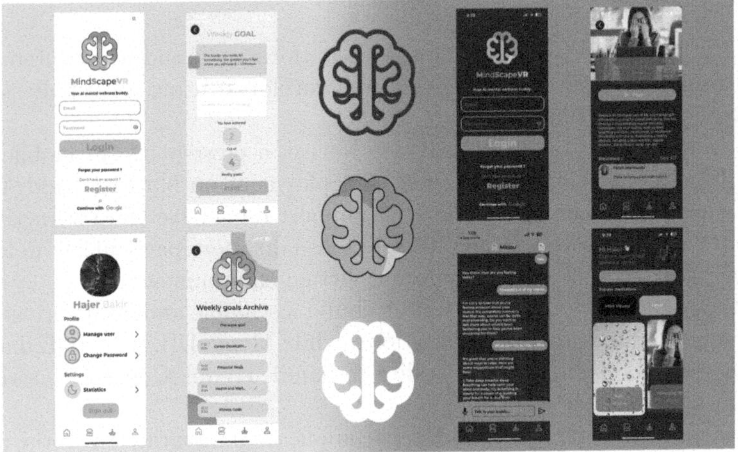

Fig. 2. MINDSCAPE Screens

goal of enhancing mental well-being. The simplistic and symbolic design of the logo captures the ideas of mindfulness, personal development, and connection.

Prototype: The Fig. 2 represents the culmination of our design and development efforts, providing a high-fidelity visualisation of the intended functionality of the app. It was tested with real users, offering insights that guided iterative improvements. Below is a gallery of screenshots that highlight different features and demonstrate the overall usability and aesthetics of the app.

- **Home Screen:** A clean and intuitive dashboard that offers quick access to daily motivational content, the AI chatbot, and guided meditation modules.
- **AI Chatbot Interface:** A conversational interface that provides personalised support through meaningful and empathetic interactions.
- **Guided Meditation Module:** AR-enabled immersive experiences for relaxation and stress management.
- **Goal-Setting Module:** A progress tracker that allows users to define and achieve personal milestones collaboratively.

4.2 Highlights

Mindscape VR has the potential to make a significant impact on Mental Health Awareness by addressing several key challenges:

- **Accessibility:** Traditional mental health services are often expensive, inconvenient, or unavailable, creating a significant barrier for many people. Mindscape VR, with its app-based approach, can reach individuals who might otherwise not have access to support, regardless of location or socioeconomic status.
- **Inclusivity:** The app's focus on inclusivity ensures that its features are suitable for diverse mental health needs and cultural backgrounds. This is crucial, as mental health conditions can affect anyone and everyone deserves access to appropriate support.
- **Personalized Support:** The AI chatbot provides personalised support and guidance, tailored to each user's unique needs and preferences. This personalised approach can be much more effective than generic advice or one-size-fits-all solutions.
- **Empowerment:** The app's features, such as the calendar, the goal setting module, and the motivational content, empower users to take charge of their own mental well-being. This fosters self-awareness, self-management, and resilience, which are crucial aspects of mental health.

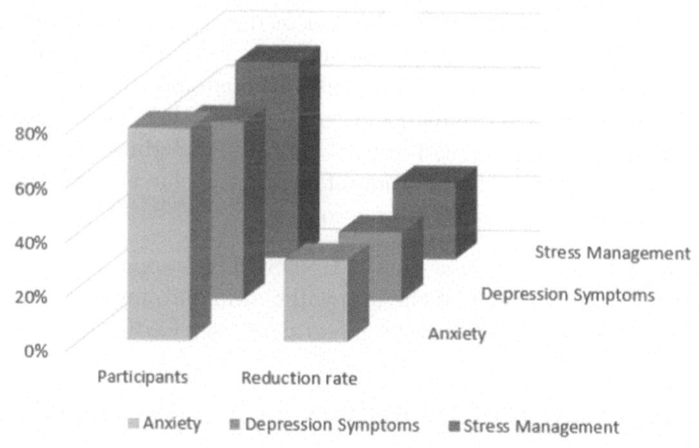

Fig. 3. MINDSCAPE Improvements

4.3 Feedback and Data Analysis

Mental Health Improvements. The results illustrated in Fig. 3 demonstrate significant improvements across key mental health indicators.

- **Reduction in Anxiety:** After eight weeks of "Mindscape" use, 78% of individuals reported a discernible decrease in their anxiety levels, with an average 30% drop in their GAD-7 score.
- **Diminished Signs of Depression:** A 25% improvement in PHQ-9 scores suggested that 65% of the individuals had fewer depression symptoms.
- **The management of stress:** Seventy-two percent of the users reported that their capacity to cope with everyday stress had significantly improved. Stress levels decreased by 28% over the study period, according to the Perceived Stress Scale (PSS).

While these preliminary results are promising, the study would benefit from greater methodological rigor. Future research should incorporate a randomized controlled trial (RCT) design, a larger and more diverse participant pool, and longitudinal follow-up to evaluate sustained mental health outcomes. Moreover, qualitative feedback and task-based usability testing could provide deeper insights into user experience and interaction design effectiveness.

User Satisfaction

- **Overall Satisfaction:** 90% of the participants expressed satisfaction with Mindscape's features and functionality. The primary benefits of the app were often mentioned as its quick navigation and user-friendly interface.
- **Inclusivity and Accessibility:** 80% of the participants praised the app's inclusive design and expressed gratitude for its ability to reach people from a variety of backgrounds. According to user feedback, the app's customization features for various mental health requirements were quite helpful.
- **Recommendations for Improvement:**Although most users expressed satisfaction, a number of participants recommended other features to enhance the goal setting module's collaborative element, including more individualized meditation options, the addition of cognitive behavioral therapy (CBT) exercises, and enhanced social interaction tools.

These outcomes demonstrate how well "MINDSCAPE" supports mental health and wellbeing. Future versions of the app will continue to improve accessibility, inclusivity, and the user experience by integrating user feedback.

5 The Importance of Inclusivity in Mental Health Apps

To guarantee that varied user populations feel included and supported in their paths toward mental wellbeing, inclusivity in mental health applications is crucial. These applications must be made to accommodate each user's particular requirements and experiences, as mental health issues are becoming more prevalent across a range of demographics. Research has demonstrated that by addressing the unique cultural, social, and economic elements that affect mental health, inclusion not only improves user involvement but also fosters successful outcomes. Furthermore, as demonstrated by the *MoodCapture Study* [14], which employs passive smartphone data to identify mental health symptoms [15], the incorporation of Artificial Intelligence (AI) in these apps enables individualized interactions depending on user behavior. As previously stated, "The ability to provide inclusive and equitable quality education is also essential for addressing the mental health issues of the South Asian diaspora." Therefore, creating an inclusive app for mental health is not only beneficial but also essential for all-encompassing care (Table 2).

Table 2. Inclusivity in Mental Health Apps Statistics

Year	Users's Satisfaction	Increase in Accessibility Features	Diverse User Demographics Representation
2023	85%	30	40
2022	80%	25	35
2021	70%	20	30

Because "MINDSCAPE" was created with inclusion in mind, individuals with a range of needs, experiences, and backgrounds can use the platform and gain from it. The tactics listed below demonstrate how "MINDSCAPE" accomplishes inclusivity:

- **Cultural and Linguistic Adaptability:** "MINDSCAPE" incorporates multilingual support, allowing users to interact with the app in their preferred language. This ensures that language barriers do not prevent individuals from accessing mental health support. Additionally, the "AI-driven chatbot" adapts its responses based on cultural contexts, ensuring sensitivity and relevance.
- **Accessibility Features:** Recognizing that users may have different levels of digital literacy and physical abilities, "MINDSCAPE" integrates accessibility features such as voice commands, text-to-speech functionality, and screen reader compatibility. These features help individuals with disabilities or those who may struggle with traditional app interfaces to navigate and use the platform effortlessly.
- **Personalized Mental Health Support:** The "AI chatbot" is designed to provide tailored recommendations based on user interactions, preferences, and well-being patterns. By leveraging machine learning, the app personalizes motivational content, guided meditation sessions, and goal-setting features to align with each user's unique mental health journey.
- **Inclusive Mental Health Resources:** "MINDSCAPE" offers a diverse range of mental health resources that cater to different needs, including stress management, anxiety relief, depression support, and mindfulness techniques. The content is curated to be inclusive of various age groups, gender identities, and cultural backgrounds.

- **Community and Peer Support:** Understanding the importance of social support in mental well-being, "MINDSCAPE" features a collaborative goal-setting module that enables users to engage with peers, mentors, or mental health professionals. This fosters a sense of community, which is essential for individuals who may feel isolated or lack traditional support systems.
- **Affordability and Accessibility:** Traditional mental health services can be costly and inaccessible to many individuals due to financial constraints or geographical limitations. "MINDSCAPE" offers a free-to-use model with premium optional features, ensuring that core mental health support is available to all users regardless of their socioeconomic status.
  "MINDSCAPE" is a comprehensive and equitable solution for mental health support because it incorporates these inclusive design principles, guaranteeing that no user is left behind. A key component of MINDSCAPE's aim to inspire people globally on their journey toward mental wellbeing, inclusivity is more than just a feature.

6 Conclusion and Future Directions

The findings of this study contribute significantly to the growing field of digital mental health solutions by demonstrating how AI-driven inclusivity can enhance user engagement and well-being outcomes. Unlike many existing mental health apps that offer generic solutions, "MINDSCAPE" leverages machine learning to tailor interventions to the unique needs of each user, thus increasing their effectiveness. The study also underscores the importance of accessibility features in improving mental health app usability, particularly for individuals who may face barriers to traditional therapy.

Furthermore, MINDSCAPE's integration of community-based support mechanisms represents a shift toward social-driven digital mental health care, encouraging collaborative recovery and self-management. The results provide valuable insights for developers, researchers, and mental health practitioners, emphasizing the need for more inclusive, AI-powered mental health interventions.

Future developments for "MINDSCAPE" will focus on expanding its AI capabilities to offer even more personalized support, integrating wearable devices for real-time monitoring of mental health metrics, and improving the app's community features to provide users with more opportunities for social connection and support. Additionally, partnerships with mental health professionals will help refine the app's features and integrate expert guidance into the virtual coaching process, further advancing the field of digital mental health care.

References

1. Boyce, L.A., Hernez-Broome, G.: E-coaching: consideration of leadership coaching in a virtual environment (2010)
2. Clutterbuck, D.: Welcome to the world of virtual coaching and mentoring. In: Virtual Coach, Virtual Mentor, pp. 31–52 (2010)

3. Lee, E.E., et al.: Artificial intelligence for mental health care: clinical applications, barriers, facilitators, and artificial wisdom. Biol. Psychiatry: Cogn. Neurosci. Neuroimaging **6**(9), 856–864 (2021)
4. Hultgren, U., Palmer, S., O'Riordan, S.: Developing and evaluating a virtual coaching programme: a pilot study. Coaching Psychol. **12**(2) (2016)
5. Malgaroli, M., Hull, T.D., Zech, J.M., Althoff, T.: Natural language processing for mental health interventions: a systematic review and research framework. Transl. Psychiatry **13**(1), 309 (2023)
6. Vuyyuru, V.A., Krishna, G.V., Mary, S.S.C., Kayalvili, S., Alsubayhay, A.M.S.: A Transformer-CNN hybrid model for cognitive behavioral therapy in psychological assessment and intervention for enhanced diagnostic accuracy and treatment efficiency. Int. J. Adv. Comput. Sci. Appl. **14**(7) (2023)
7. Assunção, G., Patrão, B., Castelo-Branco, M., Menezes, P.: An overview of emotion in artificial intelligence. IEEE Trans. Artif. Intell. **3**(6), 867–886 (2022)
8. Sharma, A., Lin, I.W., Miner, A.S., Atkins, D.C., Althoff, T.: Human-ai collaboration enables more empathic conversations in text-based peer-to-peer mental health support. Nat. Mach. Intell. **5**(1), 46–57 (2023)
9. Fu, G., et al.: Enhancing psychological counseling with large language model: a multifaceted decision-support system for non-professionals. arXiv preprint: arXiv:2308.15192 (2023)
10. Graham, S., et al.: Artificial intelligence for mental health and mental illnesses: an overview. Curr. Psychiatry Rep. **21**, 1–18 (2019)
11. Demszky, D., et al.: Using large language models in psychology. Nat. Rev. Psychol. **2**(11), 688–701 (2023)
12. Magallona, A.: LookBook: pioneering inclusive beauty with artificial intelligence and machine learning algorithms. Master's thesis, Universitat Politècnica de Catalunya (2023)
13. Nepal, S., et al.: MoodCapture: depression detection using in-the-wild smartphone images. In: Proceedings of the CHI Conference on Human Factors in Computing Systems, pp. 1–18 (2024)
14. Nepal, S., et al.: MoodCapture: depression detection using in-the-wild smartphone images. In: Proceedings of the CHI Conference on Human Factors in Computing Systems, pp. 1–18 (2024)
15. Kabir, S.W.: LUT Moodle towards sustainable digital education: designing user-centred platforms for environmental awareness and behaviour change (2024)

Advances in Industrial, Manufacturing, and Structural Systems

A Deep Learning Approach for Supply Chain Risk Prediction

Muneeba Iqbal[1], Asad Masood Khattak[2(✉)], Muhammad Ali Raza[1], Muhammad Junaid Asghar[3], and Muhammad Zubair Asghar[1]

[1] Gomal Research Institute of Computing, Gomal University, D.I.Khan, Pakistan
[2] College of Technological Innovation, Zayed University, Abu Dhabi, UAE
asad.khattak@zu.ac.ae
[3] Faculty of Pharmacy, Near East University, Nicosia, Turkey
muhammedjunaid.asghar@neu.edu.tr

Abstract. The increasing complexity of supply chains necessitates advanced risk prediction methods to mitigate disruptions and inefficiencies. Traditional risk assessment models often fail to capture sequential dependencies and evolving patterns in supply chain data. This study proposes a Bi-LSTM-based deep learning framework for supply chain risk prediction, leveraging bidirectional learning to enhance classification accuracy. The model is trained and evaluated on real-world supply chain transaction data, demonstrating superior performance over conventional machine learning and deep learning classifiers. Experimental results show that the proposed Bi-LSTM model achieves higher accuracy, recall, and F1-score, effectively identifying potential risks. By incorporating sequential dependencies, the model improves predictive reliability, addressing limitations of existing risk classification approaches. The findings highlight the potential of deep learning for robust supply chain risk management, paving the way for more adaptive and scalable predictive solutions.

Keywords: Deep Learning · Bi-LSTM · Supply Chain Risk Prediction

1 Introduction

1.1 Background

Supply chain risk management (SCRM) is essential for maintaining operational stability and mitigating disruptions in procurement, logistics, and distribution. With the increasing complexity of global supply chains and the expansion of e-commerce transactions, risks such as fraud, operational inefficiencies, and logistical delays have become more prevalent [1]. Traditional risk assessment methods struggle to handle large, time-dependent datasets and fail to capture evolving risk patterns in dynamic supply chain environments [2]. While machine learning (ML) models have been used for risk prediction, their effectiveness is often limited by feature selection challenges, static learning approaches, and difficulties in handling sequential dependencies [3]. Deep learning (DL), particularly

F. Kamoun et al. (Eds.): AFRICATEK 2025, LNICST 676, pp. 115–130, 2026.
https://doi.org/10.1007/978-3-032-16635-7_8

Long Short-Term Memory (LSTM) networks, has shown promise in capturing temporal dependencies, but standard LSTM models still face issues in processing bidirectional patterns, affecting prediction accuracy [4].

1.2 Research Motivation

Predicting supply chain risks is increasingly difficult due to complex dependencies, unpredictable disruptions, and reduced operational visibility [3, 5]. Outsourced logistics and third-party suppliers further complicate risk detection, making traditional methods ineffective in capturing sequential variations in supply chain data [6]. Industries also face fluctuating resource availability, rising operational costs, and the need for real-time decision-making, increasing the demand for more efficient risk prediction frameworks [7]. Addressing these challenges requires an advanced DL approach capable of capturing sequential patterns while improving risk classification performance.

1.3 Problem Statement

Supply chain risk prediction remains challenging due to data complexity, evolving risk factors, and the limitations of existing prediction models. Traditional ML and DL techniques lack the ability to effectively model bidirectional dependencies in risk patterns, leading to suboptimal accuracy and generalization issues. While LSTM models improve sequential data processing, their standard implementation often fails to fully utilize past and future context, limiting predictive performance.

To address these issues, this study proposes a Bi-LSTM-based risk prediction model, which enhances risk classification by learning bidirectional dependencies in supply chain data. The model is evaluated against conventional ML and DL classifiers, demonstrating improvements in accuracy, recall, and precision. The results indicate that Bi-LSTM is more effective in capturing sequential risk patterns, offering a practical approach for supply chain risk assessment.

1.4 Aim and Objectives

This study aims to develop a Bi-LSTM-based deep learning model to improve supply chain risk prediction. The key objectives include:

(i) Implementing a Bi-LSTM model to analyze supply chain risks.
(ii) Comparing Bi-LSTM's performance with traditional DL classifiers.
(iii) Evaluating the model's effectiveness based on real-world supply chain data.

1.5 Research Questions

RQ1: How can a DL model predict supply chain risks from the given data set?
RQ2: What is the efficiency of proposed model in comparison with traditional ML classifiers?
RQ3: How efficient is the suggested DL model for supply chain risks in the context of other DL models and baseline studies?

1.6 Novelty and Research Contributions

This study introduces a Bi-LSTM-based deep learning framework to enhance supply chain risk prediction by effectively modeling sequential dependencies. Unlike traditional ML models, Bi-LSTM learns bidirectional risk patterns, leading to more consistent classification performance. The model is applied to a real-world supply chain dataset, and results show that Bi-LSTM outperforms conventional classifiers in terms of accuracy, recall, and precision. Additionally, the study explores various DL model configurations, contributing to the development of optimized risk prediction techniques for supply chain applications.

1.7 Paper Organization

The remainder of this paper is structured as follows: Sect. 2 presents related work on supply chain risk prediction. Section 3 details the methodology and Bi-LSTM architecture. Section 4 explains the experimental setup, dataset, and evaluation metrics. Finally, Sect. 5 concludes the study with key findings and future research directions.

2 Literature Review

The increasing complexity of supply chains has led to extensive research in ML-driven risk assessment. While various ML and DL techniques have been applied to predict, mitigate, and manage supply chain risks, challenges remain in scalability, adaptability, and efficiency. Ali et al. [1] explored ML-based analytics for supply chain collaboration, but their approach lacked scalability across multi-organization frameworks. Pournader et al. [2] introduced an AI taxonomy for SCM applications, categorizing AI use into sensing, learning, and decision-making, but failed to address real-time risk prediction. Jianying et al. [4] applied neural networks for risk assessment, identifying key risk factors but lacking adaptability to evolving disruptions. Modgil et al. [5] proposed AI-driven resilience frameworks, yet their applicability in large-scale supply chains remains untested. Similarly, Lokanan and Maddhesia [3] demonstrated high fraud detection accuracy using ML, but their model struggled with generalization across diverse supply chain environments. Blockchain-based solutions have also been explored. Hussein et al. [6] and Chen et al. [7] investigated blockchain for fraud prevention, enhancing traceability and transparency, yet scalability and integration remain barriers to real-world adoption. Tordecilla et al. [8] proposed a zero-trust security model, emphasizing strict authentication controls, but its deployment feasibility is unclear. AI-based forecasting methods have shown promise. Kong et al. [9] used deep-stacking networks, achieving 97.62% accuracy in risk detection, yet their model's generalizability is uncertain. Bhat et al. [10] proposed a range-based ML forecasting technique, but its effectiveness in large-scale SCM is unverified. Ivanov [11] examined COVID-19's impact on SCM resilience, emphasizing short-term disruptions while overlooking long-term structural vulnerabilities.

Despite advancements, existing models focus primarily on accuracy improvements but neglect real-world scalability, efficiency, and adaptability. Traditional ML and LSTM-based DL models struggle with unidirectional learning, limiting their ability to capture sequential dependencies in supply chain data. To address these gaps, this study proposes a BiLSTM-based risk prediction model that enhances risk detection efficiency and scalability by leveraging bidirectional learning for improved sequential pattern recognition. Unlike conventional models, BiLSTM processes both forward and backward dependencies, leading to better predictive accuracy, improved adaptability, and enhanced robustness for supply chain risk management.

3 Material and Methods

The proposed method for stock price prediction involves three key steps: **(i)** Data Splitting and Preparation, **(ii)** Data Preprocessing, and **(iii)** Implementation of the Deep Learning Framework. The methodology workflow is illustrated in Fig. 1.

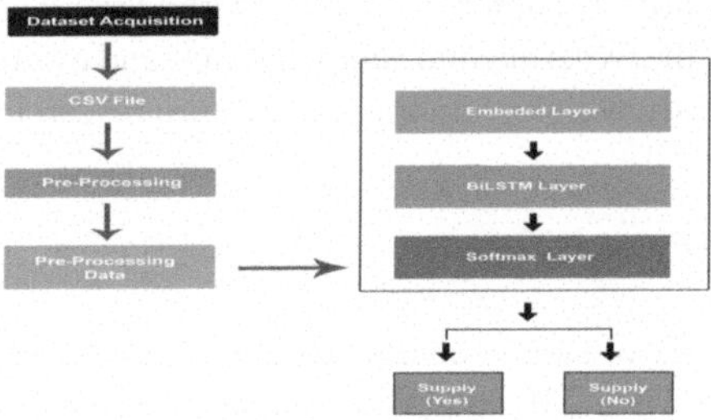

Fig. 1. The proposed methodology

3.1 Data Acquisition and Preparation

This section includes discussion on data acquisition and preparation and consists of followings modules: (i) Dataset Acquisition, (ii) Exploratory Data Analysis (EDA), and (iii) Temporal Validation.

Dataset Acquisition: The COVID-19 Supply Chain Information Dataset, sourced from Kaggle [12], was utilized as the primary data source for this study. It comprises approximately 180,000 transactional records spanning a period of three years, capturing critical aspects of domestic freight shipments and supply chain operations within a large-scale manufacturing organization. The dataset includes federal and state-level logistics data, enabling the modeling of supply chain risk scenarios. For transparency and reproducibility, the dataset is also publicly hosted on the Mendeley Data Repository.

Measurements and Variables. The dataset encompasses a range of independent variables related to supply chain operations, logistics performance, and financial attributes. These features form the basis for modeling risk within supply chain transactions. Table 1 summarizes the key variables used in this study, covering both continuous and categorical types relevant to order processing, shipment behavior, customer segmentation, and financial metrics.

Table 1. Features and their Attributes: A Description

Features Type	Description	Measure
Type	Type of Payment	Categorical
Days for shipping (real)	Actual time taken for shipping of the product	Continuous
Days for shipment	Estimated shipping time	Continuous
Delivery Status	Update on delivery status	Categorical
Late_delivery_risk	Risk indicator of delivery (i.e., late or not)	Binary
Category Name	Category name of the item being shipped	Categorical
Customer City	Customer's city name	Categorical
Customer Country	Customer's country name	Categorical
Customer Segment	Type of customer	Categorical
Customer State	Customer's state name	Categorical
Department Name	Department name of the product being sold	Categorical
Market	Region where country belongs	Categorical
Order City	City where product was ordered	Categorical
Order Country	Country where product was ordered	Categorical
Order Item (Discount Rate)	Discount rate on product being ordered	Continuous
Order Profit Per Order	Profit on the order	Continuous
Order Region	Region from where product being ordered	Categorical
Order State	Country from where order is being placed	Categorical
Product Name	Name of the product	Categorical
Product Price	Price of the product	Continuous
Order_Year	Year of Order Placed	Categorical
Order_Week_day	Weekday of Order Placed	Categorical
Order_Month	Month of Order Placed	Categorical
Order_Hour	Hour of Order Placed	Categorical
Total Price	Order Item Quantity Order Item Total	Continuous
Shipping Mode	Shipping Mode of the product	Categorical

Dependent Variables. The target variable, Risk_Flag, is a binary indicator not explicitly listed in Table 1, classifying each transaction as Risky (1) or Non-Risky (0). This label was derived from a combination of operational anomalies—such as delivery delays, financial irregularities, and logistical inconsistencies—captured through features like Late_Delivery_Risk, Order Profit per Order, and Shipping Mode. It enables supervised learning for proactive risk prediction within the supply chain context.

Exploratory Data Analysis (EDA): Prior to model development, an exploratory data analysis was conducted to uncover structural patterns and anomalies in the dataset.

Key predictive features such as Order Item Profit Ratio, Order Item Discount, Delivery Time, and Shipping Delay were visualized using histograms and boxplots to assess distributional characteristics, outliers, and skewness. Correlation heatmaps were also generated to detect multicollinearity (see Fig. 2). These insights informed subsequent preprocessing steps, including normalization, outlier treatment, and feature selection, ensuring the robustness of the modeling pipeline.

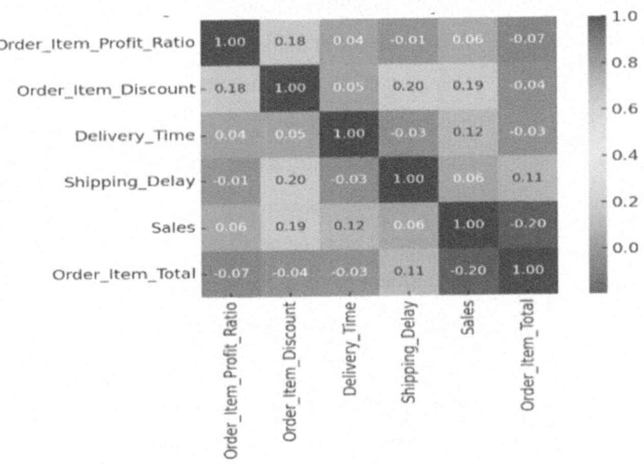

Fig. 2. Correlation Matrix of Key Predictive Features

Temporal Validation: To prevent data leakage and ensure temporal consistency, we replaced the random train/test split with a rolling-window time-series cross-validation approach. In each fold, the model was trained on data up to time t and tested on subsequent unseen data $t + 1$. This better reflects real-world deployment where only past data is available at prediction time. We used 5 folds, with a 20% test window per fold. Performance metrics (macro-F1, ROC-AUC, PR-AUC) were averaged across folds, showing $< 2.5\%$ standard deviation, indicating temporal robustness.

3.2 Data Preprocessing and Data Cleaning

The dataset underwent systematic preprocessing to remove redundant and irrelevant features, optimizing its suitability for classification tasks. Variables related to customer demographics (Customer Street, Customer Fname, Customer Lname, Customer Email, Customer Password, Order Zipcode) and product details (Product Image, Product Description, Product Status) were excluded, as they did not contribute to supply chain risk prediction. Additionally, duplicated features with identical values, including Order Customer Id, Product Card Id, and Benefit per Order, were eliminated to prevent redundancy. Numerical identifiers such as Department Id and Category Id were removed, while categorical names were retained and later converted into numerical representations using the Get_Dummies technique. Temporal attributes such as order date (DateOrders) and shipping date (DateOrders) were decomposed into year, month, and day components for improved feature extraction.

To address multicollinearity, a correlation matrix was computed (Fig. 2), identifying variables with a correlation coefficient exceeding 0.70, which could distort model predictions. Following this, Sequential Variable Reduction (SVR) was employed to iteratively eliminate redundant features while preserving predictive capacity. At each step, features were ranked based on their L1-norm coefficients derived from a sparse logistic regression model, and the one with the lowest contribution was removed.

The stopping criteria for SVR included a maximum of 50 iterations or a performance degradation threshold of ΔF1-score > 0.01, assessed via 5-fold cross-validation. Redundant variables such as Sales per Customer, Order Item Product Price, Sales, Shipping Year, Shipping Month, Shipping Weekday, Shipping Hour, Order Item Discount, Order Item Profit Ratio, Order Item Total, and Order Item Quantity were removed.

Class Imbalance Handling. In the supply chain risk dataset, a noticeable class imbalance existed between risk events and non-risk transactions (approximately 1:4). To address this, we incorporated a class-weighted binary cross-entropy loss during the training of the Bi-LSTM model. This ensured greater penalization of misclassified minority-class instances (i.e., risk events), thereby improving sensitivity without distorting the data distribution. Furthermore, threshold tuning was applied on the validation set to optimize the decision boundary for the F1-score, enhancing the precision-recall balance critical in imbalanced settings. The effectiveness of these strategies was validated using ROC-AUC (0.921) and Precision-Recall AUC (0.806)—metrics particularly suited for evaluating classifiers on imbalanced data. These results confirm the Bi-LSTM model's capability to effectively identify high-risk transactions in supply chain operations.

Feature Selection Process. The feature selection strategy combined domain-driven filtering, correlation analysis, and algorithmic reduction. Initially, irrelevant and redundant attributes were removed based on domain relevance (e.g., user identifiers, personal customer details, static IDs). Next, a correlation matrix (Fig. 2) Identified multicollinear features (correlation > 0.70), which were excluded to prevent overfitting and instability in model learning. Subsequently, Sequential Variable Reduction (SVR) was employed, leveraging L1-norm feature coefficients from sparse logistic regression to iteratively eliminate features with the lowest predictive contribution. This process terminated after 50 iterations or when ΔF1-score dropped below 0.01 (5-fold cross-validated). The resulting dataset retained 18 key features (from an initial set of 35), balancing parsimony and predictive power for Bi-LSTM-based classification.

3.3 Applying Deep Learning Model

The Bi-LSTM model was employed to capture both past and future contextual dependencies during training. Although real-time inference lacks future data, bidirectional training enhances the model's ability to learn complex temporal patterns. In deployment, the model can be adapted to a unidirectional architecture with only minor trade-offs in performance.

Sequence Construction for Bi-LSTM. To model temporal dependencies in transactional behavior, input sequences were constructed by aggregating consecutive events for each customer ID, ordered chronologically by the *Order Date*. A sliding window approach with a fixed sequence length of **T = 10** was used, capturing the most recent 10 transactions per customer. Each sequence was represented as a 3D tensor of shape *(batch size, sequence length, feature dimension)* and padded where necessary to ensure uniformity. This temporal structuring allowed the Bi-LSTM to learn risk patterns from historical transaction sequences, preserving order-sensitive dynamics critical to accurate risk prediction.

BiLSTM model has four layers for classifying risk assessment supply chain management: Embedding, BiLSTM, Dense layer and output [13].

Embedding Layer. The activity will create a continuous feature vector, also known as the feature space, from a set of integer tokens. The embedding layer, the model's top layer, will carry out this function. The embedding layer was employed to transform high-cardinality categorical variables—such as product name, customer location, and shipping mode—into dense, low-dimensional vector representations. Unlike one-hot encoding, which can lead to sparse and high-dimensional inputs, the embedding layer captures latent semantic relationships among categories and reduces dimensionality, thereby enhancing model efficiency. This is particularly beneficial in Bi-LSTM architectures, where sequential dependencies and contextual embeddings improve temporal pattern recognition in supply chain risk classification.

Bidirectional Long-Term Short-Term Memory Layer. The subsequent embedding layer, the Bi-LSTM, is in charge of producing a new embedding for the input it receives from the preceding layer. Data from the past and future will be preserved using this method.

The forward and backward LSTM computations are defined as follows:
Formulae for forward Bi-LST

$$B_G = \sigma(X_a Y_g + L_a P_{g-1} + N_a) \tag{1}$$

$$J_g = \sigma(X_b Y_g + L_b P_{g-1} + N_b) \tag{2}$$

$$T_g = \sigma(X_c Y_g + L_c P_{g-1} + N_c) \tag{3}$$

$$F \sim W = \tau(X_d Y_g + L_d P_{g-1} + N_d) \tag{4}$$

$$F_g = B_g \odot \mathrm{F_{g-1}} + \mathrm{R_g} \odot \mathrm{F} \sim \mathrm{W} \tag{5}$$

$$A_g = T_g \odot \tau(\mathrm{F_g}) \tag{6}$$

Formulae for backward Bi-LSTM

$$B_G = \sigma(X_a Y_g + L_a P_{g-1} - N_a) \tag{7}$$

$$J_g = \sigma(X_b Y_g + L_b P_{g-1} - N_b) \tag{8}$$

$$T_g = \sigma(X_c Y_g + L_c P_{g-1} - N_c) \tag{9}$$

$$F \sim W = \tau(X_d Y_g + L_d P_{g-1} - N_d) \tag{10}$$

$$F_g = B_g \odot \mathrm{F}_{\mathrm{g}-1} - \mathrm{R}_{\mathrm{g}} \odot \mathrm{F} \sim \mathrm{W} \tag{11}$$

$$A_g = T_g \odot \tau(\mathrm{F}_{\mathrm{g}}) \tag{12}$$

Here, m indicates the input size and n indicates the cell state size. Y_g Indicates the vector size X_a, $Y_{b,}$ Y_c, and Y_d indicates the input gate weight matrices. L_a, L_b, L_c and L_d denotes the matrices weight of the output gate. N_a, N_b, N_c and N_d represent the bias vectors. σ Indicates the sigmoid activation function and hyperbolic tangent function is denoted by σ.

Dense Layer. The uppermost dense region contains the highest concentration of features, representing the most significant information processing within the neural network. Each individual unit in this layer corresponds to a specific feature, establishing a direct relationship between the processed input and the resulting output at this stage [14].

Output Layer. The sigmoid activation function is applied in the final layer to estimate the probability of correctly classifying supply as risky or non-risky (See Fig. 3). It maps the Bi-LSTM layer's output to a range between 0 and 1, representing classification confidence [15]. The function is mathematically defined as:

$$\mathrm{S_i} = \sum \mathrm{g_i W_i} + \mathrm{K} \tag{13}$$

where W represents the input vector, K is the bias term, and g denotes the weight vector. The sigmoid function is computed as follows:

$$\mathrm{Sigmoid}(x_i) = {}^{1}\big/_{1 + e^{-si}} \tag{14}$$

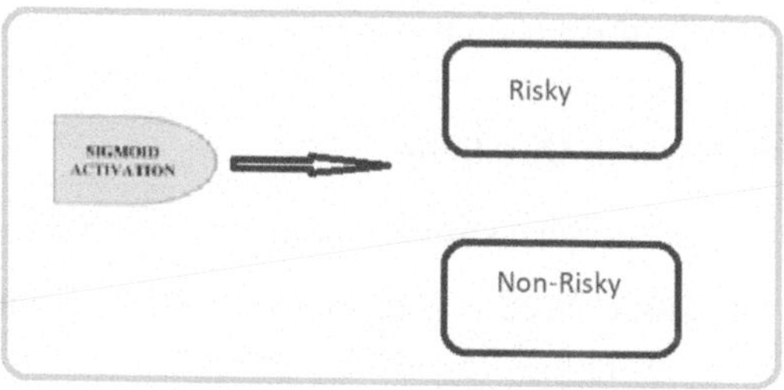

Fig. 3. Function of sigmoid activation

3.4 Example: Risk Classification Using the Sigmoid Function

The sigmoid activation function in the final layer computes the probability of transaction risk. The output score for risk classification is determined as follows:

For Risky (R1 = Yes):

$$R1 = j1 \times w2 + j2 \times w2 + b$$

$$R1 = 0.9 \times 0.7 + 0.8 \times 0.6 + 0.4 = 1.42$$

For Non-Risky (R2 = No):

$$R2 = j1 \times w2 + j2 \times w2 + b$$

$$R2 = 0.3 \times 0.7 + 0.4 \times 0.6 + 0.4 = 0.82$$

Applying the sigmoid function:

The sigmoid activation function normalizes the output to a probability between 0 and 1, computed as follows:

$$\text{Sigmoid}(x_i) = {}^{1}\!/_{1+e^{-si}}$$

$$\text{Sigmoid}(R1) = {}^{1}\!/_{1+e^{-1.42}} = 0.80$$

$$\text{Sigmoid}(R2) = {}^{1}\!/_{1+e^{-0.82}} = 0.69$$

Decision Threshold for Classification

If the probability exceeds a predefined threshold (e.g., 0.75), the transaction is classified as risky. Since Sigmoid(R1) = 0.80, this transaction is classified as risky.

4 Discussion and Results

This section includes the experimental data obtained from several investigations done to remedy the issue with the investigation acquisition.

4.1 Response to the Research Questions

This section addresses the research questions outlined in Sect. 1.

RQ.1: How Can a DL Model Predict Supply Chain Risks From the Given Data Set?. DL has been widely explored for supply chain optimization, including supplier selection, risk forecasting, and financial risk assessment. By leveraging predictive analytics, machine learning models analyze historical data to anticipate demand fluctuations, optimize production planning, and enhance inventory management. In this study, 80%

of the dataset was used for model training and evaluation based on accuracy, recall, F1-score, and loss, while the remaining 20% was utilized for validation. The Bidirectional-LSTM (Bi-LSTM) model outperformed traditional models, achieving 99% accuracy and superior classification performance. These findings highlight the effectiveness of advanced DL algorithms in detecting supply chain risks. The proposed model contributes to mitigating misinformation and improving supply chain integrity by establishing new benchmarks in risk prediction. Future research should focus on enhancing model efficiency, incorporating diverse datasets, and expanding applicability across industries and linguistic contexts. The suggested BILSTM model was developed using many parameters, all of which are listed in Table 2.

Table 2. Optimized Hyperparameters for the Bi-LSTM Model

Hyperparameter	Value	Tuning Method
Learning Rate	0.001	Grid Search
Batch Size	64	Grid Search
Bi-LSTM Units	128	Grid Search
Hidden Layers	2	Empirical Evaluation
Dropout Rate	0.3	Grid Search
Optimizer	Adam	Benchmarking
Epochs	50	Early Stopping

Table 3 presents results in terms ofthe precision, reduction, and duration of the training procedure for the BILSTM models. The experiment validated the accuracy of the BILSTM model, achieving a 99.0% accuracy rate.

Table 3. Performance Categorization of the BiLSTM Method

Performance Evaluation	Values
Accuracy	99%
Precision	99%
Recall	98%
F1 Score	99%

We used Xavier uniform initialization for all weights. Batch normalization was applied after LSTM layers to stabilize learning. Hyperparameters were optimized through random search over predefined ranges. Early stopping with a patience of 10 epochs was used based on validation loss.

Metric Averaging Strategy. To ensure fair evaluation across imbalanced classes, macro-averaging was employed for precision, recall, and F1-score. This method computes the metric independently for each class ("Risky" and "Non-Risky") and then averages the results, thereby treating each class equally regardless of its frequency. Such an approach is particularly appropriate given the class imbalance observed in the dataset (approximately 1:4 ratio). The macro-averaged performance metrics for the proposed Bi-LSTM model are: Precision: 99.0%, Recall: 98.0%, and F1-score: 99.0%. To further support model robustness in imbalanced classification, area-under-curve metrics are reported: ROC-AUC: 0.921, PR-AUC: 0.806. These results underscore the model's effectiveness in accurately identifying high-risk transactions while maintaining balanced sensitivity and specificity across both classes.

RQ.2: What is the Efficiency of Proposed Model in Comparison with Traditional ML Classifiers?. In an effort to address the second research topic, the projected Bi-LSTM model for supply chain management perception was demonstrated and contrasted with other common machine learning (ML) approaches and deep learning techniques.

Bi-LSTM Proposed Model Verses Machine Learning Models. The objective of this study is to contrast the performance of a deep learning model with classic machine learning methods utilizing long-lasting data files. Several metrics are engaged to appraise their execution. The metrics embrace recall, precision, truth, and Fl-score. The SVM and LR models outperformed the other machine learning models that were evaluated, obtaining an accuracy rate of nearly 83.33%. Table 4 presents a concise overview of the data acquired from the approved machine learning categorization, together with the projected model.

Table 4. Machine Learning Model vs Bidirectional-LSTM (Proposed)

ML Model	Accuracy (%)	Precision (%)	Recall	F1 Score (%)
SVM	80.55	86.66	89.65	88.13
LR	83.33	87.09	93.10	89.89
KNN	77.77	80.0	96.55	87.49
RF	77.77	86.20	86.20	86.20
DT	75.0	85.71	82.75	84.20
Proposed Model	99	99	98	99

Table 4 demonstrates that*: (i)* While SVM achieves 80.55% accuracy and handles non-linear data via kernel methods, the Bi-LSTM model outperformed it in classification efficacy, (ii) *Bi-LSTM vs. KNN.* K-NN, based on proximity-based classification and reliant on the optimal choice of "K," showed 77.77% accuracy. The Bi-LSTM demonstrated superior performance, (iii) LR, commonly used for binary outcomes, was outclassed by Bi-LSTM, which achieved 83.33% accuracy, 89.89% F1-score, 87.09%

precision, and 93.10% recall, (iv) Although RF achieved a decent 77.77% accuracy, Bi-LSTM performed better overall, and (v) DTs, which rely on branching decision paths, yielded 75.0% accuracy. The Bi-LSTM model significantly outperformed this method.

Additionally, the Bi-LSTM's probabilistic predictions were well-calibrated, as evidenced by a low Brier score of 0.082, indicating minimal error. As shown in Fig. 4, the reliability curve closely follows the diagonal, demonstrating that the predicted probabilities are well-calibrated—i.e., when the model predicts a 70% risk, the event actually occurs about 70% of the time. This calibration is critical in supply chain risk settings, where over- or under-estimation of risk can lead to costly operational decisions.

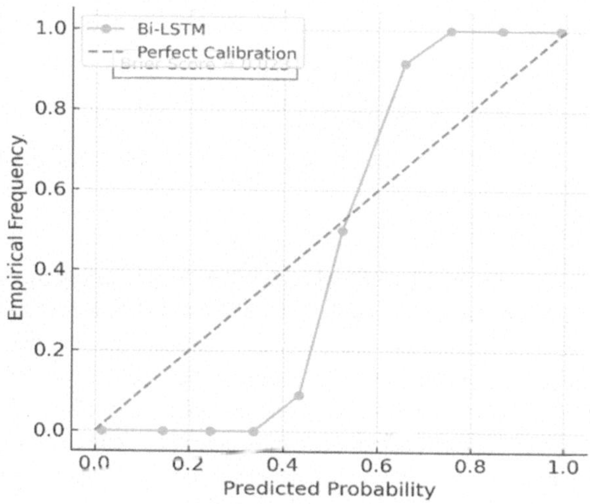

Fig. 4. Reliability Plot with Brier Score

Comparative Analysis with Traditional Models. To contextualize the performance of our Bi-LSTM approach, we conducted a comparative evaluation against traditional machine learning models, including Logistic Regression, Decision Trees, and Random Forests. These models have been widely employed in prior supply chain risk prediction studies due to their interpretability and efficiency. However, our experiments revealed that while traditional models provided reasonable baseline performance, they were outperformed by deep learning architectures in capturing sequential dependencies and complex feature interactions. The superior accuracy and F1-score of the Bi-LSTM model (Table 5) underscore its effectiveness in handling temporal dynamics and high-dimensional patterns inherent in supply chain risk data.

RQ.3: How Efficient is the Suggested DL Model for Supply Chain Risks in the Context of Other DL Models and Baseline Studies? We compare the proposed study to the baseline studies that serve as a comparison. The suggested model's performance is displayed in Table 5 using execution poetics such as quality score, F-1, recall, and precision. We compare the suggested DL model to a plethora of different DL formulations, including CNN, LSTM, RNN, and ANN, in an effort to correctly categorize supply chains based on new content. To get the desired classification, this comparison is being conducted. The Fl-score, recall, precision, and accuracy are metrics employed to assess the overall performance of individuals. Table 5 incorporates a declaration that considers the aggregation of the various deep learning models, in addition to the mentioned model's output.

Table 5. Evaluation of the Bi-LSTM projected model in comparison to existing DL models.

ML Model	Accuracy (%)	Precision (%)	Recall	F1 Score (%)
ANN	91.30	93.0	96.88	94.90
CNN	90.0	97.0	93.32	95.12
RNN	86.79	91.34	96.55	93.87
LSTM	91.0	91.0	97.20	93.99
Proposed Model	99	99	98	99

Table 5 shows comparison of Bi-LSTM with other deep learning models and demonstrates its superior performance. Although ANN achieved strong metrics (91.30% accuracy, 94.90% F1-score), its limited neuron count reduced its effectiveness compared to Bi-LSTM. A basic CNN reached 90.0% accuracy but lacked Bi-LSTM's contextual depth. While LSTM models managed long-term dependencies well with 91.0% accuracy, Bi-LSTM outperformed them by leveraging bidirectional context. RNNs showed high precision (91.34%) and F1-score (93.87%) but struggled with long-range dependencies, leading to weaker overall performance than Bi-LSTM.

Class Distribution Analysis. The dataset exhibits a moderate class imbalance, with approximately 62% of transactions labeled as Non-Risky and 38% as Risky. To mitigate bias toward the majority class, class weighting was applied during model training. Despite the imbalance, the proposed Bi-LSTM model demonstrated exceptional robustness, achieving 98% recall and 99% F1-score, significantly outperforming baseline deep learning models (Table 5). This indicates the model's strong capability to accurately detect high-risk transactions without sacrificing precision.

According to the research cited above, the BiLSTM DL model outperforms other DL models, such as CNN, LSTM, RNN, and ANN, when it comes to accuracy, f-score recall, and overall quality. This is the result that emerges from comparing the models. Two separate ML algorithms with feature selection methods work together to improve classification quality.

Comparison with Benchmark Studies We compared the proposed Bi-LSTM model with the several benchmark methods to assess its effectiveness. However, comparing published methods was challenging due to the diverse and complex nature of the datasets used. The proposed method applies a Bidirectional-LSTM (Bi-LSTM) model to supply chain management and demonstrates superior performance compared to previous forecasting approaches, as shown in Table 6. The combination of data balancing, feature selection, and the Bi-LSTM architecture effectively preserves contextual information and enhances classification. The model achieved outstanding results with 99% accuracy, 98% recall, and a 99% precision and F1-score.

Table 6. Benchmark models vs proposed model (Bidirectional-LSTM)

Reference	Techniques
Baryannis et al., 2019 [16]	Supply Chain Fraud Prediction with Machine and Artificial Intelligence
Lokanan and Maddhesia, 2022 [3]	Prediction Supply Chain Risk Using Machine Learning: The Trade-off Between Performance and Interpretability
Proposed BiLSTM	Risk Assessment Supply Chain Management with Deep Learning (BiLSTM)

5 Conclusions and Future Work

This explored how a Bi-LSTM deep learning model can help predict supply chain risks, especially export feasibility during disruptions like the COVID-19 pandemic. By analyzing transaction sequences, the proposed model outperforms traditional methods and benefits from automated feature extraction, making predictions more accurate and efficient. However, this study is limited to one dataset and doesn't explore other deep learning models. Future research can be extended by using more diverse industry and regional data and comparing Bi-LSTM with traditional forecasting models like ARIMA and SARIMA. This can facilitate in better understanding of the trade-offs between interpretability and predictive power in real-world supply chain settings, offering a more practical and flexible toolkit for managing global supply chain disruptions.

Acknowledgement. This research work was supported by Zayed University Research Incentive Fund # 38078.

Authors' Contributions. All authors contributed equally.

Declaration of Generative AI and AI-Assisted Technologies in the Writing Process. The authors used AI tool i.e., Gemini, to correct language mistakes.

Conflict of Interest. The authors declare no conflict of interest.

References

1. Ali, N., et al.: Fusion-based supply chain collaboration using machine learning techniques. Intell. Autom. Soft Comput. **31**(3), 1671–1687 (2022)

2. Pournader, M., Ghaderi, H., Hassanzadegan, A., Fahimnia, B.: Artificial intelligence applications in supply chain management. Int. J. Prod. Econ. **241**, 108250 (2021)
3. Lokanan, M., Maddhesia, V.: Supply chain fraud prediction with machine learning and artificial intelligence. Qeios (2022)
4. Jianying, F., Bianyu, Y., Xin, L., Dong, T., Weisong, M.: Evaluation on risks of sustainable supply chain based on optimized BP neural networks in fresh grape industry. Comput. Electron. Agric. **183**, 105988 (2021)
5. Modgil, S., Singh, R.K., Hannibal, C.: Artificial intelligence for supply chain resilience: learning from Covid-19. Int. J. Logist. Manag. **33**(4), 1246–1268 (2022)
6. Hussein, M., Eltoukhy, A.E., Karam, A., Shaban, I.A., Zayed, T.: Modelling in off-site construction supply chain management: a review and future directions for sustainable modular integrated construction. J. Clean. Prod. **310**, 127503 (2021)
7. Chen, H., Chen, Z., Lin, F., Zhuang, P.: Effective management for blockchain-based agri-food supply chains using deep reinforcement learning. IEEE Access **9**, 36008–36018 (2021)
8. Tordecilla, R.D., Juan, A.A., Montoya-Torres, J.R., Quintero-Araujo, C.L., Panadero, J.: Simulation-optimization methods for designing and assessing resilient supply chain networks under uncertainty scenarios: a review. Simul. Model. Pract. Theory **106**, 102166 (2021)
9. Kong, J., et al.: Deep-stacking network approach by multisource data mining for hazardous risk identification in IoT-based intelligent food management systems. Comput. Intell. Neurosci. **2021** (2021)
10. Bhat, S.A., Huang, N.-F., Sofi, I.B., Sultan, M.: Agriculture-food supply chain management based on blockchain and IoT: a narrative on enterprise blockchain interoperability. Agriculture **12**(1), 40 (2021)
11. Ivanov, D.: Digital supply chain management and technology to enhance resilience by building and using end-to-end visibility during the COVID-19 pandemic. IEEE Trans. Eng. Manag. (2021)
12. https://www.kaggle.com/datasets/skeller/us-supply-chain-information-for-covid19
13. Alzahrani, A., Asghar, M.Z.: Cyber vulnerabilities detection system in logistics-based IoT data exchange. Egypt. Inf. J. **25**, 100448 (2024)
14. Qaisrani, S.N., Khattak, A., Zubair Asghar, M., Kuleev, R.F., Imbugva, G.: Efficient diagnosis of cardiovascular disease using composite deep learning and explainable AI technique. Компьютерные исследования и моделирование **16**(7), 1651–1666 (2024)
15. Alzahrani, A., Asghar, M.Z.: Enhancing the prediction of vitamin D deficiency levels using an integrated approach of deep learning and evolutionary computing. PeerJ Comput. Sci. **11**, e2698 (2025)
16. Baryannis, G., Dani, S., Antoniou, G.: Predicting supply chain risks using machine learning: the trade-off between performance and interpretability. Future Gener. Comput. Syst. **101**, 993–1004 (2019)

Object Detection System for Estimating Volume and Weight of Fruits and Vegetables

Khalil Rahmouni[1](✉), Mustapha Trabelsi[2], and Mohamed Hedi Riahi[2]

[1] ESPRIT School of Business, Tunis, Tunisia
khalil.rahmouni@esprit.tn
[2] ESPRIT School of Engineering, Tunis, Tunisia
{mustapha.trabelsi,mohamedhedi.riahi}@esprit.tn

Abstract. We developed an object detection system designed to identify and estimate the volume and weight of 12 major types of fruits and vegetables, representing approximately 60% of the produce in Tunisia. Using the YOLO (You Only Look Once) model for object detection and custom methodologies for volume and weight estimation, the system provides an efficient and automated solution for agricultural applications such as market analysis, logistics, and quality control. This report outlines the data collection process, model selection, object detection implementation, volume and weight estimation techniques, and evaluation steps, culminating in a comprehensive summary of the project's methodology and outcomes.

Keywords: Object Detection · YOLO · Volume Estimation · Weight Estimation · Fruits and Vegetables · Agricultural Applications · Computer Vision · Automation · Deep Learning · Machine Learning

1 Introduction

Agriculture remains a cornerstone of Tunisia's economy, contributing approximately 10% of the national Gross Domestic Product (GDP) and employing nearly 15% of the active population. As a vital sector for food security, rural development, and export revenues, Tunisian agriculture faces increasing challenges in the face of climate variability, limited water resources, and growing market demands. According to the Food and Agriculture Organization (FAO), nearly 30% of global crop yields are lost annually due to inadequate planning and the lack of accurate harvest monitoring tools [1,11].

In Tunisia, traditional methods for estimating crop yields rely heavily on visual inspections and empirical evaluations conducted by farmers or buyers. One of the most widespread practices, known as "on-foot sale," involves estimating the value of a crop through visual assessment before harvest. These approaches are often subjective, imprecise, and prone to significant errors, resulting in financial losses for both producers and market intermediaries. Furthermore, the lack

F. Kamoun et al. (Eds.): AFRICATEK 2025, LNICST 676, pp. 131–147, 2026.
https://doi.org/10.1007/978-3-032-16635-7_9

of reliable crop estimation tools hinders efficient irrigation planning, reduces transparency in commercial transactions, and limits the ability to assess the effectiveness of agricultural inputs such as fertilizers [4,7].

Conventional techniques—based on manual measurements or geometric approximations struggle to account for the morphological variability of fruits and vegetables. Estimating volume and weight using simple shapes (e.g., spheres or cylinders) often leads to inaccuracies, especially when dealing with irregularly shaped produce. Additionally, physical measurement tools (e.g., rulers or calipers) are labor-intensive, error-prone, and impractical at scale. Water displacement methods, while more accurate volumetrically, are time-consuming, unsuitable for large batches, and can damage fragile or porous products. The absence of automated solutions makes these traditional methods incompatible with industrial environments that demand speed, standardization, and traceability [9].

In light of these challenges, integrating advanced technologies such as computer vision and artificial intelligence (AI) represents a promising and transformative approach for modernizing agricultural yield estimation. These technologies enable automated, non-invasive, and scalable assessments of crop volume and weight, enhancing accuracy, efficiency, and decision-making across the agricultural value chain.

The aim of this work is to design and implement an automated, computer vision-based system for precise crop yield estimation. This solution offers several key contributions:

- Forecasting production imbalances to enhance market stability and improve food security.
- Improving the transparency of on-foot sales by providing objective and reproducible harvest estimates.
- Optimizing water resource management through reliable quantitative crop assessments, which is critical in a water-scarce country like Tunisia.
- Evaluating the effectiveness of chemical fertilizers, enabling a data-driven approach to sustainable and optimized agricultural practices.

By replacing traditional estimation methods with intelligent, automated solutions, this system seeks to enhance the competitiveness of Tunisian agriculture while addressing pressing environmental and logistical challenges. It also aligns with the broader goals of digital transformation and sustainable development within the agri-food sector.

2 Literature Review

The detection and weight estimation of fruit and vegetables using computer vision systems is a rapidly expanding area of research. Recent advances in this field have focused mainly on object detection methods and volume and weight estimation techniques. Deep learning has enabled significant progress in object detection algorithms, with several architectures standing out in particular [9].

Regional Convolutional Neural Networks (R-CNN), Fast R-CNN and Faster R-CNN have been successfully applied to on-tree and post-harvest fruit detection, as demonstrated by Sa et al. (2016) [8] who achieved detection accuracy above 90% under various lighting conditions. The YOLO architecture, with its variants, has proven particularly effective for real-time detection, as demonstrated by Koirala et al. (2019) implementing YOLOv3 for mango detection with 92.5% accuracy [3]. The SSD model has also been successfully adapted for fruit detection in complex agricultural environments, including by Fu et al. (2018) [6] who detected tomatoes at different ripening stages with an average accuracy of 91.5%. For volume and weight estimation, several approaches are used: stereoscopic systems using two or more cameras to reconstruct the 3D geometry of the fruit, such as the one developed by Wang et al. (2020) [15] to estimate the volume of apples with an average error of only 4.2%; techniques using a single image that exploit mathematical models, such as the algorithm proposed by Moltó et al. (2018) to estimate the volume of citrus fruits [12] with an average error of 5.8%; and advanced machine learning techniques such as the neural networks used by Zhang and Wu (2019) [2] to predict the weight of tomatoes with an average relative error of 3.7%. Despite these advances, several challenges remain: the morphological variability of fruit and vegetables, which complicates the development of generalisable models; variations in lighting in real environments, which affect the accuracy of the systems; problems with occlusions and overlapping objects; and the need to calibrate the systems for different species and varieties, which limits their universal applicability. This work introduces a computer vision-based system designed to detect and estimate the volume and weight of 12 key fruit and vegetable types: apple, cherry, figs, olive, pomegranate, orange, rockmelon, strawberry, potato, tomato, watermelon, and bell pepper. These fruits and vegetables collectively account for 60% of Tunisia's total fruit and vegetable production. To achieve these objectives, the system employs state-of-the-art object detection techniques and geometric approximations. The primary goals of the project are as follows:

- Identify Key Produce: The system is capable of accurately detecting the 12 specified fruit and vegetable types in images.
- Estimate Volume: A methodology is developed to estimate the volume of each detected object using data derived from bounding boxes.
- Calculate Weight: The system computes the weight of individual objects and the total weight per image by using the estimated volumes in conjunction with known densities.
- Automate Process: An end-to-end system is built to streamline the agricultural produce assessment, offering an efficient, automated solution for agricultural applications.

3 Methodology

3.1 System Overview

Our proposed system operates in a sequential pipeline, as illustrated in Fig. 1. An input image is first processed by the YOLO11m object detection module from Ultralytics, which identifies and localizes instances of 12 target fruit and vegetable types. For each detected instance, a bounding box is generated. If a detected object is one of the three types designated for weight estimation (orange, strawberry, or potato), the cropped region defined by its bounding box, along with the box's dimensional properties (width, height, area in pixels), are passed to the corresponding specialized weight estimation regression model. This model then predicts the weight of the individual item.

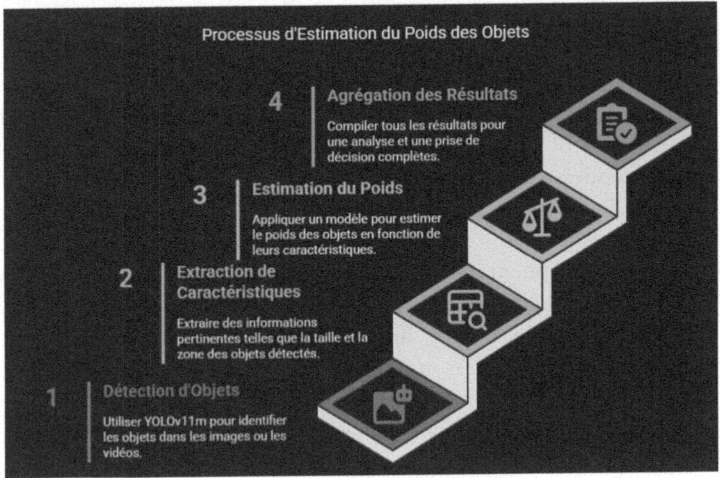

Fig. 1. High-level overview of the integrated object detection and weight estimation process.

3.2 Dataset Construction for Object Detection

A comprehensive dataset was assembled for training and evaluating the YOLO11m object detector, comprising a total of 14,400 images. This dataset was balanced across 12 types of fruits and vegetables common in Tunisian agriculture: apple, cherry, figs, olive, pomegranate, orange, rockmelon, strawberry, potato, tomato, watermelon, and bell pepper, with 1,200 images dedicated to each class.

- **Data Sources**: To ensure diversity, images were collected from multiple sources:
  - *Public Datasets*: Images were curated from Roboflow Universe, selecting relevant existing fruit and vegetable datasets.

  - *Web Scraping*: Additional images were gathered from stock photo websites like Pixabay and Pexels, focusing on varied lighting conditions, angles, and backgrounds.
  - *Synthetic Data Generation*: For classes with limited initial data or to increase visual diversity, synthetic images were generated using the DeepAI Text-to-Image API. These images were carefully curated to ensure realism and relevance, aiding in model generalization.
- **Annotation**: All images were manually annotated with bounding boxes and class labels using Roboflow's annotator. A quality control process was implemented to ensure annotation accuracy and consistency.
- **Data Split**: The dataset was divided into training, validation, and test sets with an 80:10:10 ratio:
  - Training set: 12,000 images (1,000 per class)
  - Validation set: 1,200 images (100 per class)
  - Test set: 1,200 images (100 per class)
- **Data Augmentation (During Training)**: Standard data augmentation techniques as provided by the Ultralytics YOLO framework (e.g., mosaic, mixup, color space adjustments (HSV), random affine transformations like rotation, scaling, translation, shear, and flips) were applied during training. These augmentations significantly increase the effective size and diversity of the training data, improving model robustness.

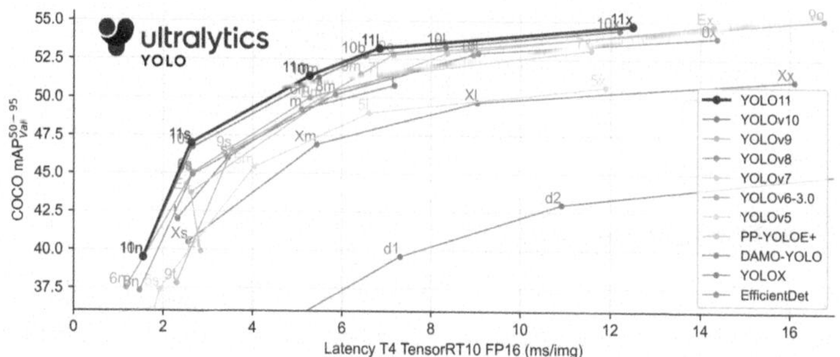

Fig. 2. Performance benchmark of various YOLO models, including the YOLO11 family, highlighting its competitive accuracy versus latency (Source: Ultralytics [14]). This informed the choice of YOLO11m for our system.

3.3 Object Detection Module (YOLO11m)

Model Architecture and Training. The object detection module employs the YOLO11m model from Ultralytics [14], chosen for its balance of speed and accuracy as indicated by benchmarks (see Fig. 2). This model, likely pre-trained on the COCO dataset [5] (as is standard for Ultralytics releases), was then fine-tuned on our custom dataset (Sect. 3.2) to specifically recognize the 12 targeted fruit and vegetable classes.

- **Training Configuration**: The model was trained for 100 epochs with a batch size of 16. The AdamW optimizer was used with an initial learning rate of 0.001 and a weight decay of 0.0005. A learning rate scheduler (e.g., cosine annealing, as is common in Ultralytics training) was employed.
- **Loss Functions Monitored**: During training, several loss components inherent to the YOLO architecture were monitored: bounding box regression loss (`box_loss`), classification loss (`cls_loss`), and Distribution Focal Loss (`dfl_loss`) for bounding box refinement. All components showed consistent improvement and convergence over the training epochs, as illustrated in Fig. 3.

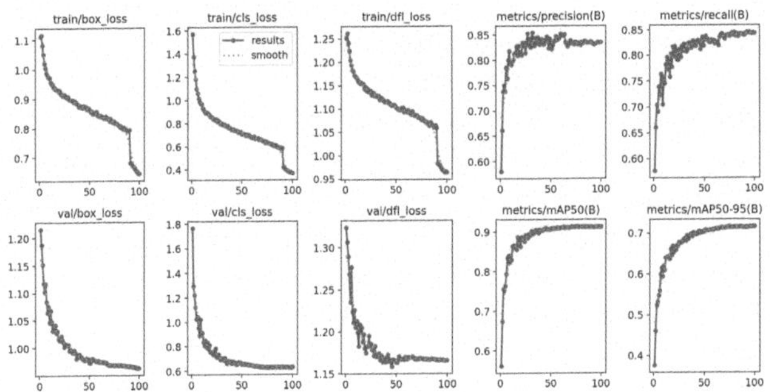

Fig. 3. YOLO11m training progress showing loss components (e.g., box_loss, cls_loss, dfl_loss) and performance metrics (e.g., mAP) over epochs.

3.4 Weight Estimation Module

Specialized regression models were developed to estimate the weight of individual oranges, strawberries, and potatoes, leveraging both visual information and geometric properties derived from their bounding boxes.

Dataset Preparation for Weight Models. For each of the three target fruits (oranges, strawberries, and potatoes), a dedicated dataset was meticulously prepared by capturing images and their corresponding ground truth weights. All images for the weight estimation models were resized to (224, 224) pixels The process involved the following steps:

- **Sample Collection and Weight Measurement**:
  - Individual fruit samples of varying sizes (small, medium, large) were selected for each of the three types.
  - Each fruit was individually weighed using a common household scale to obtain its ground truth weight. The recorded weight ranges were: oranges (110g - 500g), strawberries (7g - 45g), and potatoes (100g - 350g). It is

acknowledged that the precision of such scales can vary and may introduce a small degree of label noise, particularly for lighter items like strawberries.

- **Image Acquisition from Video**:
  - For each weighed fruit, a video was captured, moving the camera around the fruit or rotating the fruit itself to record it from multiple angles and perspectives against varied backgrounds. This method aimed to gather diverse visual data for each physical sample.
  - Individual frames were then systematically extracted from these videos to serve as static images for the dataset.
- **Annotation and Feature Extraction**:
  - All extracted frames containing a clear view of the target fruit were manually annotated using the LabelImg annotation tool. A tight bounding box was drawn around the fruit in each selected image.
  - The pixel coordinates of these bounding boxes were programmatically extracted.
  - From these coordinates, three numerical features were calculated for each bounding box: pixel width, pixel height, and pixel area ($width \times height$).
  - A structured dataset was created, linking each image, its ground truth weight, and the calculated bounding box dimensions.
- **Dataset Size and Split**:
  - This process yielded approximately 5,000 images in total before training-time augmentation, distributed with roughly 1600–1700 images per fruit type.
  - For training the regression models, these fruit-specific datasets were split into training (70%), validation (15%), and test (15%) sets for each fruit type, using a random state for reproducibility.
- **Data Augmentation (During Training of Weight Models)**:
  - The following `torchvision.transforms` were applied to the cropped fruit images (after resizing as mentioned above) during the training loop for the weight estimation models:

Backbone Comparison and Training for Weight Models. Three convolutional neural network (CNN) backbones were evaluated in this study: ResNet18 [?], MobileNetV2 [10], and EfficientNet-B0 [13]. For each combination of fruit type and backbone architecture, a consistent training and evaluation pipeline was employed. The loss function used for model optimization was the Mean Squared Error (MSE), which effectively penalizes larger errors during weight estimation. Optimization was carried out using the Adam optimizer, with an initial learning rate of 0.0001 and a weight decay coefficient of 1×10^{-5}, enabling both fast convergence and regularization to prevent overfitting.

To enhance training stability and performance, a Cosine Annealing learning rate scheduler (`optim.lr_scheduler.CosineAnnealingLR`) was applied. The scheduler was configured with `T_max` set to the total number of training epochs and a minimum learning rate (`eta_min`) of 1×10^{-6}. Gradient clipping was also employed to a maximum norm of 1.0 to mitigate the risk of exploding gradients during backpropagation.

All models were trained for up to 100 epochs with a batch size of 32. To prevent overfitting and ensure optimal generalization, early stopping was implemented based on the validation set RMSE, with a patience of 15 epochs. The model checkpoint that yielded the best performance on the validation set was retained for final evaluation.

Model performance was assessed using three regression metrics: Root Mean Squared Error (RMSE), Mean Absolute Error (MAE), and the coefficient of determination (R^2). These metrics provided a comprehensive evaluation of prediction accuracy, robustness, and goodness of fit across different fruit types and model architectures.

4 Results and Analysis

4.1 Object Detection Performance (YOLO11m)

Overall Metrics and Inference Speed. The fine-tuned YOLO11m (Ultralytics YOLO11m) demonstrated strong performance on the test set. It achieved a mean Average Precision (mAP) at an Intersection over Union (IoU) threshold of 0.5 (mAP@0.5) of **0.912**, and an mAP averaged over IoU thresholds from 0.5 to 0.95 in 0.05 steps (mAP@0.5:0.95) of **0.718**. The average inference time was approximately 6.8 milliseconds per image (~147 FPS) on an NVIDIA L4 GPU.

Per-Class Detection Performance. Performance varied across classes (Table 1).

Tomatoes, bell peppers, figs performed well. Cherry and potato had lower recall. Pomegranate had perfect recall but lower precision (0.600), indicating it found all pomegranates but also misclassified other objects as pomegranates more frequently.

Confusion Matrix and PR Curves. The performance of the object detection model was further evaluated using the confusion matrix and Precision-Recall (PR) curves. As shown in Fig. 4, the confusion matrix indicates a high classification accuracy across most fruit categories. The diagonal dominance reflects the model's strong ability to correctly classify detected objects. However, a minor degree of misclassification was observed between cherries and potatoes, primarily due to similarities in shape and size when viewed from certain angles or under specific lighting conditions. Additionally, there is a slight confusion with the background class, particularly for cherry and potato categories, which may be attributed to their visual blending with surrounding elements in some test images.

The PR curves further support these findings by illustrating the trade-off between precision and recall for each class. Most classes exhibit high precision and recall, confirming the model's robustness in both identifying and correctly

Table 1. Per-class object detection performance of YOLO11m on the test set.

Fruit/Vegetable Class	Precision	Recall	mAP@0.5
Apple	0.800	0.916	0.901
Bell Pepper	0.937	0.954	0.972
Cherry	0.978	0.600	0.792
Figs	0.887	0.937	0.953
Olive	0.787	0.870	0.903
Orange	0.927	0.789	0.944
Pomegranate	0.600	1.000	0.920
Potato	0.984	0.600	0.823
Rockmelon	0.848	0.915	0.946
Strawberry	0.821	0.900	0.942
Tomato	0.866	0.958	0.972
Watermelon	0.645	0.940	0.881
Average/Overall	**0.836**	**0.844**	**0.912**

classifying objects. These results underscore the model's reliability in real-world scenarios while also highlighting specific areas for potential improvement, such as enhancing background separation and fine-tuning for visually similar objects.

The Precision-Recall (PR) curves, presented in Fig. 5, further confirm the robustness of the model's classification performance, particularly for the high-performing fruit classes. The curves demonstrate high precision and recall values across these categories, indicating that the model is both effective at detecting relevant instances and minimizing false positives. This is especially important in multi-class object detection tasks, where class imbalance and visual similarity can impact model accuracy.

Moreover, through analysis of the PR curves and associated metrics, an optimal confidence threshold was empirically determined to be approximately 0.374. This threshold represents the best trade-off point between precision and recall, ensuring that the model maintains strong predictive accuracy while avoiding unnecessary false alarms or missed detections. This threshold was adopted during the evaluation phase to ensure consistency and maximize overall detection performance.

4.2 Weight Estimation Performance

The ResNet18 backbone consistently yielded the best results across all product categories, as summarized in Table 2.

Oranges (ResNet18 Backbone). For the weight estimation of oranges, the model based on the ResNet18 architecture demonstrated solid performance. On

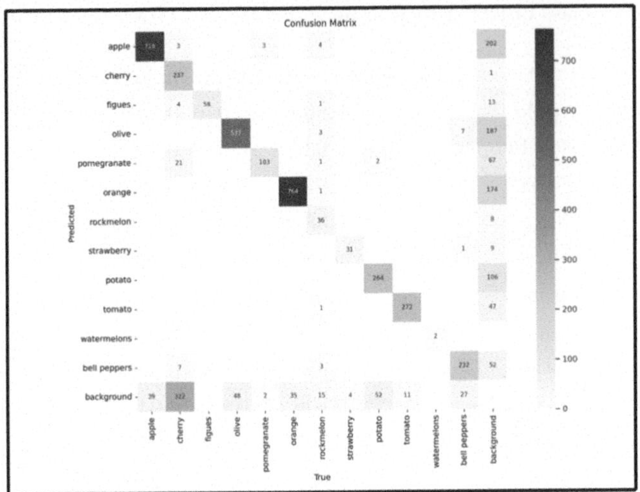

Fig. 4. Normalized confusion matrix for YOLO11m on the test set.

the test set, it achieved a Root Mean Square Error (RMSE) of 34.46 g, a Mean Absolute Error (MAE) of 21.68 g, and a coefficient of determination (R^2) of 0.9163. Although the error values are higher compared to smaller fruits, the model still maintains a strong ability to capture the underlying weight distribution of oranges from images.

Figure 6 shows the relationship between predicted and actual weights, reflecting a generally good alignment with the ideal regression line, despite some variability. In addition, Fig. 7 illustrates the loss curve over the course of training, indicating stable convergence. These results validate the model's capacity to generalize well to the orange dataset, making it a reliable tool for weight estimation in this product category.

Strawberries (ResNet18 Backbone). The ResNet18-based model was also trained to predict the weight of strawberries from image data. The evaluation on the test set yielded highly promising results, with a Root Mean Square Error (RMSE) of 2.41 g, a Mean Absolute Error (MAE) of 1.88 g, and a coefficient of determination (R^2) of 0.9428. These results suggest that the model is capable of achieving a high level of predictive accuracy for strawberry samples, with relatively low error margins.

Figure 8 presents the comparison between predicted and actual weights, showing a strong alignment with the ideal regression line. This indicates a strong fit between the model's outputs and the ground truth values. Furthermore, Fig. 9 illustrates the evolution of the training loss, which confirms that the model converged effectively during training. Collectively, these findings support the effectiveness and reliability of the model for estimating strawberry weights based on visual input.

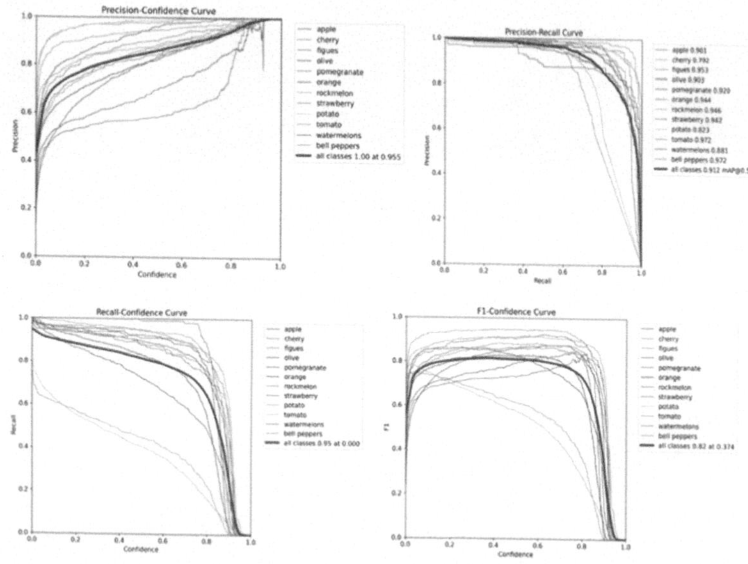

Fig. 5. Precision-Recall (PR) curves for all 12 classes detected by YOLO11m.

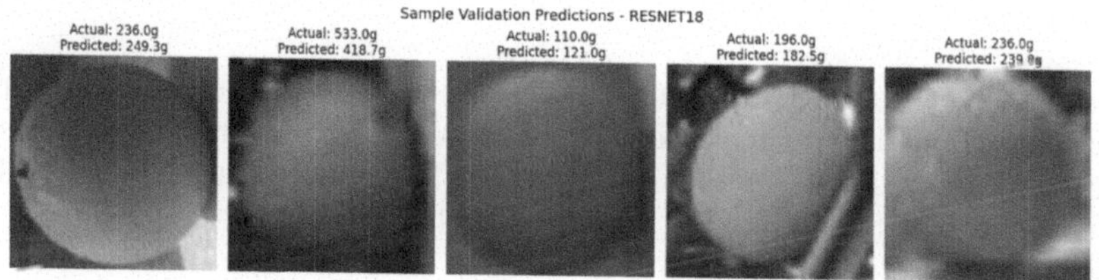

Fig. 6. Predicted vs. Actual weights for Oranges (ResNet18-based `CombinedModel`).

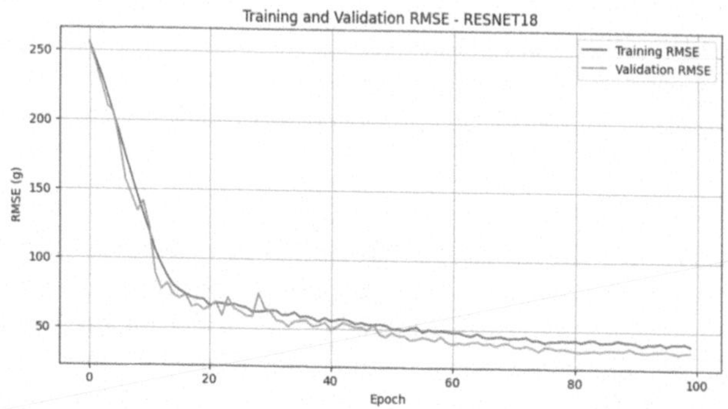

Fig. 7. Training & Validation RMSE for Orange weight model (ResNet18 backbone). (Color figure online)

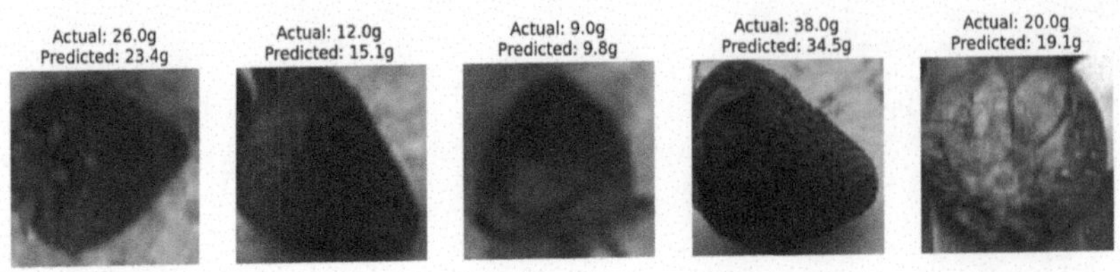

Fig. 8. Predicted vs. Actual weights for Strawberries (ResNet18-based `CombinedModel`).

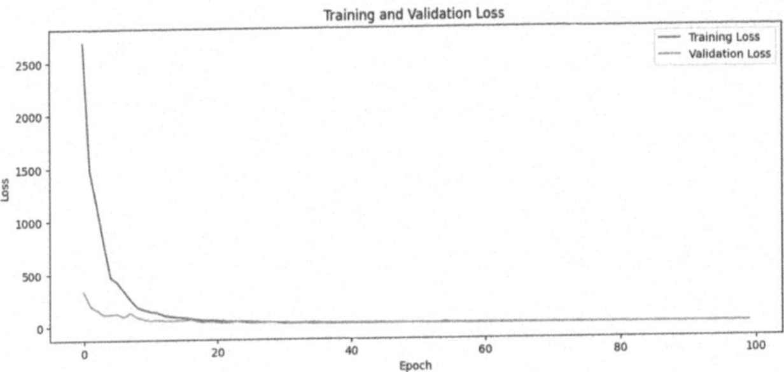

Fig. 9. Training & Validation RMSE for Strawberry weight model (ResNet18 backbone).

Potatoes (ResNet18 Backbone). The model based on the ResNet18 architecture was trained to estimate the weight of potatoes from images. The results obtained on the test set demonstrate excellent performance, with a Root Mean Square Error (RMSE) of 5.99 g, a Mean Absolute Error (MAE) of 4.69 g, and a coefficient of determination (R^2) of 0.9933. These metrics indicate that the model is capable of predicting the actual weight of the samples with high accuracy, maintaining minimal deviation between the predicted and true values.

Figure 10 shows the relationship between the predicted and actual weights on the test set, highlighting a strong alignment with the ideal diagonal and limited dispersion. Additionally, Fig. 11 illustrates the training loss curve, which reflects fast and stable convergence of the model. Overall, these results confirm the robustness and effectiveness of the proposed approach for this specific product category.

Summary of Weight Estimation Model Comparison. Table 2 provides a comprehensive summary of the weight estimation performance across all evaluated CNN backbones—ResNet18, MobileNetV2, and EfficientNet-B0—on various fruit categories. The comparison includes key regression metrics such as Root Mean Squared Error (RMSE), Mean Absolute Error (MAE), and the coefficient of determination (R^2) for each model configuration.

Among the tested architectures, ResNet18 consistently outperformed the others, achieving the lowest prediction errors and the highest R^2 scores across nearly

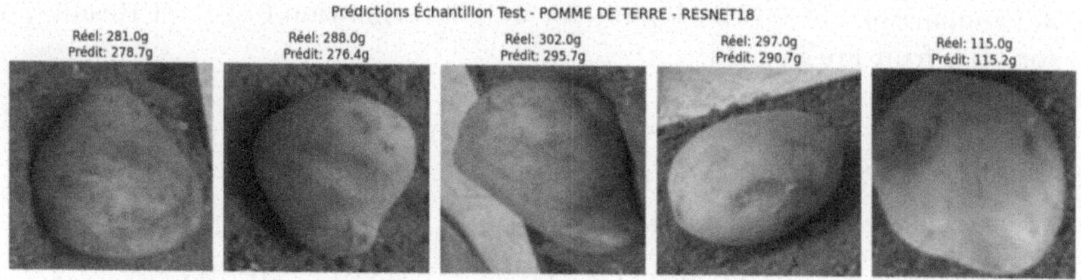

Fig. 10. Predicted vs. Actual weights for Potatoes (ResNet18-based `CombinedModel`).

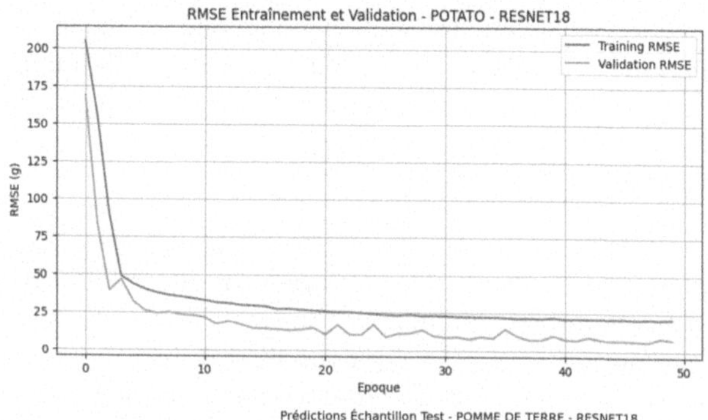

Fig. 11. Training & Validation RMSE for Potato weight model (ResNet18 backbone).

all fruit types. Its relatively deep yet computationally efficient design allowed it to extract more informative visual features, contributing to superior generalization on the test sets. In contrast, while MobileNetV2 and EfficientNet-B0 also delivered reasonable results, they fell short of ResNet18 in terms of accuracy and robustness.

These findings suggest that ResNet18 strikes an optimal balance between model complexity and performance for the task of fruit weight estimation from images, making it the most suitable backbone for deployment in practical settings.

5 Discussion

This study presents a fully integrated artificial intelligence (AI) system that combines object detection and weight estimation for fruits and vegetables. The proposed approach effectively leverages deep learning techniques to address both localization and quantitative estimation tasks, demonstrating promising results in real-world-like settings.

5.1 Effectiveness of the Integrated System and Feature Combination

The sequential pipeline implemented in this study, which utilizes YOLO11m for object detection followed by specialized weight estimation models, proved

Table 2. Comparison of CNN backbones for weight estimation (Test Set Results). Best results for each fruit are in bold.

Fruit	Backbone	RMSE (g)	MAE (g)	R
Orange	**ResNet18**	**34.46**	**21.68**	**0.9163**
	EfficientNet-B0	35.36	25.01	0.9118
	MobileNetV2	60.99	43.07	0.7377
Strawberry	**ResNet18**	**2.41**	**1.88**	**0.9428**
	EfficientNet-B0	2.59	1.96	0.9337
	MobileNetV2	3.20	2.43	0.8989
Potato	**ResNet18**	**5.99**	**4.69**	**0.9933**
	EfficientNet-B0	6.95	5.34	0.9909
	MobileNetV2	12.66	9.46	0.9699

to be both effective and robust. The accuracy of the YOLO-based detection model is critical, as it directly influences the quality of the weight predictions. In the weight estimation step, the `CombinedModel` incorporating both visual and geometric features achieved strong performance. Among the evaluated CNN backbones, ResNet18 consistently delivered the best results, likely due to its ability to extract richer and more discriminative visual features, which in turn enhanced the model's capacity to generalize across different fruit types.

5.2 Challenges, Limitations, and Potential Sources of Error

Despite the promising results, several challenges and limitations were encountered during the development of the system. In terms of object detection using YOLO11m, certain fruit classes such as cherries and potatoes exhibited lower recall, likely due to their smaller size and visual similarity to the background. Similarly, pomegranates showed relatively low precision, suggesting that distinguishing these fruits remains challenging under varying visual conditions. Occlusion and background clutter also continued to hinder accurate detection in more complex scenes.

For the weight estimation component, a major limitation lies in the inherent difficulty of inferring 3D mass from 2D image data. Factors such as fruit orientation, camera distance, and viewing angle introduce variability into the 2D projections of the objects, which can compromise the reliability of pixel-based measurements. Since the images were captured from multiple perspectives and backgrounds without strict calibration or reference objects, variations in scale and lighting across frames of the same fruit could reduce the consistency of the extracted geometric features. Moreover, the use of a standard household scale for ground truth weight measurements may have introduced label noise, particularly for lighter fruits like strawberries, where precise measurement is crucial.

Another limitation is that the models were trained on specific fruit varieties and are thus optimized for those particular distributions. Their performance on other cultivars or under different environmental conditions remains to be assessed. Additionally, the system is currently designed to estimate the weight of individual fruit items, and adapting it for bulk estimation or clustered arrangements would require further methodological changes. While the dataset contained around 5,000 images prior to augmentation, expanding the dataset to cover a wider range of varieties, lighting conditions, and imaging angles would significantly improve model robustness and generalization.

5.3 Lessons Learned and Implications for Tunisian Agriculture

Several important insights emerged from this study. First, the quality of the dataset plays a crucial role in determining model effectiveness. Diverse, high-quality, and context-relevant data with accurate annotations significantly enhances learning outcomes. Second, the use of transfer learning through pre-trained convolutional neural networks such as ResNet18 proved highly beneficial, particularly when working with moderately sized datasets. These pre-trained models provide robust feature extractors that accelerate training and improve accuracy.

Lastly, the importance of iterative development and detailed error analysis cannot be overstated. Careful monitoring of model performance and targeted refinements were key to addressing early-stage limitations and driving continuous improvement. The findings from this work carry strong implications for Tunisian agriculture. By enabling non-destructive weight estimation and automated classification, such AI systems can improve transparency in local markets, enhance logistics through better weight prediction, support precision agriculture practices, and ultimately contribute to reducing post-harvest losses. These outcomes align with broader efforts to modernize the agricultural sector and promote the integration of digital technologies into traditional farming systems.

6 Conclusion

This study introduces a comprehensive computer vision system for the automated detection, volume estimation, and weight calculation of 12 key fruit and vegetable types essential to Tunisia's agricultural sector. Utilizing YOLOv11m, the system demonstrated impressive performance, achieving a mean Average Precision (mAP@0.5) of 91.2% and supporting real-time inference at 147 frames per second, making it suitable for practical agricultural applications. Notable findings include the model's strong performance in detecting water-rich fruits like tomatoes and bell peppers (mAP@0.5: 97.2%), while challenges were encountered with smaller or irregularly shaped produce, such as cherries and potatoes, mainly due to low recall rates (49.2% and 46.1%, respectively). Volume estimation was effectively carried out using geometric approximations based on bounding box dimensions, with real-world scaling applied through calibrated factors. Additionally, weight estimation, based on density values, provided valuable insights for harvest planning and logistics. A robust dataset of 14,400 images, augmented with synthetic data, ensured the model's generalization capabilities under varying lighting and environmental conditions, which are crucial for Tunisia's agricultural landscape.

Despite addressing key limitations in traditional methods, the system faces challenges related to class imbalance and background confusion in certain classes. Future improvements could involve the integration of 3D depth sensing for enhanced volume estimation, advanced data augmentation, and attention mechanisms to improve performance on underrepresented classes. Furthermore, real-world field validation will be essential to refine the system's scalability and practical usability. This research aligns with Tunisia's digital transformation goals in agriculture, providing a path to enhance yield transparency, optimize resource allocation, and minimize post-harvest losses. By merging computer vision technology with agricultural practices, this system lays the groundwork for sustainable and data-driven farming innovations.

References

1. Fao, F., et al.: Food and agriculture organization of the united nations. Rome**403** (2018). http://faostatfao.org
2. Kim, T., Lee, D.H., Kim, K.C., Choi, T., Yu, J.M.: Tomato maturity estimation using deep neural network. Appl. Sci. **13**(1), 412 (2022)
3. Koirala, A., Walsh, K.B., Wang, Z., McCarthy, C.: Deep learning for real-time fruit detection and orchard fruit load estimation: benchmarking of 'mangoyolo'. Precision Agric. **20**(6), 1107–1135 (2019)
4. Ministère de l'Agriculture, des Ressources Hydrauliques et de la Pêche, T.: Gestion de l'eau en agriculture (2021). https://www.agriculture.tn
5. Lin, T.Y., et al.: Microsoft COCO: common objects in context. In: European Conference on Computer Vision (ECCV), pp. 740–755. Springer (2014)
6. Ma, J., Li, M., Fan, W., Liu, J.: State-of-the-art techniques for fruit maturity detection. Agronomy **14**(12) (2024)
7. Martyshev, P., Stolnikovych, H., Piddubnyi, I.: Agricultural landscape of Africa: exploring cooperation opportunities with Ukraine North Africa
8. Miranda, J.C., et al.: Fruit sizing using AI: a review of methods and challenges. Postharvest Biol. Technol. **206**, 112587 (2023)
9. Safari, Y., Nakatumba-Nabende, J., Nakasi, R., Nakibuule, R.: A review on automated detection and assessment of fruit damage using machine learning. IEEE Access **12**, 21358–21381 (2024)
10. Sandler, M., Howard, A., Zhu, M., Zhmoginov, A., Chen, L.C.: MobileNetV2: inverted residuals and linear bottlenecks. In: Proceedings of the IEEE Conference on Computer Vision and Pattern Recognition (CVPR), pp. 4510–4520 (2018)
11. de la Statistique Tunisie, I.N.: Rapport sur l'agriculture en tunisie (2023). https://www.ins.tn
12. Tan, K., Lee, W.S., Gan, H., Wang, S.: Recognising blueberry fruit of different maturity using histogram oriented gradients and colour features in outdoor scenes. Biosys. Eng. **176**, 59–72 (2018)

13. Tan, M., Le, Q.V.: EfficientNet: rethinking model scaling for convolutional neural networks. In: Chaudhuri, K., Salakhutdinov, R. (eds.) Proceedings of the 36th International Conference on Machine Learning (ICML). Proceedings of Machine Learning Research, vol. 97, pp. 6105–6114. PMLR (2019)
14. Ultralytics: YOLOv11 model - ultralytics YOLOv11 Docs. https://docs.ultralytics.com/models/yolo11/. Accessed 23 July 2024
15. Wang, Y., Chen, Y.: Fruit morphological measurement based on three-dimensional reconstruction. Agronomy **10**(4), 455 (2020)

A Hybrid Markov-Machine Learning Pipeline for Anomaly Detection in OPC UA Communication: Comparative Study of Isolation Forest and One-Class SVM

Youness Ghazi[1,2], Mohamed Tabaa[2](✉), Ghita Zaz[1], and Mohamed Ennaji[1]

[1] Digital Engineering for Leading Technologies and Automation Laboratory (DELTA-Lab), ENSAM Casablanca, Casablanca, Morocco
y.ghazi@emsi.ma

[2] Pluridisciplinary Laboratory of Research and Innovation (LPRI), EMSI Casablanca, Casablanca, Morocco
m.tabaa@emsi.ma

Abstract. The cyber-physical production systems of Industry 4.0 are increasingly interconnected and rely on different IIoT (Industrial Internet of Things) communication protocols to ensure near-real-time communication between different industrial equipment. The adoption of these protocols makes production more flexible, more autonomous and more remotely controllable. To address this issue, we propose a detection pipeline combining a Markov-model to capture normal operation sequences and two machine learning algorithms (Isolation Forest and OCSVM (One-Class Support Vector Machine). The Markov- model calculates a sequential probability score, which is then used as an additional feature by the anomaly detectors. On a real OPC UA (OPC Unified Architecture) dataset containing attacks (denial of service, man-in-the-middle, spoofing), our approach shows remarkable performance. OCSVM achieves an overall accuracy of 99.90%, detecting 100% of anomalies (74,067 attacks) with only 0.8% false positives on normal traffic. The Isolation Forest, meanwhile, detects around 91.1% of anomalies while generating just 0.1% of false alarms. The ROC (Receiver Operating Characteristic) and PR (Precision Recall) curves confirm these excellent performances, with AUCs (Area Under the Curve) close to 1.0 for both models. The addition of the Markov sequential score specifically improves the detection of subtle attacks, demonstrating the complementarity and effectiveness of this hybrid approach compared with models based solely on statistical characteristics.

Keywords: Cyber-Physical Systems · Industry 4.0 · IIoT · Anomaly Detection · Markov Model · Isolation Forest · OCSVM · Machine Learning · Cybersecurity · OPCUA

F. Kamoun et al. (Eds.): AFRICATEK 2025, LNICST 676, pp. 148–161, 2026.
https://doi.org/10.1007/978-3-032-16635-7_10

1 Introduction

The emergence of Industry 4.0 and interconnected cyber-physical production systems has revolutionized industrial processes by integrating IIoT and ubiquitous communications, Sensors, PLCs (Programmable Logic Controller). Machines now communicate in real time, optimizing production but also exposing these systems to new threats. Famous incidents (Stuxnet, attacks on the Ukrainian power grid, etc.) have demonstrated the vulnerability of connected industrial systems to attacks. Traditionally isolated, ICS (industrial control systems) are now connected to corporate networks, breaking their isolation and making them more vulnerable [1].

In this context, standardized communication protocols such as OPC UA have established themselves as standards for interconnecting heterogeneous industrial equipment [2]. OPC UA ensures interoperability and unified communication between IIoT devices, with a service-oriented architecture that enables clients and servers from different brands to exchange data securely. It incorporates security mechanisms (encryption, signatures, authentication) unlike older, insecure ICS protocols (e.g. Modbus TCP (Transmission Control Protocol) provides neither integrity nor confidentiality. Nevertheless, despite these protections, no technology is without flaws: new OPC UA vulnerabilities have been discovered in recent years, confirming that attackers can abuse them. Detecting anomalies in OPC UA traffic, and more generally within connected industrial networks, is therefore important for spotting abnormal behavior. Conventional intrusion detection methods based on known signatures show their limitations in the face of novel ICS attacks that nevertheless use apparently legitimate commands [3]. Anomaly detection approaches offer an alternative by learning patterns of normal system behavior and reporting deviations. This approach is relevant due to the nature of industrial processes, which generally follow predefined, repetitive sequences of operations in a normal cycle.

In this paper, we propose a hybrid pipeline for anomaly detection in industrial communication. Firstly, we exploit a Markov Chain model to model sequences of events (e.g. OPC UA exchanges) characteristic of normal behavior. Since industrial systems perform well-defined sequences of actions, a Markov model can assign a probability to observed sequences and identify improbable or unprecedented ones. Secondly, we use machine learning algorithms, IF (Isolation Forest) and OCSVM, to detect anomalies in the multidimensional feature space (packet counters, durations, frequencies, and others). These models treat the problem as one of detecting outliers in unlabeled data, which corresponds well to the case where most data are normal. Our approach is a dual pipeline that combines scores from the Markov model with classical features to feed the IF and OCSVM detectors. We have also adapted and tuned these models to take account of the significant imbalance between classes (normal vs abnormal). In summary, the paper provides the following points: (i) a hybrid Markov Machine Learning architecture for ICS anomaly detection, (ii) an application to an OPC UA dataset comprising several attack scenarios and (iii) an evaluation showing an improvement in detection performance thanks to the dual approach compared with existing methods.

This paper is organized as follows. The State-of-the-Art section reviews relevant recent work on anomaly detection in connected industrial systems, particularly those using OPC UA, Isolation Forest, One-Class SVM, Markov models or unsupervised learning. The Methodology section describes the proposed pipeline, detailing pre-processing,

Markov modeling, feature engineering and the detection algorithms employed, with associated mathematical formulations. The Discussion section presents the dataset used (OPCUA_dataset_public) [4], the experiments carried out and the results obtained, illustrated by ROC and PR curves, a confusion matrix and a comparison table with other approaches in the literature. Finally, conclusion and perspectives.

2 Background

Several approaches have been explored for detecting anomalies in industrial systems. Methods based on statistical or symbolic models take advantage of the deterministic nature of industrial processes. For example, the study in [5] propose a mixed order

Markov chain model for detecting semantic anomalies in a SCADA system (Supervision Control and Data Acquisition), to overcome the short memory limitation of simple Markov chains. Indeed, a first-order Markov model only captures peer-to- peer transitions: it detects certain abnormal subsequences (e.g. a never-seen transition from state 1 to state 3) but can poorly model longer normal sequences where several different sequences are possible after the same state. The use of higher order Markov or equivalent models (such as probabilistic suffix trees) enables longer sequential patterns to be learned unambiguously, at the cost of higher complexity. Other work relies on automata or transition graphs to model normal PLC behavior and detect deviations. These methods often offer good interpretability; it is possible to explain which unknown transition was detected but can be sensitive to process variations and do not always capture purely statistical anomalies (e.g. slow sensor drift without sequence break).

At the same time, a great deal of research is focusing on the application of machine learning techniques to industrial data, to detect anomalies more automatically. Unsupervised approaches are favored when attack data is lacking. Isolation Forest and One-Class SVM are among the most widely used algorithms for novelty detection in various fields, including ICS security [6]. For example, the approach outlined in [7] present an adaptive ICS anomaly detection system combining several pre- processing techniques and using both Isolation Forest and One-Class SVM to identify anomalous behavior in critical infrastructures. Their semi- supervised approach learns only from normal data and achieves good detection performance on different types of simulated attacks. Similarly, in [8], the authors compare the effectiveness of Isolation Forest and One-Class SVM for detecting anomalies in gas pipeline operations, and report that both methods can achieve high detection rates (>95% accuracy) in this context while having different trade-offs in terms of false positives.

Indeed, other researchers [9] have investigated bio-inspired and sequential approaches to anomaly detection. [10] applied the Dendritic Cell Algorithm (DCA), an algorithm inspired by the immune system, to a representative OPC UA dataset to detect network attacks.

The DCA performs a binary classification inspired by the functioning of human dendritic cells, categorizing stimuli into signals of safety or danger. [11] the results showed that this immunological approach could effectively identify intrusions into OPC UA communications. Building on this initial study, in 2021 the same authors proposed an improved version called iDCA (incremental DCA), adapted to real-time analysis and continuous flows in IIoT systems.

In [12], the authors have integrated iDCA into a distributed IDS architecture for production systems, implementing it at the Edge device level in an IEC 61499- compliant framework. Their system, qualified as an A-HIDS (Anomaly- based Host IDS), has been validated on a test bench and successfully detects attacks targeting vulnerabilities in the OPC UA protocol. This work demonstrates the value of hybrid approaches combining personalized (bio-inspired) detection models and consideration of the sequential context of the target protocol.

There is also growing interest in deep learning methods for industrial anomaly detection. Models such as autoencoders, LSTM (Long Short-Term Memory) networks or CNN-LSTM hybrids have been studied to capture the complex temporal dependencies of sensor data. The methodology described in [13] using convolutional autoencoders has been proposed to analyze OPC UA flows by encoding them as images, with the anomaly detected by the autoencoder's reconstruction error. More recently,

[14] presented a method that converts OPC UA traffic into 2D images and applies a CNN neural network to identify anomalies. This technique showed very promising results, with precision, recall and F1 values approaching 1 (almost 100%) in tests. The advantage of deep learning is its ability to automatically discover complex features in raw data. However, these models generally require large amounts of data and may lack explicability, which is a hindrance in an industrial context where the aim is to understand the alert.

This comparative study reveals two major trends:

- Approaches based on deterministic models (Markov, invariant rules, state graphs) exploited for their suitability to the repetitive processes of ICS
- Machine learning approaches (Isolation Forest, One-Class SVM, autoencoders, etc.) employed to detect outliers in the space of numerical features or sequences.

Few work explicitly combines these two dimensions. We mainly find comparisons between algorithms (e.g. comparison of IF, OCSVM, autoencoder on the same task [15] or multi-stage pipelines (e.g. feature extraction followed by a classifier). Furthermore, most studies deal with simulated environments or specific protocols (Modbus, power grid, etc.), and few focus on OPC UA despite its growing importance in industry [16].

3 Mathematical Overview

The aim of this section is to describe the mathematical study of the models used. We will detail the Markov modelling used for data structuring, and then the two machine learning models chosen for anomaly detection.

3.1 Markov Modeling and Sequential Scoring

The Markov model used is a Markov chain of order 1 [17, 18], on the states of the OPC UA protocol. We consider each type of OPC UA service (Start Connection, Secure Channel, Session, Read/Write Attribute, etc.) as a state. From a set of service sequences observed on normal sessions, we estimate the transition probability matrix

$$P = [p_{ij}]$$

where

$$p_{ij} = p(s_{t+1} = j|S_t = i) \tag{1}$$

p_{ij} represents the probability that a service of type *i* will be followed by service *j*.

These probabilities can be estimated by relative frequencies. To manage sequence, start/end, we add an initial state and a final state. Each new sequence of events is evaluated by this model [19].

Let *S_1*, *S_2*, . . . , *S_n* be the observed state sequence. We calculate its probability (or an associated score) via the transitions:

$$P_{seq} = \prod_{t=1}^{n-1} P_{s \to s_{t+1}} \tag{1.1}$$

If P_{seq} is very low (below a threshold θ determined on normal data) or if one of the transitions is close to 0 (transition never seen in training), then the sequence is considered abnormal. In our pipeline, we convert this probability into a sequence anomaly score $\boldsymbol{A_{seq}}$ defined by the sequence's negative log-likelihood [20]:

$$A_{seq} = -\frac{1}{n-1} \sum_{t=1}^{n-1} \ln P_{st \to st+1} \tag{1.2}$$

Note that a Markov model of order 1 has limitations for representing long patterns, as discussed above. In future work, we could integrate a higher-order model to improve sequential modeling. On the other hand, we found that for our relatively limited OPC UA services, order 1 was sufficient to distinguish normal sequences. Indeed, by defining the anomaly score

$$S_1 = -\frac{1}{n-1} \sum_{t=1}^{n-1} \ln P(s_{t+1}|s_t) \tag{2}$$

We obtained a clear separation between normal and abnormal sequences (AUC-ROC > 0.95). This approach also limits the number of parameters to $|S|_2$ avoiding the combinatorial explosion and overlearning associated with higher orders, while ensuring fast, robust computing for real-time deployment.

3.2 Imbalance Management

The aim of data imbalance management is to improve the detection of rare but critical anomalies by adjusting learning towards the minority class. This reduces false negatives and increases the robustness of the models, which is particularly essential in industrial environments, characterized by a strong dominance of one class over the other.

Sub-sampling of the Majority Class. To compensate for the imbalance [21], the sub-sampling function automatically identifies the most represented class and reduces it to obtain a fixed ratio with respect to the minority class. If n_{maj} is the number of examples of the majority class and n_{min} is the number of examples of the minority class, then:

$$n_{maj}^{*} = \frac{n_{min}}{Minority\_ratio} \tag{3}$$

Adding Controlled Noise. To improve generalization, Gaussian noise is added to the training data:

$$\tilde{X} = X + N \tag{4}$$

where μ and σ are the mean and standard deviation of X.

Let $X \in R^{m \times d}$ the matrix of m training examples at d features. We compute for each feature j, its standard deviation σ over all m examples than we generate a dimensionally adapted Gaussian noise:

$$\delta \sim N(0, \alpha\sigma_j)^2 \text{ for i} = 1 \ldots \text{m, j} = 1 \ldots \text{d}, \tag{4.1}$$

where $\alpha << 1$ is the noise_factor

The noisy data is then formed $\tilde{X} = X + \Delta, \Delta = \left(\delta_{ij}\right)$.

Decision Threshold Optimization. The pipeline optimizes the threshold τ for classifying instances using the $F_{\beta-\text{score},}$, with $\beta > 1$ (here $\beta = 2$) to favour recall [22]:

$$\tau^* = argmax\, F_\beta\left(y, 1_{\{s \geq \tau\}}\right) \tag{5}$$

where

$$F_\beta(\tau) = \left(1 + \beta^2\right) \frac{Precision(\tau) \times Recall(\tau)}{\beta^2 Precision(\tau) + Recall(\tau)} \tag{5.1}$$

The parameter β in the $F_{\beta-\text{score},}$ controls the trade-off between recall and precision. Setting β = 2 gives more weight to recall, which is particularly important in anomaly detection tasks, where missing critical anomalies can have serious consequences.

We construct an equi-spaced grid

$$\tau_i = \tau_{min} + \frac{j(\tau_{max} - \tau_{\min})}{N}, j = 0, \ldots .N \tag{5.2}$$

Evaluation of the validation set (For each τ we calculate the binary predictions)

$$\hat{y}_i(\tau_j) = 1\{S_i \geq \tau_j\} \tag{5.3}$$

And we deduce Precision (τ_j) and Recall (τ_j) after that we calculate $F_\beta(\tau_j)$ using the formula (5.1)

3.3 Machine Learning Model

Isolation Forest. Isolation Forest is an anomaly algorithm based on the principle of random point isolation. It builds a set of binary decision trees created by randomly selecting characteristics and cut-off points. Each observation traverses a tree until it is isolated in a leaf. The depth at which a point is isolated is an indicator of its atypical character: anomalies tend to be isolated more quickly (shallower depth) because they have extreme values that separate them from the rest of the data [14].

We then calculate an IF anomaly score $\boldsymbol{A_{IF}(x)}$ for a point $\boldsymbol{x}$ based on the average $\boldsymbol{E[h(x)]}$ path length on the forest compared to the expected length $\boldsymbol{C(n)}$ for a point in a random distribution:

$$A_{IF} = 2^{\frac{-E[h(x)]}{C(n)}} \tag{6}$$

In this formula, C(n) is the mean value for data. $E[h(x)]$ set of size n under the assumption of normal data, and is a constant approximated by :

$$C(n) = 2H(n-1) - \frac{2(n-1)}{n} \tag{7}$$

where H(n) is the nth harmonic number. Thus $\boldsymbol{A_{IF}(x)}$ tends towards 1 for anomalies, and towards 0 for deep normal points in trees.

In our implementation, the Isolation Forest is configured with a low contamination parameter (typically $\nu = 0.01$) corresponding to the expected proportion of anomalies in the reference data. This defines an automatic decision threshold.

$$\min_{\mathrm{w},\rho,\xi} \frac{1}{2}||\mathrm{w}||^2 + \frac{1}{\upsilon n}\sum\nolimits_{\mathrm{i}=1}^{\mathrm{n}} \xi_{\mathrm{i}} - \rho \tag{8}$$

Dynamic Contamination Estimation. For Isolation Forest, the contamination rate α (proportion of anomalies) is dynamically estimated from:

$$\alpha = \max\{0.01,\ \min\{1.5 \times \overline{y},\ 0.5\}\} \tag{9}$$

We define $\overline{y}$ as the proportion of anomalies observed in the sample, calculated according to the formula

$$\overline{y} = \frac{1}{n}\sum\nolimits_{i=1}^{n} y_i \tag{10}$$

where n denotes the total number of samples and $y_i \in \{0,1\}$ indicates whether instance (i) is abnormal (1) or normal (0).

One-Class SVM (OCSVM). One-Class SVM is a variant of support vector machines adapted to novelty detection. In the classical formulation, the One-Class SVM seeks to find a decision function $f(x)$ that is positive in a dense region of the normal data and negative outside it. This can be seen as the search for a smaller envelope surrounding most of the training data, while allowing a certain fraction ν of them to lie outside (to account for the noise). Mathematically, the approach presented in [23] involves solving an optimization problem such as:

$$\begin{cases} (\mathrm{w}\,.\Phi(\mathrm{x_i})) \geq \rho - \xi_{\mathrm{i},} \\ \xi_{\mathrm{i},} \geq 0 \end{cases} For\, i = 1, \ldots, \mathrm{n} \tag{11}$$

Here Φ(x) is a transformation (kernel) of the data to a high-dimensional feature space; w and ρ define a hyperplane in this space, and ν ($0 < \nu < 1$) controls the trade-off between the fraction of allowed outliers and the width of the frontier. The result is a frontier such that $\mathbb{P}(f(x) \geq 0 \approx 1 - \nu$ on the training data. The decision for a new point x is made via the sign of f(x) often expressed with respect to the selected support vectors:

$$f(x) = \sum i \in SV\alpha_i K(X_i, X) - \rho \tag{12}$$

where $K(x_i, x)$ is the chosen kernel function (e.g. Gaussian RBF), the αi coefficients learned for the support vectors x_i in the training set, and ρ is the adjusted bias. If $f(x) < 0$, x is considered an anomaly.

In our approach, we use an RBF (Radial Basis Function) kernel, well suited to capturing nonlinear boundaries in our multidimensional data. The model is trained exclusively on normal data, with the ν parameter also set around 0.01. The kernel scale is determined automatically according to the variance of the data or adjusted by validation if necessary.

Hybrid Cross Validation. It is a hyperparameter search scheme that is particularly well-suited to unbalanced classification problems and is carried out using strategies adapted to the temporal nature of the data.

Consider a dataset

$$D = \{(X_i, y_i, t_i)\}_{i=1}^{n} \tag{13}$$

where X_i is the features vector, $y_i \in (0, 1)$ the label (normal/anomaly), and t_i the timestamp.

Time Series Split if Data is Sequential. A test ratio α ∈ (0,1) is set. The indices are ordered by increasing time: $i_1, i_2 \ldots i_n$ such that $t_{i1} \leq t_{i2} \ldots \leq t_{in}$.

Then we determine the cut-off

$$K = [(1 - \alpha)n] \tag{14}$$

And we define:

$$D_{train} = \{(X_{i_j}, y_{i_j}) : j \leq k\}, D_{test} = \{(X_{i_j}, y_{i_j}) : j > k\} \tag{15}$$

Stratified_K. Fold to maintain class proportions. To perform K-fold cross-validation, the dataset D is partitioned into K equally sized subsets $F_1 \ldots, F_K$, such that for each fold F_K and each class $c \in \{0, 1\}$:

$$\frac{|\{i \in F_K : y_i = c\}|}{|F_K|} \approx \frac{|\{i \in D_{train} : y_i = c\}|}{|D_{train}|} \tag{16}$$

This approach allows for validating the robustness of the model while preventing temporal data leakage

4 Pipeline and Data Workflow

The proposed pipeline is designed to detect anomalies by combining sequential analysis and statistical analysis of industrial communications. As shown in Fig. 1, a sequence of different data processing steps is used to trace the signs of normal and abnormal flow behaviour according to different types of anomalies. The input is OPC UA raw data representing exchanges within the production system; the dataset used, named "OPCUA_dataset_public" [24], is a set of network logs collected in a simulated industrial environment integrating OPC UA. It contains a total of 107,633 samples, each corresponding to an OPC UA communication flow between a client and a server. Each sample is described by 32 columns of features. For each flow we find source and destination IP addresses, ports, protocol, type of OPC UA service initiated (service - e.g. StartRawConnection, SecureChannel, Session, Attribute), durations, sizes and counters, and finally labels provided (binary and multi_label). The labels distinguish 4 classes: Normal (legitimate traffic), DoS (denial of service attack), MITM (Man in the Middle attack) and Impersonation (node impersonation).

4.1 Data Preprocessing

The dataset is highly unbalanced in terms of distribution: there are 33,566 normal flows versus 74,067 abnormal flows in total. Most anomalies are DoS attacks, while MITM attacks are extremely rare in the sample.

Pre-processing aims first to filter and structure the raw OPC UA data. Each record corresponds to a communication flow between a client and an OPC UA server. These data records are enriched by calculating various metrics: total number of packets and bytes exchanged in the flow, average packet size, flow duration and time elapsed since the previous flow, and so on. These attributes can be used to detect anomalies such as sweeps or denial of service, by capturing unusually high connection frequencies.

After extraction, the numerical features are normalized to prevent a large-scale dimension from dominating the distance calculations of the algorithms.

Categorical features are encoded: in our implementation, we chose to convert each service type into an integer identifier and let the IF/OCSVM model treat this identifier as a numeric variable. An alternative would have been to use one-hot encoding, but this greatly increases the dimension and complexity for these algorithms; we have therefore opted to include sequential information via the Markov model rather than via full explicit encoding in the features.

4.2 Anomaly Detection Pipeline Design

For our experiments, we separated the data in such a way as to simulate a realistic unsupervised scenario: we used only normal data to train the models (Markov, IF, OCSVM) and calibrate the thresholds, then evaluated detection on a test set containing a mixture of new normal and abnormal data.

We separately evaluated Isolation Forest and One-Class SVM, both of which incorporate Markov scoring in their feature representations. Two types of complementary features are derived sequential and statistical properties of the data:

- sequences of events: the sequence of OPC UA service types used during a session
- aggregated numerical features describing each connection or flow (number of packets, bytes exchanged, flow duration, number of errors, etc.). As a result (Fig. 1), our pipeline has two parallel branches. The first branch uses a Markov model to evaluate

the probability of event sequences. This model, trained on data considered as normal, calculates a compliance score for each new sequence, based on the transition probabilities between states. The second branch uses numerical features as input to an outlier detection algorithm (Isolation Forest or One- Class SVM). In our implementation, we combine these branches by integrating the Markov score as an additional feature for the detection algorithm.

In this way, the final anomaly detector (IF or OCSVM) considers both conventional numerical attributes and an indicator of the trace's sequential consistency. The output is a detection decision: each new observation is either classified as normal or flagged as an anomaly.

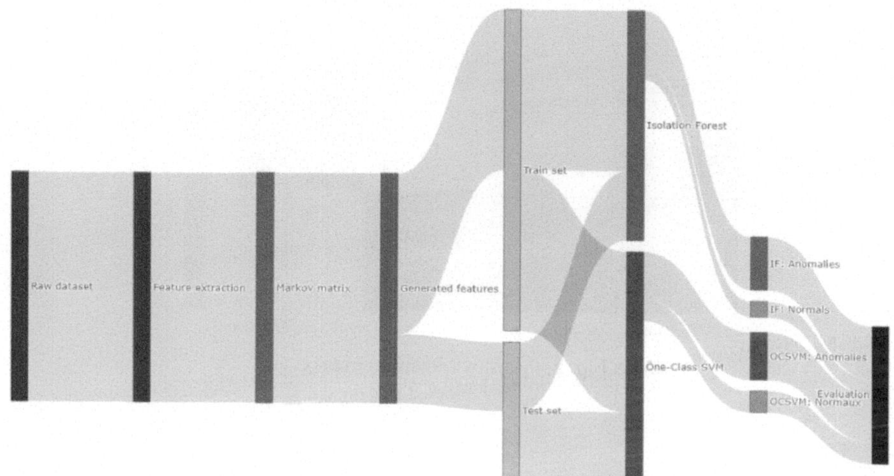

Fig. 1. Schematic of the anomaly detection pipeline for OPC UA data

5 Results and Discussion

The Markov transition matrix, Fig 2, shows that the dominant states are Attribute and StartRawConnection, in the sense that, as soon as you access them, you're likely to stay there. Secure Channel and Session are more subject to transitions between themselves or to others.

The two trained models were able to detect almost all the anomalies in the test set, with a very low alarm rate on normal traffic. The One-Class SVM proved extremely effective, identifying 100% of the 74,067 attacks present, while generating only 83 false alarms out of the 10,070 normal flows tested (i.e. ~0.8% false positives). Isolation Forest, on the other hand, missed a few anomalies but produced even fewer false positives: it detected around 91.1% of attacks (i.e. 66,445 correctly reported anomalies out of 74,067) and only falsely labeled 10 normal flows as abnormal (0.1% false positives). These results translate into excellent performance scores.

The One-Class SVM achieves an overall accuracy of around 99.90% and a recall of 100% on anomalies, with a specificity of 99.2% on normal. Isolation Forest achieves an overall accuracy of around 92.1%, a recall of ~91.1%, and a specificity of 99.90%. The areas under the ROC curve (AUC) and under the PR curve (Average Precision) approach 1.0 in both cases, indicating near-perfect performance. On the ROC curve, we can see that both models rise almost immediately to a true positive rate of 1.0 for a false positive rate close to 0 (Fig. 3).

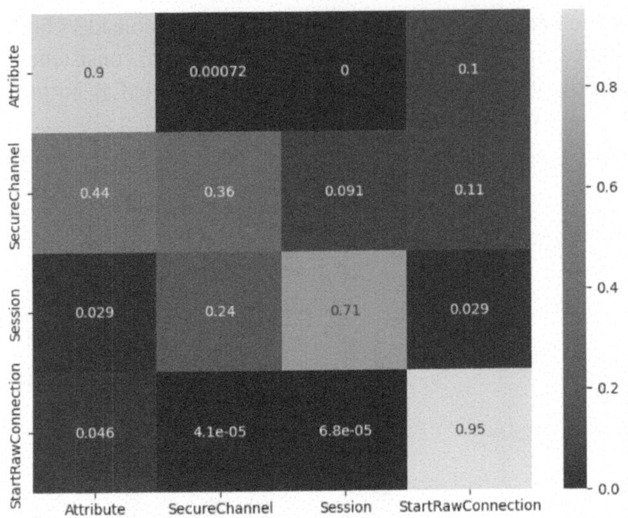

Fig. 2. Markov transition matrix

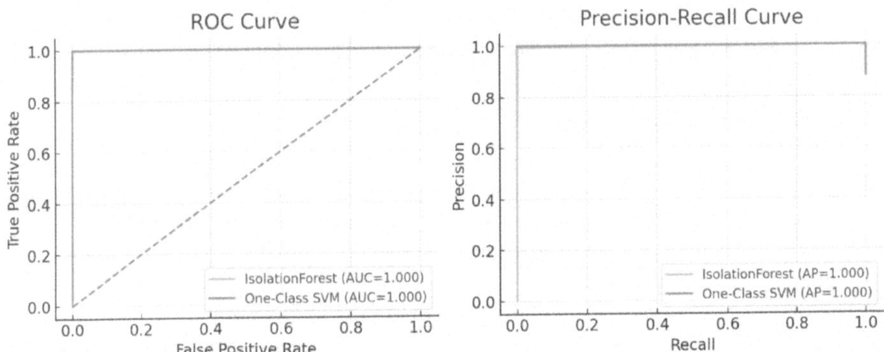

Fig. 3. ROC and PR curves for anomaly detection on OPC UA data, with Isolation Forest (orange curve) and One-Class SVM (red curve).

As shown in Table 1, The One-Class SVM achieves an AUC $\approx$ 0.9999, very slightly higher than that of the Isolation Forest (AUC $\approx$ 0.9998). The Precision-Recall curve highlights that for a recall of ~0.91 (91%), Isolation Forest maintains a precision of 100% (no false alarms for this recall level), while One-Class SVM retains a precision of

99.2% at recall 1.0 (due to the 0.8% false positives). Overall, both PR curves are almost at the ceiling (precision >99% over the entire recall range), indicating that the models clearly separate anomalies from normal data in this case study.

Table 1. Comparison of metrics between Isolation Forest and One-Class.

Metric	Isolation	One-Class SVM
Precision	0.9	1.00
Reminder	0.98	1.00
F1	0.92	0.95
F2	0.94	0.97
AUC	0.86	0.96
PR AUC	0.75	0.88

5.1 Comparative Study

Based on Table 2, we can see that several approaches achieve very high detection rates. With, the neural network approach of · PERFORMS extremely well on their OPC UA data, just as a supervised Random Forest trained on a labeled dataset reached 99% accuracy. However, our method stands out by achieving equivalent performance without strong supervised supervision (No attack examples were required to train the OCSVM) and with partial interpretability thanks to the Markov model that identifies which sequential transition caused the problem. Compared with methods based purely on a single algorithm, the Markov + OCSVM combination offers a better balance: for example, compared with the Isolation Forest alone of, we have increased sensitivity to the stealthiest attacks while maintaining a low false alarm rate. In sum, this comparison suggests that our hybrid pipeline is competitive with the best current approaches for anomaly detection in connected production systems.

Table 2. Comparison of our approach with some existing works. FP = false positives

Paper	Techniques used	Context	Performance achieved
[15]	CNN on image- encoded OPC UA	OPC UA	
[16]	traffic	(variousscenarios)	~99% precision,
[20]	Supervised binary SVM vs Random Forest	OPC UA + SVM 92%	SVM 92% accuracy
		Modbus (attacks);	RF 99% accuracy
[21]	Forest insulation + OCSVM (semi-supervised)	ICS miscellaneous (semi-synth.)	> 95% detection (Multi-attack)

(*continued*)

Table 2. (*continued*)

Paper	Techniques used	Context	Performance achieved
[24]	Mixed-order Markov chain + rules	ICS (SCADA model)	> 90% semantic attack detection
Proposed (Markov + OCSVM)	**Markov model + One-Class SVM**	**OPC UA (DoS, MITM, etc.)**	**> 99% accuracy (Recall 100%, 0.8% FP)**

6 Conclusion and Perspectives

Protecting production systems in Industry 4.0 requires the ability to rapidly detect abnormal behavior indicative of failures or attacks. In this paper, we have proposed a scientific approach combining a sequential Markov model and unsupervised machine learning algorithms (Isolation Forest, One-Class SVM) for anomaly detection in OPC UA communications. This dual approach exploits both the temporal structure of exchanges (via the Markov score) and the statistical distribution of network indicators (via IF/OCSVM), demonstrating high-level performance on a realistic dataset featuring a variety of attacks. Our results show that it is possible to achieve near-perfect detection (>99% recall) while drastically limiting false alarms (<1%) by judiciously combining these techniques. One-Class SVM enriched with Markov chain scoring proved capable of catching even subtle anomalies (such as unusual OPC UA sequences) that simpler methods might miss, without requiring training on known attacks. Future work will focus more on collecting more structured real data and testing other machine learning models.

References

1. Li, K., et al.: Rethinking the operation pattern for anomaly detection in industrial cyber-physical systems. Appl. Sci. **13**(5), 3244 (2023)
2. Rahadian, H., et al.: Open source OPC UA data traffic characteristic and anomaly detection using image-encoding based CNN. In: Proceedings ICEVT 2022. IEEE (2022)
3. Vávra, J., et al.: Adaptive anomaly detection system based on machine learning algorithms in an industrial control environment. Int. J. Criti. Infrastruct. Prot. **34**, 100446 (2021)
4. Guo, H.: Anomaly detection algorithm in ICS based on mixed-order Markov tree model. Acta Automatica Sinica **46**(1), 127–141 (2020)
5. Lukito, K., et al.: Comparison of isolation forest and one class SVM in anomaly detection of gas pipeline operation. Conference Paper, December 2023
6. Park, S., et al.: One-Class Support Vector Machines and Random Forest for Anomaly Detection in OPC UA and Modbus Data. (Experiment reported in [41])
7. Rosenberg, I., et al.: Adversarial ML attacks and defenses in the cyber security domain. ACM Comput. Surv. **54**(5), 1–36 (2021)
8. Jamal, R., et al.: Machine learning for CPS security: a survey. IEEE Access **11**, 86132–86154 (2023)
9. Khalili, A., et al.: Detecting semantic attacks in SCADA systems: a behavioral model approach. IEEE Trans. Ind. Inf. **17**(8), 5741–5751 (2021)

10. Helman, P., et al.: LAD-C: a detector for industrial process anomalies. In: NDSS Symposium (2017)
11. Pinto, F.R., Ferreira, J.C., de Carvalho, R.R.: Dendritic cell algorithm for industrial intrusion detection: a practical analysis on OPC UA traffic. In: Proceedings IEEE 29th International Symposium Industrial Electronics (ISIE), Delft, Netherlands, pp. 632–637, June 2020
12. Pinto, F.R., Campos, R., Ferreira, J.C.: Real-time incremental dendritic cell algorithm for industrial intrusion detection. Eng. Appl. Artif. Intell. **103** (2021). art. 104300
13. Pinto, F.R., Campos, R., Ferreira, J.C.: Enabling data-driven anomaly detection by design in cyber-physical production systems. Cybersecurity **5**(1), 1–20 (2022)
14. Dennler, N., et al.: Online detection of vibration anomalies using balanced spiking neural networks. In: 2021 IEEE 3rd International Conference on Artificial Intelligence Circuits and Systems (AICAS). IEEE (2021)
15. Xu, Z., et al.: Method of Cumulative Anomaly Identification for Security Database Based on Discrete Markov chain. Security and Communication Networks (2022): n. pag
16. Sorostinean, R., et al.: Anomaly detection in smart industrial machinery through hidden Markov models and autoencoders. IEEE Access **12**, 69217–69228 (2024)
17. Santos-Fernandez, E., et al.: Unsupervised anomaly detection in spatio-temporal stream network sensor data. Water Resources Res. **60**(11), e2023WR035707 (2024)
18. Shi, H., et al.: Collusive anomalies detection based on collaborative markov random field. Intell. Data Anal. **26**, 1469–1485 (2022)
19. Vojír, T., Matas, J.: Image-consistent detection of road anomalies as unpredictable patches. In: 2023 IEEE/CVF Winter Conference on Applications of Computer Vision (WACV), pp. 5480–5489 (2023)
20. Djenouri, Y., et al.: A survey on urban traffic anomalies detection algorithms. IEEE Access **7**, 12192–12205 (2019)
21. Woldaregay, A.Z., Årsand, E., Botsis, T., Albers, D., Mamykina, L., Hartvigsen, G.: Data-driven blood glucose pattern classification and anomalies detection: machine-learning applications in type 1 diabetes. J. Med. Internet Res. **21**(5), e11030 (2019). https://doi.org/10.2196/11030. PMID: 31042157; PMCID: PMC6658321
22. Chen, C., et al.: Deep anomaly detection via active anomaly search. In: Adaptive Agents and Multi-Agent Systems (2024)
23. Pinto, R.: M2M using OPC UA. Web (2020)
24. Lagogiannis, I., et al.: Unsupervised pathology detection: a deep dive into the state of the art. IEEE Trans. Med. Imaging **43**(1), 241–252 (2023)
25. Rai, S.N., et al.: Unmasking anomalies in road-scene segmentation. In: Proceedings of the IEEE/CVF International Conference on Computer Vision (2023)

Advancing Human-Robot Interaction for Smart Disassembly with Artificial Intelligence: Case of Real-Time Voice Controlled for a Cobot

Soufiane Ameur[1,2,3], Mohamed Tabaa[2](✉), Kaouter Karboub[2], Mohamed Hamlich[1], and Richard Bearee[3]

[1] CCPS Laboratory, ENSAM-C, Hassan II University, Casablanca, Morocco
[2] Pluridisciplinary Laboratory of Research and Innovation (LPRI), EMSI Casablanca, Casablanca, Morocco
m.tabaa@emsi.ma
[3] LISPEN, Arts Et Métiers Institute of Technology, Lille, France

Abstract. This paper explores the integration of Artificial intelligence (AI), in the form of advanced real time speech to text recognition models integrated to enable a cobot to interpret and act on spoken instructions autonomously. A comparative study across four workstation setups, with voice control was conducted under three key scenarios and variant inputs. Experimental results from RoboDK simulations and physical testbed experiments demonstrate that voice-controlled cobots reduce response times and improve flexibility compared to manual and traditional HRC setups. Emergency stop activation was 40–50% faster, and task adaptation required significantly less intervention. The system supported over 14 voice commands, with recognition rates ranging from 79% to 99%, depending on word complexity and structure. Commands such as "Stop" and "Repeat" achieved near-perfect accuracy while multi-word phrases showed slightly lower performance. Voice-based human confirmations were also reliably detected, contributing to logical task application. Measured inference times across selected commands ranged from 2.31 s to 2.85 s, with Real-Time Factors (RTF) consistently below 1 confirming the system's suitability for real-time deployment.

Keywords: Voice Control · Robotic Disassembly · Human Robot Interaction · embedded systems · AI

1 Introduction

Robotic disassembly has contributed significantly to recycling and remanufacturing industries through increased material recovery [1]. With industries focusing on sustainability, effective recovery and efficient disassembly of valuable materials has become crucial. Disassembly can be automated by robots to offer precision in part extraction and separation with reduced waste and lower environmental impact. Such systems are effective in processing complex and delicate components that are hazardous or difficult for

F. Kamoun et al. (Eds.): AFRICATEK 2025, LNICST 676, pp. 162–179, 2026.
https://doi.org/10.1007/978-3-032-16635-7_11

human handling. With robotics as a platform for disassembly capability, human-robot collaboration [2] has become a major factor in optimizing these processes. Merging human know-how with robotics precision offers a flexible and responsive means of disassembly. Human staff can provide insight and make judgments in situations that require dexterity or problem-solving ability while robots can perform repetitive or physically demanding operations to improve efficiency and safety. This synergy improves the capability of disassembly systems and offers new means of automating recycling and remanufacturing processes. Human-Robot Interaction (HRI) is crucial in facilitating and optimizing this cooperation [3]. By improving the communication channels between humans and robots, HRI ensures smoother coordination and task execution. Traditionally, HRI has relied on visual, tactile, or graphical interfaces, but these methods often require manual input, which can break the flow of interaction.

To address this challenge, innovative approaches are being explored to improve the user experience and streamline interaction. Among these innovations, speech-based control systems present a promising avenue for enhancing HRI. Voice manipulation allows for a hands-free, natural mode of communication, enabling human operators to issue commands and receive feedback without interrupting their focus on the disassembly task. By integrating speech as a secondary interaction modality, the collaboration between humans and robots becomes more intuitive and efficient, especially in scenarios where physical interaction is infeasible. This paper investigates the integration of voice-controlled systems into robotic disassembly to advance HRI by introducing speech as a secondary mode of interaction. Employing a speech-to-text model, the system could receive commands, alongside the ability to logically track pre-event misunderstandings, making the system highly responsive by giving feedback via a speaker.

The structure of the paper is as follows: Sect. 2 reviews the existing literature on HRI and speech-based control systems, Sect. 3 outlines the system architecture and integration process of the speech tool with the mathematical Formulation, Sect. 4 presents experimental results and discusses the implications of the findings, and Sect. 5 concludes with a look at future research directions in this field.

2 Related Works

Since voice-controlled cobots enhance HRI in Human-Robot Collaboration, several studies have explored this method from speech recognition, multimodal interaction, to real-time control in robotics. For example, Birch et al. [4] analyzed MFCC-based speech recognition with Dynamic Time Warping (DTW), highlighting its noise sensitivity in industrial settings. In Another work, Tamba et al. [5] improved humanoid ASR using deep learning models and attention-based speech recognition. Another paper from Campagna et al. [6] combined voice and gesture commands using HMM and CNN-based models to enhance trust and reduce workload in HRC. On the other hand, Rogowski [7] optimized synchronization in medical robots with Hybrid HMM-GMM speech processing while Rietz et al. [8] developed a Python-based Wizard-of-Oz interface with ROS for efficient HRI testing. Further work from Plapper et al. [9] integrated into Alexa via AWS IoT Core for voice-controlled robotic disassembly. Lai et al. [10] applied Transformer-based NLP and depth-based object detection for improved multimodal communication. Aswinbalaji et al. [11] have implemented a wireless voice-controlled robotic arm employing Zigbee for real-time command execution where Abhiram & Udupa [12] implemented a 6 DoF robotic arm incorporating MoveIt motion planning along with Gaussian Mixture Regression for voice control. A work from Lai et al. [13] presented a multimodal HRI framework fed by LLM that combines speech and posture detection. In a paper by Zhang et al. [14], they presented an LLM-driven AR puppet system featuring Open-AI's GPT together with Meta Quest 3 providing real-time control while Novoa et al. [15] demonstrated the use of LLM-based acoustic modeling and beamforming techniques for indoor ASR. A unified sensory representation format was demonstrated by Valner et al. [16], allowing modular task execution for voice and gesture-based interaction. And finally, a work from Alonso et al. [17], have exploited Google Assistant APIs along with cloud-based NLP for better performance in HRI (Table 1).

Table 1. Summarized comparative table of related works.

Authors	Technology Used	Context	Trade-offs
Birch et al. [4]	MFCC + DTW for speech recognition	Industrial speech commands	Low-cost, poor robustness to industrial noise
Tamba et al. [5]	DNN-based ASR with attention	Humanoid speech interface	requires significant training data and compute resources
Campagna et al. [6]	HMM + CNN for speech & gesture fusion	Trust-focused HRC	Multimodal improves trust; rigid model design
Rogowski et al. [7]	Hybrid HMM-GMM speech model	Medical robotics	Precise control; lacks adaptability to complex language inputs
Rietz et al. [8]	Python-based ASR + ROS Wizard-of-Oz	HRI prototyping	Good for testing; lacks scalability and real-time performance
Plapper et al. [9]	Alexa + AWS IoT Core + Lambda	Voice-based robotic disassembly	Powerful NLP; dependent on cloud, limited offline autonomy
Lai et al. [10]	Transformer NLP + depth perception	Multimodal elderly-friendly HRC	Handles ambiguity well
Aswinbalaji et al. [11]	Zigbee wireless voice control	Basic robotic arm	Simple and wireless; low noise robustness
Abhiram & Udupa [12]	MoveIt + ROS Noetic + Gaussian Mixture Regression (GMR)	6 DoF home service robot	Smooth motion planning; lacks semantic understanding in voice control
Lai et al. [13]	Encoder-decoder + posture + voice + LLM	Multimodal HRI	High interaction quality; risk of hallucination from LLM
Zhang et al. [14]	OpenAI GPT + Meta Quest 3 AR	AR-based robot puppeteering	Immersive and hands-free; requires AR gear and processing power
Novoa et al. [15]	Beamforming + DNN-HMM	Indoor mobile robots	Excellent noise robustness; lo cally deployable
Valner et al. [16]	UMRF + semantic task parsing via JSON	Modular HRI platforms	Flexible and reusable; integration complexity
Alonso et al. [17]	Google Assistant + cloud NLP	Assistive robotic interface	Reliable recognition; limited au tonomy due to cloud dependence

3 System Architecture

Our proposed system architecture for real-time voice-controlled cobots aims to improve HRI in smart disassembly processes. It integrates a voice control module with a robotic control system to support voice-based manipulation. In this section, four main sections are presented. Starting with the architecture overview providing an overall description of the system components and their interactions. Then, a speech-to-text processing section describes how voice commands are processed and converted into text using the Whisper model [18]. Next, real-time command execution describing how validated commands are passed on to the cobot along with human confirmation for execution. Finally, a mathematical formulation is provided to describe the formal models used to predict command time and error, ensuring precise task execution.

3.1 Architecture Overview

Our system consists of several interconnected components including a microphone, a loudspeaker, a speech-to-text unit, a command validation module and a UR10e cobot (As shown in Fig. 1,). As the human operator commands, the Microphone captures them before being processed in MiniForge for speech-to-text conversion. The extracted text is then filtered to eliminate any unnecessary words or errors prior to validation. Following the verification of the command, it's then passed on to the URScript module on a Raspberry Pi 5, which then interprets the command and executes it as appropriate. Such a structured workflow ensures accurate robotic control and improves the reliability of task execution.

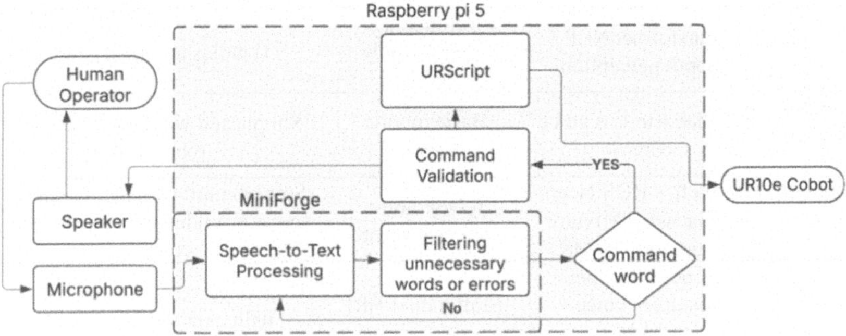

Fig. 1. Proposed System Architecture.

In Table 2, we present the summarized hardware and corresponding software layers used in the proposed system where The Raspberry Pi 5 operates on three layers, running Python 3.11 and Linux 6.1 kernel. The microphone and speaker devices are connected directly to the third layer, while the UR10e cobot is managed via URScript which is in the second layer awaiting a response from layer 3.

Table. 2 Hardware Components and Corresponding Software Layers

Hardware	Layer 1	Layer 2	Layer 3
Raspberry pi 5	Python 3.11 Kernel 6.1	Miniforge URScript	Whisper Model Linear Programming
Speaker			+
Microphone			+
UR10e		+	

3.2 Speech to Text Processing

To carry out real-time speech-to-text processing, our solution used Whisper AI as an advanced deep learning model developed by OpenAI to support automatic speech recognition (ASR). In view of Raspberry Pi's hardware constraints, we chose the miniature version of Whisper AI which balances accuracy with computational efficiency. In Table 3, we provide a comparison of the various model sizes including parameters, required VRAM and relative processing speed [19]. The Tiny model requires approximately 1 GB of VRAM making it suitable for deployment on low-power peripheral hardware such as the Raspberry Pi. Yet despite its small size it retains solid voice recognition capabilities guaranteeing efficient processing of voice commands for real-time interaction with the cobot.

Table 3. Whisper AI versions.

Size	Parameters	Required VRAM	Relative speed
Tiny	39M	~1GB	~10x
Base	74M	~1GB	~7x
Small	244M	~2GB	~4x
Medium	769M	~5GB	~2x
Large	1550M	~10GB	~1x
Turbo	809M	~6GB	~8x

In Fig. 2, we're showing the architecture of the Whisper AI model used in our system to convert the voice commands into text. The model takes the log-mel spectrogram of the spoken input and processes it through a stack of encoder and decoder blocks using a transformer architecture where cross-attention, then the decoder predicts the next tokens allowing for accurate transcription. In our use case, this enables the system to understand spoken commands like "Stop" or "Repeat" forming a reliable model base for cobot control.

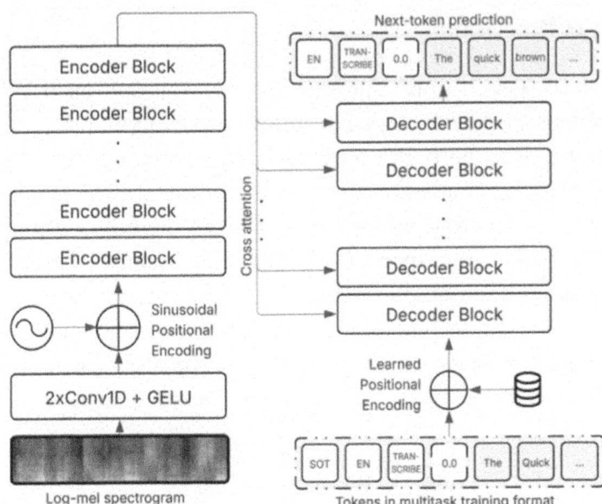

Fig. 2. Whisper Model Architecture

3.3 Real Time Command

In the context of real-time human-robot collaboration programs, easy and reliable execution of voice commands is essential to ensure transparent interaction between the human operator and the cobot. In our proposed system, we predefined a set of voice commands (Table 4) to control the cobot's actions in real time. These range from basic motion commands (Approach, Reverse, Return home…) all the way to task-specific operations (Pick + object, Place + object, Grasp, Release…) and when it receives a voice input the system processes it through Whisper AI for speech-to-text conversion. One of the key features of this system is its ability to control the cobot's actions in real time. When the command has been validated it is transmitted to the robotic control unit, where it is executed accordingly. In the event of misinterpretation or invalid instructions, error management mechanisms, such as the "Bad" command, enable corrective action within the system.

Table 4. Predefined set of voice commands.

Word	Meaning
" Activate "	Initialize the cobot.
" Pause "	Pause current action.
" Resume "	Continue the paused task.
" Stop "	Immediately halt all actions.
" Repeat "	Perform the last executed action again.
" Cancel "	Abort the current command or task.
" Pick + Object "	Instruct cobot to pick up a specified object.
" Place + Object "	Command cobot to place the specified object
" You take "	Ask cobot to grab and hold the indicated item.
" Approach "	Move closer slowly to the human operator.
" Backward "	Retreat from current position.
" Return home "	Move back to default position.
" Grab "	Close gripper.
" Release "	Open gripper.
" Bad "	Indicate incorrect action or error.
" Shutdown "	Power off the cobot safely.
" Switch + Model "	Parameter the cobot for another model.
" Yes "	Confirm and proceed with the action.
" Approach "	Move closer slowly to the human operator.
" Backward "	Retreat from current position.
" Return home "	Move back to default position.
" Grab "	Close gripper.
" Release "	Open gripper.
" Bad "	Indicate incorrect action or error.
" Shutdown "	Power off the cobot safely.
" Switch + Model "	Parameter the cobot for another model.
" Yes "	Confirm and proceed with the action.

The real-time command processing includes a human confirmation mechanism for validating unrecognized and illogical commands before they are carried out. As illustrated in Fig. 3, the system first processes the raw audio input by using the whisper model described earlier. Once errors and unnecessary words have been filtered out by the system, it compares the extracted command with the predefined command list (Table 4). If a matching command is found it is executed. Nevertheless, if the command is not logically organized nor present in the command list, the human operator is requested to confirm it. This is done by repeating the detected word with a question mark ("Activate?"). This incorporated basic expressive cues presented as a "confused" response to make the interaction more intuitive and human-friendly. If the user confirms the command, it's validated and applied with the UR10e cobot. The system waits for a human response before proceeding. This ensures operational safety and minimizes unintentional actions particularly for delicate disassembly tasks such as removing battery.

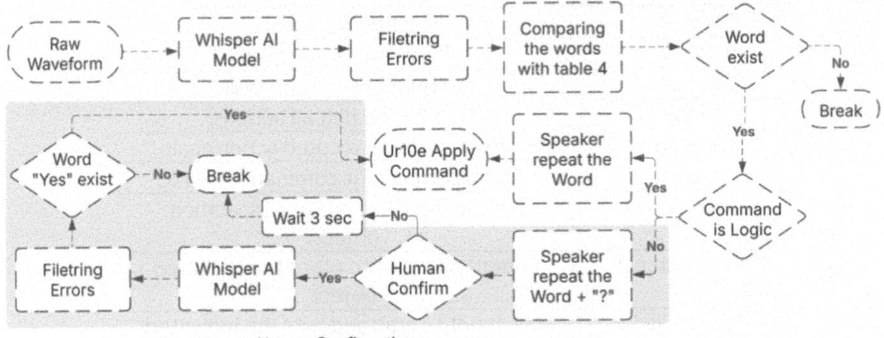

Fig. 3. Voice Command Processing with the Human Confirmation Flow.

To determine whether a command is logically valid in the execution sequence, the system employs a context-aware verification mechanism based on previous commands. As shown in Fig. 4, each newly received command (Cmd-X) is checked against a command list that has been programmed before. Certain commands such as “Pause”, “Stop”, or “Yes”… Are excluded from logical verification as they serve as standalone or confirmation actions. For other commands, the system compares the new command with the last issued command. If the sequence is consistent with expected operational logic, the system proceeds with execution. Otherwise, the system prompts the human operator for confirmation before proceeding. For instance, a “Pick Tool 1” command must logically be before a “Approach” command.

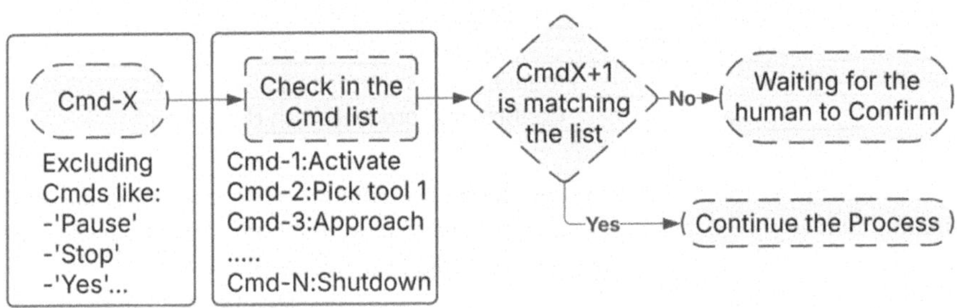

Fig. 4. Command Validation Workflow.

4 Mathematical Formulation

This section is done to define the key parameters and equations for our evaluating voice command response time, error and validation in real-time control. In Table 5, we present a critical variable that includes variables like the error rate (Evc), response time (T_r), or command validation ((Cmd)). Such metrics are ensuring a quantifying command accuracy and logical execution.

Table 5. Variables of our system.

Parameters	Meaning	Parameters	Meaning
E_{vc}	Error Rate in Voice Commands	T_{vc}	Time taken to recognize the voice command.
T_r	Response Time of the Cobot	T_{proc}	Time taken for processing
T_d	Delay Due to Human Confirmation	T_{ex}	Time taken to execute the command.
$V(Cmd)$	Command Validation	T_w	Human confirmation delay
X	Excluded Commands	T_{hc}	Human time to repeat the command
W_{er_i}	Number of incorrect commands	L	List of commands traced in the process
ω_i	Weight assigned to command	H_v	Human Validation
W_{total}	Total number of command attempts	H_{vt}	Time of Human validation
T_i	Inference process time	T_a	Audio segment duration

4.1 Error Rate in Voice Commands

The error rate ($Ev(\%)$)) measures incorrect voice commands relative to total attempts considering misheard, unrecognized, and misinterpreted inputs. Another variable of the recognition rate is computed as $100 - E_{v(\%)}$ that ensures speech model performance evaluation. A lower $E_{v(\%)}$ indicates better speech-to-text conversion reliability, essential for real-time control. The inclusion of weight factors (ω) helps adjust for the impact of different types of errors on the system's overall accuracy. For example, a longer phrase command has a lower weight than a shorter one.

$$E_{vc(\%)} = \sum_{i=1}^{N} \omega_i \frac{W_{er_i}}{W_{total}} \times 100 \tag{1}$$

$$W_{er_i} = N_{misheard} + N_{unrecognized} + N_{misinterpreted} \tag{2}$$

$$RecognitionRate_{(\%)} = 100 - (1 - \mathrm{E}_{\mathrm{vc}(\%)}) \tag{3}$$

4.2 Response Time of the Cobot

The response time (T_r) is the sum of voice recognition time (T_{vc}), processing time (T_{proc}), and execution time (T_{ex}), representing the system's latency from command input to action. Reducing Tr is crucial for achieving near-instantaneous reaction times in dynamic environments. Optimizing processing time (T_{proc}) through a more lightweight model can further enhance system performance.

$$T_r = T_{vc} + T_{proc} + T_{ex} \tag{4}$$

4.3 Command Validation and Execution Model

Command validation as explained before ensures logical execution. Commands like "*Pause*", "*Stop*" *or* "*Yes*" in list (*X*) are excluded from validation. The function (*Cmd*) assigns value "1" based on whether a command exists in the tracked list (*L*) if not, it requires human validation (H_v).

$$T_r = T_{vc} + T_{proc} + T_{ex} \tag{5}$$

$$V(Cmd) = \begin{cases} 1 & \text{if } Cmd \notin X \text{ and } Cmd + 1 \in L \\ 1 & \text{if } Cmd \in X \text{ and } Cmd + 1 \notin L \text{ and } H_v == 1 \\ 0 & \text{if } Cmd \in X \text{ and } Cmd + 1 \notin L \text{ and } H_v == 0 \end{cases} \tag{6}$$

4.4 Delay Due to Human Confirmation

The total delay time (*Td*) in executing a voice command depends on whether the command is logical or requires human confirmation. If the command is valid, the delay equals the cobot's response time (T_r). However, if the command is not logically structured, an additional waiting time (T_w) is introduced while the system requests confirmation. If the human validation time (*Hvt*) exceeds 3 s with no response, the delay includes both T_r *and* T_w, if not a Human time to repeat the command (T_{hc}) is an added ($T_d = T_r + T_w + T_{hc}$).

$$T_d = \begin{cases} T_r & \text{if } Cmd \text{ is Logic} \\ T_r + T_w & \text{if } Cmd \text{ is not logic and } H_{vt} > 3\,\text{s} \\ T_r + T_w + T_{hc} & \text{if } Cmd \text{ is not logic and } H_{vt} \leqslant 3\,\text{s} \end{cases} \tag{7}$$

4.5 Inference and Real-Time Factor Calculation

The inference process time (T_i) is the duration taken by the Whisper model to transcribe a single voice command. This time is measured from the start to the end of the model's transcription execution. Given a fixed audio segment duration (T_a) typically 3 s in this study. The Real-Time Factor (*RTF*) is computed as the ratio between the inference time and the audio duration. This reflects how efficiently the model performs relative to real-time constraints. An RTF value less than 1 indicates that the system is capable of processing faster than the incoming audio, making it suitable for real-time interaction. On the contrary, values greater than 1 signify delays that may affect responsiveness.

$$RTF = \frac{T_i}{T_a} \text{ where } T_a = 3\,\text{sec} \tag{8}$$

5 Use Case and Findings

The following section shows how voice-controlled cobots function effectively in HRC disassembly applications. The experimental purpose aims to determine the successful implementation and operational efficiency of voice commands for disassembly workstreams in situations where conventional methods prove inadequate. All four workstations shown in Fig. 5 aim to disassemble car batteries as their main purpose. The disassembly duties in Workstation 1 are entirely performed by a human worker as part of a complete manual operation. Workstation 2 makes use of an industrial cobot arm that operates without human intervention, yet it cannot respond to unexpected variations in the work environment. Workstation 3 implements a traditional human-robot collaboration system where operators must provide manual control inputs to the robot throughout the process. Our solution in Workstation 4 allows operators to control the cobot using voice commands which enhances both system reaction times for unexpected situations along with adaptability.

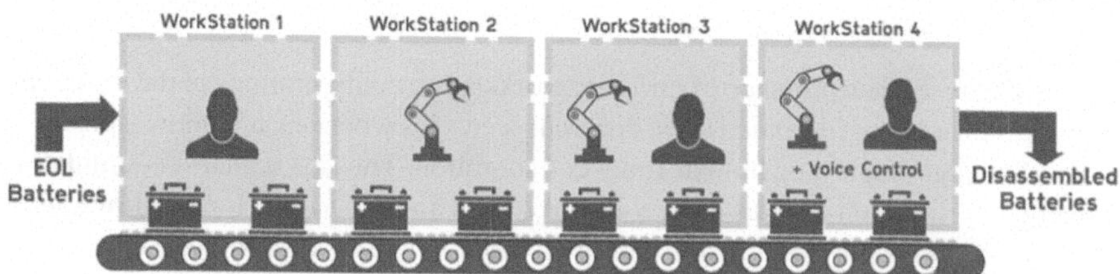

Fig. 5. Four Workstation Setups for Battery Disassembly Process (1: Human-Only, 2: Robot-Only, 3: Traditional HRC, 4: HRC + Voice Control)

Most of the workstations included in this research were simulated using RoboDK software [20] that enables accurate modeling of robotic movements and task execution during disassembly (Fig. 6, Section I). Certain scenarios were tested with real human actions for workstations 1, 3 as well as 4, to assess the real-world feasibility, time estimation and practicality of human-robot collaboration for the UR10e cobot it was replaced with a 4DOF mechanical arm as a testbed only to visualize the cobot not the applicability as in the the simulation. (Fig. 6, Section II). The combination of simulation and human trials provided a comprehensive understanding.

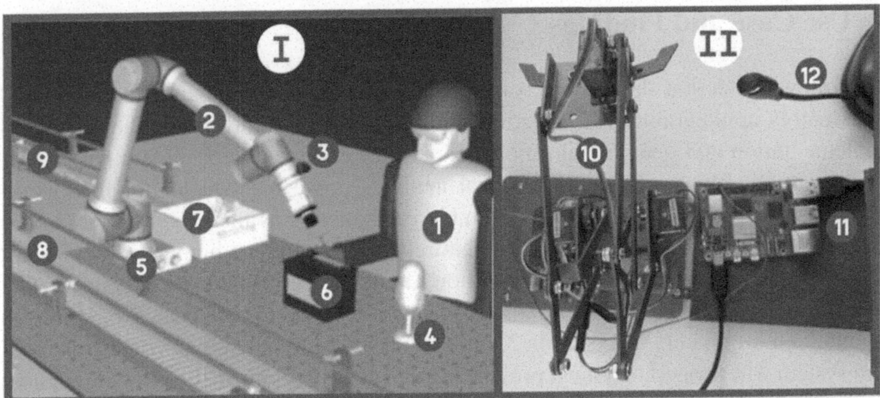

Fig. 6. Section I: Simulation Using Robodk (1: Human, 2: Ur10e, 3: Camera, 4: Microphone, 5: Speaker, 6: Battery, 7: ToolBox, 8: Input Conveyor, 9: Output Conveyor), Section II: Realistic testbed connected to Respberry Pi 5 (10: 4DOF mechanical arm KIT, 11: Raspberry pi 5, 12: Microphone)

To evaluate the performance of different workstation configurations in the disassembly process in depth we designed three different scenarios where each is addressing some critical challenges regarding human-robot collaboration. The first scenario is simulating an emergency situation such as a fire which requires an immediate stop. It allows us to test the reaction time as well as the safety measures of each workstation. The second scenario focuses on the execution of an unsuccessful task such as a stuck screw, in which the system is confronted with an unscrewing failure caused by misuse of tools or unexpected screwing conditions. Scenario 3 adds input variants requiring manual adaptation or reprogramming when the system must handle different battery brands. All three scenarios provide a structured approach to measuring the flexibility and responsiveness of each workstation within real-life disassembly conditions (Tables 6 and 7).

Table 6. The Three Proposed Scenarios

Scenario I	Scenario II	Scenario III
Fire Incident	Unsuccessful Task	Variant Inputs

Table 7. Performance of Workstations on each Scenario.

Workstation	Scenario 1	Scenario 2	Scenario 3
Workstation 1 : Human-Only	Manually stops C activates ES button	-Repeat it manually -Change Tool if needed	Adapts manually
Time	3-10s	5-10s	10-30s
Workstation 2 : Robot-Only	Detects heat but needs human intervention	Fails or pass it	Fails, needs reprogramming
Time	-	-	-
Workstation 3 : Traditional HRC	Stops but require manual emergency stop	Fails, needs human Intervention	Manual setting change
Time	5-10s	15-20s	30s-5min
Workstation 4: HRC + Voice Control	Human says "Emergency Stop !"	Stops, Human says "Repeat".	Human says "Switch + Model"
Time	3-5s	3-5s	3-5s

The following table summarizes the performance of our four workstation setups in the different scenarios with the response times obtained from RoboDK simulations with the physical test bench experiments. Variations in response times are determined by the level of automation or human intervention. In the event of a fire a human needs 3 to 10 s to detect it manually and activate the emergency stop whereas the robot can sense heat but still requires human intervention making the response time uncertain. In comparison, the traditional HRC requires 5 to 10 s since humans can take charge, while the voice-controlled cobot reacts more quickly with verbal commands. For scenario 2, the human-only workstation requires time for attempts while the robot-only system can fail or ignore the task, thus making the response time unpredictable. Using a traditional HRC system, human intervention takes 15 to 20 s but using the "Repeat" function, enabled by the voice-controlled cobot solved the problem in 3 to 5 s. For different input variants or battery brands, a human workstation adapts in 10 to 30 s while the robotic system fails, unless reprogrammed. A traditional HRC system will take 30 s to 5 min to adjust manually, just as a voice-activated cobot can adapt in 3 to 5 s with "Change model". Depending on workstation configuration and human reaction speed, such times prove that speech control can significantly improve adaptability and reaction time in disassembly tasks (Table 8).

Table 8. Recognition Rate of Words.

Word	*Recognition Rate*$_{\%}$	Word	*Recognition Rate*$_{\%}$
" Activate "	95%	" Approach "	90%
" Pause "	97%	" Backward "	88%
" Resume "	94%	" Return home "	83%
" Stop "	99%	" Grab "	93%
" Repeat "	98%	" Release "	90%
" Cancel "	97%	" Bad "	97%
" Pick + Object "	85%	" Shutdown "	93%
" Place + Object "	81%	" Switch + Model "	79%
" You take "	85%	" Yes "	98%

The recognition results indicate that short commands are more precise with words like "Stop" or "Repeat" being very reliable. On the other hand, sentences with several words such as "Switch + Model" showed lower recognition levels owing to variations in pronunciation or background noise. Movement commands such as "Approach" showed moderate accuracy, suggesting that directional words may require further optimization. Despite some variation, critical safety commands like "Stop" remained highly reliable to ensuring effective interaction in tasks.

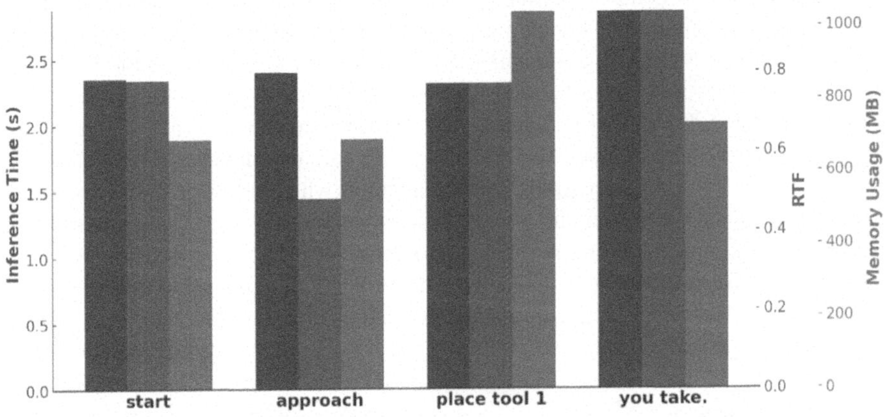

Fig. 7. Performance Metrics per Commands (Color figure online)

In Fig. 7, we have shown the performance metrics of four different voice commands as examples ("start", "approach", "place tool 1" and "you take"). The three key metrics highlighted are inference time (blue), real-time factor (red) and memory usage (green). All these commands had inference times between 2.3 and 2.8 s, indicating a relatively constant processing speed. Memory consumption in "Place tool 1" command is the most memory-intensive probably due to its multi-word structure and linguistic complexity.

RTF values remain below 1 for all commands suggesting that the system is processing faster than real time in all cases. This confirms Whisper's suitability for real-time command recognition in robotic applications.

Compared with hybrid disassembly stations, such as that by Chen et al. [21] that emphasize manual learning and predefined robot states, which limit adaptability to new tasks or spontaneous interactions. Meanwhile, Minca et al.[22] present control systems based on Petri nets in which task changes are based on rigid logic and without a natural language interface. In contrast, our system introduces real-time voice control allowing dynamic task switching together with hands-free interaction and reduced programming overhead thereby addressing the flexibility and scalability issues of previous HRC systems.

5.1 Limitations

The system's speech recognition precision can be affected by industrial noise which in turn can lead to interpretation errors. Furthermore, a set of predefined commands restricts the flexibility of processing complex instructions. Speech processing latency can impact on real-time decision-making due to response time fluctuations. Another limitation concerns the response time of the 4 approaches, which can vary depending on the architecture or the technology of the cobot. A further problem stated is the limitation of Raspberry Pi 5, to which we can only use the miniature version, which increases the response time.

6 Conclusion and Future Works

The aim of this study was to validate the contribution of voice-controlled cobots to robotic disassembly by demonstrating how voice interaction can considerably improve task flexibility and safety. Based on a benchmarking study involving different workstation configurations, our results demonstrated that the inclusion of voice commands can reduce manual intervention and streamline interaction between human operators and robots. The possibility of giving verbal commands in real time enables faster handling of emergency situations and more rapid recovery from failure along with greater adaptability to process variation thus making robotic disassembly more intuitive. Further experimental findings emphasize the fact that voice assistance is bridging the gap between fully autonomous and manually operated systems by offering a flexible alternative. As opposed to rigid preprogrammed automation, the voice-controlled cobot is able of dynamically adapting itself to different scenarios proving an invaluable tool in industries that require responsive disassembly processes. Overall, these results demonstrated that integrating voice control into robotic systems can improve both operational performance and human-robot collaboration paving the way for more interactive disassembly. Also, the system could explore larger command sets or continuous speech input, enabling more natural and flexible interaction. For instance, instead of saying "Pick Object" and then "Place Object," the operator could say, "Pick up the battery and place it in the left tray" as a single instruction. This opens new research directions in realtime natural language processing for HRC. Further future work, an optimization of response time as well as an improvement of noise filtering that should reinforce the overall accuracy of the system by exploring the integration of complementary modalities such as gesture and posture recognition alongside voice commands with a view to making interaction more flexible and multimodal. Such progress will enable a much more adaptive and collaborative disassembly process.

References

1. Foo, G., Kara, S., Pagnucco, M.: Challenges of robotic disassembly in practice. Procedia CIRP **105**, 513–518 (2022)
2. Text="CE: Unable to parse this reference. Kindly do manual structure" Ameur, S., Tabaa, M., Hamlich, M., Hidila, Z., Bearee, R.: Human-robot collaboration in remanufacturing: an application for computer disassembly. In: International Conference on Smart Applications and Data Analysis, pp. 70–84. Springer, Cham (2024)
3. Murphy, R.R., Nomura, T., Billard, A., Burke, J.L.: Human-robot interaction. IEEE Robot. Autom. Mag. **17**(2), 85–89 (2010)
4. Birch, P., et al.: Environmental effects on reliability and accuracy of MFCC-based voice recognition for industrial human-robot collaboration. Front. Robot. AI **8**, 668057 (2021)
5. Tamba, R., et al.: Comparing social robot screen and voice interfaces for smart home control. In: ACM/IEEE International Conference on Human-Robot Interaction (HRI), pp. 438–447. ACM (2023)
6. Campagna, G., et al.: Fostering trust through gesture and voice-controlled robot trajectories in industrial human-robot collaboration. In: IEEE International Conference on Robotics and Automation (ICRA). IEEE (2025)
7. Rogowski, A.: Scenario-based programming of voice-controlled medical robotic systems. Appl. Sci. **22**(9520), 1–18 (2022)
8. Rietz, A., et al.: Development of a voice-controlled human-robot interface. In: International Conference on Interactive Collaborative Robotics. LNCS, vol. 12905, pp. 108–117. Springer, Cham (2021)
9. Plapper, P., et al.: RACIR CR: combining virtual and robot assistants. In: IEEE International Conference on Emerging Technologies and Factory Automation (ETFA)
10. Lai, Y., Radke, M., Nassar, Y., Rätsch, M.: Intuitive multi-modal human-robot interaction via posture and voice. In: RoboVis 2024. LNCS. Springer, Heidelberg (2024)
11. Aswinbalaji, R., Arunraja, A.: Wireless voice-controlled robotics arm. Int. J. Emerg. Technol. Comput. Sci. Electron. (IJETCSE) **12**(4), 33–35 (2015)
12. Abhiram, T.V., Udupa, G.: Voice-controlled 6 DoF arm mobile robot in an assisted home environment. Res. Square, preprint (2024)
13. Lai, Y., et al.: NMM-HRI: natural multimodal human-robot interaction with voice and deictic posture via large language model. arXiv:2501.00785 (2025)
14. Zhang, Y., et al.: LLM-driven augmented reality puppeteer: controller-free voice-commanded robot teleoperation. arXiv:2502.09142 (2025)
15. Novoa, J., et al.: Automatic speech recognition for indoor HRI scenarios. ACM Trans. Hum.-Robot Interact. **10**(2), Article 17 (2021)
16. Valner, R., et al.: Unified meaning representation format (UMRF): a task description and execution formalism for HRI. ACM Trans. Hum.-Robot Interact. **11**(4), Article 38
17. Alonso, R., Concas, E., Recupero, D.R.: An abstraction layer exploiting voice assistant technologies for effective human–robot interaction. Appl. Sci. **11**(9165) (2021)
18. Radford, A., et al.: Robust Speech Recognition via Large-Scale Weak Supervision (2022). https://openai.com/research/whisper

19. OpenAI: Whisper - General-purpose speech recognition model. GitHub. https://github.com/openai/whisper
20. RoboDK: RoboDK – Robot Simulation and Offline Programming. https://robodk.com
21. Chen, W.H., Wegener, K., Dietrich, F.: A robot assistant for unscrewing in hybrid human-robot disassembly. In: Proceedings of 2014 IEEE International Conference on Robotics and Biomimetics (ROBIO), Bali, Indonesia, pp. 536–541 (2014)
22. Minca, E., Filipescu, A., Voda, A.: Control Eng. Pract. **31**. 50–62 (2014). https://doi.org/10.1016/j.conengprac.2014.06.005

The Maghreb in the Era of Industry 4.0: Opportunities and Challenges

Feten Teber(✉), Nadia Chagtmi, and Nejla Rejeb

Esprit School of Engineering, Ariana 2083, Tunisia
{feten.teber,nadia.chagtmi,nejla.rejeb}@esprit.tn

Abstract. The fourth industrial revolution is imposing major challenges on manufacturing organizations, affecting technological, organizational and managerial aspects all at once. The emergence of Industry 4.0, marked by advanced automation and the use of robots, is profoundly changing production processes, as well as relations within companies and with the workforce. These transformations go far beyond industry, directly influencing everyday life and the organization of work. However, despite the scale of this revolution in many regions, studies specifically addressing its impacts in the Maghreb, particularly on labor markets, manufacturing sectors and energy consumption, remain limited. The associated risks include technological unemployment, a redefinition of skills in the workforce, and a transformation of employment structures and industrial relations, all of which require immediate attention. This study seeks to analyze the potential effects of Industry 4.0 on the Maghreb region and assess its preparedness for these changes. A qualitative approach, based on case studies, was used, with in-depth interviews conducted with industry players to identify specific issues. In addition, a literature review was carried out to enrich the analysis and reinforce the reliability of the results. The aim of this method is to gain a better understanding of the challenges facing the Maghreb in the face of the technological revolution, and to formulate recommendations for improving the competitiveness of local industries.

Keywords: Industry 4.0 · Technological challenges · Labor relations · Manufacturing sectors · Energy consumption

1 Introduction

The Fourth Industrial Revolution is driving profound transformations in manufacturing sectors through the adoption of new technologies and the reconfiguration of production processes. These developments pose significant organizational, technological, and administrative challenges for industrial companies [1]. The integration of artificial intelligence, connected objects (IoT), and automation requires an adaptation of workers' skills to the production systems of the future [2]. Workflows are gradually becoming more transparent, decentralized, and flexible, reducing the hierarchical rigidity of manufacturing companies [3]. However, this transition to a digitalized environment increases the risks associated with the automation of certain jobs. According to a study by [4],

F. Kamoun et al. (Eds.): AFRICATEK 2025, LNICST 676, pp. 180–193, 2026.
https://doi.org/10.1007/978-3-032-16635-7_12

approximately 47% of jobs in the United States could be automated within the next few decades, a trend that could also affect some regions of the Maghreb. Similarly, [5] estimate that more than 25% of jobs in some geographic areas are highly threatened by automation. In future production systems, some processes will be simplified through automation, while others will become more complex and digitally integrated. This evolution will lead to a decrease in low-skilled jobs in favor of positions requiring advanced skills in data management, robotics, and artificial intelligence. Societal acceptance and the technical feasibility of these innovations will play a key role in the success of this transformation [6]. Without an adaptation of socio-economic systems, these advances could increase inequalities and threaten social cohesion. Industry 4.0 relies on the integration of advanced technologies such as industrial IoT, Big Data, artificial intelligence and robotics [7]. These changes are putting increasing pressure on economic decision-makers, who must adapt education and training policies to meet the new demands of the labor market.

In this context, the Maghreb faces a dual challenge: on the one hand, to take advantage of the opportunities offered by Industry 4.0 to boost its industrial development, and on the other hand, to overcome the obstacles linked to the infrastructure deficit, limited skills and economic uncertainties [8]. To date, few studies have examined in depth the capacity of Maghreb countries to integrate these technological transformations [9]. This research aims to assess the level of preparedness of the Maghreb for Industry 4.0 by analyzing its impacts on the labor market, the manufacturing sector and energy consumption. A qualitative methodology was adopted, combining semi-directed interviews with industrial actors and an in-depth analysis of existing literature. The objective is to identify the main challenges and levers of action for a successful transition to this new industrial era.

2 Research Overview

This section begins with an overview of existing research and publications on the application of Industry 4.0 technologies. It continues by analyzing the benefits and obstacles associated with their implementation. Finally, the analytical strategy adopted is explained in depth in the final section.

2.1 The Industry 4.0 Concept

Industry 4.0 emerged as a key concept for the digital transformation of the manufacturing sector, first introduced at the Hannover Messe in 2011. The initiative was quickly recognized as a strategic lever to modernize global industry, with Germany taking a leading position by integrating it as a national project in 2013. The goal was to develop intelligent production systems to optimize the productivity and efficiency of industrial companies [10, 11]. Industry 4.0 is distinguished by the integration of advanced technologies such as autonomous robots, machine learning, and the Internet of Things, opening up new perspectives in manufacturing [12]. Through increased digitalization of the supply chain, it promotes real-time communication between systems, objects, and human actors. This intelligent interconnection enables dynamic adaptation of products, machines and processes to changing environmental conditions, thus optimizing value creation throughout the product life cycle [13].

The technological foundations of Industry 4.0 are based on four key elements. The first is cyber-physical systems (CPS), which integrate physical and digital components using high-performance communication networks. Next comes the Internet of Things (IoT), which allows physical devices to interact and exchange data autonomously. The third pillar, the Internet of Services (IoS), makes it possible to offer digital services based on the data collected by these connected objects. Finally, smart factories leverage all of these technologies to optimize production processes, while strengthening their flexibility and ability to adapt to market changes.

According to Adetunla et al. [14], the fundamental characteristics of Industry 4.0 include virtualization, interoperability, automation, flexibility, real-time availability, service orientation, and energy efficiency. These attributes not only improve productivity, but also promote a more sustainable use of resources. This industrial revolution also brings about a socio-technical transformation of the role of humans in production systems. As Van Lopik [15] point out, all stages of the value chain must now be based on intelligent strategies based on information and communication technologies (ICT). This change not only enables the production of customized goods on a large scale, but also the reduction of resource use and the improvement of quality and operational efficiency. In conclusion, although the adoption of Industry 4.0 offers considerable benefits, it also requires a revision of human skills and organizational models to fully exploit its technological and economic potential [16].

2.2 Key Benefits of Industry 4.0

The adoption of Industry 4.0 by Maghreb companies depends on several crucial factors, which go beyond the simple understanding of the concept. According to Santos et al., Industry 4.0 allows African companies to make a direct transition from obsolete and less efficient manufacturing technologies to intelligent and advanced manufacturing models, giving them the ability to compete in the global market without following the same long industrial development path as developed countries [17]. In a context of increased global competition, companies must increase their innovation capacity, improve their productivity and reduce time to market in order to maintain their competitiveness. Industry 4.0 offers solutions to meet these challenges by integrating advanced technologies such as the Internet of Things (IoT), artificial intelligence (AI), big data and robotics, thus transforming traditional factories into interconnected ecosystems.

In addition, traditional production methods no longer meet modern industrial requirements and often generate a negative environmental impact [18]. Industry 4.0 is compatible with better management of environmental impact, allowing to reduce energy and resource consumption while improving production. By adopting Industry 4.0 technologies, companies can improve their production, reduce resource waste and increase energy efficiency. These developments not only allow significant savings, but also improve product quality and increase profitability, thus strengthening its position in the international market. Industry 4.0 represents a major strategic asset to ensure the sustainability and competitiveness of manufacturing companies on a global scale. Numerous studies highlight its significant benefits, which are grouped around several key axes, as presented in Table 1:

Table 1. Strategic Axis and Benefits of Industry 4.0.

Strategic Axis	Benefits
Economic Performance	✓ Productivity and Innovation: Industry 4.0 increases productivity and stimulates innovation [11, 12, 19–21].
	✓ New Business Models: Allows the emergence of innovative business models, agile to the market [9] [22].
Increased Competitiveness	Strategic Positioning: Strengthens competitiveness in the face of growing competition [14, 23, 24].
Sustainability and Energy Saving	Reduced Ecological Footprint: Optimizes energy consumption for greater sustainability [25–27].
Management and Decision Making	Managerial Efficiency: Offers advanced management tools and real-time analytics [15] [28, 29].

2.3 Challenges in Adopting Industry 4.0

The integration of Industry 4.0 faces several major challenges, including the need to continuously train workers to adapt to the ever-changing environments and the shortage of skilled labor [30–32]. With the emergence of new ways of working, employees could both benefit from them and suffer from their disadvantages, which could also generate conflicts within the professional environment due to the changed working conditions [30]. Another barrier frequently mentioned in the literature is the lack of financial resources, which limits the ability of companies to invest in Industry 4.0 technologies. This budgetary constraint is often accompanied by insufficient levels of standardization, a limited understanding of technological integration, and increasing concerns about data security [33, 35]. Indeed, Raj et al. [34] highlight the legal challenges posed by cybersecurity, specifying that the massive adoption of new technologies is likely to intensify concerns related to the secure management of personal data. The transition to more advanced production systems also increases the vulnerability of companies to process fragility, making the widespread adoption of Industry 4.0 even more uncertain [35]. To ensure a smooth integration of components, tools and methods, it is essential to develop flexible interfaces capable of synchronizing various technologies, processes and languages. In addition, the reliability and stability of the systems must be guaranteed to enable efficient communication between machines [35]. It also appears that many companies struggle to justify their investments in the infrastructure required for Industry 4.0, in particular due to the lack of solid business cases and convincing feasibility studies [33]. This strategic gap significantly slows down the adoption of these new technologies. Furthermore, Aheleroff [36] notes that many organizations still do not clearly perceive the potential benefits they could derive from using Industry 4.0 solutions. In addition, some researchers point to the lack of digital maturity of companies, which translates into a low capacity to integrate information technologies into industrial processes [31]. The rapid evolution of skills required in the technological field also creates a gap between the qualifications available on the labor market and those needed to fully exploit the tools of Industry 4.0 [32].

Figure 1 presents a comprehensive summary of the obstacles identified in the literature.

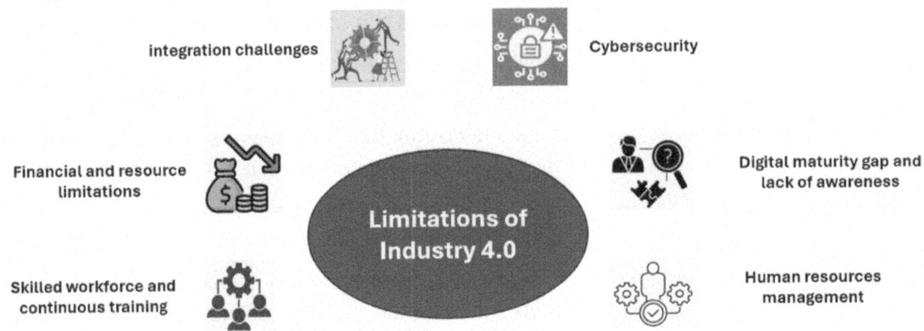

Fig. 1. Main Barriers to the Implementation of Industry 4.0

2.4 Areas for Further Research

It is crucial to analyze the extent of the application of the Industry 4.0 concept in the Arab Maghreb countries to assess its impact and measure the level of preparedness of these nations. In order to better understand the implementation of Industry 4.0 in the five largest Maghreb countries in terms of Gross Domestic Product (GDP), this study is based on the review of available research. These countries are Algeria, Morocco, Tunisia, Libya and Mauritania. Algeria, with a GDP of $224 billion, remains heavily dependent on its oil and gas sector, although agriculture, including the production of wheat, cereals and citrus fruits, also contributes significantly to the national economy. Libya, although affected by political and social issues in recent years, maintains a prominent position thanks to its significant oil and natural gas reserves, with a GDP estimated at $47 billion, mainly from the export of these resources [37]. Morocco, with a GDP of $198 billion, has a thriving agricultural sector, with significant exports of citrus fruits and olive oil, and stands out for its notable progress in the renewable energy sector. Tunisia, with a GDP of around $46,3 billion, is characterized by a dynamic tourism sector and an expanding industrial sector, particularly in the automotive and textile sectors. Finally, Mauritania, with a GDP of around $9,78 billion, relies mainly on the mining and fishing sectors. Table 2 provides an overview of the economic strength of the Maghreb region, illustrating the diverse industries contributing to the GDP of these countries.

Table 2. Maghreb Countries Ranked by GDP in 2023.

Rank	Country	GDP (billion USD)	Key Economic Sectors
1	Algeria	224	Oil and gas, agriculture (wheat, cereals)
2	Morocco	198	Agriculture (citrus, olive oil), renewable energy
3	Libya	47	Oil and gas
4	Tunisia	46,3	Tourism, industry (automotive, textiles)
5	Mauritania	9,78	Mining, fishing

Current research indicates that the adoption of Industry 4.0 in these countries faces several challenges, including the modernization of industrial infrastructures and the strengthening of digital skills, as highlighted by various studies on the subject [38, 39].

3 Methodology

3.1 Gathering of Data

This research focuses on how Industry 4.0 is perceived and its impact on the industrial sector, energy consumption and working conditions in the five main Maghreb countries, namely Algeria, Morocco, Tunisia, Libya and Mauritania. The aim was to assess the impact of this technology and the level of preparedness of these countries for its implementation. We conducted interviews and used a research method based on grounded theory. This approach consists of generating theories from systematically collected and analyzed data, in order to provide detailed explanations of a specific phenomenon [40]. As Chen (2018) explains, the purpose of grounded theory research is to elucidate events from the theoretical framework that is built as the research process progresses [41]. This method is based on a structured set of approaches to develop theories from qualitative data collection. Following this method, we collected and analyzed our data iteratively, until reaching a theoretical saturation point. The objective of this qualitative approach is to collect data by carefully observing how local actors perceive their environment. After comparing the advantages and disadvantages of focus groups and interviews, we opted for semi-structured interviews. Focus groups have disadvantages, such as unstructured responses, which complicate analysis, and responses can be influenced by social expectations related to group norms. To ensure the reliability of our results, we therefore conducted semi-structured interviews with Industry 4.0 experts in these five Maghreb countries. Our study identified three key roles in Industry 4.0. The first role is that of providers, which are the companies developing the technologies associated with Industry 4.0. The second role is that of users, namely the entities that integrate these technologies into their industrial processes. Finally, the third role, that of hybrid actors, concerns companies that play the role of both suppliers and users of Industry 4.0 technologies.

A total of seven companies operating in strategic sectors such as energy, infrastructure, and technology participated in semi-structured interviews. Their selection was guided by a qualitative approach, based on the principles of grounded theory, aimed at exploring the cases studied in depth. This number was determined based on the criterion of theoretical saturation, reached when the interviews no longer provide new information likely to enrich the analysis. These interviews made it possible to gather detailed information on the perception and integration of Industry 4.0 within the companies concerned. To strengthen the validity of the results, we also consulted works and publications by recognized experts in the field, particularly in North Africa. A structured interview guide based on existing literature was used, which allowed us to uncover unexpected aspects of Industry 4.0 and explore topics not initially anticipated. The interview was divided into two parts: the first covered general elements such as the company's organization, its history, the participants' role and experience, and the transition to Industry 4.0. The second focused on the interpretation of Industry 4.0, its impacts on employees, the challenges to be overcome, as well as organizational and managerial issues. To ensure the credibility of the results and limit bias, the anonymity and confidentiality of the participants' responses were respected. Table 3 presents the companies involved in this study, with information on their sectors of activity and their roles in the adoption of Industry 4.0.

Table 3. Information on the companies that participated in the interviews.

Company	Country	Industry Sector	Role in Industry 4.0
STMicroelectronics	Tunisia	Electronics Manufacturing	Provider
Telnet	Tunisia	IT & Consulting	Provider and user
Tunisair	Tunisia	Air Transport	User
Sonatrach	Algeria	Oil & Gas	Provider
OCP	Morocco	Fertilizers	User
ENI	Libya	Oil & Gas	Provider
Cevital	Algeria	Agribusiness	Provider and user

3.2 Analysis of Data

This study is based on a methodological approach based on grounded theory, which allows for a rigorous and detailed analysis of the interviews conducted, as well as the annual reports published on the companies' websites. This method offered great flexibility in the interpretation of the data, by allowing for the exploration of unforeseen aspects of the phenomenon studied. Thanks to this approach, it was possible to measure in a precise and nuanced manner the level of preparation of the Maghreb countries for the adoption of Industry 4.0, taking into account the specificities and challenges of each national context. The data analysis was structured around three major dimensions, in order to provide a complete vision of the issues and impacts of this transition:

- **The impact on the manufacturing industry:** This analysis focuses on the transformation of production and manufacturing processes in Maghreb companies. It explores efficiency gains, improvements in product quality, as well as the integration of advanced technologies such as automation, artificial intelligence and the Internet of Things (IoT) in production chains.

- **The impact on energy consumption:** This dimension examines how the adoption of Industry 4.0 could influence the energy needs of companies, particularly in terms of energy efficiency, reduction of consumption and integration of renewable energies in industrial processes. It also analyzes the impact on environmental sustainability and resource management.
- **The impact on the working conditions of employees:** This category examines the potential changes in tasks, required skills, and personnel management, in connection with the introduction of Industry 4.0 technologies. The objective is to assess the effects on the quality of life at work, safety, as well as the training and development of employee skills.

Figure 2 illustrates the intersection of Industry 4.0 impacts on workforce conditions, manufacturing processes, and energy efficiency in Maghreb companies.

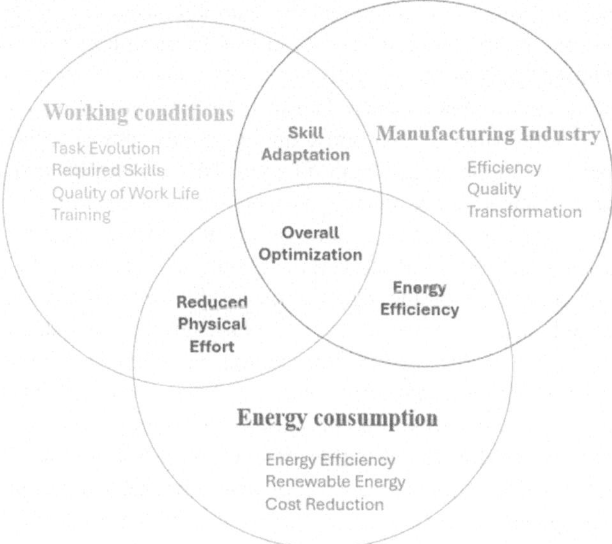

Fig. 2. Intersection of Industry 4.0 Impacts: Workforce, Manufacturing, and Energy Efficiency

4 Results and Discussion

4.1 The Impact on the Manufacturing Industry

The concept of Industry 4.0 has been well received in many organizations, although the issue of data security has emerged as a major challenge. While the integration of this technology presents undeniable opportunities, it also requires rigorous management of the information generated by production processes.

A first interviewee shared: "Currently, we only exploit a tiny fraction of production data. It is therefore imperative to target only the relevant data. By analyzing this crucial information, our company has significantly improved its decision-making. However, it is essential to limit the analysis to the data that really brings value."

A second interviewee explained: "We implemented industrial sensors to monitor temperature, vibrations and identify elements that are difficult to see. Production management is optimized thanks to I/O-Link technology, allowing direct communication with sensors and actuators. The addition of specific cameras allows real-time feedback, reducing errors and minimizing waste. These cameras have also facilitated production documentation, ensuring better traceability, enhanced quality control and more precise monitoring of machine status."

Another testimonial highlights the impact of advanced logistics technologies: "Thanks to Industry 4.0, we have managed to optimize the flow of products in real time. Our smart warehousing systems use RFID, tags and antennas to track products throughout the chain. In addition, our smart logistics systems adjust shipping routes and distribute goods according to truck loading orders." »

In light of the interviews conducted and the available research, the implementation of Industry 4.0 in the industrial sector turns out to be a complex process that requires meticulous planning. The benefits are indisputable: the quality of production improves, which leads to an increase in sales and a reduction in losses. The use of data analysis tools can provide valuable information to produce quality goods, almost without errors, thus reducing costs while eliminating production losses. This also translates into a decrease in expenses related to maintenance and repairs. The results of this transformation should quickly translate into an increase in exports and a decrease in imports. Industry 4.0, combined with other technological innovations, could also increase the share of high value-added products in global trade [42]. For successful implementation, it is essential that government policies, integrated innovation plans, training and skills development initiatives be strengthened. In addition, the integration of external knowledge by the manufacturing sector promotes innovation and the exploration of new business models. In order to maximize the benefits of technological innovation, companies must excel in the dissemination of information within their organization and across their value networks, going beyond their direct relationships with consumers and suppliers. Industry 4.0 thus opens new perspectives for optimizing production by fully exploiting advanced technologies, while reducing resource consumption.

4.2 The Impact on Energy Consumption

Based on the interviews conducted and available research, the sustainability of Industry 4.0 in the Maghreb appears to be closely linked to energy consumption management.

A company manager explained: "The energy consumption of Industry 4.0 technologies is quite high. In order to limit this consumption, we installed a wireless sensor network, which is both efficient and cost-effective, to monitor and reduce our energy consumption within the factory."

Concerning the energy sector in the region, an expert commented: "The Maghreb has great potential to deploy renewable energy solutions, but the sector is still developing. Energy has always been a key element of economic and social progress, and insufficient energy resources are a major obstacle to this development. However, the introduction of Industry 4.0 could encourage governments to modernize their energy infrastructure, which could attract new investments."

Another interviewee added: "In the context of Industry 4.0, energy efficiency is not limited to battery management. By optimizing downtime, technologies such as Machine Metrics can save energy and increase process efficiency. In addition, solutions such as fuel cells, used to store energy in data centers, can significantly reduce energy consumption. The deployment of Industry 4.0 therefore represents an opportunity for the Maghreb to strengthen its energy efficiency."

Research has highlighted the importance of energy networks in supporting the rise of Industry 4.0. With its deployment, energy demand will increase and improving electricity networks will be essential. The Maghreb, in particular, faces challenges in terms of access to electricity, especially in rural areas and some fragile regions. In Algeria, Tunisia or Libya, although infrastructure is growing, millions of people still do not have reliable access to electricity. It is therefore crucial to integrate energy management tools to ensure efficient consumption and support the implementation of Industry 4.0. Specialists advocate the adoption of an approach based on the Internet of Things (IoT) to better understand and anticipate the energy consumption of industrial systems. This method could allow companies in the Maghreb to reduce their energy footprint and improve their energy management [43]. However, despite the promises of Industry 4.0, many digitalization initiatives in the region do not yet effectively integrate energy management. As companies gradually become aware of the importance of energy in their operations, data centers, which are large consumers of energy, are raising major concerns. One solution to counter this problem could be the adoption of fuel cells, which would allow energy storage and ensure continuity of operations in the event of a failure, thus reducing dependence on excessive energy consumption. This represents a major opportunity for the Maghreb industry to move towards more sustainable energy management.

4.3 The Impact on the Working Conditions of Employees

Following interviews with seven Industry 4.0 technology experts and an in-depth analysis of the websites of ten other companies operating in the Maghreb region, several key findings emerged. Participants highlighted that the adoption of Industry 4.0 technologies could lead to the disappearance of low-skilled jobs, due to the integration of key components such as sensors, data, information and operations.

One interviewee expressed concerns about the impact of the introduction of robots and machines, which could radically transform the nature of work and the skills required, potentially increasing unemployment.

Another interviewee mentioned that the substitution of human labor with robots and digital technologies is accompanied by a desire to overcome labor shortages by optimizing productivity. Many companies expressed their intention to leverage Industry 4.0 technologies to address this challenge.

However, another speaker identified a major obstacle. According to him, one of the biggest challenges in integrating Industry 4.0 technologies is the lack of skilled labor. He stressed that training and upgrading current employees is a complex and costly task, requiring both time and considerable financial investments. At the same time, he stressed that, although the digitalization of industrial processes offers substantial financial benefits, such as reduced operational costs and better inventory management, the initial investment required for the adoption of these technologies could slow down some companies. The budget constraint is therefore an important factor to take into account, especially in an economic context where each investment is closely scrutinized

Furthermore, another expert mentioned organizational resistance and poor management of the transformations induced by Industry 4.0, another significant obstacle. According to him, many companies are not yet ready to embrace this technological transition. He explained that tensions have arisen within organizational units, where conflicting interests have clashed with a lack of understanding of new technologies and a general apprehension of the unknown. These elements have led to resistance to change, both among middle managers and lower-level employees. This participant also highlighted that, with the rise of digitalization, some employees fear for their professional future, not feeling sufficiently trained to adapt to the new requirements. Finally, he noted that the roles of middle managers will also undergo a significant change: they will have to take on new responsibilities, often more complex, which will require more specialized and in-depth skills.

This study highlights that information and communication technologies (ICT) are the fundamental basis of Industry 4.0. Integrating these principles from an early age into the education system, from primary school to university, is crucial to prepare the future generation of workers. The transformation of work environments will lead to the disappearance of some traditional professions, while others, more specialized and requiring advanced technological skills, will emerge [44, 45]. Although the adoption of Industry 4.0 generates new jobs, unemployment could also increase in Maghreb countries that will take longer to integrate this digital revolution, due to a mismatch between the current skills of the workforce and the needs of industrial sectors. The first Maghreb countries to successfully transition to Industry 4.0 will probably have a positive impact on the unemployment rate in the long term, provided that this transition is done in an inclusive and rapid manner. It is essential for governments and businesses in these countries to conduct a comprehensive assessment of the benefits and risks associated with this new technological era, in order to better prepare their labor markets. Since the first industrial revolution, Maghreb countries have faced a growing demand for skilled workers. The fourth industrial revolution will be no different: it will lead to the disappearance of certain professions while changing existing ones. For example, sectors such as information technology, data analytics, cybersecurity, and robotics are expected to experience strong growth in the coming years. Jobs such as artificial intelligence specialists, data analysts, cybersecurity engineers, and advanced industrial maintenance experts are expected to thrive in the near future [46]. However, some currently sought-after professions, such as machine learning engineers or Internet of Things (IoT) specialists, could become obsolete if the digital transition is not managed properly [47].

It is therefore essential that Maghreb countries address the risk of unemployment growth due to automation and new technologies by implementing appropriate strategies for training, reskilling and integrating the skills needed for Industry 4.0. This proactive approach is essential to avoid massive technological unemployment and ensure sustainable and inclusive growth in the region.

5 Conclusion

This paper explores the existing literature and presents the results of interviews conducted with seven Maghreb companies that have integrated Industry 4.0 technologies. The aim is to assess the region's readiness for the fourth industrial revolution and its impact on industrial sectors and labor market dynamics. Our results suggest that Industry 4.0 offers interesting prospects for the deployment of advanced monitoring and control systems, which play a key role in the sustainability and efficiency of decision-making processes. We observed divergent perceptions regarding risks and opportunities, both among users of the technology and suppliers. In Maghreb countries where Industry 4.0 is already being adopted, the reduction in unit costs has improved export competitiveness while reducing dependence on imports. However, while Industry 4.0 promotes innovation and information technologies, it also leads to a decrease in low-skilled jobs, with an increase in opportunities in the fields of design and technology development. Despite its potential for economic growth, major challenges remain, particularly in terms of data security and energy consumption. Organizational resistance, mainly linked to the fear of job losses, highlights the need for a deep reform of education systems in the region. It is therefore essential that Maghreb countries quickly reform their education systems, in order to adapt them to the requirements of Industry 4.0 and strengthen their competitiveness on the international scene, thus contributing to the strength of the regional economy.

References

1. Müller, J.M., Buliga, O., Voigt, K.: The role of absorptive capacity and innovation strategy in the design of industry 4.0 business models-a comparison between SMEs and large enterprises. (3) 1–11 (2020)
2. Büchi, G., Cugno, M., Castagnoli, R.: Smart factory performance and industry 4.0. Technol. Forecast. Soc. Change. **150** (2019, 2020)
3. Pina, A., Ferrão, P., Fournier, J., Lacarrière, B., Le Corre, O.: Industry 4.0 technology implementation impact to industrial sustainable energy in Indonesia: a model conceptualization (2019)
4. Frey, C., Osborne, M.: The Future of Employment: how Susceptible Are Jobs to Computerisation? (2017)
5. Horváth, D., R. Z.: Szabó: driving forces and barriers of industry 4.0: do multinational and small and medium-sized companies have equal opportunities? Technol. Forecast. Soc. Change. **146**(June), 119–132 (2019)
6. Karl, S., Backhaus, H., D.: Nadarajah: investigating the relationship between industry 4.0 and productivity: a conceptual framework for. Malays. Manuf. **00** (2019)
7. Ghobakhloo, M.: Industry 4.0, digitization, and opportunities for sustainability. J. Clean. Prod. **252**, 119869 (2020)
8. Manda, M.I., Dhaou, S.B.: Responding to the challenges and opportunities in the 4th industrial revolution in developing countries. In: Proceedings of the 12th International Conference on Theory and Practice of Electronic Governance (ICEGOV2019), pp. 244–253, Melbourne, VIC, Australia (3-5 Apr 2019)
9. Castelo-Branco, F., Cruz-Jesus, Oliveira, T.: Assessing industry 4.0 readiness in manufacturing: evidence for the European Union. Comput. Ind. **107**, 22–32 (2019)
10. Stief, P., Dantan, J., Etienne, A., Siadat, A.: Deriving Essential Components of Lean and Industry 4.0 Assessment Model for Manufacturing SMEs (2019)

11. Benešová, A., Hirman, M.: Determination of Changes in Process Management within Industry 4.0. **00**(2019) (2020)
12. Henao-hernández, I., et al.: Control and monitoring the Industry Control manufacturing the Industry. **10**, 195–200 (2019)
13. Imran, S., Szczerbicki, E., Sanin, C.: Proposition of the methodology for data acquisition, analysis and visualization in support of industry 4.0. **00** (2019)
14. Adetunla, A.O., Barenji, A.V., Barenji, R.V.: Developing manufacturing execution software as a service for small and medium size enterprise. In: Proceedings of the International Conference on Industrial Engineering and Operations Management., 8-10 March (2016)
15. Van Lopik, K., et al.: Developing augmented reality capabilities for industry 4.0 small enterprises: lessons learnt from a content authoring case study. Comput. Ind. **117**, 103208 (2020)
16. Lass, S., Gronau, N.: A factory operating system for extending existing factories to industry. Comput. Ind. **115** (2020)
17. Santos, L., Brittes, G., Fabián, N., Germán, A.: The expected contribution of industry 4.0 technologies for industrial performance. Int. J. Prod. Econ. **204**(8), 383–394 (2018)
18. Doltsinis, S., Ferreira, P., Mabkhot, M.M., Lohse, N.: A decision support system for rapid ramp-up of industry 4.0 enabled production systems. Comput. Ind. **116** (2020)
19. Kamble, S., et al.: Industry 4.0 and its impact on productivity and innovation. J. Ind. Eng. Manag. **12**(3), 27–44 (2019)
20. Raj, R., et al.: Technological advancements and their impact on the industry. Int. J. Manuf. Technol. **28**(4), 55–67 (2019)
21. Ahmed, A., et al.: Adoption of industry 4.0 technologies: challenges and opportunities. J. Manuf. Process. **34**(2), 120–133 (2019)
22. Singh, A., et al.: Business transformation through industry 4.0. J. Bus. Res. **75**(6), 40–58 (2019)
23. Sharpe, M., et al.: Strategic positioning in the age of industry 4.0. Manag. Sci. **65**(7), 65–78 (2019)
24. Namasudra, S., et al.: Enhancing competitive advantage through innovation. J. Competitiveness Stud. **29**(2), 91–102 (2020)
25. Imran, M., et al.: Energy optimization in industry 4.0: a sustainable approach. Renewable. Energy J. **48**(5), 231–241 (2019)
26. Stief, D., et al.: Industrial sustainability through energy-efficient systems. Energy Rep. **5**(4), 233–245 (2019)
27. Santos, M., et al.: Environmental impact and energy savings in industry 4.0. Environmental. Eng. J. **22**(3), 98–111 (2018)
28. Jorge, A., et al.: Managerial efficiency in the digital age. Manag. Organ. Rev. **14**(6), 204–215 (2020)
29. Lui, S., et al.: Real-time decision-making systems in industry 4.0. J. Oper. Manag. **40**(2), 76–87 (2020)
30. Environment: energy-efficient through-life smart design, manufacturing and operation of ships in an industry 4.0 environment. **2012**, 1–13 (2017)
31. Liu, X.L., Wang, W.M., Guo, H., Barenji, A.V., Li, Z., Huang, G.Q.: Industrial blockchain based framework for product lifecycle management in industry 4.0. **63**(November), 2019 (2020)
32. Kadir, B. A., Broberg, O., Souza, C.: Current research and future perspectives on human factors and ergonomics in industry 4.0. Comput. Ind. Eng. **137**, (July 2019).
33. Prause, R., Kumar, A., Hughes, E., Ghobakhloo, M.: Prioritizing barriers to industry 4.0 adoption: financial constraints, standardization, data security and workforce implications. Comput. Ind. Eng. **171**, 108428 (2022)

34. Raj, A., Dwivedi, G., Sharma, A., Beatriz, A., De Sousa, L.: Barriers to the adoption of industry 4.0 technologies in the manufacturing sector: an inter-country comparative perspective. Int. J. Prod. Econ. (Nov 2019)
35. Kamble, S.S., Gunasekaran, A., Sharma, R.: Analysis of the driving and dependence power of barriers to adopt industry 4.0 in Indian manufacturing industry. Comput. Ind. **101**(May), 107–119 (2018)
36. Aheleroff, S., et al.: IoT-enabled smart appliances under industry 4.0: a case study. Adv. Eng. Inform. **43** (Feb 2020)
37. Ben Salah, F.L., et al.: Economic analysis of the oil and gas sector in Libya. Energy Policy. **39**, 4879–4886 (2020)
38. Haddad, M.C., et al.: Digital transformation in Maghreb countries: the road ahead. J. Ind. Eng. **50**, 110–122 (2021)
39. Bouzid, T., et al.: Barriers and opportunities for industry 4.0 adoption in North Africa. Int. J. Technol. Manag. **65**(2), 128–145 (2021)
40. Ma, F.: Research of evolution mechanism of network group event based on grounded theory under micro blog platform. J. Netw. Comput. Appl. **39**(5), 678–684 (2015)
41. Chen, C.: Research on the incentive mechanism of Hidilao hotpot's employees based on grounded theory. In: Proceedings of the International Conference on Business Management, pp. 118–130 (2018)
42. Systems, I.M.: Industry 4.0 roadmap for Mexico and lessons for South Africa. In: Proceedings of the Industry 4.0 Conference, pp. 1–10 (2019)
43. Author, F.: Policy implications of the 4th industrial revolution for the cultural and creative economy. Journal. (Dec 2018)
44. Moraes, E.B., et al.: Integration of industry 4.0 technologies with education 4.0: advantages for improvements in learning. Interact. Technol. Smart Educ. **20**(2), 271–287 (2023)
45. Grassi, A., Guizzi, G., Santillo, L.C., Vespoli, S.: A semi-heterarchical production control architecture for industry 4.0-based manufacturing systems. J. Ind. Eng. Manag. **24**, 43–46 (2020)
46. Aghimien, D.O., Matabane, K., Aigbavboa, C., Oke, A.E.: Industry 4.0 diffusion in the south African construction industry – construction professionals' perspective. In: Proceedings of the South African Construction Conference (Sept 2019)
47. Meredith, J.R., Pilkington, A.: Assessing the exchange of knowledge between operations management and other fields: some challenges and opportunities. J. Oper. Manag. **60**(2), 47–53 (2018)
48. The Impacts of the Fourth Industrial Revolution on Jobs and the Future of the Third Sector. pp. 1–25, (Jan 2016)

Human Beings at the Heart of Education 4.0 and Lean Management: A Synergy for Industrial Competitiveness

Douae Dbaich[1,2], Aziza Mahil[1], and Mohamed Tabaa[2](✉)

[1] LIASMAD FSJES Ain sbaa Casablanca, Casablanca, Morocco
[2] LPRI Lab EMSI Casablanca, Casablanca, Morocco
m.tabaa@emsi.ma

Abstract. This article describes how companies in the industrial sector are leveraging key competencies to strengthen their Lean Management initiative, contributing to their competitiveness and sustainability. The aim is to improve their ability and expertise to adapt to market change, innovate, maintain their competitive edge and reduce the risks associated with economic uncertainty. Companies set objectives by analyzing the synergies between these areas, identifying key competencies and assessing their impact on Lean Management. Our approach borrows these elements from a range of articles and reviews by experts in Lean Management, Industry and Education 4.0. We exploit technological mutations linked to artificial intelligence, aimed at developing systems and algorithms for creating programs, personalizing employee training, analyzing data on learner performance and identifying trends that predict future actions. These are techniques that highlight the need for an organizational learning culture in professional development, responding to the problem of adapting employees to technological change, the CDIO approach, creating an educational revolution 4.0. These discussions place the human being at the heart of Lean Management 4.0, hence the importance of continuous improvement and adaptation to change for sustainable competitiveness.

Keywords: Education 4.0 · Industry · Program · Lean management · Artificial Intelligence

1 Introduction

This paper highlights two sectors that have been characterized by the integration of advanced technology such as Artificial Intelligence, automation, databases... into the production process. This integration has profoundly revolutionized economic and social models. These two sectors are joined by a model known as CDIO, forming a solid triangle to meet the challenges and issues facing industry on the one hand, and education on the other.

If the industrial sector has created intelligent factories capable of contributing to the optimization of production processes, human resources and financial resources (cost

F. Kamoun et al. (Eds.): AFRICATEK 2025, LNICST 676, pp. 194–205, 2026.
https://doi.org/10.1007/978-3-032-16635-7_13

reduction), it has not only limited itself to the technical know-how with which it attempts to maintain growth in production, but has also extended itself to making tasks more creative and solving complex production-related problems. These are the principles on which Lean Management is based [1].

In parallel with the industrial sector, Education 4.0 has sought to offer a pedagogical model that puts students at the center of their educational project, by further encouraging a dynamic based on collaboration and the acquisition of technical, personal and social skills. The aim is to turn students into responsible talents capable of adapting to the paradigm shift imposed by the integration of new technology tools [2]. To answer the question: "How can the synergies between core competencies, the CDIO approach, Education 4.0 and artificial intelligence technologies sustainably strengthen Lean Management initiatives in the industrial sector?" We have highlighted the role that companies can play in raising awareness and training employees to use, firstly, the skills they have acquired to adapt to the new context created by the use of technological tools, whether in the industrial or educational sector, and secondly, to call on external skills (core business) to meet market needs.

The need to innovate in order to adapt to new technologies sets the scene for training establishments. This staging is then defined in training programs centered on the reality of daily life within organizations [3].

Indeed, this new approach attempts to create a bridge between universities 4.0 on the one hand, and industry on the other. To this end, the CDIO model has emerged as a tool offering a teaching method capable of meeting the demands and challenges of the industrial sector. Unlike the traditional approach, the CDIO model focuses on learning by doing. This concept enables learners to Design, Develop, Implement and Operate complex programs and systems [4].

To address the problem posed, this study adopts an exploratory qualitative approach, based on a narrative review of the literature. The aim is to analyze the synergies between key competencies, the CDIO model, Education 4.0 and artificial intelligence technologies in the context of Lean Management.

2 State of Art

In the context of Lean Management, this section explores the theories, methodologies and practices that have shaped this approach over time. By analyzing the work of pioneers and recent contributions, we can better understand how key competencies and technological innovations, such as artificial intelligence, are influencing the development and application of Lean Management in the industrial sector [5].

2.1 Education 4.0 and Skills:

Based on the idea that Education 4.0 refers to an evolution in learning and research. This evolution has been characterized by the integration of information and communication technologies, and in a very relaxed way. In this evolving context, learners are seeking to develop their skills to succeed in a world that has become digitalized par excellence.

Indeed, learners now need to have a good command of IT tools in order to acquire good practice in using them. We're highlighting some educational software, e-learning platforms and other applications that we call interactive. In the absence of this skill, it seems very difficult to understand digital information, to interpret it and then to analyze it, or even to have the ability to assess the credibility of sources gathered online. Hence the need to seek out specialized skills that enable them to decipher and analyze it, such as the notion of leadership, considered one of the key skills [6]. Learners need to take the initiative in questioning the information they gather, analyzing problems simply and effectively, and developing innovative and creative solutions. This must be done in a collaborative and virtual environment, so that learners are increasingly exposed to an environment where online collaboration is essential. As a result, these learners are obliged to develop their skills in terms of communication, collaboration and team spirit: it's a question of increasing their personal competencies. Indeed, the use of different media, online writing, virtual presentation and participation in online exchanges calls for soft skills and abilities. This leads us to the idea that learners are called upon to master multiple languages for various reasons, which are defined in their confrontation with programming, media languages and other digital communication styles and figures [7].

In addition to the above, digital information highlights other mandatory skills such as entrepreneurship, information management and adaptability. Indeed, Education 4.0 fosters the development of entrepreneurial intelligence, awareness and imagination, encouraging learners to take the initiative and even instilling in them the spirit of risktaking known as calculation on the one hand, and leading them to demonstrate their relevance online, hence the importance of this type of skill in the field of research and information management; otherwise known as database management on the other. In other words, candidates in Education 4.0 need to have a good understanding of how to gather information, store it, organize it and then interpret it.

One of the aims of Education 4.0 is to develop in learners a spirit of perseverance and sustainability, with a view to adapting to society's technological evolutions. It aims to prepare young people to succeed in this new digital world by providing them with a range of skills: technical skills, cognitive skills and socio-emotional skills [8].

2.2 Lean Management Principles:

Lean Management is defined as a management approach that aims to maximize customer value, while minimizing resource waste. To achieve this, it calls on fundamental principles linked to various fields, notably education, and in particular the context of Education 4.0. This integrates new technologies to enhance learning [9].

Among the foundations of Lean Management weaving potential links with Education 4.0 we cite the following elements:

Continuous Improvement (Kaizen Theory): Kaizen is a method that promotes the idea that small, regular changes can lead to significant improvements over time. As such, it emphasizes the constant effort to identify and solve even the smallest problems. The Kaizen method therefore emphasizes a culture of improvement where processes are constantly evaluated, analyzed and refined to eliminate waste.

Applied to education, the Kaizen method implies a commitment to the continuous improvement of teaching and/or learning methods and styles, using new, innovative educational technologies. This enables the use of new pedagogical approaches using knowledge and know-how transfer tools while optimizing the learning experience, such as Education 4.0 [10].

Just in Time: One of the main aims of Lean Management is to minimize, if not get rid of, unnecessary stockpiling in terms of waste, and also to provide the necessary resources at the right time and in the right quality, in order to cope with tasks efficiently [11].The use of new technology enables students and/or learners to access educational resources that are relevant to today's context, such as: e-learning platforms, online courses and exercises, educational and sports games.

Reducing Waste: Lean Management is part of a quality approach that aims, among other things, to identify and eliminate all unnecessary elements that add no value to the final product or service. The use of technology in Education 4.0 aims to eliminate waste in processes either in terms of time, energy, materials... The objective is to optimize processes to make them efficient. This is the aim of Education 4.0 [1]

Staff Involvement: Lean Management recognizes the importance of the active participation of all members of the organization, whatever their hierarchical level: workers, supervisors, managers Its aim is to involve all staff in decision-making and process improvement. Education 4.0 is part of this approach, which aims to encourage the participation of all stakeholders: teachers, students or learners and parents [12]. New interactive teaching methods (learning platforms) can only play a role in strengthening the participation of the latter.

Workflow: Promoting a smooth, continuous flow of work is a fundamental principle of Lean Management, helping to avoid interruptions and delays caused by humans or machines. Following the example of this Lean Management principle, Education 4.0 also opts for the inclusion of new educational technologies that can promote the flow of information, making it easier for students and/or learners to access content and learning activities on a continuous basis, regardless of time or place [4].

Standardization: Lean Management, with reference to the Kaizen method, encourages the standardization of processes. By "standardization" we mean the creation of standards that can be improved over time, with the aim of maintaining consistency within the same process.

Education 4.0 can in turn integrate educational standards into e-learning platforms, for example, while guaranteeing conformity in the quality of educational content and assessments [4]. Integrating the above principles of Lean Management into Education 4.0 will undoubtedly create an effective, even efficient, learner-centered learning environment adapted to the changing needs of the so-called modern world.

2.3 Employability and Agility:

Responding to market demands requires an approach that is flexible and geared to the real needs of learners. To achieve this, education needs to be personalized, using strategies that can be implemented to better align students' skills with market demands. These strategies can be listed as follows:

Market Needs Analysis: the Aim of this Operation is Twofold:

- Carry out an in-depth analysis of skills on the one hand, and the qualifications required by the labor market in the various sectors of activity on the other.
- Collaborate with organizations: companies, trade associations and other stakeholders to understand both current and future market trends [13].

Program Development: The aim is to design flexible curricula that enable learners to personalize their study and/or career paths according to their interests and the requirements of the job market; and to integrate specialized modules, content and courses to meet specific demand-driven needs, particularly in the industrial sector [6].

Use of Educational Technologies: This strategy involves integrating new technologies such as e-learning and virtual and augmented reality simulations to create interactive and engaging experiences. It also uses adapted platforms to make content more specialized according to the skills and needs of each student or learner [1].

Experiential Learning: Based on the idea that you can only learn by doing, Education 4.0, through this strategy, promotes experiential learning by integrating learners into internships, practical projects and even providing them with opportunities to work within organizations in programs on the one hand; and encouraging partnerships with companies from different sectors to offer students concrete experiences related to their field of study [6].

Tutoring, Mentoring and Coaching: Through this strategy, Education 4.0 is attempting to set up Tutoring and Mentoring programs with all stakeholders including industry professionals to better guide students in their personal development. On the one hand, this strategy extends to offering these students Coaching services to help them better define their career goals and acquire the necessary personal skills.

Competency-Based Assessment: Competency-based assessment is an effective method because it focuses on practical and professional skills, not just on memorizing teaching approaches and styles. In fact, this type of assessment uses projects, case studies and simulations to reflect the real challenges encountered in the workplace.

Continuing Education: Instilling the importance of lifelong learning into the minds of learners provides them with opportunities for lifelong learning in general and their professional lives in particular, enabling them to remain relevant and effective in the job market. Indeed, recognizing students' acquired experience means enhancing the skills they need by perfecting them in the field.

Working with Industry: It's important to establish a real partnership with companies based on a win-win strategy to ensure that educational content is aligned with real market needs. A strategy conceived as a bridge between school and the job market. For this reason, it is essential to call on professionals as speakers and trainers to share their expertise with young people [14].

Market Trends: It is essential to maintain a constant watch on market trends and adjust educational programs accordingly. This monitoring enables Education 4.0 to integrate new skills and emerging technologies into curricula in sufficient quantity, quality and time.

By personalizing education, educational establishments can better prepare young learners for the specific requirements of the job market, thus promoting their employability and professional success.

The Lean Management approach stems from the Lean Manufacturing principle, which plays a crucial role in enhancing the employability and agility of young people, teams and organizations [15]. Indeed, this approach can contribute to and cover both aspects, namely employability and agility, through:

Identifying and Developing Key Skills: Lean Management encourages the identification of key competencies by drawing up an inventory of the specific skills needed to achieve the organization's objectives. This operation can be applied at individual level to help workers define the key competencies in their field of activity. Through this approach, Education 4.0 aims to boost employability by directing young people towards specific skills in high demand on the job market.

Continuous Improvement and Agility: Based on the idea that the Kaizen approach, which promotes continuous improvement, aims to create a culture of agility within organizations, teams are increasingly encouraged to identify continuous improvement opportunities and adapt quickly to change. This adaptability is reinforced by implementing rapid adjustment cycles while experimenting with new approaches [11].

Reducing Waste and Optimizing Resources: Faced with waste in both production and operational processes, Lean Management enables efficient use of human, material and financial resources. This optimization plays a very important role in enhancing employability, by enabling young people and teams of workers to be productive in an efficient and productive way.

Customer Focus and Adaptability: Lean Management's focus on customer value encourages companies to become more customer-oriented. This orientation influences individuals to better understand the real needs of customers, be they companies, employers or partners, and thus to respond rapidly to changes in customer or market expectations.

Collaborative Working: It should be emphasized that Lean Management requires close collaboration between team members to promote open and transparent communication [16].

Visual Management: The use of visual boards is one of the best practices in Lean Management, as it promotes transparency in operations and projects, which enhances employability by creating a climate of trust and responsibility, both individual and collective, a much sought-after quality in the job market [9].

Versatile Training: Lean Management encourages greater versatility in employees, otherwise known as "high potential": the set of hidden skills that do not fall within the remit of certain job. This leads us to the idea that these employees are trained to be competent in several fields and not specialized in just one. Through versatility, Education 4.0

reinforces employability and offers individuals greater flexibility to adapt to different situations and professional responsibilities.

The integration of all the above Lean Management principles into organizational culture and individual practices. Education can develop skills and adapt them to today's job market, while fostering the agility needed to meet job/profile fit [10].

2.4 The Contribution of the CDIO Process in the Education Sector:

Referring to the previous section, we can say that in this context described as agile, where companies are looking for talent capable of adapting quickly to new professional situations and successfully leading teams, CDIO (Conceive, Develop, Implement, Operate) is an innovative pedagogical approach designed to transform learners' skills (Fig. 1).

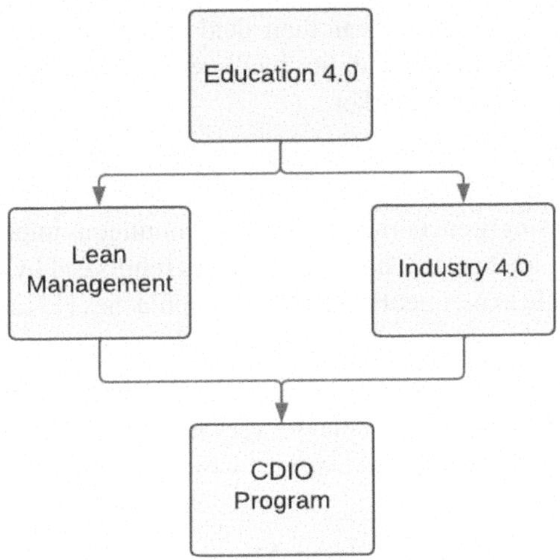

Fig. 1. The bridge from university to industry

This approach acts as a tool for organizing pedagogical work within training establishments. This is achieved by proposing a number of projects directly related to industrial issues in general, and educational issues in particular.

This pedagogical approach, based on the CDIO process, enables learners to acquire and develop consistent personal and professional theoretical skills. The relevance of this process makes it a bridge between the professional industrial sector and the academic, educational sector.

In addition to theoretical knowledge, CDIO as a process of design, development, implementation and operation focuses on key technical skills such as communication, problem-solving, teamwork and leadership. These skills enable students to take responsibility for their own training, particularly in terms of managing their own projects. This autonomy remains essential in preparing for a future professional career based on educational issues that are both real and interdisciplinary. This last feature encourages students to adopt a global vision that takes into account the interactions between the stakeholders in the education system.

To understand the four phases of the process in question, its integration into learning programs and its impact on the environment. Indeed, the adoption of this process aims to define the needs and specifications of the programs taught, and to highlight the dayto-day problems relating to these programs. The aim is to be able to create lesson plans and schemes on the one hand, and to use the algorithms and models needed to carry out projects on the other. This realization calls for tests to make the product or educational system more consistent.

It should be stressed that the integration of the CDIO process into teaching programs extends over long periods (term, semester, etc.), depending on the nature of the teaching objectives set. In fact, the application of this process is based on real-life case studies, with the aim of encouraging students to assimilate critical thinking, as well as on practical work to apply students' theoretical skills, and finally on simulations so that learners can explore multiple learning situations enabling them to make the right choices.

The implementation of the CDIO process as we have just explained cannot take place without the conditions and requirements prior to its use, i.e. pedagogical workspaces for each team, the tools and software needed to carry out educational projects, and finally a strong partnership with all stakeholders in the education sector: ministry, local authority, academy, educational or training establishment, association...

By this innovative and skill-transforming aspect, the CDIO process offers a new and interesting alternative to traditional teaching methods in order to better prepare young students for the challenges of tomorrow.

3 Result and Discussion

By integrating new advanced technologies such as artificial intelligence and virtual and augmented reality, one can decide on the harmonization of education 4.0 in general and in the industry sector in particular with the principles of Lean Management, and this to develop a set of adequate skills in the professional world of today and the future. The development of learners in this context, which is considered to be innovative, enables them to acquire new advanced technological skills that help them adapt to a constantly changing digital environment [17].

It should be stressed that focusing on the notion of adaptability and agility can only encourage proactive attitudes to change on the one hand, and to strengthen the ability of students to become familiar with rapid changes in the labour market.

Also, one of the key features to highlight this approach that we call innovative is defined in critical thinking and problem solving. Young students develop their ability to analyse professional situations, assess tasks performed and provide elements of answers to problems encountered in an active and effective manner [18]. This development cannot take place without the integration of Lean Management principles based on quality and operational efficiency.

In this innovative context, we cannot do without the notion of collaboration and teamwork which occupies a central place alongside interdisciplinary projects and online platforms that stimulates the development of individual and collective communication skills in a part of the concept of time management and operational efficiency which are part of the general philosophy of Lean Management based on the elimination of waste on the other hand. Indeed, young students are trying to develop their practical skills in a way that takes time management into account in order to contribute to greater productivity [19].

In addition to the above, it should be said that education 4.0 highlights an important element that is defined in self-direction in learning. This is an element that has the role of further strengthening the continuous learning mentality, one of the characteristics on which the philosophy of continuous improvement of Lean Management is based. The students' location at the heart of their learning makes them future leaders capable of leading complex projects by working with other teams. This character is initiated by the adoption of the CDIO process which represents a kind of bridge between the world of training and the professional world.

We cannot close without recalling an essential and centrifugal element around which the principle of continuous learning, which is the client, rests. The latter requires a very thorough understanding of these needs, knowing that this reflection around it is at the heart of the principles of Lean Management which focus on creating value for the client, Process optimization and cost reduction [20].

Ultimately, education 4.0 when aligned with the principles of Lean Management offers students a quality training that is qualified as versatile with technological skills, critical thinking, agility, collaboration, time management, self-direction and customer orientation. These skills can only prepare them in an effective way by allowing them to evolve in a dynamic professional world aimed at operational efficiency, the very objective of this new approach called education 4.0.

The integration of Lean, Education 4.0, artificial intelligence and CDIO frameworks into change management is not straightforward. Despite growing interest and the potential for transformational impact, structural limitations remain. Firstly, the multiskilled nature of CDIO is both an asset and a liability. It is an intersection of management, engineering, education and digital technologies, each with vocabularies, theoretical frameworks and approaches that are often incommensurable and very difficult to harmonize.

Moreover, not all concepts are treated in the same way. Apart from the abundance of literature and industrial practices on Lean management, Education 4.0 and the CDIO approach are not yet accepted in a large number of institutions. At the other extreme, artificial intelligence (AI) exists mostly in prototype form in educational or industrial contexts. On the other hand, the application of these approaches faces innumerable problems at the strategic level, such as a lack of willingness to change, a lack of basic digital skills, an insidious budget and an imbalance… the mismatch… the gap between educational and technological infrastructure and industry standards. Regimes. When it comes to design and implementation challenges, understanding geographical and cutural issues is just as tricky

4 Conclusion

The present reflection, subject of our article: "Human Beings at the Heart of Education 4.0 and Lean Management: A Synergy for Industrial Competitiveness" is the importance of acquiring specific skills in order to strengthen Lean Management. Reinforcement using advanced technological tools from the industrial sector.

Artificial Intelligence as an innovative tool that provides for the personalization of employee training and performance analysis. Among these advanced tools is the CDIO process, which aims to innovate in the education sector as well as in the industrial sector. This innovation is reflected in the identification and development of specific skills to cope with changes in the training and education paradigm [7]. This change requires, of course, a pedagogical approach and where a better organized learning culture to allow the acquisition of new skills in question.

We also note that the tools of advanced technology, already discussed, are not intended as a training support in the industrial sector in general and in the educational sector in particular but they are seen as a trigger for change in teaching practices in a way that is described as profound. We are referring here to the so-called revolutionary process in the field of CDIO education and this through the implementation of projects related to the experience of learners within universities and employees in companies [21]. This symmetry is based on the notion of adaptation to change, which becomes essential in this constantly changing professional context; and therefore continuous improvement, which aims to contribute to the strengthening of the competitiveness of organizations whether industrial or educational and thus promotes the emergence of new innovative solutions.

In conclusion, we can say that the CDIO process is at the heart of this change in the industrial and educational paradigm as an essential tool for improving the performance and adaptability of actors in both sectors. This thus offers a future vision qualified as innovative in order to bring the sense of organization to companies on the one hand and training institutions on the other hand in order to face the challenges of the digital age [22].

References

1. Ciolacu, M.I., Binder, L., Svasta, P., Tache, I., Stoichescu, D.: Education 4.0 – jump to innovation with IoT in higher education. In: 2019 IEEE 25th International Symposium for Design and Technology in Electronic Packaging (SIITME), pp. 135–141. IEEE, Cluj-Napoca, Romania (Oct 2019). https://doi.org/10.1109/SIITME47687.2019.8990825
2. Guppy, N., Verpoorten, D., Boud, D., Lin, L., Tai, J., Bartolic, S.: The post-COVID-19 future of digital learning in higher education: views from educators, students, and other professionals in six countries. Brit. J. Educ. Tech. **53**(6), 1750–1765 (2022). https://doi.org/10.1111/bjet.13212
3. Ariyo Okaiyeto, S., Bai, J., Xiao, H., College of Mechanical and Electrical Engineering, Qingdao Agricultural University, Qingdao 266126, China: Generative AI in education: to embrace it or not? Int. J. Agric. Biol. Eng. **16**(3), 285–286 (2023). https://doi.org/10.25165/j.ijabe.20231603.8486

4. Cen, J., Fu, F., Yang, Y., Yan, J., Li, J.: Distant or local? The roles of knowledge search on general purpose technology innovation in emerging industries. J. Innov. Knowl. **8**(2), 100331 (2023). https://doi.org/10.1016/j.jik.2023.100331
5. Abad-Segura, E., González-Zamar, M.-D., Infante-Moro, J.C., Ruipérez García, G.: Sustainable Management of Digital Transformation in higher education: global research trends. Sustainability. **12**(5), 2107 (2020). https://doi.org/10.3390/su12052107
6. Bonfield, C.A., Salter, M., Longmuir, A., Benson, M., Adachi, C.: Transformation or evolution?: education 4.0, teaching and learning in the digital age. Higher Educ. Pedagogies. **5**(1), 223–246 (2020). https://doi.org/10.1080/23752696.2020.1816847
7. Almeida, F., Simoes, J.: The role of serious games, gamification and industry 4.0 tools in the education 4.0 paradigm. Cont. Ed. Technolo. **10**(2), 120–136 (2019). https://doi.org/10.30935/cet.554469
8. Adeel, S., Daniel, A.D., Botelho, A.: The effect of entrepreneurship education on the determinants of entrepreneurial behaviour among higher education students: a multi-group analysis. J. Innov. Knowl. **8**(1), 100324 (2023). https://doi.org/10.1016/j.jik.2023.100324
9. Frimousse, S., Horts, C.-H.B.D.: L'art Du Prompt: Une Compétence À Maîtriser Pour Les Futurs Chercheurs En Sciences De Gestion. Manag. Data Sci. (2023). https://doi.org/10.36863/mds.a.24326
10. Huu, D.N., et al.: Towards the higher education 4.0 – characteristics and criteria. PaM. **34**(4) (2018). https://doi.org/10.25073/2588-1116/vnupam.4160
11. Petrolo, D., Fakhar Manesh, M., Palumbo, R.: Unpacking business, management, and entrepreneurship education online: insights from a hybrid literature review. Int. J. Manag. Educ. **21**(2), 100812 (2023). https://doi.org/10.1016/j.ijme.2023.100812
12. B. Himmetoglu, D. Aydug, and C. Bayrak, Education 4.0: defining the teacher, the student, and the school manager aspects of the revolution Turk. Online J. Dist. Educ., vol. 21, no. Special IssueIODL, pp. 12–28., Jul. 2020, https://doi.org/10.17718/tojde.770896.
13. Das, S., Kleinke, D., Pistrui, D.: Reimagining engineering education: does industry 4.0 need education 4.0? In: 2020 ASEE Virtual Annual Conference Content Access Proceedings, Virtual on Line: ASEE Conferences, p. 35136 (Jun.2020). https://doi.org/10.18260/1-2-35136
14. Goh, P.S.-C., Abdul-Wahab, N.: Paradigms to drive higher education 4.0. IJLTER. **19**(1), 159–171 (Jan. 2020). https://doi.org/10.26803/ijlter.19.1.9
15. Neaga, I.: Applying industry 4.0 and education 4.0 to engineering education. PCEEA. (Nov. 2019). https://doi.org/10.24908/pceea.vi0.13859
16. Laura Icela, G.-P., María Soledad, R.-M., Juan Antonio, E.-G.: Education 4.0 maturity models for society 5.0: systematic literature review. Cogent Bus. Manag. **10**(3), 2256095 (2023). https://doi.org/10.1080/23311975.2023.2256095
17. Ji, M., Jiao, Y., Cheng, N.: An innovative decision-making scheme for the high-quality economy development driven by higher education. J. Innov. Knowl. **8**(2), 100345 (2023). https://doi.org/10.1016/j.jik.2023.100345
18. Wang, K., Li, B., Tian, T., Zakuan, N., Rani, P.: Evaluate the drivers for digital transformation in higher education institutions in the era of industry 4.0 based on decision- making method. J. Innov. Knowl. **8**(3), 100364 (Jul. 2023). https://doi.org/10.1016/j.jik.2023.100364
19. Baidoo-Anu, D., Ansah, L.O.: Education in the era of generative artificial intelligence (AI): understanding the potential benefits of ChatGPT in promoting teaching and learning

20. Lozano, R., Merrill, M., Sammalisto, K., Ceulemans, K., Lozano, F.: Connecting competences and pedagogical approaches for sustainable development in higher education: a literature review and framework proposal. Sustainability. **9**(10), 1889 (2017). https://doi.org/10.3390/su9101889
21. Oliveira, K.D.S., De Souza, R.A.C.: Digital transformation towards education 4.0. Inf. Educ. (2021). https://doi.org/10.15388/infedu.2022.13
22. Mynbayeva, A., Sadvakassova, Z., Akshalova, B.: Pedagogy of the twenty-first century: innovative teaching methods. In: Cavero, O.B., Llevot-Calvet, N. (eds.) New Pedagogical Challenges in the 21st Century - Contributions of Research in Education. InTech (2018). https://doi.org/10.5772/intechopen.72341

Identifying Electrochemical Parameters of PEMFC Fuel Cells by Artificial Intelligence: Methods, Results and Industrial Perspectives

Mohamed Selmene Ben Yahia(✉)

ESPRIT School of Engineering, ZI. Chotrana II, P. O. Box 160-2083, Tunis, Tunisia
medselmene.benyahia@esprit.tn

Abstract. Faced with the climate emergency and the energy transition, proton exchange membrane fuel cells (PEMFC) represent a key solution for clean electricity production from hydrogen. However, their mass deployment is hampered by technical challenges, notably membrane moisture management and early detection of failures (flooding, dehydration). This paper explores the use of artificial intelligence (AI) to optimize the identification of critical electrochemical parameters (ohmic resistance, double-layer capacitance) via impedance spectroscopy.

Traditional methods, while accurate (squared error $\sim 10^{-8}$), suffer from prohibitive computation times (2–3 h) and an inability to predict failures in real time. To remedy this, hybrid approaches combining genetic algorithms (GA) and neural networks (LSTM, CNN) reduce analysis time to less than 10 min, with an accuracy adapted to industrial needs ($\sim 10^{-6}$). A case study demonstrates that a CNN model achieves 98% accuracy in flooding detection, thanks to automated Nyquist diagram analysis.

In addition, the integration of digital twins enables dynamic simulation of PEMFCs, optimizing their performance and anticipating aging. Future prospects include Edge AI for embedded monitoring, data federation for generalizable models, and adaptive twins coupled with recurrent networks. These advances position AI as a key pillar for accelerating the adoption of PEMFCs in electric vehicles and stationary storage systems, supporting Europe's transition to hydrogen, whose automotive market is expected to grow by 14.1% by 2032.

Keywords: PEMFC · artificial intelligence · impedance spectroscopy · predictive maintenance · digital twin

1 Introduction

Proton Exchange Membrane Fuel Cells (PEMFCs) represent a promising technology for clean and efficient energy conversion, particularly in the context of reducing greenhouse gas emissions and enabling the hydrogen economy. Their ability to operate at low temperatures, coupled with high power density and fast start-up times, makes them attractive for a wide range of applications, including transportation, stationary power systems, and portable electronics.

F. Kamoun et al. (Eds.): AFRICATEK 2025, LNICST 676, pp. 206–219, 2026.
https://doi.org/10.1007/978-3-032-16635-7_14

However, despite these advantages, the widespread deployment of PEMFCs faces several technical challenges. One of the most critical issues lies in the accurate and real-time identification of key electrochemical parameters, such as ohmic resistance, charge transfer resistance, and double-layer capacitance. These parameters are essential for monitoring the health and performance of the fuel cell, detecting faults like flooding or membrane drying, and implementing predictive maintenance strategies.

Traditional methods for parameter identification, such as equivalent circuit modeling and impedance spectroscopy, although accurate, are often computationally intensive and not suitable for real-time applications. In this context, Artificial Intelligence (AI) techniques offer a powerful alternative for faster and more scalable parameter estimation and fault diagnosis.

The objective of this paper is to propose a novel approach that combines AI methods—specifically Genetic Algorithms (GA), Long Short-Term Memory (LSTM) networks, and Convolutional Neural Networks (CNN)—to enable fast, accurate, and interpretable identification of PEMFC electrochemical parameters from impedance spectroscopy data. The study aims to reduce computational time, improve prediction accuracy, and demonstrate the ability of AI models to detect and classify fuel cell faults in real-time settings. Furthermore, the paper discusses the implementation of digital twins and the potential of Edge AI to enhance the monitoring and control of fuel cells in embedded systems.

By integrating advanced AI models into the analysis pipeline, this work contributes to bridging the gap between laboratory-based diagnostics and real-world, deployable fuel cell management systems.

2 PEMFC Structure and Operation

The Proton Exchange Membrane Fuel Cell (PEMFC) [1] is based on a precise architecture combining three key components:

- The Nafion® membrane, a proton-conducting polymer that separates the electrodes and regulates hydration.
- The porous electrodes (GDL, Gas Diffusion Layers), coated with catalysts (platinum), ensuring gas diffusion (H_2 at the anode, O_2 at the cathode) and electrochemical reactions.
- The bipolar plates, etched with channels, which distribute the reagents and evacuate the water produced.

Details of a cell are shown in Fig. 1. It includes the membrane (1) with the annealing anode and cathode. These are made up of the activation layer (2) of porous carbon, the diffusion layer containing platinum particles platinum (3) particles, and the bipolar plates for current collection and gas supply gas supply (4). These elements are discussed in greater detail below [3].

These components enable complex physico-chemical phenomena to take place:

- Gas diffusion: Hydrogen and oxygen pass through the GDL to reach the catalytic sites.

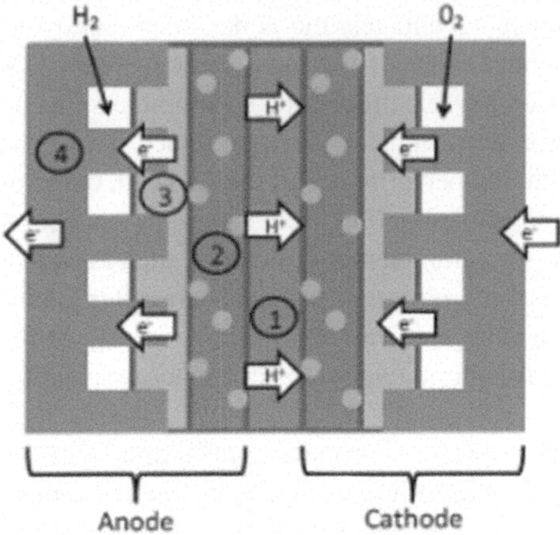

Fig. 1. Detail of a cell [2].

- Proton transfer: H^+ ions migrate through the wet membrane, while electrons flow through the external circuit, generating a current.
- Water management: electro-osmosis drives water from the anode to the cathode, while condensation can cause flooding, affecting performance.
- However, these mechanisms induce voltage losses:
- Activation losses: slower reactions at the electrodes (especially the cathode).
- Ohmic losses: membrane and interface resistance.
- Concentration losses: Limitation of high-current gas diffusion [3].

1: Fluidic phenomena: gas flow
2: Gas diffusion
3: Electrochemical phenomena + diffusion
4: Ohmic phenomena: proton transport
5: Water transport
6: Thermal phenomena: heat flow

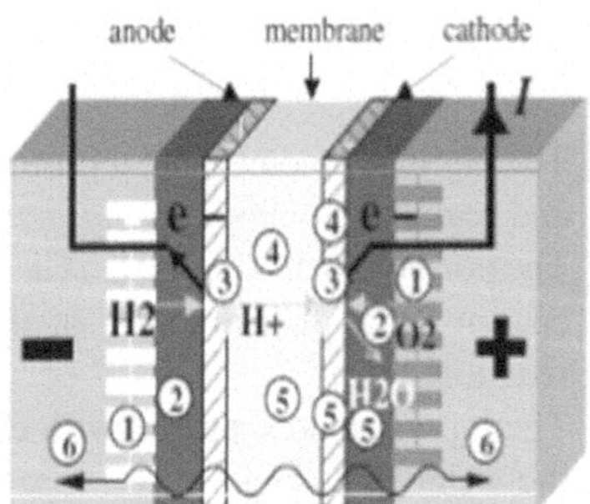

Fig. 2. General description of electrochemical phenomena in a cell [3]

Detailed modeling of these phenomena is essential to optimize the efficiency (>50%) and durability (>10,000 h) of PEMFCs, particularly in mobile applications (electric vehicles) or stationary applications (energy storage).

3 Identification Methods: Complex Impedance Modeling & Experimental Results

Dynamic characterization of PEMFC fuel cells relies on precise impedance measurement methods:

- Potentiostatic method: A low-amplitude sinusoidal voltage is imposed on the cell, and the resulting current is measured. This approach, coupled with a frequency analyzer, extracts the impedance response over a wide range (0.1 Hz - 100 kHz) [4].
- Load modulation: A sinusoidal disturbance is superimposed on the operating current, simulating real load variations. This less invasive method is suitable for systems in continuous operation [5].

The results are visualized via a Nyquist diagram, where the real part of the impedance is plotted against its imaginary part, revealing capacitive arcs (charge transfer) and resistive segments (ohmic losses).

3.1 Electrochemical Impedance Spectroscopy (EIS)

Electrochemical impedance spectroscopy (EIS) is a non-invasive method widely used to characterize the dynamic properties of PEMFC fuel cells. By applying a low-amplitude sinusoidal signal over a range of frequencies (typically from 0.1 Hz to 100 kHz), this technique measures the complex impedance response $Z(\omega) = \frac{V(\omega)}{I(\omega)}$ where V(ω)and I(ω)represent voltage and current respectively in the perturbed regime [6].

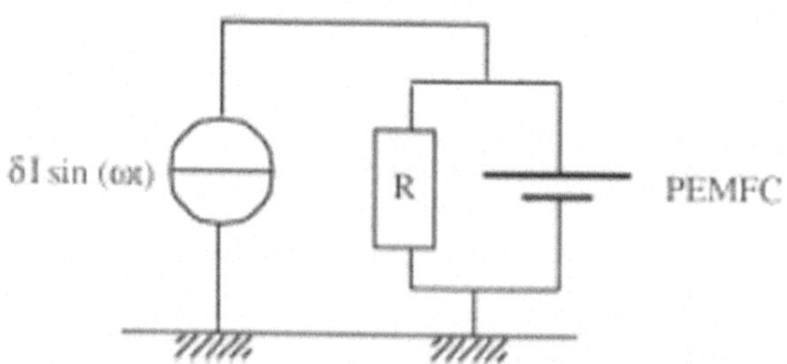

Fig. 3. Principle of electrochemical impedance spectroscopy [6]

The spectra obtained, often visualized via Nyquist diagrams (real vs. imaginary part), make it possible to extract key parameters such as the ohmic resistance of the membrane (RM), the charge transfer resistance (RT), and the double layer capacitance (CDC). These parameters reflect the internal state of the cell, such as membrane hydration or the efficiency of electrochemical reactions [7].

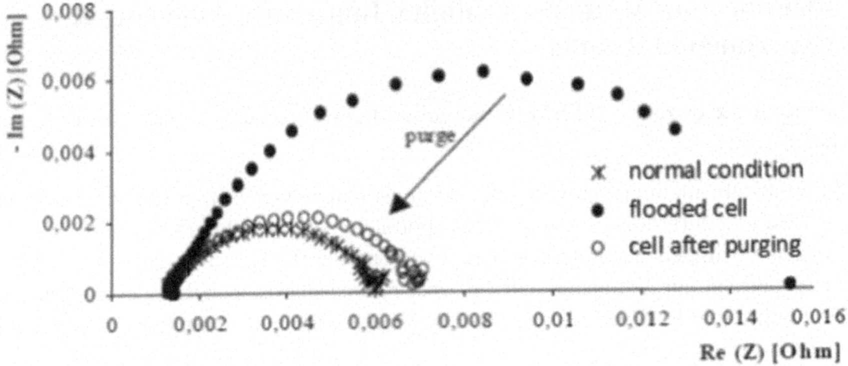

Fig. 4. Nyquist representation of the state of the cell in the event of flooding [8].

3.2 The Randles Model

To interpret EIS data, the Randles model is commonly used as a simplified equivalent electrical circuit. This model combines [9]:

- A series resistance (RM), representing ohmic losses (membrane, contacts).
- A parallel branch combining RT (charge transfer resistance at the electrodes) and CDC (capacitance associated with the electrode-electrolyte interface).

Although simplistic, this circuit captures the dominant mid-frequency phenomena and facilitates parameter identification via optimization tools.

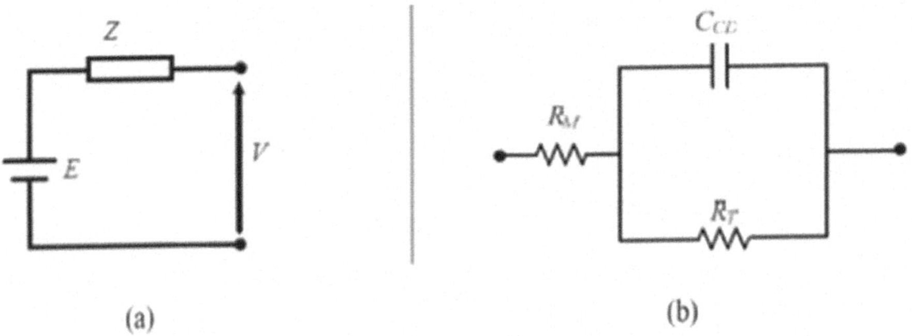

Fig.5. Simple fuel cell model [10]. (a) Representation of a fuel cell by a voltage source associated with its electrical impedance. (b) Simple cell impedance.

To interpret the spectroscopy data, the Randles circuit is used as a simplified equivalent electrical model:

- R_M: Overall ohmic resistance, including membrane and electrical contacts.
- R_T // C_{DC}: Parallel branch modeling the charge transfer resistance (RT) and the double-layer capacitance (C_{DC}), linked to charge accumulation at electrode-electrolyte interfaces.

Total impedance is expressed as [11]:

$$Z(\omega) = R_M + \frac{R_T}{1 + \mathrm{j}\, R_T C_{DC} \omega} \quad (1)$$

This model can be used to describe the frequency behavior of the battery, in particular the transition between ohmic (high-frequency) and capacitive (low-frequency) regimes.

3.3 Experimental Results

Experimental validation was carried out on a Nexa Ballard 1.26 kW [12], instrumented for high precision measurements:

- Identified parameters:
- $R_M = 10\, m\Omega$, membrane resistance.
- $R_T = 90\, m\Omega$, transfer resistance.
- $C_{DC} = 300\, uF$, double layer capacitance.

3.4 Limits of Traditional Approaches

- High computation time

Least-squares parameter identification relies on iterative optimization to minimize the discrepancy between experimental data and the model. This procedure, although accurate, becomes time-consuming for complex systems (e.g. multi-frequency models or multi-cell stacks), limiting its use in real-time [13].

The convergence curves for RM, RT and CDC [14, 15] are shown in Figs. 6, 7 and 8.

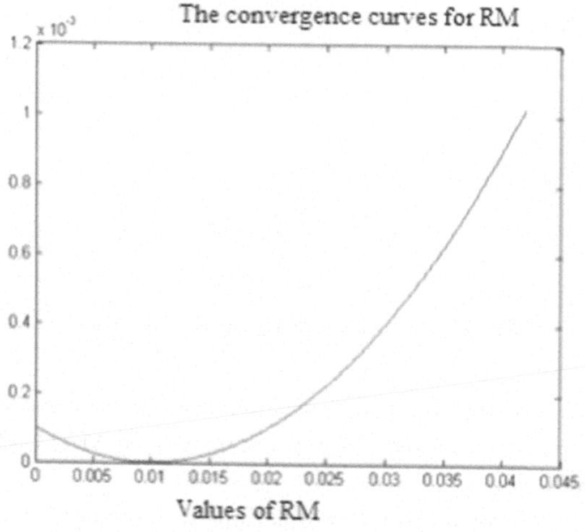

Fig. 6. The convergence curves for RM

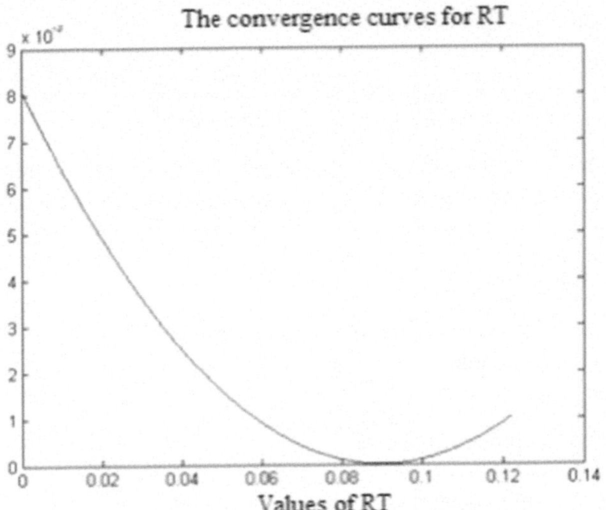

Fig. 7. The convergence curves for RT

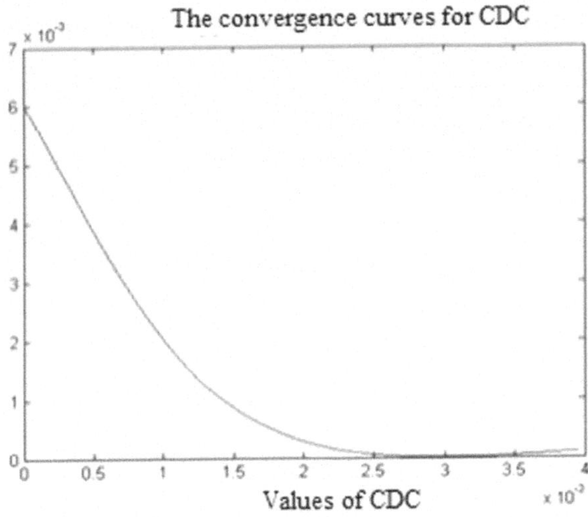

Fig. 8. The convergence curves for CDC

The mean square error between the measured data and the model was reduced to 10–8 thanks to an optimization algorithm implemented in MATLAB, confirming the robustness of the method.

These results demonstrate the ability of the Randles model to diagnose faults such as flooding (increase in RT) or dehydration (increase in RM), paving the way for predictive maintenance of hydrogen energy systems [16].

- Difficulty of real-time prediction

Traditional approaches struggle to anticipate critical failures (e.g. flooding, drought) under dynamic conditions (variable loads, frequent start-ups). The latency between data acquisition, spectrum analysis and parameter adjustment makes these methods ill-suited to applications requiring immediate responsiveness, such as electric vehicles or backup systems.

These constraints are motivating the development of hybrid methods, combining physical models and artificial intelligence, to speed up parameter identification and improve diagnostic robustness [17].

4 Integration of Artificial Intelligence (AI)

4.1 Parameter Optimization Using Genetic Algorithms

Genetic algorithms (GAs) offer a powerful alternative to traditional optimization methods such as least squares. Inspired by natural selection, these algorithms explore the space of potential solutions via crossover, mutation and selection operations. Their main advantage lies in their ability to avoid local minima and converge towards a global optimum, even for complex or non-linear models. In the context of PEMFCs, libraries such as DEAP (Distributed Evolutionary Algorithms in Python) are used to tune RM, RT and CDC parameters from experimental impedance spectra. For example, a population of candidate solutions (parameter sets) is evolved over hundreds of generations, reducing computation time by 50% compared with conventional iterative methods [18].

4.2 Machine Learning for Impedance Prediction

Neural networks are revolutionizing the prediction of electrochemical parameters, combining speed and accuracy. Trained on synthetic data generated by simulation (e.g. virtual impedance spectra for various battery states), these models learn to map frequency signals directly to RM, RT and CDC parameters. An LSTM (Long Short-Term Memory) architecture, specialized in time sequences, is particularly well suited to modeling frequency dependencies in impedance spectra. Once trained, the network provides results in real time (a few milliseconds), eliminating the need for costly iterative calculations [19].

4.3 Predictive Diagnostics Using Deep Learning

Deep learning is used to anticipate critical failures (flooding, corrosion, dryness) through automated analysis of Nyquist spectra. A convolutional neural network (CNN), such as an adapted version of ResNet-18, is trained on a database of annotated spectra (e.g. 10,000 spectra labeled "healthy", "flooded", or "dehydrated"). The model learns to identify subtle patterns in capacitive arcs or diagram deformations, achieving 98% accuracy in cross-validation. These predictions enable proactive maintenance, reducing downtime and repair costs [20].

4.4 Digital Twin for Real-Time Simulation

A digital twin of the fuel cell integrates real-time data streams (temperature, humidity, current) to faithfully simulate its physical behavior. This dynamic model, powered by on-board sensors, virtually reproduces the cell's responses under different operating conditions (e.g. load variations, extreme temperatures). Key benefits include:

- Virtual testing: Evaluation of control strategies (e.g. humidity management) without risk to the physical system.
- Lifetime prediction: Estimation of membrane degradation via historical data analysis.
- Energy optimization: Real-time adjustment of parameters to maximize yield.

AI-Electrochemistry synergy: These hybrid approaches, combining physical models and AI, transform the management of PEMFCs, making them more adaptable to demanding applications such as electric vehicles or smart microgrids [21, 22].

5 Results and Synthesis

5.1 Comparison of Traditional Methods and AI

Traditional parameter identification methods, such as least squares, offer high accuracy (10–8) but require prohibitive computation time (2–3 h) for complex systems, limiting their use in real time. Conversely, hybrid approaches combining genetic algorithms (GA) and machine learning (ML) reduce this time to less than 10 min, with slightly lower accuracy (10–6), but sufficient for industrial applications. The strength of AI lies in its predictive capability, enabling failures (flooding, corrosion) or variations in performance to be anticipated thanks to the analysis of complex patterns in the data. For example, a model trained on historical impedance spectra can predict membrane degradation several cycles before its physical manifestation, offering a critical window of intervention.

Table 1. Comparative study from two identification method

Criterion	Least-square	IA (AG + ML)
Calculation time	2–3 h	10 min
Accuracy	10^{-8}	10–6
Prediction capability	Limited	High

5.2 Case Study: CNN Flooding Detection

An experimental study was carried out on 500 impedance spectra (250 normal, 250 flooded) from a PEMFC cell subjected to over-wetting conditions [23]. A convolutional neural network (CNN), based on an adapted ResNet-18 architecture, was trained to classify these spectra. The model achieved 98% accuracy in cross-validation, demonstrating its ability to identify subtle signatures such as widening Nyquist arcs or reduced capacitive slope, indicators of flooding. To enhance transparency, Grad-CAM heat maps have been generated, highlighting the frequency regions (e.g. low frequencies < 1 Hz) most influential in network decision-making. This visualization enables engineers to validate results and adjust maintenance protocols [24].

5.3 Future Prospects

- Edge AI and TinyML: The integration of lightweight models (e.g. quantized neural networks) on embedded microcontrollers (STM32, Raspberry Pi Pico) will enable real-time monitoring without relying on the cloud. For example, a TinyML system could analyze impedance spectra locally and alert in case of flooding risk, even in isolated environments (vehicles, drones).
- Data federation: Inter-laboratory collaboration using frameworks such as Flower or TensorFlow Federated would enable models to be trained on distributed and heterogeneous datasets, while preserving confidentiality. This approach would improve the generalizability of algorithms, particularly for stacks of different technologies (SOFC, AFC) [25, 26].
- Adaptive Digital Twins: Coupling digital twins with recurrent neural networks (RNN) would enable simulation of long-term parameter evolution (e.g. catalyst aging) and optimization of preventive replacement strategies [27, 28].

5.4 Industrial Implications

These advances position AI as a central pillar for the transition to hydrogen, reducing operational costs (predictive maintenance) and accelerating the deployment of reliable batteries in key sectors such as heavy transport or stationary storage.

- An example from Europe:

In 2022, the European automotive fuel cell market was estimated at $0.5 billion, with forecasts indicating an average annual growth rate of 14.1% between 2023 and 2032. Fuel cells are electrochemical systems that generate electricity through the reaction of hydrogen with oxygen, emitting only water as a by-product. They serve as an on-board power source for vehicles by converting chemical energy directly into electrical energy. The market's expansion is supported by the growing development of hydrogen-related infrastructure and by substantial public and private investments in hydrogen refueling stations, which are key to encouraging the adoption of fuel cell vehicles (FCVs) [29].

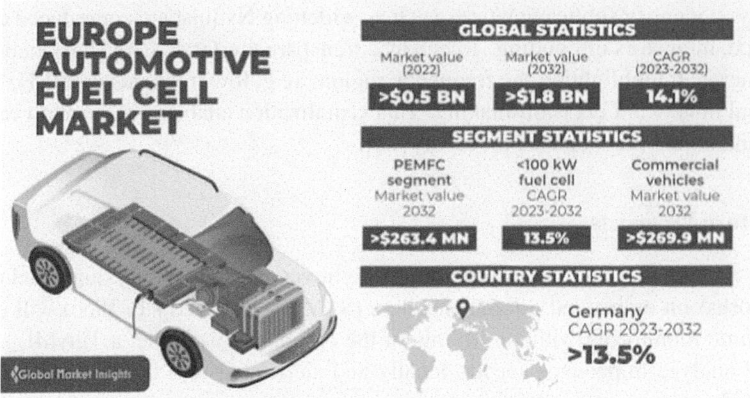

Fig. 9. The statistics of Europe market for automotive fuel cells [29]

Proton Exchange Membrane Fuel Cells (PEMFCs) are projected to reach a market value of USD 263.4 million by 2032. This growth is largely driven by supportive government regulations that encourage the adoption of environmentally sustainable technologies, alongside continuous innovations in fuel cell engineering. Rising investment in hydrogen refueling infrastructure and increasing consumer demand for low-emission vehicles are also key factors accelerating the integration of fuel cells in the automotive industry.

In terms of power output, the segment of fuel cells rated below 100 kW is expected to expand at an approximate annual rate of 13.5% through 2032. Their advantages—such as reduced weight, lower production costs, and faster refueling—make them more efficient than many alternatives. Technological advancements, together with financial support mechanisms like subsidies and incentives, are expected to further stimulate market adoption. The growing use of fuel cells in applications such as electric bicycles, unmanned aerial vehicles (UAVs), and various utility vehicles will also contribute to overall market expansion [29].

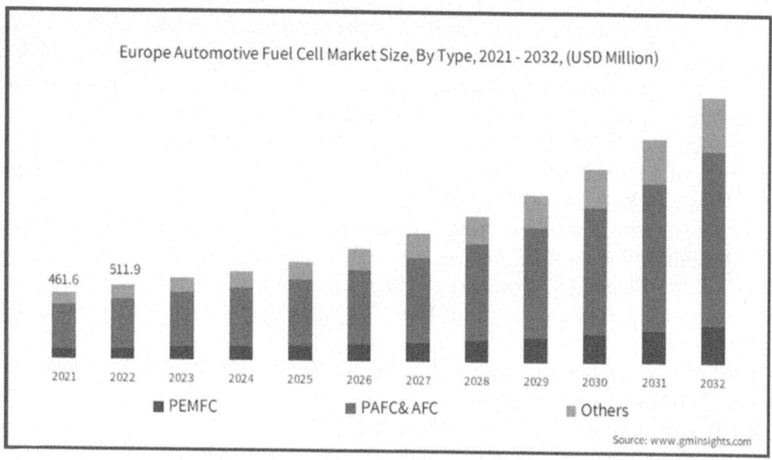

Fig. 10. Europe Automative Fuel Cell Market Size, by Type, 2021–2023 [29]

6 Conclusion

The integration of artificial intelligence into PEMFC fuel cell analysis marks a major step forward in overcoming the limitations of traditional methods. By combining genetic algorithms, neural networks (LSTM, CNN) and digital twins, AI enables rapid (~10 min) and reliable identification of electrochemical parameters, while anticipating critical failures such as flooding with 98% accuracy. These innovations transform predictive maintenance and optimize the durability of PEMFCs, essential for mobile and stationary applications. With promising prospects (Edge AI, data federation), AI is catalyzing the transition to hydrogen in Europe, where the PEMFC market is expected to grow by 14.1% by 2032. In this way, the alliance between electrochemistry and AI is paving the way for clean, efficient and resilient energy, aligned with the climate and industrial imperatives of the XXIe century.

References

1. Azib, T.: Contribution à l'Etude d'Electro-générateurs à Pile à Combustible Conceptions d'Architectures et de Leurs Commandes. Doctoral thesis, Université Paris Sud XI, Faculté des Sciences d'Orsay (December 2010)
2. https://www.ballard.com/
3. Busquet., S.: Etude d'un système autonome de production d'énergie couplant un champ photovoltaïque, un électrolyseur et une pile à combustible : Réalisation d'un banc d'essai et de modélisation", Thesis, Ecole des Mines de Paris (December 2003)
4. Marchand, M.: Water management in fuel cells. Thesis, Institut national polytechnique de Gronoble (November 1998)
5. Blunier, B.: Modelling of motor-compressors for air management in fuel cell systems - simulation and experimental validation, Thesis, Université de Technologie de Belfort-Montbéliard (December 2007)
6. Frappé, E.: Fault-tolerant static converter architecture for 30kW modular power-traction fuel cell generator". Doctoral dissertation, French Institute of Transport and Planning Science and Technology (December 2012)

7. Fontes, G.: Modeling and characterization of the PEM battery for the study of interactions with static converters. Thesis, Institut National Polytechnique de Toulouse (September 2005)
8. Gerbaux., L.: Modelling of a hydrogen/air fuel cell and experimental validation experimental. Doctoral thesis, Institut National Polytechnique de Grenoble (1996)
9. Yahia, M.S.B., Allagui, H., Mami, A.: The Identification of Randles Impedance Model Parameters of a PEM Fuel Cell by the Least Square Method. Inter. J. Adv. Comput. Sci. Appli. (IJACSA) **8**(8), 345~354 (2017)
10. Zandi., M.: Contribution au pilotage des sources hybrides d'énergie électrique. University of Nancy Institut National Polytechnique de Lorraine thesis. November (2010)
11. Yahia, M.S.B., Allagui, H., Bouaicha, A., Mami, A.: Fuel cell impedance model parameters optimization using a genetic algorithm. Inter. J. Electr. Comput. Eng. (IJECE) **7**(1), 184~193 (2017)
12. Sélmene, B.Y.M., Wahib, A., Hatem, A., Abdelkader, M.: Modeling and parameters identification of PEM Fuel cell for application to a hybrid vehicle system» le nom du livre (Book name) : Research Trends \Challenges Phys. Sci. (2021)
13. Chaouali, H., Othmani, H., Yahia, M.S.B., Mezghani, D., Mami, A.: Energy management strategy of a PV/Fuel cell/supercapacitor hybrid source feeding an off-grid pumping station. Inter. J. Adv. Compute. Sci. Appli. (IJACSA) **8**(8), 250~257 (2017)
14. Sélmene, B.Y.M.: Validation of no-linear model of electrochemical impedance of a PEM fuel cell using the EIS Spectrum Analyzer. In: participation à la conférence internationale the 9th International Conference on Sciences of Electronics, Technologies of Information and Telecommunications (2022 IEEE SETIT)
15. Wahib, A., Samir, G., Sélmene, B.Y.M., Hatem, A., Abdelkader, M.: Supervisory control design for a PEM fuel cell electric vehicle» participation à la conférence internationale. KIn: The 12th International Renewable Energy Congress (IREC 2021)
16. Mennola, T., Mikkola, M., Noponen, M., Hottinen, T., Lund, P.: Measurement of ohmic voltage losses in individual cells of a PEMFC stack. J. Power Sources **112**, 261–272 (2002)
17. Deseure, J., Thivel, P.-X., Marchesillo, M.: Méthodes de caractérisation d'une pile à combustible. article by institut universitaire de technologie 1, université joseph fourrier de gronoble (2008)
18. Diard, J.-P., Glandut, N., Le Gorrec, B., Montella., C.: Application des mesures d'impédances aux piles à combustible. In: 17th Forum on Electrochemical Impedances, Paris , pp. 33–50 (2005)
19. Cooper, K.R., Smith, M.: Electrical test methods for on-line fuel cell ohmic resistance measurement. J. Power Sources **160**, 1088–1095 (2006)
20. Karamer, B: .Mesure par spectroscopie de l'impédance d'une pile à combustible en charge. DEA Report UHP Nancy1, France
21. Yahia, M.S.B., Andari, W., Allagui, H., Mami, A.: Nonlinear Modeling Impedance Electrochemical of PEM Fuel Cell. participation à la conférence internationale on Sciences and Techniques of Automatic control & computer engineering (STA 2017)
22. Andari, W., Yahia, M.S.B., Allagui, H., Mami, A.: Modeling and Simulation of PEM Fuel Cell/Supercapacitor hybrid power sources for an electric vehicle. participation à la conférence internationale The 8th International Renewable Energy Congress (IREC 2019)
23. Yuan, X.-Z., Song, C.: Wang, H., Zhang, J.: Electrochemical Impedance Spectroscopy in PEM Fuel Cells Fundamentals and Applications
24. Yahia, M.S.B., Allagui, H., Mami, A.: Parameters Identification of the PEM fuel cell impedance model. In: World Symposuim on Mechatronics Engineering & Applied Physics (WSMEAP'2015) 11–13 June 2015 Sousse, Tunisia (2015)
25. Yahia, M.S.B., Allagui, H., Mami, A.: The frequency behavior of the electrochemical model fuel cell by impedance spectroscopy. In: The 7th International Renewable Energy Congress - IREC (IREC'2016), 22–24 March 2016 Hammamet, Tunisia (2016)

26. Rouane, A., Aglzim, E.-H., Kraemer, El-moznine, R.: Impedance measurement of a fuel cell on load. In: 9th International Conference Electrical Power Quality and Utilisation, Barcelona (October 2007)
27. Agalzim, E-H., Rouane, A., El-Moznine, A.R.: An electronic measurement instrumentation of the impedance of a loaded fuel cell or battery. Sensors 2007 (ISSN 1424–8220 © 2007 by MDPI www.mdpi.org/sensors)
28. Aglzim, E.-H., Rouane, A., Nadi, M., Kourtiche, D.: Signal processing for the impedance measurement on an electrochemical generator. Sensors & Transducers J. 90, Special Issue, 150–159 (2008)
29. https://www.gminsights.com/industry-analysis/europe-automotive-fuel-cell-market

Machine Learning-Based Prediction of Aluminium Metal Matrix Composite Properties Reinforced with Biomass Ash

Adekunle Adeleke[1](✉), Praise Nwachukwu[1], Feranmi Ayonitemi Oyedare[2], Seun Jesuloluwa[1], Temitayo Ogedengbe[1], and Peter Ikubanni[3]

[1] Department of Mechanical Engineering, Nile University of Nigeria, Abuja, FCT, Nigeria
adekunle.adeleke@nileuniversity.edu.ng

[2] Waste to Wealth Research Group, Nile University of Nigeria, Abuja, Nigeria

[3] Department of Mechatronics Engineering, Bowen University, Iwo, Osun, Nigeria

Abstract. Conventional experiments play a crucial role in determining the thresholds at which biomass ash addition begins to adversely affect the mechanical properties of composites. These experiments are often costly and limited to the specific biomass ash analysed. In contrast, Machine Learning (ML) models provide a robust and scalable alternative. First, they learn how the mechanical properties of materials are influenced by the various oxides present in biomass. Then, they generate models that capture the interactions between these oxides and their effects on the mechanical properties of composites, specifically Aluminium Metal Matrix Composites (AMMCs) in this case. This study investigates the influence of biomass ash on AMMCs using a dataset of 317 observations and 35 variables. Machine Learning (ML) models predict mechanical properties based on oxide compositions. Lasso regression, Least Squares Boosting, and Neural Networks were evaluated for accuracy, precision, and robustness at varying performance levels (high, moderate, and low), with the Least Squares Boosting model demonstrating superior predictive performance. Interpretability tools, Partial Dependency Plots and Response Surface Methodology, show that the oxide interactions of SiO_2, MgO & CaO enhanced the hardness, Al_2O_3 and Fe_2O_3 improved tensile strength, while SiO_2 & Al_2O_3 improved elongation.

Keyword: AMMCs · Machine Learning · Regression Models

1 Introduction

Traditional characterization methods for Metal Matrix Composites (MMCs) reinforced with biomass-derived oxides have depended on techniques like Universal Testing Machines to assess their mechanical properties [1, 2]. Although these approaches provide useful insights, they can be time-consuming, expensive, and restricted to specific material compositions. The swift progress in computational tools within engineering research has greatly improved the analysis and optimization of material properties. This

F. Kamoun et al. (Eds.): AFRICATEK 2025, LNICST 676, pp. 220–239, 2026.
https://doi.org/10.1007/978-3-032-16635-7_15

study posits that biomass ash oxides demonstrate intricate nonlinear interactions with the mechanical properties of AMMCs, utilizing machine learning (ML) models as an efficient alternative to conventional experimental techniques. In the Metal Matrix Composites (MMCs) field, where critical mechanical properties include the strength-to-weight ratio, tribological behavior, and corrosion resistance, ML models present a data-driven methodology for understanding and predicting the impact of reinforcement materials [3]. With the growing demand for sustainable and cost-effective materials, researchers have investigated biomass ash use as a reinforcement in MMCs, given its abundance and the significant strengthening oxides it contains, such as SiO_2, Fe_2O_3, Al_2O_3, and MgO. Research has shown that incorporating biomass ash can improve mechanical properties while lowering production costs, making it a feasible alternative to traditional reinforcement materials [4]. Understanding the complex nonlinear relationship between biomass oxides on the mechanical properties of AMMCs is the subject of this paper.

1.1 Literature Review

Several experimental investigations have highlighted the potential of biomass ash in aluminium MMCs. Osunmakinde et al. [5] reinforced aluminium powder with varying weights of coconut shell ash, rice husk ash, and cassava peel ash, observing increased hardness (64.27%), and tensile strength (33.60%) but reduced impact energy (22.60%). Similarly, the integration of ultra-fine breadfruit hull ash particles (500 nm) into A2009 (Al-Si-Fe) alloy via the stir-casting method resulted in an ultimate tensile strength of 202.67 MPa from 175 MPa and a yield strength of 182.42 MPa from 150 MPa, though with a reduction in impact energy. Other studies have explored agro-residues such as palm kernel shells, bean pods, corn cobs, and coconut husks, showing promising improvements in mechanical performance due to their oxide compositions. Despite these advancements, the dependence on experimental methods limits the scope of research, as findings are restricted to the specific biomass types analysed. Machine learning offers a transformative solution by leveraging large datasets to model the relationships between oxide composition and mechanical properties, allowing for more generalized predictions. By training ML models on extensive experimental data, researchers can identify optimal reinforcement compositions, predict material behaviour under different conditions, and develop efficient design strategies without the need for exhaustive laboratory testing [6, 7].

This study explores the application of ML models, including Lasso Regression, Least Squares Boosting, and Neural Networks, to predict the mechanical properties of aluminium MMCs reinforced with biomass ash. These models provide insights into how oxide compositions influence material behaviour, offering a scalable approach to material optimization. Furthermore, interpretability tools such as Partial Dependency Plots and Response Surface Methodology will be employed to analyse nonlinear oxide interactions and will help optimize composite formulations. By integrating ML into material design, this research aims to advance the development of sustainable MMCs, reducing experimental costs while enhancing predictive accuracy in composite engineering.

Table 1: Summary of Features used to build Regression Models

	Features/variables	Mean (%wt)	Count
	Biomass Type	–	22
	Aluminum Type	–	10
	Biomass	6	–
Impurities found in Aluminum	SiC	4.96	90
	Cu	2.09	34
	Si	4.64	38
	Mg	0.99	52
	Al2O3	2.48	35
	Graphite	1.26	32
	Tungsten	2.00	9
Oxides	SiO_2	57.963	–
	Al2O3	7.14	–
	Fe2O3	3.32	–
	CaO	4.41	–
	MgO	0.85	-
	TiO_2	0.44	–
	Na_2O	0.38	–
	K_2O	1.17	–
	P2O5	0.70	–
	MnO	0.36	–
	Mechanical Property	Mean	Observations
	Hardness	94.0	299
	Tensile strength	150.0	287
	Elongation	8.3	110

2 Methodology: Oxides Exploration, Regression Models, and Model Optimization

2.1 Data Resourcing and Oxide Exploration

To develop robust machine learning models for predicting the mechanical properties of aluminium metal matrix composites (AMMCs) reinforced with biomass ash, a dataset of 317 observations and 35 variables was sourced from peer-reviewed literature, including Scopus, Google Scholar, Science Direct, and Semantic Scholar. This dataset is then represented as a system of linear equations, $\boldsymbol{Ax} = \boldsymbol{b}$ in this case, the system is overdetermined, meaning there are more equations than unknowns, with solutions approximated by minimizing errors in x. Three machine learning models: Least Squares Boosting, Lasso Regression, and Neural Networks, to capture interactions between biomass ash oxides and the mechanical properties of the composites. Model optimization involves parameter tuning to improve performance and generalization [6, 8, 9]. The evaluation metrics include Root Mean Square Error (RMSE), R-squared accuracy, and Mean Absolute Error (MAE). The dataset features essential biomass attributes such as oxide composition, weight percentage of the composite, and physical properties like oxide density, correlating them with mechanical properties like tensile strength and hardness, as illustrated in Table 1. Interpretability tools, including Partial Dependency Plots and Response Surface Methodology, are utilized to analyze oxide interactions and their effects on composite behavior. The dataset, compiled from 62 literature sources, examines the weight percentages (%wt.) of biomass ash, oxides, and impurities as independent variables. The mechanical properties derived from these three categories serve as the dependent variables. This comprehensive dataset includes 22 distinct types of biomass ash and their corresponding references, which are detailed in Table 2. Missing data is handled by removing incomplete rows to preserve data fidelity and retain meaningful trends. In some cases, missing values were calculated using the mean or average values. Thereafter, the dataset is explored to identify outliers, notable trends, and correlations.

Table 2. Biomass Ash Types and Corresponding References

Biomass Ash Type	Count	References
Aloe Vera Powder	1	[10]
Baggase Ash (BA)	15	[11, 12]
Bamboo Leaf Ash (BLA)	6	[13, 14]
Cassva Peel Ash (CPA)	5	[5, 15]
Coconut Shell Ash (CSA)	30	[16–21]
Corn Cob Ash	4	[22]
Eggshell Powder	37	[23–25]
Flyash (FA)	49	[26–34]
Green Plantain Peel Ash (GPPA)	6	[35]
Groundnut Shell ash (GSA)	14	[13, 36]
Locust Bean Pod Ash	4	[37, 38]
Melon Shell Ash	4	[39]
Maize Stalk Ash	5	[40]
Palm Kernel Shell Ash (PKSA)	17	[41–44]
Peanut Shell Ash (PSA)	6	[45]
Quarry dust	4	[13]
Rice Husk Ash (RHA)	71	[11, 13, 46–55]
Red Mud	12	[56, 57]

(continued)

Table 2. *(continued)*

Biomass Ash Type	Count	References
Sawdust Ash (SDA)	3	[1]
Bean pod (n.p)	4	[58]
Breadfruit Hull Ash	6	[59]
Periwinkle	14	[60, 61]

Oxides Correlation. Spearman's rank correlation in Eq. (1) was used due to its effectiveness in handling non-linear and monotonic relationships equally, accommodating outliers.

$$\rho = 1 - \frac{6\sum d_i^2}{n\left(n^2 - 1\right)} \tag{1}$$

where d_i is the difference between the ranks of the two variables, and n is the number of observations.

Understanding Outliers: Outliers were identified using the Interquartile range IQR after performing the Henze-Zirkler multivariate normality test (HZ-test), which gave lognormal mean and variance values of -0.0416 and 0.0296, respectively, and a p-value $\ll 0.05$, indicating that the multivariate oxide data is not normally distributed. The HZ-test statistic is given by Eq. (2).

$$HZ = \frac{1}{n}\sum_{i=1}^{n}\left(X_i - \overline{X}\right)^T S^{-1}\left(X_i - \overline{X}\right) \tag{2}$$

where $\mathbf{X}_i$ is the i-th observation, $\overline{\boldsymbol{X}}$ is the mean vector, and $\mathbf{S}$ is the sample covariance matrix.

IQR, a non-parametric approach to identify outliers. Data points beyond $Q_3 + 1.5 \times IQR$ are flagged as outliers using Eq. (3).

$$IQR \approx 1.348\sigma \tag{3}$$

Here, 1.348σ provides an approximation of the IQR to the standard deviation.

Understanding the Data Structure in Lower-Dimensional Space.
Multidimensional scaling (MDS), shown in Fig. 1, is a visual representation of the multivariate data structure on a 2-dimensional plane, maintaining the rank order of dissimilarities while transforming the matrix of pairwise distances to identify clusters or patterns.

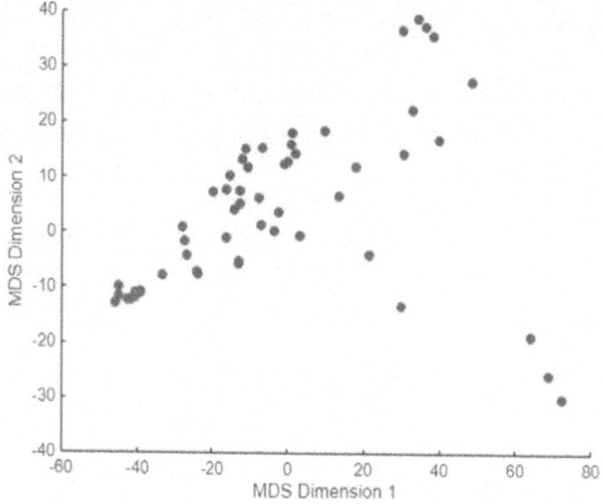

Fig. 1. MDS with Strain Criterion of oxides

This is achieved by using Eq. (4).

$$\mathbf{A} = \mathbf{J}\mathbf{D}\mathbf{J}^T \tag{4}$$

where **A** is the matrix with coordinates, **D** is the matrix of squared distances, and **J** is the centering matrix of vectors defined by Eq. (5).

$$\mathbf{J} = \mathbf{I} - \frac{1}{\mathbf{n}}1 \tag{5}$$

I is the identity matrix, **1** is a matrix of ones, and ***n*** is the number of observations.

2.2 Overview of Mechanical Properties

The analysis forecasts trends in the mechanical properties of the data. The number of mechanical properties observations is shown in Table 1. Indicates researchers' focus when incorporating biomass particles into the metal matrix. Senthilraj et al. [62] emphasized efforts to improve the strength of the aluminum matrix, acknowledging the need for practical reinforcements due to the growing demand for fuel-efficient and lightweight materials that can reduce CO emissions. Investigating the aluminum types used in the dataset literature also showed that researchers have a clear preference for studying the effects of biomass on the Al-6xxx series (Al-Mg-Si) Al6061 and Al6063 alloys, with medium strength constitute 61.22% of the 10 categories of aluminum samples analyzed.

2.3 Regression Models

Linear and nonlinear regression models facilitate problem-solving by minimizing the error in the solution x, ensuring that for linear models, Eq. (6) applies, while for nonlinear models, Eq. (7) holds.

$$\mathbf{A}x = \mathbf{b} \tag{6}$$

and for non-linear models:

$$\mathbf{A}\psi(x) = \mathbf{b} \tag{7}$$

where ψ represents a higher-dimensional basis to capture the non-linear data structure in the data. For simplicity, ψ is not considered in this explanation of regression models. The objective of linear regression is to minimize the error or difference between Ax – b as expressed in Eq. (8).

$$\underset{x}{\operatorname{argmin}}\|\mathbf{A}x - b\|_2^2 < \varepsilon \tag{8}$$

where ϵ is the error threshold. The solution is found by minimizing the error in x, such that the system is expressed by Eq. (9).

$$\mathbf{A}x \approx \mathbf{b} \tag{9}$$

This approach allows models to recognize patterns within the data structure that generalize effectively to new field data. Models vary in optimization parameters, such as learning rates and solver algorithms, as well as structural components, including regularization techniques, loss functions, and interpretability. Given that the system is overdetermined, with more data points than parameters, i.e., (m > n), the solution is constrained, minimizing the risk of overfitting and improving generalization. The models employed in this analysis, namely Lasso regression, Least Squares Boosting, and Neural Networks, are summarized according to robustness, tendency to overfit, and hyperparameters used in Table 3.

Both linear and nonlinear models are utilized based on the outcomes of the exploratory analysis, incorporating insights from the MDS plot which suggested possible positive linear correlations and indicates clustering at the bottom-right ranging between -40 to -20 on the y-axis, and 60 to 80 on the x-axis, and another cluster at the top right (40, 40) implying the need for non-linear models to capture data trends better and produce more accurate predictions.

Table 3. Overview of Regression Models: Characteristics and Analysis Parameters

Regression Model	Model Type	Hyperparameters	Model Robustness	Over-fitting	Cross-Val	One-Hot Encoding
Lasso Linear	Linear Model	alpha = 0.1 Max. Iter = 1000	High	Low	-	Yes

(continued)

Table 3. (*continued*)

Regression Model	Model Type	Hyperparameters	Model Robustness	Over-fitting	Cross-Val	One-Hot Encoding
Least Squares Boosting	Non-Linear Model	No. of Learners = 2000; Learning rate = 0.01 Minimum Leaf size = 8	High	Moderate	k = 5	No
Neural Network	Non-Linear Model	1st Layer = 10; 2nd Layer = 100 3rd Layer = 10 Activation = ReLU Lambda (λ) = 0.4	Moderate	High	k = 5	No

Lasso Regression. is the only linear model used in this analysis, requiring one-hot encoding to handle categorical variables in the extracted data. It employs the l_1-norm (a way to measure the length of a vector, by summing absolute values of its components) for regularization, which promotes sparsity in the solution. This inherent attribute mitigates overfitting, enhancing the model's robustness against outliers. In a high-dimensional, overdetermined system, a significant portion of the data information is embedded within a lower-dimensional structure, effectively reducing noise and eliminating occlusions that often manifest as outliers. The objective function for Lasso regression is represented in Eq. (10).

$$\underset{x}{\text{argmin}}\|\mathbf{A}x - \mathbf{b}\|2 + \lambda\|X\|1 \tag{10}$$

Least Squares Boosting (LSBoost). Boosting algorithms, such as Least Squares Boosting (LSBoost), are ensemble methods that iteratively construct models, aiming to minimize errors at each stage. These techniques exhibit a slower rate of overfitting compared to traditional models, as they prioritize correcting errors from previous iterations rather than attempting to fit the entire dataset simultaneously. A key characteristic of boosting is its emphasis on data points that are difficult to classify, as opposed to those that are easily classified. Conceptually, there is an analogy between boosting and cross-validation (Sect. 3); while their objectives differ, both involve iterative learning processes with a focus on error reduction, and ultimately, a weighted average of predictions is produced. This approach is the backbone behind achieving sparse solutions in ensemble models. It sequentially trains weak learners, typically decision trees (h_m), see Eq. (11), to correct the residuals of the previous model.

$$h_m(x) = \sum_{j=1}^{Jm} c_j 1\left(x \in R_j\right) \tag{11}$$

where J_m is the number of leaf nodes in the tree at stage m (number of learners), R_j is the region of partition defined by the tree, c_j is the average residual in region R_j, and **1** indicates if $x \in R_j$. This minimizes the least square error, shown in Eq. (12).

$$\sum\nolimits_{i \in R_j} \left(r_i^{(m)} - c_j\right)^2 \tag{12}$$

LSBoost uses the learning rate and the minimum leaf to regularize the model and prevent overfitting. More learners m improves accuracy, but can lead to overfitting. The lower the value of the learning rate η, the less prone the model will be to overfitting and the more robust. Since one-hot encoding inflates dimensionality, it is not used with LSBoost. The sum of all the predictions while using LSBoost results in Eq. (13).

$$F_M(x) = F_0(x) + \sum_{m=1}^{M} \eta hm(x) \tag{13}$$

where M is the number of learners, in this case M = 2000; and h_m are the weak decision trees, and η is the learning rate.

Neural Networks. Neural networks produce highly non-linear models, especially due to the number of hidden layers. This model is also known as the black-box model, making it difficult to understand and interpret variable relationships. Inspired by biological nervous systems, the network is built by combining several layers based on the size of the dataset. The higher the value of the regularization strength, or lambda, the sparser the solution. Cross-validation is also used to prevent overfitting. The output of the neural network Eq. (14).

$$y = f\left(b + \sum_{i=1}^{n} w_i x_i\right) \tag{14}$$

where w_i is the weight or strength of a neuron, b is a bias, and f is the activation function, in this case, the ReLU function. Lasso regression was chosen for its ability to handle high-dimensional data with regularization, thereby reducing overfitting. Least Squares Boosting was selected due to its iterative refinement process, which enhances predictive accuracy. Neural Networks were included to explore deep, nonlinear feature interactions, though their interpretability remains a limitation [8, 9].

2.4 Preventing Overfitting and Promoting Sparse Solutions

Robust models often benefit from sparse solutions, which identify key features by minimizing non-zero elements in the vector x. Techniques like one-hot encoding, k-fold cross-validation, and regularization enhance robustness and performance. Regularized models in this study make use of the L_1 norm, penalizing the sum of the absolute values of the solution vector λ, expressed as Eq. (15).

$$\lambda \sum_{i=1}^{n} |x_i| \tag{15}$$

Non-linear models handle categorical data better than linear models, making one-hot encoding unnecessary, whereas linear models often require it to improve accuracy.

2.5 Evaluation Metrics

The models are evaluated using the Root Mean Square Error (RMSE), R-squared (R^2) accuracy, and the Mean Absolute Error (MAE). The Root Mean Square Error (RMSE) and the Mean Absolute Error (MAE) both measure the extent to which $\mathbf{A}x = \mathbf{b}$ or $\mathbf{A}\psi(x) = \mathbf{b}$, where $\mathbf{b}$ represents the actual value being predicted. The RMSE is more sensitive to larger error values, but normalizes these values by taking the square root. Conversely, MAE gives equal weight to all errors and is more sensitive to smaller deviations. R-squared accuracy, also known as the coefficient of determination, ranges between 0 and 1, with the goal being an R^2 value as close to 1 as possible without overfitting. The formulas for these evaluation metrics—RMSE, R^2 accuracy, and MAE—are provided as Eqs. (16–18).

$$RMSE = \sqrt{\frac{1}{n}\sum_{i=1}^{n}(b_i - Ax_i)^2} \tag{16}$$

$$R^2 = 1 - \frac{\sum_{i=1}^{n}(b_i - Ax_i)^2}{\left(b_i - \overline{b}\right)^2} \tag{17}$$

$$MAE = \frac{1}{n}\sum_{i=1}^{n}|b_i - Ax_i| \tag{18}$$

where b is the actual value of the system, Ax is the predicted value, and $\hat{}b$ is the mean of the actual values

2.6 Interpretability Analysis

Local and global interpretability analyses are employed to explain the model behaviour. Global analyses, such as Partial Dependence Plots (PDP), examine features independently, without considering potential correlations or interactions. Response Surface Methodology (RSM) plots help visualize the interactions between features and their consequent effects on the model's predictions. These techniques reveal patterns within the feature space and identify the features with the most significant influence on the model output.

3 Results and Discussion

3.1 Exploratory Data Analysis Results and Interpretation

The box plot of the oxides shown in Fig. 2 indicates that silicon dioxide SiO_2 is symmetrical with no outliers from its median at 57.963 $wt\%$. It ranges from 0.0724 $wt\%$ to 97.095 $wt\%$ and is the only oxide feature that is not skewed. It is the most abundant in most oxide in the biomass ash residues; conversely, magnesium oxide MgO averages as the least abundant, and is closely followed by sodium dioxide (Na_2O).

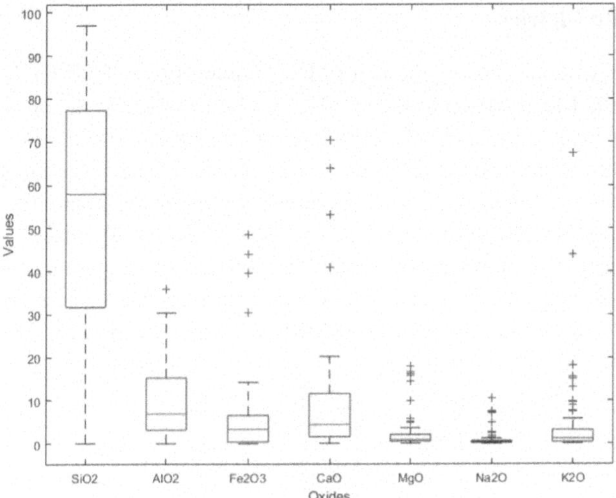

Fig. 2. Box Plot of Oxides

The parallel plot in Fig. 3 is used to understand the outliers in the box plot better. The plot indicates that SiO_2 is most abundant in Rice Husk Ash (RHA), having up to 97.095 *wt%* of the biomass. Fernandes et al. [63], in 2016, remark that RHA, which accounts for 4% of rice paddy weight, can have silicon dioxide ranging between 90.02 - 96.71 *wt%*. RHA is closely followed by Palm Kernel Shell Ash (PKSA), at 96.09% of SiO_2. Studies by Imoisili et al. [64] in 2020 present data on the synthesis of palm kernel shell ash, indicating that silicon dioxide SiO_2 can attain up to 96.83 *wt%* of PKSA. A notable trend is observed in CaO-rich oxides— periwinkle and eggshell, both have little to no silicon dioxide. A characterization study by [65] in 2018 revealed that while silicon dioxide amounts to only 0.363 *wt%*, CaO extracted from calcinated $CaCO_3$ could take up to 90 *wt%* in eggshell biomass. A 2021 article by Haddad et al. [66] and Samuel et al. [67] in 2024 noted that CaO takes up to 70 *wt%* and 63.8 *wt%* in periwinkle and eggshell powder, respectively, which is very similar to the values in the plot. In aluminium oxide Al_2O_3, the outlier is breadfruit hull ash, which, according to chemical characterization studies by Aigbodion et al. [68] and Nwajiobi et al. [69], is rich in aluminium oxide. Other biomass types that have observable trends are Coconut shell ash (CSA), which has the highest amount of Magnesium oxide (MgO) at a percentage weight of 18.

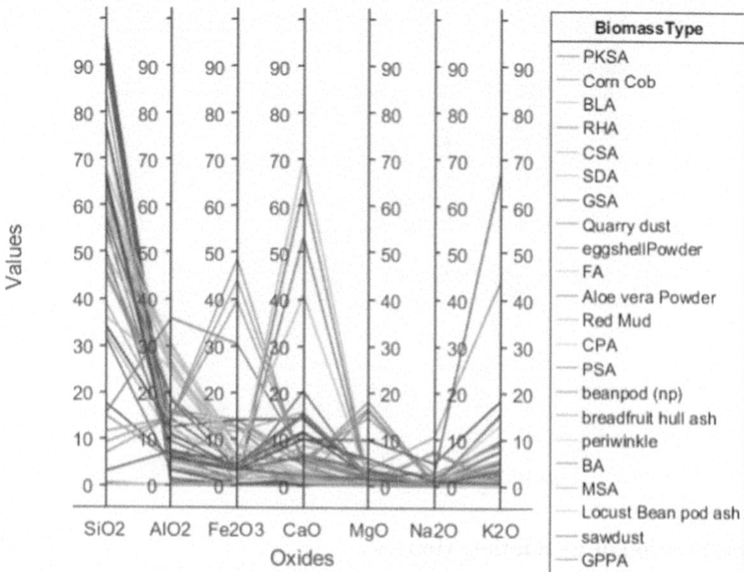

Fig. 3. Parallel Plot of Oxides

CSA also has remarkable amounts of Aluminium oxide at 16 *wt%*, which is more than twice the average, and Potassium oxide (K_2O) as high as 43.98 *wt%*. Kumar et al. [70] and Madakson et al. [71] placed the percentage of magnesium in coconut shell ash between 13 -16.2 *wt%*. Red Mud, another notable biomass, has a high concentration of Iron oxides (Fe_2O_3) and sodium oxide (Na_2O). Nath et al. [72] corroborate this in their study, where the Iron oxide content of solid waste from aluminium industries was found to range between 48–54 *wt%*. Green Plantain Peel Ash (GPPA) has a high concentration of Potassium oxide at 67.34 *wt%*. In 2018, [73] aimed to find renewable alternatives to potassium hydroxide and assessed the potential of plantain. In their study, K_2O is the most dominant oxide in plantain peel ash at 54.2 *wt%*. Finally, it can be observed that biomass types of RHA and PKSA, rich in SiO_2, the most abundant oxide, 8 times more abundant than the next most abundant oxide, have lower concentrations of other oxides. Conversely, biomass ashes rich in other less abundant oxides have relatively low amounts of silicon, e.g., GPPA, Red Mud, periwinkle, eggshells, etc.

Further examining the relationship between each oxide, using the Spearman correlation in Fig. 4, validates some useful trends seen in the parallel plot. The strong negative correlation between SiO_2 and other oxides suggests that biomass types rich in SiO_2 have lower proportions of other strengthening oxides, such as Al_2O_3 and Fe_2O_3. This could be attributed to the natural abundance of silica in agricultural residues like rice husk ash, which inversely affects the concentration of other oxides. The strong positive correlation between Al_2O_3 and Fe_2O_3 likely stems from their common occurrence in mineral-rich biomass sources, which contribute to mechanical reinforcement in AMMCs.

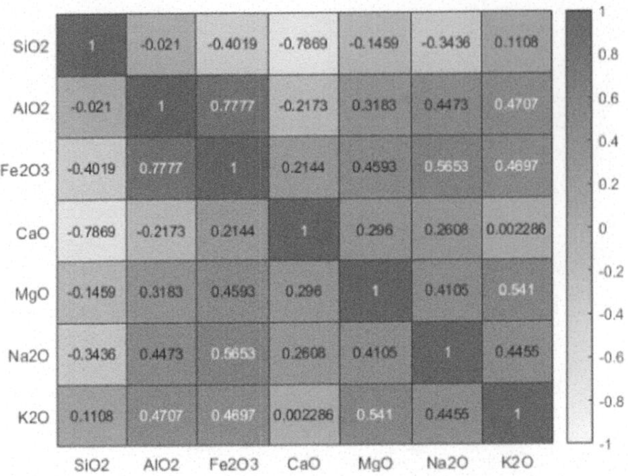

Fig. 4. Spearman's Correlation of Oxides

3.2 Interpretation of Evaluation Metrics

The results in Table 4. Shows that the Least Square Boosting model outperforms the other models for all mechanical properties, and the Lasso Linear model performs the worst for all mechanical properties, further justifying the need for more robust models that capture complex, nonlinear data correlations between the oxides and mechanical properties as explained in Sect. (2.3).

Table 4. Evaluation metrics for the Mechanical Properties

Regression Model	Hardness			Tensile Strength			Elongation		
	RMSE	*R2*	MAE	RMSE	*R2*	MAE	RMSE	*R2*	MAE
Lasso Linear	20.23	0.60	14.56	39.79	0.47	27.75	5.704	0.61	4.41
Least Squares Boosting	16.182	0.74	10.28	20.14	0.92	13.67	3.149	0.88	2.202
Neural Network	23.389	0.47	15.73	31.33	0.81	18.43	6.479	0.56	4.197

3.3 Model Evaluation Using Partial Dependence Plots

The PDP plot for hardness, tensile strength, and elongation is shown in Fig. 5, illustrating the complex non-linear relationships between the oxides and each mechanical property as captured by the boosting model.

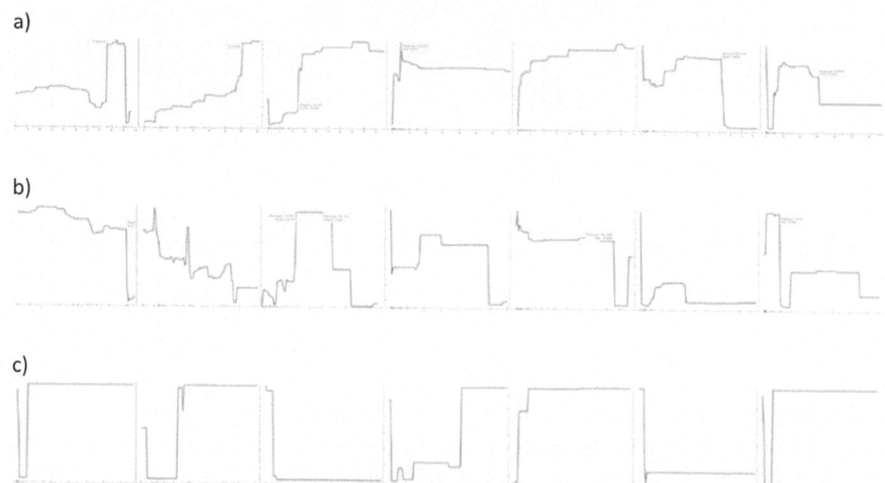

Fig. 5. Least Square Boosting results for (a) Hardness, (b) Tensile Strength, and (c) Elongation. L-R: SiO_2, Al_2O_3, Fe_2O_3, CaO, MgO, Na_2O, K_2O.

The PDP for hardness Fig. 5a, indicates that Fe_2O_3 and MgO have an immediate and consistently positive impact on hardness. Conversely, Al_2O_3 shows a gradual positive effect over a broader range of compositions. SiO_2, CaO, Na_2O, and K_2O initially enhance the mechanical properties; however, beyond specific thresholds, they exhibit a counteractive effect. These critical points occur at approximately 90 *wt%*, 7 *wt%*, 6.5 *wt%* and 30 *wt%* for SiO_2, CaO, Na_2O, and K_2O, respectively. It is important to note that SiO_2 has a noticeably high positive effect within the range of $78 \leq wt\% \leq 90$, while CaO remains beneficial up to 6.5 wt%. For tensile strength Fig. 5b, the continuous addition of oxides to the metal matrix generally results in a decline. However, Fe_2O_3 shows a positive trend in tensile strength within the range of $14 \leq wt\% \leq 24$. Similarly, CaO, K_2O and Na_2O demonstrate localized positive correlations at $18 \leq wt\% \leq 30$, $15 \leq wt\% \leq 55$, and $1.2 \leq wt\% \leq 4$, respectively. Beyond these ranges, most oxides exhibit an overall negative influence on tensile strength.

Elongation shown in Fig. 5c trends negatively with increasing MgO and Na_2O content. However, after surpassing approximately 10 *wt%* of Al_2O_3, elongation begins to exhibit a positive trend, suggesting a threshold-dependent behaviour. These findings show the complex relationship between oxide composition and mechanical properties and drive the quest to understand how these oxides combine to influence mechanical properties.

3.4 Model Evaluation Using Response Surface Methodology

The evaluation of oxide combinations using Response Surface Methodology (RSM) aims to determine the optimal mixture that positively influences mechanical properties. This is particularly crucial since biomass ashes are typically not added in isolation.

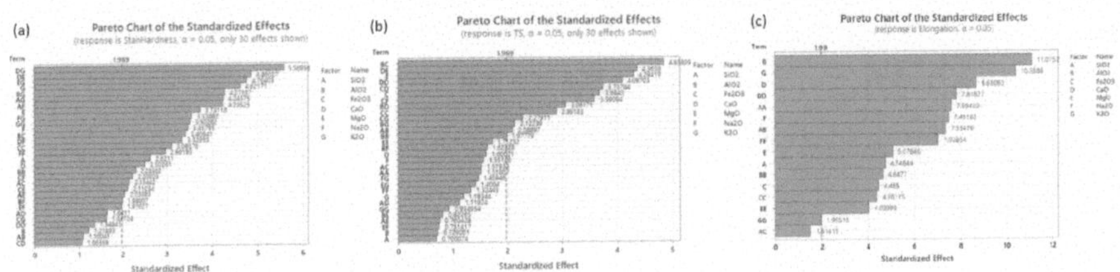

Fig. 6. Response Surface Methodology for Hardness, Tensile Strength, and Elongation

Hardness: The combination of CaO and K_2O has the most significant positive impact on hardness, with a significance level of $\alpha = 0.05$ and an impact value of 5.5696. The next most influential combination is CaO and MgO, with an impact value of 4.8603, followed by MgO and K_2O, which has an impact value of 4.76403, shown in Fig. 6.

Tensile Strength: The Pareto chart of standardized effects for tensile strength reveals that Al_2O_3 and Fe_2O_3 exhibit the strongest impact, with an effect value of 4.8381, followed by the combination of CaO and MgO.

Elongation: Al_2O_3 also exhibits the highest standardized effect value for elongation, at 11.0752, followed by K_2O, which has a standardized effect value of 10.3888. Figure 6 indicates that all oxides and oxide combinations, except for the interaction between K_2O and SiO_2-Fe_2O_3, exceed the threshold value of 1.99, signifying their importance in influencing elongation.

4 Conclusion

In this paper, we have investigated the influence of biomass ash oxides on AMMCs using machine learning techniques. The MDS plot supports our hypothesis that the mechanical properties of AMMCs have complex, nonlinear relationships with the oxides present in biomass ash. Among the models used, the nonlinear models outperformed the linear models according to the evaluation metrics. Correlation analysis revealed a strong negative relationship between SiO_2 and CaO, yet both improved hardness and elongation properties, indicating they can serve as substitutes within the thresholds indicated in the results. Tensile strength, on the other hand, required more localized oxide concentrations to improve, with Al_2O_3 and Fe_2O_3 highlighting the importance of this study and the need for further precision when introducing oxides to AMMCs. Response Surface Methodology (RSM) further refined oxide interactions, demonstrating key synergies, such as CaO, MgO for hardness, Al_2O_3 Fe_2O_3 for tensile strength, and SiO_2, Al_2O_3 for elongation. These findings provide a comprehensive understanding of the influence of biomass ash oxides on AMMCs, offering a robust and scalable alternative to conventional experiments.

References

1. Daniel, I.M., Chun, H.J., Karalekas, D.: Characterization of metal matrix composites. Contractor Report NASA-CR-195381, NASA, Washington, D.C. (1994). https://ntrs.nasa.gov/citations/19950012525
2. Adeleke, A.A., Ikubanni, P.P., Odusote, J.K., Olujimi, B.B., Okolie, J.A.: Influence of sawdust ash on the microstructural and physicomechanical properties of stir-cast Al6063/sda matrix composite. Inter. J. Adv. Manufact. Technol. **127**(5–6), 2523–2536 (2023). https://doi.org/10.1007/s00170-023-11700
3. Characterization of aluminium matrix composites (aa6061/b4c) fabricated by stir casting technique. Mater. Today: Proc. **2**(4), 2984–2990 (2015). https://doi.org/10.1016/j.matpr.2015.07.282,
4. Adeleke, A.A., Okolie, J.A., Ogbaga, C.C., Ikubanni, P.P., Okoye, P.U., Akande, O.: Machine learning model for the evaluation of biomethane potential based on the biochemical composition of biomass. Bioenergy Res. **17**(1), 731–743 (2024). https://doi.org/10.1007/s12155-023-10681-9
5. Osunmakinde, L., Asafa, T.B., Agboola, P.O., Durowoju, M.O.: Development of aluminum composite reinforced with selected agricultural residues. Discov Mater 3(1) (2023). https://doi.org/10.1007/s43939-023-00069-z
6. Brunton, S.L., Kutz, J.N.: Data-Driven Science and Engineering: Machine Learning, Dynamical Systems, and Control. Cambridge University Press, 1 edn. (2019). https://doi.org/10.1017/9781108380690
7. Pali, M.C., Schnass, K.: Dictionary learning—from local towards global and adaptive. arXiv preprint arXiv:1804.07101 (2018)
8. Hoefler, T., Alistarh, D., Ben-Nun, T., Dryden, N., Peste, A.: Sparsity in deep learning: Pruning and growth for efficient inference and training in neural networks. J. Mach. Learn. Res. **22**(241), 1–124 (2021)
9. Liu, S., Wang, Z.: Ten lessons we have learned in the new "sparseland": A short handbook for sparse neural network researchers. arXiv preprint arXiv:2302.02596 (2023)
10. Gireesh, C.H., Prasad, K.G.D., Ramji, K., Vinay, P.V.: Mechanical characterization of aluminium metal matrix composite reinforced with aloe vera powder. Mater. Today: Proc., 3289–3297 (2018). https://doi.org/10.1016/j.matpr.2017.11.571
11. Usman, A.M., et al.: A comparative study on the properties of al-7%sirice husk ash and al-7%si-bagasse ash composites produced by stir casting. Inter. J. Eng. Sci. 3(8), 1–7 (2014). https://www.theijes.com
12. Imran, M., Khan, A.R.A., Megeri, S., Sadik, S.: Study of hardness and tensile strength of aluminium-7075 percentage varying reinforced with graphite and bagasse-ash composites. Resource-Efficient Technol. **2**(2), 81–88 (2016). https://doi.org/10.1016/j.reffit.2016.06.007
13. Alaneme, K.K., Bodunrin, M.O., Awe, A.A.: Microstructure, mechanical and fracture properties of groundnut shell ash and silicon carbide dispersion strengthened aluminium matrix composites. J. King Saud Univ. Eng. Sci. **30**(1), 96–103 (2018). https://doi.org/10.1016/j.jksues.2016.01.001
14. Kumar, B.P., Birru, A.K.: Microstructure and mechanical properties of aluminium metal matrix composites with addition of bamboo leaf ash by stir casting method. Trans. Nonferrous Metals Soc. China **27**(12), 2555–2572 (2017). https://doi.org/10.1016/S1003-6326(17)60284-X
15. Olaniran, O., Babatunde, O.: Influence of silicon carbide-cassava peel ash weight ratio on the mechanical and tribological characteristics of al-mg-si alloy hybrid composites. J. Chem. Technol. Metallurgy, 56(5), 1082–1088 (2021). https://www.researchgate.net/publication/353523370

16. Blessing, U., Franklin, T., Gregory, O.: Determination of mechanical properties of coconut shell ash reinforced aluminium metal matric composite (2022). https://www.researchgate.net/publication/372101572
17. Yekinni, A.A., Bello, S.K., Bajela, G.G., Adigun, I.A.: Effect of coconut shell ash and graphite particles on microstructure and mechanical properties of recycled aluminium composites. Inte. J. Adv. Sci. Res. Eng. **06**(10), 61–71 (2020). https://doi.org/10.31695/ijasre.2020.33904
18. Saldanha, J.X., Singh, J., Pinto, G.M.: Effect of coconut shell ash and sic particles on mechanical properties of aluminium based composites. Am. J. Mater. Sci. **2017**(4), 112–115 (2017). https://doi.org/10.5923/j.materials.20170704.09
19. Daramola, O.O., Adediran, A.A., Fadumiye, A.T., Daramola, O.O., Adediran, A.A., Fadumiye, A.T.: Evaluation of the mechanical properties and corrosion behaviour of coconut shell ash reinforced aluminium (6063) alloy composites (2022). http://lejpt.academicdirect.org
20. Mangalore, P., Akash, Ulvekar, A., Abhiram, Sanjay, J., Advaith: mechanical properties of coconut shell ash reinforced aluminium metal matrix composites. In: AIP Conference Proceedings, vol. 2080, p. 020014 (2019). https://doi.org/10.1063/1.5092897,
21. Lakshmikanthan, P., Prabu, B.: Mechanical and tribological behaviour of aluminium al6061-coconut shell ash composite using stir casting pellet method. J. Balkan Tribol. Associat. **22**(4-I), 400–4018 (2016) http://www.scibulcom.net/
22. Fatile, O., Fatile, O.B., Akinruli, J.I., Amori, A.A.: Microstructure and mechanical behaviour of stir-cast al-mg-sl alloy matrix hybrid composite reinforced with corn cob ash and silicon carbide. Intern. J. Eng. Technol. Innovat. **4**(4), 251–259. (2014). https://www.researchgate.net/publication/279192238
23. Dwivedi, S.P., Sharma, S., Mishra, R.K.: Effects of waste eggshells and sic addition in the synthesis of aluminum hybrid green metal matrix composite. Green Process. Synth. **6**(1), 113–123 (2017). https://doi.org/10.1515/gps-2016-0119
24. Hassan, S.B., Aigbodion, V.S.: Effects of eggshell on the microstructures and properties of al–cu–mg/eggshell particulate composites. J. King Saud Univ. Eng. Sci. **27**(1), 49–56 (2015). https://doi.org/10.1016/j.jksues.2013.03.001
25. He, Y., Che, D., Ouyang, X., Niu, Y.: Surface properties of eggshell powder and its influence on cement hydration. Materials **15**(21), 7633 (2022). https://doi.org/10.3390/ma15217633
26. Prasad D.S., Krishna, A.R.: Production and Mechanical Properties of A356.2 /RHA Composites. Inter. J.Adv. Sci. Technol. **33**, 51–58, (2011). https://www.researchgate.net/publication/284651427
27. Narasaraju, G., Raju, D.L.: Characterization of hybrid rice husk and fly ash-reinforced aluminium alloy (alsi10mg) composites. Mater. Today: Proc. 3056–3064 (2015). https://doi.org/10.1016/j.matpr.2015.07.245
28. Saha, M.: Fly ash composites: A review arXiv preprint arXiv:2202.11167 (2022) https://arxiv.org/pdf/2202.11167
29. Kanth, U.R., Rao, P.S., Krishna, M.G.: Mechanical behaviour of fly ash/sic particles reinforced al-zn alloy-based metal matrix composites fabricated by stir casting method. J. Market. Res. **8**(1), 737–744 (2019). https://doi.org/10.1016/j.jmrt.2018.06.003
30. Juang, S.H., Li, C.F.: Influence of different addition ratios of fly ash on mechanical properties of adc10 aluminum matrix composites. Metals (Basel) 12(4) (2022). https://doi.org/10.3390/met12040653
31. Boopathi, M.M., Arulshri, K.P., Iyandurai, N.: Evaluation of mechanical properties of aluminium alloy 2024 reinforced with silicon carbide and fly ash hybrid metal matrix composites. Am. J. Appl. Sci. **10**(3), 219–229 (2013). https://doi.org/10.3844/ajassp.2013.219.229
32. Kumarasamy, S.P., Vijayananth, K., Thankachan, T., Muthukutti, G.P.: Investigations on mechanical and machinability behavior of aluminum/flyash cenosphere/gr hybrid composites processed through compocasting. J. Appli. Res. Technol. **15**(5), 430–441 (2017). https://doi.org/10.1016/j.jart.2017.05.005

33. Selvam, J.D.R., Smart, D.S.R., Dinaharan, I.: Synthesis and characterization of al6061-fly ashp-sicp composites by stir casting and compocasting methods. Energy Proc. **34**, 637–646 (2013). https://doi.org/10.1016/j.egypro.2013.06.795
34. Wessley, G.J.J., Franklin, A.G., Vijay, S.J.: Fabrication and mechanical characterization of stir cast aa6063-borosilicate-fly ash hybrid metal matrix composites. Inter. J. Eng. Technol. **7**(3.6), 101 (2018). https://doi.org/10.14419/ijet.v7i3.6.14949
35. Ben, F., Amodu, F.R., Olubambi, P.A.: Influence of green plantain peel ash and alumina reinforcement on the physio-mechanical properties of aluminium matrix hybrid composites. Mater. Sci. Forum **1107**, 33–45 (2023). https://doi.org/10.4028/p-5CdJMw
36. Singh, J., Suri, N.M., Verma, A.: Affect of mechanical properties on groundnut shell ash reinforced al6063. Inter. J. Technol. Res. Eng. **2**(11), 2347–4718 (2015). www.ijtre.com
37. Bawa, M.A., Umaru, O.B., Abur, B.T., Salako, I., Jatau, J.S.: Effect of locust bean pod ash on the hardness and wear rate of heat treated a356 alloy metal matrix composite for production of automobile brake rotor. Inter. J. Res. Publications **57**(1) (2020). https://doi.org/10.47119/IJRP100571720201325
38. Adama, A.Y., Jimoh, Y.A., Kolo, S.S.: Effect of locust bean pod ash on compaction characteristics of weak sub grade soils. Inter. J. Eng. Sci. Invention **2**(1), 2319–6729 (2013). www.ijesi.org
39. Suleiman, I.Y., Salihu, S.A., Mohammed, T.A.: Investigation of mechanical, microstructure, and wear behaviors of al-12%si/reinforced with melon shell ash particulates. Int. J. Adv. Manuf. Technol. **97**(9–12), 4137–4144 (2018). https://doi.org/10.1007/s00170018-2157-9
40. Oghenevweta, J.E., Aigbodion, V.S., Nyior, G.B., Asuke, F.: Mechanical properties and microstructural analysis of al–si– mg/carbonized maize stalk waste particulate composites. J. King Saud Univ. Eng. Sci. **28**(2), 222–229 (2016). https://doi.org/10.1016/j.jksues.2014.03.009
41. Aigbodion, V.S., Ezema, I.C.: Multifunctional a356 alloy/pksanp composites: microstructure and mechanical properties. Defence Technol. **16**(3), 731–736 (2020). https://doi.org/10.1016/j.dt.2019.05.017
42. Edoziuno, F.O., Adediran, A.A., Odoni, B.U., Utu, O.G., Olayanju, A.: Physico-chemical and morphological evaluation of palm kernel shell particulate reinforced aluminium matrix composites. Mater. Today: Proc., 652–657 (2021). https://doi.org/10.1016/j.matpr.2020.03.641
43. Okoro, A.M., Oladele, I.O.: The effect of palm kernel shell ash on the mechanical properties of as-cast aluminium alloy matrix composites (2016). https://www.researchgate.net/publication/326316583
44. Ikubanni, P.P., Oki, M., Adeleke, A.A., Omoniyi, P.O.: Synthesis, physico-mechanical and microstructural characterization of al6063/sic/pksa hybrid reinforced composites. Sci. Rep. **11**(1), 14845 (2021). https://doi.org/10.1038/s41598-021-94420-0
45. Refaai, M.R.A., Reddy, R.M., Venugopal, J., Rao, M.V., Vaidhegi, K., Yishak, S.: Optimization on the mechanical properties of aluminium 8079 composite materials reinforced with psa. Adv. Mater. Sci. Eng. **2022** (2022). https://doi.org/10.1155/2022/6328781
46. Prasad, D.S., Krishna, A.R: Fabrication and characterization of a356.2-rice husk ash composite using stir casting technique. Inter. J. Eng. Sci. Technol. **2**(12), 7603–7608 (2010)
47. Saravanan, S.D., Senthilkumar, M., Shankar, S.: Effect of particle size on tribological behavior of rice husk ash-reinforced aluminum alloy (alsi10mg) matrix composites. Tribol. Trans. **56**(6), 1156–1167 (2013). https://doi.org/10.1080/10402004.2013.831962
48. Sarkar, S., Bhirangi, A.: Mechanical characterization of aluminium metal matrix composite reinforced with aloe vera powder. Mater. Today: Proc. 3289–3297 (2018). https://doi.org/10.1016/j.matpr.2017.11.571

49. Adediran, A.A., Alaneme, K.K., Oladele, I.O., Akinlabi, E.T.: Microstructural characteristics and mechanical behaviour of aluminium matrix composites reinforced with si-based refractory compounds derived from rice husk. Cogent Eng. **8**(1) (2021). https://doi.org/10.1080/23311916.2021.1897928
50. Alaneme, K.K., Adewale, T.M., Alaneme, K.K.: Influence of rice husk ashsilicon carbide weight ratios on the mechanical behaviour of al-mg-si alloy matrix hybrid composites Tribol. Indust. **35**(2), 163–172 (2013), www.tribology.fink.rs
51. Arora, G., Sharma, S.: A comparative study of aa6351 mono-composites reinforced with synthetic and agro waste reinforcement. Int. J. Precis. Eng. Manuf. **19**(4), 631–638 (2018). https://doi.org/10.1007/s12541-018-0076-1
52. Prasad, D.S., Krishna, S.A.P.R., Prasad, D.S., Krishna, A.R.: Production and mechanical properties of a356.2 /rha composites (2011), https://www.researchgate.net/publication/284651427
53. Prasad, D.S., Shoba, C., Ramanaiah, N.: Investigations on mechanical properties of aluminum hybrid composites. J. Market. Res. **3**(1), 79–85 (2014). https://doi.org/10.1016/j.jmrt.2013.11.002
54. Gladston, J.A.K., Sheriff, N.M., Dinaharan, I., Selvam, J.D.R.: Production and characterization of rich husk ash particulate reinforced aa6061 aluminum alloy composites by compocasting. Trans. Nonferrous Metals Soc. China **25**(3), 683–691 (2015). https://doi.org/10.1016/S1003-6326(15)63653-6
55. Muralimohan, R., Kempaiah, U.N.: Seenappa: Influence of rice husk ash and b4c on mechanical properties of adc 12 alloy hybrid composites. Mater. Today: Proc. **5**(11), 25562–25569 (2018). https://doi.org/10.1016/j.matpr.2018.10.363
56. Kumar, B.P.: Evaluation of mechanical properties of aluminium alloy 7075 reinforced with silicon carbide and red mud composite. Inter. J. Eng. Res. General Sci. **2**(6), 1081–1088 (2014). www.ijergs.org
57. Singla, Y.K., Chhibber, R., Bansal, H., Kalra, A.: Wear behavior of aluminum alloy 6061-based composites reinforced with sic, al2o3, and red mud: a comparative study. JOM **67**(9), 2160–2169 (2015). https://doi.org/10.1007/s11837-015-1365-0
58. Atuanya, C.U., Aigbodion, V.S.: Evaluation of al–cu–mg alloy/bean pod ash nanoparticles synthesis by double layer feeding–stir casting method. J. Alloy. Compd. **601**, 251–259 (2014). https://doi.org/10.1016/j.jallcom.2014.02.086
59. Atuanya, C.U., Ibhadode, A.O.A., Dagwa, I.M.: Effects of breadfruit seed hull ash on the microstructures and properties of al-si-fe alloy/breadfruit seed hull ash particulate composites. Results Phys. **2**, 142=–149 (2012). https://doi.org/10.1016/j.rinp.2012.09.003
60. Nwabufoh, M.N.: A. Master's thesis, Ahmadu Bello University (2015)
61. Umunakwe, R., Olaleye, D.J., Oyetunji, A., Okoye, O.C., Umunakwe, I.J.: Assessment of the density and mechanical properties of particulate periwin-kle shell-aluminium 6063 metal matrix composite (pps-almmc) produced by two-step casting (2021)
62. Senthilraj, K., Rajamurugan, G.: Corrosion, fatigue, and wear performance of friction stir welded aluminum metal matrix composites: a review. Trans. Indian Inst. Met. **76**(12), 3201–3218 (2023). https://doi.org/10.1007/s12666-023-03038-5
63. Fernandes, I.J., et al.: Characterization of rice husk ash produced using different biomass combustion techniques for energy. Fuel **165**, 351–359 (2016). https://doi.org/10.1016/j.fuel.2015.10.086
64. Imoisili, P.E., Ukoba, K.O., Jen, T.C.: Synthesis and characterization of amorphous mesoporous silica from palm kernel shell ash. Boletín de La Sociedad Española de Cerámica y Vidrio **59**(4), 159–164 (2020). https://doi.org/10.1016/j.bsecv.2019.09.006
65. de O. Spelta, J.S., de S. Galdino, A.G.: Bioceramic composite: Hen's eggshell characterization and main applications. Revista Ifes Ciência **4**(1), 9–20 (2018). https://doi.org/10.36524/ric.v4i1.323

66. Haddad, B., et al.: Synthesis and characterization of egg shell (es) and egg shell with membrane (esm) modified by ionic liquids. Chemical Data Collections **33**, 100717 (2021). https://doi.org/10.1016/j.cdc.2021.100717
67. Samuel, A.E., Kamba, S.Y., Samaila, D.S., Ilesanmi, N.Y.: Preparation and characterization of periwinkle shell based chitosan-kenaf fibre copolymer and its derivatives for selective binding of cu (ii) and zn (ii) ions from electroplating effluent. J. Appl. Sci. Environ. Manag. **28**(3), 853–863 (2024). https://doi.org/10.4314/jasem.v28i3.25
68. Aigbodion, N.: Characterization of breadfruit seed hull ash for potential utilization in metal matrix composites for automotive application. Eng. Environ. Sci. Mater. Sci. (2012)
69. Nwajiobi, C.C., Otaigbe, J.O.E., Oriji, O.: Physicochemical, spectroscopic and tableting properties of microcrystalline cellulose obtained from the african breadfruit seed hulls. Afr. J. Biotech. **18**(18), 371–382 (2019). https://doi.org/10.5897/AJB2019.16791
70. Kumar, A., et al.: The utilisation of coconut shell ash in production of hybrid composite: Microstructural characterisation and performance analysis. J. Clean. Prod. **398**, 136494 (2023). https://doi.org/10.1016/j.jclepro.2023.136494
71. Madakson, P., Apasi, A.: Characterization of coconut shell ash for potential utilization in metal matrix composites for automotive applications, n.d
72. Nath, H., Sahoo, A.: A study on the characterization of red mud. Inter.. Appli. Bio-Eng. **8**(1), 1–4 (2014). https://doi.org/10.18000/ijabeg.10118
73. Omoniyi, K.I., Nwokem, N.C., Usman, Y.O., Idowu, O.O.: An assessment of the potential of plantain peel ash as a potash biocatalyst for producing reducing sugar from phoenix dactylifera seed pit. Moroccan J. Chem. **7**(1) (2018). http://revues.imist.ma/?journal=morjchempage=login

AI-Powered System for Detecting Structural Pathologies in Civil Engineering Using CNNs: Aigis

Ghanem Gharbi and Afif Beji(✉)

School of Engineering, ESPRIT, 1, 2 rue André Ampère, Pôle Technologique, El Ghazala, 2083 Ariana, Tunisia
ghanem.gharbi@esprit.tn, afif.beji@esprit.tn

Abstract. Structural pathologies, such as cracks, spalling concrete, and corrosion, pose significant challenges in civil engineering (CE), threatening the safety and longevity of infrastructures. Traditional inspection methods rely heavily on manual expertise, are time-intensive, and often fail to detect defects at an early stage. These limitations underscore the need for innovative automated solutions. To address these limitations, we developed Aigis, an AI-based system designed to detect and diagnose structural pathologies. Leveraging a Convolutional Neural Network (CNN) trained on annotated images, Aigis identifies critical defects with high accuracy. To ensure its practical applicability, the system integrates international engineering standards (such Eurocodes) to classify the severity of detected pathologies. This combination of AI and engineering norms transforms Aigis from a mere detection tool into a comprehensive diagnostic system. The methodology involves data collection and annotation using Label Studio, model training with a balanced dataset of real pathology images, and integration of Eurocode thresholds to enhance diagnostic accuracy. Initial tests yielded a validation accuracy of 87%, with promising results observed in real-world evaluations. Aigis demonstrates significant potential for scalability and efficiency. By automating pathology diagnostics, it reduces reliance on manual inspections, enhances structural safety, and promotes preventive maintenance.

Keywords: Structural integrity · pathologies · cracks · spalling concrete · corrosion · artificial intelligence · machine learning · Convolutional Neural Networks · TensorFlow Lite · mobile application · structural health monitoring · predictive maintenance · Eurocodes

1 Introduction

Aging infrastructures present significant challenges for many developing countries, particularly Tunisia, impacting both public safety and economic stability. The country's infrastructure quality has notably declined over the past decade; according to the World Economic Forum rankings, Tunisia was positioned 33rd

F. Kamoun et al. (Eds.): AFRICATEK 2025, LNICST 676, pp. 240–256, 2026.
https://doi.org/10.1007/978-3-032-16635-7_16

globally in 2008 but fell to 82nd by 2017 [1]. This deterioration underscores the critical need for effective assessment and rehabilitation strategies to ensure the safety and functionality of public structures. Traditional inspection methods, while widely used, are time-consuming, labor-intensive, and prone to inconsistencies due to varying environmental conditions and human subjectivity [2]. As a result, there is a growing demand for automated, accurate, and scalable solutions to assess structural integrity. Recent advancements in computer vision and deep learning (DL) have enabled AI-driven pathology detection, offering a promising alternative to manual inspections. Convolutional Neural Networks (CNNs), in particular, have demonstrated remarkable accuracy in detecting structural anomalies, often exceeding 90% in controlled settings [3]. By leveraging these advancements, AI-based vision systems can automate structural assessments, reduce human error, and enhance early detection of critical defects such as cracks, spalling concrete, and corrosion. In this research, we propose an AI-powered pathology detection model specifically tailored for civil infrastructure. Our model, trained on a diverse dataset, achieved a 87% validation accuracy, demonstrating strong potential for real-world deployment. This study encompasses:

- The creation of a robust dataset capturing structural defects under varied conditions.
- The development and optimization of a deep learning model for pathology detection.
- The integration of the model into a user-friendly application, providing actionable insights to engineers and field professionals.

By combining state-of-the-art deep learning techniques with practical implementation, this work aims to modernize structural inspection, improving safety, efficiency, and decision-making in infrastructure maintenance across developing regions.

2 Existing Methods for Pathology Detection

The detection of structural pathologies, such as cracks, spalling concrete, and corrosion, remains a critical challenge in civil engineering. Accurate identification and timely intervention are essential to ensure the safety and longevity of buildings, infrastructure as well as protecting human lives. Over the years, various detection methods have been employed, including manual inspections, non-destructive testing (NDT) techniques, and early digital tools. While each approach offers a set of advantages, their shortcomings emphasize the urgent necessity for innovative alternatives and more sophisticated and reliable solutions [4].

2.1 Manual Inspection: Strengths, Limitations and Solutions

Historically, Manual inspection has been the most widely used method for identifying structural pathologies and assessing structural integrity. This process involves engineers or inspectors visually examine structures, often supplemented by basic tools such as measuring tapes and flashlights. While this approach offers a straightforward and cost-effective approach, it is highly dependent on the expertise and experience of the inspector, introducing a significant degree of subjectivity. Despite its simplicity, manual inspection uncovers considerable limitations. First, it is time-intensive, particularly for large-scale structures like bridges, high-rise buildings, or dams. Second, it often fails to detect micro-level defects or subsurface damage, which can escalate into critical issues if left unaddressed. For example, a study by the Federal Highway Administration (FHWA) reported that over 60% of structural failures in bridges were directly linked to defects that have been overlooked during routine manual inspections (FHWA, 2020). Additionally, certain environments pose accessibility challenges, such as confined spaces or high elevations, where thorough manual examination could be potentially impractical or unsafe. These drawbacks emphasize the need for more reliable and scalable solutions in structural pathology detection.

The constraints related to conventional approaches highlight the need for creative an innovative solutions to pathology detection. AI-based detection tools present a promising alternative, offering several key advantages [5]:

- Consistency: Automated systems eliminate the variability associated with human subjectivity, ensuring assessment's uniformity.
- Efficiency: AI can process and analyze large datasets in real time, reducing inspection durations.
- Scalability: AI models can be integrated across mobile and web platforms, enabling on-site diagnostics for various applications.

The development of AI-driven intelligent pathology detection systems, as proposed in this study, represents a transformative step toward enhancing reliability, improving safety, and modernizing structural assessment practices. By leveraging deep learning techniques, these systems provide a scalable and trustworthy alternative that outperforms traditional inspection methods, meeting the industry's increasing demand for greater precision and efficiency.

2.2 AI in Civil Engineering

Artificial Intelligence is revolutionizing civil engineering by enhancing traditional practices and offering innovative solutions to long-standing challenges. AI-driven technologies including machine learning (ML), deep learning (DL), and computer vision enable the automation of labor-intensive tasks, improving efficiency, accuracy and scalability in areas like structural health monitoring, design optimization, and construction management. For instance, AI-powered tools analyze data from sensors embedded in bridges and buildings to detect stress, strain, and vibrations in real-time, while computer vision algorithms process images to identify structural defects like cracks, corrosion, or spalling concrete. These capabilities not only reduce human error but also allow for scalable assessments of large infrastructures, often using drone-captured imagery and enable cost-effective, continuous monitoring of extensive civil assets [6–8].

Beyond structural diagnostics, AI plays a crucial role in sustainable construction by optimizing material usage and predicting the environmental impact of designs, aligning with global sustainability goals [9]. Moreover, AI-driven models have been integrated into disaster risk assessment, using both historical and real-time data to predict natural hazards and simulate the resilience of structures under extreme conditions.

Despite its transformative potential, the widespread adoption of AI in civil engineering is hindered by several challenges and obstacles. High-quality annotated datasets are essential for training models; yet acquiring such data may be time-consuming and costly. Additionally, the complexity of deep learning models often leads to "black box" behavior, making them difficult to interpret and even trust in critical applications. Integration with traditional workflows and the lack of AI expertise in the industry further complicate implementation and large-scale deployment.

Looking ahead, AI's potential in civil engineering is vast and immensely promising. The development of digital twins—virtual replicas of physical structures—can facilitate proactive maintenance, while autonomous drones and robotic arms could conduct real-time repairs. Interdisciplinary integration with technologies like Building Information Modeling (BIM) and Geographic Information Systems (GIS) promises to reshape how infrastructure is designed, monitored and managed. By addressing current limitations, AI has the potential to not only enhance efficiency and reduce costs but also to ensure safer and more sustainable infrastructure for future generations [10,11].

2.3 Research Gap

Despite advancements in AI applications for civil engineering, several critical gaps persist. Traditional inspection methods, such as manual assessments and non-destructive techniques (NDT), are limited by scalability, cost, and accuracy [12]. Existing AI models often focus narrowly on specific pathologies, such as cracks, neglecting other critical issues like spalling and corrosion. Additionally, many AI models rely on imbalanced or limited datasets, reducing their robustness and generalizability to diverse structural conditions.

Another key gap is the lack of alignment with international standards, which are crucial for defect classification and severity assessment in real-world applications. Deployment challenges also persist, as AI tools are rarely tested in field conditions where environmental factors, such as lighting and weather, can degrade performance [13].

Finally, AI interpretability remains a significant barrier. Engineers often struggle to trust "black-box" models, limiting their practical adoption. Addressing these issues requires balanced datasets, alignment with industry standards, and transparent, field-deployable tools. This research seeks to bridge these gaps by developing an AI-driven pathology detection system that prioritizes transparency and practical application [14].

3 Methodology

3.1 Data Collection, Preprocessing and Annotation

In this project, data collection played a pivotal role in developing an effective AI model for structural pathology detection. A total of 3,608 images were collected from multiple sources to ensure a diverse and representative sample of structural pathologies. Crack images were sourced from Mendeley [15], corrosion images were obtained from GitHub [16], and spalling concrete images were accessed via Roboflow [17]. These images were curated to encompass various environmental conditions, lighting scenarios, and angles to improve the robustness and generalizability of the model. A subset of the dataset was created by selecting 902 images from each source to guarantee balanced and equal representation across structural pathologies as shown in Table 1. To prepare the dataset for training, annotations were performed using Label Studio, a versatile open-source tool for labeling data. Each image was meticulously annotated to precisely mark the exact regions corresponding to specific structural pathologies.

Table 1. Dataset distribution across structural pathologies.

Pathology Type	Number of Images	Percentage (%)	Conditions Represented
Cracks	902	25%	Varying widths, in-door/outdoor, different orientations
Spalling Concrete	902	25%	Different severity levels, lighting variations
Corrosion	902	25%	Rust intensity, environmental conditions
Normal/No pathology	902	25%	Clean surfaces, varying textures, lighting conditions
Total	3608		

3.2 AI Model Development

To develop a robust pathology detection model for structural analysis, we initially selected VGG16, a widely used Convolutional Neural Network (CNN) architecture developed by the Visual Geometry Group at the University of Oxford [18,19]. VGG16's structured architecture, consisting of 16 weight layers with small 3×3 convolutional filters and max-pooling layers, made it a suitable candidate for transfer learning. Its pre-trained weights on ImageNet, a dataset containing over 1.2 million images across 1,000 classes, provided a strong initialization, particularly beneficial given our relatively small dataset of 3,608 images. We modified the original classification head by replacing it with a custom network tailored to detect three types of structural pathologies: cracks, corrosion, and spalling concrete. This involved removing the fully connected layers and introducing a Flatten layer, a Dense layer with 512 neurons, a Dropout layer for regularization, and a final Dense layer with three output neurons. To retain the general features learned from ImageNet, we applied a freezing mechanism to the lower layers, ensuring that only the newly added layers were trained.

To leverage the pre-trained knowledge of VGG16 while adapting it to our dataset, we froze the lower convolutional layers, ensuring that only the newly added layers were trainable.

However, despite these adaptations, several challenges emerged when using VGG16. The model exhibited signs of overfitting, even with extensive data augmentation techniques such as rotation, flipping, and zooming. Additionally, its fixed receptive fields limited its ability to capture complex structural features, particularly in detecting corrosion patterns. Furthermore, the computational inefficiency of VGG16 made it less practical for high-resolution structural images, as training times were significantly longer compared to more modern architectures. To overcome these limitations, we transitioned to ResNet50, a deep CNN architecture that leverages residual learning through skip connections [20]. ResNet50, with its 50-layer depth, offers improved feature extraction capabilities while mitigating the vanishing gradient problem through its residual blocks [21]. These skip connections allow information to bypass certain layers, preventing degradation in deep networks and enhancing gradient flow during backpropagation [22]. This architectural advancement enables more effective learning of complex visual patterns, making ResNet50 particularly suitable for detecting fine-grained structural anomalies such as corrosion and spalling. Compared to VGG16, ResNet50 offers several advantages:

- Deeper architecture: Its deeper network structure enhanced feature extraction and representation of complex structural patterns.
- Residual connections: Refined gradient flow, accelerated convergence, and mitigated vanishing gradient issues.
- Enhanced generalization: Distinguished subtle pathology variations.
- Computational efficiency: Reduced parameter complexity and optimized training times.
- Scalability: Demonstrated effectiveness and better versatility across various computer vision tasks.

By integrating ResNet50 into our pathology detection model, we achieved improved generalization, reduced overfitting, and enhanced computational efficiency, making it a more suitable framework and practical solution for our structural health monitoring application.

Hyperparameter Optimization. Hyperparameter optimization played a crucial role in refining the performance of the ResNet50-based model by systematically adjusting key parameters such as the learning rate, batch size, number of epochs, and regularization techniques. Initially, the learning rate was set to 0.001 to enable substantial weight updates in the early stages of training, while a batch size of 32 was selected to balance computational efficiency and convergence speed. The model was trained for 20 epochs, leveraging the Adam optimizer for its adaptive learning rate and momentum-based updates. During training, early stopping was implemented to prevent overfitting and unnecessary computation by halting training when validation loss failed to improve for a set number of epochs, ensuring an optimal balance between generalization and efficiency. Additionally, a learning rate scheduler, ReduceLROnPlateau, was employed to enhance model stability and convergence by dynamically reducing the learning rate when validation loss showed no improvement. To further refine performance, various regularization strategies were employed, including increasing dropout to 0.7 to mitigate overfitting, incorporating batch normalization to stabilize training and improve generalization, and employing extensive data augmentation techniques such as rotation (up to 25°), zooming (up to 30%), horizontal and vertical shifts (up to 15%), and horizontal flipping.

As summarized in Table 2, the final optimized configuration involved a reduced learning rate of 0.0001 for finer weight updates in later epochs, an increased number of epochs to 50 for sufficient iterations without overfitting, the Adam optimizer for improved convergence, categorical cross-entropy as the loss function suitable for multi-class classification, an intense augmentation strategy to enhance model robustness, and early stopping with a patience parameter of 8 to prevent unnecessary computations when no improvements were observed. These optimizations led to significant improvements in model performance, including reduced overfitting, as evidenced by a minimal gap between training and validation accuracies, increased robustness to unseen data through advanced augmentation techniques, and improved convergence stability through dynamic learning rate adjustments. Collectively, these strategies refined the ResNet50-based model, making it highly effective for detecting structural pathologies in civil engineering applications.

3.3 Integration of Eurocode Standards

To align structural health monitoring (SHM) predictions with internationally recognized engineering norms, the developed AI model incorporates Eurocode standards, which provide rigorous guidelines for evaluating structural integrity, diagnosing pathologies, and recommending interventions. By embedding Eurocode principles within the AI framework, the system enhances regulatory compliance with standardized practices while enabling automated, data-driven diagnostics. Additionally, an interactive feature leveraging the OpenAI API was implemented to bridge gaps in the model's diagnostic depth, allowing users to query detected pathologies and receive actionable guidance.

Pathology-to-Eurocode Mapping Framework. The AI model detects structural pathologies (e.g., cracks, corrosion, spalling) and systematically maps them to Eurocode guidelines via a rule-based layer. While time constraints limited the current implementation to foundational rules, the framework establishes measurable thresholds for preliminary compliance checks. Key mappings include:

Table 2. Optimized hyperparamter configuration for ResNet50-based pathology detection model.

Hyperparameter	Values	Explanation
Learning Rate	0.0001	Reduced dynamically to allow finer updates in later epochs
Epochs	50	Ensured sufficient iterations for convergence without overfitting
Optimizer	Adam	Adaptive optimizer for faster convergence
Loss Function	Categorical Cross-Entropy	Suitable for multi-class classification
Dropout	0.7	Reduced overfitting by deactivation 70% of neurons randomly during training
Augmentation	Intense	Enhanced robustness with rotations, shifts, flips, and zooms
Early Stopping	Patience = 8	Prevented overfitting by stopping training early when no improvements were observed
Learning Rate Scheduler	ReduceLROnPlateau	Adjusted learning rate dynamically based on validation loss trends

- Cracks in concrete (Eurocode 2: EN 1992-1-1): Crack width estimated from annotated training data, triggers alerts. Cracks exceeding 0.3 mm are flagged as critical; narrower cracks are monitored for progression.
- Corrosion (Eurocode 3: EN 1993-1-4): Any detected corrosion prompts an inspection recommendation, though severity classification remains an area for future enhancement through environmental data integration and rust pattern analysis.
- Spalling concrete (Eurocode 2: EN 1992-1-1): Spalling is deemed critical if annotations reveal exposed reinforcement or significant material loss. Future enhancements will incorporate concrete cover thickness metrics for risk evaluation.
- Structures without detected pathologies are classified as "normal" but include routine inspection reminders to ensure sustained compliance.

Interactive Diagnostics via OpenAI API. To compensate the model's current limitations in Eurocode-compliant severity assessment, an OpenAI API-driven interface was integrated. This feature enables users to submit contextual queries (e.g., "What repairs are suitable for a 0.5 mm crack?") and receive responses synthesized from Eurocode standards, engineering best practices, and the model's outputs. For example:

- Crack-related queries return severity explanations, repair methods (e.g., epoxy injection), and monitoring protocols.

- Corrosion or spalling inquiries generate preventative measures (e.g., protective coatings, cathodic protection) along with suggested inspection schedules.

This hybrid approach—combining automated detection with interactive consultation—enhances diagnostic utility, empowering engineers to make informed maintenance decisions despite the model's nascent rule-based system.

Limitations and Future Directions. While the current implementation prioritizes foundational compliance checks, it still requires refinement to fully align with Eurocode's nuanced requirements. Future work will integrate environmental sensors (e.g., humidity, chloride exposure) for corrosion severity classification and LiDAR-derived concrete cover measurements for spalling risk assessment. Expanding the rule-based system with probabilistic models could further improve diagnostic accuracy, enabling dynamic adaptation to site-specific conditions. This integration of Eurocode standards, AI-driven detection, and interactive guidance represents a scalable paradigm for SHM, balancing regulatory compliance with user-centric innovation.

4 Results

This section presents a detailed performance evaluation of the pathology detection model, supported by various metrics, visualizations, and real-world testing. The results are designed to offer a comprehensive understanding of the model's strengths and weaknesses, offering valuable insights for future improvements, refinement and optimization in subsequent iterations.

4.1 Model Performance

The performance of the pathology detection model was evaluated using several key metrics, including accuracy, precision, recall, F1-score, and a confusion matrix. These metrics provide an in-depth view of the model's effectiveness in identifying different structural pathologies.

4.2 Key Metrics

Table 3 summarizes the key performance metrics for the model based on the evaluation conducted on the test dataset:

The results indicate that the model effectively detects pathologies with a high level of overall accuracy. The close alignment between validation accuracy and training performance suggests a well-generalized model.

The accompanying graph illustrates the training loss and validation loss of our model over a series of epochs, alongside an indicator for early stopping (Fig. 1).

Table 3. Evaluation Metrics of the Pathology Detection Model on the Test Dataset.

Evaluation metric	Value
Accuracy	86.73%
Loss	0.1825
Validation Loss	0.1768
Validation Accuracy	87.26%

- The training loss (Blue line) remains consistently low and stable across all epochs, indicating that the model is fitting the training data well. There is no noticeable increase or fluctuation encountered in this line.
- The validation loss (Orange line) initially decreases, reflecting successful learning. Meanwhile, after reaching its minimum around epoch 3, the validation loss tends to increase significantly, particularly after epoch 10. This suggests the onset of overfitting, where the model starts to memorize the training data instead of generalizing to unseen data.
- The red dashed line marks the point at which early stopping was triggered. This mechanism prevents further training once the validation loss ceases to improve, ensuring that the model maintains its generalization ability while avoiding overfitting.

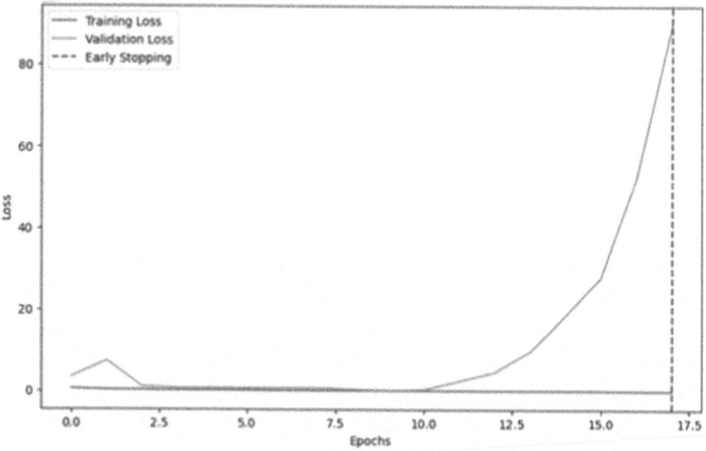

Fig. 1. Training and Validation Loss with Early Stopping Over Multiple Epochs.

The early stopping mechanism worked effectively, as it halts training when the validation loss started to increase, preventing the model from overfitting. The stability of the training loss compared to the sharp rise in validation loss confirms that the model could overfit the data if training continued.

Figure 2 shows the training and validation accuracies over a series of epochs.

- Training accuracy starts at a relatively high value and steadily continues to improve, eventually stabilizing at a value close to 1.0. This indicates that the model performs very well on the training data and learns effectively.
- Validation accuracy rises sharply and appears to peak around epoch 9. Beyond this point, it starts to drop significantly, falling to a much lower value by epoch 10 and stabilizing at a very poor accuracy level.

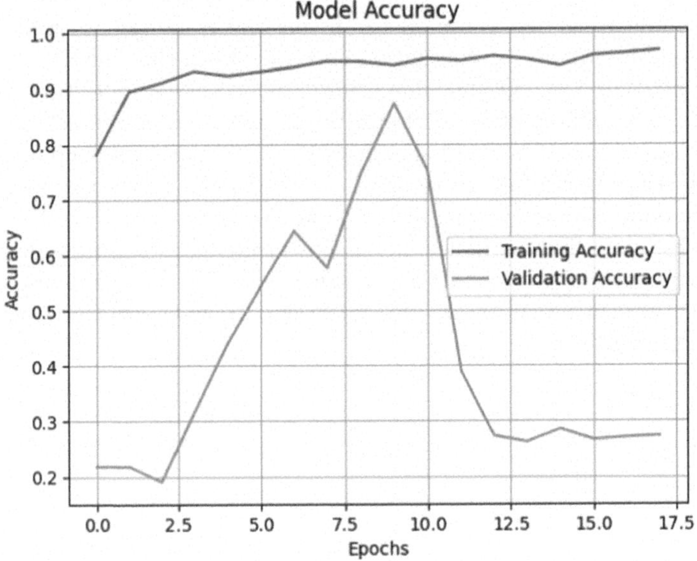

Fig. 2. Model Accuracy trends Over Multiple Epochs.

This discrepancy between training and validation accuracy is an obvious indication of overfitting; the model learns patterns in the training data that do not generalize well to the validation data. The model could have benefited from early stopping around epoch 9, where validation accuracy peaked. Extending training beyond this point leads to a significant drop in generalization performance. The graph reflected a well-performing model in the training set but highlighted the need for better generalization to mitigate overfitting.

4.3 Pathology-Specific Metrics

To evaluate the performance of the model on each specific type of pathology, we computed precision, recall, and F1-score for each category as shown in Table 4. These metrics provide a more granular understanding of how well the model detects each pathology type:

Table 4. Performance Metrics For Each Pathology Category.

Pathology	Precision	Recall	F1-score	Support
Corrosion	0.93	0.85	0.89	181
Cracks	0.80	0.93	0.86	192
Spalling	0.81	0.73	0.77	157
Normal Structure	0.95	0.96	0.96	192

- Corrosion: The model demonstrated a high precision of 93% in detecting corrosion, indicating that it rarely misclassified other pathologies as corrosion. However, its recall was slightly lower at 85%, suggesting that some instance of corrosion were missed during detection. This points the need to further refinement to improve the sensitivity in capturing all corrosion-related cases.
- Cracks: The model achieved a relatively balanced performance for cracks, with a precision of 80% and a recall of 93%. While the recall indicates that the model was able to identify most of the cracks, there was still some misclassified (with a lower precision). The model might benefit from additional refinement to reduce false positives.
- Spalling: Spalling concrete had the lowest performance, with a recall of 73%, which shows that the model had difficulty detecting all instances of spalling. However, its precision was higher at 81%, indicating fewer false positives. Misclassifications between spalling and cracks were more frequent, suggesting that the model may struggle to distinguish between these two visually similar pathologies, requiring further feature enhancement.
- Normal Structure: The highest performance was observed for the detection of normal structures, with a precision of 95% and a recall of 96%. This indicates that the model is very effective at identifying undamaged structures, which is crucial for accurately categorizing non-pathological samples and minimizing false alarms.

4.4 Confusion Matrix Analysis

The confusion matrix illustrated in Fig. 3, offers a more detailed view of the model's classification performance across all pathology categories. By visualizing the true positives, false positives, true negatives, and false negatives, we can identify key areas where the model may have underperformed.

- Normal structures were consistently detected with high accuracy and minimal misclassifications.
- Corrosion was mostly correctly identified, though some cases were misclassified as cracks or spalling.
- Cracks was commonly confused with spalling, leading to some misclassifications, particularly in cases with less obvious crack feature.

- Spalling faced the greatest challenge in detection, with several instances being misclassified as cracks or even corrosion.

These observations reveal areas for improvement, particularly in improving the model's ability to distinguish between spalling and cracks, as well as increasing its sensitivity to subtle corrosion cases.

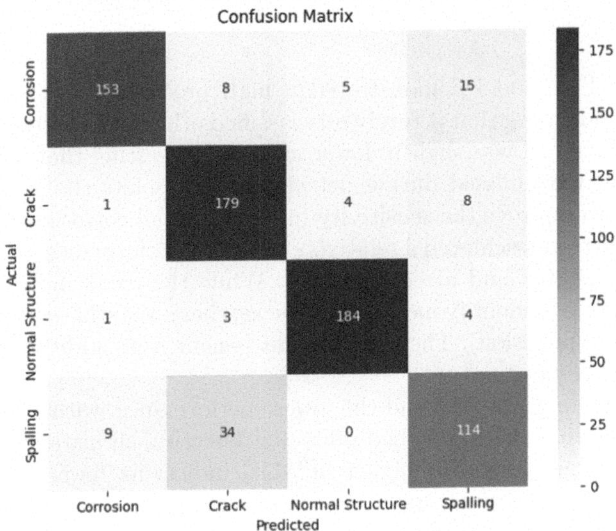

Fig. 3. Confusion Matrix.

4.5 Overall Performance

To summarize the model's overall performance across all categories, we computed the macro average for precision, recall, and F1-score as presented in Table 5. These macro averages provide an unbiased evaluation and a balanced view of the model's performance by treating each pathology equally, regardless of the class distribution.

Table 5. Evaluation Metrics of the Pathology Detection Model on the Test Dataset.

Evaluation metric	Value
Macro Average Precision	0.87
Macro Average Recall	0.87
Macro Average F1-score	0.87

These results indicate that the model performs well across all categories, achieving a balanced trade-off on precision and recall. The overall F1-score of 0.87 shows that the model effectively minimizes both false positives and false negatives, offering a reliable solution for pathology detection.

5 Comparative Analysis with Related Work

To place the current model's performance in context, we compared it with findings from recent literature. Arafin et al. conducted a comprehensive study on concrete pathology classification using deep learning, achieving segmentation accuracy in the range of 86%–91% across various defect types [23].

Their model—based on an InceptionV3 CNN classifier pretrained on ImageNet—reported the following key results:

- Crack detection F1-score: 95.66%.
- Spalling detection F1-score: 89.43%.
- Overall accuracy: 91%.
- Precision: 83%.
- Recall: 100%.

Guo et al. developed MCD-Net, a multi-path CNN model for detecting metal corrosion. Their model achieved an F1-score of 84.53% on a public corrosion dataset, surpassing other conventional deep learning methods such as U-Net, Deeplabv3+, and Swin-U-Net, which reported F1-scores between 76.89% and 81.69% [24].

In contrast, our model achieved a higher corrosion F1-score of 89%, suggesting better detection accuracy. Although Guo et al.'s model emphasizes speed and practical deployment, our approach balances performance across multiple pathology types, offering higher precision in corrosion detection and consistent classification in normal structure and cracks.

While our model demonstrates competitive performance, particularly in detecting cracks and normal structures, it underperforms in spalling detection relative to Arafin et al. Their model's exceptional recall of 100% suggests superior generalization, possibly due to more advanced feature extraction or better data augmentation. Our model, though effective and computationally efficient, shows room for improvement in handling more complex and subtle defect patterns, especially spalling.

Nonetheless, our use of early stopping and robust validation ensures generalizability and makes the model suitable for deployment in resource-constrained environments where interpretability and speed are prioritized over absolute precision.

6 Conclusion

The primary objective of this study was to develop a robust and efficient AI-driven system for detecting structural pathologies in civil engineering, with a particular emphasis on cracks, corrosion, and spalling concrete. By integrating deep learning techniques with a carefully curated and balanced dataset, this study demonstrated the feasibility of automated pathology detection with a high accuracy. The proposed model achieved an overall accuracy of 86.73%, with a validation accuracy of 87.26%, underscoring its potential for real-world applications.

A key contribution is the alignment of AI-based defect classification with Eurocode guidelines, particularly in crack width diagnostics, positioning Aigis as a decision-support tool rather than a simple classifier. In contrast to studies relying on extensive proprietary or imbalanced datasets [7,8], Aigis achieves competitive performance using a modest, balanced dataset, enhanced through transfer learning and augmentation.

Furthermore, the integration of conversational AI—leveraging models like OpenAI's GPT—enhances user engagement and interpretability. However, this component remains experimental and requires further evaluation in operational contexts.

Despite these contributions, several limitations must be acknowledged. These include the need for validation in complex real-world scenarios and the extension to broader structural codes and pathology types. Future work should explore, among other directions, severity assessment, temporal analysis, and predictive maintenance.

Overall, Aigis advances the application of AI in structural health monitoring by bridging engineering standards, usability, and data challenges, setting the stage for intelligent, scalable infrastructure assessment.

References

1. World Economic Forum: The Global Competitiveness Report 2019. Report No. 12345-WEF (2019). https://www3.weforum.org/docs/WEFTheGlobalCompetitivenessReport2019.pdf. https://openknowledge.worldbank.org/server/api/core/bitstreams/b137066e-2e97-5bc3-bfa5-5114181ddcd5/content
2. AlHamaydeh, M., Ghazal Aswad, N.: Structural health monitoring techniques and technologies for large-scale structures: challenges, limitations, and recommendations. In: Practice Periodical on Structural Design and Construction 27 (2022). https://doi.org/10.1061/(ASCE)SC.1943-5576.0000703
3. Nex, F., et al.: Structural building damage detection with deep learning: assessment of a state-of-the-art CNN in operational conditions. Remote Sens. **11**(23), 2765 (2019). https://doi.org/10.3390/rs11232765
4. Kim, B., Cho, S.: Automated vision-based detection of cracks on concrete surfaces using a deep learning technique. Sensors **18**(10), 3452 (2018). https://doi.org/10.3390/s18103452
5. de Nogueira Diniz, J.C., et al.: A method for detecting pathologies in concrete structures using deep neural networks. Appl. Sci. **13**(9), 5763 (2023). https://doi.org/10.3390/app13095763
6. Avci, O., Abdeljaber, O., Kiranyaz, S.: An overview of deep learning methods used in vibration-based damage detection in civil engineering. In: Grimmelsman,

K. (ed.) Dynamics of Civil Structures, Volume 2. CPSEMS, pp. 93–98. Springer, Cham (2022). https://doi.org/10.1007/978-3-030-77143-0_10
7. Zhang, L., et al.: A review of the research and application of deep learning-based computer vision in structural damage detection. Earthq. Eng. Eng. Vibr. **21**(1), 1–21 (2022). ISSN: 1993-503X. https://doi.org/10.1007/s11803-022-2074-7
8. Zou, Q., et al.: DeepCrack: learning hierarchical convolutional features for crack detection. IEEE Trans. Image Process. **28**(3), 1498–1512 (2019). https://doi.org/10.1109/TIP.2018.2878966
9. Regona, M., et al.: Artificial intelligence and sustainable development goals: systematic literature review of the construction industry. Sustain. Cities Soc. **108**, 105499 (2024). ISSN: 2210-6707. https://doi.org/10.1016/j.scs.2024.105499
10. Pan, Y., Zhang, L.: Integrating BIM and AI for smart construction management: current status and future directions. Arch. Comput. Methods Eng. **30**, 1081–1110 (2023). https://doi.org/10.1007/s11831-022-09830-8
11. BibLus Editorial Team: Generative AI in Civil Engineering: Applications, Benefits, and Future Challenges (2025). https://biblus.accasoftware.com/en/ai-in-civil-engineering-6-application-examples-all-the-advantages-and-new-challenges-for-the-future/?utmsource=chatgpt.com
12. Ye, X.W., et al.: A review on deep learning-based structural health monitoring of civil infrastructures. Smart Struct. Syst. **24**, 567–585 (2019). https://doi.org/10.12989/sss.2019.24.5.567
13. Taghi, S., et al.: Vision-based autonomous structural damage detection using data-driven methods (2024). https://doi.org/10.48550/arXiv.2501.16662
14. Serhii, N.: Enhanced Model Tree Application Framework for Developing Interpretable AI in Construction Engineering. Master's thesis (2020). https://doi.org/10.7939/r3-va9b-1r71
15. Hamed, J., et al.: Cracks in Concrete Structures (CICS) Dataset. Mendeley Data **V1** (2023). https://doi.org/10.17632/9brnm3c39k.1
16. Sun, P.: Phase5 Capstone-Project: CORROSION dataset. GitHub (2024). https://github.com/pjsun2012/Phase5Capstone-Project/tree/main/data/CORROSION. Accessed 12 Dec 2024
17. CViSSLab. ZhangDataset. Roboflow Universe (2024). https://universe.roboflow.com/cvisslab/zhang-3seb8. Accessed 12 Dec 2024
18. Simonyan, K., Zisserman, A.: Very deep convolutional networks for large-scale image recognition. In: International Conference on Learning Representations (ICLR) (2015). https://arxiv.org/abs/1409.1556
19. Arif, M.A.: Understanding VGG16: a powerful deep learning model for image recognition. A comprehensive guide to the VGG16 architecture, its applications, and how to use it in your projects (2023). https://smuhabdullah.medium.com/understanding-vgg16-a-powerful-deep-learning-model-for-image-recognition-d40b074fd01c
20. He, K., et al.: Deep residual learning for image recognition. In: IEEE Conference on Computer Vision and Pattern Recognition (CVPR) (2016). https://arxiv.org/abs/1512.03385
21. Wisdomml. Understanding ResNet-50 in Depth: Architecture, Skip Connections, and Advantages over other Networks (2023). https://wisdomml.in/understanding-resnet-50-in-depth-architecture-skip-connections-and-advantages-over-other-networks/
22. Mukherjee, S.: The annotated ResNet-50: Explaining how ResNet-50 works and why it is so popular (2022). https://medium.com/towards-data-science/the-annotated-resnet-50-a6c536034758

23. Arafin, P., Muntasir Billah, A.H.M., Issa, A.: Deep learning-based concrete defects classification and detection using semantic segmentation. Struct. Health Monitor. **23**(1), 383–409 (2024). https://doi.org/10.1177/14759217231168212
24. Guo, J., Wang, L., Hua, L.: Efficient metal corrosion area detection model combining convolution and transformer. Appl. Sci. **14**(21), 9900 (2024). https://doi.org/10.3390/app14219900

Smart Cities and Smart Agriculture

Enhancing Food Security Through Intelligent Decision Support: A Crop Decision Framework for Small-Scale Farmers in South Africa

Naledi Thothela(✉), Elisha Markus, and Muthoni Masinde

Central University of Technology, Bloemfontein, South Africa
nthothela@cut.ac.za

Abstract. Food security remains a critical challenge in Africa, exacerbated by climate change, resource mismanagement, and inefficiencies in agricultural decision-making. This paper introduces the Decision Support System (DSS) Framework, an intelligent decision support system designed to optimize agricultural productivity and resource allocation. By leveraging data analytics, machine learning, and IoT integration, the framework provides actionable insights for small-scale farmers, policymakers, and agribusiness stakeholders. The study evaluates the framework's effectiveness in predictive crop management, supply chain optimization, and real-time decision-making. Our results indicate that the IACDSS framework significantly enhances agricultural resilience and food production efficiency, positioning it as a transformative tool for AgriTech and food security initiatives.

Keywords: Artificial Intelligences (AI) · Indigenous Knowledge (IK) · Machine Learnings (ML) · Crop decision-making · Small-scale farmers · Sensor technology

1 Introduction

Agriculture plays a pivotal role in Africa's economy, contributing significantly to employment and food production. However, food security challenges persist due to erratic climate patterns, poor resource distribution, and outdated farming techniques. The integration of AgriTech solutions, such as data-driven decision support systems, has the potential to mitigate these challenges.

Small-scale agriculture plays a crucial role in global food security, particularly in Sub-Saharan Africa, where nearly 80% of food production comes from smallholder farmers [1]. However, these farmers face numerous challenges, including climate unpredictability, limited access to modern agricultural technology, and reliance on Indigenous Knowledge (IK) for decision-making [2]. The impact of climate change has further exacerbated the vulnerability of smallholder farming communities, with frequent droughts and erratic rainfall reducing crop yields and increasing food insecurity [3, 4].

To address these challenges, Information and Communication Technologies (ICTs) and data-driven approaches such as Artificial Intelligence (AI) and Machine Learning (ML) have emerged as viable solutions [5, 6]. ML-based decision support systems

F. Kamoun et al. (Eds.): AFRICATEK 2025, LNICST 676, pp. 259–273, 2026.
https://doi.org/10.1007/978-3-032-16635-7_17

can provide data-driven insights on optimal crop selection, leveraging climatic and soil (edaphic) data to improve farming decisions [7, 8]. Despite the increasing adoption of AI in precision agriculture, the integration of IK into ML-driven agricultural decision support systems remains an underexplored area [9]. Traditional farming communities continue to rely on generational knowledge of weather patterns and soil conditions, which, if systematically combined with AI models, can enhance decision accuracy and promote technology adoption [10, 11].

This study proposes an Intelligent Agro-Climate Decision Support System (IACDSS) that integrates IK with ML techniques to improve pre-planting crop selection for small-scale farmers in Pietermaritzburg, South Africa. The system utilizes supervised learning algorithms to analyse edaphic and climatic data and provides farmers with accurate recommendations on the best crops to plant [12, 13]. The research aims to bridge the gap between modern AI-driven farming and traditional knowledge systems, ensuring that smallholder farmers benefit from cutting-edge technological advancements while maintaining trust in their ancestral farming practices [14].

The remainder of this paper is structured as follows: Sect. 2 provides a review of related work on AI applications in agriculture and Indigenous Knowledge systems. Section 3 details the methodology, including data collection and ML model training. Section 4 presents the results, while Sect. 5 discusses the implications and potential scalability of the proposed framework. Section 9 concludes the study and outlines future work.

2 Related Literature

2.1 Mobile Technology in Sub-Saharan Africa

Information and Communication Technologies (ICTs), particularly mobile technology, have become a crucial tool for bridging the digital divide in Sub-Saharan Africa. Despite progress in internet accessibility, Africa continues to lag behind other regions in terms of digital inclusion [1]. However, mobile phone penetration has significantly increased, with over 63% of the population using mobile devices as their primary means of internet access [2]. Mobile phones offer cost-effective solutions, enabling farmers to receive agricultural advisories, weather forecasts, and market prices in real-time [3]. The widespread availability of mobile phones makes them an ideal platform for deploying decision support systems (DSS) to assist small-scale farmers [4]. Various mobile applications, such as DrumNet in Kenya, have demonstrated success in linking smallholder farmers with financial institutions and input suppliers, ultimately improving productivity and income generation [5].

2.2 Mobile Technology in Agriculture

Mobile technology has revolutionized agricultural decision support systems by facilitating real-time communication and enhancing access to critical information [6]. Farmers use mobile-based applications to access weather updates, pest control measures, and precision farming insights. However, despite the potential benefits, adoption rates remain low among small-scale farmers due to technological illiteracy, affordability constraints, and scepticism toward digital tools [7]. Decision support tools tailored to smallholder farmers must address these challenges by integrating local knowledge and user-friendly interfaces [8]. The DrumNet platform has proven that mobile advisory services can improve agricultural decision-making, but more research is needed to enhance adoption at scale [9].

2.3 Indigenous Knowledge and Its Role in Small-Scale Farming

Indigenous Knowledge (IK) plays a critical role in agricultural decision-making among small-scale farmers. Rooted in centuries of observation and experience, IK systems help farmers predict weather patterns, soil fertility, and crop suitability [10]. This knowledge is typically passed down through generations, incorporating environmental cues such as animal behaviour, plant phenology, and cloud formations to guide planting and harvesting decisions [11]. Despite the growing reliance on modern technologies, IK remains a primary tool for decision-making in many rural farming communities [12]. Research indicates that over 80% of smallholder farmers in Kenya, Zambia, and Zimbabwe continue to use IK for their agricultural decisions, highlighting its enduring relevance [13]. However, as climate change intensifies, traditional forecasting methods may require scientific reinforcement through data-driven decision support systems [14].

2.4 Integrating Indigenous Knowledge with ICTs for Agricultural Decision Support

The integration of IK with ICT-based decision support systems can improve the adoption of AI-driven tools in small-scale farming. Studies suggest that combining AI with IK enhances the accuracy and reliability of agricultural predictions, particularly for climate variability and soil conditions [15]. Decision support frameworks such as ITIKI (Indigenous Knowledge and Technology Integration for Climate Information) have successfully integrated traditional knowledge with AI-based climate forecasting models, improving smallholder resilience to droughts [16]. By embedding IK into machine learning algorithms, farmers are more likely to trust and adopt AI-driven agricultural solutions [17]. This hybrid approach ensures that technology remains culturally relevant and contextually applicable [18].

2.5 Decision Support Systems for Small-Scale Farmers

Decision Support Systems (DSS) are essential for optimizing crop selection, yield prediction, and farm management. DSS platforms typically rely on satellite data, IoT sensors, and predictive analytics to assist farmers in decision-making [19]. However, in Sub-Saharan Africa, DSS adoption remains limited due to high costs, limited internet connectivity, and lack of localized solutions [20]. To address these challenges, mobile-based DSS with offline functionality and IK integration have been proposed as viable alternatives [21]. Previous studies have demonstrated that AI-driven DSS can significantly enhance agricultural efficiency, but further research is needed to refine these models for smallholder adoption [22].

2.6 Application of Artificial Intelligence in Agriculture

Artificial Intelligence (AI) and Machine Learning (ML) are transforming agriculture by enabling real-time crop monitoring, yield prediction, and disease detection [23]. AI models can process vast amounts of climatic and edaphic data to optimize decision-making [24]. Recent studies indicate that machine learning algorithms such as Support Vector Machines (SVM) and Artificial Neural Networks (ANN) have achieved high accuracy in predicting crop suitability [25]. However, AI adoption remains low due to a lack of farmer trust, high implementation costs, and limited access to training [26]. To overcome these barriers, AI models must be designed to be explainable, accessible, and adaptable to small-scale farming conditions [27].

2.7 The Role of Fuzzy Inference Systems in Crop Decision Support

Fuzzy Inference Systems (FIS) have been explored as an alternative AI-driven decision support tool for agriculture. These systems allow for uncertainty handling and linguistic-based decision-making, making them highly adaptable to imprecise farming conditions [27]. Studies have demonstrated that FIS-based models can improve crop disease diagnosis and optimize planting schedules [9]. The ITIKI framework successfully leveraged fuzzy logic and AI to deliver localized weather forecasting for small-scale farmers, demonstrating its potential for broader agricultural applications [27].

2.8 Summary and Research Gap

While substantial progress has been made in AI-driven agriculture, a critical gap remains in the integration of Indigenous Knowledge (IK) with machine learning models for small-scale farming. Existing DSS platforms do not sufficiently incorporate local knowledge systems, leading to low adoption rates among rural farmers. This study seeks to bridge this gap by developing an Intelligent Agro-Climate Decision Support System (IACDSS) that integrates AI-driven predictions with IK-based decision-making. By doing so, this research contributes to the growing field of context-aware, culturally relevant agricultural decision support tools.

3 Methodology

This study follows an inductive research approach, focusing on the integration of Machine Learning (ML) and Indigenous Knowledge (IK) to develop a pre-planting crop selection framework for small-scale farmers. The methodology consists of four primary phases: data collection and pre-processing, machine learning model development, framework implementation, and evaluation of system performance (Fig. 1).

3.1 Data Pre-processing

The study utilized three main data sources: Indigenous Knowledge (IK) from local farmers and climatic data from the South African Weather Service (SAWS) and edaphic data

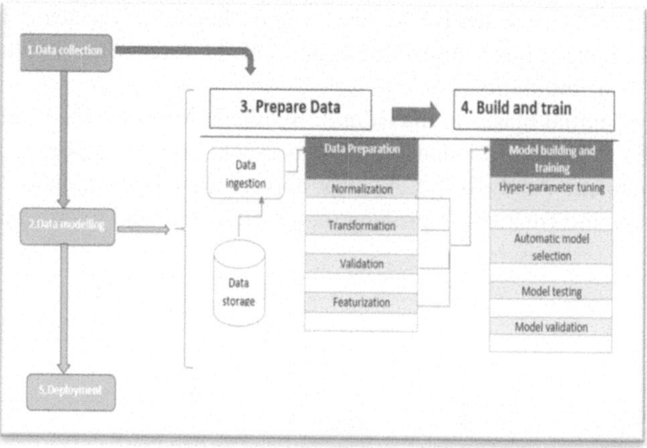

Fig. 1. Machine learning process

from official agricultural records. Structured questionnaires and focus group discussions were conducted with 50 small-scale farmers in Pietermaritzburg to document traditional farming practices, weather prediction techniques, and local indicators of soil fertility. The collected IK data were transcribed, categorized, and mapped against historical climatic patterns for validation [1, 2].

Historical climatic data for the previous 15 years were obtained from the South African Weather Service (SAWS). The key variables included temperature, rainfall and humidity. Edaphic data were obtained from the Department of Agriculture, Land Reform, and Rural Development (DALRRD). These variables included soil pH, and nutrient levels, namely nitrogen, phosphorus, and potassium, as well as Temperature, Humidity and rainfall for 5 chosen crops in the area. To address inconsistencies in data sources, missing values were managed using mean imputation techniques, and feature scaling was applied using MinMax normalization to standardize data distributions [25].

Data augmentation was utilized to develop a synthetic dataset comprising of 750 labelled records using this available data, and the planting calendar for the area. A train-test split of 80% training and 20% test was used to train the model.

3.2 Model Development

A multi-class classification approach was employed to determine the most suitable crops for specific climatic and soil conditions. The algorithm selection process is shown in Fig. 2. Five ML models were considered: Decision Trees, Random Forest, Gradient Boosting, K-Nearest Neighbors (KNN), and Support Vector Machines (SVM). After evaluating model performance using 10-fold cross-validation on the training set, Random Forest and KNN achieved the highest training accuracy of 100%, while SVM achieved an accuracy of 99% [5]. However, upon evaluation on the test set, SVM exhibited a more consistent generalization performance with slightly better robustness against overfitting compared to Random Forest and KNN. Feature importance analysis using 10-fold cross-validation revealed that temperature, rainfall, and soil pH were the most influential factors in determining crop suitability [6].

To address potential biases in the dataset, Synthetic Minority Over-sampling Technique (SMOTE) was used to balance underrepresented crop categories. Additionally, Principal Component Analysis (PCA) was applied to reduce dimensionality while preserving critical information, improving model efficiency and interpretability [7, 8].

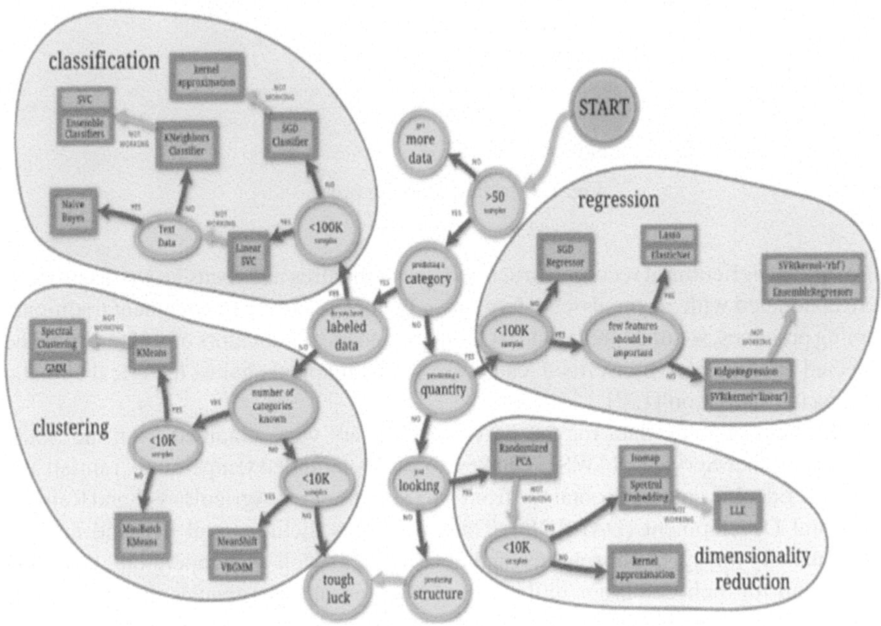

Fig. 2. Machine learning process for Algorithm selection [27]

4 Framework Implementation

The Intelligent Agro-Climate Decision Support System (IACDSS) was developed as a mobile-based application to provide farmers with real-time crop recommendations. The system integrates:

ML predictions based on climate and soil conditions.

IK validation mechanisms, ensuring alignment with traditional knowledge.

A reconciliation mechanism where conflicting recommendations are resolved through expert consultation or intercropping alternatives [9].

The application was designed with a user-friendly interface, supporting multiple South African languages and delivering results via SMS notifications and in-app messages for accessibility in low-internet regions [10] (Fig. 3).

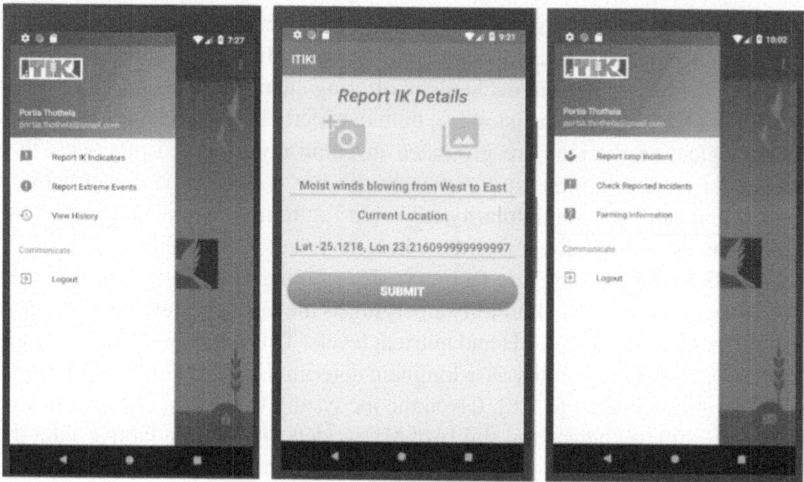

Fig. 3. Mobile application interface

5 Evaluation of System Performance

Model performance was assessed using accuracy, precision, recall, and F1-score metrics. Additionally, a user acceptance study was conducted with 20 farmers to evaluate the system's ease of use, reliability, and perceived benefits. The results indicated a 78% adoption willingness rate, with farmers expressing confidence in recommendations that aligned with IK [12].

6 Discussion

The findings of this study highlight the potential of integrating Machine Learning (ML) with Indigenous Knowledge (IK) to enhance pre-planting crop selection for small-scale farmers in South Africa. While Random Forest and KNN models achieved 100% accuracy on the training data, further evaluation indicated possible overfitting, as SVM maintained strong generalization with an accuracy of 99% and more balanced precision-recall performance on the test data, demonstrating the robustness of AI-driven decision support systems in agriculture [1]. These findings align with prior studies on the effectiveness of ML in precision agriculture, where AI-driven models have significantly improved prediction accuracy and farming efficiency [2, 28]. However, this study contributes uniquely by incorporating IK, ensuring that technological advancements are both contextually relevant and culturally acceptable to local farmers.

A key contribution of this study lies in the integration of Indigenous Knowledge (IK) into the decision-making process of the IACDSS. Unlike conventional systems that treat local knowledge as informal or anecdotal, our framework treats IK as a validation and reconciliation layer, rather than a direct input to the machine learning (ML) model. Specifically, once the ML model generates a crop recommendation based on climate and edaphic data, the system independently consults a knowledge base built from structured farmer interviews and encoded rules derived from IK. If the IK and ML recommendations align, the result is communicated directly to the user. In cases of disagreement, the system triggers a reconciliation mechanism, offering alternatives such as intercropping suggestions or escalating the decision to a human expert. This layered approach ensures that technological predictions are grounded in culturally accepted practices, thereby enhancing user trust, adoption, and system credibility. Importantly, this structure also promotes explainability and modularity, allowing future improvements to either the AI or IK components without disrupting the whole system.

The significant role of climatic factors in determining crop suitability was evident, with rainfall, temperature, and humidity emerging as the most critical variables, surpassing edaphic factors such as soil pH and nutrient levels. This aligns with previous studies that emphasize climate variability as a dominant determinant of agricultural productivity in rain-fed farming systems [4, 28]. Given the increasing frequency of extreme weather patterns due to climate change, the ability of ML models to provide adaptive, data-driven insights can support resilience in small-scale farming communities [6].

Furthermore, the integration of IK into the decision-making process proved valuable in enhancing model acceptance among farmers. Many smallholder farmers rely on generational knowledge to make planting decisions, and previous studies have noted the reluctance to adopt AI-based agricultural tools due to trust issues and digital illiteracy [29]. By incorporating IK alongside AI-driven recommendations, this study bridges the gap between traditional knowledge systems and modern precision agriculture. When ML and IK predictions aligned, farmers expressed greater confidence in the system, increasing the likelihood of technology adoption. Conversely, when discrepancies arose, the reconciliation mechanism, offering expert consultation or intercropping alternatives, provided a flexible and farmer-inclusive solution. Compared to existing research, this study builds on prior work by introducing a hybrid AI-human framework for agricultural decision support. Previous studies have explored ML in agriculture [9], soil fertility optimization [10], and mobile-based precision farming. However, the integration of IK with ML for pre-planting crop selection remains an underexplored area. This research extends the body of knowledge by demonstrating that AI-driven agricultural solutions can be more effective when co-developed with local communities, aligning with global trends towards participatory technology design (Table 1).

Table 1. Summary of Accuracy scores

Model name	Accuracy score
Decision Tree	0.991
Random Forest	1.00
Gradient Boosting	0.991
K-Nearest Neighbour	1.00
Support Vector Machine:	
Linear function	0.995
Radial Bias Function	1.00
Polynomial Function	1.00

The user evaluation involved a structured questionnaire administered to 20 small-scale farmers from the target community, selected to represent diverse demographics in age, gender, education, and farming experience. The questionnaire combined Likert-scale and open-ended questions to assess trust, usability, and perceived value of the IACDSS system. Questions focused on the farmers' ability to interpret and accept recommendations derived from both Indigenous Knowledge and AI predictions. Trust was measured by gauging agreement with statements such as "I believe the system's recommendation matches traditional methods" and "I feel confident acting on suggestions from the application." Usability was assessed based on accessibility, language, and ease of understanding. Cronbach's Alpha for internal consistency was calculated at 0.97, indicating high reliability of the instrument. While responses were generally positive, one limitation was the small sample size and reliance on self-reported data, which may not fully capture behavioural outcomes in real-world field settings.

Despite these promising findings, some limitations must be acknowledged. First, due to COVID-19 restrictions, real-world field testing was limited, and validation relied on historical and synthetic datasets rather than real-time sensor data. Future research should incorporate Internet of Things (IoT)-based soil sensors to enhance real-time data accuracy [14]. Additionally, while the model performed well for the Pietermaritzburg region, expanding the dataset to include multiple agro-ecological zones will improve generalizability and robustness [15]. Another challenge lies in addressing the digital divide, while mobile-based decision support tools increase accessibility, some farmers may require training to maximize the benefits of AI-driven recommendations [29].

Future research should focus on three key areas. First, longitudinal studies should be conducted to measure the real-world impact of the IACDSS framework over multiple cropping seasons. Second, multi-label classification should be explored to optimize inter-cropping recommendations, an important practice among smallholder farmers. Third, improving AI interpretability by developing more interpretable models with clear justifications for predictions will enhance trust and adoption among end users [18]. Finally, integrating remote sensing data, such as satellite imagery, can further improve predictive accuracy and scalability [18].

Finally, this study demonstrates that integrating ML with IK offers a novel, scalable, and contextually relevant solution to enhance pre-planting crop selection for smallholder farmers in South Africa. By combining data-driven insights with traditional agricultural wisdom, the IACDSS framework provides a pathway toward more resilient and sustainable farming practices. While challenges such as field validation, dataset expansion, and digital literacy remain, the findings lay a foundation for future AI-driven agricultural innovations that are both scientifically rigorous and locally appropriate. This research contributes to ongoing efforts to bridge the gap between technological advancements and real-world farming needs, offering a model that can be adapted to other regions facing similar agricultural challenges (Table 2).

Table 2. Model Hyperparameter setting

Model	Hyperparameter	Value
Decision Tree	Criterion	Gini impurity
	Max Depth ('max_depth')	10
	Min Samples Split ('min_samples_split')	4
	Min Samples Leaf ('min_samples_leaf')	2
	Random State	42
Random Forest	Number of Trees ('n_estimators')	200
	Criterion	Gini impurity
	Max Depth ('max_depth')	15
	Min Samples Leaf ('min_samples_leaf')	2
	Bootstrap	True
	Random State	42
Gradient Boosting	Number of Estimators ('n_estimators')	150
	Learning Rate	0.05
	Max Depth ('max_depth')	4
	Subsample	0.8
	Loss Function	Multiclass deviance (log loss)
	Random State	42
K-Nearest Neighbors	Number of Neighbors ('n_neighbors')	7
	Distance Metric	Euclidean
	Weight Function	Distance
Support Vector Machine	Kernel	RBF
	Regularization Parameter ('C')	10.0
	Gamma	Auto
	Decision Function Shape	One-vs-Rest

7 Functionality of the IACDSS

As illustrated in Fig. 4, the IACDSS model integrates climatic data (a) and edaphic data (b), which are processed through a machine learning algorithm to generate predictive outputs for optimal crop selection (x) for planting. Indigenous Knowledge (IK) is not treated as a direct input feature to the machine learning model; rather, it functions as an independent knowledge system that operates alongside the ML prediction module. Specifically, IK is incorporated at the validation and reconciliation stages of the Intelligent Agro-Climate Decision Support System (IACDSS).

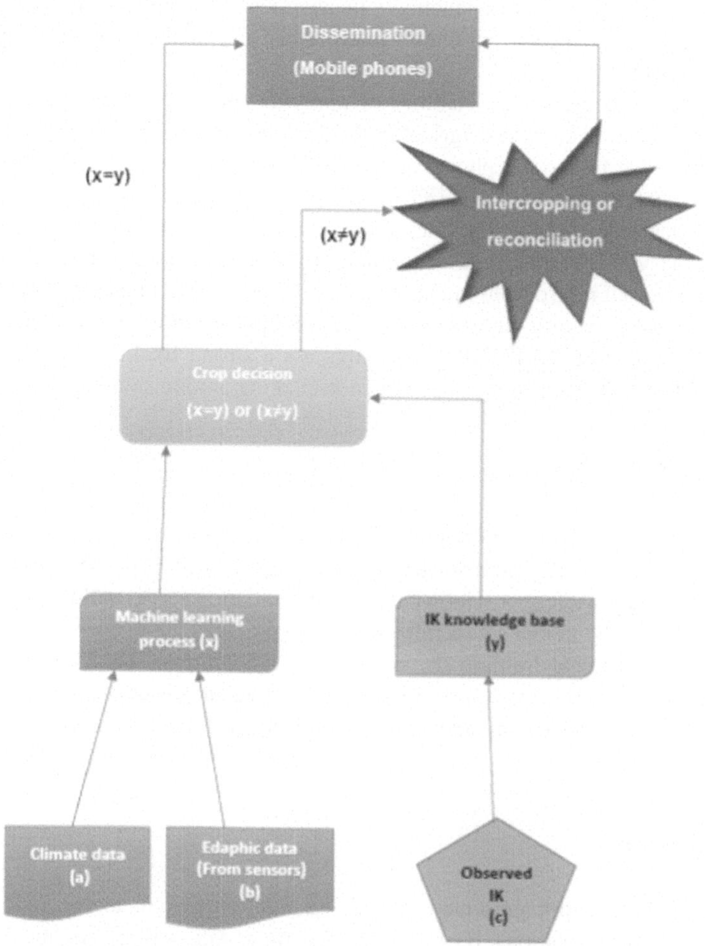

Fig. 4. The Intelligent Agro-Climate Decision support System representation

During the inference phase, the ML model predicts the optimal crop (x) based on climatic and edaphic features. Separately, an IK-based rule engine, constructed from structured interviews and encoded farming heuristics, generates its own crop suggestion (y). These two outputs are then compared:

If the ML and IK predictions agree ($x = y$), the recommendation is forwarded directly to the farmer.

If they disagree ($x \neq y$), the system invokes a reconciliation mechanism. This may involve:

A fallback to intercropping suggestions.

Referral to a human agricultural expert for final decision.

Future versions will support fuzzy logic scoring to quantify confidence in each recommendation stream.

This hybrid architecture ensures that AI recommendations are aligned with culturally embedded decision practices, enhancing both accuracy and user trust. By separating the ML and IK processes, the system retains interpretability and allows modular updates to either component.

The results underscore the viability of applying machine learning techniques to agro-climatic data for improved agricultural decision support. This research highlights the innovative use of mobile phones as collaborative tools in delivering agricultural solutions, as exemplified by the ITIKI framework [30, 31]. The ITIKI framework has empirically demonstrated that the integration of Indigenous Knowledge with scientific modelling can yield reliable rainfall predictions. This successful synthesis forms the foundational basis for the development of the Intelligent Agro-Climate Decision Support System (IACDSS). As rainfall forecasting is a prerequisite for informed crop selection, the proven efficacy of the ITIKI system suggests a strong likelihood of comparable success for the IACDSS in supporting decision-making among small-scale farmers.

8 Future Considerations

To enhance robustness, future iterations of the system will incorporate real-time IoT soil sensors for continuous data updates and explore deep learning approaches to improve predictive accuracy. Moreover, a larger-scale field validation across multiple regions will further strengthen the model's generalizability and practical application [32].

This methodological framework provides a scalable approach for integrating AI with Indigenous Knowledge, ensuring that technological advancements in precision agriculture remain contextually relevant and accessible to smallholder farmers in South Africa and beyond.

9 Conclusion

The IACDSS Framework presents a promising solution for enhancing food security through AgriTech innovations. By providing real-time, data-driven insights, the framework empowers farmers and agricultural stakeholders to make informed decisions, leading to increased productivity and sustainability. As Africa continues to embrace digital transformation in agriculture, frameworks like IACDSS will play a crucial role in ensuring long-term food security (Table 3).

Table 3. Summary of classification reports

Model	Category	Precision	Recall	F1-Score	Support
Decision tree	Tomatoes	1.0	0.958	0.979	48
	Potatoes	1.0	1.0	1.0	47
	Peppers	0.956	1.0	0.977	43
	Maize	1.0	1.0	1.0	44
	Beans	1.0	1.0	1.0	43
Random Forest	Tomatoes	1.0	1.0	1.0	48
	Potatoes	1.0	1.0	1.0	47
	Peppers	1.0	1.0	1.0	43
	Maize	1.0	1.0	1.0	44
	Beans	1.0	1.0	1.0	43
Gradient Boosting	Tomatoes	1.0	0.958	0.979	48
	Potatoes	1.0	1.0	1.0	47
	Peppers	0.956	1.0	0.977	43
	Maize	1.0	1.0	1.0	44
	Beans	1.0	1.0	1.0	43
Support Vector Machine Linear	Tomatoes	1.0	1.0	1.0	41
	Potatoes	1.0	1.0	1.0	43
	Peppers	1.0	0.968	0.984	31
	Maize	1.0	1.0	1.0	40
	Beans	0.978	1.0	0.989	45
K-Nearest Neighbour	Tomatoes	1.0	1.0	1.0	21
	Potatoes	1.0	1.0	1.0	30
	Peppers	1.0	1.0	1.0	30
	Maize	1.0	1.0	1.0	21
	Beans	1.0	1.0	1.0	23

Acknowledgments. We extend our gratitude to CSIR for partnering and contributing to this research and the development and testing of the IACDSS Framework.

The authors have no competing interests to declare that are relevant to the content of this article.

References

1. Manjula, A., Narsimha, G.: XCYPF: a flexible and extensible framework for agricultural crop yield prediction. In: Proceedings of 2015 IEEE 9th International Conference on Intelligent control systems. ISCO 2015 (2015). https://doi.org/10.1109/ISCO.2015.7282311
2. Masinde, M.: MAS-DEWS: a multi-agent system for predicting Africa's drought. In: Proceedings of International Joint Conference on Neural Networks, vol. 2015-September (2015). https://doi.org/10.1109/IJCNN.2015.7280837
3. Masinde, M.: IoT applications that work for the African continent: innovation or adoption?. In: Proceedings - 2014 12th IEEE International Conference on Industrial Informatics. INDIN 2014, pp. 633–638 (2014). https://doi.org/10.1109/INDIN.2014.6945587

4. Kabbiri, R., Dora, M., Kumar, V., Elepu, G., Gellynck, X.: Mobile phone adoption in agri-food sector: are farmers in Sub-Saharan Africa connected?. Technol. Forecast. Soc. Change **131**(December 2016), 253–261 (2018). https://doi.org/10.1016/j.techfore.2017.12.010
5. Nyamane, S., Elbasit, M.A.M.A., Obagbuwa, I.C.: Harnessing Deep Learning for Meteorological Drought Forecasts in the Northern Cape, South Africa, vol. 2024 (2024). https://doi.org/10.1155/2024/7562587
6. Milovanović, S.: The support and contribution of mobile technologies and applications to agriculture. Acta Agric. Serbica **28**(56), 75–86 (2023). https://doi.org/10.5937/aaser2356075m
7. Phelan, D.C., et al.: Advancing a farmer decision support tool for agronomic decisions on rainfed and irrigated wheat cropping in Tasmania. Agric. Syst. **167**(September), 113–124 (2018). https://doi.org/10.1016/j.agsy.2018.09.003
8. Westermann, O., Förch, W., Thornton, P., Körner, J., Cramer, L., Campbell, B.: Scaling up agricultural interventions: case studies of climate-smart agriculture. Agric. Syst. **165**(June), 283–293 (2018). https://doi.org/10.1016/j.agsy.2018.07.007
9. Masinde, M., Abu-Mahfouz, A., Thothela, N.P., Markus, E.: A framework for an intelligent agro-climate decision support system for small-scale farmers in Swayimane. In: 2023 3rd International Conference on Electrical, Computer, Communications and Mechatronics Engineering (ICECCME), Tenerife (2023). https://doi.org/10.1109/ICECCME57830.2023.10253285
10. APRO Software: Why Machine Learning Is Agriculture's New Best Friend - APRO Software. https://apro-software.com/machine-learning-agriculture/. Accessed 25 Sept 2021
11. Meroni, M., Waldner, F., Seguini, L., Kerdiles, H., Rembold, F.: Yield forecasting with machine learning and small data: what gains for grains?. Agric. For. Meteorol. 308–309(April) (2021). https://doi.org/10.1016/j.agrformet.2021.108555
12. Chlingaryan, A., Sukkarieh, S., Whelan, B.: Machine learning approaches for crop yield prediction and nitrogen status estimation in precision agriculture: a review. Comput. Electron. Agric. **151**(June), 61–69 (2018). https://doi.org/10.1016/j.compag.2018.05.012
13. Liakos, K.G., Busato, P., Moshou, D., Pearson, S., Bochtis, D.: Machine learning in agriculture: a review. Sensors (Switzerland) **18**(8), 1–29 (2018). https://doi.org/10.3390/s18082674
14. Toseef, M., Khan, M.J.: An intelligent mobile application for diagnosis of crop diseases in Pakistan using fuzzy inference system. Comput. Electron. Agric. **153**(August), 1–11 (2018). https://doi.org/10.1016/j.compag.2018.07.034
15. Masinde, M.: An innovative drought early warning system for sub-saharan Africa: integrating modern and indigenous approaches. African J. Sci. Technol. Innov. Dev. **7**(1), 8–25 (2015). https://doi.org/10.1080/20421338.2014.971558
16. Thothela, N.P., Markus, E.D., Masinde, M., Abu-Mahfouz, A.M.: A survey of intelligent agro-climate decision support tool for small-scale farmers: an integration of indigenous knowledge, mobile phone technology and smart sensors. Lect. Notes Netw. Syst. **154**, 715–730 (2021). https://doi.org/10.1007/978-981-15-8354-4_71
17. Sternberg, R.J.: Intelligence. Dialogues Clin. Neurosci. **14**(1), 19–27 (2012). https://doi.org/10.7551/mitpress/9780262062749.003.0018
18. Kganyago, M., Adjorlolo, C., Mhangara, P., Tsoeleng, L.: Optical remote sensing of crop biophysical and biochemical parameters: an overview of advances in sensor technologies and machine learning algorithms for precision agriculture. Comput. Electron. Agric. **218**(November 2022), 108730 (2024). https://doi.org/10.1016/j.compag.2024.108730
19. Seeds for Africa: Kwazulu Natal Vegetable Planting Chart – Seeds for Africa. https://www.seedsforafrica.co.za/pages/kwazulu-natal-vegetable-planting-chart. Accessed 17 Aug 2021
20. Sondhi, P.: Feature construction methods: a survey. Sifaka. Cs. Uiuc. Edu. **69**, 70–71 (2010)

21. Zhong, Z., Zheng, L., Kang, G., Li, S., Yang, Y.: Random erasing data augmentation. In: AAAI 2020 - 34th AAAI Conference on Artificial Intelligence, pp. 13001–13008 (2020). https://doi.org/10.1609/aaai.v34i07.7000
22. DALRRD: Department of Agriculture, Land Reform and Rural Development > Branches > Agricultural Production, Health & Food Safety > Plant Production > Production Guidelines > Pguidelinesarchieve. https://www.dalrrd.gov.za/Branches/Agricultural-Production-Health-Food-Safety/Plant-Production/Production-Guidelines/Pguidelinesarchieve. Accessed 17 Aug 2021
23. Pozdnoukhov, A., Kanevski, M.: Machine learning algorithms for analysis and modeling of geospatial data. Geomathematics GIS Anal. Resour. Environ. Hazards - Annual Conference on International Association for Mathematical Geosciences. IAMG 2007, no. January 2007, pp. 216–219 (2007)
24. Elsayed, A., Rixon, S., Levison, J., Binns, A., Goel, P.: Application of classification machine learning algorithms for characterizing nutrient transport in a clay plain agricultural watershed. J. Environ. Manag. **345**(September), 118924 (2023). https://doi.org/10.1016/j.jenvman.2023.118924
25. "Feature Scaling | Standardization vs Normalization. https://www.analyticsvidhya.com/blog/2020/04/feature-scaling-machine-learning-normalization-standardization/. Accessed 03 Oct 2021
26. Pedregosa, F., Weiss, R., Brucher, M.: Scikit-Learn: Machine Learning in Python, vol. 12, pp. 2825–2830 (2011)
27. Singh, P., Singh, M.K., Singh, N., Chakraverti, A.: IoT and AI-based intelligent agriculture framework for crop prediction. Int. J. Sens. Wirel. Commun. Control **13**(3), 145–154 (2023). https://doi.org/10.2174/2210327913666230509144225
28. Masinde, M., Bagula, A., Muthama, N.: Implementation roadmap for downscaling drought forecasts in Mbeere using ITIKI. In: International Telecommunication Union – Proceedings of 2013 ITU Kaleidoscope Academic Conferences, Build Sustainable Communities, K 2013, pp. 63–70 (2013). http://www.scopus.com/inward/record.url?eid=2-s2.0-84881272297&partnerID=tZOtx3y1
29. Zul Azlan, Z.H., Junaini, S.N., Bolhassan, N.A., Wahi, R., Arip, M.A.: Harvesting a sustainable future: An overview of smart agriculture's role in social, economic, and environmental sustainability. J. Clean. Prod. **434**(December 2023), 140338 (2024). https://doi.org/10.1016/j.jclepro.2023.140338
30. Muthoni, M.E.: ITIKI: Bridge Between African Indigenous Knowledge and Modern Science on Drought Prediction. University of Cape Town (2012). https://doi.org/10.1080/19474199.2012.683444
31. Masinde, M., Thothela, P.N.: ITIKI Plus: a mobile based application for integrating indigenous knowledge and scientific agro-climate decision support for Africa's small-scale farmers. In: 2019 IEEE 2nd International Conference on Information Computer and Technology. ICICT 2019, pp. 303–309 (2019). https://doi.org/10.1109/INFOCT.2019.8711059
32. Qazi, S., Khawaja, B.A., Farooq, Q.U.: IoT-Equipped and AI-enabled next generation smart agriculture: a critical review, current challenges and future trends. IEEE Access **10**, 21219–21235 (2022). https://doi.org/10.1109/ACCESS.2022.3152544

Temperature and Humidity Chipless RFID Sensors Using Smart Materials for Agritech Applications

Maha Added[1](✉), Nadia Chagtmi[1], Karima Rabaani[2], and Noureddine Boulejfen[3]

[1] ESPRIT School of Engineering, Z.I. Chotrana II, 2083 Tunis, Tunisia
maha.added@esprit.tn
[2] Microwave Electronic Research Laboratory, University of Tunis el Manar, Tunis, Tunisia
[3] Military Research Center, Military Air Base Aouina, Tunis, Tunisia

Abstract. This paper presents chipless RFID sensors for temperature and humidity monitoring, leveraging smart materials to enhance their sensitivity and performance. The sensors use slow-wave reflective resonators, offering a compact and passive solution. For temperature sensing, a low-loss RO3210 substrate is used, chosen for its strong thermal dependence of the dielectric constant, which enables the detection of specific temperature thresholds. For humidity sensing, Kapton is employed as the sensing material due to its high sensitivity to moisture-induced permittivity changes. A comprehensive theoretical analysis, supported by electromagnetic simulations, has been conducted. The results confirm the effectiveness of the proposed sensors and highlight their potential for applications in agricultural technology (Agritech).

Keywords: Chipless RFID sensor · Internet of Things (IoT) · smart material · Agritech

1 Introduction

Agritech, short for agricultural technology, involves the application of technology and innovation to enhance agricultural practices, processes, and products. It covers a broad spectrum of tools, technologies, and methods aimed at improving the efficiency, sustainability, and profitability of farming and food production. A key area within Agritech is the Internet of Things (IoT), which often relies on RFID sensors to gather crucial environmental data such as humidity and temperature.

In recent years, chipless RFID sensors have attracted growing interest from researchers across various IoT-related fields, including Agritech. This rising attention stems from their extremely low cost and the simplicity of their fabrication processes. Chipless RFID sensors offer a promising solution for large-scale, low-cost environmental monitoring in agricultural applications.

To enable real-time sensing capabilities, chipless sensors often incorporate smart materials as core components. These materials exhibit changes in their physical properties in response to variations in specific environmental parameters. Consequently, these

F. Kamoun et al. (Eds.): AFRICATEK 2025, LNICST 676, pp. 274–287, 2026.
https://doi.org/10.1007/978-3-032-16635-7_18

property changes directly affect the sensor's electromagnetic behavior, allowing it to detect and monitor environmental conditions effectively.

In [1], Rogers RT/Duroid® 6010.2LM was utilized as a smart material to develop a chipless multiparameter sensor capable of both temperature sensing and crack detection. The sensor design incorporates "U"- and "L"-shaped resonators, operating within the 2–8 GHz frequency range. Additionally, a circular microstrip patch antenna was employed for crack characterization.

In [2], a chipless RFID humidity sensor was introduced, utilizing Polyvinyl Alcohol (PVA) film as smart material. The sensor operates within the 1–2 GHz frequency range. A ring-shaped antenna, coated with Rogers RT/Duroid® 5880, serves as the reflector. For effective humidity sensing, the PVA film is strategically placed at the center of the antenna structure.

Another chipless RFID humidity sensor for smart packaging applications has been presented in [3]. The sensor comprises a metallic Electric-Field-Coupled (ELC) resonator on a 168 μm thick Rogers 4350 substrate, covered with a 50 μm thick Nafion NRE-212 membrane sensitive to humidity. Operating in the 1–2 GHz frequency range, it exhibits high sensitivity in low humidity conditions (1–10% RH), with a frequency shift of approximately 11 MHz and a significant reduction in signal intensity. This design enables non-invasive, wireless monitoring of package integrity by detecting internal humidity changes.

In [4], both humidity and temperature chipless RFID sensor is printed on a paper substrate using zinc conductive lines and beeswax encapsulation. It includes two spiral resonators: one for temperature sensing at 1.2 GHz and one for humidity sensing at 2.0 GHz, coated with konjac glucomannan. The sensor shows a −1.35 MHz/°C shift for temperature and up to −8 MHz/%RH for humidity. It is fully biodegradable, degrading in compost within 70 days.

This paper presents chipless RFID sensors designed for temperature and humidity monitoring. The temperature sensor, detailed in the following section, employs the low-loss RO3210 substrate, known for its sensitivity to temperature variations. In contrast, the humidity sensor utilizes Kapton 500 HN polyimide film, which responds to changes in humidity levels. The high-quality factor slow-wave resonator (SW-resonator), developed in our previous work [5], was utilized as the radar cross section (RCS) reflector in both sensor designs. For each sensor, the investigation began with a detailed examination of the physical properties of the smart material used. This was followed by a theoretical analysis and electromagnetic simulations to assess how variations in temperature and humidity influence the sensor's electromagnetic responses. The research is wrapped up with a final discussion of the results.

2 RFID Chipless Temperature Sensor

This section presents a chipless RFID sensor developed for temperature detection. The sensor leverages a temperature-sensitive dielectric substrate as a smart material, allowing it to detect specific temperature thresholds. The study will begin with a characterization of the substrate's properties. Subsequently, the sensor's structure will be described in detail, followed by an analysis of its electromagnetic behavior across varying temperature levels.

2.1 Smart Material Description (RO3210 Substrate)

The operating principle of the proposed chipless temperature sensor is based on the temperature-dependent properties of the substrate. Each substrate is characterized by its thermal coefficient of dielectric constant (TCεr), which quantifies how the relative permittivity (εr) changes with temperature. The sensor exploits this behavior by etching its resonator onto a substrate with a significant TCεr, enabling effective detection of temperature variations.

As temperature changes, the relative permittivity of the substrate (εr) varies accordingly, resulting in a shift in the resonator's resonance frequency. Consequently, each temperature level corresponds to a distinct resonance frequency, allowing temperature detection without the need for an integrated chip.

To ensure high sensitivity to temperature changes, various low-loss substrates with notable TCεr values were evaluated. Among them, the RO3210 substrate was selected due to its superior performance. RO3210 exhibits a TCεr of −459 ppm/°C over the temperature range of 0 °C to 100 °C. It has a thickness (H) of 1.28 mm. At 23 °C, its relative permittivity (εr) is 10.8, and the dissipation factor (tanδ) is 0.0027 [6].

Figure 1 illustrates the variation of the substrate's relative permittivity (εr) as a function of temperature (T), based on the TCεr.

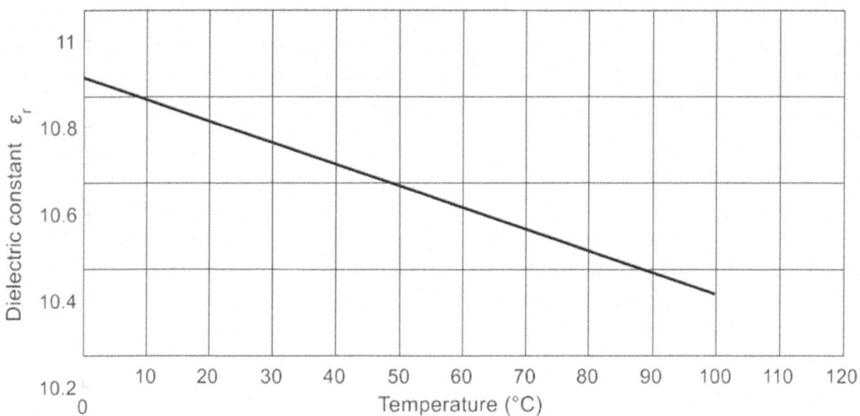

Fig. 1. The change of the relative permittivity εr of RO3210 according to the temperature value

Additionally, the change of the relative permittivity of RO3210 according to the temperature value can be expressed as follow:

$$\varepsilon r(T) = -0.005 * T + 10.92 \quad (1)$$

As it is shown in the figure, the relative permittivity (εr) decreases as temperature increases, demonstrating an inverse relationship between εr and temperature. For the temperature range of 0 °C to 100 °C, εr varies from 10.92 to 10.42, with each temperature level corresponding to a specific permittivity value.

2.2 Structure Description

The SW-resonator, developed in our previous work [5], serves as the fundamental resonator in the proposed chipless sensor. The structure is designed using the RO3210 substrate to resonate within the X-band frequency range. To determine the fundamental dimensions of the SW-resonator, the substrate parameters provided in the datasheet [6] were used: $\varepsilon r = 10.8$ at 23 °C, $\tan\delta = 0.0027$, and thickness $H = 1.28$ mm. For this initial calculation, the substrate's sensitivity to temperature variation was disregarded.

As outlined in [5], the initial step involves calculating the parameters of a half-wave dipole antenna designed to resonate at the target frequency. To achieve resonance around 8.6 GHz, a half-wave dipole antenna with a length of 6.65 mm and a width of 0.55 mm was designed. The following step applies the slow-wave technique to the previously designed half-wave dipole antenna to determine the dimensions of the corresponding SW-resonator, as detailed in [5].

The resulting SW- resonator is illustrated in Fig. 2. The structure features a microstrip line loaded with four shunt stubs to increase its electrical length. All dimensions are detailed in the figure, and the overall size of the proposed chipless temperature sensor is 6×4 mm^2.

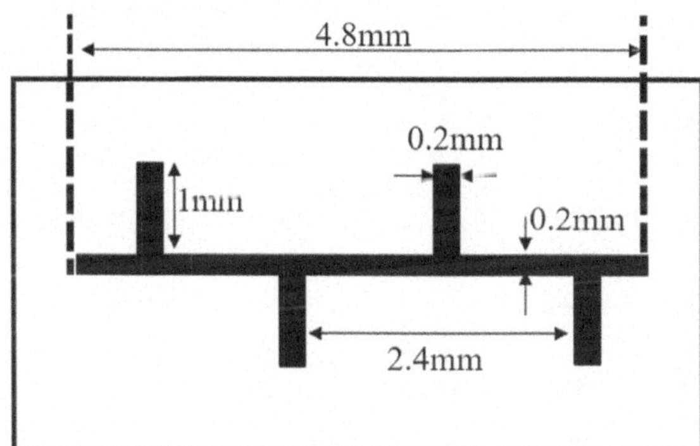

Fig. 2. The chipless temperature sensor based on SW-resonator designed using the RO3210 substrate.

2.3 The Electromagnetic Behavior of the Proposed Chipless Temperature Sensor

This section analyzes the electromagnetic behavior of the proposed SW-resonator, with a focus on its response to temperature variations. The analysis is divided into two parts: a theoretical study and electromagnetic simulations.

Theoretical Study

The following theoretical analysis aims to evaluate the electromagnetic behavior of the proposed chipless sensor under varying temperature conditions.

The resonance frequency of the proposed SW-resonator f_{res} can be calculated using the Eq. (2) [7]:

$$f_{res} = \frac{c}{2*L*\sqrt{\varepsilon_{eff}}} \tag{2}$$

Here, c is the speed of light (c = 299 792 458 m/s), ε_{eff} is the effective dielectric constant and L is the length of the correspondent half-wave dipole antenna, as calculated and presented in the previous section.

Regarding ε_{eff} value, it can be calculated using the following equations [8]:

For $\frac{W}{H} \leq 1$:

$$\varepsilon_{eff} = \frac{\varepsilon_r + 1}{2} + \frac{\varepsilon_r - 1}{2}\left[\left(1 + \frac{12.H}{W}\right)^{-\frac{1}{2}} + 0.04\left(1 - \frac{W}{H}\right)^2\right] \quad (3)$$

For $\frac{W}{H} > 1$:

$$\varepsilon_{eff} = \frac{\varepsilon_r + 1}{2} + \frac{\varepsilon_r - 1}{2}.\left(1 + \frac{12.H}{W}\right)^{-\frac{1}{2}} \quad (4)$$

where W denotes the width of the associated half-wave dipole resonator, while H and εr represent the thickness and relative permittivity of the substrate, respectively. Equations (1) through (4) were used to calculate the variation in the resonance frequency of the SW-resonator in response to temperature changes, as illustrated in Fig. 3.

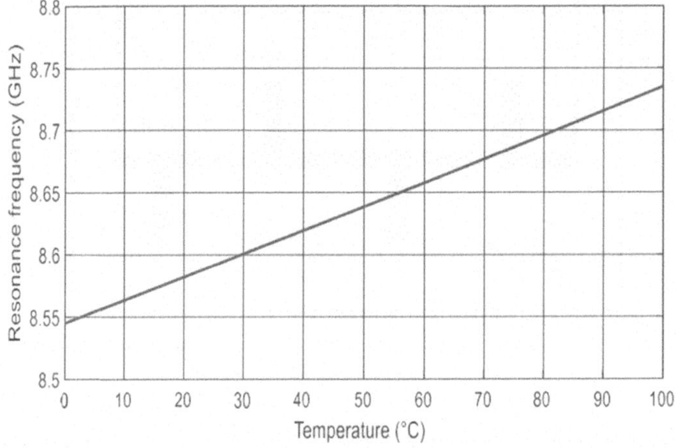

Fig. 3. The calculated resonance frequencies of SW-resonator depending on temperature.

As illustrated in Fig. 3, the resonance frequency of the proposed sensor varies linearly with temperature. Over the range of 0 °C to 100 °C, the resonance frequency shifts from 8.545 GHz to 8.736 GHz.

Theoretically, the sensor requires a frequency bandwidth of 191 MHz to cover this temperature range, corresponding to an average frequency shift of approximately 1.9 MHz per degree Celsius.

Electromagnetic Simulation Study

This section presents a simulation study of the sensor's electromagnetic behavior. The proposed sensor is illuminated with a linearly polarized plane wave and simulated using CST STUDIO SUITE. The reflected signal is captured by probes placed 30 cm from the structure, and the radar cross section (RCS) is used as the performance evaluation metric.

Based on Eq. (1), the relative permittivity (ϵ_r) of the RO3210 substrate was used as a parameter for the parametric simulations. Each ϵ_r value corresponds to a specific temperature threshold. The structure was simulated using ϵ_r values of 10.92, 10.82, 10.72, 10.62, 10.52, and 10.42, which correspond to temperature thresholds of 0 °C, 20 °C, 40 °C, 60 °C, 80 °C, and 100 °C, respectively. The simulated RCS responses of the proposed sensor at various temperature thresholds are shown in Fig. 4.

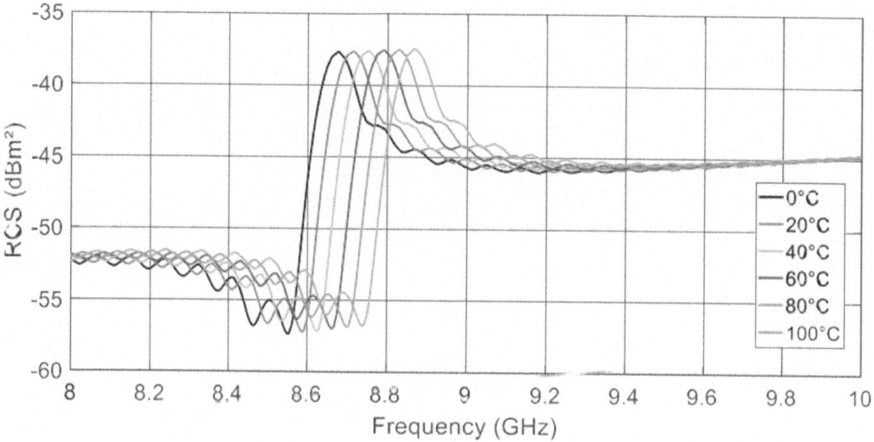

Fig. 4. The simulated Radar Cross Section (RCS) of the chipless sensor under different temperature thresholds

As clearly demonstrated, a distinct resonance frequency is detected for each temperature threshold, while the signal shape and RCS level remain unchanged. The temperature thresholds and their corresponding resonance frequency values are presented in Table 1.

Based on the extracted values, a frequency band of 190 MHz, spanning from 8.551 GHz to 8.741 GHz, is needed to cover the temperature range from 0 °C to 100 °C. Additionally, a consistent shift of 38 MHz between successive resonance frequencies was observed, resulting in a frequency shift (Δf) of 1.9 MHz/°C.

Table 1. Temperature thresholds and their correspondent resonance frequencies

Temperature threshold (°C)	Resonance frequency (GHz)
0	8.551
20	8.589
40	8.627
60	8.665

(continued)

Table 1. *(continued)*

Temperature threshold (°C)	Resonance frequency (GHz)
80	8.703
100	8.741

Furthermore, as clearly shown in Fig. 5, there is a strong agreement between the theoretical study and the simulation results. This alignment highlights the reliability and accuracy of the obtained results, reinforcing the effectiveness of the proposed chipless temperature sensor.

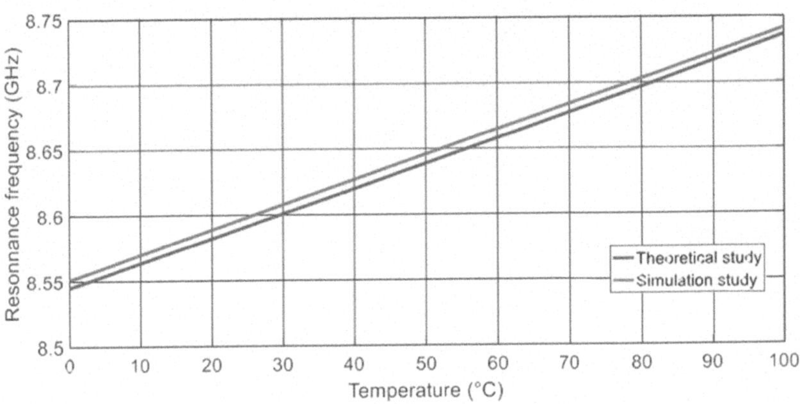

Fig. 5. Comparison of theoretical and simulated resonance frequency variations as a function of temperature thresholds.

The sensing process has been analyzed using the SW-resonator, with both theoretical and simulation results showing promising outcomes.

3 RFID Chipless Humidity Sensor

This section presents a chipless RFID humidity sensor. The smart material used in the proposed sensor is the Kapton substrate, which is well-known for its sensitivity to variations in relative humidity. The investigation follows the same phases as the previously discussed temperature sensor study.

3.1 Smart Material Description (Kapton 500 HN Film)

The operating principle is based on the use of Kapton 500 HN polyimide film as a smart material. Manufactured by DuPont, Kapton 500 HN is a flexible, low-loss dielectric material renowned for its mechanical robustness and thermal stability across a broad temperature range (−269 °C to +400 °C). It is particularly sensitive to changes in relative humidity (RH), which makes it a suitable candidate for humidity sensing applications. As reported in its technical datasheet [9], this polyimide film demonstrates a linear variation in its dielectric properties in response to RH changes. Specifically, up to frequencies of 3 GHz, its relative permittivity (Ɛr-Kapton) increases linearly with the ambient relative humidity, as described by Eq. (5) [10]:

$$\varepsilon\text{r-Kapton (RH)} = 0.008 * \text{RH} + 3.05 \tag{5}$$

Thus, for a relative humidity range of 0% to 100%, Kapton's relative permittivity changes from 3.05 to 3.85, respectively. This property of Kapton has been leveraged to develop a humidity sensor.

3.2 Structure Description

Figure 6 presents the design of the proposed chipless humidity sensor, showing both the top view (Fig. 6(a)) and the side view (Fig. 6(b)). The sensor's architecture is based on the Slow-Wave resonator configuration, previously introduced in our earlier work [5], which serves as the foundational structure for this design.

As illustrated in Fig. 6, a single SW-resonator is placed atop a stack of two dielectric substrate layers:

- The first substrate layer comprises a 125 μm-thick Kapton 500 HN polyimide adhesive tape (H_{kapton}), whose dielectric constant (Ɛr-Kapton) is sensitive to changes in environmental RH, as detailed earlier.
- The second layer is a 0.83 mm-thick Rogers RO4003 substrate (Ɛr = 3.55, tanδ = 0.0027), used to improve the resonance quality factor [5]. Its properties are not affected by changes in ambient humidity.

The concept consists in printing the SW-resonator onto the Kapton 500 HN film using conductive ink, followed by bonding the film onto the RO4003 substrate. As the relative permittivity of Kapton changes with humidity levels, it alters the electromagnetic characteristics of the SW-resonators, which are consequently affected by the relative humidity.

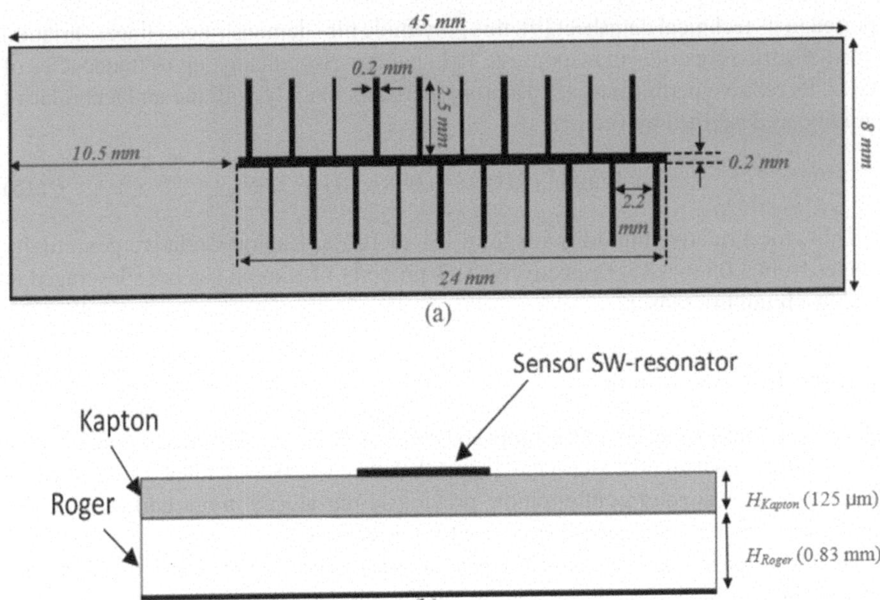

Fig. 6. The dimensions of the chipless humidity sensor (a) Top view (b) side view

Considering that the physical properties of Kapton, as discussed in the previous section, are applicable within a frequency range up to 3 GHz, the sensing SW- resonator has been designed to resonate around 2.3 GHz. The SW-resonator shown in Fig. 6 corresponds to a half-wave dipole antenna with a length of L = 40 mm and a width of W = 1.24 mm [5]. Dimensions of the proposed SW-resonator are provided in Fig. 6 (a).

3.3 The Electromagnetic Behvior of the Proposed Chipless Humidity Sensor

This section presents a theoretical study, and electromagnetic simulations conducted to examine the effect of relative humidity variations on the electromagnetic response of the proposed humidity sensor.

Theoretical Study

The objective of this study is to evaluate the resonance frequency of the SW-resonator under different relative humidity conditions. Accordingly, the resonance frequency of the associated half-wave dipole antenna was computed for RH values ranging between 0% and 100%.

For this purpose, four steps have been followed:

- *Step 1:* The correlation between Kapton's relative permittivity and ambient relative humidity (εr-Kapton = f(RH)) is defined by Eq. (5). As previously mentioned, within the 0% to 100% RH range, εr-Kapton increases from 3.05 to 3.85, respectively.
- *Step 2:* The overall relative permittivity of the substrate, comprising both Kapton and Rogers layers ($\varepsilon_{r-hom} = f(\varepsilon_{r-Kapton}, \varepsilon_{r-Roger})$), has been determined using the

following equation [11]:

$$\varepsilon_{r-hom} = \frac{H_{kapton} + H_{Roger}}{\frac{H_{kapton}}{\varepsilon_{r-Kapton}} + \frac{H_{roger}}{\varepsilon_{r-Roger}}} \tag{6}$$

H_{kapton} and H_{roger} correspond to the thicknesses of the Kapton and Rogers layers, respectively. Similarly, $\varepsilon_{r\text{-}Kapton}$ and $\varepsilon_{r\text{-}Roger}$ refer to their respective relative permittivities. Since the relative permittivity of Kapton ($\varepsilon_{r\text{-}Kapton}$) is influenced by changes in the ambient relative humidity (RH), the overall effective permittivity of the combined multilayer substrate ($\varepsilon_{r\text{-}hom}$) is inherently dependent on the RH conditions of the environment. Consequently, variations in humidity directly impact the dielectric behavior of the substrate as a whole, due to the humidity-sensitive nature of the Kapton layer.

- *Step 3:* The effective dielectric constant, ε_{eff}, which varies with $\varepsilon_{r\text{-}hom}$ and consequently depends on the relative humidity (RH), was determined by applying Eqs. (5), (3), and (4). Here, W denotes the width of the associated half-wave dipole antenna (W = 1.24 mm), and H corresponds to the total thickness of the multilayer substrate, calculated as the sum of the Kapton and Rogers layers' thicknesses ($H = H_{kapton} + H_{roger} = 0.955$ mm).
- *Step 4:* The resonance frequency of the SW-resonator was determined using Eq. (2), where L corresponds to the length of the associated half-wave dipole antenna (L = 40 mm). Given that the effective dielectric constant, $\varepsilon_e$ff, is a function of relative humidity, the resonance frequency consequently exhibits a dependency on ambient humidity levels.

Following the methodology described above, the variation of the SW-resonator's resonance frequency with respect to relative humidity levels is presented in Fig. 7.

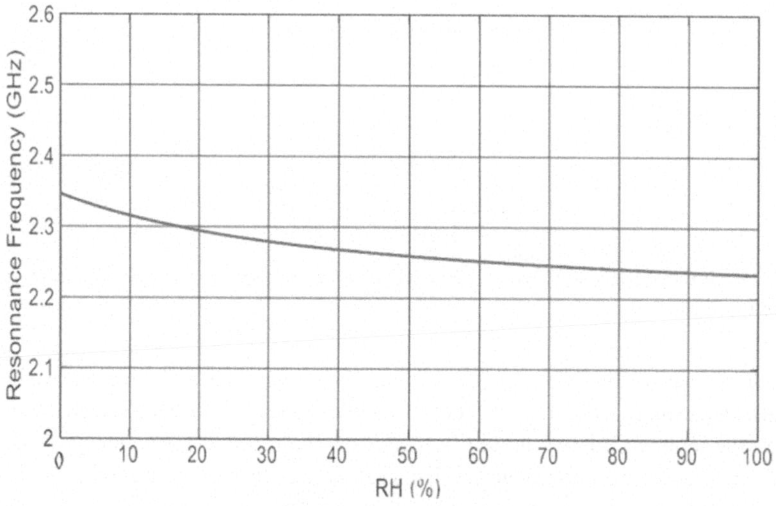

Fig. 7. The calculated resonance frequencies of the SW-resonator depending to the relative humidity level

For a relative humidity range from 0% to 100%, the resonance frequency of the corresponding half-wave dipole antenna varies from 2.348 GHz to 2.235 GHz, respectively. Therefore, a frequency range of 113 MHz is required to cover the entire range of relative humidity levels. Additionally, a non-linear variation in the resonance frequency has been observed. The resonance frequency changes more significantly at lower relative humidity levels, while at higher humidity levels, the frequency stabilizes. This indicates that the resonator exhibits greater sensitivity at lower relative humidity levels compared to higher ones.

Electromagnetic Simulations Results

To validate the theoretical study on the effect of relative humidity variation on the electromagnetic behavior of the proposed humidity sensor, electromagnetic simulations were conducted using CST STUDIO SUITE. The proposed sensor is illuminated by a linearly polarized plane and the reflected signal is measured using probes positioned 30 cm from the structure, and the radar cross section (RCS) is employed as the primary performance evaluation metric.

The relative permittivity of Kapton ($\varepsilon_{r\text{-}Kapton}$) corresponding to relative humidity levels of 0%, 20%, 40%, 60%, 80%, and 100% was calculated using Eq. (5). Subsequently, several simulations of the SW-resonator were performed with the calculated values of $\varepsilon_{r\text{-}Kapton}$. The results of these simulations are presented in Fig. 8.

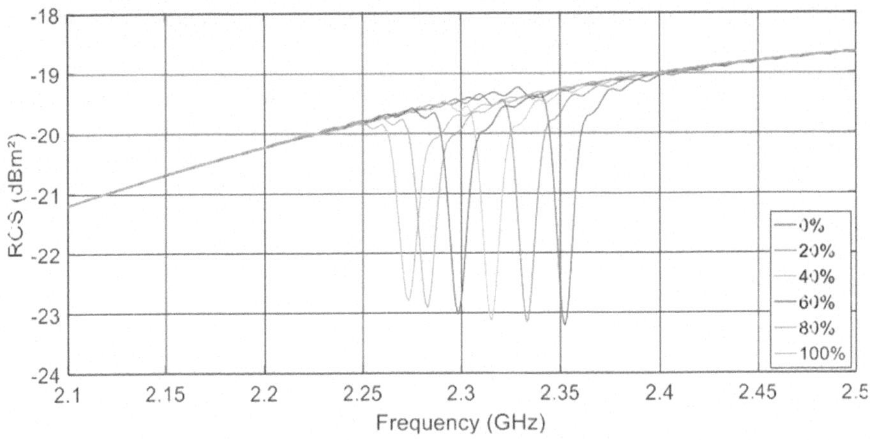

Fig. 8. The simulated Radar Cross Section RCS of the proposed sensor in different relative humidity thresholds

The figure shows the RCS responses of the SW-resonator at different relative humidity levels. A distinct resonance frequency has been detected for each relative humidity level. As the ambient relative humidity increases, the resonance frequency of the SW-resonator shifts to lower frequencies. The corresponding relative humidity levels and their resonance frequency values are presented in Table 2.

Table 2. The relative humidity level and their correspondent resonance frequencies

Relative humidity level (%)	Resonance frequency (GHz)	Frequency shift (MHz)
0	2.355	-
20	2.333	22
40	2.315	18
60	2.298	17
80	2.283	15
100	2.273	10

A frequency span of 82 MHz, extending from 2.355 GHz down to 2.273 GHz, is necessary to encompass relative humidity levels ranging from 0% to 100%. Notably, the frequency shift is more significant at lower humidity values. For a RH range of 0% to 20%, a frequency shift of 22 MHz is observed, while a shift of only 10 MHz is noted for a RH range of 80% to 100%. This indicates that the sensitivity of the SW-resonator decreases as the ambient relative humidity increases, which aligns with the findings from the theoretical study.

A comparison between theoretical and simulated results is presented in Fig. 9.

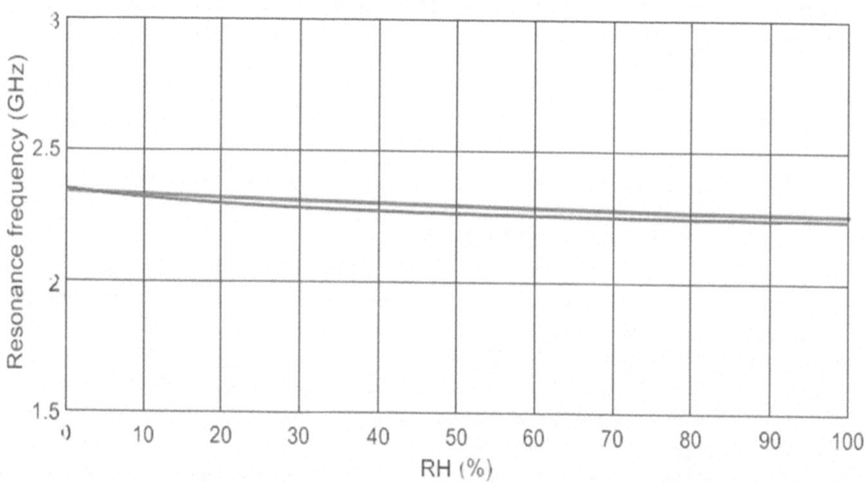

Fig. 9. Theoretical modeling (blue curve) and numerical simulation (red curve) with respect to variations in relative humidity. (Color figure online)

As shown in the figure, there is good agreement between the simulation results and theoretical study. However, the frequency range needed to cover relative humidity levels from 0% to 100% has decreased from 113 MHz in the theoretical analysis to 82 MHz in the simulations. This discrepancy may be attributed to errors arising from the non-dispersive model used to calculate the effective dielectric constant (Ɛeff) in the

Theoretical analysis, combined with the approximation of the effective relative permittivity as defined in Eq. (6), reveals a certain degradation in performance. However, the simulated frequency bandwidth remains sufficiently broad to enable reliable humidity sensing, especially when evaluated relative to benchmarks established in prior studies.

4 Conclusion

This paper proposes compact, passive, low-cost planar chipless RFID sensors for temperature and humidity monitoring. The temperature-sensitive, low-loss RO3210 substrate and the humidity-sensitive Kapton 500HN polyimide film are utilized as smart materials for parameter detection. The SW-resonator is integrated as the core reflector to generate the sensor's frequency resonances. The relationship between the physical properties of each smart material and the corresponding monitored parameter has been clarified. The sensor structures are then described, highlighting their compact sizes. Additionally, both theoretical studies and electromagnetic simulations have been conducted and thoroughly discussed, demonstrating strong agreement between the obtained results. The results are promising; however, experimental measurements are needed to validate and strengthen the findings of the investigation.

The proposed sensors, with their compact design and low cost, offer considerable potential for applications in Agritech, especially in environmental monitoring for precision farming. Identification functionality can be integrated into these sensors by adding extra resonators.

References

1. Javed, N., Azam, M.A., Amin, Y.: Chipless RFID multisensor for temperature sensing and crack monitoring in an IoT environment. IEEE Sens. Lett. **5**(6), pp. 1–4 (2021). Art. 6001404. https://doi.org/10.1109/LSENS.2021.3083218
2. Wang, B., Li, Y., Gao, F., Han, B., Chen, C., He, J.: Design and characterization of a passive wireless chipless RFID humidity sensor. In: Proceedings 2023 International Conference Information Technology (ICIT), Amman, Jordanie, août 2023, pp. 647–651 (2023). https://doi.org/10.1109/ICIT58056.2023.10225940
3. Marchi, G., Mulloni, V., Gaiardo, A., Valt, M., Donelli, M., Lorenzelli, L.: A chipless RFID humidity sensor for smart packaging applications. Proceedings **97**(1) (2024). Art. 46. https://doi.org/10.3390/proceedings2024097046
4. Bourely, J., et al.: Degradable and printed microstrip line for chipless temperature and humidity sensing. Adv. Electron. Mater. **10**(11) (2024). Art. no. 2400229. https://doi.org/10.1002/aelm.202400229
5. Added, M., Boulejfen, N., Svanda, M., Ghannouchi, F.M., Vuong, T.-P.: High-performance chipless radio-frequency identification tags: using a slow-wave approach for miniaturized structure. IEEE Antennas Propag. Mag. **61**(4), 46–54 (2019). https://doi.org/10.1109/MAP.2019.2920664
6. Rogers Corp advanced connectivity solutions (ACS) products, consulté le 10 septembre 2023. https://www.rogerscorp.com/acs/products.aspx
7. Rizzi, P.A.: Microwave Engineering Passive Circuits, pp. 152–154. Pearson, New York (2007)

8. Sadiku, M.N.O., Musa, S.M.: Comparison of dispersion formulas for microstrip lines. In: Proceedings IEEE SoutheastCon, March 2004. https://doi.org/10.1109/SECON.2004.1287946
9. DuPont: Kapton® HN thermal adhesive polyimide film, consulté le 10 septembre 2023. https://www.dupont.com/products/kapton-hn.html
10. Karmakar, N.C., Saha, J.K., Amin, E.M.: Chipless RFID Sensors. John Wiley & Sons, Hoboken, NJ, (2015). https://doi.org/10.1002/9781119078104
11. Radonic, V., Birgermajer, S., Kitic, G.: Microfluidic EBG sensor based on phase-shift method realized using 3D-Printing technology. Sensors **17** (2017). Art. 892. https://doi.org/10.3390/s17040892

AI-Enhanced Intelligent Transplantation Machine Based on IoT for Optimized Plant Growth

Hazem Kalboussi(✉)

M2M Team, ESPRIT School of Engineering, Tunis, Tunisia
Hazem.kalboussi1@esprit.t

Abstract. Advanced technologies are increasingly being integrated into modern agriculture to maximize crop yields and reduce operational costs. This paper presents the design and implementation of an AI-enhanced intelligent transplantation machine based on the Internet of Things (IoT). The proposed system utilizes smart sensors and an automated control unit to optimize transplantation parameters such as depth, spacing, and orientation based on realtime environmental data. Preliminary testing and simulations indicate a potential increase in seedling survival rate by 30% and a 25% reduction in transplantation time. This research introduces a scalable, sustainable solution aligned with the objectives of precision agriculture and highlights the potential for further improvements through AI-driven predictive analytics.

Keywords: Artificial Intelligence (AI) · Internet of Things (IoT) · Smart Agriculture · Transplantation Automation · Precision Agriculture · Autonomous Systems · Environmental Sensing

1 Introduction

The rapid development of intelligent technologies has transformed various sectors, including agriculture [1]. Precision agriculture is growing as more effective and datadriven farming techniques replace conventional ways. Drones, sensors, and automated equipment are just a few of the cutting-edge instruments and methods used in precision agriculture to maximize crop yields, minimize resource waste, and enhance overall farm management. One key aspect of this transition is optimizing the transplantation process, which is crucial for ensuring healthy plant growth and maximizing crop output [2].

Modern agriculture is undergoing a transformation driven by technological innovations, notably in the fields of Artificial Intelligence (AI) and the Internet of Things (IoT). These technologies are enabling more precise, data-driven farming methods that enhance productivity and sustainability.

In developing countries, the adoption of AI and IoT technologies in agriculture faces several systemic challenges, including financial constraints, inadequate digital

F. Kamoun et al. (Eds.): AFRICATEK 2025, LNICST 676, pp. 288–296, 2026.
https://doi.org/10.1007/978-3-032-16635-7_19

infrastructure, and limited technical expertise. Addressing these barriers is essential to ensure widespread deployment and impact.

One critical area of focus is the transplantation process, which is often performed manually and is prone to inefficiencies such as improper depth, uneven spacing, and mechanical damage to seedlings. These limitations affect crop uniformity and yield. Although this study touches upon the transplantation problem early on, it must also address it consistently throughout the paper to maintain thematic alignment.

Moving young plants or seedlings from one place to another, usually from a nursery to a field or greenhouse, is known as transplantation, and it is an essential farming technique [3]. Plant growth, survival rate, and farm productivity are all directly impacted by transplantation success. However, conventional transplantation techniques often involve inefficiencies including uneven seedling placement, incorrect planting depth, and insufficient spacing, all of which can lead to suboptimal growth and reduced yields [4–6].

In [7], an innovative solution integrating IoT and AI for automated crop management in urban farming is proposed. This approach enables real-time monitoring and intelligent decision-making, which could enhance systems such as an AI-driven transplantation machine to optimize plant growth through data-driven practices. In [8], an intelligent system for automated plant cultivation using IoT in hydroponics is presented, emphasizing energy efficiency, Wi-Fi-based data transmission, and microcontroller integration. However, it does not specifically address AI-enhanced transplantation. Similarly, in [9], a smart agriculture system leveraging IoT for soil analysis and deep learning for pest detection is explored, focusing on real-time nutrient monitoring and pest management rather than transplantation automation. An IoT-based hydroponic system for lettuce cultivation is described in [10], utilizing Arduino and Raspberry Pi for real-time monitoring and control, yet it does not specifically consider AI-driven transplantation mechanisms.

This research addresses the limitations identified in prior works by proposing an intelligent transplantation system that integrates the Internet of Things (IoT) to enhance precision and operational efficiency. The system utilizes IoT-based sensors to monitor critical soil parameters, including temperature, humidity, and moisture content, in real time. An automated control unit processes this data and dynamically adjusts the machine's operation to ensure optimal transplantation conditions for different plant species. By leveraging these technologies, the proposed system aims to minimize human error, reduce labor costs, and facilitate the relocation of plants to environments that maximize growth potential.

To further improve system performance, this study envisions the integration of artificial intelligence (AI) in future developments. AI capabilities could enable predictive analysis, allowing the system to anticipate environmental changes and proactively adjust transplantation strategies. The combination of IoT and AI presents a promising path way toward a fully autonomous and adaptive system, capable of revolutionizing modern agricultural practices through continuous learning and optimization. Beyond validating the feasibility of this intelligent transplantation system, this research also examines its potential for large-scale adoption within the agricultural sector. The proposed technology has the potential to significantly enhance crop productivity, promote sustainable farming practices, and contribute to the advancement of precision agriculture by improving the accuracy, efficiency, and adaptability of the transplantation process.

2 Literature Review

Smart agriculture systems leveraging IoT and AI have been extensively studied in recent years. For instance, [7] proposed a system for automated crop management in urban settings using real-time data collection and decision-making. Similarly, [8] developed an intelligent hydroponic system, but without addressing transplantation. Table 1 summarizes recent relevant works and highlights the distinctions of our proposed solution.

Table 1. Comparison of related smart agriculture systems.

Study	Technology	AI	Focus Integration	Transplantation Support
[7]	IoT + AI	Urban farming	Yes	No
[8]	IoT	Hydroponics	No	No
[9]	IoT + DL	Soil analysis, pest detection	Yes	No
Ours	IoT + AI	Transplantation automation	Yes	Yes

Our contribution differs by directly targeting transplantation optimization, supported by real-time environmental sensing, automated mechanical execution, and envisioned AIenhanced decision-making.

3 System Architecture

The modular architecture of the intelligent transplanting machine is made up of multiple subsystems, each of which adds to the machine's overall effectiveness and functionality. In addition to the IoT sensors, automated control system, and actuators, this system also integrates solar panels for sustainable power supply, making it an eco-friendly solution for modern agriculture as shown in Fig. 1.

The system consists of several key components working together to ensure efficient and sustainable transplantation. It includes a range of IoT sensors, such as the Riko M30 PSC3018 inductive sensor, which ensures accurate positioning by detecting metallic objects, and the DAR 02 D51 sensor, which provides precise measurements of an object's position to guarantee optimal planting depth and spacing. Additional environmental sensors monitor soil moisture and temperature, aiding in the assessment of ideal planting conditions. The system is controlled by an automated control system that analyzes sensor data and adjusts parameters like depth, spacing, and orientation in real-time to match agronomic requirements and soil conditions. Actuators physically perform the transplantation process with minimal human involvement, ensuring accuracy and efficiency. Solar panels are incorporated to provide sustainable power, reducing dependence on non-renewable energy sources while maintaining energy efficiency. Furthermore, the system features a communication module based on the MQTT protocol, enabling remote

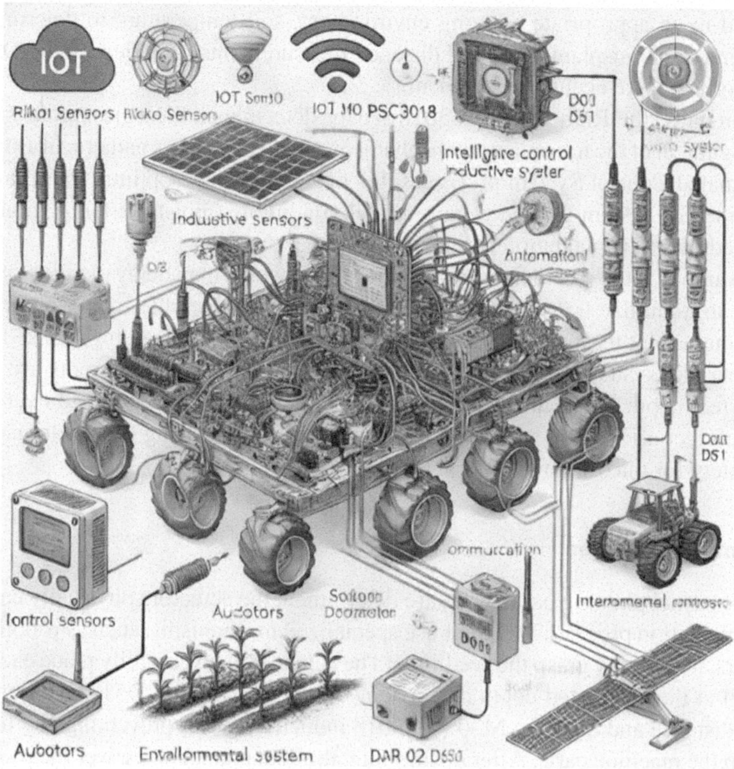

Fig. 1. Intelligent transplantation machine (illustration generated using AI tools). (The real prototype is provided in Fig. 3, while Fig. 1 offers a conceptual AIgenerated visualization).

monitoring and control of the machine via a central cloud platform. This allows farmers to track sensor readings and system diagnostics, adjust, and receive over-the-air updates, ensuring the system remains up-to-date and functional.

4 Machine Operation

To guarantee accurate and efficient planting, the intelligent transplantation machine combines adaptive systems, decision-making algorithms, and real-time data collection. The entire procedure is automated, requires very little human involvement, and is made to adapt quickly to shifting field circumstances.

4.1 Data Collection

The system utilizes several IoT sensors to collect data before startup, including the Riko M30 PSC3018 inductive sensor, the DAR 02 D51 sensor, and environmental sensors such as soil moisture, temperature, and humidity. These sensors continuously monitor various aspects of the soil and environment, including soil moisture to ensure plants are moved to an appropriate growing environment, soil temperature to determine the optimal time for transplantation, and distance measurements provided by the DAR 02 D51 sensor to ensure accurate placement.

Additionally, the Riko M30 PSC3018 sensor detects metallic objects to ensure the proper alignment of the transplanting mechanism. Once the sensors gather real-time data, the Automated Control System processes this data to calculate optimal transplantation parameters. The system evaluates current soil conditions (moisture, temperature, pH, etc.) and adjusts transplantation parameters accordingly.

For example, if the soil moisture is too low, the machine may delay planting or adjust the depth to minimize transplant shock, and if the soil temperature is not optimal, the machine may adapt its speed to reduce potential damage to the seedlings. Based on the sensor data, the system calculates the ideal planting depth, ensuring roots are placed at the correct depth for healthy growth, optimal planting spacing to avoid overcrowding, and correct orientation for directional growth plants, ensuring each plant is placed appropriately for maximum growth potential.

4.2 Planting Execution

Once the optimal planting parameters are determined, the actuators physically carry out the transplantation process. They first use specialized mechanisms, such as robotic arms or grippers, to securely grasp the seedlings. The actuators then carefully place each plant in the soil at the calculated depth and spacing, with the DAR 02 D51 sensor ensuring accurate distance and the Riko M30 PSC3018 inductive sensor preventing any interference from the machine parts. After positioning, the actuators gently cover the roots with soil to provide stable support and minimize transplant shock. The system operates in a dynamic, adaptive mode, constantly receiving feedback from the sensors during the process. Based on this feedback, the control system makes real-time adjustments, such as modifying the planting depth if the soil is harder or softer than expected, recalibrating plant spacing if uneven terrain is detected, or adapting the planting strategy in response to environmental changes like temperature fluctuations. Additionally, the system detects and corrects errors automatically, such as repositioning a misaligned seedling without human intervention.

4.3 Remote Monitoring and Adjustment

The communication module, based on the MQTT protocol, allows the system to continuously transmit real-time data, including sensor readings and operational status, to a central cloud platform. This enables farmers to remotely monitor the machine's performance and intervene when necessary. Through a user interface, farmers can make remote adjustments to the system based on the data provided, such as modifying the machine's parameters if a specific area of the field has different soil conditions. The system will automatically implement these changes in real-time. Additionally, the system can receive over-the-air firmware updates and troubleshooting support, ensuring it remains up to date with the latest features and improvements.

4.4 AI Integration and Data Flow

In future implementations, AI will be integrated into the system to enable predictive decision-making. Supervised learning models trained on historical environmental data and crop outcomes will allow the machine to recommend optimal transplantation strategies. The primary data sources include soil moisture, temperature, humidity, and plant positioning, all gathered through embedded sensors. These insights will be processed to adjust transplantation parameters in real time. To better illustrate this workflow, a system-level process flowchart (Fig. 2) will be added to demonstrate how data collection, analysis, actuation, and feedback correction are coordinated.

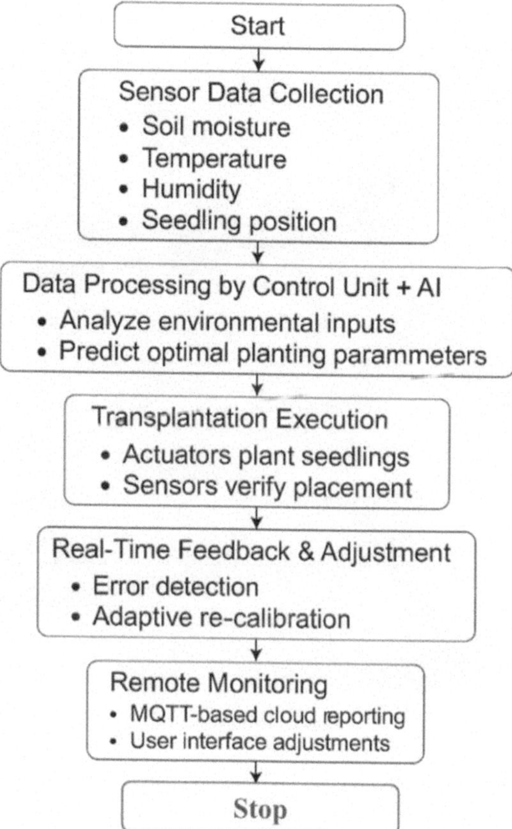

Fig. 2. Machine system-level process flowchart

5 Results and Explanation

To evaluate the performance of the intelligent transplantation machine in real agricultural environments, tests will be conducted on various crops to assess key performance indicators, such as transplantation effectiveness and plant survival rates. Preliminary models and simulations suggest that the system will outperform traditional methods in several ways. By adjusting transplantation conditions in realtime, including planting depth, spacing, and environmental factors, the system aims to enhance seedling health and promote stronger root systems, which is expected to increase the plant survival rate by 30%. Additionally, the automated control system and real-time adjustments based on sensor data are anticipated to reduce transplantation time by approximately 25%, improving operational efficiency. This time saving will allow for quicker deployment over larger areas, ultimately boosting productivity across the field. The system is designed to be energy self-sufficient via solar power. Although the design aims for cost-effectiveness suitable for rural deployment—with an estimated unit cost under $500—this aspect has not yet been tested or validated in real-world conditions.

Fig.3. Prototype

6 Conclusion

The intelligent transplantation machine is a significant improvement in precision agriculture because it combines IoT sensors, automated control systems, actuators, and solar panels to optimize plant placement and increase plant survival rates. It enables real-time modifications depending on environmental data, resulting in improved crop growth.

However, significant limitations remain, such as the fact that the system has yet to be tested in real-world field circumstances. Furthermore, real-time data collecting might be improved to enable more precise agricultural decision-making. These aspects must be addressed in order to test the system's performance under different environmental circumstances and assure its scalability.

For future work, numerous tangible enhancements can be considered:

- **Large-scale testing:** By implementing the system on a variety of agricultural operations, the system's robustness and reliability may be validated in realworld scenarios.
- **Integration with existing agricultural services:** By integrating the machine with existing digital farming systems, it can be adopted and used more effectively in the context of integrated farm management.
- **Energy efficiency improvements:** Future versions could include alternate energy sources such as wind or kinetic energy, as well as high-capacity energy storage systems, to assure continuous operation regardless of solar availability.
- **AI integration:** The addition of AI could improve planting tactics, autonomously estimate planting timings, and anticipate maintenance requirements, resulting in a more efficient and adaptive system.

In conclusion, while this technology has considerable potential for precision agriculture, additional enhancements are required to optimize its benefits and ensure its usefulness in real-world and diverse circumstances.

Acknowledgments. The author received financial support from ESPRIT University. This backing had a substantial impact on the success of our initiative.

Additionally, portions of the manuscript were edited and refined using ChatGPT, a large language model developed by OpenAI, to improve clarity and coherence.

References

1. Harakannanavar, S.S., Joshitha, T., Thejashree, V., Dedipya: Intelligent agriculture using machine learning and internet of things. In: International Conference on Data Science and Network Security (ICDSNS), Tiptur, India, pp. 1–5 (2023)
2. Marinello, F., et al.: The path to smart farming: innovations and opportunities in precision agriculture. Agriculture (2023). https://doi.org/10.3390/agriculture13081593
3. Sánchez-Molina, J.A., Rodríguez, F., Moreno, J.C., Sánchez-Hermosilla, J., Giménez, A.: Robotics in greenhouses. Scoping review. Comput Electron. Agric. **219**, 108750 (2024). https://doi.org/10.1016/j.compag.2024.108750
4. Ishizaki, S.M., et al.: Development of a transplanter-based transplanter for vegetable seedlings cultured in a cuttable nursery mat. J. Agric. Eng. (2024)
5. Genty, N.R., Dominic, J.M.J.: AI-powered autonomous plant-growth optimization system that automatically adjusts input variables to yield desired harvest traits (2019). https://www.freepatentsonline.com/y2021/0027057.html
6. Sharma, K., Shivandu, S.K.: Integrating artificial intelligence and internet of things (IoT) for enhanced crop monitoring and management in precision agriculture. Sens. Int. **5**, 100292 (2024). https://doi.org/10.1016/j.sintl.2024.100292
7. Konar, M.: Integrating IoT and AI for automated crop with smart urban farming, pp. 454–462 (2024). https://doi.org/10.1109/innocomp63224.2024.00080

8. Zemskov, K.V., Sidorina, V.A., Bulatova, E.G.: Intelligent system development for plant cultivation complex by means of the internet of things concept. Intell. Syste. Prod. (4), 68–74 (2023). https://doi.org/10.22213/2410-9304-2023-4-68-74
9. Kumar, K.A., Aju, D.: An internet of thing-based agribot (IoT-agribot) for precision agriculture and farm monitoring. Int. J. Educ. Manage. Eng. **10**(4), 33–39 (2020). https://doi.org/10.5815/IJEME.2020.04.04
10. Gomathi, M., Monika, G.A., Nachammai, M., Saranya, A., Deva Priya, R.S.: AI driven interactive agri bot providing real-time assistance in cultivation and market linkages. Int. J. Multidiscip. Res. **6**(2) (2024). https://doi.org/10.36948/ijfmr.2024.v06i02.18409

A Bibliometric Review of the Application of Artificial Intelligence in Emergency Care Units: Trends and Research Agenda

Tebogo Bokaba[1(✉)], Tsholofelo Mokheleli[1], and Patrick Ndayizigamiye[2]

[1] Department of Applied Information Systems, University of Johannesburg, Johannesburg 2006, South Africa
{tbokaba,tsholofelom}@uj.ac.za

[2] Centre for Applied Data Science, University of Johannesburg, Johannesburg 2006, South Africa
pndayizigamiye@uj.ac.za

Abstract. This study explores the application of artificial intelligence (AI) in emergency care units (ECUs) between 1999 and 2024 through a bibliometric analysis using the Scopus database. The findings highlight a steady rise in AI-related publications, marked by an 18.56% annual growth rate from 2012 to 2023, despite a decline in citations from 2018 to 2024. The United States and China emerged as leading contributors. Thematic insights reveal that "accident and emergency medicine" is part of niche but underdeveloped themes, while "ultrasound" and "point-of care ultrasound" are gaining prominence. The absence of well-established core themes in the motor theme quadrant suggests room for development, although AI, deep learning, and emergency medicine are beginning to gain traction. A proposed research agenda includes the use of AI for real-time monitoring, patient flow optimization, resource forecasting, predictive analytics, and enhancing documentation and communication in ECUs.

Keywords: Artificial Intelligence · Bibliometric Analysis · Emergency Care Units · Research Agenda

1 Introduction

Emergency care units (ECUs) are critical components of healthcare systems worldwide, acting as the first point of care for acute medical conditions, traumas, and other urgent health crises [1]. Effective management of emergencies is vital to save lives and reduce the long-term impact of acute health events on patients. The complexity and urgency of decision-making in ECUs require innovative approaches to enhance care delivery, patient outcomes, and operational efficiency [2]. In recent years, artificial intelligence (AI) has shown the potential to improve emergency medicine [3,4]. AI technologies, including machine learning (ML), natural language processing (NLP), and computer vision, are being

F. Kamoun et al. (Eds.): AFRICATEK 2025, LNICST 676, pp. 297–312, 2026.
https://doi.org/10.1007/978-3-032-16635-7_20

leveraged to support diagnostic processes, predict patient outcomes, optimise treatment pathways, and manage hospital resources more effectively [5–7]. Integrating AI into ECUs represents a paradigm shift, promising to enhance the precision and speed of emergency care services while addressing the challenges of workload management and diagnostic complexities [8,9].

In many developing regions, particularly in low- and middle-income countries (LMICs), ECUs face severe challenges such as understaffed medical teams, lack of access to specialists in rural areas, and outdated or absent triage systems [10]. These systemic issues often result in delayed diagnoses and preventable fatalities. AI technologies, ranging from diagnostic tools to decision-support systems, can alleviate these challenges by automating routine assessments, enabling remote diagnostics, and improving resource allocation in low-resource settings [11].

The primary focus of this study is to conduct a bibliometric analysis of research on the application of artificial intelligence (AI) in emergency care units (ECUs) from 1999 to 2024. The study aims to identify key publication trends, influential authors, sources, and countries, as well as emerging research themes and gaps. Recent trends in AI research applied to emergency care show an important area of study for healthcare practitioners, researchers, and the broader medical community, as it has significant implications for improving patient care and operational efficiency. AI technologies enable faster and more accurate diagnostics, improve treatment outcomes, and optimise resource allocation in high-pressure environments. For example, studies have shown that AI can significantly reduce the time to diagnose critical conditions such as sepsis and heart attacks, potentially lowering mortality rates and enhancing patient outcomes [12,13]. This study proposes a research agenda and explores future directions for AI applications in ECUs.

2 Review of Background Concepts

Integrating AI into ECUs can help optimise healthcare delivery and patient outcomes in critical care settings [8,14]. This section discusses the critical role of ECUs in the healthcare system and AI technologies' capabilities.

2.1 Emergency Care Units in Healthcare

Information and Communication Technologies (ICTs) have historically been crucial in improving emergency care delivery, particularly through electronic health records, telemedicine, and digital triage systems [15]. These technologies laid the foundation for more advanced innovations, such as AI, which now promise to revolutionise emergency medical services.

ECUs are pivotal as the initial point of contact for patients facing acute medical crises. However, they often face systemic challenges in delivering timely and effective care, especially in high-pressure and resource-constrained environments. Common issues include overcrowding, prolonged waiting times, and limited access to specialist care—factors that can severely impact patient outcomes

[16,17]. These operational pressures are particularly pronounced in LMICs, where ECUs are frequently understaffed and overburdened. Studies such as Campos, Souza, and Alves [18] and Oliveira et al. [16] illustrated the adaptations required during routine operations and health crises like the COVID-19 pandemic. Moreover, violence against staff—often triggered by long waiting times and a shortage of available beds—has been documented, highlighting urgent safety and efficiency concerns [18]. To address these challenges, various technological and process innovations have been explored. For example, Lean Healthcare approaches and enhanced educational platforms have shown promise in improving patient flow and staff capabilities [19,20]. In parallel, emerging technologies such as the Internet of Things (IoT) have demonstrated significant potential in automating routine monitoring tasks and enabling real-time clinical response [21].

The integration of AI, alongside IoT and Lean models, represents a transformative opportunity for ECUs. AI can support dynamic triage, optimise resource allocation, and improve real-time decision-making, thus directly addressing many of the current operational inefficiencies. In addition, as Giske et al. [20] highlights, ECUs serve as important educational platforms for medical and nursing students, and AI integration can further enrich this environment through advanced decision-support systems. As noted by Nazir et al. [22] and Sandhu and Aoun [23], AI has the potential to make ECUs not only more efficient but also safer for both patients and staff by reducing overload, mitigating risk, and enhancing care delivery.

2.2 Artificial Intelligence

AI, encompassing a broad range of technologies from ML algorithms to advanced predictive analytics, has become a catalyst for transformation across numerous sectors [7,24], with healthcare being one of the most impactful [25,26]. This subsection focuses on the application of AI within ECUs, emphasising its role in operations, diagnostics, treatment protocols, and care management.

Safiya Parvin and Saleena [12] conducted a systematic review spanning 2015 to 2022 across major databases, namely, Scopus, Web of Science, and PubMed. As highlighted in their analysis, they found that ML and deep learning (DL) models are highly effective in the early detection of sepsis, as evidenced by robust Area Under the Receiver Operating Characteristic Curve (ROC Curve) performance. The findings showed the substantial potential of ML and DL technologies to enhance diagnostic accuracy in critical care settings. Rocha et al. [27] using over 2.7 million medical records, demonstrated that AI-driven data models in ECUs could significantly enhance epidemiological surveillance by predicting pandemic outbreaks up to 72 days in advance. This approach surpasses traditional methods, which typically rely on manual data collection and analysis, delayed reporting, and less sophisticated predictive modelling, thus showcasing AI's capacity to transform public health responses by providing early warnings and enabling timely interventions during health crises. Their study highlights the critical role of ECUs in utilising advanced technology to manage and mitigate pandemic impacts effectively.

In addition, Kajanan et al. [28] demonstrated the application of ML in refining the diagnostic accuracy of arterial blood gas (ABG) tests in ECUs. By implementing several supervised ML models, including extreme gradient boosting (XGBoost), the study achieved high diagnostic accuracy, significantly aiding in identifying types of respiratory failure. The success of XGBoost, confirmed through K-fold cross-validation, highlights the potential for ML to enhance diagnostic precision in emergency care settings.

Finally, Lequertier et al. [29] explored the potential of DL to enhance hospital operational efficiencies by predicting the length of stay (LOS) in ECUs. The study, which used over 1.14 million records of patient admissions at six university hospitals, utilised a feed-forward neural network (FFNN) that leveraged extensive administrative data, including demographics, diagnoses, medical procedures, and socioeconomic factors. The FFNN significantly outperformed traditional models like random forest (RF) and logistic regression (LR) in predicting LOS, achieving an accuracy of 0.94 and a Cohen's kappa of 0.94. These metrics showed the DL model's precision and reliability compared to the lower scores from RF and LR, highlighting its effectiveness in providing fine-grained predictions that could optimise care scheduling and resource allocation in emergency care settings. The successful implementation of this DL model could enhance the quality of patient care by enabling more accurate and efficient planning and management of hospital resources.

These studies demonstrate the transformative potential of AI in enhancing the efficiency and effectiveness of emergency care. By integrating advanced AI technologies, ECUs can improve patient outcomes and pave the way for innovations that could reshape future emergency medical practices. The continuous application of AI in ECUs represents a promising frontier for improving immediate patient care and setting new standards in healthcare technology. Recent advancements in Generative AI (Gen-AI) and Large Language Models (LLMs) are transforming emergency care. Arslan et al. [30] found that ChatGPT and Copilot matched or outperformed nurses in triaging high-acuity patients, with ChatGPT achieving 66.5% accuracy. These tools offer consistent performance across demographics, enhance decision-making, reduce bias, and streamline communication in overcrowded settings.

3 Methodology

This study utilised the Scopus database to search for articles to be included in the bibliometric analysis. Scopus is renowned for its comprehensive coverage and multidisciplinary focus, encompassing a wide range of peer-reviewed journals, conference papers, and book chapters. Scopus is essential for conducting a holistic review of any scientific domain, especially one as interdisciplinary as AI in healthcare [31]. In addition, Scopus's advanced indexing, citation tracking features, reliability and data quality make it an ideal source for conducting bibliometric analyses.

The study's data was collected from the Scopus database on 28th March 2024, covering 1999 to 2024. The following search string was utilised to extract data: ("Artificial Intelligence" OR "machine learning" OR "deep learning") AND ("emergency care" OR "emergency department" OR "emergency crisis unit" OR "Triage" OR "Emergency Medicine") using the title, abstract and keywords. Document titles and abstracts were reviewed during data extraction, and documents published in languages other than English were excluded, resulting in 2,020 documents. These documents were analysed using the Biblioshiny tool, a web-based interface for the Bibliometrix R-package, which allows for comprehensive bibliometric analysis. The summary of extracted data was as follows: documents (2,020), average citation per document (11.26), sources (834), authors (10,343), authors' keywords (3,574), and annual growth (18.56%).

4 Results and Discussion

This section presents and discusses the results obtained from the analysis of the 2,020 documents identified.

4.1 Annual Production by Article and Citation

Figure 1 is divided into the number of articles (a) and total citations (b) per year. Figure 1a shows the annual distribution of the 2,020 documents from 1999 to 2024 in AI applications in ECU research. It highlights a fluctuating trend with increasingly variable periods that started in 2006 and ended in 2011. From the 2,020 documents, it is revealed that there was a steady increase in publications from 2012 through to 2023, with 1,920 documents contributing 95.05% and an overall annual growth rate of 18.56%. Figure 1b shows a notable fluctuation of citations between 2002 and 2018, with a peak in citations in 2009, followed by a sharp decrease in citations from 2019 to 2023. It is important to note that the apparent drop in publications after 2023 may be due to indexing delays for 2024 in Scopus. Similarly, the decline in citations after 2018 likely reflects the typical time lag required for newer studies to gain recognition and accumulate citations. This trend may also indicate that, as research in AI continues to evolve, only a limited number of publications at the intersection of AI and Emergency Care have emerged as authoritative or widely cited between 2018 and 2024.

4.2 Most Relevant Sources

Table 1 presents the top 10 most cited sources in the application of AI in ECU. The sources published 344 documents, with *PLoS One* ranked as the leading source with 54 published documents. It is followed by *Science Reports* with 49 documents, *Journal of Medical Internet Research* with 36 documents, *Lecture Notes in Computer Science (Including Subseries Lecture Notes in Artificial Intelligence and Lecture Notes in Bioinformation)* and *Studies in Health Technology and Informatics*, both with the same number of documents, that is, 34.

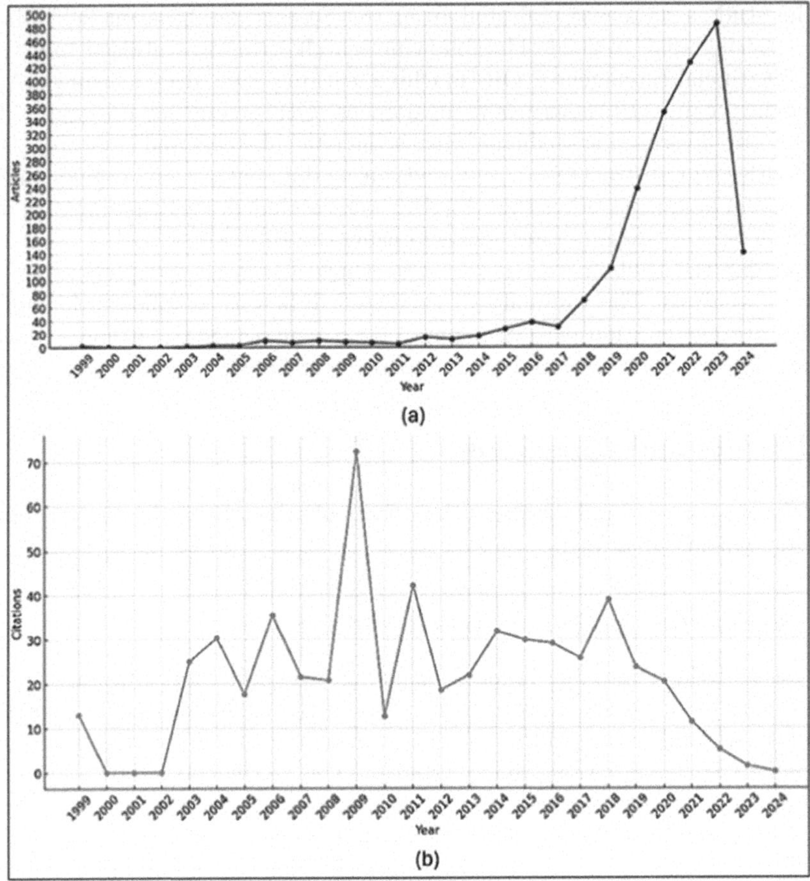

Fig. 1. Distribution of publications and citations over time. (a) Annual number of articles published; (b) Annual number of citations received.

Table 1. Top 10 most cited sources.

S/No.	Sources	Articles
1	PLoS One	54
2	Scientific Reports	49
3	Journal of Medical Internet Research	36
4	Lecture Notes in Computer Science (Including Subseries Lecture Notes in Artificial Intelligence and Lecture Notes in Bioinformation)	34
5	Studies in Health Technology and Informatics	34
6	International Journal of Medical Informatics	33
7	American Journal of Emergency Medicine	29
8	BMJ Open	26
9	JMIR Medical Informatics	25
10	Jama Network Open	24

4.3 Most Relevant Authors

From 1999 to 2024, 10 343 authors participated in research on the application of AI in ECU, with only 81 single-authored documents. Table 2 presents the top 10 relevant authors with Liu N having the highest publication count of 25 documents, Taylor RA having the highest citation count of 156, and Liu N and Taylor RA having the same h-index of 10. Overall, it is shown that the top five most relevant authors are Liu N, Taylor RA, Ong MEH, Lee S and Kim D. The concentration of influential publications and citations among the top authors, notably Liu N and Taylor RA, highlights a core group of researchers driving research on the application of AI in ECUs. This dominance suggests that the field benefits significantly from their contributions, foundational to the ongoing development and understanding of AI technologies in emergency medical settings. Their work not only advances the scientific discourse but also sets benchmarks for future research in this critical area of healthcare.

Table 2. Top 10 Most Relevant Authors

S/No.	Authors	Articles	Citation	H_index
1	Liu N	25	73	10
2	Ong MEH	24	60	9
3	Lee S	18	40	6
4	Cha WC	16	24	5
5	Taylor RA	16	156	10
6	Kim D	14	30	5
7	Kim JH	14	31	6
8	Klang E	14	28	5
9	Kim J	13	30	5
10	Ho AFW	12	36	7

4.3.1 Author Collaboration Network

Figure 2 shows the collaboration network among the top 50 authors of research in the application of AI in ECUs, featuring 15 distinct clusters. Notably, the clusters with the largest nodes include those centred around Liu N and Ong MEH, the most relevant contributors, as depicted in Sect. 4.3, indicating their central roles in the network and their extensive collaborative engagements. In addition, the grey cluster prominently features Cha WC, the fourth most cited author, highlighting their significant connections within this research cluster. The author collaboration network shows the interconnected nature of this field, with key researchers forming strong collaborative ties that facilitate the exchange of ideas and drive the field's advancements.

4.4 Most Relevant Affiliations

Table 3 shows the top 10 affiliations contributing the most to research on the application of AI in ECU, with a total of 908 documents. *Harvard Medical School* in the United States of America (USA) had the highest number of publications, with 169 documents, followed by the *University of California* (USA) with 113 documents, the *University of Toronto* (Canada) with 96 documents, *Fondazione Policlinico Universitario A. Gemelli Irccs* (Rome) with 78 documents, and the *National University of Singapore* (Singapore) with 78 documents. The results corroborate with those in Table 4, with the USA being the leading country in this research.

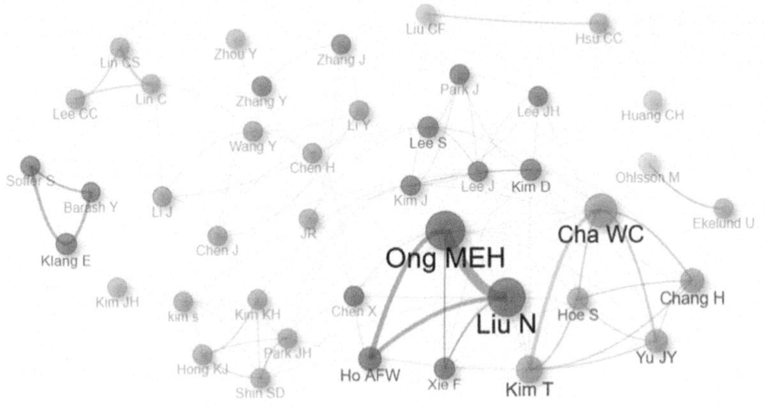

Fig. 2. Author collaboration network.

Table 3. Top 10 Most Relevant Affiliations

S/No.	Affiliation	Articles
1	Harvard Medical School	169
2	University of California	113
3	University of Toronto	96
4	Fondazione Policlinico Universitario A. Gemelli IRCCS	78
5	National University of Singapore	78
6	Mayo Clinic	77
7	Medical University of South Carolina	77
8	Stanford University	77
9	Sungkyunkwan University School of Medicine	73
10	Tel Aviv University	70

4.5 Corresponding Authors Countries

In exploring the global dynamics of research in the application of AI in ECUs, the analysis delved into single-country publications (SCPs) and multiple-country publications (MCPs), which assess the scope of international collaboration in this domain. The SCPs reveal the contributions of individual countries, showing national research strengths. MCPs illustrate cross-border collaborations, highlighting global efforts and the significance of international partnerships in advancing AI in healthcare [32,33].

Table 4 reveals that the USA, China, Korea, Canada, and the United Kingdom are the foremost contributors to AI research in ECUs, ranked by the number of published articles. The variation in MCP ratios further highlights the differing extents of international collaboration. Spain and Canada have the highest inclination towards cross-border research partnerships, indicating diverse strategies in advancing AI applications in healthcare across countries.

Table 4. Top 10 corresponding authors countries

S/No.	Country	Articles	Citation	SCP	MCP	Freq	MCP_Ratio
1	USA	586	8864	506	80	0.29	0.137
2	China	168	1235	134	34	0.083	0.202
3	Korea	106	901	96	10	0.052	0.094
4	Canada	91	926	66	25	0.045	0.275
5	United Kingdom	88	894	65	23	0.044	0.261
6	Australia	60	586	47	13	0.03	0.217
7	Italy	58	640	44	14	0.029	0.241
8	Spain	45	628	32	13	0.022	0.289
9	India	43	116	35	8	0.021	0.186
10	France	41	558	31	10	0.02	0.244

4.6 Most Cited Documents

The top 10 most cited documents in the application of AI in ECUs have citations ranging from 179 to 367. Table 5 reveals that Lindsey et al. [34] have 367 citations, Taylor et al. [13] have 321 citations, followed by Ahmed and Alkhamis [35], Fleuren et al. [36], Raita et al. [37], Mao et al. [38], and Levin et al. [39] each have citations above 200.

The top-cited documents on the application of AI in ECUs reflect the various applications of AI across diverse aspects of emergency care. From enhancing diagnostic accuracy in fracture detection to predicting in-hospital mortality among sepsis patients, these studies show AI's role in improving diagnostics, operational efficiency, and patient outcomes. The common trend identified in the top-cited

Table 5. Most cited articles in AI application in ECU

S/No.	Author/Year	Title	Sources	Citations
1	Lindsey et al. (2018)	Deep neural network improves fracture detection by clinicians	National Academy of Sciences	367
2	Taylor et al. (2016)	Prediction of in-hospital mortality in emergency department patients with sepsis: A local big data-driven, machine learning approach	Academic Emergency Medicine	321
3	Ahmed & Alkhamis (2009)	Simulation optimisation for an emergency department healthcare unit in Kuwait	European Journal of Operational Research	290
4	Fleuren et al. (2020)	Machine learning for the prediction of sepsis: A systematic review and meta-analysis of diagnostic test accuracy	Intensive Care Medicine	285
5	Raita et al. (2019)	Emergency department triage prediction of clinical outcomes using machine learning models	Critical Care	210
6	Mao et al. (2018)	Multicentre validation of a sepsis prediction algorithm using only vital sign data in the emergency department, general ward, and ICU	BMJ Open	205
7	Levin et al. (2018)	Machine-learning-based electronic triage more accurately differentiates patients with respect to clinical outcomes compared with the emergency severity index	Annals Emergency Medicine	204
8	Chang et al. (2018)	Hybrid 3D/2D convolutional neural network for hemorrhage evaluation on head CT	American Journal of Neuroradiol-ogy	186
9	Koyner et al. (2018)	The development of a machine learning inpatient acute kidney injury prediction model	Critical Care Medicine	180
10	Horng et al. (2017)	Creating an automated trigger for sepsis clinical decision support at emergency department triage using machine learning	PLoS One	179

documents is the application of ML and deep neural networks in emergency medicine. The significant citations these articles have received highlight the academic and clinical importance of AI technologies in advancing emergency care practices.

4.7 Thematic Map - Author Keywords

The thematic map in Fig. 3 categorises research themes that emerged from studies on the application of AI in ECUs into niche and basic themes. The thematic map categorises research themes into distinct quadrants reflecting their development status and research activity. These themes are divided into Motor themes, which are central and well-developed within the field; Niche themes, specialised and developed within a smaller community; Emerging or declining themes, indicating emerging or declining areas of research; and Basic themes, foundational topics that strengthen broader research connections [40,41]. The absence of emerging or declining themes in the thematic map of AI in ECUs suggests a mature field with stable research interests.

Niche themes like "accident & emergency medicine" and "information technology" indicate specialised yet less developed areas, whereas "ultrasound" and "point-of-care ultrasound" suggest growing interest. As noted, the absence of themes in the Emerging or Declining quadrant suggests a stable or maturing research landscape. The Basic themes quadrant highlights foundational topics such as "artificial intelligence," "deep learning," and "emergency medicine," emphasising their importance in this research domain. In addition, "machine learning," "emergency department," and "triage" underline core, evolving aspects of AI application in emergency care. The Motor Theme Quadrant was empty, indicating a lack of well-developed and central themes within the research; however, AI, DL, and emergency medicine are slightly moving into this quadrant. This map reflects a research domain grounded in essential AI technologies, pointing to specialised areas for potential growth.

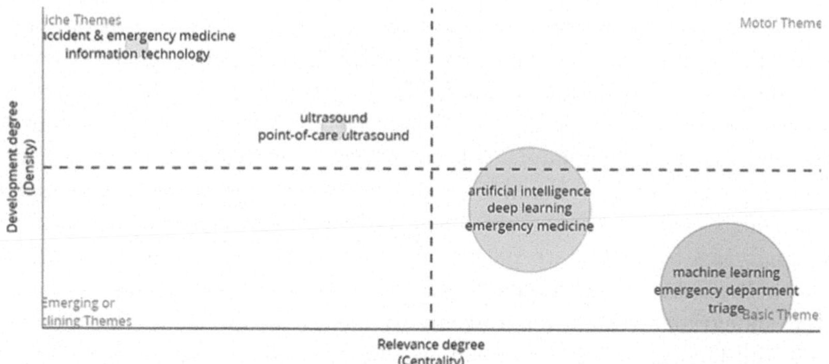

Fig. 3. Thematic map.

5 Identification of Research Agenda in the Application of AI in ECU Research

This bibliometric analysis conducted on the application of AI in ECU research spanning from 1999 to 2024 highlights this field's expansive growth and evolving landscape. With a significant increase in the total number of publications and citations over the years, this study demonstrates the growing interest in the application of AI technologies in emergency care. The thematic analysis, particularly the thematic map and thematic evolution, uncovers both foundational and niche themes, reflecting the multifaceted applications of AI in ECUs. Identifying a research agenda from this analysis points to several opportunities and gaps. There is a clear opportunity to further explore and innovate in the niche areas identified, such as the application of ultrasound technologies and information technology in emergency care [42,43]. While currently less developed, these areas can potentially contribute to operational efficiency in ECUs. In addition, the evolving themes around ML and AI show a sustained interest in these technologies' significant role in advancing emergency medicine [28,29].

However, the absence of emerging or declining themes suggests a potential gap in identifying and nurturing new research areas within the application of AI in emergency care. This gap represents an opportunity for future research to explore uncharted territories through interdisciplinary collaborations that could bring fresh perspectives and innovative solutions to persistent challenges in ECUs. For example, AI applications can be pivotal in addressing overcrowding by optimising patient triage processes and improving patient flow management [20], and reducing long waiting times by automating administrative tasks, thereby improving resource allocation [29]. These applications can enhance operational efficiency and improve patient satisfaction and outcomes. Aligning these potential AI applications with the operational challenges detailed in Sect. 2 reinforces the necessity for a focused exploration of AI's capabilities within the ECU environment. Moreover, the concentration of research contributions from a core group of countries and authors indicates the need for broader international collaboration to diversify research perspectives and approaches in this domain.

While the application of AI in ECU research is growing, there is a crucial need to deepen and broaden research efforts. Deepening involves pushing the boundaries in established areas like ML and DL in diagnostics and patient care. Broadening, on the other hand, calls for exploratory research into underdeveloped domains, including AI-enabled real-time triage and prioritisation systems that enhance clinical response efficiency. Future work should also explore predictive analytics to anticipate patient deterioration and enable early intervention, as well as AI-driven forecasting models that support dynamic staff and resource allocation in high-demand environments. In addition, the integration of LLMs and GenAI into ECU workflows can streamline clinical documentation and enhance communication across medical teams. These directions can help shape a more adaptive, intelligent, and equitable emergency care infrastructure globally.

6 Conclusion

The bibliometric analysis of AI applications in ECUs revealed significant advancements in enhancing diagnostic precision, operational efficiency, and overall patient care. ML and DL technologies notably improved the early detection and management of critical conditions like sepsis, signalling AI's important role in emergency care. The increase in AI-related research since 2012 shows a growing academic and clinical interest in leveraging AI to address complex healthcare challenges. While this indicates a mature field, the absence of emerging or declining themes suggests unexplored avenues for interdisciplinary collaborations for innovative solutions in ECUs. In addition, international contributions emphasise the need for global collaboration to diversify research perspectives and drive future innovations. Integrating AI in ECUs addresses systemic challenges such as overcrowding and enhances educational platforms within these units. There is a need for continued research to fully harness AI's potential in emergency care settings, paving the way for improved patient outcomes and operational efficiencies in healthcare delivery.

The authors acknowledge the reliance on data exclusively from the Scopus database, which, despite its extensive coverage, could have omitted relevant studies indexed in other databases. The focus on English-language publications also potentially excluded significant research in other languages. The thematic analysis is limited to available literature and may not fully capture emerging trends that have not been extensively published or indexed.

References

1. Al Owad, A., et al.: Integrated Lean Six Sigma and Kotter change management framework for emergency healthcare services in Saudi Arabia. Benchmark. Int. J. (2023). https://doi.org/10.1108/BIJ-05-2023-0335
2. Chacón-Encalada, G., Jaramillo-Mediavilla, L., Rivera-Montesdeoca, W., Suárez-Zambrano, L., García-Santillán, I.: Detection of space and time patterns in the ECU 911 integrated security system using data mining techniques. In: Salgado Guerrero, J.P., Chicaiza Espinosa, J., Cerrada Lozada, M., Berrezueta-Guzman, S. (eds.) TICEC 2021. CCIS, vol. 1456, pp. 61–74. Springer, Cham (2021). https://doi.org/10.1007/978-3-030-89941-7_5
3. Kapil, S.: Emergency medicine in the digital age: AI-assisted critical care. Indus J. Med. Health Sci. **1**(01), 117–126 (2023). https://induspublishers.com/IJMHS/article/view/59
4. Ramlakhan, S., et al.: Understanding and interpreting artificial intelligence, machine learning and deep learning in emergency medicine. Emerg. Med. J. **39**(5), 380–385 (2022). https://doi.org/10.1136/emermed-2021-212068
5. Liu, Z., et al.: Listening to mental health crisis needs at scale: using natural language processing to understand and evaluate a mental health crisis text messaging service. Front. Digit. Health **3** (2021). https://doi.org/10.3389/fdgth.2021.779091
6. Lobo, A., et al.: Better medical efficiency by means of hospital bed management optimization a comparison of artificial intelligence techniques. In: Moniz, N., Vale, Z., Cascalho, J., Silva, C., Sebastião, R. (eds.) EPIA 2023. LNCS, pp. 260–273 (2023). https://doi.org/10.1007/978-3-031-49011-8_21

7. Mbuya, E., et al.: A multiclass approach to predicting diabetes using machine learning. In: Proceedings of the ACIS (2023). https://aisel.aisnet.org/acis2023/140
8. Al Badawi, A.K., Nashwan, A.J.: The future of prehospital emergency care: embracing AI applications in ambulance services. Int. Emerg. Nurs. **72**, 101385 (2024). https://doi.org/10.1016/j.ienj.2023.101385
9. Wu, T.-C., Ho, C.-T.B.: Blockchain revolutionizing in emergency medicine: a scoping review of patient journey through the ED. Healthcare **11**(18), 2497 (2023). https://doi.org/10.3390/healthcare11182497
10. Silva, L.O.J.E., et al.: Emergency medicine in Brazil: historical perspective, current status, and future challenges. Int. J. Emerg. Med. **14**, 79 (2021). ISSN: 1865-1372. https://doi.org/10.1186/s12245-021-00400-6
11. El-Kareh, R., Sittig, D.F.: Enhancing diagnosis through technology. Crit. Care Clin. **38**, 129–139 (2022). ISSN: 07490704. https://doi.org/10.1016/j.ccc.2021.08.004
12. Safiya Parvin, A., Saleena, B.: Analysis of machine learning and deep learning prediction models for sepsis and neonatal sepsis: a systematic review. ICT Express **9**(6), 1215–1225 (2023). https://doi.org/10.1016/j.icte.2023.07.007
13. Taylor, R.A., et al.: Prediction of in-hospital mortality in emergency department patients with sepsis: a local big data driven, machine learning approach. Acad. Emerg. Med. **23**(3), 269–278 (2016). https://doi.org/10.1111/acem.12876
14. Hosseini, MM., et al.: The aspects of running artificial intelligence in emergency care; a scoping review. Arch. Acad. Emerg. Med. **11**(1), e38 (2023). https://doi.org/10.22037/aaem.v11i1.1974
15. Tonetto, L.M., et al.: Information and communication technologies in emergency care services for patients with COVID-19: a multi-national study. Int. J. Prod. Res. **61**, 8384–8400 (2023). ISSN: 0020-7543. https://doi.org/10.1080/00207543.2021.1967501
16. Junior, A.D.O.S., et al.: Musculoskeletal pain during and after SARS-CoV-2 infection and healthcare utilization: a cross-sectional study. BMC Musculoskeletal Disord. **24**(1), 685 (2023). https://doi.org/10.1186/s12891-023-06794-z
17. Camilo, D.G.G., et al.: Multi-criteria analysis in the health area: selection of the most appropriate triage system for the emergency care units in natal. BMC Med. Inf. Decis. Making **20**(1), 38 (2020). https://doi.org/10.1186/s12911-020-1054-y
18. Campos, I.C.M., Souza, M.S., Alves, M.: Violence in the daily work of healthcare professionals in an emergency care unit. Revista Ga cha de Enfermagem **44** (2023). https://doi.org/10.1590/1983-1447.2023.20230001.en
19. Bonamigo, A., et al.: Optimizing patient flow in emergency care units and lean healthcare. Lean Healthcare, 167–185 (2023). https://doi.org/10.4018/979-8-3693-0458-7.ch007
20. Giske, S., et al.: Mapping interaction quality for nursing and medical students in primary care placement in municipal emergency care units: a systematic observational study. Front. Med. **11** (2024). https://doi.org/10.3389/fmed.2024.1181478
21. Al Mudawi, N.: Integration of IoT and fog computing in healthcare based the smart intensive units. IEEE Access **10**, 59906–59918 (2022). https://doi.org/10.1109/ACCESS.2022.3179704
22. Nazir, T., et al.: Artificial intelligence assisted acute patient journey. Front. Artif. Intell. **5** (2022). https://doi.org/10.3389/frai.2022.962165
23. Sandhu, A.K., Aoun, M.: Understanding the impact of AI-driven automation on the workflow of radiologists in emergency care settings. Adv. Intell. Inf. Syst. **8**(2), 1–17 (2019)

24. Mokheleli, T., Museba, T.: Machine learning approach for credit score predictions. J. Inf. Syst. Inf. **5**(2), 497–517 (2023). https://doi.org/10.51519/journalisi.v5i2.487
25. Kaul, D., Raju, H., Tripathy, B.K.: Deep learning in healthcare. Stud. Big Data **91**. https://doi.org/10.1007/978-3-030-75855-4_6
26. Monselise, M., Yang, C.C.: AI for social good in healthcare: Moving towards a clear framework and evaluating applications. In: Proceedings - 2022 IEEE 10th International Conference on Healthcare Informatics, ICHI 2022. pp. 470–471 (2022). https://doi.org/10.1109/ICHI54592.2022.00072
27. Rocha, H.A.L., et al.: COVID-19 outbreaks surveillance through text mining applied to electronic health records. BMC Infect. Dis. **24**(1), 359 (2024). https://doi.org/10.1186/s12879-024-09250-y
28. Kajanan, S., et al.: Classify the outcome of arterial blood gas test to detect the respiratory failure using machine learning. In: 2022 International Conference on Decision Aid Sciences and Applications (DASA), pp. 1139–1143 (2022). https://doi.org/10.1109/DASA54658.2022.9765012
29. Lequertier, V., et al.: Length of stay prediction with standardized hospital data from acute and emergency care using a deep neural network. Med. Care **62**(4), 225–234 (2024). https://doi.org/10.1097/MLR.0000000000001975
30. Arslan, B., et al.: Evaluating LLM-based generative AI tools in emergency triage: a comparative study of ChatGPT Plus, Copilot Pro, and triage nurses. Am. J. Emerg. Med. **89**, 174–181 (2025). ISSN: 0735-6757. https://doi.org/10.1016/J.AJEM.2024.12.024. https://www.sciencedirect.com/science/article/pii/S0735675724007071
31. Pranckut, R.: Web of science (WoS) and Scopus: the titans of bibliographic information in today's academic world. Publications **9**(1), 12 (2021). https://doi.org/10.3390/publications9010012
32. Shi, Z., et al.: Current trends and future directions of global research on wastewater to energy: a bibliometric analysis and review. Environ. Sci. Pollut. Res. **31**(14), 20792–20813 (2024). https://doi.org/10.1007/s11356-024-32560-2
33. Sweileh, W.M., et al.: Bibliometric analysis of worldwide publications on multi-, extensively, and totally drug resistant tuberculosis (2006 2015). Multidisc. Respir. Med. **11**(1), 45 (2016). https://doi.org/10.1186/s40248-016-0081-0
34. Lindsey, R., et al.: Deep neural network improves fracture detection by clinicians. Proc. Nat. Acad. Sci. **115**(45), 11591–11596 (2018). https://doi.org/10.1073/pnas.1806905115
35. Ahmed, M.A., Alkhamis, T.M.: Simulation optimization for an emergency department healthcare unit in Kuwait. Eur. J. Oper. Res. **198**(3), 936–942 (2009). https://doi.org/10.1016/j.ejor.2008.10.025
36. Fleuren, L.M.. et al.: Machine learning for the prediction of sepsis: a systematic review and meta-analysis of diagnostic test accuracy. Intensive Care Med. **46**(3), 383–400 (2020). https://doi.org/10.1007/s00134-019-05872-y
37. Raita, Y., et al.: Emergency department triage prediction of clinical outcomes using machine learning models. Crit. Care **23**(1), 64 (2019). https://doi.org/10.1186/s13054-019-2351-7
38. Mao, Q., et al.: Multicentre validation of a sepsis prediction algorithm using only vital sign data in the emergency department, general ward, and ICU. BMJ Open **8**(1), e017833 (2018). https://doi.org/10.1136/bmjopen-2017-017833
39. Levin, S., et al.: Machine-learning-based electronic triage more accurately differentiates patients with respect to clinical outcomes compared with the Emergency Severity Index. Ann. Emerg. Med. **71**(5), 565–574.e2 (2018). https://doi.org/10.1016/j.annemergmed.2017.08.005

40. Misra, V.P., Mishra, P.K., Sharma, A.: Artificial intelligence in education emerging trends, thematic analysis application in lifelong learning. In: 2023 IEEE Asia-Pacific Conference on Computer Science and Data Engineering (CSDE), pp. 1–6 (2023). https://doi.org/10.1109/CSDE59766.2023.10487664
41. Rodríguez-Sabiote, C., et al.: Active learning in an environment of innovative training and sustainability. Mapping of the conceptual structure of research fronts through a bibliometric analysis. Sustainability **12**(19), 8012 (2020). https://doi.org/10.3390/su12198012
42. Amaral, C.B., Ralston, D.C., Becker, T.K.: Prehospital point-of-care ultrasound: a transformative technology. SAGE Open Med. **8**, 205031212093270 (2020). https://doi.org/10.1177/2050312120932706
43. Shagerdi, G., Ayatollahi, H., Hemmat, M.: Emergency care for the elderly: a review of the application of health information technology. Health Policy Technol. **11**(1), 100592 (2022). https://doi.org/10.1016/j.hlpt.2021.100592

An Improved Fire Detection and Classification System

Eustace M. Dogo[1(✉)], Tebogo Bokaba[2], Joshua Onu[1], and Bentem Terence[1]

[1] Department of Computer Engineering, Federal University of Technology, Minna, Nigeria
eustace.dogo@futminna.edu.ng

[2] Department of Applied Information Systems, University of Johannesburg, Johannesburg, South Africa

Abstract. Fires cause significant damage and destruction to many individuals every year globally, necessitating improved approaches to fire detection and classification. This paper presents a multi-sensor system that detects and classifies fire using a camera and several gas and temperature sensors based on the nature of the burning material. It also dispatches notifications about the fire source and determines and executes an appropriate response to the detected fire. The study investigated three machine learning models (Neural Networks, Random Forest, and K-Nearest Neighbours) and three pre-trained Convolutional Neural Network models (VGG16, MobileNetV2, and EfficientNetBO) for sensor and image data classification, respectively, in indoor fire detection. Random Forest and VGG16 were the best performing models for sensor and image classification tasks. The results obtained show that the sensor data classifier obtained an accuracy of 99.35%, while the image classifier had an accuracy of 95.83%, with identical values for precision and recall. The overall system response time was measured to be approximately 15 s on average, demonstrating a fairly quick and accurate response in determining the nature of fires in indoor environments.

Keywords: Fire detection · fire classification · gas sensors · image · machine learning · deep learning · fire response system · IoT

1 Introduction

Fire detection is a popular field of study within the vast field of electrical and electronics engineering, with good reason, since the dawn of civilization, man has experienced both the benefits and hazards of fires, with the hazards usually leading to large-scale loss of lives and property. An unfortunate side effect of uncontrolled fires is the smoke and volatile organic compounds (VOCs) produced alongside the intense heat, with some studies showing that the inhalation of these substances is the leading cause of fatalities in fires, rather than the heat of the flames [1]. It is worth noting that not all fires are alike, as the nature of various materials when set aflame can lead to vastly different flame characteristics, affecting the colour of the flame, the intensity of heat produced by the flame, and especially its smoke content. These different characteristics may be used to infer the source of a fire, and possibly the materials involved [2].

F. Kamoun et al. (Eds.): AFRICATEK 2025, LNICST 676, pp. 313–330, 2026.
https://doi.org/10.1007/978-3-032-16635-7_21

The majority of fire detection systems follow two major philosophies, requiring either the use of a variety of sensors to observe extreme temperature changes and increases in smoke concentration, or the repurposing of traditional surveillance systems to recognise fire colours and outlines in real-time [3]. Sensor-based approaches typically use two or more sensors with simple inference algorithms to detect fires, while vision-based approaches tend to use one or more cameras for fire detection.

Flame colours, in particular, serve as a useful metric for differentiating materials that are on fire, although the temperature of a fire also plays a part in the eventual colour of the flame, with hotter flames generally producing lighter colours. However, some commonly known metals produce distinctive flame colours, such as Barium (green), Sodium (yellow), Copper (blue-green), and Strontium (red) [4].

Another common method for determining the combustible material in a fire outbreak is the isolation and identification of the individual components making up its smoke and gaseous emissions. Various gases such as carbon monoxide (CO), carbon dioxide (CO2), nitrogen monoxide (NO), oxygen (02), hydrogen cyanide (HCN), along with other volatile organic compounds (VOCs) such as benzene, formaldehyde, and 1,3-Butadiene is also present in fires [5–7]. Many of these emissions are produced in the early stages of fires, providing a method for the detection of fire outbreaks before they reach a critical point [8].

A standardised system for the classification of fires exists, based on the type of materials and combustion fuel. The system uses letters to represent different types of fires, primarily for the quick identification of the correct flame retardant to use for extinguishing the fire [9]. The use of the correct extinguisher is crucial as some flame retardants have negative effects when used on the wrong type of fire, e.g. electrocution from water on electrical fires, or explosions from water on flammable metal fires. Class A fires generally involve combustible materials like wood, paper, cloth and some common plastics; Class B represents flammable liquids like petrol although some territories designate class B for flammable gases such as LPG and propane; Class C for electrical fires emanating from live wires and electrical components; Class D for flammable metals such as magnesium and sodium; and finally, Class F for oil fires generally involving cooking oils and fats [9, 10].

This study presents a mechanism for detecting and classifying fires based on their gas concentrations, temperature, and flame images. The primary contributions of this study are as follows: 1) Designing and implementing hardware consisting of six different gas sensors, a camera, and a temperature sensor for fire data collection. 2) Modelling and training three different machine learning (ML) algorithms for fire-type classification based on sensor data. 3) Developing three different pre-trained Convolutional Neural Network (CNN) architectures for fire colour classification from associated images. 4) Developing a notification and response system to facilitate fire mitigation and damage control. 5) Evaluating the system's performance based on accuracy, precision, and recall metrics, as well as the system's response time.

The rest of the paper is organised as follows: The review of related works section provides an overview of relevant research projects carried out in the field of fire detection and classification. The system design section details the software and hardware configurations of the system, the results section presents the outcome of system testing, while the discussion of results section interprets and provides context for the collected results. Finally, the conclusion and future work section summarises the findings of this paper and suggests areas for future research.

2 Review of Related Works

At the forefront of technological advancements in this decade is the rise of ML algorithms and artificial intelligence (AI). These concepts are being applied in almost every aspect of technology, and this is also the case in the area of fire detection, ranging from purely sensor-driven to image-based systems. Early works show CNNs as being suitable for processing video and image-based fire detection [11], while comparisons of Support Vector Machines (SVMs), Decision Trees (DTs), Logistic Regression (LR) and Multi-Layer Perceptron (MLP) for sensor network data produced accuracies of up to 99.97% using MLPs [12].

To speed up training and improve real-world performance of image-based fire detection, some approaches have employed transfer learning and lightweight architectures. Faster R-CNN with Inception V2 delivered 92.4% fire-detection accuracy despite its poor smoke detection by leveraging pre-trained weights [13]. Transfer-learned MobileNet and Visual Geometry Group (VGG) models can be used to overcome imbalanced datasets mimicking real-world fire scenarios, to reach accuracies of 98.48% and 99.15% in just ten epochs [14]. For resource-constrained and low-energy devices, inverted residual blocks, depth-wise and octave convolutions can cut Floating Point Operations per Second (flops) by 97% and parameters by 59%, while still reaching 84.36% accuracy across three still fire image datasets [15]. A bespoke "E-FireNet" (a trimmed, kernel-optimized VGG16) further demonstrated 98% accuracy, 100% precision and a 99% F1 score on early-fire imager [16].

Pure sensor-network studies also continue, with [17] showing a sensor array tracking H_2, CO, CO_2, VOCs, particulate matter, UV, temperature and humidity to achieve 73% baseline classification accuracy of wood, cotton, cable and candle fires by integrating TrAdaBoost and sensor-position boosting. Dynamic time-warping on sensor time series plus k-out-of-p voting in a Nearest Neighbour classifier reduced false alarms and pinpointed fire-start times more precisely [18]. Large scale wireless sensor networks using multiple sensor nodes employing methane, propane, liquefied petroleum gas (LPG), CO, and H2 sensors to relay radio frequency (RF) collected data to a leader node for early wildfire alerts [19].

Hybrid architectures merge sensor and vision data to cut false alarms and raise accuracy. One design combined Adaboost-LBP feature selection with multiple MLPs and a downstream CNN, to reach an overall accuracy of 99% [20]. Another Raspberry Pi-based solution uses OpenCV to detect heat, light intensity and motion indicative of a fire [21], while pure-vision setups illustrated the trade-off between speed and bounding-box completeness in image-based fire detection [22]. Region-based CNNs in conjunction with still frame inputs from security cameras, augmented with LSTM, capture temporal dynamics to distinguish fires over sequences, is another approach explored [23], with a lean transfer-learning CNN approach increasing accuracy from 87.4% to 96.3% in surveillance footage [24].

Efforts are underway to create autonomous systems that not only detect fires but also combat the fires. The studies in [25–27] propose systems to reduce the dangers involved in combating fires through remote autonomous systems to detect fires, ascertain their source and deliver the deterrent fluid to extinguish the flame. Both approaches employ mobile units to aid detection and extinguishment at the fire source. In other studies in [28–31] employed a wider Internet of Things (IoT) system to serve as an early response system, taking action based on the severity of the detected fire outbreak using ventilation systems, notification systems and water support sprinkler systems to prevent suffocation and mitigate fire damage. The authors in [32] combine this method with Unmanned Aerial Vehicle (UAV) technologies for wildfire detection.

2.1 Research Gaps and Challenges in Existing Literature

The review process of recent works carried out in the field of fire detection and classification revealed several challenges faced and some potential improvements for future approaches to implement. The major challenges encountered during the implementation of previous systems include: 1) False alarms and misidentifications of fires in unfavourable weather conditions using vision-based detection systems. 2) Nuisance effects in sensor based detection systems. 3) Absence of integrated notification and response mechanisms for outbreak mitigation.

Along with the challenges identified in previous systems, a number of potential improvements were also pinpointed. Some of these improvements pertain to sensor technologies used for fire detection, ML models, the size and nature of employed datasets, and integrated response mechanisms for fire mitigation. The identified research gaps are:

1) The fusion of sensor-based and vision-based technologies for fire detection and classification. 2) The employment of remote processing for more complex fire detection and classification tasks. 3) Performance evaluation of classification models based on their response times. 4) Utilising multiple extinguisher types to handle a greater variety of fire situations. 5) Identifying other suitable ML algorithms.

3 System Design

3.1 Hardware Design

A block diagram of the fire detection and response system is provided in Fig. 1 and is composed of six units required to carry out the intended function of the overall system, as listed below:

1) Microcontroller: The ESP32 is the central data collector, notification centre, and decision maker of the system, responsible for sensor data collection, data transmission for processing, notification triggering, and response execution.
2) Sensor Array: Consists of the MQ-2, 3,5,7,8, and 135 gas and the temperature sensor used to detect various gases and smoke conditions in active fire situations.
3) Camera: The camera for taking pictures of active flames for colour extraction purposes. The camera selected for use is the ESP32-CAM module.

4) Notification Mechanism: The user warning system using the Telegram messaging API, a dedicated Telegram Bot and HTTP requests.
5) Pumping System: The early response system consists of a set of extinguisher fluids, containers, DC pumps and pipes.
6) Remote PC/Server: The remote system running the two TensorFlow-developed classification models for detecting the nature of the burning material.

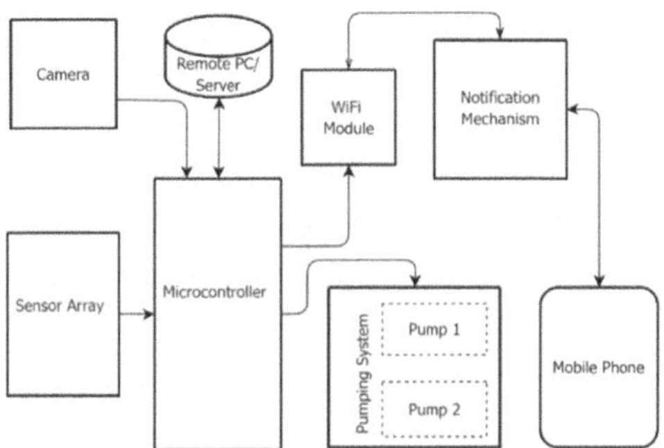

Fig. 1. Block diagram of the fire detection and response system

3.2 Software Design

The software employed in this study encompasses the notification mechanism, the remote server and the communication system, in addition to the trained ML models.

Notification Mechanism. The flowchart of the notification and response system is provided in Fig. 2. This system module begins its operation when a processing result is received from the Cloud PC, and a simple evaluation is then performed to determine the nature of the received response for further action. All communications between the ESP32 and external devices are carried out through HTTP requests and API calls.

Evaluation of the nature of the received response triggers the sending of an appropriate pre-crafted message, detailing the most likely fire class, with additional information on supplementary fire fighting actions that may be taken. These messages are transmitted directly to registered phone numbers through the popular Telegram messaging service.

The evaluated response is also integral in the selection of the appropriate extinguisher fluid to be used. The inferred class of fire prompts the ESP32 microcontroller to send a control signal to the selected relay of the pump system, closing the circuit, and allowing the DC pump to continuously pump out extinguisher fluid until the fire is quenched or the fluid has been exhausted.

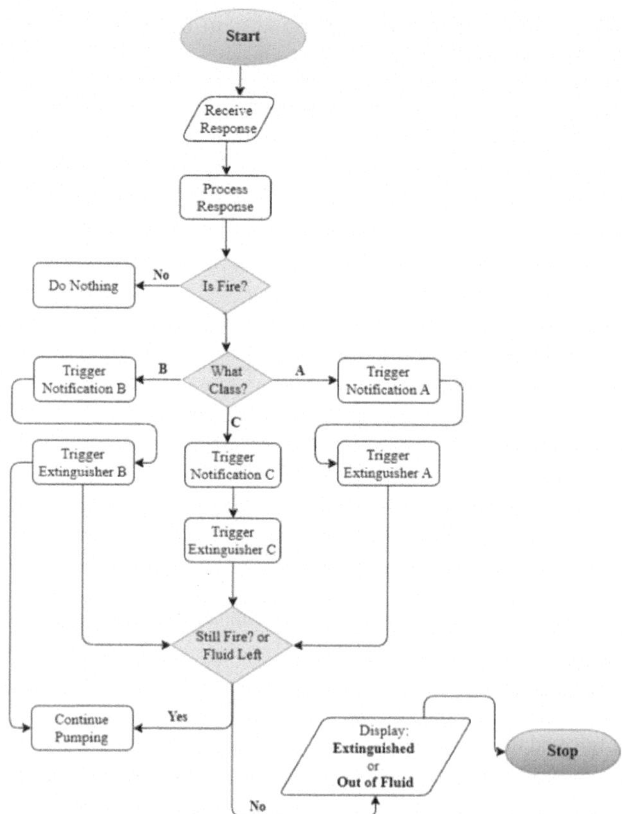

Fig. 2. Response system flow chart

Trained ML Models. The development of the classification models required key processes such as data collection, feature extraction, and model training. The process involved in the building of the complete classification system is detailed as follows:

Data Collection. As no publicly available datasets for the sensor data exist to fulfil the needs of this study, the data for model training was collected by setting fire to several test materials to obtain sensor values for the purpose of classification. The data collection tests were conducted 20 times per material, with corresponding flame images collected for their colours. The data was collected over a two-week period in a controlled environment. The image dataset for this study was sourced from several online sources, coupled with a large number of publicly available images for some of the more exotic flame colours produced by special burning materials, which may also be found in residential settings. Tables 1 and 2 detail the distributions of the collected data samples.

Table 1. Sensor data sample distribution

Fire Class	Number of Sensor Samples
Background ("No-Fire")	244
Class A (Wood, Paper)	313
Class B (LPG)	235
Class C (Cable)	218

Table 2. Fire image sample distribution

Fire Colour	Number of Samples
Orange	109
White	62
Blue	68

Data Pre-processing. The captured images were scaled down to a uniform 240 × 240 resolution size for consistency of results and to conform to the VGG16 input parameter requirements. For the purpose of model training, rotations, zooms, and skews were also performed on the image dataset to supplement its comparatively small data size of 300 images covering 3 different fire scenarios.

Model Architecture. Random Forest (RF), NN, and K-Nearest Neighbours (KNN) were the three models selected and evaluated for the sensor classification modelling. They were selected due to their suitability for numerical data and have shown good accuracy ratings across several tested models. For the image classification model, three pre-trained CNN models, namely VGG16, MobileNetV2, and EfficientNetB0, were adopted for their better performance compared to other pre-trained CNN models for this kind of task.

Model Training. TensorFlow, a popular DL library, along with sci-kit-learn and other Python software packages, were used to implement and train both the pre-trained CNN and ML models. The data was pre-processed, and mean normalisation was used to make the distribution closer to a standard normal distribution. An 80-20 split was used for training and validation. Both numerical and categorical features were used in training the model, with categorical features being one-hot encoded. The Data models were trained to classify instances into one of four classes, while the pre-trained CNN models were trained to classify fire images into one of three major classes: Orange, White and Blue.

Training Details and Hyperparameter Selection. Three models were trained on tabular sensor data: a neural network with three hidden dense layers (64, 128, 256 units, all using ReLU activations), a Random Forest with 50 trees, and a K-Nearest Neighbours model with 8 neighbours. The neural network output layer used SoftMax activation to classify among multiple fire scenarios, with categorical cross-entropy loss, an Adam optimizer and a batch size of 64 over 25 epochs. The pre-trained model's weights were frozen initially to extract features, followed by a custom head consisting of a convolutional block (two Conv2D layers with 128 filters, ReLU activation, and MaxPooling), a global average pooling layer, dense layers of 64 and 128 units with ReLU, and a Dropout layer (rate = 0.3). The final layer used SoftMax for multi-class fire classification. The model was compiled using the Adam optimizer with a default learning rate of 0.001 and categorical cross-entropy loss. Training ran for 10 epochs with early stopping using a patience value of 5, with manual fine-tuning of hyperparameters employed to obtain the best results (Table 3).

Table 3. Hyperparameters for the pretrained models

Hyperparameter	Value
Pretrained Weights Frozen	Yes (initially)
Convolutional Filters	128
Convolutional Layers	2 (Conv2D)
Activation Function	ReLU
Pooling	MaxPooling + GlobalAveragePooling
Dense Layers Units	64, 128
Dropout Rate	0.3
Output Activation	SoftMax
Loss Function	Categorical Crossentropy
Batch Size	32
Optimizer	Adam
Learning Rate	0.001 (default setting)
Epochs	10
Early Stopping Patience	5
Hyperparameter Tuning	Manual

Decision Fusion. Rule-based Logic was employed to fuse the results of the sensor and image-based models for fire classification. The sensor model provides one of four fire types, while the image model returns results as one out of three fire hues. Logical rules based on fire classification descriptions and safety standards were applied to map these inputs to the appropriate fire classes. Fig. 3 shows the logic for the fusion of models, Table 4 shows the fusion logic matrix and Fig. 4 shows the framework followed for the entire classification modelling.

```
Rule 1:
IF Sensor = "Background" AND
   FlameColor IN ["orange","white","blue"] AND
THEN → Background

Rule 2:
IF Sensor = "Class A" AND
   FlameColor = "blue" AND
THEN → Class B Fire

Rule 3:
IF Sensor = "Class A" AND
   FlameColor IN ["orange", "white"] AND
THEN → Class A Fire

Rule 4:
IF Sensor = "Class B" AND
   FlameColor IN ["orange","blue", "white"] AND
THEN → Class B Fire

Rule 5:
IF Sensor = "Class C" AND
   FlameColor = "blue" AND
THEN → Class B Fire

Rule 6:
IF Sensor = "Class C" AND
   FlameColor = IN ["orange", "white"] AND
THEN → Class C Fire
```

Fig. 3. Rule-based fusion logic

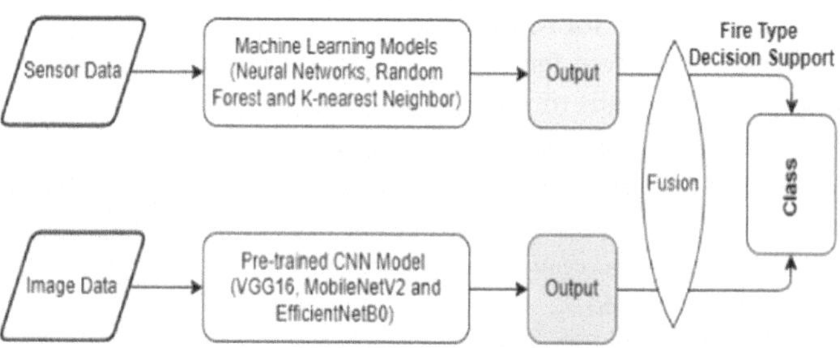

Fig. 4. Classification framework modelling

Table 4. Fusion logic outcomes

Colour/Class	Background	Class A	Class B	Class C
Orange	**Background**	Class A fire	**Class B fire**	Class C fire
Blue	Background	**Class B fire**	Class B fire	**Class B fire**
White	**Background**	Class A fire	**Class B fire**	Class C fire

Remote PC/Server. The microcontroller communicates its polled values to the server through periodic HTTP requests to the server's POST endpoints. The server is a fairly standard implementation of the C# Minimal Web API standard, with two dedicated POST routes for collecting sensor data and receiving image data. The server runs the appropriately trained model on the received values, receives this result and stores it for later retrieval. To this end, a single GET endpoint is provided for the microcontroller to obtain the results of the processed data for further action.

3.3 The System's Principle of Operation

The system starts its operation by continuously polling values from the sensor array, which consists of various gas sensors and a temperature and humidity sensor. Increases in concentrations of the target gases are detected and measured using the apparent changes in the sensitivity of the sensing element of the gas sensors. These polled gas concentration values are transmitted at intervals to the cloud PC to ascertain the current fire status of the environment. The parameters are fed as inputs into the RF model to obtain the correct classification of the type of fire. The current values of the sensor array are also displayed on the LCD screen for local viewing and review.

Received responses other than the default "Background" result of the sensor data classification model will trigger the ESP32-CAM module to take a photograph of the flame in its vicinity. The image is transmitted to the cloud PC for further processing using the ESP32-CAM's built-in Wi-Fi module. The image is then fed as an input into a pre-trained CNN model to obtain the correct fire colour, which will prove useful in the fire investigation process. The result from the classification process is then transmitted to the ESP32 microcontroller for response execution.

The received response from the Cloud PC triggers the notification system, which consists of a series of API calls to send pre-constructed messages tailored to the exact type of response. The notifications are sent directly to the mobile phones of the users using the messaging service Telegram. The received response is also used to trigger a relay and power the DC pump to the appropriate extinguisher fluid to quench the fire. The extinguisher fluid is to be continuously pumped until it is depleted, or the fire has been successfully extinguished.

3.4 Performance Metrics

The metrics used to evaluate the system are detailed in this section. The metrics selected for evaluating the proposed ML models include accuracy, precision, and recall), while the response time and message delivery frequency are the metrics for evaluating the entire designed system.

The formulas for these metrics are presented in Eqs. (1) to (5)

$$\text{Accuracy} = \frac{\text{TP} + \text{TN}}{\text{TP} + \text{TN} + \text{FP} + \text{FN}} \tag{1}$$

$$\text{Precision} = \frac{\text{TP}}{\text{TP} + \text{FP}} \tag{2}$$

$$\text{Recall} = \frac{\text{TP}}{\text{TP} + \text{FN}} \tag{3}$$

$$\text{ResponseTime} = \frac{\sum_{1}^{N} T_i}{N} \tag{4}$$

$$\text{Delivery Frequency} = \frac{N_D}{N_D + N_F} \tag{5}$$

where TP represents the number of True Positives; FP represents the number of False Positives; TN represents the number of True Negatives; FN represents the number of False Negatives; T_i represents the individual Response Times; N represents the number of recorded Response Times; N_D represents the number of Delivered Messages; and N_F represents the number of Undelivered Messages.

4 Results

This section details and discusses the results obtained. The results of the fire detection framework are presented first, followed by the outcome of the model training, testing, and validation. Lastly, the notification and response mechanism of the entire system is evaluated.

4.1 Sensor Data Classification Models

Three ML algorithms were trained and tested to properly classify detected fire types based on sensor data. The selected models were RF, NN, and KNN, displaying varying levels of accuracy.

Neural Network. The accuracy and loss results of the model training are presented in Fig. 5a and Fig. 5b, with a final validation accuracy of 98.08% and a validation loss of 0.0565.

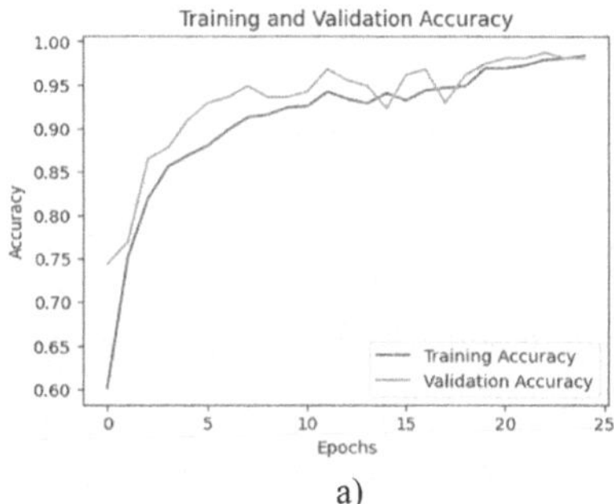

a)

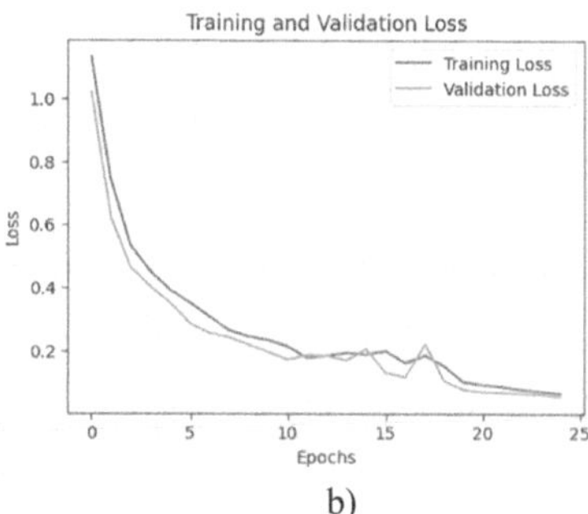

b)

Fig. 5. Training and validation of NN model: a) accuracy result; b) loss result

K-Nearest Neighbours (KNN). The KNN implementation utilised eight neighbours and recorded an accuracy rate of 96.15%.

Random Forest (RF). The RF implementation is configured with 50 DTs, producing a final accuracy of 99.35%.

Model Evaluation. The final comparison of the accuracies of the trained models is provided in Table 5.

Table 5. Model performance metrics

Model	Accuracy	Precision	Recall
RF	99.35%	98.92%	98.58%
KNN	96.15%	96.21%	96.21%
NN	98.08%	98.70%	97.74%

4.2 Image Data Classification Models

Due to the relative sparseness of the collected data set consisting of coloured fire images, three pre-trained CNN models were selected for the colour classification based on their memory and processing requirements. These three models were VGG16, MobileNetV2, and EfficientNetBO.

Model Evaluation. The final accuracies of the three pre-trained models tested for use in the flame colour recognition task are presented in Table 6.

Table 6. Comparison of the pre-trained CNN models' accuracies

Model	Accuracy
VGG16	95.83%
EfficientNetB0	93.06%
MobileNetV2	78.43%

4.3 Fused Classification System Result

Using the previously defined fusion logic, the rule-based system for model output combination achieved an accuracy of 91.58% after 50 tests (Table 7).

Table 7. Model accuracy comparisons

Model	Accuracy
VGG16	95.83%
RF	99.35%
Fused Model	91.58%

4.4 Notification Delivery and System Response Time

The total time taken for the sensor data to be received, processed, and for a notification to be sent out and a response provided by the microcontroller was measured in consecutive tests. The measured responses are presented in Table 8, and a sample of this message system result is presented in Fig. 6.

Table 8. Measured system response time

Test attempt	Response time (seconds)	Message delivered
1	20	Yes
2	19	Yes
3	14	Yes
4	16	Yes
5	12	Yes
6	11	Yes
7	13	Yes
8	14	Yes
Average Response Time	14.88	100% message delivery rate

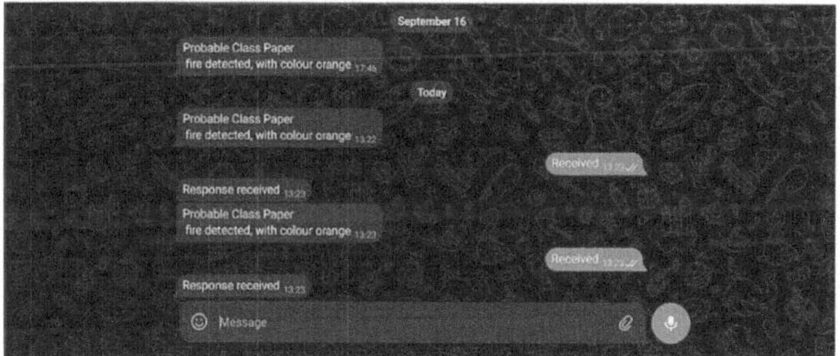

Fig. 6. Delivering notifications interface

5 Discussion of the Results

This section offers further insights into the findings presented in the previous section regarding the data and image classification models. In addition, it includes a comprehensive evaluation of the entire system and summarizes the key results obtained.

5.1 The Sensor Data Classification Model

The RF was the model selected at the end of the model training and validation process for use in the final system, as it performed the best in all selected test metrics (accuracy, recall and precision). Its accuracy of 99.35% is greater than both the 98.09% and 96.15% of the NN and KNN implementations, respectively. Further testing in new environments with new readings under differing conditions also produced consistently accurate classification results.

5.2 The Image Data Classification Model

VGG16. The pre-trained VGG16 model was loaded with an image input of shape (224, 224, 3), with the top layer excluded and an "ImageNet" weight used. The base model was set to not be trainable, with two further convolutional layers added, two dense layers (64, 128), and a max pooling, global average pooling, and drop-out layer added. The accuracy graph of the training and validation process of the VGG16 pre-trained model is provided in Fig. 7.

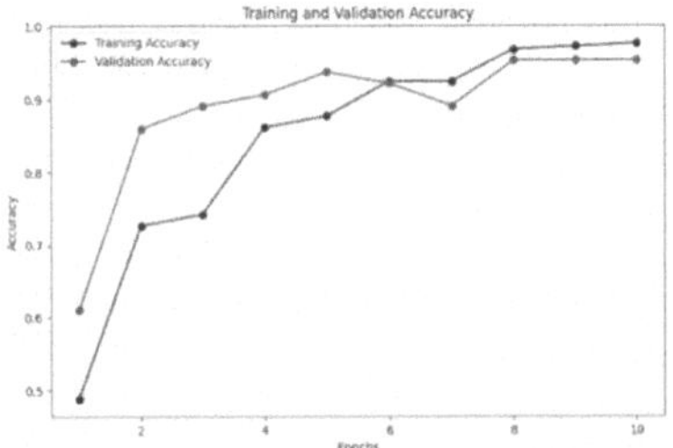

Fig. 7. Training and validation accuracy for VGG16 model

MobileNetV2. The MobileNetV2 uses much of the same implementation structure as the VGG16 pre-trained model, with the only difference being the adjusted learning rate employed during model training. The accuracy of the training and validation process is presented in Fig. 8.

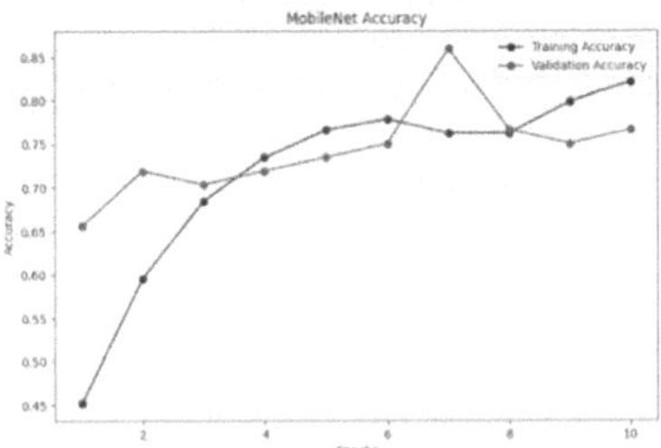

Fig. 8. Training and validation accuracy for MobileNetV2 model

EfficientNetBO. Using the same layer configuration structure as the VGG16 and the MobileNetV2 implementations, acceptable training and testing accuracies were obtained for the EfficientNetB0 model. The graph of the training and validation accuracies is provided in Fig. 9.

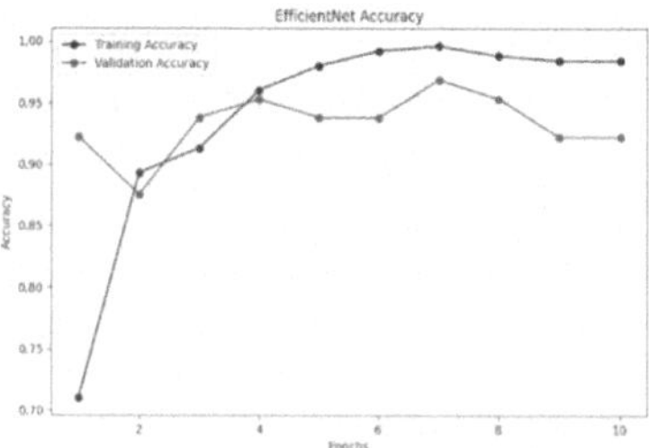

Fig. 9. Training and validation accuracy for the EfficientNetBO model.

The VGG16 model was selected as the most suitable for use at the end of the validation and testing process as it displayed better accuracy when presented with real-world fire scenario images, correctly classifying 95.83% of presented images, and representing the highest recorded validation accuracy of the three models.

VGG16 may have outperformed the EfficientNeBO and MobileNetV2 due to its lowered sensitivity to data distribution shifts making it more suitable for smaller datasets, as it reaches convergence faster without intensive tuning.

5.3 System Response Time and Notification Delivery

The average response time of the system was measured to be approximately 15 seconds, with a 100% message delivery rate using the Telegram instant messaging platform in the presence of a fairly stable internet connection. The initial measured response times were observed to be higher than subsequent measurements due to delays arising from system start-up. The assigned pump systems were correctly triggered when the corresponding responses were returned by the remote PC.

The implemented fire detection framework exhibits exceptional sensitivity to changes in gas concentration and room temperature, quickly and consistently providing instantaneous readings for accurate point-in-time-based inference of Fire or Non-fire and subsequently fire type classification situations.

5.4 Summary of the Results

The RF model was used to perform classification on the collected sensor data, with a recorded accuracy of 99.35%, while the VGG16 model was selected for use for the vision based classification model, with a recorded accuracy of 95.83%. The Telegram instant messaging platform was selected to ensure message delivery, with a simple extinguisher delivery mechanism to demonstrate viability in fire mitigation applications.

5.5 Limitations

While image and sensor fusion models show high accuracy in controlled environments, their real-world performance can be significantly affected by various factors:

- The training of the models in controlled environments limits its applicability in varying settings as a result of nuisances and environmental differences.
- Sensor readings are highly location-dependent; further distances may mean the correct gas concentrations are not detected.
- Rare or unusual fire types, including compound materials, may be underrepresented in training data, leading to poor classification performance in those cases.

6 Conclusion and Future Work

An automated fire detection and classification system with integrated notifications and early response mechanisms was successfully developed and evaluated. Specially designed classification models were implemented to complement the assembled fire detection system, showing acceptable performance. The 99.35% and 95.83% accuracy rates of the two employed models indicate the system's ability to perform highly accurate classification with minimal errors. It is important to note that while the system's performance is commendable, further steps can still be taken to further enhance system performance and general applicability. The system has the potential to be scaled up to handle more domestic and industrial fire scenarios, ensuring the safety of lives and property in a wide range of environments.

Based on the findings from the development, testing, and evaluation of the improved fire detection and classification system, the following recommendations are made: 1) Expand the range of detection for early fire situations. Future research could explore the viability of fire classification based on effectiveness and cost. 2) Focus on data collection in a wider variety of fire scenarios to enhance the robustness and general applicability of fire classification systems. 3) Utilise collected data to improve classification systems based on user feedback. 4) Integrate fire classification systems into existing building sprinkler systems to maximise extinguisher area coverage and effectively combat a wider variety of fire situations. 5) Implement multiple notification mechanisms to ensure timely reception of fire outbreak information. 6) Assess the relationships between the constituent gases in smoke to identify more suitable gas sensors for us.

References

1. Ketcherside, D.T., et al.: Effects of wildfire smoke on volatile organic compound (VOC) and PM2.5 composition in a United States Intennountain western valley and estimation of human health risk. Atmos. (Basel) **15**(10) (2024)
2. Diaconu, B.M.: Recent advances and emerging directions in fire detection systems based on machine learning algorithms. Fire **6**(11), 441 (2023)
3. Sulthana, S.F., Wise, C.T.A., Ravikumar, C.V., Anbazhagan, R., Idayachandran, G., Pau, G.: Review study on recent developments in fire sensing methods. Institute of Electrical and Electronics Engineers Inc. (2023)
4. Sadek, R., et al.: Novel colored flames via chromaticity of essential colors. Defence Technol. **15**(2), 210–215 (2019)
5. Fent, K.W., et al.: Firefighters' urinary concentrations of VOC metabolites after controlled residential and training fire responses. Int. J. Hyg. Environ. Health **242**, 113969 (2022)
6. Gutmacher, D., Hoefer, U., Wallenstein, J.: Gas sensor technologies for fire detection. Sens. Actuat. B Chem. **175**, 40–45 (2012)

7. Vorwerk, P., Kelleter, J., Muller, S., Krause, U.: Distance-based analysis of early fire indicators on a new indoor laboratory dataset with distributed multi-sensor nodes. Fire **6**(8) (2023)
8. Solorzano, A., et al.: Early fire detection based on gas sensor arrays: multivariate calibration and validation. Sens. Actuat. B Chem. **352** (2022)
9. Baballe, M.A., Abdullahi, A.Y., Bello, M.I., Sani, S.A.: Fire extinguisher types and applications. PHO-J. Adv. Res. Sci. Eng. **1**(12), 08–13 (2024)
10. Boraas, S.: Choose the right extinguisher for class B fire suppression. Eng. Min. J. **219**(4), 78–79 (2018)
11. Geetha, S., Abhishek, C.S., Akshayanat, C.S.: Machine vision based fire detection techniques: a survey. Springer (2021)
12. Secilmis, A., Aksu, N., Dael, F.A., Shayea, I., El-Saleh, A.A.: Machine learning based fire detection: a comprehensive review and evaluation of classification models. Int. J. Vis. Inform. Vis. **7**(3–2), 1982–1988 (2023)
13. Pincott, J., Tien, P.W., Wei, S., Kaiser Calautit, J.: Development and evaluation of a vision based transfer learning approach for indoor fire and smoke detection. Build. Serv. Eng. Res. Technol. **43**(3), 319–332 (2022)
14. Dua, M., Kumar, M., Singh Charan, G., Sagar Ravi, P.: An improved approach for fire detection using deep learning models. In: 2020 International Conference on Industry 4.0 Technology, I4Tech 2020, pp. 171–175. Institute of Electrical and Electronics Engineers Inc. (2020)
15. Ayala, A., Fernandes, B.J.T., Cruz, F., Macedo, D., Zanchettin, C.: Convolution optimization in fire classification. IEEE Access **10**, 23642–23658 (2022)
16. Dilshad, N., Khan, T., Song, J.S.: Efficient deep learning framework for fire detection in complex surveillance environment. Comput. Syst. Sci. Eng. **46**(1), 749–764 (2023)
17. Alqourabah, H., Muneer, A., Fati, S.M.: A smart fire detection system using IoT technology with automatic water sprinkler. Int. J. Electr. Comput. Eng. **11**(4), 2994–3002 (2021)
18. Baek, J., et al.: Real-time fire detection system based on dynamic time warping of multichannel sensor networks. Fire Saf. J. **123** (2021)
19. Saeed, F., Paul, A., Karthigaikumar, P., Nayyar, A.: Convolutional neural network based early fire detection. Mu/timed. Tools Appl. **79**(13–14), 9083–9099 (2020)
20. Gowri, D., et al.: Image processing based fire detection by using raspberry PI. J. Eng. Sci. **14**(06) (2023)
21. Dasari, P., Krishna, G., Reddy, J., Gudipalli, A.: Forest fire detection using wireless sensor networks. Int. J. Smart Sens. Intell. Syst. **13**(1), 1–8 (2020)
22. Ramasubramanian, S., Muthukumaraswamy, S.A., Sasikala, A.: Fire detection using artificial intelligence for fire-fighting robots. In: International Conference on Intelligent Computing and Control Systems (2020)
23. Kim, B., Lee, J.: A video-based fire detection using deep leaming models. Appl. Sci. (Switz.) **9**(14) (2019)
24. Mahmoud, H.A.H., Alharbi, A.H., Alghamdi, N.S.: Time-efficient fire detection convolutional neural network coupled with transfer leaning. Intell. Autom. Soft Comput. **31**(3), 1393–1403 (2022)
25. Sharma, A., Singh, P.K., Kumar, Y.: An integrated fire detection system using IoT and image processing technique for smart cities. Sustain. Cities Soc. **61** (2020)
26. Samkari, Y., Guedri, K., Oreijah, M., Munshi, S., Azam, S.: Designing and testing of a smart firefighting device system (LAHEEB). JAES Int. J. Robot. Autom. (JJRA) **9**(2), 143 (2020)
27. Islam, M.M.: Autonomous and wireless control fire fighter robot. Autom. Control Intell. Syst. **9**(4), 97 (2021)
28. Rehman, A., et al.: Smart fire detection and deterrent system for human savior by using internet of things (IoT). Energies (Basel) **14**(17) (2021)
29. Teja, D., Kiran, M.S., Sudheer, A.V., Reddy, I.A.K., Jyothi, K.: LoT based fire detection and automatic water sprinkler system. Int. J. Eng. Appl. Sci. Technol. **6**(12), 312–317 (2022)

30. Vorwerk, P., Kelleter, J., Millier, S., Krause, U.: Classification in early fire detection using multi-sensor nodes-a transfer leaming approach. Sensors **24**(5) (2024)
31. Hossain, M.A., Roy, H.S., Kbondakar, M.F.K., Sarowar, M.H., Hossainline, A.: Design and implementation of an IoT based fire fighting and affected area monitoring robot. In: International Conference on Robotics, Electrical and Signal Processing Techniques, pp. 552–556 (2021)
32. Komalapati, N., Yarra, V.C., Kancharla, L.A.V., Shankar, T.N.: Smart fire detection and surveillance system using IoT. In: Proceedings - international Conference on Artificial intelligence and Smart Systems, JCAJS 2021. Institute of Electrical and Electronics Engineers Inc., pp. 1386–1390 (2021)

Transforming Real Estate Pricing in Tunisia: A Machine Learning Framework with Perspectives on Large Language Models

Wissal Neji(✉), Naouel Boughattas, Faten Ziadi, Sarra Zouari, and Sarra Abidi

Esprit School of Engineering, Tunis, Tunisia
wissal.neji@Esprit.tn, {naouel.boughattas,faten.ziadi}@esprit.tn

Abstract. Today's Tunisian real estate market platforms do not provide sufficient information for those seeking to make well-informed property buying decisions. Moreover, retrieving this information is challenging, as it exists in different places and is presented and structured in heterogeneous ways. This data should be cleaned, stored, and modeled in a flexible data structure, enabling the centralization of relevant real estate offers. The use of classical machine learning (ML) methods presents several challenges, particularly in terms of data preparation are complex. An application was developed using ML algorithms for data preprocessing, classification, feature extraction, and price estimation, achieving a classification accuracy of 85% and a recommendation precision of 0.79 using cosine similarity over TF-IDF. In addition, this article explores the potential impact of incorporating Large Language Models (LLMs) to further refine text analysis, particularly in handling the Tunisian dialect and automating data preprocessing. While LLMs were not yet integrated into the current implementation, their prospective use is discussed as a future direction to improve the interpretation of listing descriptions, extract key features, and reduce manual intervention. This work provides a practical contribution to real estate analysis in Tunisia and outlines perspectives for enhancing future systems with advanced language technologies.

Keywords: Tunisian Real Estate · Data Preparation · AI

1 Introduction

In a Tunisian real estate market in constant evolution, access to reliable, centralized information represents a major challenge for buyers, sellers, and investors. With prices continuing to rise, the search for properties to suit individual needs is becoming more and more complex, and the traditional buying process is becoming longer and more cumbersome. In fact, despite the presence of numerous agencies and online platforms, users still find it difficult to quickly identify properties that match their criteria. The search often relies on calls to agencies, multiple visits, and associated costs, making the experience both tedious and inefficient.

F. Kamoun et al. (Eds.): AFRICATEK 2025, LNICST 676, pp. 331–345, 2026.
https://doi.org/10.1007/978-3-032-16635-7_22

Currently, property ads are scattered across several platforms, with heterogeneous data formats and structures that are difficult to exploit. What is more, essential information such as inflation and interest rates are rarely uploaded. Some ads include missing or incorrect data, making decision-making difficult.

Facing these challenges, the development of a web application that centralizes real estate ads, corrects, and restructures the information in a homogeneous way becomes a necessity. Such a platform, available 24/7, would automate real estate market operations by providing advanced functionalities such as advanced search, real-time price analysis, personalized alerts, and transaction transparency.

The use of classical ML algorithms presents several challenges, particularly in terms of data preparation, where the handling of outliers, the encoding of categorical variables, and the structuring of nonstandardized data are particularly complex [2]. In addition, the analysis of real estate listing descriptions is hampered by the variability of the Tunisian dialect, making it challenging for traditional models to extract accurate information.

In this work, a web application is proposed to improve the real estate search experience. The proposed solution uses web scraping techniques to collect data from several online sources, ensuring a comprehensive and current repository of property listings. Once gathered, the data is processed through rigorous cleaning methods to correct entry errors and fill in missing information, standardizing various formats into a unified structure. Additionally, the application employs machine learning algorithms to estimate property prices accurately, while its recommendation engine offers property suggestions tailored to each customer's search history.

Preliminary results are promising. This approach has led to a satisfactoty price estimation accuracy and enhanced personalized recommendations. Furthermore, the streamlined data cleaning process has significantly reduced manual intervention and processing time. This integrated solution not only simplifies the property search process but also equips users with reliable insights and customized guidance, ultimately redefining decision-making in the Tunisian real estate market.

The emergence of LLMs offers a new approach, facilitating both understanding of the Tunisian dialect and automation of data preprocessing. These models improve the interpretation of ads descriptions, extract key features [12], and reduce the need for cumbersome manual cleaning processes.

In this article, the potential impact of integrating these emerging LLMs into the current work is also explored. The evaluation focuses on how their inclusion can further refine text analysis, enhance feature extraction from property ads, and streamline the overall data processing workflow. Ultimately, this investigation seeks to improve price estimation accuracy and the effectiveness of personalized property recommendations.

This article is organized as follows. It begins with an Introduction that focuses on the challenges in the Tunisian real estate market. Next, the Background and Related Work is reviewed to highlight existing approaches and their limitations.

The Proposed Framework is then presented. Following this, the Results and Discussion section showcases the findings and insights. The Methodology section details the process, starting with Data Collection and proceeding to Data Preprocessing, which encompasses address preprocessing, text processing, NLP and classification, feature extraction, and the recommendation system. This is complemented by the Experimental Results. The challenges of using traditional ML methods are further discussed, and the rise of LLMs in real estate valuation is explored. The article concludes with a summary of the contributions and perspectives for future research.

2 Background and Related Work

The objective assessment of a property's value is a complex task, requiring the consideration of multiple parameters, such as property quality, location, the state of the real estate market and other factors. Real estate appraisal is not an exact science: depending on the theoretical approaches adopted and the methods employed, the results can differ considerably. Traditionally, the stakeholders involved call on real estate experts, whose expertise enables them to select, adapt and apply the most appropriate valuation method. However, with the rise of artificial intelligence (AI), this process has become more accessible and accurate.

A large number of research studies have explored the use of AI to refine property valuation, exploiting advanced machine learning and predictive analytics algorithms. These new approaches make it possible to automate valuation, improve the accuracy of estimates and optimize decision-making in the real estate market. In this context, a study presented in [7] explores the application of machine learning to real estate price prediction through a literature review. It examines different approaches, including neural networks, ensemble methods and advanced regression techniques, while highlighting some limitations, such as the lack of exploration of hybrid models combining ML and econometrics.

A study conducted in [6] focuses on forecasting real estate prices in Izmir using classification methods. For their part, the authors in this work [1] applied 14 machine learning algorithms, including Random Forest (RF), with 10-block cross-validation, to model house prices using data from online ads in Istanbul.

In [9], a comparison between regression models and neural networks (NNs) for predicting real estate rents in Japan showed that ANNs offered better performance, particularly with large datasets. Meanwhile, the study in [8] analyzed the use of machine learning to estimate property prices in Italy, testing three models: ElasticNet, XGBoost and artificial neural networks (ANNs). The results revealed that ANN provided the most accurate estimates, particularly for mid-to low-range properties.

In [3], the author compares several real estate price prediction methods, including convolutional neural networks (CNNs), decision trees and the k-nearest neighbor algorithm (KNN). The study in [11] uses machine learning algorithms, in particular linear regression, to predict property prices.

The analysis in [5] applies three machine learning algorithms: Support Vector Machine (SVM), RF and Gradient Boosting Machine (GBM) in Hong Kong. The

Table 1. Related work summary

Used AI models	Advantages	Challenges
Statistical approach based on discriminant analysis, Turkey, Izmir [6]	The discriminant functions developed were able to correctly classify 78.3% of properties	Many factors influence the price of a property, and it can be difficult to establish a clear model
14 different algorithms, including random forest, Turkey, Istanbul [1]	- Automated approach to real estate data collection and price estimation, reducing the need for manual intervention -Multiple artificial intelligence algorithms enable comparison and selection of the best performing model	Collection and treatment of large volumes of data from a variety of online sources
Nearest Neighbor Gaussian Processes and Deep Neural Network, Japan [9]	Better accuracy with large samples	-Large number of data sets (in excess of 1 million) -Integration of spatial dependency of housing for prediction
ElasticNet, XGBoost and Artificial Neural Network, Italy [8]	The simplicity of the proposed model enables users to predict house prices with various data sets	Lack of data for the most expensive houses leading to reduced model accuracy
CNN, KNN and Decision Trees, Can be applied to various real estate markets around the world [3]	The use of these AI techniques helps to better predict real estate prices by using techniques adapted to the available data	-Overfitting -Modelling accurately the complex interactions between different property characteristics -The presence of irrelevant or incorrect data
Linear Regression, KNN and Random Forest, India [11]	-A price estimation with 85% accuracy. - Adaptability where the methodology can be adopted to other real estate markets with appropriate adjustments	Property prices are affected by a variety of factors, making it difficult to estimate them accurately
SVM, RF and GBM Hong Kong [5]	RF and GBM algorithms offer better prediction than traditional methods and can significantly reduce overfitting	Algorithms such as GBM and RF require longer computation times, which can be a challenge given available resources and time con-straints
Decision Trees, Linear Regression, SVR and Lasso Regression [4]	-Adaptability -More precise estimation with the used models	The complexity of interpreting relationships between characteristics and real estate prices for complex models, since they can act as a black box

results show that RF and GBM outperform SVM in terms of accuracy, although the latter still performs well for fast predictions. Finally, the authors of [4] evaluate several housing price prediction algorithms, including decision trees, linear regression, support vector regression (SVR) and Lasso regression. They stress the importance of the choice of input variables in improving the accuracy of predictive models.

In summary, Table 1 offers a comprehensive overview of prior efforts and highlights the persistent gaps, especially in adapting models to heterogeneous and dialect-specific data.

Building on these insights, the proposed framework is presented in the next section which aims to address these challenges by integrating structured automation, ML pipelines, and emerging LLM capabilities.

3 Proposed Framework

As described in the previous section, the review of the state of the art highlights the inherent complexity of real estate valuation and the limitations of current approaches, despite the rise of artificial intelligence techniques. These studies show that, although traditional and hybrid models offer interesting performances, challenges remain, particularly in terms of heterogeneous data management and forecast accuracy.

It is in this context that a structured and integrated approach is proposed, aimed at automating data collection and processing, optimizing predictive modeling, and centralizing information for a more refined analysis of the Tunisian real estate market. The project is structured into several distinct phases, each designed to ensure the systematic collection, processing, and analysis of data, ultimately leading to the development of a robust predictive model and an interactive platform for end-users.

Phase 1- Automated Data Collection and Monitoring: In the initial phase, data will be collected using automated mechanisms to ensure efficiency and scalability. These mechanisms will include automated update systems to maintain the relevance and accuracy of the data over time. To effectively manage these processes, a web-based monitoring service will be implemented. This service will play a critical role in overseeing the automated systems, ensuring their proper functioning, and providing real-time insights into data collection activities.

Phase 2- Data Exploration and Transformation: The second phase focuses on exploring the collected data and applying necessary transformations to clean and standardize it. This step is crucial to ensure data consistency and quality, which are foundational for subsequent analysis and modeling. Techniques such as data normalization, handling missing values, and removing inconsistencies will be employed to prepare the dataset for further processing.

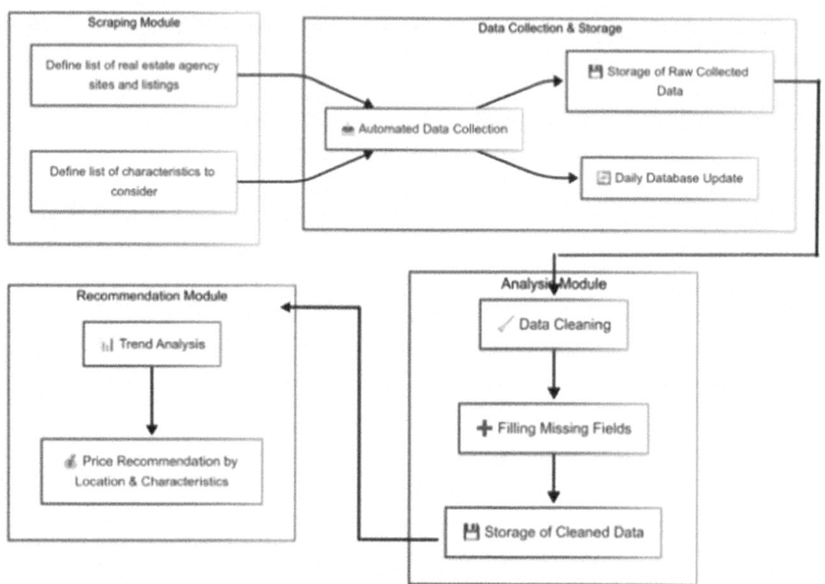

Fig. 1. The proposed Framework.

Phase 3- Predictive Model Development: Even in cases where certain data points, such as property descriptions, may be incomplete, a predictive model will be developed to address these gaps. The model will be designed to classify textual descriptions of property listings into relevant categories, such as kitchen features, square footage, or price. This classification will enable the construction of a comprehensive dataset, even when some information is initially absent. The predictive model will serve as a key tool in enhancing the dataset's completeness and usability.

Phase 4- Centralized Data Compilation and Analysis: Once the data has been compiled and enriched through the predictive model, the next phase involves creating a centralized platform for users to search and analyze potential real estate investments. This platform will provide buyers with insightful tools to evaluate properties based on the compiled data. Additionally, a key objective of this phase is to establish a reliable database for analyzing real estate prices, which will serve as a valuable resource for market trend analysis and decision-making.

Phase 5- Interactive Dashboard and Web Platform Development: In the final phase, interactive dashboards will be created to present the results of the data analysis and price predictions. These dashboards will be accessible via a web-based platform, offering users an intuitive and visually engaging way to explore the data. The platform will enable buyers to make informed decisions by providing them with clear, actionable insights derived from the project's analytical outputs.

The proposed solution, as outlined in the Fig. 1, encapsulates a comprehensive approach to data collection, transformation, predictive modeling, and user-centric presentation. By following this structured methodology, the project aims to deliver a powerful tool for real estate analysis, empowering buyers with the information they need to make informed investment decisions.

4 Results and Discussion

This section presents the results and a detailed discussion of the methodology implemented in this study. It begins with an overview of the used techniques and model, followed by the experimental results that demonstrate the effectiveness of the proposed approach. Finally, the discussion section analyzes the outcomes and highlights the strengths and limitations of the approach.

4.1 Methodology

Building upon the structured approach outlined in the proposed framework, this section details the methodological steps undertaken to implement the system effectively. The success of the platform relies on the quality and completeness of the collected data, making the first phase—automated data collection—a critical component. Here, the techniques and tools used to scrape real estate listings from multiple sources are detailed, ensuring a comprehensive and structured dataset. This step lays the groundwork for the subsequent phases, including data preprocessing, predictive modeling, and centralized analysis, ultimately leading to the development of an interactive platform for end-users.

Data Collection. To gather property advertisements, web scraping was employed, a technique that allows for the automated extraction of data from various websites using specialized scripts or programs. In our case, Python's powerful tools was used, such as Scrapy, Selenium, and BeautifulSoup. After evaluating these options, Scrapy is selected for its efficiency and ability to handle more complex scraping tasks. Scrapy uses selectors (either XPath or CSS) to extract data, and XPath was preferred for its flexibility in pinpointing specific parts of the HTML document.

An items.py file was created to define the elements to be extracted and identified 10 websites for scraping. This process led to the creation of 10 individual spiders, each responsible for a different site. However, it was necess to remove three websites from the list due to issues like blocking or unreliable price data. After scraping, the collected data in JSON and Excel files was stored, which allowed to easily compare the number of ads across different platforms. Despite some challenges, the process was highly successful, with the majority of the advertisements being scraped accurately and with minimal loss of data.

The scraping results across various real estate websites are summarized in Table 2.

Table 2. Scraping Results Across Different Real Estate Websites

Website	Number of Ads on the Site	Number of Ads Extracted	Scraping Duration
Affare	24,365	24,365	1:41 min
Ayoub	293	271	6 min
casamed	This site is not reliable	This site is not reliable	This site is not reliable
Dahmen Immobilier	787	785	20 min
Home Sweet Home	1,123	1,123	30 min
Houni	28,887	28,867	6 h
immoland	157	157	3 min
Immo / jemeloge	Scraping prohibited	Scraping prohibited	Scraping prohibited
Jumia	1,919	1,919	40 min

Data Preprocessing: Following the data preprocessing phase, which focused on cleaning and standardizing the collected information, the specific techniques used for addressing and processing the various types of data was detailed. The next subsections provide a detailed look at how address preprocessing and text processing was handled, two critical steps in ensuring the data's accuracy and relevance for subsequent analysis.

Address Preprocessing. This phase focused on cleaning and standardizing unstructured data, with particular emphasis on address normalization. Missing fields such as locality, delegation, and governorates were addressed by referencing the official addresses provided by The Tunisian Post. To automate the identification and correction of errors, Natural Language Processing (NLP) techniques, specifically the Entity Ruler in SpaCy, were employed to recognize and rectify named entities.

The application of Named Entity Recognition (NER) through SpaCy facilitated the detection of key components, such as localities, within addresses. For the imputation of missing values, the NER model was enhanced by integrating a custom dictionary of Tunisian addresses, ensuring more accurate extraction and correction. Furthermore, gaps in features was identified and addressed such as heating and bathroom data, ensuring the dataset was properly prepared for subsequent analysis.

Figure 2 represent the results obtained after the adress correction phase.

	Adresse	Gouvernorat	delegation	localite
0	EL MENZAH 9, ARIANA, TUNISIE	TUNIS	EL MENZAH	EL MENZAH 9
1	MORNAG, TUNISIE	BEN AROUS	MORNAG	MORNAG
2	LA MARSA, TUNISIE	TUNIS	LA MARSA	
3	EL MENZAH 5, ARIANA, TUNISIE	TUNIS	EL MENZAH	EL MENZAH 5
4	BIZERTE, TUNISIE	BIZERTE	BIZERTE NORD	BIZERTE
...	...	...	...	...
1117	BORJ LOUZIR, ARIANA, TUNISIE	ARIANA	LA SOUKRA	BORJ LOUZIR
1118	BEN AROUS, TUNISIE	BEN AROUS	BEN AROUS	BEN AROUS
1119	GAMMARTH, TUNISIE	TUNIS	LA MARSA	GAMMARTH
1120	LA MANOUBA, TUNISIE	MANOUBA		
1121	MORNAG, TUNISIE	BEN AROUS	MORNAG	MORNAG

Fig. 2. Adressing preprocessing results.

Text Processing: In this phase, the text data of the ads description was cleaned and structured by removing special characters, punctuation, and HTML tags. Descriptions were standardized by converting textual representations of numbers (e.g., "one" or "two") into their corresponding numeric values. Part-of-speech tagging and pattern matching techniques were employed to identify and eliminate adjectives preceding nouns, thereby ensuring the accurate extraction of features such as room counts.

NLP and Classification: For property classification, several machine learning algorithms was explored to identify the most suitable approach for accurately categorizing property descriptions. Initially, Long Short-Term Memory (LSTM) networks was tested , a type of Recurrent Neural Network (RNN) designed to capture long-range dependencies in sequential data. LSTMs are well-suited for tasks involving time-series or text data, as they can retain information over extended sequences. However, during experimentation, overfitting was encountered, where the model performed well on the training data (97%) but poorly on the validation set (62%), likely due to the complexity of the model and the relatively small dataset.

To address this issue, SpaCy's TextCategorizer was used, a pre-built machine learning model designed for text classification tasks. The TextCategorizer uses a convolutional neural network (CNN) architecture, which is effective in extracting high-level features from text and generalizing well to various text classification tasks. Unlike LSTM, which relies heavily on sequential data processing, SpaCy's model is optimized for efficiency and scalability in handling structured text data.

The model was trained on a dataset consisting of 2,000 labeled property descriptions in both French and Arabic. These descriptions were categorized into various property-related features, such as room count, type of property, and amenities. By focusing on these key elements, the aim was to improve the accuracy and relevance of the property classification. The switch to SpaCy's TextCategorizer resulted in better generalization and more reliable performance across both languages, leading to improved classification accuracy in the real estate data.

After analyzing our data, a small portion of descriptions was found in Tunisian dialect, so they were classified under the Arabic language category. Then, a dictionary in Tunisian was created to facilitate feature extraction.

Feature Extraction: In this step, specialized functions was developed to systematically extract crucial property attributes, such as the number of bathrooms, kitchens, and parking spaces, from the textual descriptions. The extraction process relied on pattern matching and keyword identification to accurately capture these features. For handling keywords related to air conditioning and heating, the Levenshtein distance algorithm was employed, which is particularly useful for identifying approximate string matches. This algorithm calculates the minimum number of single-character edits (insertions, deletions, or substitutions) required to transform one string into another, making it ideal for detecting variations in spelling or terminology used in property descriptions.

The Levenshtein distance between two strings is computed using dynamic programming with a matrix D, where $D[i][j]$ represents the minimum cost to transform the first i characters of one string into the first j characters of another.

$$D[i][j] = \begin{cases} 0 & \text{if } i = 0 \text{ and } j = 0, \\ i & \text{if } j = 0, \\ j & \text{if } i = 0, \\ \min \begin{cases} D[i-1][j] + 1, \\ D[i][j-1] + 1, \\ D[i-1][j-1] + c \end{cases} & \text{otherwise.} \end{cases}$$

where $c = 0$ if $A[i] = B[j]$, otherwise $c = 1$.

By incorporating Levenshtein distance, minor discrepancies in keyword representation, such as typos or different phrasing, were effectively accounted for, thereby enhancing the accuracy of feature extraction.

Figure 3 illustrates the results of applying our feature extraction model to extract outdoor amenities and the number of existing kitchens from the textual descriptions of property advertisements. Prior to the application of the model, none of the advertising platforms provided these details as structured fields.

Recommendation System: The design of the recommendation system focused on aligning property features with user preferences to provide personalized and relevant property suggestions. Initially, key property attributes was transformed, such as location, size, and amenities, into a structured format that could be easily compared across different listings. To quantify the relevance of each property in relation to its features, the TF-IDF (Term Frequency-Inverse Document Frequency) Vectorizer was used, a widely-used technique in natural

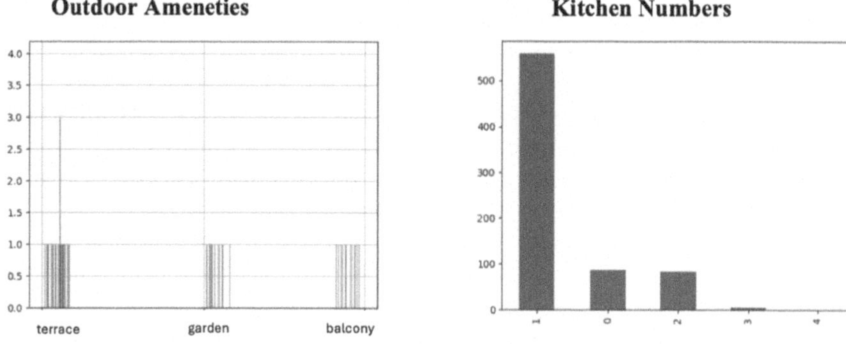

Fig. 3. Feature Extraction Results.

language processing. TF-IDF evaluates the importance of each feature by considering how frequently it appears in a given property description relative to its frequency across the entire dataset. This helps prioritize unique features that distinguish properties.

After vectorizing the property features, Cosine Similarity was employed, a metric that measures the cosine of the angle between two vectors in a multi-dimensional space. Cosine similarity ranges from -1 to 1, with 1 indicating that two properties are identical in terms of their feature profiles. By using this metric, the closeness between properties was determined, enabling them to be ranked according to how similar they are to the user's preferences.

Based on this similarity ranking, the system selected the 30 most relevant properties, presenting them to the user in an ordered list. The recommendation process ensures that users receive personalized property suggestions, with a focus on those that best match their specific criteria. This approach leverages both user input and property attributes to deliver accurate and tailored recommendations, enhancing the overall user experience.

4.2 Experimental Results

The performance of both the NLP classification model and the recommendation system was thoroughly evaluated. After training the classification model and processing the property data, the accuracy of feature extraction and classification was assessed using metrics such as accuracy, precision, recall, and F1-score. These metrics provided a comprehensive evaluation of the model's effectiveness in identifying and classifying key property features.

To evaluate the recommendation system, the cosine similarity was computed between property descriptions, which allowed us to rank properties according to their relevance to the user's preferences. The mean average precision (MAP) wad also measured of the top 10 recommendations, which showed strong relevance in the suggestions.

The classification model achieved an accuracy of 85%, with a precision of 83%, recall of 87%, and F1-score of 85%. Meanwhile, the recommendation system showed a mean average precision of 0.79 for the top 10 recommendations.

Error analysis revealed that the model occasionally struggled with ambiguous or incomplete property descriptions, especially when key features were omitted. These challenges slightly lowered the model's performance in certain cases but did not significantly impact overall results.

To further validate the system's practical impact, several case studies were conducted to assess its effectiveness in real estate decision-making. The case studies demonstrated that the NLP-based feature extraction significantly improved the accuracy and relevance of property listings, and the recommendation system was successful in delivering personalized suggestions.

These results validate the effectiveness of the proposed system and indicate its potential for improving real estate decision-making.

4.3 Discussion

The integration of advanced data analytics into property data significantly improves market transparency by delivering more reliable and precise information. This enables consumers to make well-informed decisions, as they have access to comprehensive and accurate property details. Consequently, this fosters a more equitable and transparent real estate market.

Furthermore, enhanced property data contributes to economic growth by supporting more effective decision-making in areas such as property transactions, investments, and urban development. Access to detailed and accurate data can lead to better resource allocation and more informed investment strategies. Additionally, it plays a pivotal role in cultural and social development, as it empowers individuals with a broader array of property options. This increased access can ultimately contribute to improved community planning and more sustainable urban development practices.

5 Challenges Using Traditional ML Methods

To analyze real estate market data in Tunisia, several challenges related to both data quality and the use of the Tunisian dialect are encountered. In the current absence of an official centralized database for real estate transactions, data is scraped from several sites. Each site can organize its data in a unique way. This requires adapting extraction techniques to the specificities of each source.

Extracted data often miss essential information on surface area, price per square meter and precise location. Prices too can be very high or very low, leading to errors or fraudulent ads. This requires data cleansing and pre-processing.

A feature engineering step is also required to convert all categorical data into numerical data such as property type (apartment, villa, land) and model geographical factors such as neighborhood quality, proximity to services as well as economic factors (interest rates, inflation, etc.) which impact on the evolution of the real estate market although they are rarely integrated into the model.

Many ads are written in a mixture of Tunisian dialect, French and Arabic, with different spellings for the same word (e.g. "dar", "daar" for "house") and informal abbreviations ("S+3" for an apartment with living room and 3 bedrooms). Prices themselves are written in several forms ("three hundred thousand dinars", "300TD" or "300 thousand TD"). The Description field in the ad often includes subjective expressions ("very beautiful house" or "strategic location") that are difficult to quantify, as well as local references ("near Bab Souika market"), which are not directly geolocated. NLP models can be used to extract and structure certain information, but these models remain unable to understand the Tunisian dialect because they have been trained only on the French or Arabic language.

6 Future Work: Toward Integrating Large Language Models (LLMs)

Although this paper focuses on classical ML algorithms for real estate price prediction, the potential integration of Large Language Models (LLMs) represents an important direction for future work. Their capabilities offer promising avenues for automating complex NLP tasks, especially in low-resource and dialect-rich contexts like Tunisia. The use of LLMs can greatly simplify the data preparation process [10]. They can detect and correct spelling mistakes, recognize abbreviations, standardize units (converting "300 thousand dinars" into "300,000 TD" and harmonizing surface area formats in m^2), identify duplicates and detect anomalies (abnormally high or low prices). They can also automatically extract important features and classify ads according to predefined types.

Thanks to their capacity to handle under-resourced languages and dialects, LLMs are able to identify different linguistic variations of the same word and understand the context of ads written in the Tunisian dialect. This enables the detection of implicit features such as the type of property, its condition, its standing, etc. This makes it possible to generate complete, standardized and well-structured descriptions. What's more, the Tunisian dialect can be translated into any language, enabling us to address a wider interbational audience.

For instance, an LLM could be prompted with: "Extract the number of rooms and the surface area in square meters from the following Tunisian Arabic property description":

دار في حي الخضراء، فيها زوز بيوت ، مساحتها ١٢٠ متر، فيها سخان و كليماتيزور

Expected output: "rooms": 2, "surface": 120 LLMs can be used to generate attractive, detailed property descriptions, ensuring consistency and quality in ads. Chatbots powered by LLMs can be set up to respond instantly to customer queries 24/7, answer questions, schedule visits and provide information on the purchasing and rental processes [10]. They can also generate personalized emails and messages to customers based on their preferences and search history, automate the creation of contracts and other personalized legal documents, and synthesize long documents such as changes to regulations or planning laws [10]. Thanks to LLMs, websites can integrate market analysis and investment advice for the most loyal customers.

Going a step further, LLMs can create training material for new agents, assess customer satisfaction and identify areas for improvement.

7 Conclusion and Perspectives

In this paper, a method was presented for predicting real estate prices in Tunisia using classical ML algorithms. The proposed method was evaluated through classification and recommendation tasks, achieving a classification accuracy of 85% and a mean average precision of 0.79 in the recommendation system. This implementation highlights the challenges encountered in the proposed approach, particularly regarding the data preparation process, the presence of Tunisian dialect in ads, and natural language processing to extract missing information and enrich property descriptions.

The potential of Large Language Models (LLMs) was also discussed, and an analysis was carried out of their advantages for real estate price prediction methods, particularly in automating data preparation and handling unstructured and dialectal textual data This analysis demonstrated that the integration of LLMs will enable ads to be processed efficiently and instantaneously, regardless of their nature, and will automate the data pre-processing step, thereby improving the accuracy of estimates.

Despite all the benefits outlined above, LLMs need to be integrated into real estate prediction systems using a hybrid approach that combines the strengths of traditional ML models with the advanced capabilities of LLMs: pre-processing textual data with LLMS to generate structured features, then injecting them into classic ML models to benefit from their efficiency in statistical modeling and prediction based on these structured features.

In the subsequent phase, efforts will be directed toward:

- Expand our database to include new ads extracted from other websites and social networks (there's a growing trend towards publishing ads on social networks)
- Integrate LLMs (which can be optimized to become specialized in real estate) into the proposed model to automate and accelerate the data preparation process and the textual data analysis
- Integrate economic data influencing real estate market trends, such as inflation and interest rates.
- The proposed method will be extended from the Tunisian context to a global context. An application is envisioned that will enable the user to access real estate data anywhere in the world: by selecting the region of interest on the world map, an immediate update of the interface and the analysis will be performed, enabling real estate prices to be tracked in real time with customized recommendations.

References

1. Aydemir, E., Aktürk, C., Yalçınkaya, M.A.: Yapay zekâile konut fiyatlarının tahmin edilmesi. Turkish Stud. **15**(2), 183–194 (2020). https://doi.org/10.29228/TurkishStudies.43161
2. Baldominos, A., Blanco, I., Moreno, A.J., Iturrarte, R., Bernárdez, Ó., Afonso, C.: Identifying real estate opportunities using machine learning. Appl. Sci. **8**(11), 2321 (2018). https://doi.org/10.3390/app8112321
3. Chen, Z.: Integrating machine learning techniques for real estate analysis. Highlights Sci. Eng. Technol. **92**, 252–256 (2024). https://doi.org/10.54097/cvn9mr84
4. Dhar, T.: A literature review on using machine learning algorithm to predict house prices. Int. Res. J. Adv. Sci. Hub **5**(05S), 132–137 (2023). https://doi.org/10.47392/irjash.2023.S017
5. Ho, W.K.O., Tang, B.S., Wong, S.W.: Predicting property prices with machine learning algorithms. J. Prop. Res. **38**(1), 48–70 (2021). https://doi.org/10.1080/09599916.2020.1832558
6. Kuru Erdem, M., Yiğit Erdem, O., Calis, G.: Sale price classification models for real estate appraisal. Revista de la Construcción **20**(3), 440–451 (2021). https://doi.org/10.7764/rdlc.20.3.440
7. Mathotaarachchi, K.V., Hasan, R., Mahmood, S.: Advanced machine learning techniques for predictive modeling of property prices. Information **15**(6), 295 (2024). https://doi.org/10.3390/info15060295
8. Rampini, L., Re Cecconi, F.: Artificial intelligence algorithms to predict italian real estate market prices. J. Property Invest. Finance **40**(6), 588–611 (2022). https://doi.org/10.1108/JPIF-08-2021-0073
9. Seya, H., Shiroi, D.: A comparison of residential apartment rent price predictions using a large data set: kriging versus deep neural network. Geogr. Anal. **54**(2), 239–260 (2022). https://doi.org/10.1111/gean.12283
10. Szumilo, N., Wiegelmann, T.: Real estate insights AI: real estate's new roommate–the good, the bad and the algorithmic, vol. 42 (2024). https://doi.org/10.1108/JPIF-01-2024-0001
11. Vyas, R., Sharma, J.: An algorithm to predict real estate price using machine learning. Asian J. Comput. Sci. Technol. **12**(1), 31–34 (2023). https://doi.org/10.51983/ajcst-2023.12.1.3592
12. Zhao, Y., Gao, H.: Utilizing large language models for information extraction from real estate transactions. arXiv preprint (2024). https://doi.org/10.48550/arXiv.2404.18043

Emerging Technologies for Higher Education

Artificial Intelligence in Higher Education: A Framework for Enhancing Metacognition through Human–Machine Collaboration

Meriem Chichti(✉), Faten Tebourbi, and Chaima Ayari

ESPRIT School of Business, Tunis, Tunisia
{meriem.chichti,ayari.chaima.messaad}@esprit.tn,
feten.tebourbi@Esprit.tn

Abstract. This research examines the nexus of emerging technologies, metalearning, and critical pedagogy in higher education, assessing the potential of AI-supported learning to promote metacognitive abilities in Business English and UX Design classes. As artificial intelligence transforms learning environments, it becomes increasingly crucial to enable learners to assume control over their learning activities. We conducted mixed-methods research with 80 students studying Business English at Esprit Business School and 100 students studying UX Design at Esprit Engineering School.

Structured learning activities aligned with clear objectives encouraged students to identify gaps, refine strategies, and assess their progress. Pre- and post-test surveys (based on the MAI) measured changes in confidence, strategy use, and AI's impact, while an ethnographic study captured how UX Design students used AI for creative problem-solving. Results show that framing AI as a collaborative partner enhances learning but requires structured guidance to avoid overreliance. To address this, we propose a three-phase framework—preparation, collaboration, reflection—that supports responsible, effective AI use. Integrating metalearning, AI, and critical pedagogy, this approach fosters adaptive, reflective learners for a technology-driven world.

Keywords: Emerging technology · Metalearning · Artificial Intelligence · Human-AI-Human

1 Introduction

In contemporary education, emerging technologies such as artificial intelligence (AI) are transforming the way knowledge is acquired, processed, and applied [1]. Equipping learners to take ownership of their learning is increasingly important as AI reshapes educational settings. This study explores how metalearning—the process of knowing and managing one's learning [2] —collides with AI to propel metacognitive skills in Business English and UX Design education. The process is student-centered, involving students in tasks that enhance thinking ability and promote critical self-assessment of

F. Kamoun et al. (Eds.): AFRICATEK 2025, LNICST 676, pp. 349–364, 2026.
https://doi.org/10.1007/978-3-032-16635-7_23

their strength, methodology, and confidence [3]. Rooted in critical pedagogy [4], these tasks are presented within explicit objectives so that students can recognize flaws and refine their process; however, there remain difficulties in achieving the full cooperative potential of AI. Our mixed-method study, conducted during 2024–2025, involved 80 Business School students learning Business English and 100 Engineering School students learning UX Design with specialization in creative problem-solving.

Pre- and post-test surveys, adapted from the Metacognitive Awareness Inventory (MAI) [5], measured changes in confidence, strategy development, metacognitive growth, and AI's role in Business English, whereas an ethnographic investigation examined UX Design students' engagements with AI. Though artificial intelligence is presented as an ethical collaborator designed to enhance capabilities [6], our research indicates a necessity for organized direction to advance beyond sheer mechanistic use. We suggest a triadic framework—preparation, collaboration, and reflection—to guide educators and students in strategically using AI [7]. Blending metalearning, AI, and critical pedagogy, this framework cultivates reflective and adaptive learners for a technology-integrated future.

2 Impact of Emerging Technologies on Metalearning

Metalearning, the process of understanding and optimizing one's own learning strategies [2], is increasingly influenced by emerging technologies, particularly artificial intelligence (AI). Traditionally defined as "learning how to learn" [3], metalearning involves self-regulation, cognitive strategy selection, and adaptive learning techniques. However, with the rise of AI-driven educational tools, this process now extends beyond individual cognition to human-AI collaboration.

Furthermore, the integration of AI adds another dimension to metalearning—critical AI literacy. Learners must develop metacognitive skills for self-regulation while also learning to assess AI's potential and constraints, questioning the validity, ethical impli- cations, and contextual relevance of its outputs rather than passively accepting them [6]. This aligns with [8] self-regulated learning model, where students actively plan, monitor, and evaluate their strategies, now expanded to scrutinize AI-generated insights. In our research context, this framework enables students to interrogate AI's role across domains—such as generating UX proto- types or tailoring language exercises—enhancing their reflective analysis

In the domain of User Experience (UX) design, metalearning manifests as designers iteratively refine their craft by analyzing user feedback and adapting methodologies. In the context of emerging technologies and metalearning, Schön's reflexive model [9] is adapted to new dynamics. AI tools allow us to integrate real-time reflection by analyzing data and suggesting optimizations. However, reflection on action remains essential: designers need to look back to evaluate the relevance of AI recommendations, identify its biases and adjust their own decision-making process. In this way, Schön's model [9] helps us to understand how metalearning is evolving in the digital age, combining the human capacity for critical reflection with the analytical efficiency of emerging technologies. This interplay between human metacognition and machine intelligence represents a frontier where metalearning transcends individual cognition to col- laborative human-AI systems.

Our approach emphasizes that students must develop metacognitive skills to assess AI's strengths and limitations, ensuring they remain active agents in their learning process.

2.1 AI as a Collaborative Tool

The state-of-the-art reflects a growing integration of AI in education, with tools like learning analytics dashboards [10] and adaptive systems [11] offering real-time data on student progress. Yet, our research stresses that students must be taught to leverage these tools collaboratively [12]. found that AI-enhanced educational platforms increased engagement when students were encouraged to question the system's logic. Comparing different groups of learners, they found that those who were encouraged to analyze and criticize the AI's decisions developed a finer understanding of how it worked and adjusted their learning strategies more effectively.

Drawing on [13] insights into intelligent educational systems, the most evident influence of artificially intelligent technologies lies in their ability to personalize learning experiences directly. However, beyond this, they have spurred the development of innovative pedagogies and teachers' practices. These emerging ap- proaches, enabled by advancements in AI, empower educators to support students and facilitate learning opportunities in ways that were largely impractical before such tech- nologies existed. For instance, [13] highlights how AI-driven analytics can in- form adaptive teaching strategies, allowing teachers to tailor guidance and enhance student engagement more effectively than traditional methods permitted.

2.2 The Challenges of Metalearning in the Era of Emerging Technologies

Implementing this vision faces hurdles. Over-reliance on AI remains a risk, particularly among students conditioned to trust technology [6]. Additionally, fostering critical metalearning requires teacher training and curricular redesign, which may strain resources [14]. Cultural factors also matter students from hierarchical educational traditions may hesitate to challenge AI outputs [15].

However, the challenge for the metalearning future in education is to provide students with the tools they require to navigate the role with AI in all fields. Emerging technologies such as virtual reality [16] might simulate AI-driven scenarios - for example, refining a UX prototype or debating the feedback from an AI tutor - fostering real-time critique. Open access AI initiatives [17] promise broader access, ensuring that this approach reaches diverse learners. In this sense, teachers need to cultivate pedagogical strategies that leverage the potential for AI retaining the intellectual rigor to question it, positioning metalearning as the bridge between technological innovation and human agency.

3 Collaborative UX and Artificial Intelligence: A Transformative Alliance

3.1 The Rise of Collaborative UX: AI as a Catalyst for Innovation

User Experience (UX), defined as the comprehensive set of interactions between a user and a product or service [18], has traditionally been shaped by specialized design teams. Recently, however, there has been a notable shift towards participative and collaborative design methodologies. This transformation is exemplified by the integration of artificial intelligence (AI) tools into UX design processes. According to a study by the Nielsen Norman Group (2023), 72% of UX teams that have adopted AI tools report significant improvements in their output.

Furthermore, research from the Massachusetts Institute of Technology (2023) [19], indicates that teams utilizing AI assistants experience a 25% increase in creative potential, underscoring the synergistic potential of collaborative UX and AI.

Additionally, a study from Stanford University (2024) [20], demonstrates AI's role as a mediator in design teams, facilitating the synthesis of ideas and aiding in the convergence towards optimal solutions. These findings collectively suggest that the integration of AI is redefining the landscape of UX design through enhanced collaboration and creativity.

3.2 Collaborative User Experience (UX) Design and the Emergence of the Human-AI Experience (HAX)

Collaborative User Experience (UX) design is a foundational concept in the development of enriched user interactions, traditionally centered on the cooperative efforts of human designers. This paradigm, however, extends beyond conventional human collaboration by integrating artificial intelligence (AI) as a key participant. This fusion of human and AI capabilities gives rise to what we term the Human-AI Experience (HAX). The HAX model emphasizes the essential synergy between human designers and AI systems across the design and development lifecycle. Within this framework, AI transcends its traditional role as a passive tool, instead functioning as an active col- laborator, thereby fostering a dynamic and interactive partnership in the design process. John Maeda, Vice President of Design and AI at Microsoft, articulates a set of fun- damental principles aimed at improving user experiences by integrating artificial intel-ligence (AI) co-pilots into applications [21].

Central to this framework is the Human-AI Experience (HAX) model, conceptualized as a "co-pilot" paradigm. Within this model, the human assumes the role of the "pilot," while the AI serves as the "cooperator." This collaborative relationship is strongly tied to human expertise and skills, with the AI positioned to complement, en- hance, and support decision-making processes rather than supplant them.

The effectiveness of this co-piloting dynamic hinges on the proficiency of the human pilot. Consequently, the objective of collaborative User Experience (UX) design is to foster a robust partnership between humans and AI. Achieving this requires AI systems that prioritize respect for human input, maximize the advantages of intelligent interaction, and provide iterative guidance toward user goals with confidence. The HAX model finds practical expressions in AI interfaces such as ChatGPT 4, Grok 3, and Deepseek R1. These systems solicit user feedback following each interaction to assess the utility of their responses, emphasizing the critical role of continuous feedback and user engagement in shaping decision-making outcomes. This mechanism reinforces the principle that AI augments, rather than replaces, user autonomy.

Empirical evidence supports this approach. Research, including a meta-analysis conducted by Harvard (2024) [22], demonstrates that AI does not displace but rather enriches the core principles of collaborative UX as established by [23]. Teams that effectively integrate these technologies while preserving a collaborative ethos consistently achieve superior results, underscoring the value of synergistic human-AI partnerships.

4 Context and Methodological Approach

4.1 Methodology: Pre- and Post-Test Design for Assessing Metacognition

To assess students' metalearning and metacognitive awareness, we carried out mixed-method research spanning Spring 2024 to February 2025 on 180 Esprit school students in two formats: a quantitative survey for Business English (80 Business school students) and an ethnographic observational study for UX Design (100 Engineering School students in the WEB specialization). The institutional review board approved the research, and all participants were asked for and provided their informed consent to participate in the surveys and other research activities. To protect student privacy, all responses and data were anonymized.

The purpose of this study was to investigate how AI tools influence metacognitive development in the contexts of business education and UX design. This research adds to existing studies on AI in education [1] and metacognition [24].

Following the Metacognitive Awareness Inventory (MAI) [5], these questionnaires addressed self-awareness and strategy control using AI tools on reading, writing, and design tasks, examining AI's impact on shaping metacognitive development in the context of business education. The study was conducted across two modules: The Business English module targeted language capacity and communications, while UX Design focused on AI-supported creative problem-solving.

For Business English, 80 students completed pre- and post-tests with three MAI-aligned sections:

(1) Knowledge About Cognition Knowledge About Cognition, such as declarative knowledge (e.g., awareness of strengths and weaknesses in AI task work), procedural knowledge (e.g., understanding of strategies for working with AI outputs), and condi- tional knowledge (e.g., understanding of contexts in which AI tools are most useful);
(2) Cognition Regulation such as planning (e.g., development and confidence in AI use plans), monitoring (e.g., how often to review AI results), debugging strategies (e.g., confidence to manage ambiguous AI results), and information management (e.g., struc- turing AI-provided information);
(3) Engagement and Reflection assessing the perceived balance of human versus AI contribution and confidencein utilizing AI tools, with the post-test adding an evaluation

component (e.g., reflecting on AI's overall contribution and emotional influences. The pre-test (prior to February 21, 2025) consisted of an AI-free research task, followed by Likert-scale (1 = "Very poorly" to 5 = "Very well") and open-ended questionnaires regarding strengths, strategy, and confidence. The post-test (February 23, 2025) stu- dents did the task using AI tools in order to compare results, responding to a second survey with the samemeasures. For UX Design, an ethnographic study in Spring 2024 observed 100 Web-specialized students throughout project stages, analyzing perceptions and interactions with AI tools via mini-groups of 5, facilitated by teachers, with team journals monitoring progress. The process involved several steps. Firstly, the students were introduced to AI tools applied in specific stages of the UX process so that they could get first-hand experience with the contribution of such technology in different stages of the UX design process. Secondly, they were given the liberty to experiment and evaluate other tools based on their own preferences and project needs. The objective of combining these two studies is to examine the advent of this new global technology, sampling our Esprit students—by analyzing metacognitive de- velopment involving AI supports, thereby ensuring full acceptance of this innovative change in tertiary education.

This study was conducted at two schools with specific modules (Business English and UX Design). As a result, further research is required to determine if these findings apply to other educational settings or disciplines.

4.2 Results of Quantitative Survey

The quantitative analysis of pre- and post-test surveys conducted with 180 students reveals statistically significant changes in their understanding and use of AI in educational contexts.

1. Improvement in Analytical Thinking and Organizational Skills
   The proportion of students identifying "analytical synthesis" and "organizational skills" as strengths increased by 6.2% in the post-test. A McNemar's test for paired proportions confirmed this difference to be statistically significant ($p = 0.031$), with a Cohen's g effect size ≈ 0.25, indicating a small to moderate effect. This suggests a positive shift in students' capacity for structured reasoning and information management through AI.
2. Emergence of Strategic Thinking and Autonomy
   New cognitive categories such as "strategic planning" (5.7%) and "autonomy and independence" (4.6%) emerged in the post-test. While these responses were absent in the pre-test and thus not statistically testable in a paired design, their appearance reflects a qualitative evolution in students' perceptions, emphasizing greater self-direction and decision-making confidence.
3. Decrease in Time Efficiency as a Primary Concern
   The emphasis on time-saving dropped from 18% in the pre-test to 11.5% in the post-test. A chi-square test confirmed the difference to be significant ($\chi 2 = 4.15$, $p = 0.042$), with a Cramer's $V = 0.22$, indicating a small effect size. This shift implies that students began to view AI not merely as a productivity tool but also as a means for enhancing cognitive depth.

4. Reliability of Measurement Instruments
   Several Likert-scale items assessing AI-related competencies (e.g., critical thinking, organization, autonomy) were grouped into thematic dimensions. Internal consistency for these dimensions was acceptable, with a Cronbach's alpha of 0.74, indicating a satisfactory level of reliability in measuring students' evolving attitudes.

These quantitative findings underscore a significant shift in how students conceptualize and interact with AI. Moving beyond a functional or time-saving view, students increasingly recognize AI's potential for supporting metacognitive engagement, including strategic thinking, autonomy, and analytical reasoning. This confirms that when meaningfully integrated into learning, AI can act as a catalyst for deeper cognitive and self-regulated learning processes.

4.3 Results of Ethnographic Observational Survey

The table below summarizes and highlights the contributions and limitations of AI in the UX process during observation, underlining the importance of a thoughtful and critical use of these tools.

Observations of 100 UX Design students across Spring 2024 projects outlined AI's contributions and limitations (see table below). AI aided research (e.g., data aggregation) and transcription (e.g., real-time notes), accelerating tasks, but lacked depth in ideation (e.g., superficial ideas) and analysis (e.g., uncontextualized insights). Students often used AI mechanically, rarely validating outputs, which reduced creativity and raised reliability concerning echoing prior studies [6]. While AI facilitated problem identification and prototyping, over-reliance dulled innovation, under- scoring the need for the collaboration phase to foster critical engagement. This suggests AI's potential as a partner is unrealized without structured guidance, reinforcing the framework's value in enhancing metacognition and adaptability (Table 1).

Table 1. Observations on Student-IA Collaboration Through the Stages of the UX Process.

UX Process Stage	Student-AI Colla-boration Capabi-lity	Observed Re- sults	Identified Limitations and Issues
Documentary Research	AI assists students in collecting and aggregating information.	Automated execution of tasks with- out critical validation.	Unverified information, risk of errors and bias in selected sources.
Ideation	Generation of ideas based on student queries.	AI responses remain superficial and sometimes inconsistent.	Lack of collaborative and creative spirit among team members, failure to adhere to ideation methodologies (e.g., brainstorming, de- sign thinking).

(*continued*)

Table 1. *(continued)*

UX Process Stage	Student-AI Colla-boration Capabi-lity	Observed Re- sults	Identified Limitations and Issues
Documentation	Adapting UX do- cuments (forms, user scenarios).	Automated task execution, lacking in-depth reflection.	Produced documents are vague, lack personalization, and fail to meet the specific pro- ject needs.
Interview Notes	Real-time docu- mentation of con- versations.	Speeds up note-taking process.	Risks of misunderstandings and misattribution of comments to the wrong speakers.
Interview Transcription & Synthesis	Automatic generation of summaries and extraction of key themes.	Smart topics and custom summary templates helped students focus on the analytical part.	Unverified results, higher error rates for certain languages or accents, potential omissions.
Data Sorting and Analysis	Organization and grouping of raw data into thematic categories.	Facilitates the identification of general trends.	Frequent errors, manual re-sorting required to ensure relevance and re- liability.
Quantitative Analysis	Automation of descriptive statistical data analysis.	Time-saving for extracting figures.	Statistics produced without thorough verification, risk of biased in- terpretation.
Qualitative Analysis	Helps identify key trends and insights.	Accelerates the analysis process.	Lack of contextualiza- tion and in-depth interpretation of results, risk
			of erroneous conclusions.

4.4 Results of Ethnographic Observational Survey

Ethnographic observations were conducted during Spring 2024 across UX design workshops involving 100 undergraduate students. A structured grid was used to record student behaviors, verbal interactions, and tool usage across all stages of the UX process. The observation was non-participant and carried out by two researchers over a 6-week period. All field notes were thematically coded using an inductive approach. Categories were defined based on recurring patterns such as: mechanical AI use, lack of critical validation, and dependence on automated outputs.

This coding was carried out manually and cross-validated by two coders to ensure intersubjective agreement. The themes were then mapped against the stages of the UX process to identify where and how AI tools supported or limited students' engagement.

A recurrent theme was the automated use of AI without critical questioning. For instance, during the ideation stage, one observer noted:

"One student told her teammate: 'Let's just ask ChatGPT for five ideas and pick the best. We don't have time to brainstorm.'"

Similarly, in the documentation phase, students used AI to auto-generate content with little adaptation:

"The persona descriptions were copy-pasted from AI with minimal editing. When asked why, a student answered: 'It sounds professional enough. Why change it?'"

Another revealing moment was during user interviews, where students relied on AI for summarization:

"After uploading the transcript, they didn't verify the summary. When asked, one student said: 'It looks fine. I trust the tool to get the gist.'" These behaviors reflect a lack of critical distance, echoing concerns in the literature (Selwyn, 2022), and raising pedagogical questions on digital literacy and metacognitive engagement.

Despite these limits, AI tools facilitated several phases of the UX process, particularly in data aggregation, prototyping, and problem identification. However, over-reliance reduced creativity and sometimes led to factual errors or superficial conclusions. This over-automation also impacted the collaborative spirit of teams, as tools often replaced rather than augmented discussion.

In conclusion, while AI tools provided logistical advantages, their uncritical use highlighted the need for structured pedagogical frameworks that develop students' capacity for critical thinking, interpretive judgment, and ethical reflexivity in digital design contexts.

4.5 Interpretations and Recommendations

There is major potential in the integration of AI tools in higher education, but they need to be guided in their intended use in a structured way that maintains a balance between automation and analytic thinking. A well-defined role is fundamental to avoid over- dependence and to ensure that their potential is fully exploited. Survey results revealed a strong need among students for interactive, structured learning, accompanied by precise guidelines on the use of AI tools. This approach would not only optimize their effectiveness, but also limit their possible deviations. Finally, education must evolve to foster the development of critical thinking in response to AI-generated results while actively working to mitigate the inherent biases of these technologies. It is also essential to explore new pedagogical models of triadic collaboration—Human (student) - AI - Human (student)—that emphasize complementarity and exchange between artificial intelligence and human expertise, as illustrated in the revised figure above. This automation represents only a small facet of generative AI; therefore, integrating it as a collaborative partner should be aimed at cultivating a more complex critical and analytical mindset. Such an approach will ultimately enhance decision-making and drive innovation in education.

The Integration of AI in Higher Education: Towards a Triadic Model Inspired by Houssaye's Pedagogical Triangle: The emergence of artificial intelligence tools in education is revolutionizing learning dynamics. However, this potential can only be fully realized if integrated within a structured pedagogical framework that maintains a delicate balance between technological efficiency and cognitive depth [25]. pedagogical triangle - built upon the fundamental interactions between teacher, learner, and knowledge - provides a particularly relevant lens through which to conceptualize this integration. Transposing this model to the digital age reveals a renewed triadic approach where AI becomes an active mediator in the pedagogical re- lationship, without compromising the primacy of human reflection (Figs. 1 and 2).

Fig. 1. Diagram of the educational triangle of Jean Houssaye (1988)

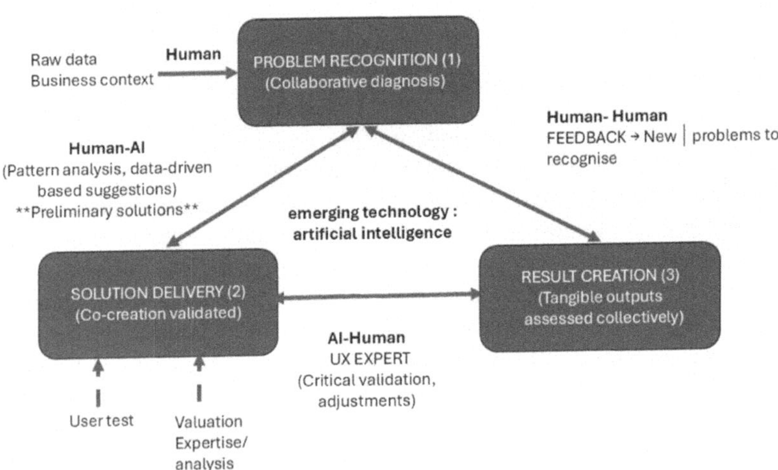

Fig. 2. Proposed The Metalearning Triad: Recognition, Delivery, Creation

Collaborative Diagnosis: The Foundation of Augmented Pedagogy: The first phase of the process, corresponding to the teacher-student vertex of the original triangle, is being reconfigured by emerging technologies. Traditionally, identifying learning difficulties relied primarily on interpersonal exchanges and pedagogical intuition. AI now introduces an unprecedented analytical dimension. By processing massive datasets, it can reveal patterns often imperceptible to human observation: recurring error types across a cohort, abnormally long response times on specific exercises, or unexpected correlations between conceptual difficulties.

This diagnostic capability doesn't replace human interaction but complements it syn- ergistically. Consider an economics course where an AI system detects that 65% of students consistently fail to apply price-elasticity concepts in complex case studies. When presented to the instructor through clear visualizations, this data enables more targeted dialogue with students. During tutoring sessions, rather than proceeding through trial-and-error, the teacher can immediately address potential gaps in prerequi- site mathematical knowledge, often uncovering previously unnoticed struggles with logarithmic functions.

Solution co-Creation: AI as Pedagogical Partner: The second phase, aligned with Houssaye's teacher-knowledge relationship, undergoes perhaps more radical transformation. Modern AI, particularly through advances in natural language processing and content generation, can produce remarkably relevant educational resources: exercises tailored to each learner's precise level, multiple reformulations of theoretical concepts, or personalized learning pathways.

This co-creation phase thus represents a delicate equilibrium where educators must simultaneously: Leverage AI's information processing power, maintain critical distance from its proposals and contextualize generated resources according to their discipline's specific academic culture

Collective Evaluation: the Virtuous Cycle of Continuous Improvement: The third component, corresponding to Houssaye's student-knowledge relationship, gains a novel collaborative dimension [9]. work on reflective practice becomes particularly relevant here: evaluating human-AI co-created pedagogical solutions can- not be a one-directional process but must involve continuous feedback loops.

5 Course Design and Pedagogical Refinements

To enhance students' metalearning (awareness of their own learning processes) while using AI, the curriculum should be adapted to guide students beyond basic AI usage toward higher-order thinking skills (analysis, evaluation, and creation). By leveraging Bloom's taxonomy, we can structure future learning outcomes and teaching strategies that deepen students' engagement with AI for lifelong learning.

5.1 Pedagogical Refinements

Explicit Metalearning Activities: Integrating explicit metalearning activities is essential to help students develop critical thinking about their use of AI tools. One approach is to include self-reflection tasks where students analyze the impact of AI on their critical thinking, for example, by answering questions such as: "How has AI influenced my approach in this project?" Additionally, implementing an AI learning journal could be beneficial. Students would document their use of AI tools, identified errors, and improvements made, allowing them to track their progress and adjust their practices accordingly.

Introduction to AI Tools: The introduction of AI-specific training modules is es- sential to ensure an informed and critical use of these tools. Students must be trained to evaluate AI-generated outcomes, particularly through fact-checking, source analysis, and the identification of algorithmic biases. It is also crucial to integrate an ethical di- mension into this education by addressing topics such as data privacy, algorithmic transparency, and the impact of automated decisions on UX processes.

Scenario and Problem-Based Learning: Scenario-based and problem-based learning is an effective approach to helping students understand how to strategically inte- grate AI into the learning process. Real-world-inspired simulations could be imple- mented, where students must use AI to solve complex problems while considering its limitations. Additionally, peer assessment tasks would be introduced to encourage students to analyze and critique AI-enhanced work. This approach fosters a deeper un- derstanding of both the benefits and limitations of these technologies within a collabo- rative framework.

Fostering Autonomy in Learning for more Focused and in-Depth Coaching by the Teacher: Instead of considering AI as a simple executor of tasks, it is important to en- courage its use as a thinking partner. Students should be encouraged to refine and per- sonalize the results generated by AI, rather than blindly accepting them. This approach fosters the development of a more advanced critical and analytical mindset. In addition, AI-enhanced peer teaching could be an innovative solution: students would explain some concepts to their peers using AI as a support tool, thus supporting a better under- standing of knowledge and active learning. In this context, the teacher guides and sup- ports the team in the collaboration between students and AI.

These pedagogical adjustments aim to transform AI into a true educational ally, enabling students to acquire not only technical skills, but also critical analysis skills and an ethical approach to its use. For teachers, this approach allows them to coach students throughout the project, especially in overburdened classrooms.

5.2 Pedagogical Framework: Guiding Students to Collaborate with AI across Domains

To position AI as a collaborative partner in the learning process, we propose a three-phase framework for teachers to guide students in any domain. This process—Pre-Task Preparation, Collaborative Task Execution, and Post-Task Reflection and Synthesis—draws from our study's findings and best practices in AI-enhanced education [7]. It aims to shift students' perception of AI from a passive tool to an active collaborator, fostering metalearning by encouraging planning, critical evaluation, and self-regulation. Below, we outline each phase with specific steps, examples, and domain-adaptable strategies (Fig. 3).

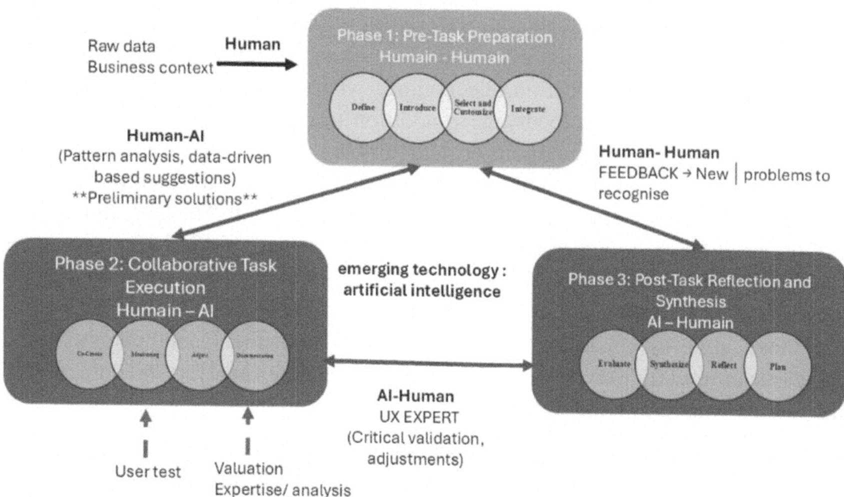

Fig. 3. Proposed Pedagogical Framework: Guiding Students to Collaborate with AI Across Domains

Phase 1: Pre-Task Preparation: Phase 1 prepares students to collaborate with emerging technologies like AI, as tested with Business English and UX Design learners, by setting goals (e.g., enhancing writing coherence or UX prototypes), selecting tools ethically (considering biases and privacy), and anticipating AI's role, building confidence in their learning process. To begin, teachers facilitate discussions where students articulate their objectives, such as improving writing coherence in Business English, generating design prototypes in UX, or analyzing data trends in science. Co-defining these objectives ensures students perceive AI as a tool that supports their learning rather than dictates it. Next, teachers introduce AI as a collaborator by explaining its capabilities—such as generating ideas and providing feedback—and its limitations, including potential biases and the need for human verification. In this step, AI is framed as a teammate rather than an authority. The selection and customization of AI tools follows where students and teachers collaboratively choose domain-specific AI applications. To reinforce this process, students briefly test these tools and discuss their alignment with their goals, fostering ownership and critical awareness of AI's role. Finally, students plan how they will integrate AI into their work, outlining specific usage strategies before revising manually or practicing dialogue with an AI chatbot. Teachers provide a structured template, such as "Tool, Purpose, Expected Outcome," to encourage deliberate AI integration and avoid over-reliance on automation.

Phase 2: Collaborative Task Execution: In this phase, students engage in active partnership with AI, emphasizing critical interaction and real-time metacognitive monitoring. They work alongside AI to produce outputs—whether writing a text, designing a prototype, or solving a problem—treating AI as a contributor rather than the sole provider. An iterative collaboration approach is encouraged, where students refine AI-generated content by adding their interpretations or insights. Teachers prompt students to periodically assess AI outputs for accuracy and alignment with their learning goals using a structured checklist evaluating relevance, clarity, and originality. This reflective monitoring helps prevent passive reliance on AI and fosters critical thinking. Then, Teachers introduce peer evaluation checkpoints, where students exchange work with classmates to receive human feedback in addition to AI-generated insights. This human-to-human interaction strengthens critical thinking skills and prevents over-reliance on AI, reinforcing that AI should be an augmentation tool rather than a replacement for human judgment. As students interact with AI, they adjust their strategies dynamically, modifying prompts or switching tools based on performance. If AI outputs are unhelpful, students work together to troubleshoot issues, strengthening collaborative problem-solving skills. For additional reflection, students document their AI interactions in a learning log, capturing key moments of revision, tool adjustments, and insights gained. This log is later used for peer review sessions, where students analyze and compare their AI interaction strategies with classmates.

Phase 3: Post-Task Reflection and Synthesis: The final phase emphasizes deepening students' metalearning through self-reflection, peer feedback, and synthesis of AI-generated content with their own contributions. Students begin by evaluating AI's role in their learning, using guided reflection questions such as "What worked?" and "What didn't?" They rate AI's usefulness and justify their assessments, reinforcing critical evaluation skills. To integrate AI contributions with human insights, students engage in peer synthesis activities where they discuss how AI supported their work and where human creativity made a difference. For instance, a Business English student might reflect on how AI improved sentence structure but required human intervention for nu- ance, while a UX student might discuss blending AI-generated mockups with original design elements. These peer discussions help students recognize the value of human creativity and collaborative input alongside AI-generated assistance. Beyond task-specific reflections, students analyze their metalearning gains by answering prompts such as "What did I learn about my learning process?" or "How did AI help me adjust my approach?" These reflections are shared in small groups, where students provide peer feedback on each other's learning strategies, fostering cross-disciplinary insights and best practices.

Finally, students plan for future AI integration, proposing refinements such as using more precise prompts, incorporating peer review earlier, or balancing AI reliance with human evaluation. This phase concludes with a peer feedback exchange, where students review and comment on their classmates' proposed strategies, helping them refine their approach for future learning tasks. By embedding peer evaluation throughout the process, this framework ensures that students develop both AI literacy and essential human-human collaboration skills enhancing their capacities while developing the metacognitive skills. Through structured interactions with AI and their peers, students enhance critical thinking, adaptability, and self-regulated learning—key components of metalearning in the 21st century.

6 Conclusion

This study explored the relationship between students and artificial intelligence (AI) tools in higher education, focusing on the metacognitive dimensions associated with the emergence of these technologies. Drawing on the "UX Design" and "English for

Business" modules, and involving a sample of 180 students, we obtained both qualitative and quantitative results.

The results revealed that students encounter several obstacles in establishing an effective triadic collaboration between themselves, the teacher and the AI. In particular, these difficulties are linked to a lack of familiarity with AI tools, leading to mechanical and non-reflexive use, often limited to the execution of predefined tasks without any real understanding. Furthermore, analysis has shown that AI-generated answers are rarely verified by students, compromising the reliability of the process and complicating decision-making.

These findings underline the need to design a pedagogical framework aimed at strengthening collaboration between students, teacher and AI, in a dynamic that goes beyond mere technical execution, to foster critical analysis, appropriation of tools and genuine co-construction of knowledge. Moreover, AI tools like socially assistive robots must be designed with learning theories to enhance human learning without fostering dependency, which could undermine self-regulation. Additionally, AI cannot replace teachers' irreplaceable human skills—empathy, compassion, and interpersonal communication—which are critical for understanding students' needs and fostering positive learning environments. Sustainable efforts are needed to extend AI and learning analytics to support teachers in complex collaborative settings, as current applications remain limited.

Thus, this article proposes a pedagogical strategy integrating AI as a collaborator in its own right, taking into account both the results of the study and the rapid evolution of generative AI technologies. However, given that this research is based on a limited sample of 180 students, it would be pertinent to conduct further research action in various disciplinary contexts in order to assess the effectiveness of this process more widely and through longitudinal studies in diverse fields like STEM (e.g., AI-assisted coding) and humanities (e.g., AI-scaffolded text analysis) to validate the framework's adaptability. By tackling these challenges, this framework can advance an ethical, inclusive AI pedagogy that strengthens collaborative and regulatory capacities for students and educators.

References

1. Zawacki-Richter, O., Marín, V.I., Bond, M., et al.: Systematic review of research on artificial intelligence applications in higher education – where are the educators? Int. J. Educ. Technol. High. Educ. **16**, 39 (2019). https://doi.org/10.1186/s41239-019-0171-0
2. Biggs, J.B.: The role of metalearning in study processes. Brit. J. Educ. Psychol. **55**(3), 185–212 (1985)
3. Flavell, J.H.: Metacognition and cognitive monitoring: a new area of cognitive-de- velopmental inquiry. Am. Psychol. **34**(10), 906–911 (1979)
4. Freiré, P.: The adult literacy process as cultural action for freedom. Harv. Educ. Rev. **40**(2), 205–225 (1970). https://doi.org/10.17763/haer.40.2.q7n227021n148p26
5. Schraw, Dennison, R.S.: Assessing metacognitive awareness. Contemp. Educ. Psychol. **19**(4), 460–475 (1994).I SSN 0361-476X). https://doi.org/10.1006/ceps.1994.1033
6. Selwyn, N.: Education and Technology: Key Issues and Debates, 3rd edn. Bloomsbury Publishing (2022)
7. Kukulska-Hulme, Agnes, et al.: Whitelock, Denise and Zhang, Shuai. Innovating Pedagogy 2021: Open University Innovation Report 9. The Open University, Milton Keynes. (2021)

8. Zimmerman, B.J.: Attaining self-regulation: a social cognitive perspective. In: Boekaerts, M., Pintrich, P.R., Zeidner, M. (eds.) Handbook of Self-Regulation, pp. 13–39. Academic (2000)
9. Schön, D.A.: The Reflective Practitioner: how Professionals Think in Action. Basic Books (1983)
10. Jivet, I., Scheffel, M., Drachsler, H., Specht, M.: Awareness is not enough: pitfalls of learning analytics dashboards in the educational practice. In: Lavoué, É., Drachsler, H., Verbert, K., Broisin, J., Pérez-Sanagustín, M. (eds.) Data Driven Approaches in Digital Education. EC-TEL 2017 Lecture Notes in Computer Science(), vol. 10474. Springer, Cham (2017). https://doi.org/10.1007/978-3-319-66610-5_7
11. Chen, X., Zou, D., Cheng, G., Xie, H.: Artificial intelligence-assisted personalized language learning. In: Systematic Review and co-Citation Analysis, pp. 241–245 (2021)
12. Baker, Ryan & Siemens, G.: Educational data mining and learning analytics. (2014). https://doi.org/10.1017/CBO9781139519526.016.B. https://www.researchgate.net/publication/316628053_Educational_data_mining_and_learning_analytics
13. Sharma, P., Hannafin, M.: Scaffolding in technology-enhanced learning environments. Interact. Learn. Environ. **15**(1), 27–46 (2007). https://doi.org/10.1080/10494820600996972
14. Veenman, M.V.J., Van Hout-Wolters, B.H.A.M., Afflerbach, P.: Metacognition and learning: conceptual and methodological considerations. Metacogn. Learn. **1**(1), 3–14 (2006)
15. Hadwin, A.F., Järvelä, S., Miller, M.: Self-regulation, co-regulation, and shared regulation in collaborative learning environments. In: Schunk, D.H., Greene, J.A. (eds.) Handbook of Self-Regulation of Learning and Performance, 2nd edn, pp. 83–106. Routledge (2018)
16. Moyón, C., Bastidas-González, K., Figueroa, M., Policarpo, E.: Virtual reality as a tool for training communication skills in higher education students. Revista de Gestão Social e Ambiental. **18**, e07085 (2024). https://doi.org/10.24857/rgsa.v18n4-144
17. UNESCO.: Artificial intelligence in education: Challenges and opportunities for sus- tainable development. UNESCO Publishing. 2019. https://unesdoc.unesco.org/ark:/48223/pf0000366994
18. Norman, D.: The Design of Everyday Things (Revised and expanded ed.). Basic Books. (2013)
19. Massachusetts Institute of Technology (MIT): The impact of AI assistants on crea- tive potential in design teams. MIT Press (2023).
20. Stanford University.:AI as a mediator in collaborative design: Enhancing idea synthe- sis. Stanford Design Press. (2024).
21. https://theglobalcollege.com/news/john-maeda-inaugurates-2023-school-year/
22. Harvard University: Meta-analysis on AI integration in collaborative design teams. Harvard Research Press(2024).
23. Sanders, E. B.-N., Brown, B., & Nielsen, J.: Collaborative UX in the age of AI: Prin- ciples and practices. O'Reilly Media. (2023).
24. Matsuda, N., Weng, W., Wall, N.: The effect of metacognitive scaffolding for learning by teaching a teachable agent. Int. J. Artif. Intell. Educ. **30**, 1–37 (2020). https://doi.org/10.1007/s40593-019-00190-2
25. Houssaye, J.: Pedagogy and didactics: A reflection on concepts. De Boeck Supérieur. (1993).

Evaluation of Large Language Models in Simulating Real-World Engineering Scenarios and Decision Making: A Comparative Study of ChatGPT-4o, Gemini, and Perplexity

Faouzi Kamoun[1](✉), Farkhund Iqbal[2], Heni Abidi[3], and Aymen Ben Brik[3]

[1] ESPRIT School of Business, ESPRIT School of Engineering, Ariana, Tunisia
faouzi.kammoun@esprit.tn
[2] College of Technological Innovation, Zayed University, Abu Dhabi, UAE
[3] ESPRIT School of Business, Ariana, Tunisia

Abstract. Integrating real-world simulations and decision-making scenarios through case studies has been shown to enhance students' critical thinking and problem-solving skills. Prior research highlighted a gap in faculty capacity to create or access such materials, an issue particularly acute in developing countries. This research explores the potential of three prominent LLMs, namely ChatGPT-4o, Gemini 2.0, and Perplexity, to generate high-quality case studies for graduate engineering education. In this study, we define a high-quality engineering case study as one that is narratively rich, embeds socio-technical and multidisciplinary perspectives, presents an open-ended practical problem, includes plausible and data rich role-playing scenarios, and supports active learning and reflective thinking.

Our evaluation employs a multi-layered methodology combining: (1) a linguistic analysis using standard NLP metrics; (2) automated mixed-method assessments using four LLMs; and (3) mixed-method evaluation by three Subject Matter Experts (SMEs). Our findings revealed that while Perplexity produced the most readable content, it failed along with Gemini to meet the minimum required word count. The SMEs unanimously ranked ChatGPT-4o as superior across all performance dimensions. This study reveals several LLM limitations, such as limited narrative flow, lack of depth, compelling storytelling and academic rigor, failure to meet explicit instructional requirements, and instances of fake or inaccurate citations. These challenges reinforce the necessity for a "human-in-the-loop" approach. Our study offers a balanced and evidence-based perspective on the role of LLMs in augmenting, rather than replacing, human expertise in case study development.

Keywords: Emerging Technologies · Applied Computing · Computer-managed Instruction · Experiential Learning · Large Language Models · Generative AI · NLP · Natural Language Processing · Case Studies · Engineering Education · Decision-making · Critical Thinking

F. Kamoun et al. (Eds.): AFRICATEK 2025, LNICST 676, pp. 365–393, 2026.
https://doi.org/10.1007/978-3-032-16635-7_24

1 Introduction

Exposing students to experiential learning opportunities has been recognized as a cornerstone pedagogical approach to bridge the gap between theoretical knowledge and practical, hands-on problem-solving, which is particularly vital in the context of engineering education [1]. Experiential learning is a hands-on approach that exposes students to real-world experiences through active participation and reflective thinking on experience. This approach has been proven to facilitate deeper understanding of the subject matter [2], stimulate critical thinking and problem-solving [3], foster adaptability competencies [1], boost students' intrinsic motivation [4] and enhance employability [5]. Experiential learning can take many forms such as laboratory work, internships, field trips, capstone and integrated projects, community service activities, workshops, simulations, and role playing.

Exposing engineering students to rich case studies that simulate real-life scenarios, coupled with role-playing and decision-making activities, is particularly enlightening as an inductive experiential teaching strategy [6]. Such an exposure can potentially allow students to practice decision-making and develop critical thinking and problem-solving skills while considering the broader context pertaining to ethics and sustainable development [7].

Although case studies hold significant potential, engineering faculty are not generally well positioned to seize these opportunities for many reasons:

- Engineering graduates are recruited and rewarded for solving problems, so they should be trained on how to solve workplace problems. However, engineering problems are inherently complex, ill-defined, and multi-disciplinary [8]. This makes it difficult for faculty to propose authentic case studies that simultaneously replicate real-world scenarios and at the same meet specific learning outcomes without making oversimplifying assumptions [9].
- Engineering faculty might not have any professional experience or access to up-to-date engineering trends and solutions [10, 11]. This makes it challenging for them to develop authentic case studies that reflect current industry practices.
- Creating meaningful and up to date case studies is a resource-intensive endeavor for faculty members [12]. Heavy workload, limited time and resources, lack of Problem Based Learning (PBL) training and the over-focus of faculty promotion policies on research productivity at the expense of pedagogical innovation amplify the opportunity cost for faculty to invest in developing authentic case studies [12].
- Although there are some publicly available engineering case studies, faculty members often struggle to find cases that align with their course learning outcomes.
- Most publicly available case studies are developed in the context of developed countries. As a result, faculty in developing regions, particularly in Africa, face challenges in finding case studies that are both contextually relevant and globally oriented.
- Limited financial resources constrain Higher Education Institutions (HEIs) in developing countries from subscribing to premium case study collections offered by major publishers such as Emerald and Harvard Business Review (HBR). These collections, while valuable, often come at a prohibitive cost that many universities in low-income regions cannot afford.

Recent developments in Generative Artificial Intelligence (GAI) have stimulated a growing interest in leveraging Large Language Models (LLMs) to enhance students' learning and faculty teaching. Within the realm of AI in Education (AIEd), these models enable a variety of applications, including profiling and prediction, intelligent tutoring systems, assessment and evaluation, and adaptive learning [13]. While the potential of AI-driven conversational models to create teaching content has been the subject of growing interest, the application of these models to generate authentic case-studies and simulation scenarios remains largely unexplored, particularly in the field of engineering education.

Despite certain inherent limitations, the selected LLMs are generally well poised to serve as co-producers of engineering case studies for at least two main reasons:

First, they have the capability to mine and synthesize large amounts of information from multiple and diverse sources to help synthesize complex engineering scenarios and generate engineering case studies, thus reducing the workload for faculty to develop these studies from scratch.

Second, as engineering problems often require interdisciplinary knowledge, LLMs can integrate various disciplines into simulations and role-playing, showcasing the multifaceted aspects of real-world engineering problems. In doing so, LLMs can potentially train students to develop intricate judgment skills when exposed to muddy situations or ethical dilemmas.

Rooted in established interdisciplinary concepts and educational theories such as constructivism, experiential learning, Augmented Intelligence (AuI) and co-creation, and situated cognition theory, this study aims to explore the potential usage and the relative merits of three prominent LLMs, namely ChatGPT-4o (OpenAI), Gemini 2.0 Flash (Google) and Perplexity Free Tier version (Perplexity AI) in generating case studies that simulate real-world engineering scenarios and decision making. We position the usage of LLMs as co-producers for crafting case studies as a potential opportunity to democratize access to quality case studies in developing countries. To achieve this goal, we use a conversational analysis approach coupled with a multi-layered assessment methodology.

The remainder of this paper is organized as follows: Sect. 2 presents a literature review of related studies. Section 3 details the research methods and procedures. Section 4 presents the results of our study, while Sect. 5 provides a detailed discussion of these findings. Finally, Sect. 6 presents a summary of the key research results, their implications, and some suggestions for future research.

2 Literature Review and Research Contribution

The merits of exposing students to case studies, simulated engineering scenarios and decision-making processes are manifolds: Provision of authentic and safe learning environments [14], development of critical thinking and problem-solving skills that are transferable to real-world contexts [15], exposure to simulated ethical dilemmas [16], development of project management competencies [17], enhancement of students' engagement and motivation that can potentially lead to better learning outcomes [18], and the broadening of the educational outcomes to cover emerging global, economic, environmental, sustainability, and societal trends [19]. In particular, role-play simulations, meant to mimic real decision-making scenarios, are effective methods for students to practice critical thinking and decision making [20].

We conducted a literature review by exploring a range of scholarly publications related to our research topic, utilizing pertinent keywords across major academic databases including Google Scholar, IEEE Xplore, ScienceDirect, and ACM Digital Library. Our literature review revealed the scarcity of related contributions, although a few studies have been reported in healthcare (e.g., [21–24]) and management education (e.g., [25]). The reader is referred to these studies and the references cited therein for a more comprehensive review of earlier research.

This research makes the following main contributions:

- Unlike most previous studies that focused on the application of a single LLM (predominantly ChatGPT) for case study generation, thereby limiting the generalizability of their findings, this research examines the relative merits of three major LLMs (ChatGPT-4o, Gemini 2.0, and Perplexity) using a multi-layered mixed-methods approach, offering a more comprehensive assessment of their effectiveness in generating case studies. Such comparative analysis is essential, as each LLM operates on distinct architectures, training data, and optimization strategies, which can significantly influence the quality, coherence, contextual accuracy, and adaptability of the generated case study. Hence by evaluating multiple LLMs, this research provides a more comprehensive understanding of LLM-generated case studies, offering richer empirical insights into their relative strengths, effectiveness, and limitations. Such an approach enhances the generalizability of findings and informs best practices for leveraging LLMs to generate relevant case studies. In addition, while the relative efficacity of LLMs in the medical and health science field has been explored by some studies (e.g. evaluation of: ChatGPT-3.5, ChatGPT-4, and Claude 2 in breast cancer analysis [26], ChatGPT, BARD, and Bing AI in Rhinoplasty diagnosis [27], ChatGPT-4, Gemini, Copilot, Chatsonic, and Perplexity in Keratoconus diagnosis [28]), the assessment of their relative merits in case-study generation remains an underexplored research topic.
- To the best of our knowledge, this is the first reported contribution that explores the potential capabilities and the relative merits of three prominent LLMs in generating case studies within the specific context of engineering education.
- Drawing on established interdisciplinary concepts, theories, and approaches that are detailed later in this section, this study investigates the use of three LLMs to simulate real-world scenarios and decision-making in engineering education. This is particularly significant for HEIs in developing countries, where financial constraints often hinder access to scarce proprietary case study collections.
- We offer a balanced perspective on the use of LLMs for engineering case study generation by highlighting their merits and critically examining the limitations they present in educational settings.

Our research is rooted in and guided by the following established concepts, theories, and frameworks:

- Constructivist learning theory [29, 30] which posits that humans construct new knowledge through experimentation and reflections, rather than by the passive consumption of information through knowledge transmission. This theory guided the design phase of this research by prompting the LLMs to embed scenarios to expose students to complex technical and non-technical engineering problems and ethical situations.
- Situated cognition theory [31] that emphasizes that learning knowledge and skills should take place in contexts that reflect the way they will be used in real life. The theory promotes the idea of immersing learners into situations that mimic the context where their ideas and behaviors will be applied [29], which is the anchor of case study.
- Augmented Intelligence (AuI) and co-creation [33, 34]: AuI emphasizes a collaborative model where humans and AI work together to enhance cognitive performance and problem solving through a co-creation process. In doing so, humans and AI work to iteratively refine tasks, goals, and solutions. AuI promotes the design principle of "human in the loop", underscoring the importance of human oversight to assess the accuracy and relevance of the generated.

3 Methods and Procedures

This exploratory study employs a comparative evaluation of three advanced large language models (LLMs), namely ChatGPT-4o, Gemini 2.0, and Perplexity, to assess their effectiveness in generating high-quality case studies that simulate advanced real-world engineering role playing and decision-making scenarios. The study spanned from 10 January 2025 to 20 March 2025. Our research methodology unfolds in three distinct stages: case study generation, automated LLM-based evaluation, and expert assessment.

We contextualized our study within the setting of the graduate course "Managing Big Data Projects". This course aims to provide students with a comprehensive understanding of the technical and managerial aspects of managing big data projects, while raising awareness of the broader ethical and legal implications. The Course Learning Outcomes (CLOs) are as follows:

CLO1: Demonstrate proficiency in applying advanced big data technologies and tools.

CLO2: Develop and demonstrate advanced project management skills specifically tailored for big data projects.

CLO3: Apply principles of data governance and ethics in the context of big data projects.

CLO4: Apply analytical and critical thinking skills to solve complex problems pertaining to managing big data projects.

Being an integral part of the coursework, the case study is designed as a team project to mainly assess CLOs 2, 3, and 4.

3.1 Case Study Generation

To ensure a standardized comparison, a set of structured engineering prompts was carefully designed to guide each LLM in producing a case study. These prompts were crafted to elicit realistic and relevant engineering scenarios, ensuring that all models worked under the same input conditions. The resulting case studies were then collected for subsequent evaluation.

The general framework that guided the case study generation is depicted in Fig. 1. The framework has been developed based on best practices in interacting with AI-driven conversational models and it has been guided by the concepts, theories and frameworks described in the previous section.

Given the complexities involved in co-creating a detailed high-quality case study and to not overwhelming the LLMs with multiple tasks, we opted for a task decomposition approach using an incremental approach, as depicted in Fig. 1.

We started by providing the context and general guidelines first and then proceed iteratively to refine the case study by incorporating additional explicit instructions.

Our framework integrates advanced prompt engineering techniques to improve the quality, specificity, and effectiveness of our interactions. Recall that prompt engineering is an emerging field that aims to achieve the optimal LLM's output by recognizing the inherent capabilities, limitations, and the operational contexts within which these models operate to craft effective prompts [35].

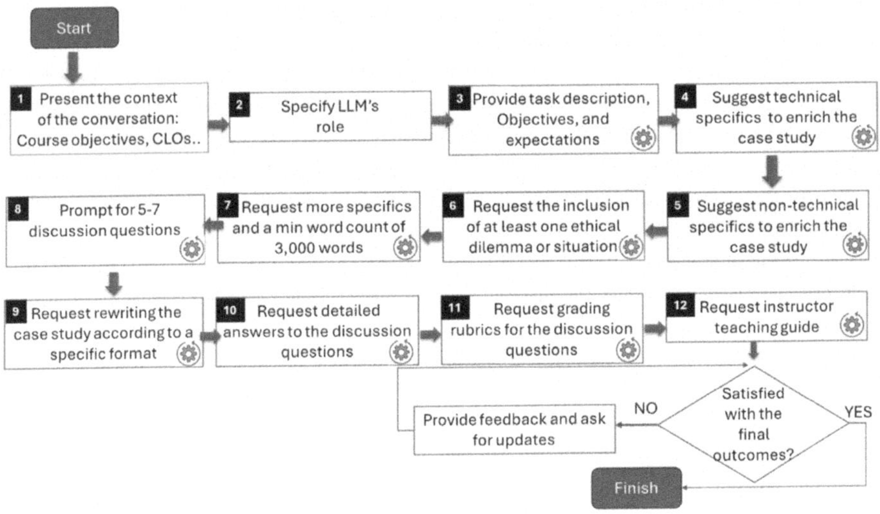

Fig. 1. Framework to guide the conversation with LLMs

As shown in Fig. 1, we started in steps 1–2 by elaborating few "system messages", also known in prompt engineering as context-setting messages to set the stage of the conversation and help guide the LLM's behavior and tone. During this first stage, we provided each LLM with the general context of the intervention, including general information about the course objectives, CLOs, and targeted audience. We also stated our expectations and highlighted our aim to collaborate with each LLM in co-producing a comprehensive case study that aligns with the stated course objectives and CLOs.

The above "systems messages" are then followed by "user messages" (steps 3–12 in Fig. 1) to drive the conversation forward by instructing each LLM to respond to specific prompts. For this conversational prompting stage, we invested the necessary time and effort to make sure that our prompts are thought out in advance, as opposed to being spontaneous stream of ad hoc thought questions. This helped us in meeting the attributes of good engineering prompts, namely precision, clarity, relevance, critical stimulation, practical applicability, and reflective provocation [36].

Besides prompting each LLM to generate the content for the case study, we also requested it to (1) propose 5–7 thought-provoking discussion questions along with their answers and grading rubrics (steps 8, 10, and 11 respectively), (2) rewrite the case according to a standard case-study format (step 9), and (3) produce the case study's instructor teaching guide (step 12). It should be noted that the last round of cross-checking and refinement that assesses user satisfaction and subsequent updates was bypassed in this study to maintain consistency across experimental conditions and ensure a direct comparison of the generated LLMs' outputs.

Due to space constraints, the 12 initial prompts used to evaluate the efficacy of ChatGPT-4o, Gemini 2.0, and Perplexity in generating the case study are not included herein, but they can be retrieved from the supplementary material (***prompts.pdf***) [37].

3.2 Automated Evaluation Using LLMs

Following case study generation, an automated evaluation process was conducted using LLMs as assessors. Alongside the three models used for content creation, Grok (xAI) was introduced as an independent evaluator. We developed explicit prompts to instruct each LLM to assess each of the generated case studies using a 1–5 Likert scale (1 = Poor, 5 = Excellent) across multiple performance metrics as shown in Table 1.

In addition to numerical ratings, we prompted each of the four LLM assessors to provide qualitative feedback, highlighting the key strengths and weaknesses of each generated case study. This dual-layered evaluation aimed to capture both quantitative performance metrics and qualitative insights into the generative capabilities of each model. To minimize potential bias in the evaluation process, each LLM assessor was tasked with assessing each of the three generated case studies without being informed of their origin.

3.3 Expert Evaluation

To further enrich the validity of our research findings, an independent expert review was conducted through an online survey, providing an external assessment of the quality of the generated case studies. Three Subject Matter Experts (SMEs) independently assessed the case studies using the same evaluation criteria listed in Table 1. These experts were also asked to provide both numerical ratings and written feedback, highlighting the strengths, weaknesses, and areas for improvement of each generated case study, along with their overall evaluation. Their assessments served as a benchmark for comparison with the LLM-generated evaluations, ensuring a more balanced and credible analysis. To

Table 1. Performance metrics for the automated evaluation of LLM-generated cases study

Performance metric	Usefulness
Relevance & accuracy	Measures the degree to which the case study aligns with the given topics and instructions while being free of misinformation and hallucinations
Structural coherence	Measures the extent to which the case study adheres to a logical structure
Depth of analysis	Measures the LLM's ability to go beyond surface-level narratives and explanations to provide meaningful insights and synthesis
Logical consistency of argumentation	Measures the extent to which arguments are logically developed and maintain coherence in reasoning, ensuring a structured and progressive flow of ideas
Citation quality	Measures the correctness and appropriateness of the references provided (if any), which is a proxy indicator of academic rigor and credibility
Linguistic fluency	Measures the extent to which the generated case study fulfills readability, fluency and grammatical correctness criteria
Creativity & originality	Measures the extent to which the LLM can go beyond generating generic content to providing unique perspectives, insights and novel ideas
Readability and engagement	Measures how easily the case study can be read and understood, while also evaluating its ability to capture the student's interest

ensure objectivity and minimize potential bias, we employed a blind evaluation method in which ChatGPT-4o, Gemini, and Perplexity were anonymized as LLM1, LLM2, and LLM3, respectively. This approach concealed the identity of the model that generated the case study, hence minimizing the risk of any model-specific bias or predisposition.

The complete questionnaire used for the SME survey is provided in the supplementary material (***SME_Questionnaire.pdf***) [37].

3.4 Natural Language Processing (NLP) Linguistic Assessment

To add more rigor and objectivity to our comparative performance evaluation, we have incorporated standard Natural Language Processing (NLP) metrics for linguistic assessment, including sentence length, readability standards, syntactic depth, and lexical diversity, among others. These are illustrated in Table 2.

We developed custom Python scripts designed to process each generated case study as input and compute the NLP metrics as output.

3.5 Data Analysis

The collected ratings from LLM-based assessments, expert evaluations, and NLP linguistic standard calculations were analyzed through a mixed-methods approach. Descriptive statistics were computed to identify patterns in model performance across the different evaluation dimensions. Additionally, qualitative content analysis was performed on the descriptive feedback to extract recurring themes regarding the advantages and limitations of each LLM in generating the case study.

4 Results

4.1 Generated Case Studies

Due to space limitations, the complete case studies generated by ChatGPT-4o, Gemini 2.0, and Perplexity are available in the supplementary material (***case_chatgpt.pdf***), (***case_gemini.pdf***), and (***case_perplexity.pdf***), respectively [37]. Table 3 summarizes the key highlights of each case study.

The faculty study guide, answers to case study questions and grading rubrics are available in the supplementary material (***guide_chatgpt.pdf***), (***guide_gemini.pdf***), and (***guide_perplexity.pdf***) [37]. Due to lack of space, their assessment is not included herein.

Table 3. Case Study Highlights

LLM	Case study title	Application domain	Core ethical dilemma
ChatGPT-4o	DataPulse Innovations: A Case Study in managing Big Data Projects	Data analytics services	Should DataPulse prioritize aggressive data monetization (even if it means potentially compromising privacy standards), to meet pressing revenue targets?
Gemini 2.0	Project Heartbeat: Predicting Heart Failure Readmission at health Insights Inc.	Healthcare Business Intelligence	Given that the company has discovered a racial bias in the predictive model against African American patients, should it proceed with or delay the pilot study?

(*continued*)

Table 3. (*continued*)

LLM	Case study title	Application domain	Core ethical dilemma
Perplexity	Smart Healthcare Analytics for pandemic Preparedness: A Detailed Case Study	Smart real-time pandemic outbreak prediction	Should Synergy Health Solutions leverage its Smart Pandemic Outbreak Prediction System to fulfill the Department of Public Health's request to integrate law enforcement data for predicting crime hotspots, knowing that this could reinforce existing biases in law enforcement?

4.2 Evaluation of Case Studies by LLM Assessors

Tables 4, 5 and 6 show the quantitative assessment results reported by the LLM assessors for the case studies generated by ChatGPT-4o, Gemini 2.0, and Perplexity, respectively. A consolidated summary of the mean scores is illustrated in Table 7.

Table 4. LLM Assessment– **ChatGPT-4o** Case Study

Metric	Assessor				
	ChatGPT-4o	Gemini 2.0	Perplexity	Grok	
	Rating (1–5)	Rating (1–5)	Rating (1–5)	Rating (1–5)	Mean ± SD
Relevance & Accuracy	5	5	5	5	5 ± 0
Structural Coherence	5	5	5	5	5 ± 0
Depth of Analysis	5	4	4	4	4.25 ± 0.5
Logical Consistency	5	5	5	5	5 ± 0
Citation Quality	4	4	3	4	3.75 ± 0.5
Linguistic Fluency	5	5	5	5	5 ± 0
Creativity & Originality	4	4	4	4	4 ± 0

(*continued*)

Table 4. (*continued*)

Metric	Assessor				
	ChatGPT-4o	Gemini 2.0	Perplexity	Grok	
	Rating (1–5)	Rating (1–5)	Rating (1–5)	Rating (1–5)	Mean ± SD
Readability & Engagement	4	4	4	5	4.25 ± 0.5

Table 5. LLM Assessment– **Gemini** Case Study

Metric	Assessor				
	ChatGPT-4o	Gemini 2.0	Perplexity	Grok	
	Rating (1–5)	Rating (1–5)	Rating (1–5)	Rating (1–5)	Mean ± SD
Relevance & Accuracy	5	5	5	5	5 ± 0
Structural Coherence	5	5	5	5	5 ± 0
Depth of Analysis	5	4	4	4	4.25 ± 0.5
Logical Consistency	5	5	5	5	5 ± 0
Citation Quality	3	3	2	4	3.0 ± 0.8
Linguistic Fluency	5	5	5	5	5 ± 0
Creativity & Originality	4	4	4	5	4.25 ± 0.5
Readability & Engagement	4	4	4	5	4.25 ± 0.5

Table 6. LLM Assessment– **Perplexity** Case Study

Metric	Assessor				
	ChatGPT-4o	Gemini 2.0	Perplexity	Grok	
	Rating (1–5)	Rating (1–5)	Rating (1–5)	Rating (1–5)	Mean ± SD
Relevance & Accuracy	5	5	5	5	5 ± 0
Structural Coherence	5	5	5	5	5 ± 0

(*continued*)

Table 6. (*continued*)

Metric	Assessor				
	ChatGPT-4o	Gemini 2.0	Perplexity	Grok	
	Rating (1–5)	Rating (1–5)	Rating (1–5)	Rating (1–5)	Mean ± SD
Depth of Analysis	5	4	4	4	4.25 ± 0.5
Logical Consistency	5	5	5	5	5 ± 0
Citation Quality	4	4	4	4	4.0 ± 0
Linguistic Fluency	5	5	5	5	5 ± 0
Creativity & Originality	5	4	4	5	4.5 ± 0.57
Readability & Engagement	4	4	5	5	4.5 ± 0.57

Table 7. LLM Assessment– Case Study Average Scores

	Case Study		
	ChatGPT-4o	Gemini 2.0	Perplexity
	Average Rating ± SD	Average Rating ± SD	Average Rating ± SD
Relevance & Accuracy	5 ± 0	5 ± 0	5 ± 0
Structural Coherence	5 ± 0	5 ± 0	5 ± 0
Depth of Analysis	4.25 ± 0.5	4.25 ± 0.5	4.25 ± 0.5
Logical Consistency	5 ± 0	5 ± 0	5 ± 0
Citation Quality	3.75 ± 0.5	3.0 ± 0.8	4.0 ± 0
Linguistic Fluency	5 ± 0	5 ± 0	5 ± 0
Creativity & Originality	4 ± 0	4.25 ± 0.5	4.5 ± 0.57
Readability & Engagement	4.25 ± 0.5	4.25 ± 0.5	4.5 ± 0.57

Table 2. NLP-based metrics for linguistic assessment

NLP metric	Usage and interpretation
Sentence Length	We used the **Mean Sentence Length** (**MSL**) which is defined as the average number of words per sentence. The expected range is 15–25 words per sentence for formal writing. MSL below 10 indicates simplistic writing, while MSL greater than 30 indicates convoluted writing
Readability Standards	We used three common readability metrics: **Flesch-Kincaid Grade Level (FGL)**: It reflects the complexity of the case study. The expected range is 10–14 for academic readability **Flesch Reading Ease Score (FRES)**: It indicates on a scale of 0 to 100, the readability of the case study, with a higher score translating to easier comprehension. The expected range is 30–60 for formal writing **The Coleman-Liau Index (CLI)**: It indicates the education level required to understand the case study. The CLI is based on the average number of letters and sentences per 100 words. Lower CLI scores (below 8) indicate simple, easy-to-read text, which is a proxy indicator for ease of accessibility but could signal oversimplification of complex engineering concepts. High CLI scores (above 12), on the other hand, indicate complex writing that may be appropriate for advanced readers but could hinder accessibility and engagement
Lexical and Syntactic Complexity	We used the **Type-Token Ratio (TTR)** Lexical Diversity metric, defined as the ratio of unique words to total words. Higher TTR values infer richer (more diverse) vocabulary usage
Lexical diversity	We used two metrics to assess lexical diversity: **DISTINCT-1: Unigram diversity** – Higher values suggest a more varied use of individual words **DISTINCT-2: Bigram diversity** – Higher values indicate a greater variety of word pairs and phrase structures

(*continued*)

Table 2. (*continued*)

NLP metric	Usage and interpretation
Coherence and fluency	We used **Perplexity (PPL)** score to assess coherence and fluency. Lower values correspond to more coherent and predictable (or fluent) text, inferring that the model is more confident in its predictions, suggesting better performance. PPL provides a more intuitive measure than traditional cross-entropy metric
Sentence structures complexity	We used **Syntactic Depth (SD)** which represents the complexity of sentence structures, measured by analyzing syntactic tree depth or embedding levels in linguistic parsing, with higher SD values indicating more complex, nested, and sophisticated constructions. While a low SD infers simple, direct sentences for enhanced clarity, it can indicate lack of depth. A high SD value on the other hand infers sophisticated sentence structures which can reduce accessibility and increase cognitive load. A moderate SD value balances readability and engagement
Sentence structure and phrasing Diversity	We used the **Self-BLEU Score (SBC)** which evaluates diversity among sentences. A high SBC indicates that the case study is overly repetitive, hence lacking variation in expression, potentially making it monotonous and less engaging for readers. A very low SBC may indicate excessive variation, making the case study incoherent, while a moderate SBC suggests that the case study maintains a balance between coherence and variation, ensuring both readability and engagement

In addition to providing quantitative ratings for each of the eight-performance metrics, we prompted each LLM assessor to identify the associated strengths and weaknesses and provide suggestions for further improvement. A condensed summary of identified weaknesses is presented in Table 8.

Table 8. Summary of Feeback Provided by the LLM Assessors

	Case Study		
	ChatGPT-4o	Gemini 2.0	Perplexity
Relevance & Accuracy	Could include additional industry-specific data	Could include additional real-world statistics	The Usage of fictional elements, while illustrative, may slightly diverge from real-world specificity
Structural Coherence	Technical details section is dense	Provide brief summaries at the start of each section	Some sections are dense, which might challenge readers who prefer more succinct structure
Depth of Analysis	Expand the financial implications of the transformation for greater depth	Could benefit from deeper quantitative analysis and more elaboration on data preprocessing techniques	Certain areas could benefit from deeper exploration of stakeholder implications for alternative strategies. Potential long-term societal impacts of the "predictive policing" dilemma could be expanded

(*continued*)

Table 8. (*continued*)

	Case Study		
	ChatGPT-4o	Gemini 2.0	Perplexity
Logical Consistency	Transitions between highly technical and managerial sections could be made smoother	Some transitions between highly technical and managerial discussions could be streamlined for improved flow	The integration of the predictive policing dilemma, while intriguing, might appear abrupt to some readers
Citation Quality	Lacks in-text citations, which might be expected in an academic context	Lacks in-text citations to sources	Some citation formats are inconsistent and lack detailed author or publication information. Need to explicitly connect the references to specific points within the case study
Linguistic Fluency	Some sentences are lengthy	Some sentences are long and complex	Occasional complex sentence structures may challenge non-expert readers
Creativity & Originality	Incorporate more novel insights	Include more innovative narrative techniques to further boost originality. The ethical dilemma of AI bias is a frequently discussed topic	The ethical dilemma of "predictive policing," while important, is a frequently discussed topic
Readability & Engagement	Dense technical jargon may be challenging for non-expert audiences	Technical density and complexity may overwhelm readers with little familiarity with healthcare data systems	The high level of detail and technical language may overwhelm readers not familiar with the subject matter

4.3 NLP Linguistic Assessment Results

The NLP linguistic assessment results are presented in Table 9.

Table 9. NLP Linguistic Assessment Results

NLP metric	ChatGPT-4o Case Study	Gemini 2.0 Case Study	Perplexity Case Study
Total number of words	3081	2447	2300
Number of unique words	1451	1199	1308
Total number of sentences	184	138	420
Mean Sentence Length (MSL)	16.74	17.73	5.48
Readability Standards:			
Flesch-Kincaid Grade Level (FGL)	17.24	15.56	17.0
Flesch Reading Ease Score (FRES)	20.32	22.39	34.42
Coleman-Liau Index (CLI)	20.24	20.05	21.43
Lexical and Syntactic Complexity:			
Type-Token Ratio (TTR)	0.47	0.49	0.56
Lexical diversity:			
DISTINCT-1 Unigram diversity	0.47	0.49	0.56
DISTINCT-2 Bigram diversity	0.89	0.89	0.93
Coherence and fluency:			
Perplexity (PPL)	21.62	36.06	18.13
Sentence structures complexity:			
Syntactic Depth (SD)	6.67	6.91	4.62
Sentence structure & phrasing Diversity:			
Self-BLEU Score (SBC)	0.09	0.10	0.12

4.4 Quantitative Evaluation by SMEs

Tables 10, 11 and 12 show the quantitative assessment results reported by the three Subject Matter Experts (SME1, SME2, SME3) for the case studies generated by ChatGPT-4o, Gemini 2.0, and Perplexity, respectively. A consolidated summary of the mean scores is illustrated in Table 13 and Fig. 1.

Table 10. SME Assessment– **ChatGPT-4o** Case Study

	SME1	SME2	SME3	
	Rating (1–5)	Rating (1–5)	Rating (1–5)	Mean ± SD
Relevance & Accuracy	5	5	5	5.0 ± 0
Structural Coherence	4	4	5	4.33 ± 0.57
Depth of Analysis	4	4	4	4.0 ± 0
Logical Consistency	5	4	5	4.66 ± 0.57
Citation Quality	3	2	4	3.0 ± 1
Linguistic Fluency	5	5	5	5.0 ± 0
Creativity & Originality	4	4	4	4.0 ± 0
Readability & Engagement	3	4	4	3.66 ± 0.57

Table 11. SME Assessment– **Gemini 2.0** Case Study

	SME1	SME2	SME3	
	Rating (1–5)	Rating (1–5)	Rating (1–5)	Mean ± SD
Relevance & Accuracy	4	5	5	4.66 ± 0.57
Structural Coherence	4	4	4	4.0 ± 0
Depth of Analysis	3	3	3	3.0 ± 0
Logical Consistency	4	4	4	4.0 ± 0
Citation Quality	1	1	1	1.0 ± 0
Linguistic Fluency	5	4	4	4.33 ± 0.57
Creativity & Originality	4	3	5	4.0 ± 1
Readability & Engagement	3	3	3	3.0 ± 0

Table 12. SME Assessment– **Perplexity** Case Study

	SME1	SME2	SME3	
	Rating (1–5)	Rating (1–5)	Rating (1–5)	Mean ± SD
Relevance & Accuracy	2	2	3	2.33 ± 0.57
Structural Coherence	3	3	2	2.66 ± 0.57
Depth of Analysis	2	3	3	2.66 ± 0.57
Logical Consistency	3	2	3	2.66 ± 0.57
Citation Quality	0	1	1	0.66 ± 0.57
Linguistic Fluency	4	3	3	3.33 ± 0.57
Creativity & Originality	3	3	4	3.33 ± 0.57
Readability & Engagement	2	2	2	2.0 ± 0

Table 13. SME Assessments– Case Study Average Scores

	Case Study		
	ChatGPT-4o	Gemini 2.0	Perplexity
	Average Rating ± SD	Average Rating ± SD	Average Rating ± SD
Relevance & Accuracy	5.0 + 0	4.66 ± 0.57	2.33 ± 0.57
Structural Coherence	4.33 ± 0.57	4.0 ± 0	2.66 ± 0.57
Depth of Analysis	4.0 ± 0	3.0 ± 0	2.66 ± 0.57
Logical Consistency	4.66 ± 0.57	4.0 ± 0	2.66 ± 0.57
Citation Quality	3.0 ± 1	1.0 ± 0	0.66 ± 0.57
Linguistic Fluency	5.0 ± 0	4.33 ± 0.57	3.33 ± 0.57
Creativity & Originality	4.0 ± 0	4.0 ± 1	3.33 ± 0.57
Readability & Engagement	3.66 ± 0.57	3.0 ± 0	2.0 ± 0

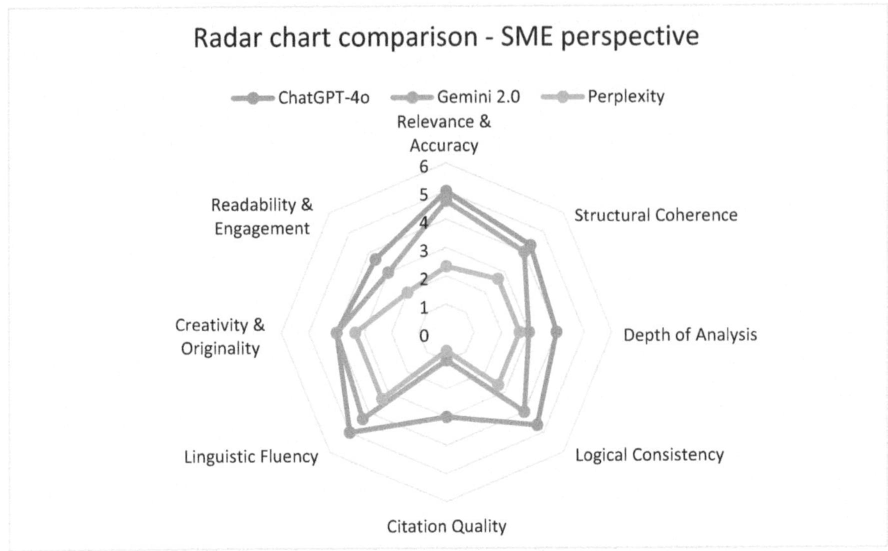

Fig. 2. SMEs' average ratings of LLM-generated case studies across 8 dimensions

In addition to requesting quantitative ratings for each of the eight-performance metrics, we asked each SME assessor to outline the associated strengths and weaknesses, provide suggestions for improvement, and provide an overall assessment of the suitability of the generated case study for potential course adoption. A condensed summary of this feedback is presented in Table 14. Detailed explanations can be retrieved from supplementary material (***SME_feedback.pdf***) [37].

Table 14. Summary of Key Strengths, Weaknesses and Suggestions as Reported by the SMEs

	Case Study		
	ChatGPT-4o	Gemini 2.0	Perplexity
Key recurring strengths	Comprehensive Coverage & Structure Meets the 3,000-word requirement Holistic Approach: Goes beyond technical details to incorporate organizational, managerial, and ethical considerations Strong Implementation Plan with clear criteria for measuring effectiveness Stakeholder-Centric Analysis Up-to-Date and Relevant Technological Integration Well-Executed Big Data Management Discussion Engaging Ethical Considerations	Real-world relevance, showing significant practical value Innovative application domain Effective implementation plan: Holistic Approach: Goes beyond technical details to incorporate organizational, managerial, and ethical considerations Multiple stakeholder perspectives and emphasis on the role of leadership Relevant and engaging ethical issues	Simulated a realistic fictional scenario Clear and consistent flow Relevant discussion questions Balanced integration of technical and ethical aspects Practical appendices: Engaging subject choice
Key recurring weaknesses	Surface-level writing Lack of narrative storytelling Prescriptive tone Editing issues Lack of reflective analysis Overuse of bullet points and short sentences Outdated references Insufficient practical examples Weak academic rigor Unresolved ethical dilemma	Word count issue: The case study fails to meet the required minimum word count of 3,000 words Unreliable references Lack of engaging storytelling Inadequate technical coverage Vague recommendations Overly prescriptive: Poor supporting material Excessive bullet points and short sentences: Several instances of repetitive content Structural issues	Word count issue Failure to address core technical problems Citation issues Simplistic writing Lack of depth Lack of creativity Failure to engage students Unoriginal ethical issue Missing conclusion No implementation plan or alternative solutions

(*continued*)

Table 14. (*continued*)

	Case Study		
	ChatGPT-4o	Gemini 2.0	Perplexity
Key areas for improvement	Offer multiple technical solutions for students to explore, fostering critical thinking Deepen analysis Adopt a more narrative-driven style Include more supporting material and data for students to analyze Reorganize structure: Move Sect. 2.3 after 3.2 for better logical flow and clarity Strengthen citations and replace general references with peer-reviewed articles and verifiable sources	Make the conclusion more reflective, incorporating deep, open-ended questions to encourage critical thinking Incorporate captivating narrative elements to increase engagement Enhance storytelling: Develop technical content: Detail machine learning models:	Rewrite with narrative style and enrich with deeper discussions Provide insightful conclusion Replace non-academic references with peer-reviewed sources Incorporate more challenges related to Big Data techniques, addressing complexities such as scalability, latency, and other technical hurdles
Suitability for adoption?	The case study is **not suitable for use in its current form**, as it requires thorough editing and refinement to meet academic standards, including robust citations, real-world examples, and solution-oriented analysis, to be effective for graduate-level engineering education	The case study is **not suitable in its current form** and requires major revisions, including strengthening the technical details, improving the structure, adding supporting materials, and incorporating relevant references to meet academic standards and enhance its credibility	The case study is **not suitable in its current form** and requires major rework, including more technical depth, reliance on peer-reviewed sources, and revisions to meet academic standards and scholarly rigor

5 Discussions

We start our discussion by a general observation that the LLMs demonstrated inconsistencies in adhering to our specific structured instructions outlined in Fig. 1. In fact, the LLMs tended to restructure or rewrite the case study as opposed to incrementally refining prior outputs. These limitations are attributed to the fact that unlike humans, LLMs lack persistent memory across sessions and interactions. LLMs primarily rely on regressive language modeling, leveraging probabilistic predictions to generate future words and sentences based on learned patterns from extensive training data, rather than strictly adhering to predefined formatting or instructional constraints [38]. Moreover, like most transformer-based architectures, these models are constrained by finite context windows, which limit the amount of text they can process in a single query and hence their ability to maintain dialogue coherence over longer interactions. For instance, ChatGPT-4o supports a maximum context window of 8,192 tokens per query, Perplexity (Free Tier) is limited to 4,000 tokens, while Gemini 2.0 Flash extends this capacity to 1 M tokens, encompassing both input text and generated responses. When these context thresholds are exceeded, the models truncate earlier segments of the conversation to accommodate new inputs and outputs.

The results of the NLP-based textual analysis, as summarized in Table 9, yield several significant observations regarding the quality and stylistic characteristics of the generated case studies:

- Neither Gemini nor Perplexity adhered to the stipulated minimum word count of 3,000 words. Perplexity employed more than twice the number of sentences used by ChatGPT-4o, yet these sentences were considerably shorter, with an average length of 5.48 words compared to 16.74 words per sentence in the ChatGPT-4o output. This difference highlights Perplexity's preference for brevity over syntactic elaboration.
- In terms of textual accessibility and reader comprehension, Perplexity produced the most readable content, achieving a Flesch Reading Ease (FRE) score of 34.42 which is substantially higher than those of ChatGPT-4o (20.32) and Gemini (22.39). This relatively higher FRE score is largely attributable to Perplexity's reliance on very short, yet concise sentence structures. Furthermore, the Flesch-Kincaid Grade Level and Coleman-Liau Index scores for all three models indicate that the generated case studies possess appropriate academic readability, targeting an audience of graduate-level engineering students.
- Perplexity exhibited the greatest syntactic simplicity while maintaining lexical richness, as evidenced by the highest Type-Token Ratio (TTR) of 0.56. Its reliance on short, direct sentences contributed to higher syntactic clarity and coherence, further supported by its superior performance on Perplexity (PPL) and syntactic depth metrics. In contrast, ChatGPT-4o and Gemini produced outputs with more complex syntactic structures, balancing clarity with depth of content and engagement.
- The same brevity that improved readability in Perplexity's output also introduced stylistic drawbacks. The repetition of similar sentence patterns resulted in a relatively higher Self-BLEU score of 0.12, indicating reduced stylistic diversity and a more monotonous tone. In comparison, ChatGPT-4o and Gemini delivered outputs that were stylistically more varied and thus potentially more engaging to human readers.

The evaluation results presented in Tables 4 through 6 reveal a strong level of agreement among the four LLM assessors. The aggregate ratings summarized in Table 7 indicate no clear overall leader among the three LLMs in terms of case study generation quality. However, a notable exception emerged in the "quality of citations" metric, where Gemini received the lowest average score (3.0), trailing behind ChatGPT-4o (3.75) and Perplexity (4.0).

When these LLM-generated evaluations (Tables 4–7) are compared against the SME assessments (Tables 10–13), a critical disparity becomes evident. In fact, the automatic LLM assessors exhibited a tendency toward score inflation, consistently assigning high marks and displaying limited discrimination across the eight evaluation dimensions. This uniformity suggests a form of scoring leniency that may limit the utility of LLMs for nuanced peer-style critique.

In contrast, as illustrated in Fig. 1, the SME evaluations demonstrated strong inter-rater reliability and produced a more differentiated and critical appraisal. The SMEs clearly identified ChatGPT-4o as the superior performer across all assessed dimensions of case study generation, with Gemini following, and Perplexity consistently scoring lowest. These findings highlight the continued necessity of expert human oversight in assessing educational content quality.

The qualitative feedback provided by both the LLM and SME assessors, as summarized in Tables 8 and 14 respectively, offered invaluable insights that complemented our quantitative findings. This narrative evaluation showcased both the strengths and the persistent limitations inherent in each of the three LLMs when it comes to generating case studies. These are further discussed below.

Among the three evaluated models, ChatGPT-4o emerged as the most comprehensive performer, being the only LLM to have met the 3,000-word minimum requirement. Its output demonstrated a holistic perspective, addressing not only technical aspects but also integrating organizational, managerial, and ethical considerations, while effectively capturing diverse stakeholder viewpoints. The generated case study featured a well-articulated implementation strategy and clearly defined Key Performance Indicators (KPIs) in full alignment with the structure and expectations of real-world engineering case development.

However, these strengths were accompanied by several limitations. Notably, certain sections of the generated content adopted a prescriptive tone and exhibited surface-level analysis, falling short of the narrative richness and contextual nuance characteristic of high-quality case studies. Furthermore, while references were included, many were outdated and not explicitly cited within the body of the text. The absence of in-text citations raises legitimate concerns regarding Intellectual Property (IP) and copyright compliance, particularly given that LLM output may be derived from patterns found in copyrighted training data, without formal attribution or referencing of the source origin.

Nevertheless, within the context of our study (which is focused on non-commercial, educational use) we argue that the deployment of ChatGPT-4o falls under the "fair use" doctrine. The explicit disclosure of the LLM involvement, combined with the academic intent and absence of commercial gain, aligns with prevailing interpretations of fair educational use.

Gemini 2.0 distinguished itself through the real-world relevance and practical applicability of its generated case study. Much like ChatGPT-4o, Gemini adopted a holistic approach by incorporating multiple stakeholder perspectives and addressing ethical considerations that were both timely and engaging. The case featured a well-structured implementation plan with clearly defined success criteria, contributing to its pedagogical robustness. The ethical dilemma presented in the case was particularly relevant, engaging and well-aligned with typical challenges faced in engineering projects.

Despite these merits, several limitations were observed. First, Gemini's generated case study fell short of the required minimum 3,000-word threshold, hence limiting the depth and development of its arguments. Moreover, most of the references included were drawn from websites rather than peer-reviewed academic literature, which raises concerns about the scholarly credibility and long-term educational value of the content. Gemini's overreliance on bullet points and short sentences disrupted the narrative flow of the case and weakened the storytelling and immersive quality that are expected in typical case studies. This stylistic approach enhanced clarity but diminished student engagement by diluting the complexity required for critical reflection and discussion. Additionally, the technical dimension of the case lacked rigor, offering limited exploration of problem-solving pathways or alternative engineering solutions. These shortcomings suggest that while Gemini showed potential for quickly crafting accessible and practical case study, its current formulation lacks the depth and scholarly rigor needed for graduate-level engineering instruction.

Perplexity was consistently ranked lowest by the three SMEs across all eight performance dimensions, highlighting several critical shortcomings in its ability to generate pedagogically effective case studies. Despite this, the model did present a thematically relevant and engaging scenario that simulated a plausible real-world situation, potentially offering a foundation for learner engagement. Furthermore, the integration of ethical considerations alongside technical elements and the inclusion of well-crafted discussion questions reflected a commendable attempt to support critical reflection.

However, these strengths were significantly undermined by structural and content-related limitations. Most notably, Perplexity relied heavily on very short, simplistic sentences (often presented in bullet-point format) which severely diminished the case study's narrative coherence and storytelling depth. It provided the shortest case study among all three models and failed to address core technical complexities, particularly those inherent to Big Data implementation projects. The content offered minimal depth and no exploration of alternative approaches or solution pathways.

The case study generated also lacked a clear implementation plan and ended abruptly without a formal conclusion. Most concerning, the case study showed serious citation issues, including some non-existent fake references, improperly cited authors, and incomplete titles. These serious limitations confirm the well-documented potential of LLMs for citation unreliability and hallucinations [39].

When asked whether the three LLM-generated case studies were ready for adoption in their current form, all three SMEs unanimously agreed that they were not. Each case study, while demonstrating potential, requires significant post-processing, and academic refinement to meet the rigor and pedagogical expectations of graduate-level engineering education. This finding underscores the critical importance of maintaining a "human-in-the-loop" approach when integrating LLMs into educational content development.

Rather than viewing LLMs as autonomous content generators, we argue that these systems are best positioned as collaborative tools. They can provide a foundational draft for a more iterative, human-led case study co-creation process. This approach holds considerable promises to accelerate the generation of quality case studies. To guide educators in integrating LLM-generated case studies ethically and responsibly, we recommend positioning these tools as co-pilots rather than as automated replacements for instructional design.

While a more detailed examination of this human-AI co-creation model is the subject of ongoing research, our findings suggest that the framework introduced in Fig. 1 serves as a valuable guide for optimizing the co-creation of case studies with the assistance of LLMs. Grounded in the principles of augmented intelligence and co-creation [33, 34], this approach reinforces the idea that artificial intelligence is most impactful when it complements rather than replaces human expertise, ensuring that content remains contextually relevant, technically sound, and pedagogically meaningful. In addition, the prompt engineering framework, depicted in Fig. 1, can be operationalized through an interactive and user-friendly software application to reduce human workload.

6 Conclusion

This study represents the first reported contribution that aimed to explore the relative merits and limitations of Large Language Models (LLMs) in generating contextually rich case studies tailored for graduate-level engineering education. Our comparative analysis revealed that ChatGPT-4o exhibited the highest potential in crafting comprehensive case studies that can potentially support experiential learning and foster critical thinking and decision-making.

Our research showed that LLM-generated case studies require thorough human oversight, including rigorous fact-checking, stylistic refinement, and narrative enhancement, before being integrated into educational settings. Issues such as limited contextual memory, citation inaccuracies, and superficial coverage persist across models, reinforcing the necessity of manual intervention.

Our research contributes to the growing body of evidence on the transformative potential of LLMs in equipping future engineers with the skills needed to address complex, interdisciplinary, and ethically nuanced engineering challenges and experiential learning experiences.

This study has many limitations. For instance, it has a narrow scope, restricted to a single course context, three prominent LLM architectures, and a limited pool of three SMEs, which limits the reliability and generalization of its findings. Future research should aim to broaden this scope by incorporating additional LLMs such as Copilot, DeepSeek, and Grok, while also engaging a more diverse and extensive panel of assessors. Furthermore, the assessments provided by the three subject matter experts are subject to inherent human biases, particularly given their awareness that the case studies were generated by large language models.

We also call on AI developers and technology providers to enhance their models' context awareness, reliability, and responsiveness to specific instructional requirements, especially in the context of rigorous academic settings.

While LLMs are not yet ready to independently generate publishable or classroom-ready case studies, they hold tremendous promise as co-creative collaborators. With proper frameworks, human oversight, and ethical and responsible usage, LLMs are poised to become beacons of hope for educators in developing countries, enabling the cost-effective access to high-quality, locally contextualized case studies and democratizing access to innovative pedagogical teaching instruments.

Acknowledgment. The authors acknowledge the assistance of ChatGPT-4.0, which was used to aid in the editing, proofreading, and enhancement of the readability of the Introduction, Discussions, and Conclusion sections of this manuscript. While the AI tool contributed to refining the language and improving the clarity of the text, all interpretations, conclusions, and the final content remain the sole responsibility of the authors.

References

1. Kolb, D.A.: Experiential Learning: Experience as the Source of Learning and Development. FT Press, Upper Saddle River (2014)
2. Kolb, A.Y., Kolb, D.A.: Learning styles and learning spaces: enhancing experiential learning in higher education. Acad. Manag. Learn. Educ. **4**(2), 193–212 (2005). https://doi.org/10.5465/AMLE.2005.17268566
3. Moon, J.A.: A Handbook of Reflective and Experiential Learning: Theory and Practice. Routledge, London (2004). https://doi.org/10.4324/9780203416150
4. Deci, E.L., Vallerand, R.J., Pelletier, L.G., Ryan, R.M.: Motivation and education: the self-determination perspective. Educ. Psychol. **26**(3–4), 325–346 (1991). https://doi.org/10.1207/s15326985ep26034_6
5. Hart, J.: Interdisciplinary project-based learning as a means of developing employability skills in undergraduate science degree programs. J. Teach. Learn. Grad. Employability **10**(2), 50–66 (2019)
6. Prince, M.J., Felder, R.M.: Inductive teaching and learning methods: definitions, comparisons, and research bases. J. Eng. Educ. **95**(2), 123–138 (2006). https://doi.org/10.1002/j.2168-9830.2006.tb00884.x
7. ABET: Criteria for Accrediting Engineering Programs, 2022–2023. https://www.abet.org/accreditation/accreditation-criteria/criteria-for-accrediting-engineering-programs-2022-2023/. Accessed 4 Apr 2025
8. Jonassen, D., Strobel, J., Lee, C.B.: Everyday problem solving in engineering: lessons for engineering educators. J. Eng. Educ. **95**, 139–151 (2006). https://doi.org/10.1002/j.2168-9830.2006.tb00885.x
9. Kolmos, A., Fink, F.K.: The Aalborg PBL model: progress, diversity and challenges. In: Krogh, L. (ed.) pp. 9–18. Aalborg University Press, Aalborg (2004)
10. Craig, N., Tennant, S., Murray, M., Forster, A., Pilcher, N.: The role of experienced practitioners in engineering education: the end of an era? In: Proceedings of the Sixth International Symposium on Engineering Education (ISEE 2016), pp. 264–272. University of Manchester, Manchester (2016)
11. Mills, J.E., Treagust, D.F.: Engineering education—is problem-based or project-based learning the answer. Australas. J. Eng. Educ. **3**(2), 2–16 (2003)

12. Chen, J., Kolmos, A., Du, X.: Forms of implementation and challenges of PBL in engineering education: a review of literature. Eur. J. Eng. Educ. **46**(1), 90–115 (2021)
13. Zawacki-Richter, O., Marín, V.I., Bond, M., Gouverneur, F.: Systematic review of research on artificial intelligence applications in higher education–where are the educators? Int. J. Educ. Technol. High. Educ. **16**(1), 1–27 (2019)
14. Gredler, M.E.: Games and simulations and their relationships to learning. In: Jonassen, D.H. (ed.) Handbook of Research on Educational Communications and Technology, pp. 571–581. Lawrence Erlbaum, Mahwah, NJ (2004)
15. Jonassen, D.H.: Toward a design theory of problem solving. Educ. Technol. Res. Dev. **48**(4), 63–85 (2000). https://doi.org/10.1007/BF02300500
16. Martin, D.A., Conlon, E., Bowe, B.: Using case studies in engineering ethics education: the case for immersive scenarios through stakeholder engagement and real-life data. Australas. J. Eng. Educ. **26**(1), 47–63 (2021)
17. Geithner, S., Menzel, D.: Effectiveness of learning through experience and reflection in a project management simulation. Simul. Gaming **47**(2), 228–256 (2016)
18. Wankel, C., Blessinger, P.: Increasing student engagement and retention using immersive interfaces: virtual worlds, gaming, and simulation. In: Cutting-Edge Technologies in Higher Education, vol. 6 Part C, pp. 369–379. Emerald Group Publishing Limited (2013). https://doi.org/10.1108/S2044-9968(2012)000006C023
19. McGibbon, C., Van Belle, J.P.: Integrating environmental sustainability issues into the curriculum through problem-based and project-based learning: a case study at the University of Cape Town. Curr. Opin. Environ. Sustain. **16**, 81–88 (2015)
20. Visscher, K.: Experiencing complex stakeholder dynamics around emerging technologies: a role-play simulation. Eur. J. Eng. Educ. (2023). https://doi.org/10.1080/03043797.2023.2196940
21. Sai, S., Gaur, A., Sai, R., Chamola, V, Guizani, M., Rodrigues, J.J.P.C.: Generative AI for transformative healthcare: a comprehensive study of emerging models, applications, case studies, and limitations. IEEE Access **12**, 31078–31106 (2024). https://doi.org/10.1109/ACCESS.2024.3367715
22. Mohapatra, D.P., et al.: Leveraging Large Language Models (LLM) for the plastic surgery resident training: do they have a role? Indian J. Plast. Surg. **56**(5), 413–420 (2023). https://doi.org/10.1055/s-0043-1772704
23. Chang, C.Y., Lee, T.H., Park, J.W., Kim, M.: Facilitating nursing and health education by incorporating ChatGPT into learning designs. Educ. Technol. Soc. **27**(1), 215–230 (2024). https://www.jstor.org/stable/48754852
24. Olla, P., Elliot, L., Abumeeiz, M., Pardalis, E.: Ask and you shall receive: taxonomy of AI prompts for medical education. Res. Square, 1–18 (2024). https://doi.org/10.21203/rs.3.rs-3750487/v1
25. Singh, J., Samborowski, L., Mentzer, K.: A human collaboration with ChatGPT: developing case studies with Generative AI. In: Proceedings of the ISCAP Conference (ISCAP 2023), vol. 2473 (2023)
26. Deng, L., et al.: Evaluation of large language models in breast cancer clinical scenarios: a comparative analysis based on ChatGPT-3.5, ChatGPT-4.0, and Claude2. Int. J. Surg. **110**(4), 1941–1950 (2024)
27. Seth, I., et al.: Comparing the efficacy of large language models ChatGPT, BARD, and Bing AI in providing information on rhinoplasty: an observational study. Aesthetic Surg. J. Open Forum **5**, ojad084 (2023)
28. Reyhan, A.H., Mutaf, Ç., Uzun, İ., Yüksekyayla, F.: A performance evaluation of large language models in keratoconus: a comparative study of ChatGPT-3.5, ChatGPT-4.0, Gemini, Copilot, Chatsonic, and Perplexity. J. Clin. Med. **13**(21), 6512 (2024)

29. Piaget, J.: To Understand is to Invent: The Future of Education. Grossman Publishers, New York, NY (1973)
30. Jonassen, D.H.: Designing constructivist learning environments. In: Reigeluth, C.M. (ed.) Instructional-Design Theories and Models: A New Paradigm of Instructional Theory, vol. 2, pp. 215–239. Lawrence Erlbaum Associates, Mahwah, NJ (1999)
31. Brown, J.S., Collins, A., Duguid, P.: Situated cognition and the culture of learning. Educ. Res. **18**(1), 32–42 (1989)
32. Schell, J.W., Black, R.S.: Situated learning: an inductive case study of a collaborative learning experience. J. Ind. Teach. Educ. **34**, 5–28 (1997)
33. Dellermann, D., Calma, A., Lipusch, N., Weber, T., Weigel, S., Ebel, P.: The future of human-AI collaboration: a taxonomy of design knowledge for hybrid intelligence systems. arXiv preprint arXiv:2105.03354 (2021)
34. Xue, J., Hu, B., Li, L., Zhang, J.: Human-machine augmented intelligence: research and applications. Front. Inf. Technol. Electron. Eng. **23**(8), 1139–1141 (2022)
35. Amatriain, X.: Prompt design and engineering: Introduction and advanced methods. arXiv preprint arXiv:2401.14423 (2024)
36. Heston, T.F.: Prompt engineering for students of medicine and their teachers. arXiv preprint arXiv:2308.11628, 1–196 (2023)
37. Supplementary material for: Evaluation of Large Language Models in Simulating Real-world Engineering Scenarios and Decision Making: A Comparative Study of ChatGPT-4o, Gemini, and Perplexity. figshare. Online resource. https://doi.org/10.6084/m9.figshare.28735043.v1. https://doi.org/10.6084/m9.figshare.28735043. Accessed 4 Apr 2025
38. Lund, B.D., Wang, T., Mannuru, N.R., Nie, B., Shimray, S., Wang, Z.: ChatGPT and a new academic reality: artificial intelligence-written research papers and the ethics of large language models in scholarly publishing. J. Assoc. Inf. Sci. Technol. **74**(5), 570–581 (2023)
39. Lin, S., Hilton, J., Evans, O.: TruthfulQA: measuring how models mimic human falsehoods. arXiv preprint arXiv:2109.07958 (2021)

Harnessing Generative AI to Enhance Critical Thinking and Active Learning in a Second-Year English Language Project for Engineering Students: A Case Study

Mayssa Souissi(✉)

COGED Department, ESPRIT- Higher Private School of Engineering and Technology, Tunis, Tunisia
mayssa.souissi@esprit.tn

Abstract. This paper investigates the application of generative Artificial Intelligence (AI) in enhancing critical thinking and active learning within a project-based learning (PBL) English language project for second-year engineering students. As engineering education evolves, proficient communication skills have become essential, requiring innovative strategies to engage students effectively. Generative AI offers opportunities to transform traditional language instruction through adaptive, personalized learning experiences. By leveraging tools like ChatGPT, Grammarly, and Padlet, the study demonstrates how AI can foster critical thinking and linguistic competencies, facilitating interactive and engaging learning environments. A mixed-methods approach, including a survey and a case study at Esprit School of Engineering, evaluates students' use of generative AI and its impact on learning outcomes. The findings highlight the benefits, challenges, and ethical considerations of integrating AI into education, proposing a framework for effective implementation. This research contributes to the discourse on sustaining educational excellence in engineering through interdisciplinary applications of AI.

Keywords: Generative AI · Engineering Education · Project-Based Learning · English Language Education · Critical Thinking · Active Learning

1 Introduction

Second-year engineering students often deprioritize transversal subjects like English, focusing instead on technical disciplines. This trend presents challenges for educators aiming to develop essential soft skills, including critical thinking and communication, which are vital for professional success in engineering. While technical expertise remains crucial, soft skills have become indispensable for employability and adaptability in today's dynamic job market. However, students' reliance on generative AI tools, such as ChatGPT and Grammarly, for completing language tasks raises concerns about their critical thinking and problem-solving development.

F. Kamoun et al. (Eds.): AFRICATEK 2025, LNICST 676, pp. 394–410, 2026.
https://doi.org/10.1007/978-3-032-16635-7_25

Generative AI, when thoughtfully integrated into pedagogical practices, can address these challenges by fostering higher-order thinking skills through adaptive and personalized learning environments. Project-Based Learning (PBL), recognized for promoting collaboration and real-world problem-solving, provides an ideal context for embedding generative AI tools to enhance critical engagement with language tasks. Recent studies by Holmes et al. (2019) and Rolando et al. (2021) highlight that AI tools can encourage critical reflection and personalized learning, particularly when integrated into PBL approaches. Similarly, Zawacki-Richter et al. (2020) emphasizes the role of AI in augmenting collaborative and interactive learning environments, making them more engaging and effective for engineering students.

This paper explores the application of AI-driven tools within a collaborative e-book project, wherein students create content to encourage physical activity among peers. By employing tools like ChatGPT for ideation, Grammarly for linguistic refinement, and Padlet for collaboration, this study examines how AI can bridge the gap between technical and transversal skill development.

The choice to focus on second-year engineering students is intentional. At this stage in their academic journey, students at Esprit School of Engineering begin engaging with more complex, collaborative projects that require both technical understanding and communicative competence. They have some prior exposure to AI tools, though often in an unstructured or informal way. This makes them a pedagogically strategic group for introducing structured AI-supported learning, particularly in transversal subjects like English where critical thinking and reflection are essential but often underdeveloped.

This research addresses two central questions:

1. How does generative AI enhance critical thinking and active learning in a PBL setting?
2. What are the ethical considerations of integrating AI into educational practices?

By answering these questions, this paper contributes to a broader understanding of AI's role in fostering critical thinking and active learning, emphasizing its potential in inter-disciplinary education.

2 Literature Review

2.1 The Role of AI in Education

Artificial Intelligence (AI) is increasingly becoming a transformative force in education, enabling personalized learning experiences, adaptive feedback, and enhanced student engagement. Research by Holmes et al. (2019) and Zawacki-Richter et al. (2020) underscores the capability of AI-driven tools to cater to diverse learner needs, fostering both cognitive and affective learning domains. Generative AI tools, such as ChatGPT and Grammarly, provide students with innovative ways to refine their ideas, improve writing skills, and engage in meaningful learning activities. Moreover, Luckin (2022) argues that AI systems amplify educational outcomes when integrated with targeted instructional strategies, emphasizing the role of educators in optimizing these tools for deeper learning.

2.2 Generative AI and Critical Thinking in Education

Generative AI tools are not only useful for technical comprehension but also for promoting critical thinking. Research by McLaren et al. (2020) demonstrates that AI can support higher-order cognitive processes by encouraging students to evaluate diverse perspectives and reflect on their reasoning. ChatGPT, for instance, enables learners to explore multiple viewpoints on a given topic, fostering critical analysis and problem-solving skills. Furthermore, real-time feedback provided by AI systems enhances students' ability to refine their ideas iteratively, an essential component of critical thinking (Rolando et al., 2021).

2.3 Project-Based Learning (PBL) and Active Learning

PBL has been widely acknowledged for its capacity to engage students in hands-on, real-world projects that improve learning outcomes. Studies by Zawacki-Richter et al. (2020) and Perrotta et al. (2021) highlight how AI tools, when integrated into PBL settings, can facilitate active learning by providing immediate feedback, suggesting resources, and offering alternative problem-solving approaches. These tools encourage students to take ownership of their learning while fostering collaboration and communication within project teams. For engineering students, this approach not only enhances technical competencies but also reinforces transversal skills such as teamwork and adaptability.

2.4 Ethical Considerations in AI Integration

The integration of AI into education brings with it significant ethical concerns, including data privacy, bias, and the potential over-reliance on technology. Holmes et al. (2019) caution that biased algorithms may lead to inequitable learning experiences, while Zawacki-Richter et al. (2020) emphasize the need for transparent AI systems that prioritize fairness and inclusivity. Additionally, concerns about data security and intellectual property rights necessitate clear guidelines for responsible AI use in educational contexts. By addressing these issues, educators can ensure that AI integration enhances learning without compromising ethical standards.

2.5 Generative AI in English Language Education for Engineers

For engineering students, proficiency in English is crucial for global collaboration and professional communication. Generative AI tools, such as Grammarly and ChatGPT, have demonstrated their ability to improve students' language skills by offering real-time grammar correction, sentence restructuring suggestions, and creative writing prompts. McLaren et al. (2020) note that such tools encourage learners to critically evaluate linguistic choices, fostering both language proficiency and cognitive engagement. By embedding these tools in a PBL framework, students develop technical and communication skills simultaneously, addressing a key gap in engineering education research.

2.6 Significance of Study

Although generative AI tools have been explored in various educational contexts, limited research exists on their application in PBL settings for English language learning among engineering students. This study aims to bridge that gap by examining how these tools facilitate critical thinking, improve language competencies, and promote active engagement with learning materials. By addressing both pedagogical benefits and ethical challenges, this research provides practical recommendations for integrating AI into interdisciplinary education.

3 Materials and Methods

A mixed-methods approach was adopted to evaluate the integration of generative AI tools into a project-based learning (PBL) English language project. This section outlines the survey design, observation methodology, data analysis process, and tools used to gather and interpret comprehensive data.

3.1 Survey Design

A 13-item questionnaire was developed specifically for this study to evaluate students' familiarity with generative AI, usage patterns, perceived effectiveness, and ethical concerns. The instrument was entirely self-designed to align with the project's pedagogical objectives and classroom context, rather than adapted from pre-existing validated tools. While no formal pilot study was conducted, the questionnaire was reviewed by two faculty members to ensure clarity, alignment with research objectives, and content validity. The full set of survey items is included in the appendix for transparency and future replication.

To assess the internal consistency of the survey, Cronbach's Alpha was calculated and yielded a coefficient of 0.84, indicating good reliability. The questionnaire was distributed online via Microsoft Forms, which automatically collected responses and generated basic visual summaries. Data were retrieved once at the end of the two-week collection period (covering Weeks 2 and 3 of the observation phase), and analyzed using Microsoft Excel. Descriptive statistics, namely frequency counts, mean scores, and percentages—were used to interpret the data. As the study's aim was exploratory rather than inferential, no advanced statistical tests were conducted.

Participation was voluntary, and all students were informed about data confidentiality and their right to withdraw at any time.

The survey consisted of five key sections:

Demographic Information: Captured basic participant details (e.g., age, gender) to contextualize the analysis.

Familiarity with Generative AI: Students rated their familiarity with generative AI on a 1–5 Likert scale (1 = not familiar, 5 = very familiar).

Usage Patterns: Participants indicated how often and in what ways they used tools like ChatGPT (for drafting content and idea generation) and Grammarly (for language refinement). This data provided insight into real-world AI application within academic settings.

Perceived Effectiveness: Students evaluated AI's impact on their learning. Example items included:

o"Generative AI tools help me think more critically about my writing."

o"Using ChatGPT helps me develop better ideas for English tasks." Responses were collected using a 1–5 Likert scale.

Ethical Considerations: Students were asked whether they were concerned about the ethical implications of using AI (e.g., bias, plagiarism, data privacy). If they answered "yes," they were prompted to explain their concerns in an open-ended format.

A limitation of using self-report data is the potential for social desirability bias, where respondents might give answers, they perceive as more acceptable. While this limitation was not fully controlled, students were reassured that their answers were anonymous and would not affect their grades.

While this study highlights the use of ChatGPT, it is important to clarify that this tool was not mandated by the instructor or predetermined by the project. Students were given full autonomy to select the AI tools they preferred for completing their tasks. As part of the survey, they were asked to report which generative AI tools they used during the project. ChatGPT and Grammarly emerged as the most frequently mentioned platforms, indicating organic adoption rather than directed use.

Although open-source alternatives such as OpenAssistant or other freely available models exist, no student reported using them. This may be due to a combination of factors, including limited awareness, lower accessibility, or more complex user interfaces compared to widely known commercial tools. As a result, the focus of the analysis reflects the actual tools students engaged with during the course.

3.2 Case Study Observation

The observation was conducted over a four-week period during the first term at Esprit School of Engineering. The task required students to create a detailed electronic book (E-book) focused on physical activities designed to encourage their peers to work out, using both informative and descriptive language. Generative AI tools were integrated into the project to assist students in developing content that met these objectives. The observation focused on students' use of AI tools, their engagement with the project tasks, and teacher-student interactions. The observation methodology is detailed as follows:

Week 1: Students were introduced to the project objectives, deliverables, and evaluation *criteria. They were trained in using generative AI tools such as ChatGPT for content drafting and Grammarly for grammar and style enhancement. A brainstorming session was held to outline the E-book structure.

Week 2: Students began drafting the E-book content with support from generative AI tools. Teachers monitored their use of these tools, providing feedback on the initial drafts.

Week 3: Students refined their content based on feedback and incorporated images, diagrams, and formatting. Teachers observed their engagement levels and interaction patterns.

Week 4: Final revisions were made, and students presented their E-books. Teachers documented their observations regarding the quality of the final product and students' reflections on the use of AI tools.

Observations focused on students' usage of AI tools, their problem-solving approaches, and their collaboration during the project. Teachers maintained detailed field notes and recorded instances of AI tool application, including how students used ChatGPT for idea generation and Grammarly for real-time writing support. Engagement levels were assessed through direct interactions and classroom discussions.

4 Findings

4.1 Data Collection and Analysis:

The survey was administered to a target population of 100 s-year engineering students across three classes at Esprit School of Engineering, with 51 responses received, yielding a response rate of approximately 51%. This response rate provides a substantial basis for deriving meaningful insights, especially given the exploratory nature of this study.

While the data captures trends and perspectives from over half of the surveyed population, the response rate reflects participation dynamics that could influence the findings, such as self-selection bias. Students with a stronger interest or experience in the subject matter may have been more inclined to participate, potentially shaping the results in a specific direction.

The analysis, conducted using descriptive statistics, offers a valuable snapshot of the surveyed group's familiarity, usage, and perceptions of effectiveness regarding the subject matter. Future research with a larger or more randomized sample could further validate these findings and expand their applicability. Nevertheless, the current sample provides a solid foundation for identifying key trends and drawing preliminary conclusions.

4.1.1 Demographic Information

The demographic breakdown of the respondents is as follows:

Gender Distribution: Of the 51 responses, 17 were from female students, and the remaining 34 responses were from male students.

Age Range: Six respondents were aged between 25 and 34 years, while the remaining 45 respondents were aged between 18 and 24 years.

4.1.2 Familiarity and Usage Patterns

The data indicates that a significant number of students are aware of generative AI, with familiarity ratings predominantly falling between 3 and 4, as shown in Fig. 1. This suggests moderate engagement with these tools, reflecting their growing presence in education.

Usage patterns, as demonstrated in Fig. 2., reveal that nearly 55% of respondents frequently utilize generative AI tools for generating ideas, while 39% use them for grammar correction. These applications of generative AI align with the pedagogical goals of improving communication skills in engineering contexts. However, only 6% of students use these tools for drafting texts.

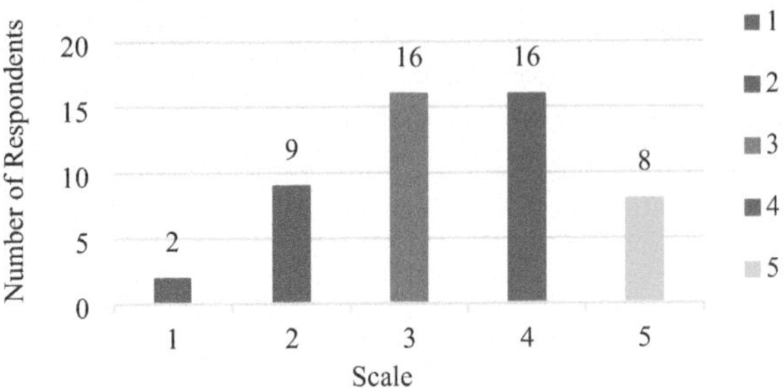

Fig. 1. Familiarity levels with generative AI

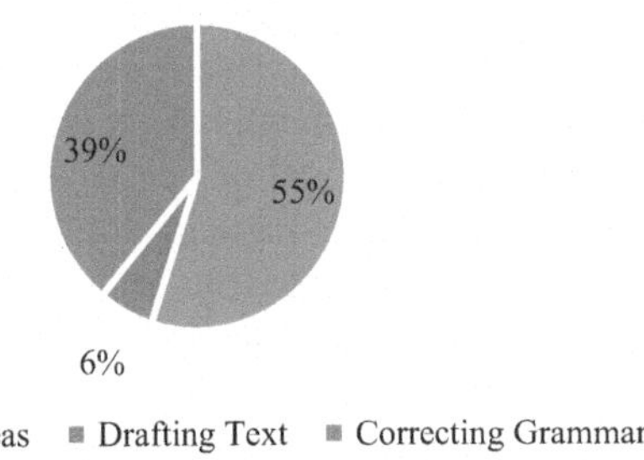

Fig. 2. Use of Generative AI

4.1.3 Perceptions of Effectiveness

Students rated the effectiveness of generative AI in enhancing critical thinking and language skills with an average score of around 3.5. This indicates a generally positive perception; however, it also points to the necessity for more structured guidance on effectively leveraging these tools. The moderate scores imply that while students recognize the utility of generative AI, they may not fully understand how to integrate it into their learning processes. Table 1 summarizes the key insights from the findings, reflecting students' perceptions of generative AI's effectiveness in their learning experiences.

Table 1. Evaluation Summary of Key Skills and Engagement in Class

Aspect	Average Score	Interpretation
Effectiveness in critical thinking	3.3	Moderate effectiveness; need more guidance
Effectiveness in language skills	4.0	Generally positive perception: higher utility recognized
Engagement in class	3.4	Mixed feelings about engagement; improvement needed

4.1.4 Benefits and Drawbacks

The qualitative responses highlight several benefits, including increased efficiency and support for creativity. However, a notable concern is the potential for over-reliance on AI, which students fear could diminish their critical thinking skills and foster a sense of laziness in academic work. Ethical concerns regarding data privacy and bias were also prevalent, suggesting that while students are enthusiastic about AI tools, they are acutely aware of the associated risks. Table 2 encapsulates the students' views.

Table 2. Perceived Benefits and Drawbacks of Technology-Assisted Learning Tools

Aspect	Benefits	Drawbacks
Time efficiency	Saves time on assignments, allowing focus on ideas	May lead to procrastination and laziness
Creativity enhancement	Assists in brainstorming and generating ideas	Discourages active creative thinking
Writing support	Improves grammar and writing quality	May produce inconsistent or biased content
Personalized learning	Tailors content to individual needs	Can create dependence on technology
Learning support	Provides access to diverse resources	Reduces intellectual engagement and effort

4.1.5 Ethical Considerations

As indicated in Fig. 3., approximately 59% of respondents expressed concerns about the ethical implications of using generative AI, particularly regarding issues such as data privacy, bias, and academic integrity.

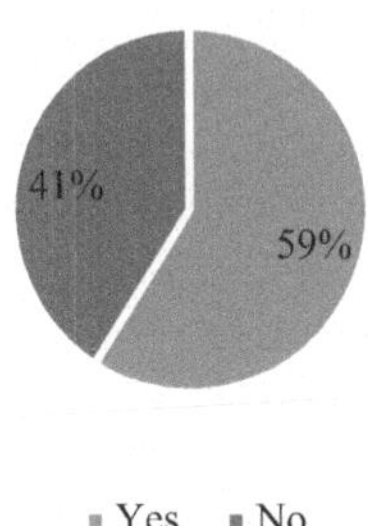

Fig. 3. Ethical Implications of Using Generative AI

Concerns about bias in AI outputs and the protection of personal data are critical considerations that educators must address when integrating these technologies into curricula. This insight underscores the need for institutions to implement clear guidelines for responsible AI use in educational settings. Table 3 depicts the nuanced perspectives students hold regarding the ethical implications of generative AI.

Table 3. Key Concerns and Reassurances Surrounding AI Use in Education

Aspect	Concerns	Reassurances
Data Privacy	Fears of sensitive information exposure	Not sharing sensitive data; acceptance of data sharing as common
Bias and Discrimination	Risk of AI perpetuating existing biases	Belief that ethical issues can be managed
Dependence on AI	Over-reliance could diminish critical thinking	Some view reliance as manageable with moderation
Academic Integrity	Risk of plagiarism and authenticity issues	No significant counterarguments noted
Intellectual Property	Concerns about copyright infringement	Acknowledgment of ongoing challenges

4.2 Case Study Observation

The observation was conducted over a four-week period during the first term at Esprit School of Engineering. The task required students to create a detailed e-book focused on physical activities designed to encourage their peers to work out, using both informative and descriptive language. Generative AI tools were integrated into the project to assist students in developing content that aligned with these objectives. The observation focused on students' use of AI tools, their engagement with the project tasks, the quality of their outputs, and teacher-student interactions. Specific attention was given to how critical thinking was evaluated and improved throughout the project.

Week 1: Initial Exploration of AI Tools:

In the initial week, students began exploring AI tools by using them to generate descriptions of physical activities. However, they relied heavily on AI-generated outputs without much critical reflection. For example, an AI-generated description of a cardio workout read:

"Perform high knees for 60 s to elevate your heart rate and improve cardiovascular endurance."

Students often accepted this content as final without questioning its relevance or tone. To address this, I introduced AI tools through a guided demonstration and encouraged students to experiment and critique AI outputs. Despite this guidance, students initially displayed minimal critical engagement, often passively accepting AI outputs as sufficient.

Week 2: Structured Guidelines for Critical Engagement:

By the second week, I implemented structured guidelines to help students critically assess and integrate AI content. This approach has noticeably improved student involvement. For instance, one student used ChatGPT4 to draft an exercise description for a stretching routine. The AI output stated:

"Sit on the floor with your legs extended. Lean forward to touch your toes, keeping your back straight. Hold this position for 30 s."

The student revised this to:

"Sit on the floor with your legs stretched out in front of you. Slowly lean forward to touch your toes, breathing deeply. Keep your back straight and hold for 30 s. Feel the stretch in your hamstrings and lower back."

Through this process, students began editing AI-generated materials to better align with personal experiences and project objectives. This iterative editing process demonstrated a shift toward more active, critical engagement with AI outputs.

Week 3: Collaborative Refinement and Feedback:

In the third week, the focus shifted to collaborative work and feedback. Students worked in groups to refine their e-book sections, incorporating peers and teacher feedback into their revisions. Groups that used AI thoughtfully produced more cohesive and contextually relevant content, blending AI input with their personal ideas.

For example, one group generated a technical description of an aerobic exercise using AI, which lacked accessibility for non-technical peers. After feedback, they modified the content to include simplified explanations and encouraging language. Group discussions and teacher critiques emphasized evaluating AI-generated content for coherence, tone, and relatability. This collaborative process further enhanced students' critical thinking as they evaluated both their peers' and their own work.

Week 4: Final Submissions and Reflections:

In the final week, students submitted their complete e-books and reflected on their projects. The most successful projects balanced AI-generated content with students' own knowledge, using AI as a supportive tool rather than a replacement. For example, one group integrated AI content about yoga poses but personalized it by adding real-life photos and testimonials from peers who practiced the routines. Conversely, groups that overly depended on AI produced sections that felt disconnected or overly technical, highlighting the limitations of uncritical AI use.

Students' reflections revealed a growing awareness of the importance of evaluating AI outputs critically. They acknowledged that while AI provided a strong starting point, their own edits and contextual additions significantly improved the quality and relevance of their work.

4.2.1 Demonstrating Critical and Reflective Thinking

As students engaged with AI-generated content, they were encouraged to critically assess and revise outputs rather than accept them at face value. For example, when ChatGPT suggested, "Perform high knees for 60 s to elevate your heart rate," students were prompted to evaluate tone, clarity, and appropriateness. One student revised this to, "Do high knees for 60 s to warm up your body before more intense movements. Keep your arms active and lift your knees to waist height." This demonstrated not only an understanding of the exercise but also an adaptation of content for peer comprehension.

Students also completed reflection prompts such as "How did using AI change the way you approached this task?" or "What would you improve in the AI's suggestion and why?" These tasks pushed learners to move beyond passive use and actively question, refine, and personalize AI outputs.

4.2.2 Evaluation of Critical Thinking

To evaluate students' critical thinking, the researcher used metrics that assessed their ability to modify AI-generated content, align it with project objectives, and balance AI input with personal contributions. These metrics as depicted in Table 4, were applied throughout the observation period, with key observations recorded for each metric.

Table 4. Key Observations Per Metric

Metric	Description	Observation
Degree of Modification	The extent to which students edited and refined AI-generated content	Students moved from minimal edits in Week 1 to substantial revisions in Week 2. For example, one group transformed a technical AI-generated description into an engaging, relatable section tailored to their peers
Relevance to Project Objectives	How well the final content aligned with the task requirements and audience needs	By Week 3, most groups ensured their e-books reflected project goals, blending AI outputs with personal inputs. For instance, a stretching routine was adapted with personal anecdotes and practical tips, increasing its relevance to the audience
Justification of Edits	The ability to explain why specific modifications were made to AI-generated outputs	In Week 4 reflections, students provided detailed explanations for their edits. One student noted that the original AI description lacked clarity for beginners, prompting the inclusion of step-by-step instructions and motivational prompts

(continued)

Table 4. (*continued*)

Metric	Description	Observation
Balance of AI Input and Personal Contributions	*The extent to which students used AI as a supportive tool rather than relying on it entirely*	Groups that relied on AI exclusively produced overly formal or disconnected content. Successful projects integrated AI outputs while adding visuals, testimonials, and personal anecdotes, showcasing critical engagement
Collaboration and Peer Feedback	The degree to which students engaged in peer discussions and incorporated feedback to improve their work	Collaborative feedback sessions in Week 3 helped students critically assess their peers' work and refine their own sections. For example, one group revised a yoga routine description to simplify terminology after peer suggestions

4.3 Conclusion of the Materials and Methods

The combined results from the survey and case study observation provide a comprehensive understanding of how second-year engineering students engage with generative AI in their English language project. The survey revealed that while students are moderately familiar with AI tools, many still lack the proficiency to use them effectively, a finding corroborated by the classroom observation, where students initially relied heavily on AI-generated content with minimal critical evaluation. However, as the project progressed and structured guidance was provided, students began to critically engage with AI, balancing it with their own input to produce higher-quality work. Those who relied less on AI showed deeper learning and better project outcomes, while over-reliance on AI led to less coherent results. These insights highlight the importance of teacher guidance and structured use of AI tools to enhance student learning, pointing to the need for teaching strategies that foster critical engagement with AI and the development of ethical frameworks for its integration into the curriculum.

5 Discussion

The findings from both the survey and case study observation reveal important insights into the use of generative AI in a PBL environment, specifically within an English language project for second-year engineering students. These insights add depth to the current body of research on AI in education, highlighting the nuanced role of AI in enhancing critical thinking and active learning when structured guidance is provided.

5.1 Comparison with Existing Research

The survey results indicate that while students are moderately familiar with generative AI tools, their proficiency in effectively utilizing them remains limited. This finding aligns with previous studies, such as those by Zawacki-Richter et al. (2019), who noted that AI is often seen by students as a convenient tool for generating ideas or completing simple tasks but is rarely used to its full potential in promoting deeper learning. The lack of critical engagement with AI-generated content reflects a broader trend in educational technology, where students frequently use AI as a passive resource rather than an active learning tool (Holmes et al., 2021).

Moreover, the moderate effectiveness scores for AI in enhancing critical thinking in this study are consistent with research suggesting that without structured guidance, students may struggle to leverage AI for complex cognitive tasks. Luckin et al. (2016) emphasize that AI, while powerful, requires targeted instructional support to foster critical thinking and problem-solving skills, particularly in non-technical subjects. This underscores the need for educators to not only introduce AI tools into the curriculum but also to integrate frameworks that teach students how to critically evaluate and refine AI-generated outputs.

What sets this study apart is its focus on using AI in a transversal subject like English within an engineering curriculum. While AI applications in education have primarily been concentrated in technical and scientific disciplines (Baker & Smith, 2019), the current research demonstrates the relevance of AI in language learning, an area that has been relatively underexplored. This interdisciplinary approach aligns with the growing call for AI to be applied across a broader range of educational contexts, including those that cultivate communication and critical thinking skills essential for engineering students (Aoun, 2017). By examining how generative AI can enhance both language and cognitive skills, this study contributes to the evolving discourse on AI's role in holistic education.

5.2 AI as a Catalyst for Reflective and Problem-Solving Skills

The findings reveal that generative AI, when supported by structured guidance, encouraged students to adopt a more reflective stance toward their work. Rather than using ChatGPT or Grammarly as final-output tools, students gradually learned to treat them as drafting assistants. This process promoted metacognitive awareness, as students began to question the suitability of tone, vocabulary, and audience impact. In group settings, they debated AI outputs and offered each other edits, indicating a shift toward problem-solving through collaborative critique. These behaviors are consistent with existing literature on AI's potential to scaffold reflective thinking (McLaren et al., 2020) and support iterative learning processes.

5.3 Significance of Teacher Facilitation

A key observation in this study is the critical role of teacher guidance in transforming AI from a passive content generator to an active learning tool. Initially, students relied heavily on AI-generated content without critically assessing its quality or relevance, a common issue in AI-enhanced learning environments. However, as structured guidance was introduced, students began to integrate their own insights with AI outputs, leading to more meaningful engagement and higher-quality project outcomes. A structured approach was implemented to encourage students to critically evaluate AI-generated outputs. Students were guided to review content for relevance, accuracy, and personal resonance. During weekly group sessions, students received specific prompts to question AI output, such as: 'Does this reflect your perspective?' or 'How can you make this more engaging for your peers?' These strategies helped shift AI use from passive consumption to active learning. This finding emphasizes the importance of not merely introducing AI tools but also embedding clear instructional strategies to foster critical thinking, which existing literature often overlooks.

5.4 Teacher Preparedness and Pedagogical Support

A key challenge in implementing AI-enhanced learning is ensuring that instructors are adequately prepared to guide students in the pedagogical use of these tools. In this study, no formal training was provided to teachers beyond initial project briefings. While instructors were familiar with the basic functions of ChatGPT and Grammarly, there was limited structured guidance on how to scaffold student engagement with these tools or integrate AI critically into their feedback practices. This lack of formal preparation represents a limitation of the study and highlights an important area for future improvement. Structured teacher training sessions—focused on both the technical use of AI tools and pedagogical strategies for encouraging critical evaluation—would likely enhance the consistency and depth of AI integration in similar projects.

5.5 Ethical Implications and Pedagogical Strategies

Ethical concerns surrounding AI use, including data privacy and potential biases in AI-generated content, were highlighted by the survey responses. These concerns are in line with broader discussions in educational technology research. Recent studies underscore the importance of integrating ethical considerations into AI education. Porayska-Pomsta et al. (2024) discuss how AI in education (AIED) can influence learning and teaching practices, emphasizing the need to address socio-cultural biases and moral dilemmas inherent in AI systems. The observational data suggests that, with proper moderation, students can mitigate these risks by balancing AI's benefits with critical oversight. The study's emphasis on ethical awareness as a teaching point offers a new pedagogical angle—by integrating discussions of AI's limitations into the curriculum, educators can prepare students to be more conscientious and responsible users of technology.

5.6 Novel Application in Language Learning for Engineers

One of the unique contributions of this research is its application of generative AI in an English language project for engineering students—a novel interdisciplinary approach. While AI is typically associated with STEM education, this study shows its effectiveness in developing language and communication skills, which are crucial for well-rounded engineering education. The successful use of AI in the PBL project illustrates the adaptability of AI tools across disciplines, adding to the growing evidence that AI can serve as a bridge between technical and transversal skills.

5.7 Future Directions

The findings from this research point to several future directions. First, further exploration of AI's role in enhancing language skills in non-language disciplines could provide new insights into interdisciplinary learning. Additionally, the development of a framework for integrating AI tools into the curriculum, one that includes both critical engagement and ethical considerations, would help guide future implementations. Lastly, longitudinal studies could assess the long-term impact of generative AI on students' learning outcomes and critical thinking abilities. The study suggests a phased framework for AI integration in language curricula to maximize its educational potential. This framework includes initial exploration, where students become familiar with AI capabilities; guided critical engagement, where students analyze and refine AI generated content; and independent application, where students use AI tools as supplements rather than crutches. Additionally, integrating discussions on ethical considerations, such as data privacy and responsible usage, is essential to prepare students as conscientious technology users.

6 Conclusion

This study highlights the potential of generative AI to enhance critical thinking and active learning in a project-based English language project for engineering students. The findings from both the survey and case study observation reveal that while students are moderately familiar with AI tools, their proficiency in using them effectively remains limited. Structured guidance played a crucial role in helping students critically engage with AI, leading to better project outcomes and deeper learning. The study also emphasizes the need to address ethical concerns, such as data privacy and potential over-reliance on AI, when integrating these tools into educational settings. Ultimately, this research demonstrates that generative AI, when thoughtfully incorporated into the curriculum, can be an asset in fostering both language and cognitive skills among engineering students, contributing to a more holistic approach to education.

Acknowledgements. I would like to express my sincere gratitude to Dr. Faouzi Kammoun, Deputy General Manager of Esprit School of Business and Head of Esprit Tech Department for his ongoing support and trust. I also extend my thanks to all respondents who participated in this study, as well as to Esprit School of Engineering for providing a supportive environment for this research.

Appendix

Survey.

1. How old are you?

Under 18.

18–24.

25–34.

2. Have you heard of generative AI before this project?

Yes.

No.

3. If yes, how would you rate your familiarity with generative AI? (1–5 scale, with 1 being not familiar at all and 5 being very familiar).

4. In what context have you used generative AI before?

5. How often do you use generative AI tools for your coursework?

Never.

Rarely.

Sometimes.

Often.

Always.

6. Which generative AI tools have you used?

7. For what purposes do you use generative AI in your English class?

Generating ideas.

Drafting text.

Correcting grammar.

8. How effective do you find generative AI tools in enhancing your critical thinking skills? (1–5 scale, with 1 being less effective and 5 more effective).

9. How effective do you find generative AI tools in improving your English language skills? (1–5 scale, with 1 being less effective and 5 more effective).

10. Do you feel more engaged in class when using generative AI tools? (1–5 scale, with 1 being less engaged and 5 more engaged).

11. What are the benefits and drawbacks of using generative AI in your English class.

12. Are you concerned about the ethical implications of using generative AI (e.g., bias, data privacy)?

Yes.

No.

13. If yes, please elaborate on your concerns.

References

Aoun, J.E.: Robot-Proof: Higher Education in the Age of Artificial Intelligence. MIT Press (2022)

Anderson, L.W., Krathwohl, D.R.: A Taxonomy for Learning, Teaching, and Assessing: A Revision of Bloom's Taxonomy of Educational Objectives. Pearson (2022)

Baker, T., Smith, L.: Educ-AI-tion rebooted? Exploring the future of artificial intelligence in schools and colleges. Nesta (2019). https://www.nesta.org.uk/report/educ-ai-tion-rebooted/

Holmes, W., Bialik, M., Fadel, C.: Artificial intelligence in education: Promises and implications for teaching and learning. Center for Curriculum Redesign (2019). https://curriculumredesign.org/wp-content/uploads/AI-in-Education-Promises-and-Implications_June2019.pdf

Holmes, W., Bialik, M., Fadel, C.: Artificial Intelligence in Education: Promises and Implications. Center for Curriculum Redesign (2022)

Luckin, R.: Intelligence Unleashed: An Argument for AI in Education. Pearson (2022). https://www.pearson.com/uk/educators/schools/news-and-policy/2022/03/intelligence-unleashed.html

McLaren, B.M., Scheuer, O., Wiggins, C.: The impact of AI-driven tools on problem-solving and critical thinking in educational contexts. Educ. Tech. Res. Dev. **68**(4), 2109–2127 (2020). https://doi.org/10.1007/s11423-020-09788-3

Seo, K., Tang, J., Roll, I., Fels, S., Yoon, D.: The impact of artificial intelligence on learner–instructor interaction in online learning. Int. J. Educ. Technol. High. Educ. **18**(1), 1–23 (2021). https://doi.org/10.1186/s41239-021-00292-9

Porayska-Pomsta, K., Holmes, W., Nemorin, S.: The ethics of AI in education. Journal of Artificial Intelligence in Education. Advance online publication (2024). https://arxiv.org/abs/2406.11842

Rolando, F., Piazza, M., de Bono, S.: The impact of AI in education: a study of generative tools in enhancing student engagement and learning. J. Educ. Technol. Soc. **24**(1), 40–53 (2021)

Zawacki-Richter, O., Anderson, T., Brouns, F.: AI applications in education: the promise and challenges of integrating generative AI tools in learning environments. Int. J. Educ. Technol. High. Educ. **17**(1), 32–46 (2020). https://doi.org/10.1186/s41239-020-00223-8

Zawacki-Richter, O., Marín, V. I., Bond, M., Gouverneur, F.: Systematic review of AI applications in higher education. Int. J. Educ. Technol. High. Educ. **20**(1) (2023). Article 12. https://doi.org/10.1186/s41239-023-00378-w

Securing Higher Education Through DevSecOps Framework

Manel Medhioub(✉) and Mohamed Ridha Boulares

ESPRIT School of Engineering, Tunis, Tunisia
{manel.madhioub,mohamedridha.boulares}@esprit.tn

Abstract. In an increasingly digital landscape, higher education institutions rely on robust information systems security as a foundation for operational success and long-term resilience. As these institutions adopt advanced technologies to enhance pedagogical, research, and administrative functions, safeguarding such systems becomes imperative. The rising demand for rapid deployment of secure and dependable software solutions has led to greater interest in DevSecOps within both industry and academia. In this context, the present study introduces a DevSecOps-oriented framework specifically designed to address cybersecurity challenges in higher education environments. The framework integrates automated security testing, continuous compliance validation, and centralized vulnerability management to strengthen institutional system resilience. The contributions of this work are threefold: (1) the formulation of a structured methodology for embedding security within DevOps pipelines; (2) the development of a centralized vulnerability tracking and remediation mechanism; and (3) the evaluation of the framework's effectiveness in mitigating threats. Results show that the proposed approach improves the security posture of academic infrastructures by reducing exposure and enhancing incident response. Ultimately, this research highlights the strategic importance of adopting DevSecOps practices to build a more adaptive and resilient cybersecurity posture in higher education.

Keywords: Devsecops Framework · Security · Higher Education

1 Introduction

1.1 Background Information

Institutions of higher education are increasingly relying on digital systems in various fields including teaching, research, and administration. This growing dependency has made them prime targets for cyber threats. Universities manage vast amounts of sensitive information, including student records, financial data, and innovative research, which makes them attractive to cybercriminals seek to exploit such data for identity theft, financial fraud, or competitive advantage. Cyberattacks on universities can result in significant financial losses, disrupt

F. Kamoun et al. (Eds.): AFRICATEK 2025, LNICST 676, pp. 411–424, 2026.
https://doi.org/10.1007/978-3-032-16635-7_26

critical services, expose confidential information, and damage institutional reputations. Higher education institutions face diverse cyber threats including data breaches, denial-of-service (DoS) attacks, ransomware, malware infections, malicious insiders, exploitation of vulnerabilities by external users, and risks associated with cloud providers [1]. In addition, the dynamic and decentralized nature of higher education - characterized by frequent user turnover, diverse roles, and distributed governance - presents unique security challenges [2]. Recent data highlight the growing severity of these threats: the education sector experienced a 157% increase in malware attacks in 2022 and ranked first in malware volume at the end of 2023 [3].

The standard security strategy typically involves adding protective measures at the end of the software development process, a method that has proven counterproductive, increasing both vulnerabilities and costs. To address these issues, adopting a more proactive and cohesive strategy has become essential. DevSecOps can enhance the resilience of educational environments against emerging cyberattacks, thus fostering a safer learning experience for students and faculty alike. Recent studies indicate that the successful adoption of DevOps, with its focus on collaboration and continuous improvement, can be strengthened by incorporating security measures early in the development process [4,5].

1.2 Research Objectives

The aim of this work is to implement a DevSecOps framework in higher education by evaluating its advantages, challenges, and adoption strategies. Given the increasing complexity of cyber threats targeting universities, integrating security into software development and deployment processes is essential. This research considers key security challenges facing higher education institutions, such as data breaches, insider threats, and vulnerabilities in cloud-based learning environments. It evaluates the relevance of DevSecOps in academia by analyzing how automation, continuous monitoring, and secure coding practices can strengthen cybersecurity defenses. Furthermore, this study defines a structured framework for implementing DevSecOps within university Information Technology (IT) environments, emphasizing security automation, compliance enforcement, and a collaborative security culture. It presents best practices and recommendations for strengthening cybersecurity frameworks, including tool selection, security awareness, and governance models aimed at continuous improvement. Through these objectives, this research demonstrates how DevSecOps can effectively protect sensitive data, maintain regulatory compliance, and fortify the security of higher education institutions. The paper is organized as follows: Sect. 2 reviews related work on DevSecOps in higher education; Sect. 3 introduces the DevSecOps approach and proposes a tailored framework; Sect. 4 applies this framework in a university environment, detailing a proposed pipeline and implementation strategies; and Sect. 5 concludes with key findings and future research directions.

2 Related Work

The progressive reliance on digital infrastructure in higher education has highlighted an increase in cybersecurity risks, prompting researchers to explore new security frameworks. Several studies have already explored the application of security measures within university IT environments and the role of DevSecOps in mitigating these threats. Ahmed and Francis [6] highlighted the limitations of traditional DevOps practices, demonstrating that security is often neglected and left until late in the development cycle, leading to vulnerabilities that necessitate intensive rework. The research in question emphasized the need for a proactive security approach that would integrate security measures right from the start of the development lifecycle with the aim of preventing security flaws before deployment. Li and Zalialetdzinau [7] explored the role of DevSecOps in the digital transformation of education. They highlighted its potential in making e-learning platforms more secure as well as protecting sensitive academic data. Their study demonstrated how combining both automated security checks and continuous vulnerability assessments greatly contributed to a more resilient IT infrastructure for universities. Other studies focused on the implementation challenges of DevSecOps in academic settings of which issues, such as lack of skilled security professionals, resistance to change within IT departments, and the complexity of integrating security tools into existing workflows, can be mentioned. Although global standards like NIST SP 800–50, ISO/IEC 27001, and CIS Controls offer valuable guidance on security awareness and risk management, they are not specifically tailored to the structural, operational, and cultural specificities of higher education institutions. This often limits their practical effectiveness when applied without customization [2]. These challenges highlight the need for tailored strategies with the intent of facilitating the adoption of DevSecOps in higher education [8]. This section establishes the foundation for our research by reviewing existing literature on cybersecurity challenges in universities and the role of DevSecOps in addressing these issues. The following sections will build upon these insights to propose a structured approach for implementing DevSecOps.

3 The DevSecOps Approach

DevSecOps represents the integration of development, security, and operations. It assigns the responsibility for application security to the team by embedding security practices and decisions at the same pace as development and operational activities. For organizations already applying a DevOps model, a transition toward DevSecOps is necessary to reach greater effectiveness in security. A DevSecOps framework employs tools that incorporate security into applications from the outset, rather than adding it randomly at a later stage. This is particularly relevant for the implementation of security measures within university IT systems, where DevSecOps contributes to reducing risks, limiting vulnerabilities, and aligning security with both IT and business objectives [6].

3.1 The Impact of DevOps on Development

In recent years, organizations have undergone significant transformations in development and process management. The transition from dynamically provisioned shared resources to cloud computing has provided major advantages in terms of speed, flexibility, and cost efficiency, thereby accelerating application development. The adoption of agile and DevOps methodologies has further enhanced this progress. Specifically, DevOps—centered on unifying development and IT operations within a single framework—has supported more frequent feature releases while improving application stability [6]. However, security has not kept pace with this rapid transformation, as traditional methods were not designed to test code at the speed required by DevOps. As a result, security has become one of the biggest challenges for fast-paced application development [6]. One of the sectors that need to improve the security of their application development is higher education, due to the sensitivity of their data and infrastructure. This makes the adoption of DevSecOps particularly beneficial for this sector.

3.2 Benefits of DevSecOps

One of the key benefits of DevSecOps in higher education is the automation of security practices from the beginning of the software development process. By embedding security controls early in the development lifecycle, universities can significantly reduce the risk of human errors that might introduce vulnerabilities. Automated security testing, including static and dynamic code analysis, dependency scanning, and infrastructure-as-code security checks, ensures that potential weaknesses are identified and mitigated before deployment. This proactive approach is particularly beneficial for university IT teams managing large-scale learning management systems, big data, research platforms, and administrative software. Another major benefit is the reduction in manual work for security engineers, allowing them to focus more on defining and enforcing security policies. [6]. By implementing DevSecOps, universities can also benefit from faster software delivery cycles, ensuring that educational platforms remain up-to-date with the latest security patches and feature enhancements. This improves not only security but also the overall user experience for students and faculty. Furthermore, centralized security monitoring and incident response mechanisms enable universities to detect and respond to cyber threats in real time, minimizing the potential impact of data breaches and system compromises. The integration of DevSecOps in higher education enhances the security posture of institutions, ensures compliance with evolving cybersecurity regulations, and enables a more resilient and efficient IT infrastructure that supports academic and research activities.

3.3 DevSecOps Framework for Higher Education

We propose a DevSecOps framework specifically designed for the higher education sector. It is a fully virtualized environment that integrates a suite of tools to analyze and secure an application throughout its entire lifecycle, from initial development to deployment. The framework follows a three-layered architecture, The infrastructure Layer is responsible for establishing a secure environment, whether in the cloud or on-premises. It ensures that identity and access management (IAM) policies are properly configured to control user permissions and authentication mechanisms. Additionally, it enforces network security policies such as firewalls, intrusion detection systems (IDS), and secure communication protocols to protect sensitive data and prevent unauthorized access. This layer serves as the foundation for secure application development and deployment.

The Development and Deployment Layer focuses on integrating security within the software development lifecycle by implementing Continuous Integration/Continuous Deployment (CI/CD) pipelines. Security tools are embedded within these pipelines to automate key processes such as static code analysis, vulnerability scanning, and compliance enforcement. These measures help identify and mitigate security risks early in the development process, reducing potential vulnerabilities before the application reaches production. By integrating security from the beginning, this layer ensures that security is not an afterthought but an integral part of the development workflow.

The Monitoring and Incident Response Layer is essential for maintaining continuous security oversight and ensuring rapid detection and response to threats. This layer leverages real-time security monitoring tools to analyze system activities and detect anomalies or potential security breaches. Automated threat detection mechanisms, such as Security Information and Event Management (SIEM) solutions, enhance visibility into security events. In the event of an incident, predefined response strategies, including automated alerts and incident containment measures, enable quick mitigation to minimize damage and downtime. This proactive approach strengthens the overall security posture of the application environment.

3.4 Implementation Strategy

Educational institutions can enhance their resilience against security threats by adopting standardized practices and tools, as suggested by the IEEE, ensuring that security is embedded in every phase of the software development process [9] To effectively integrate DevSecOps, universities should adopt the following key strategies:

- **Security by Design:** Embed security at every stage of the software development lifecycle, from code development to deployment.
- **Automation of Security Controls:** Utilize automated testing tools such as SonarQube, Snyk, and OWASP ZAP for vulnerability assessment and compliance checks.
- **Security Training and Awareness:** Conduct regular training programs for developers and IT staff on secure coding practices and DevSecOps methodologies [10].
- **Governance and Compliance:** Align security policies with regulatory frameworks such as GDPR, ISO 27001, and NIST to ensure compliance [11].

4 Applying DevSecOps in a University Environment

4.1 Proposed DevSecOps Pipeline for Higher Education

It is important to note that while the pipeline description begins at the code cloning phase, DevSecOps practices ideally start even earlier, during project planning and requirements analysis. In the context of higher education, this pipeline is designed to be used by students, researchers, and the IT department responsible for the development, deployment, and maintenance of software applications within the institution. Therefore, we assume that the codebase has already been created or is actively being developed and available in a version control system, such as Git. Git is a widely used distributed version control system that allows teams to track changes, collaborate efficiently, and manage source code repositories. The pipeline is triggered based on this existing codebase, and serves to integrate security from that point forward in a pedagogical or operational context for Higher Education.

To upgrade the security of software development in universities, we propose a DevSecOps pipeline that meets the needs of higher education institutions. The pipeline seeks to integrate security at each stage of the development lifecycle which will, in turn, ensure continuous monitoring, compliance enforcement, and rapid threat mitigation. The proposed pipeline is illustrated in Fig. 2.

As shown in Fig. 2, the proposed 12-stage DevSecOps pipeline integrates security at every phase of the application lifecycle, from development to deployment. Each stage fulfills a specific requirement, and all security analysis stages generate detailed reports to enhance visibility and compliance.

This 12-stage pipeline was designed by adapting best practices from existing DevSecOps reference architectures commonly found in DevSecOps documentations (e.g., practical-devsecops [12], OWASP [13] Fig. 1, and Microsoft Learns DevSecOps guidelines [14]). However, it was specifically tailored to address the needs of higher education institutions, where ease of deployment, resource constraints, and pedagogical data's severity were key design considerations.

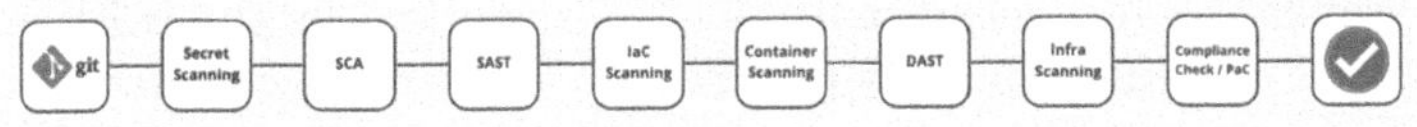

Fig. 1. Proposed DevSecOps Pipeline by the OWASP DevSecOps Guideline.

The process begins with Code Cloning, where the latest version of the source code is retrieved from a version control system such as Git. Once the code is available, Secrets Management ensures that sensitive information—including API keys, credentials, and tokens—is securely handled to prevent exposure. The next step, SAST (Static Application Security Testing) Analysis, involves scanning the source code for vulnerabilities and insecure coding practices before execution, generating a comprehensive security report. Similarly, IaC (Infrastructure as Code) Analysis evaluates infrastructure configuration files (such as

Terraform and Kubernetes manifests) for security misconfigurations, ensuring a secure deployment environment and producing a corresponding report.

Following the analysis phases, the pipeline proceeds with Build and Artifacts Deployment, where the application is compiled, dependencies are resolved, and artifacts are generated and stored. These artifacts are then used to create Docker Images, ensuring that the application is properly packaged with all necessary dependencies in a controlled environment. To maintain container security, Container Analysis is performed to detect vulnerabilities, outdated dependencies, and misconfigurations, generating another security report.

Once the containers are secured, Kubernetes Cluster Provisioning and Configuration takes place, where a Kubernetes cluster is set up and configured to host the application securely. The Application Deployment stage then deploys the containerized application into the Kubernetes cluster, making it accessible to users and further security testing. Post-deployment, DAST (Dynamic Application Security Testing) Analysis is performed to identify vulnerabilities by simulating real-world attacks, such as SQL injection and cross-site scripting (XSS), and generating an in-depth security report.

To ensure traceability and compliance, all security reports generated throughout the pipeline are managed in the final stages. Reports Archiving securely stores the analysis reports for future reference and audits, while Reports Centralization consolidates these reports into a secure and accessible system, facilitating visibility and security monitoring.

This pipeline enables proactive vulnerability detection, compliance enforcement, and continuous monitoring by integrating security at every stage of the application lifecycle.

By situating this pipeline in a higher education environment, it serves not only as a technical solution for securing institutional software but also as a practical tool to promote secure development practices among developers and IT professionals. It reflects realistic development scenarios often encountered in academic settings, where code may already exist and requires structured, secure deployment mechanisms.

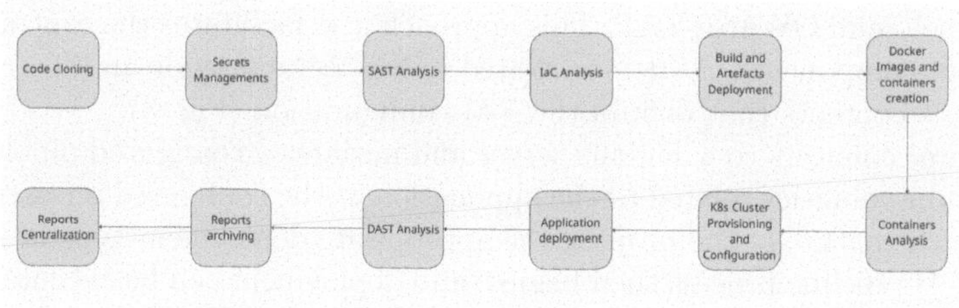

Fig. 2. Proposed DevSecOps Pipeline for Higher Education.

4.2 Security Benefits and Compliance Considerations

Integrating security across the development lifecycle, the proposed DevSecOps pipeline delivers key benefits:

- **Reduces the risk of security breaches** by identifying vulnerabilities in the early stages.
- **Automates compliance** with regulatory frameworks such as *GDPR, ISO 27001, and NIST.*
- **Enhances collaboration** between the development, security and operations teams, fostering a security-first culture.
- **Minimizes deployment delays** by seamlessly integrating security into CI/CD workflows.

In addition to these benefits, the adoption of DevSecOps in higher education institutions provides a structured and proactive approach to cybersecurity. By automating security controls and fostering a security-aware development culture, universities can significantly reduce their exposure to cyber threats. To evaluate the effectiveness of the DevSecOps framework, institutions can monitor the following Key Performance Indicators (KPIs):

- Mean Time to Remediate (MTTR) vulnerabilities
- Percentage of security flaws detected before production
- Compliance audit success rate
- Reduction in security incident occurrences post-implementation

4.3 Implementation and Validation

We have set up a test environment to demonstrate the results of our DevSecOps framework. We started by configuring our Jenkins server, which is deployed as a local Vagrant virtual machine. Then, we installed Ansible and Terraform for automated configuration and provisioning. To optimize resource consumption and ensure smooth processing, we used a containerized environment for various tools in the DevSecOps pipeline, including SonarQube, Nexus, Trivy, Snyk, Kube-Bench, and OWASP ZAP. This approach also facilitates the centralization of different components. As demonstrated in Fig. 2, we provide an illustration of the server's contents that defines the VM configuration (Fig. 3).

The user connects to a Jenkins server and initiates a configured pipeline that detects vulnerabilities related to the application or the configured infrastructure. Based on the nature of the project, the appropriate deployment type is selected. The CI/CD pipeline process then begins, and deployment can be executed either on a private Kubernetes infrastructure or on the public cloud using Azure AKS. Security reports are automatically sent to an issue manager server, where they are centralized and can be easily accessed. Figure 9 illustrates the overall process of the project (Fig. 4).

One of the most critical aspects of a DevSecOps environment is the ability to centralize and manage security reports generated by various security tools. This

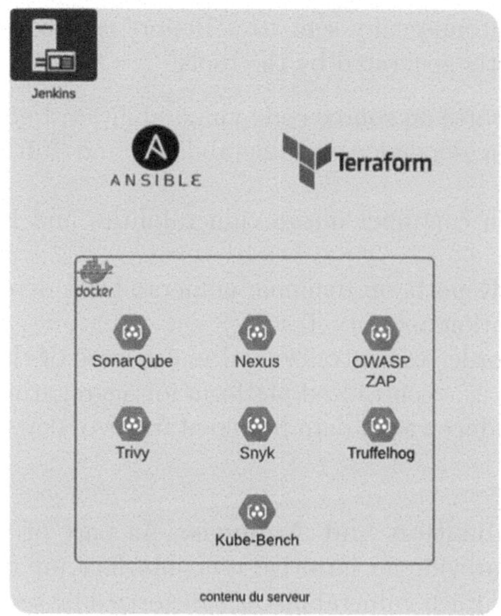

Fig. 3. Jenkins Server Content.

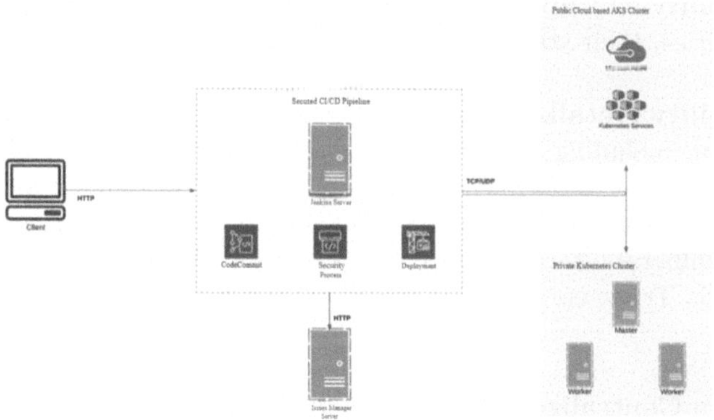

Fig. 4. Physical architecture.

centralization provides a comprehensive overview of security issues, facilitates the prioritization of fixes, and ensures proactive risk management. In our framework, we have integrated DefectDojo as the centralized vulnerability management platform to collect, analyze, and track vulnerabilities detected by tools such as SonarQube, Snyk, Trivy, OWASP ZAP, and others, while providing recommendations for remediation.

Collection of Vulnerability Reports: The various security tools used in our DevSecOps pipeline generate detailed reports on detected vulnerabilities.

These reports are automatically sent to a Report centralized manager. Below are examples of reports generated by the tools:

- **SonarQube:** Reports on source code vulnerabilities, bugs, and code smells.
- **Snyk:** Reports on dependency vulnerabilities and Infrastructure as Code (IaC) files.
- **Trivy:** Reports on container image vulnerabilities and Kubernetes configurations.
- **OWASP ZAP:** Reports on dynamic vulnerabilities detected during DAST (Dynamic Application Security Testing).
- **DefectDojo:** In order to centralize and make sense of the collected reports, DefectDojo serves as a centralized platform for aggregating and parsing security reports to produce visual data representations of detected vulnerabilities.

Centralized Visualization and Analysis: As part of this work, we have used DefectDojo to provide an intuitive user interface for visualizing and analyzing vulnerabilities. Each vulnerability is categorized by severity (critical, high, medium, low) and type of vulnerability (e.g., SQL injection, XSS, misconfiguration, etc.). All of these data are centralized within a single server which offers:

- **Vulnerability Dashboard:** A centralized dashboard displays all detected vulnerabilities, their status (open, in progress, resolved), and their potential impact.
- **Vulnerability Details:** For each vulnerability, DefectDojo provides detailed information, including a description of the vulnerability, the affected file or component, the severity and CVSS (Common Vulnerability Scoring System) score of the vulnerability, and recommendations for remediation. It categorizes the vulnerabilities based on the tools that detected them (e.g., SonarQube, Snyk, Trivy, etc.).

Example of a Centralized Report: To further illustrate the centralized management of security reports, below is an example of a vulnerability detected by **Trivy Kube-Bench** and managed in DefectDojo. This example highlights how vulnerabilities are tracked, prioritized, and remediated within the platform.

Vulnerability Overview

- **Vulnerability**: Worker Node Security Configuration Issue (CIS Benchmark).
- **Severity**: High.
- **Description**: The configuration file `/etc./kubernetes/kubelet.conf` on worker nodes has overly permissive file permissions (e.g., 644 instead of 600). This could allow unauthorized users to access or modify the Kubernetes configuration, potentially leading to security breaches.
- **Recommendation**: Restrict the file permissions to `600` using the command:

```
chmod 600 /etc/kubernetes/kubelet.conf
```

- **Status**: Open (assigned to the operations team for remediation).

DefectDojo Workflow

1. **Detection**: The vulnerability was detected by **Trivy Kube-Bench** during a Kubernetes cluster scan. Trivy identified the misconfiguration and generated a report, which was automatically imported into DefectDojo.
2. **Centralized View**: In DefectDojo, the vulnerability is displayed in the **Active Findings** section, as shown in the screenshot below. The platform provides a detailed breakdown of the issue, including its severity, description, and recommended mitigation steps.
3. **Remediation Tracking**: The vulnerability is assigned to the operations team for remediation. DefectDojo tracks the status of the issue, allowing teams to monitor progress and ensure timely resolution.
4. **Historical Data**: DefectDojo also provides historical data on vulnerabilities, as shown in the screenshot below. This allows teams to analyze trends, identify recurring issues, and improve security practices over time.
5. **Mitigation Steps**: Once the vulnerability is resolved, the team updates its status in DefectDojo. The platform records the mitigation steps taken, ensuring a complete audit trail for compliance and reporting purposes (Figs. 5, 6 and 7).

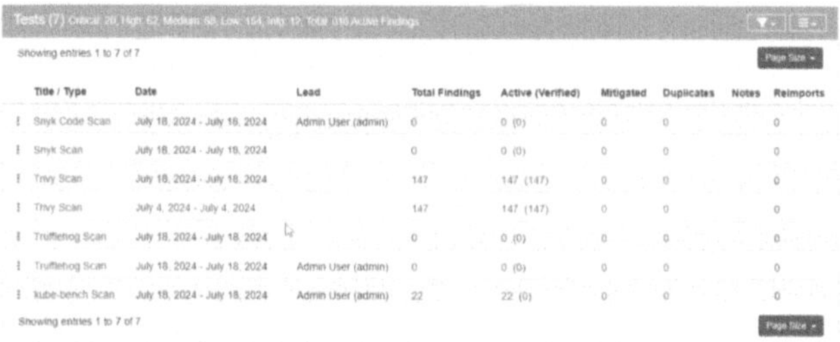

Tests (7)

Showing entries 1 to 7 of 7

Title / Type	Date	Lead	Total Findings	Active (Verified)	Mitigated	Duplicates	Notes	Reimports
Snyk Code Scan	July 18, 2024 - July 18, 2024	Admin User (admin)	0	0 (0)	0	0		0
Snyk Scan	July 18, 2024 - July 18, 2024		0	0 (0)	0	0		0
Trivy Scan	July 18, 2024 - July 18, 2024		147	147 (147)	0	0		0
Trivy Scan	July 4, 2024 - July 4, 2024		147	147 (147)	0	0		0
Trufflehog Scan	July 18, 2024 - July 18, 2024		0	0 (0)	0	0		0
Trufflehog Scan	July 18, 2024 - July 18, 2024	Admin User (admin)	0	0 (0)	0	0		0
kube-bench Scan	July 18, 2024 - July 18, 2024	Admin User (admin)	22	22 (0)	0	0		0

Showing entries 1 to 7 of 7

Fig. 5. Active Findings in DefectDojo.

Benefits of Centralized Reporting: The centralized management of vulnerabilities through DefectDojo offers significant benefits, especially within a university setting where the protection of sensitive data and compliance with regulatory standards are of prime importance. By consolidating vulnerability reports from multiple tools into a single platform, DefectDojo enables teams to effectively prioritize high-risk issues. This, in turn, ensures that critical and high-severity vulnerabilities are addressed without delay.

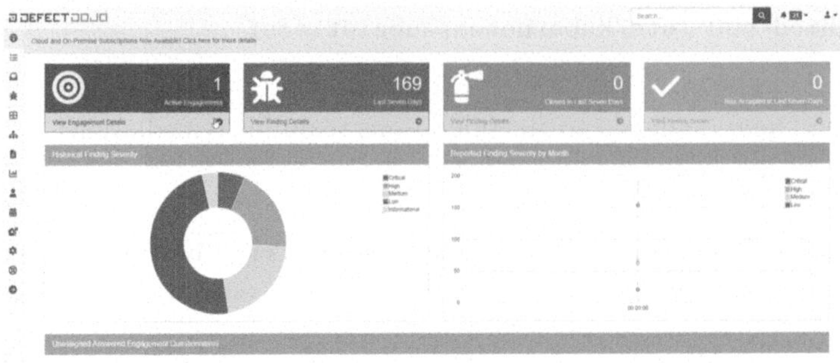

Fig. 6. Historical Finding Severity in DefectDojo.

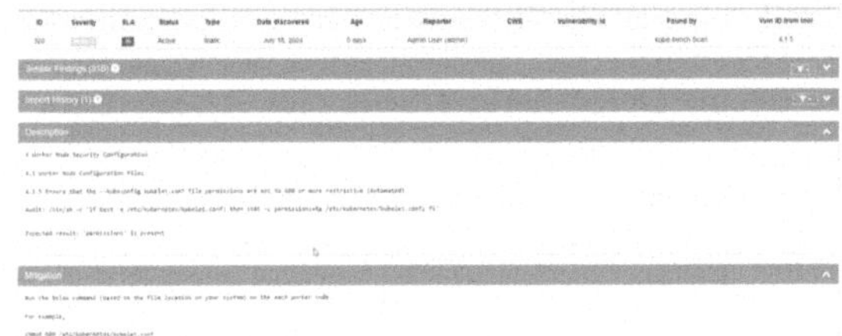

Fig. 7. Mitigation Steps for a Vulnerability in DefectDojo.

Such prioritization is crucial in an academic environment, where resources may be limited and security incidents can have serious consequences. In addition, the platform allows teams to track progress seamlessly, providing real-time visibility into the status of vulnerabilities from detection to resolution. This transparency strengthens collaboration among development, security, and operations teams, aligning with the core principles of DevSecOps.

Furthermore, DefectDojo's ability to generate detailed reports and audit trails supports compliance with regulatory frameworks such as ISO 27001 and GDPR—which are especially relevant in higher education institutions responsible for handling sensitive student and research data. By streamlining vulnerability management and fostering a proactive security culture, centralized reporting not only enhances the security posture of university applications but also accelerates the adoption of DevSecOps practices, ensuring that security is integrated throughout every stage of the software development lifecycle.

4.4 Criteria of Tools Selection

The selection of security tools for our DevSecOps pipeline was based on several criteria: open-source availability, ease of integration into CI/CD workflows, active community support, and relevance in both academic and enterprise environments. For example, SonarQube was chosen for static code analysis due to its flexibility and support for multiple programming languages. Trivy and Kube-

Bench were selected for container and Kubernetes security auditing, as they offer lightweight, developer-friendly scans. Snyk complements Trivy by focusing on open-source dependency vulnerabilities, while OWASP ZAP covers dynamic application testing through automated runtime scans. Nexus is integrated for artifact storage with built-in vulnerability intelligence.

Compared to enterprise DevSecOps frameworks, our approach emphasizes simplicity and accessibility—key factors in higher education settings, where teams often include students, researchers, and IT staff with varying levels of security expertise. While enterprise solutions frequently rely on premium tools and complex integrations, our framework strikes a balance between effectiveness and resource efficiency. Additionally, the use of centralized reporting via DefectDojo, along with role-based access for students, researchers, and IT staff, enhances visibility and traceability throughout all stages of the pipeline. This centralized strategy is especially beneficial in academic environments that prioritize hands-on training, knowledge sharing, and reproducible secure development practices.

5 Conclusion

This paper outlines a DevSecOps framework designed for higher education institutions, focusing on adaptability, scalability, and integrated security throughout software development. The framework facilitates proactive vulnerability detection, efficient remediation, and compliance with regulations like GDPR and ISO 27001. Centralizing vulnerability reports using tools such as DefectDojo improves visibility and risk management, addressing the unique challenges universities face in protecting sensitive data. Future work will involve integrating advanced modules, including Identity and Access Management and AI-driven threat detection, as well as developing user-friendly interfaces for non-technical users. Emerging technologies will enhance security through automated anomaly detection and customized configurations. By adopting this framework, universities can reduce cyberattack risks, ensure compliance, foster security awareness, and securely accelerate digital transformation. This approach is crucial for strengthening academic institutions' cybersecurity and preparing them for future challenges.

References

1. Alexei, A., Alexei, A.: Cyber security threat analysis in higher education institutions as a result of distance learning. Int. J. Sci. Technol. Res. **10**(3), 128–133 (2021). https://www.ijstr.org/final-print/mar2021/Cyber-Security-Threat-Analysis-In-Higher-Education-Institutions-As-A-Result-Of-Distance-Learning.pdf
2. Armas, R., Taherdoost, H.: Building a cybersecurity culture in higher education: proposing a cybersecurity awareness paradigm. Information **16**(5), 336 (2025). https://doi.org/10.3390/info16050336
3. Sonicwall, J.: Sonicwall Cyber Threat Report. SonicWall, Milpitas (2023)

4. Dai, Q., Huang, H., Li, J., Mao, et al.: Revisit security in the era of DevOps : An evidence-based inquiry into DevSecOps industry. The Institution of Engineering and Technology (2023). https://core.ac.uk/download/614003691.pdf
5. Mumtaz, M.H.: Digital transformation in software development : success factors, challenges, and impacts in transitioning from waterfall to devops in industry (2024). https://core.ac.uk/download/630298611.pdf
6. Ahmed, F., Francis, M.: Integrating Security with DevSecOps: Techniques and Challenges University of Birmingham (2019)
7. Li, Y., Zalialetdzinau, A.: Attemps of scientific reflection on the role of e-learning of the future in the area of digital transformation: new opportunities and experiences with DevSecOps (2022)
8. Craiger, J.P., Lindamood-Craiger, L., Zorri, D.M.: Cyber supply chain risk management: implications for the SOF future operating environment. Scholarly Commons (2021). https://core.ac.uk/download/475666563.pdf
9. Pereira, R., Prates, L.: DevSecOps practices and tools. Springer (2025). https://core.ac.uk/download/639870019.pdf
10. Gonzalez, D.N.: The state of practice for security unit testing: towards data driven strategies to shift security into developer's automated testing workflows. RIT Scholar Works (2021). https://core.ac.uk/download/481497710.pdf
11. Blum, D.: Rational Cybersecurity for Business. Springer Science and Business Media LLC (2021). https://core.ac.uk/download/478116273.pdf
12. Practical DevSecOps, DevSecOps lifecycle – key phases documentation. https://www.practical-devsecops.com/devsecops-life-cycle/
13. OWASP. OWASP DevSecOps guideline. https://owasp.org/www-project-devsecops-guideline/
14. Microsoft learn. security in DevOps (DevSecOps). https://learn.microsoft.com/en-us/devops/operate/security-in-devops

NextLearn: A Context-Aware Adaptive Learning Platform

Faten Ziadi, Naouel Boughattas(✉), Wissal Neji, and Malek Naghmouchi

Esprit School of Engineering, Tunis, Tunisia
{faten.ziadi,naouel.boughattas,wissal.neji,malek.naghmouchi}@esprit.tn

Abstract. With the advances in artificial intelligence and the digital transformation of education, it is becoming essential to harness these technologies to enhance student learning. Today, education faces several major challenges, especially adapting the learning pace to each student's needs. It is also essential to consider individual preferences and personalities, as these factors directly influence the process of knowledge acquisition. Furthermore, disparities in academic levels often lead to learning gaps, leaving some students struggling. To address these challenges, we recognized the significance of implementing a solution that can support and enhance learning, whether for students with academic difficulties or those facing psychological barriers. This paper proposes the design of an adaptive learning platform for the first-year students at Esprit (Private Higher School of Engineering and Technology), to help them reinforce their knowledge. The platform provides an intelligent environment that assesses students' academic skills and their personal features through an interactive conversational agent powered by generative AI that provides personalised real-time support, from initial skills assessment to customised learning recommendations. The proposed model lays the groundwork for future pilot studies and integration with advanced business intelligence tools to enhance academic engagement and improve first-year student retention.

The solution is currently under development and integrates several modules for visualization and tracking, course management, and the recommendation system. In this article, we present the chatbot part of the solution, designed to evaluate student skills using quizzes, answer their questions, and recommend personalized support to reinforce their skills.

Keywords: Adaptive learning · chatbot · generative AI

1 Introduction

As digital technologies rapidly evolve, students are increasingly faced with the challenge of adapting to new learning environments. In fact, motivating learners and encouraging them to actively participate in their training is a central challenge for higher education establishments [23]. At the same time, the growing integration of Information and Communication Technologies (ICT) is profoundly

F. Kamoun et al. (Eds.): AFRICATEK 2025, LNICST 676, pp. 425–437, 2026.
https://doi.org/10.1007/978-3-032-16635-7_27

changing teaching practices and redefining student expectations [5]. The rise of educational technologies, such as artificial intelligence (AI) and adaptive learning is also opening up new prospects for personalizing teaching and making learning more interactive and engaging. Thanks to advances in AI, it is becoming possible to adapt educational content in real time to the specific needs of each student, thus promoting a more effective and individualized educational experience.

However, many factors influence student engagement, including the motivational climate established by the teacher, pedagogical style and the opportunity to learn at an appropriate rhythm [27]. Traditional teaching approaches, such as lecture-based teaching, are showing their limitations and can lead to cognitive saturation [24]. It therefore becomes crucial to diversify teaching methods to maintain a balance between autonomy and support, thus fostering lasting student involvement.

These factors have a particular impact on first-year students at Esprit, who face specific challenges in their transition to higher education. Lack of academic preparation, integration difficulties and the variety of learning needs complicate their adaptation. Some start with a basic level, while others enroll late, making it difficult for them to follow a traditional course. Faced with this heterogeneity, it becomes essential to offer adapted teaching resources to guarantee a fair and effective educational experience.

Artificial intelligence and adaptive learning are promising solutions to meet these challenges [9]. By combining personalization and adaptability, these technologies make it possible to adjust pedagogical content to the specific needs of each student, offering tailor-made support and promoting a more effective and engaging learning experience.

In this context, our project aims to explore the potential of these emerging technologies to encourage a teaching experience more adapted to the specific needs of each student. More specifically, we propose to develop a digital platform for personalized and interactive learning. This platform is based on advanced technological tools, including a conversational agent, to assess students' skills, weaknesses and learning preferences. On this basis, tailored teaching resources, such as interactive courses, explanatory videos and targeted exercises, will be offered to each learner. Our project also integrates a BI-based tracking system to collect and analyze progress data. Dashboards will give students and teachers a clear view of how skills are evolving, with predictive analysis to anticipate needs or risks such as dropping out.

This platform aims to go beyond the limits of traditional consolidation by offering tailored support for students. It will not just fill gaps, but also encourage autonomy, reinforce skills and prepare students to meet academic and professional challenges.

This project is part of a process of sustainable educational transformation. It aims to improve the quality of learning while offering effective, individualized support to students, enabling them to reach their full potential and actively contribute to a demanding academic and professional environment.

This document is structured as follows: Sect. 2 describes the main challenges facing first-year students in Higher Education. Section 3 is devoted to emerging technologies in higher education, including generative artificial intelligence and chatbots, and includes a review of some existing solutions. Section 4 describes our proposed adaptive learning platform. A discussion and an overview of future perspectives are provided in Sect. 5. Section 6 is devoted to the conclusion.

2 First-Year Student Challenges in Higher Education

The transition to higher education presents first-year students with a unique set of challenges that can significantly impact their academic performance and overall well-being. One prominent issue is the diversity of learning styles prevalent in university classrooms. Students come from varied educational backgrounds and possess distinct preferences for how they absorb and process information. However, many higher education institutions employ a one-size-fits-all teaching approach that may not align with these individual needs. For instance, while some students thrive in interactive, discussion-based settings, others may perform better with structured lectures or independent study. The variety in learning preferences (visual, auditory, kinesthetic, and beyond) requires that teaching methodologies be sufficiently adaptable to engage all students effectively. When these diverse preferences are not addressed, students can experience frustration, disengagement, and diminished academic confidence underscoring the need for more inclusive and flexible pedagogical strategies. The challenges observed during the rapid transition to online learning environments in the COVID-19 pandemic further highlight how inadequate pedagogical adaptations can hinder success. Recognizing and accommodating diverse learning styles is crucial not only for improving student engagement but also for enhancing overall academic outcomes, as supported by research utilizing learning analytics to tailor assessments and feedback [31].

Compounding these challenges is the problem of inadequate academic preparation. Many first-year students enter university without the essential skills and foundational knowledge required to navigate the independent, self-directed learning environment of higher education [4]. The gap between high school, which often emphasizes rote learning and standardized testing, and the critical thinking, analytical writing, and self-directed study demanded at college can leave students feeling overwhelmed and underprepared. This academic skills gap is particularly acute among students from underrepresented backgrounds or rural communities, where resource constraints further limit access to tailored preparatory support. Moreover, the shift toward active learning methods such as problem-based learning (PBL) has exposed additional difficulties for those accustomed to traditional memorization techniques, thereby necessitating a deeper engagement with self-directed learning practices. Addressing these inadequacies may require curricular reforms at the secondary level, alongside robust support mechanisms in higher education, including bridging courses and tutoring services.

In addition to preparation issues, integration issues further complicate the transition for first-year students. Many, particularly international students, must contend with differences in academic backgrounds and cultural norms. Language barriers, unfamiliar teaching styles, and varying academic expectations can lead to misunderstandings, academic struggles, and feelings of isolation. Moreover, cultural adjustments such as adapting to new social norms and establishing relationships in an unfamiliar environment can significantly heighten stress.

Late enrollment, whether due to administrative delays, financial constraints, or personal circumstances, compounds these problems by causing students to miss essential orientation programs and early networking opportunities. Such integration challenges often result in social and emotional difficulties, leaving students feeling isolated and anxious. Addressing these issues calls for tailored support measures, including cultural orientation, language assistance, and mentorship programs that foster a sense of community and belonging.

In conclusion, navigating the transition to higher education presents significant challenges for first-year students, encompassing inadequate preparation, mismatched learning styles, and integration difficulties. The academic landscape often overwhelms newcomers as they strive to adapt to unfamiliar norms and establish connections within their academic community. Programs designed to ease this transition, such as the immersive module reported in our evaluation, can positively influence students social integration and academic preparedness [30]. However, the effectiveness of such interventions may vary, prompting critical reflection on their capacity to align with students expectations and future academic demands. Furthermore, innovative learning models, like the online learning-assisted framework, can support students' mastery of core competencies through tailored assessments, thereby addressing mismatched learning styles. Ultimately, a multifaceted approach is essential to bolster the success of first-year students during this pivotal period, ensuring they are well-equipped for their academic journeys ahead.

3 Emerging Technologies in Higher Education

In this section, we first present an overview of generative artificial intelligence and conversational agents in the field of education, and explore the potential benefits of adaptive learning systems and personalized pedagogical approaches. We conclude with a review of some existing solutions illustrating the concrete integration of these technologies in educational environments.

3.1 Overview of Generative AI and Conversational Agents in Education

Generative artificial intelligence and conversational agents are transforming the field of education by enhancing learning, engaging students and automating administrative tasks.

LLMs stimulate creativity by proposing innovative project ideas, assist in the writing of documents [19] and produce attractive multimedia content. They can dynamically generate quizzes and assessments according to the required level of difficulty, as well as summaries and personalized course materials adapted to the target audience, such as international students or students with difficulties or handicaps (voice synthesis, Braille transcription, automatic subtitling for educational videos) [3]. They can provide automatic homework correction with instant feedback. To increase student motivation and engagement, they help generate educational games tailored to students' needs and send reminders for various deadlines.

Conversational agents provide intelligent tutoring by answering students' questions and explaining key course concepts, helping to guide them through the learning process and enabling teachers to concentrate on teaching and personal support instead of administrative tasks. They can also suggest exercises and learning paths based on each student's performance and pace, promoting adaptive learning. Administrative support can also be handled by chatbots, which generate answers about deadlines and available resources. Thanks to their natural language support, students can ask questions in natural language and receive explanations adapted to their levels [3]. To train students to argue and defend their ideas, they can access debates and discussions with AI avatars.

Several studies have highlighted the importance of these conversational agents and analysed their advantages, disadvantages and prospects for use. For example, in [14], the authors examine their impact on education. Furthermore, the authors in [26] demonstrates that advanced chatbots, such as ChatGPT, make learning more interactive and personalised, improving student engagement and facilitating progression, while raising ethical and technological challenges.

To optimise their efficiency, chatbots need to be integrated with teaching tools, i.e. adaptive learning platforms. This integration represents a major advance in education, offering an innovative solution to support learners throughout their academic career.

3.2 Potential Benefits of Adaptive Learning Systems and Personalized Pedagogical Approaches

Based on AI techniques, adaptive learning systems and personalized pedagogical approaches enable the adaptation of teaching to the specific needs of each learner. These approaches offer numerous benefits for students, teachers and the education system.

Adaptive learning systems ensure that each learner progresses at his own pace : by identifying his learning gaps, personalized materials adapted to his level and learning style will be proposed, with immediate feedback on their responses, promoting rapid progress. This adjustment of difficulty levels avoids repetitive failure, which reduces frustration and discouragement. The use of interactive and immersive learning methods (interactive quizzes, simulations, videos, educational games) reinforces the involvement and motivation of students, who can follow their progress in real time, encouraging autonomy and perseverance.

Adaptive learning systems enable students with different learning rhythms to reach their full potential by adapting content for learners with specific needs (learning disabilities, handicaps, language difficulties), for example by providing new options such as text-to-speech, automatic translation and content adaptation according to the learner's profile.

3.3 Existing Solutions

The adaptive learning approaches in literature were based on different types of algorithms including Linearization [1], Ant Colony Optimization [2] [18], Genetic Algorithm [13] [15] [25], Machine Learning [32] [11], Neural Networks [17] [20] [21] [28] [29], Reinforcement Learning [16], and Generative Adversarial Networks [7].

In [8], the authors presented a mixed sequential Quant-Qual adaptative learning method combined with a flipped classroom approach. This method defines the role of the professor before and after the session, and is based essentially on interactions with the student, the self-regulation of the learning and the microlearning. The method was evaluated on 4 courses which are: Computational Thinking, Physics I, Physics II, and Fundamental Mathematical Modelling. Authors concluded that to achieve a successful adaptative learning system, we must incorporate didactic strategies, adequate implementation model, and the appropriate technology.

In [15], The genetic algorithm was used to identify the most appropriate learning activities for learners in accordance with their profiles, ensuring efficient resolution of the adaptative learning problem.

In [22], Light gradient Boosting Machine (LGBM) was used for feature selection and extraction to improve learning and predict students' academic performance based on their learning styles and other associated features in a virtual learning environment.

A linearization algorithm was used in [1] to suggest a learning path based on an Educational Concept Map (ECM). This allowed to personalize the resources identified for each student, based on his evaluation and learning objectives.

In [6], ML algorithms were used to analyse the individual needs and preferences of each learner and generated a personalized learning path with customized content. They also provided customized resources and recommendations via a chatbot.

The unsupervised learning algorithm based on an optimized version of K-means presented in [10], was used to cluster MOOC (Massive Open Online Course) forums learners and help instructors personalize their learning strategies.

In [12], The ANNs were used to identify students' learning styles based on their interactions and navigations in the e-learning application and make predictions of their learning styles.

A Reinforcement Learning algorithm was proposed in [7] to optimize the learning path and learning objects: Decisions that optimize the learning experience are rewarded, while the system can be penalized for sub-optimal decisions.

GANs are used to quickly adjust the learners' models, in order to improve the training process.

4 Design of Our Context-Aware Adaptive Learning Platform

In this section, we present our approach, designed as a solution to address all the problems encountered by the First-Year Students in ESPRIT.

4.1 Description of Our Context-Aware Adaptive Learning Platform

The architecture of our contextual adaptive learning platform is presented in Fig. 1. Student interactions are assisted by an intelligent chatbot: The student data is analysed through a classification phase, enabling precise level assignment. A dynamic recommendation process then proposes adaptive resources tailored to the specific needs of each learner. The platform will be equipped also with an advanced monitoring dashboard that allows the visualization of students' progress. By combining automation and human intervention, this intelligent platform aims to optimize learning, promote student engagement and enhance academic success for the First-Year Students in ESPRIT.

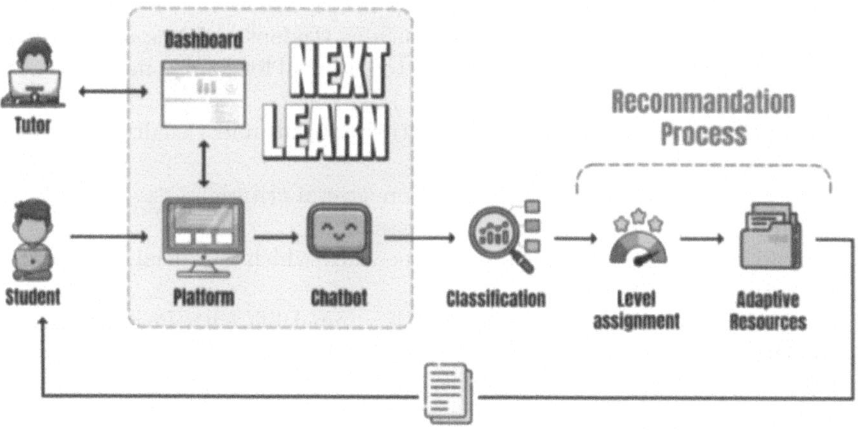

Fig. 1. NextLearn platform architecture.

4.2 Functional Requirements of the Chatbot

The chatbot is the key element of our platform, playing a crucial role in supporting students throughout their course. Its main functionalities include:

- Automatic assessment: Once connected to the platform, students pass a quiz to assess their level in a specific course. This assessment enables students to identify their strengths and weaknesses so that learning can be adapted appropriately.

- Personalised learning recommendations: At the end of the quiz, the chatbot indicates the student's level, i.e. beginner, intermediate or advanced. It then suggests appropriate teaching resources depending on their level and the skills to be reinforced (videos, courses, interactive exercises, etc.).

- Conversational support and personalised monitoring: In addition to the recommendation system, the chatbot interacts with students in real time to answer their questions, clarify concepts and guide them towards targeted exercises. It suggests remedial activities based on identified gaps and encourages students to make gradual progress. It monitors learning progress and notifies students when they are ready to move on to the next level.

4.3 Technical Architecture of the Chatbot

To ensure smooth, intelligent interaction with students, the chatbot is based on a robust technical architecture incorporating artificial intelligence algorithms, dynamic databases and optimized communication interfaces. Here's a detailed presentation of its technical architecture:

1. Database : We chose PostgreSQL for its advanced data management capabilities, which perfectly match the chatbot's needs, namely:

-Optimized storage for complex data such as student answers, MCQs, etc.

- Efficient query execution: Indeed, this tool is ideal for joining multiple tables (e.g. students, tutors, MCQs, answers, etc.).

- Compatibility with Power BI, facilitating analysis and visualization of student performance.

2. Backend : We chose FastAPI based on several criteria:

- High performance for fast query processing.

- Support for multiple queries simultaneously, which is crucial for an interactive chatbot.

- Ease of integration, where FastAPI is compatible with PostgreSQL and ChromaDB, ensuring a seamless architecture.

3. Natural language Processing: We opted for LLM - Llama3.2 & Ollama for the following reasons:

- Open-source model

- Runs locally without subscription or paid access to an external API.

- Secure where no information is sent to third-party servers, guaranteeing confidentiality.

4. Retrieval-Augmented Generation (RAG) which improves the relevance of answers by retrieving information from a knowledge base before generating a question.

5. Data storage: We use ChromaDB to enhance question search and analysis. This choice is due to :

- Semantic indexing, enabling questions to be searched according to their meaning, rather than by exact keywords.

- Integration with LangChain for improved MCQ generation and personalized recommendations.

6. File management: As our course materials are in PDF format, we chose PyMuPDF with Pandas to extract data from an excel file. This file contains details about the database contents. these tools are used due to their:

- Lightweight and powerful, enabling rapid processing of PDF files.

- Accurate, ensuring precise extraction, preserving text structure and correctly recovering MCQs.

- Efficient in identifying tables and layouts for optimal data organization.

We present in Fig. 2 a diagram illustrating the functional and technical architecture of the resulting chatbot.

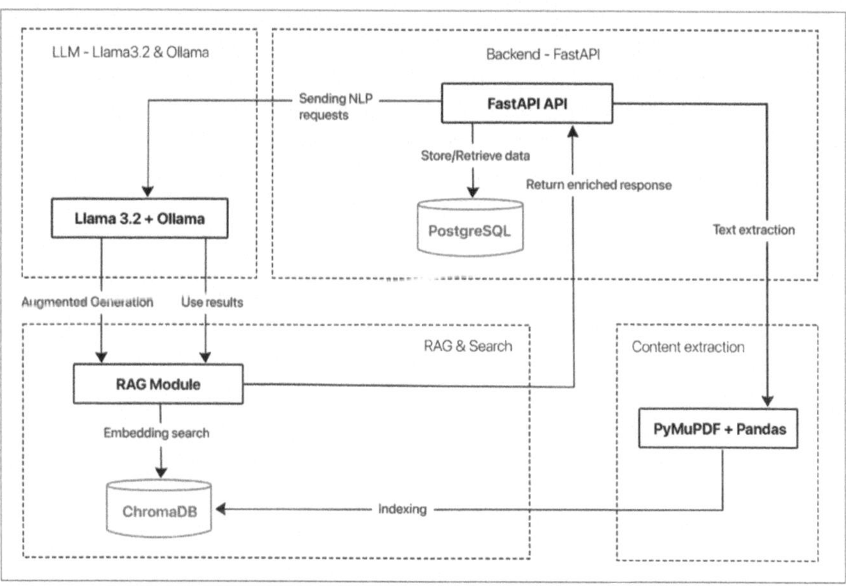

Fig. 2. Functional and technical architecture of the chatbot.

The chatbot operates using FastAPI to handle user requests and coordinate exchanges with the various modules. When a request is sent, FastAPI forwards it to Llama 3.2 via Ollama to process and generate a relevant response. To enhance the accuracy and relevance of responses, the chatbot integrates a RAG (Retrieval-Augmented Generation) system that retrieves relevant information from ChromaDB, a vector database optimizing semantic search. Structured data, such as interaction histories and references to information sources, are stored in PostgreSQL via FastAPI. In addition, PDF and Excel documents are analyzed using PyMuPDF and Pandas, then indexed in ChromaDB for easy access to enrich the responses generated.

5 Discussion and Future Directions

Personalisation plays a crucial role in education, enabling resources to be adapted to the specific needs of students while taking into consideration their personalities and learning styles. The integration of chatbots into educational platforms enables real-time interaction, making learning more dynamic, engaging and accessible to all.

In order to increase the engagement of our students, the chatbot developed, as the first step of our project, offers the following advantages:

- Accessibility and availability: the chatbot is constantly accessible enabling students to learn at their own rhythm. This accessibility also fosters continuous interaction, preventing isolation and encourages learners's active participation.

- Increased motivation thanks to instant, personalised feedback: The chatbot enables students to receive immediate feedback on their skill level. For example, a beginner can receive simplified explanations, while an advanced student will be offered more in-depth content.

The chatbot developed in our project was learned and tested on a specific module, Procedural Programming 1: A module dedicated to teaching the C language to first-year engineering students at Esprit. The chatbot was trained on this module to evaluate its performance. Initial tests with a group of students are encouraging. The chatbot can answer questions accurately, rank students according to their skill level, and recommend appropriate resources based on the results obtained.

The system evaluation can be based on several dimensions: relevance (answer accuracy, quality of recommendations), technical performance (average response time, CPU/memory usage), user engagement (number of interactions, retention rate), and RAG-specific metrics such as vector search precision and embedding quality. Our system achieved an overall accuracy rate of 83.72% (108 out of 129 correct answers). It can answer each question in under three seconds, with an average CPU usage of 17% and memory consumption of 518.74 MB.

The test phase is still ongoing, and our next steps for improving the chatbot are as follows:

- Large-scale deployment: where we plan to host the chatbot on a server to ensure accessibility to a wider audience.

- Learning improvement: Gradually integrate new questions and user interactions to improve the relevance of answers.

- Extension to other courses: Develop chatbots adapted to various modules to cover a wider range of subjects.

Our next steps for the development of the platform include:

- Development and integration: Finalize the front-end and back-end, ensure their seamless integration, and integrate the chatbot.

- Implementation of the BI part: Develop an interactive dashboard enabling teachers and students to access analytical visualizations of learning.

6 Conclusion

First-year students face a variety of challenges that impact their engagement and success. Some have diverse learning styles, while others suffer from inadequate academic preparation. International students also have to adapt to cultural and educational differences, while those enrolling late have less time to integrate and keep up with the course rhythm. In light of these factors, our project consists of developing an adaptive learning platform for first-year students at Esprit, to help them strengthen their skills. Its main aim is to make learning more motivating, optimize knowledge retention and reduce the drop-out rate, while offering personalized support to these students in difficulty.

As a first step, we developed a generative chatbot able to assess both the academic skills and personal characteristics of students. This agent classifies them according to their level and learning style, offering them adapted resources such as interactive courses, targeted videos and personalized exercises.

The next stages of our project include the continuous improvement of the chatbot by enriching it with our course resources. Once the front-end interface has been finalized, we will proceed with its integration and deployment. In addition, we will develop the BI part of the dashboard to provide teachers and students with detailed visualizations of learning progress and engagement.

References

1. Adorni, G., Koceva, F.: Educational concept maps for personalized learning path generation. In: AI* IA 2016 Advances in Artificial Intelligence: XVth International Conference of the Italian Association for Artificial Intelligence, Genova, Italy, November 29–December 1, 2016, Proceedings XV. pp. 135–148. Springer (2016). https://doi.org/10.1007/978-3-319-49130-1_11
2. Ahmad, K., Maryam, B.I., Molood, A.E.: A novel adaptive learning path method. In: 4th International Conference on e-Learning and e-Teaching (ICELET 2013), pp. 20–25. IEEE (2013). https://doi.org/10.1109/ICELET.2013.6681639
3. Ali, F., et al.: Let the devil speak for itself: should chatgpt be allowed or banned in hospitality and tourism schools? J. Global Hosp. Tourism **2**(1), 1–6 (2023). https://doi.org/10.5038/2771-5957.2.1.1016
4. Austria-Cruz, M.C.: Academic stress and coping strategies of filipino college students in private and public universities in central luzon. Int. J. Adv. Eng. Manag. Sci. **5**(11), 603–607 (2019). https://doi.org/10.22161/ijaems.511.6
5. Bharti, R., Pomal, K., Ahmed, M., Singh, C.B.: Transformative impact of ICT on education: leveraging technology and communication to enhance teaching and learning. Feedback Int. J. Commun.**1**(3), 131–141 (2024). https://doi.org/10.62569/fijc.v1i3.39
6. Davies, J.N., Verovko, M., Verovko, O., Solomakha, I.: Personalization of e-learning process using ai-powered chatbot integration. In: International scientific-practical conference, pp. 209–216. Springer (2020). https://doi.org/10.1007/978-3-030-58124-4_20
7. El Lakkah, S., Alimam, M.A., Seghiouer, H.: Adaptive e-learning system based on learning style and ant colony optimization. In: 2017 intelligent systems and

computer vision (ISCV), pp. 1–5. IEEE (2017). https://doi.org/10.1109/ISACV.2017.8054963

8. Green, T.D., Donovan, L.C.: Learning anytime, anywhere through technology: reconsidering teaching and learning for the imaker generation. The Wiley handbook of teaching and learning, pp. 225–256 (2018). https://doi.org/10.1002/9781118955901.ch9
9. Gyonyoru, K.I.K.: The role of ai-based adaptive learning systems in digital education. J. Appl. Tech. Educ. Sci. **14**(2), 380–380 (2024). https://doi.org/10.24368/jates380
10. Hou, X., Lei, C.U., Kwok, Y.K.: Op-dci: a riskless k-means clustering for influential user identification in mooc forum. In: 2017 16th IEEE International Conference on Machine Learning and Applications (ICMLA), pp. 936–939. IEEE (2017). https://doi.org/10.1109/ICMLA.2017.00-34
11. Joy, J., Raj, N.S., VG, R.: Ontology-based e-learning content recommender system for addressing the pure cold-start problem. ACM J. Data Inf. Qual. **13**(3), 1–27 (2021). https://doi.org/10.1145/3429251
12. Kolekar, S.V., Sanjeevi, S.G., Bormane, D.S.: Learning style recognition using artificial neural network for adaptive user interface in e-learning. In: 2010 IEEE International conference on computational intelligence and computing research, pp. 1–5. IEEE (2010). https://doi.org/10.1109/ICCIC.2010.5705768
13. Krechetov, I., Romanenko, V.: Implementing the adaptive learning techniques.(2 (eng)),pp. 252–277 (2020). https://doi.org/10.17323/1814-9545-2020-2-252-277
14. Labadze, L., Grigolia, M., Machaidze, L.: Role of ai chatbots in education: systematic literature review. Int. J. Educ. Technol. High. Educ. **20**(1), 56 (2023). https://doi.org/10.1186/s41239-024-00461-6
15. Lhafra, F.Z., Abdoun, O.: Integration of evolutionary algorithm in an agent-oriented approach for an adaptive e-learning. Int. J. Electr. Comput. Eng. **13**(2), 1964–1978 (2023). https://doi.org/10.11591/ijece.v13i2.pp1964-1978
16. Li, X., Xu, H., Zhang, J., Chang, H.h.: Optimal hierarchical learning path design with reinforcement learning. ApPl. Psychol. Measur. **45**(1), 54–70 (2021). 10.1177/0146621620947171
17. Lin, J., Zhao, Y., Gao, T., Liu, C., Pu, H.: Micro-video learning resource portrait and its application. In: Human Centered Computing: 6th International Conference, HCC 2020, Virtual Event, December 14–15, 2020, Revised Selected Papers 6, pp. 302–307. Springer (2021). https://doi.org/10.1007/978-3-030-70626-5_32
18. Liu, S., Chen, S., Meng, H.: A dynamic mining algorithm for multi-granularity user's learning preference based on ant colony optimization. In: Intelligence Science I: Second IFIP TC 12 International Conference, ICIS 2017, Shanghai, China, October 25-28, 2017, Proceedings 2, pp. 133–142. Springer (2017). https://doi.org/10.1007/978-3-319-68121-4_14
19. Lo, C.K.: What is the impact of chatgpt on education? a rapid review of the literature. Educ. Sci. **13**(4), 410 (2023). https://doi.org/10.3390/educsci13040410
20. Lu, T., et al.: A framework of ai-based intelligent adaptive tutoring system. In: 2021 16th International Conference on Computer Science Education (ICCSE), pp. 726–731. IEEE (2021). https://doi.org/10.1109/ICCSE51940.2021.9569273
21. Murtaza, M., Ahmed, Y., Shamsi, J.A., Sherwani, F., Usman, M.: Ai-based personalized e-learning systems: issues, challenges, and solutions. IEEE access **10**, 81323–81342 (2022). https://doi.org/10.1109/ACCESS.2022.3193938
22. Nazempour, R., Darabi, H.: Personalized learning in virtual learning environments using students' behavior analysis. Educ. Sci. **13**(5), 457 (2023). https://doi.org/10.3390/educsci13050457

23. Neji, W., Boughattas, N., Ziadi, F.: Exploring new ai-based technologies to enhance students'motivation. Issues Inf. Sci. Inf. Tech. **20** (2023). https://doi.org/10.28945/5149
24. Omelicheva, M.Y., Avdeyeva, O.: Teaching with lecture or debate? testing the effectiveness of traditional versus active learning methods of instruction. PS: Polit. Sci. Polit. **41**(3), 603–607 (2008). https://doi.org/10.1017/S1049096508080815
25. Pu, D., Zhou, Z.: Teaching path generation model based on machine learning. In: 2021 6th International Conference on Computational Intelligence and Applications (ICCIA), pp. 26–30. IEEE (2021). https://doi.org/10.1109/ICCIA52886.2021.00013
26. Rane, N.: Chatbot-enhanced teaching and learning: implementation strategies, challenges, and the role of ChatGPT in education. Challenges, and the Role of ChatGPT in Education (2023). https://doi.org/10.2139/ssrn.4603204
27. Ryan, R.M., Deci, E.L.: Intrinsic and extrinsic motivation from a self-determination theory perspective: definitions, theory, practices, and future directions. Contemp. Educ. Psychol. **61**, 101860 (2020). https://doi.org/10.1016/j.cedpsych.2020.101860
28. Saito, T., Watanobe, Y.: Learning path recommender system based on recurrent neural network. In: 2018 9th international conference on awareness science and technology (iCAST), pp. 324–329. IEEE (2018). https://doi.org/10.1109/ICAwST.2018.8517231
29. Tian, Y., Sun, Y., Zhang, L., Qi, W.: Research on mooc teaching mode in higher education based on deep learning. Comput. Intell. Neurosci. **2022**(1), 8031602 (2022). https://doi.org/10.1155/2022/8031602
30. Turner, R., et al.: Easing the transition of first year undergraduates through an immersive induction module. Teach. High. Educ. **22**(7), 805–821 (2017). https://doi.org/10.1080/13562517.2017.1301906
31. Williams, P.: Assessing collaborative learning: big data, analytics and university futures. Assess. Eval. Higher Educ. **42**(6), 978–989 (2017). https://doi.org/10.1080/02602938.2016.1216084
32. Zhou, T.F., Pan, Y.Q., Huang, L.R.: Research on personalized e-learning based on decision tree and rete algorithm. In: 2017 International conference on computer systems, electronics and control (ICCSEC), pp. 1392–1396. IEEE (2017). https://doi.org/10.1109/ICCSEC.2017.8446741

Use of a Retrieval-Augmented Generation (RAG) Chatbot for First-Year Engineering Education at ESPRIT

Hiba Maalaoui(✉) and Yahya Samet

ESPRIT School of Engineering, Ariana, Tunisia
{hiba.maalaoui,samet.yahya}@esprit.tn

Abstract. Recent advancements in generative artificial intelligence (AI) have opened up new opportunities in higher education. A large number of studies have explored the use of educational chatbots in the fields of science, technology, engineering, and mathematics. Although some research has incorporated elements for personalized or adaptive learning, there is still a need for further study on the design and evaluation of personalized adaptive learning chatbots. The focus of this study is the development of an educational chatbot using large language models (LLMs) and retrieval augmented generation (RAG) for the Project 1A module at Esprit (Private Engineering and Technology School). The goal is to improve the learning experience through personalized educational support. The chatbot provides customized assistance, real-time feedback, and adaptive learning paths, acting as an additional tutor for first year engineering students, guiding them through their projects and providing immediate answers and explanations based on course content. This research highlights the potential of enhanced RAG methods to advance the use of LLMs in the module and represents a promising approach to overcoming current challenges in the field.

Keywords: Chatbots · Retrieval-Augmented Generation (RAG) · large language models (LLMs) · AI in Education · Chatbot technology · adaptive learning

1 Introduction

First-year engineering students often face several challenges in their transition to higher education. They must quickly adapt to a demanding academic environment, from understanding complex technical concepts to managing their time efficiently. These difficulties can impact their learning experience and overall performance. However, with the right support systems and learning strategies, students can overcome these obstacles and build a strong foundation for their engineering studies. Among the first proposed solutions, the use of intelligent learning systems has emerged as a key approach and has become more prevalent in education over the past few decades. However, many learners still struggle to navigate the vast number of available resources. E-learning platforms are constantly digitizing materials to address diverse educational needs, but without appropriate guidance, selecting the most relevant content can be challenging. As the number of learners

F. Kamoun et al. (Eds.): AFRICATEK 2025, LNICST 676, pp. 438–449, 2026.
https://doi.org/10.1007/978-3-032-16635-7_28

and resources grows, it becomes increasingly difficult for educators to provide effective support. This highlights the need for an adaptive learning system that can handle complex queries and deliver personalized, relevant resources to students seeking assistance [1].

So adaptive learning is an educational approach that adapts the learning experience to each student's unique needs, interests, and preferences. In contrast to traditional teaching methods, adaptive education tailors the curriculum, pace of instruction, and learning environment to each student's specific strengths, weak nesses, and goals [2]. Additionally, the educational landscape has undergone significant large-scale transformations, driven primarily by rapid technological advancements and the growing demand for personalized learning experiences.

Research on technology, especially artificial intelligence (AI) and, more particularly, generative AI-driven adaptive learning, has demonstrated positive outcomes, particularly in improving learner engagement and academic performance in various fields, including science, technology, engineering, mathematics, and language learning.

From a technological perspective, chatbots are increasingly being used to provide adaptive learning experiences. However, many studies that incorporate adaptive learning components do not explicitly refer to a specific design framework or theoretical model for implementing adaptive learning. Educational chatbots are predominantly applied in various domains, including technology, mathematics, language learning, administrative support, and professional training [3, 4].

In this context general AI chatbots, such as ChatGPT, Gemini, and other large language models (LLMs) have emerged as promising educational solutions. These tools excel at offering detailed explanations, practical examples, and assistance in solving complex problems. However, their implementation in academic environments has exposed notable limitations, including frequent mismatches between generated answers and course content, lack of contextual alignment with specific programs, and imprecise or irrelevant responses to poorly formulated or ambiguous student queries. These shortcomings hinder their effectiveness in addressing the nuanced needs of learners within structured academic contexts [5, 6].

In addition, LLMs have played a significant role in driving natural language processing, providing significant advances in text generation, comprehension, and interpretation. By leveraging massive datasets and advanced deep learning architectures, particularly transformer models, LLMs can generate human-like text and perform a wide range of tasks with remarkable accuracy. As these models continue to evolve, their applications promise to drive further innovation and efficiency in many domains [7].

In this context, Retrieval-Augmented Generation (RAG) has emerged as a powerful framework that integrates the capabilities of large language models (LLMs) with external knowledge sources. While LLMs are powerful at generating coherent and contextually relevant text, they face challenges in providing accurate, up-to-date, and domain-specific information due to their reliance on static training data. RAG addresses these limitations by integrating a query mechanism that allows models to access external databases or knowledge sources in real-time, improving the accuracy and relevance of answers.

Combining retrieval and generation in educational chatbots opens up new opportunities for applications such as question answering, summarization, and dialogue systems. This dynamic and adaptive approach to content generation has the potential to reshape adaptive learning and provide more personalized and context-aware educational experiences.

In light of this, this paper presents SDLearn, an adaptive learning chatbot based on LLMs and the RAG framework, designed to support first year computer science engineering students at Esprit (Private Engineering and Technology School) in the project 1A module. This module is intended for first year computer engineering students. It focuses on the development of a C language video game in a team during the second semester, using an active learning approach.

SDLearn is designed to enhance students' learning experience by leveraging AI-driven adaptability to address diverse educational needs. The chatbot aims to provide personalized learning support, helping students effectively navigate the challenges of the module. To begin, we will provide a comprehensive overview of the previous theoretical foundations, ensuring a smooth transition between the role of generative AI in education and the concept of adaptive learning.

The rest of this article is divided into five connected sections. Section 2 presents the literature review providing relevant background and related studies. Following that, Sect. 3 outlines the architecture and methodology of our approach. Section 4 details the evaluation of the solution. In Sect. 5, we discuss the limitations of our work, propose directions for future research and conclude the paper.

2 Literature Review

In this section, a literature review on chatbots is conducted. Chatbots have become an important technology in the evolution of human-computer interaction, evolving from simple rule-based chatbots to sophisticated AI models.

2.1 From Rule-Based to AI-Powered: The Evolution of Chatbot Technology

Chatbot technology has grown significantly over the years, starting with rule-based systems that used predetermined scripts and rules to interact with users. A key example of this approach was ELIZA, developed by Joseph Weizenbaum in 1966 [8].

As the need for more adaptive and context-aware responses grew, retrieval-based chatbots appeared. Based on user input, these systems select responses from a predefined set. ALICE (Artificial Linguistic Internet Computer Entity), developed by Richard Wallace in 2007, is a well-known example of this approach [9].

In contrast to traditional retrieval-based systems, which rely on fixed responses, generative chatbots can generate new responses on the fly. A major advance in this area was the introduction of the Sequence-to-Sequence (Seq2Seq) model by Sutskever, Vinyals, and Le in 2014 [10], which significantly improved the capability of chatbots to generate coherent and contextually relevant discussions.

More advances were made with the transformer model, a revolutionary neural network architecture proposed by Vaswani. in 2017. This model revolutionized natural language processing by enabling more efficient and sophisticated text generation.

With the integration of pre-trained language models, such as the GPT (Generative Pre-trained Transformer) series from OpenAI, the field of generative chatbots has advanced even further. These models greatly enhance the chatbot's ability to produce highly coherent and contextually appropriate responses, having been trained on large amounts of text data and fine-tuned for specific tasks.

The most recent advance in chatbot technology is the appearance of large language models (LLMs), such as Meta Llama-2, OpenAI's GPT-3.5 and GPT-4, and Mistral. Based on the Transformer architecture, these models are trained on massive datasets from the web and other diverse text corpora. They expand the potential of AI-powered conversational systems even further.

2.2 Large Language Models

A significant advance in computational linguistics has been the development of large language models (LLMs), such as GPT-4, LLAMA3, and PaLM. These models are built on Transformer-based architectures [11]. They have large parameter spaces, which often reach hundreds of billions. They are transforming the field of Natural Language Processing (NLP) because their core functionality is based on the self-attention mechanism, which enables them to excel in both language understanding and language generation.

LLMs use a variety of Transformer architectures and pre-training strategies. These include decoder-only models (e.g., GPT-2, GPT-3), encoder-only models (e.g., BERT, RoBERTa), and encoder-decoder models such as BART. These architectures can process sequential data in a highly efficient manner, capturing complex textual dependencies while allowing for optimized parallelization. In addition, LLMs include prompting techniques and in-context learning that improve text generation by exploiting contextual cues. This capability enables them to generate coherent, contextually relevant responses, facilitating dynamic question-answer interactions [12].

2.3 Retrieval Augmented Generation

Pre-trained LLMs are excellent at acquiring large amounts of knowledge, but they are unable to update or extend their memory, which can lead to problems such as hallucinations. To reduce this problem, hybrid approaches such as Retrieval-Augmented Generation (RAG) have been introduced [13, 14]. The RAG framework combines retrieval models with generative LLMs to significantly improve the accuracy and relevance of generated responses.

Chatbots' ability to generate relevant responses relies primarily on retrievers, with generators playing a secondary role. With recent advances, LLMs have nearly perfected their ability to extract the necessary information from a given context and generate contextually appropriate responses.

As illustrated in Fig. 1, the RAG framework consists of three key components: the knowledge base, the retriever model, and the generator model.

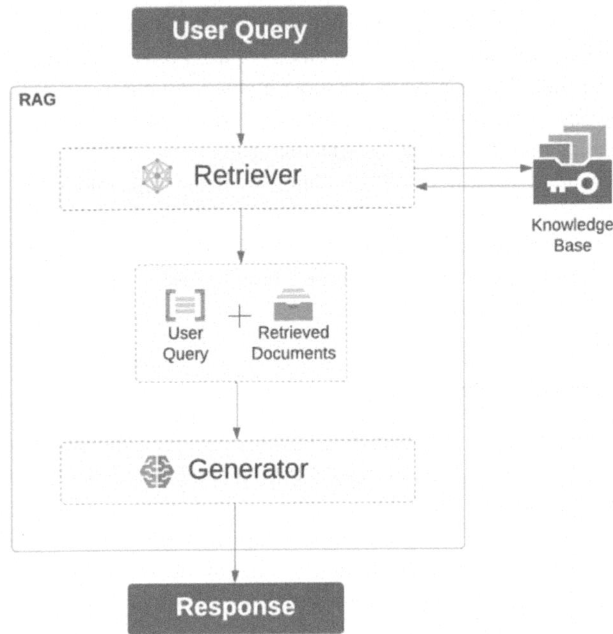

Fig. 1. Retrieval- and rule-based architecture

3 Methodology

3.1 Research Design

This section outlines our experimental setup to explore the potential and challenges of integrating LLM-based RAG into Esprit's projet 1A module. Our experiments are designed to evaluate the feasibility of using LLM-based RAG as a teaching companion.

The chatbot is called SDLearn. It is an educational companion specifically designed to support first year computer science engineering students in the Projet 1A module at Esprit. This module follows an active pedagogical approach rooted in problem-based learning and aims to guide students in the collaborative development of a video game in C during their second semester.

SDLearn includes several key features to enhance the learning experience. It automates the retrieval of educational resources by accessing ESPRIT's internal databases and relevant web content using scraping tools. Through advanced semantic analysis, the chatbot identifies and recommends the most relevant resources based on AI-driven models. It also provides intelligent, personalized responses to students' queries, ensuring tailored support. An easy-to-use, modern interface also facilitates seamless navigation and a streamlined learning experience.

3.2 Creating a Dataset

Leverage the Resources of the Project 1A Module

To help students throughout their projects, we offer a variety of official documents and educational materials. These resources include detailed tutorials, sample guidelines, workshops, presentations, module sheets, project briefs and best practices. SDLearn uses this content as the basis for personalized support. The aim is to tailor the learning experience based on the specific needs of the module, the desired learning outcomes and to provide guidance that is tailored to each student's needs.

Web Scraping for Sxternal Sducational Resources

The Project 1A module requires students to work in teams to develop a 2D video game using the SDL (Simple Direct Media Layer) library. The exploration of this library is a self-learning phase with only the support of a coach. However, we have noticed that some of the students are struggling with the overwhelming amount of resources available online, which can lead to anxiety. To address this, we have implemented web scraping to gather additional content from various online sources, including SDL documentation, programming tutorials and developer forums. This scraped content enriches the knowledge base with external insights and solutions, providing students with a wider range of information to support their learning.

Data Preprocessing

Both project 1A resources and externally scraped content are pre-processed to ensure that they are properly formatted and standardized for efficient retrieval. This process includes text cleaning, data segmentation, and preparation for embedding to ensure that the information is organized and optimized for effective use.

Storing the Embeddings in a Eector Database

We convert textual information from both the project 1A resources and scraped content into vectorized representations using embedding models text embedding 3 large. These embeddings are stored in a vector database Pinecone to allow similarity searches based on student queries.

3.3 RAG Architecture

The Fig. 2 illustrates the chatbot's functionality, demonstrating its ability to adapt to the context of the module and personalize the learning process. Leveraging the RAG framework, the chatbot retrieves relevant context from a vector database, integrating module-provided documentation with external resources. This approach ensures that students receive precise, contextually enriched responses to their queries related to game development.

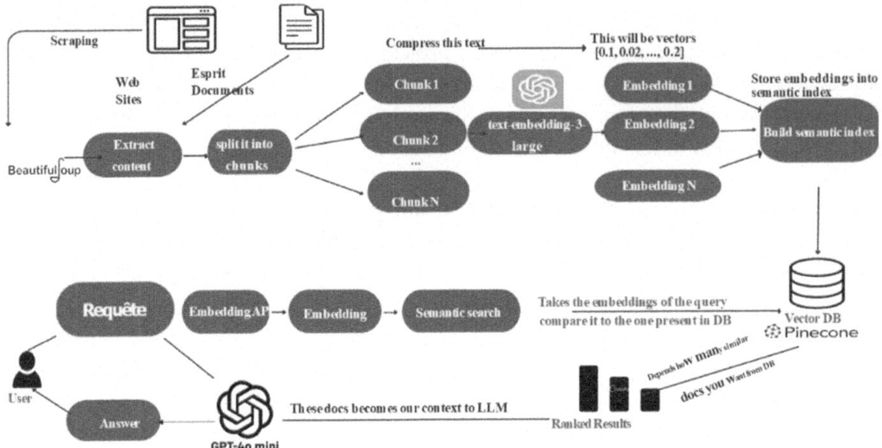

Fig. 2. SDLearn Chatbot Architecture

User

The chatbot is tailored to meet the needs of two distinct user groups: students and teachers, each with a dedicated interface and functionality, teachers and students, each with their own interface. The teacher interface enables them to manage student accounts by adding, modifying, viewing or deleting them. In addition, teachers can access student feedback and questions, allowing them to identify strengths and weaknesses in the learning process. Teachers, especially newcomers, can also benefit from the chatbot's capabilities. It offers answers to a wide range of questions, both technical (functionalities, functional prototypes, source code corrections, etc.) and pedagogical. The chatbot is multimodal, accepting both text and image-based questions. It provides comprehensive and versatile support. Once the account is created, each student receives a link with their account details, which they can then modify.

The chatbot can answer pedagogical questions (module structure, evaluation plan, grading weight, etc.) as well as technical questions related to video game development. But to be consistent with the intended learning results, the bot will not provide source code directly to the learner. Rather, they provide an algorithmic and methodical approach to solving a problem.

User Query

The system starts with a user query, typically related to a specific aspect of project development, such as game design, programming, or debugging. As the chatbot is multimodal, it accepts queries in the form of text, images or source code.

In the pilot phase, approximately 1,500 students interacted with the chatbot in a temporally distributed manner. To manage the cost associated with embedding generation, usage was limited to six questions per student per day. For improved reliability and system stability, the chatbot was deployed using a Microsoft Azure Business account.

Embedding Model

The user's query is processed through the embedding model, text-embedding-3-large, which converts the textual input into high-dimensional vector representations. These vectors capture the semantic meaning of the query, allowing for efficient similarity matching.

Vector Database

The vector representations of the user's query are used to search the Pinecone vector database. Pinecone stores embeddings of both Esprit-provided documents and external educational resources (obtained through web scraping). The database retrieves the top K relevant documents based on their similarity to the query.

Prompt Creation

The original query, combined with the relevant context retrieved from the vector database, is used to form a prompt. This prompt is designed to provide comprehensive and relevant information to answer the user's question or address their game development issue.

Language Model

The prompt is fed into the GPT-4o-mini, a powerful language model trained on a mix of public and synthetic datasets. The model generates responses that are accurate, detailed, and contextually grounded based on the prompt.

Answer Generation

The LLM generates a detailed response, offering solutions, code snippets, tutorials, or recommendations tailored to the user's query. The answer might involve step-by-step guidance on project programming, game design tips, or troubleshooting advice.

The Fig. 3 illustrate the user interfaces of the chatbot.

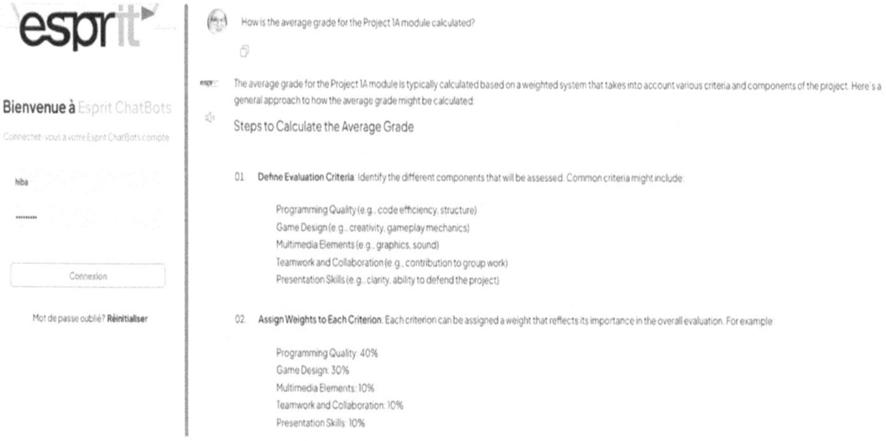

Fig. 3. User interfaces of the chatbot

4 Evaluation

RAG architectures have become the preferred approach for enriching LLMs with contextual information to reduce hallucinations. Yet, RAG systems are not immune to this problem, especially when the retrieval mechanism is unable to provide sufficient or relevant context, which then affects the generated responses of the LLM.

To systematically evaluate and reduce hallucinations in our RAG system, we leverage TruLens, a powerful evaluation tool designed to provide detailed feedback on the performance of language models, particularly in RAG systems. TruLens provides the ability to analyze and visualize the behavior of QA models, helping to identify and address potential shortcomings in the retrieval and generation processes. It helps in assessing the quality of responses by considering several dimensions:

- **Context relevance** Measures how relevant the response is to the given context or query. The first step in any RAG application is retrieval; ensuring the quality of this process is critical. Any retrieved context needs to be relevant to the input query, as it will directly affect how the LLM responds. If irrelevant information is included, it may contribute to hallucinations. TruLens facilitates the evaluation of context relevance by exploiting the structure of the serialized data set, allowing a more accurate assessment of the retrieval process.
- **Groundedness:** Ensures that the responses are based on actual retrieved documents. After the context is retrieved, it is then formed into an answer by an LLM. LLMs are often prone to stray from the facts provided, exaggerating or expanding to a correct-sounding answer. To verify the groundedness of our application, we can separate the response into individual claims and independently search for evidence that supports each within the retrieved context.
- **Answer relevance** Evaluate the response's overall relevance to the question. The last step, our response still needs to helpfully answer the original question. We can verify this by evaluating the relevance of the final response to the user input.

The Fig. 4 illustrate the RAG triad of metrics used in the evaluation framework.

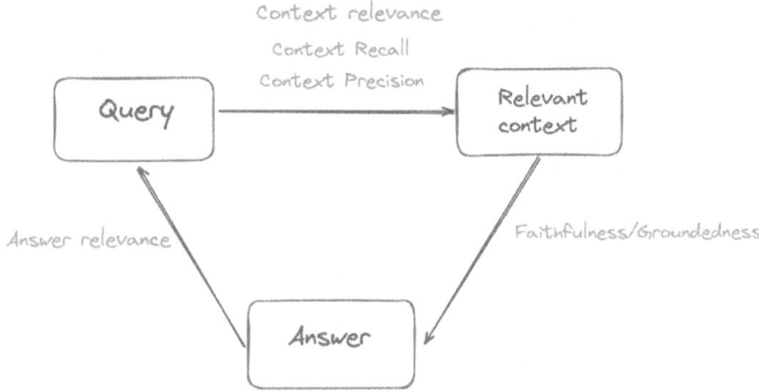

Fig. 4. RAG evaluation

4.1 Performance and Moderation Analysis of SDLearn-RAG vs SDLearn-Without RAG

This study compares two models SDLearn-RAG and SDLearn without-RAG analyzing their performance based on cost efficiency, relevance, latency, and moderation metrics. The SDLearn-RAG model utilizes retrieval-augmented generation (RAG), providing contextual information during query generation, while SDLearn-without-RAG operates without such augmentation. The results reveal key insights into their relative performance, particularly in handling moderation and cost efficiency.

- **Cost efficiency**: SDLearn-without-RAG proves more cost-efficient, with a total cost of $0.11 for 5 records, compared to $0.39 for SDLearn-RAG. The difference in cost is directly related to the token usage. SDLearn-without-RAG consumes 1.91k tokens, while SDLearn-RAG utilizes approximately 11.2k tokens. The use of additional tokens in SDLearn-RAG is attributed to the retrieval of external contextual data, which contributes to a more comprehensive, albeit costlier, response generation.
- **Latency:** Both models exhibit comparable average latencies, with values ranging from 5 to 14 s across the test samples. SDLearn-RAG demonstrates slightly higher latency due to its retrieval mechanism, but this latency remains within acceptable performance thresholds for real-time applications.
- **Moderation** SDLearn-RAG shows slightly higher reliability in moderation, particularly in handling complex queries that might touch upon sensitive content. For instance, the moderation for hate speech remains within acceptable limits across all records, though SDLearn-without-RAG occasionally flags slightly higher risks (e.g., 0.00016 vs. 0.0001).
- **Contextual relevance** The retrieval-augmented nature of SDLearn-RAG enhances the model's ability to provide contextually accurate and relevant answers, reflected in a relevance score of 0.8, compared to 1.0 for SDLearn-without-RAG. While the latter achieves perfect relevance, the inclusion of external context by SDLearn-RAG, despite its impact on cost and tokens, improves the depth and accuracy of the responses. Without retrieval, SDLearn-without-RAG may struggle with more complex or ambiguous queries, as it does not have access to external information that could enhance its responses. This leads to potential gaps in contextual accuracy, especially in cases where deeper knowledge is required.

5 Conclusion

Recent developments in AI and Generative AI have led to their integration into the field of education, opening up new possibilities for improving teaching and learning. Large Language Models (LLMs), with their advanced natural language processing capabilities, have further enhanced these capabilities by enabling sophisticated tasks such as text generation, comprehension, and interpretation.

Integrating adaptive, AI-based chatbots into education represents a turning point in how students will be supported throughout their academic journey. These chatbots offer personalized assistance, providing real-time answers, guiding students through complex topics, and suggesting resources tailored to their needs. These investments increase student engagement, ensure timely and tailored support, and contribute to a more effective and engaging learning experience. This transformation is poised to reshape the education landscape by providing students with more personalized, responsive, and effective guidance.

Building on this foundation, our study observed significant improvements in the LLM's ability to solve specific types of problems and provide accurate answers. However, we also identified limitations in enhancing its reasoning capabilities across all scenarios. To address these challenges, the most promising approach moving forward involves fine-tuning the LLM and implementing our proposed solutions to further enhance its performance and adaptability in educational applications. This includes refining dataset creation methods, optimizing interaction strategies, and incorporating advanced techniques like Corrective RAG, Graph RAG, and Hybrid RAG. By continuing to innovate and refine these strategies, we aim to expand the capabilities of LLMs in education, ultimately benefiting both students and educators.

In conclusion, while challenges remain the further advancement and improvement of adaptive chatbots hold immense promise for transforming education, offering more personalized and effective learning experiences for all.

References

1. Udupi, P.K., Malali, P., Noronha, H.: Big data integration for transition from e-learning to smart learning framework. In: Proceedings of the 3rd MEC International Conference on Big Data and Smart City (ICBDSC), pp. 1–4 (2016). https://doi.org/10.1109/ICBDSC.2016.7460379
2. Shemshack, A., Spector, J.M.: A systematic literature review of person alized learning terms (2020). https://doi.org/10.1186/s40561-020-00140-9 Smart Learning Environments
3. Kuhail, M.A., Alturki, N., Alramlawi, S., Alhejori, K.: Interacting with educational chatbots: a systematic review. Educ. Inf. Technol. **28**(1), 973–1018 (2023)
4. Kumar, J.A.: Educational chatbots for project-based learning: Investigating learning outcomes for a team-based design course. Int. J. Educ. Technol. High. Educ. **18**(1) (2021). https://doi.org/10.1186/s41239-021-00302-w
5. Meyer, J.G., et al.: ChatGPT and large language models in academia: opportunities and challenges. BioData Mining **16**(1), 20 (2023). https://doi.org/10.1186/s13040-023-00339
6. Orenstrakh, M.S., Karnalim, O., Suarez, C.A., Liut, M.: Detecting LLM generated text in computing education: A comparative study for ChatGPT cases (2023). arXiv preprint arXiv:2307.07411
7. Kaddour, J., Harris, J., Mozes, M., Bradley, H., Raileanu, R., McHardy, R.: Challenges and applications of large language models (2023). arXiv preprint arXiv:2307.10169 (2023)
8. Weizenbaum, J.: ELIZA—a computer program for the study of natural language communication between man and machine. Commun. ACM **9**(1), 36–45 (1966). https://doi.org/10.1145/365153.365168
9. Wallace, R.S.: The Anatomy of A.L.I.C.E. In Springer eBooks, pp. 181–210 (2007b). https://doi.org/10.1007/978-1-4020-6710-5_13
10. Sutskever, I., Vinyals, O., Le, Q.V.: Sequence to sequence learning with neural networks. In: Proceedings of the 27th International Conference on Neural Information Processing Systems -Volume 2 (NIPS'14). MIT Press, Cambridge, MA, USA, pp. 3104–3112 (2014)
11. Vaswani, A., et al.: Attention is all you need. Adv. Neural Inf. Process. Syst. **30** (2017)
12. Chang, Y., et al.: A survey on evaluation of large language models. ACM Trans. Intell. Syst. Technol. **15**(3), 1–45 (2024)

13. Lewis, P., et al.: Retrieval augmented generation for knowledge-intensive NLP tasks. Adv. Neural. Inf. Process. Syst. **33**, 9459–9474 (2020)
14. Petroni, F., Rocktäschel, T., Lewis, P., Bakhtin, A., Wu, Y., Miller, A.H., Riedel, S.: Language models as knowledge bases? arXiv preprint arXiv:1909.01066 (2019)

A Systematic Review of Artificial Intelligence in Predicting Undergraduate Degree Completion

Lizzy Ofusori[1(✉)], Tebogo Bokaba[2], and Eustace M. Dogo[3]

[1] Centre for Applied Data Science, University of Johannesburg, Gauteng, South Africa
lofusori@uj.ac.za

[2] Department of Applied Information Systems, University of Johannesburg, Gauteng, South Africa
tbokaba@uj.ac.za

[3] Department of Computer Engineering, Federal University of Technology, Minna, Niger State, Nigeria
eustace.dogo@futminna.edu.ng

Abstract. Artificial Intelligence (AI) is increasingly being leveraged to predict undergraduate degree completion, with the goal of enhancing educational outcomes and student support services. This study systematically reviews the AI techniques employed in this domain and explores how student characteristics have been effectively linked to academic success. Following PRISMA guidelines, a systematic literature review was conducted using the Scopus database. Out of 221 peer-reviewed articles initially identified, 51 were deemed relevant after screening. The findings reveal that a variety of AI methods drawing on academic performance, demographic factors, and behavioral data have been successfully applied to forecast degree completion among undergraduates.

Keywords: Undergraduate degree · higher education · Artificial Intelligence · PRISMA · degree completion

1 Introduction

Student assessment is crucial in determining eligibility for degree completion, as it helps in identifying students who are likely to fail or pass [1]. While degree completion is a major milestone, it can be challenging to achieve. According to Pelima, Sukmana and Rosmansyah [2], student retention and timely graduation have continued to remain a major concern for administrators and faculty. Moreso, delayed graduation can lead to increased financial burdens for both students and the university. Graduating on time means completing all required coursework and the number of credits within the expected timeframe for the degree program. However, Mabel and Britton [3], using administrative data from Florida and Ohio to conduct an event history analysis on the dropout process, found that one-third of college dropouts left after completing three-quarters or more of the credits needed for a bachelor's degree. In addition, undergraduates are also taking longer to earn baccalaureate degrees, particularly at public institutions in the District of Columbia [4].

F. Kamoun et al. (Eds.): AFRICATEK 2025, LNICST 676, pp. 450–465, 2026.
https://doi.org/10.1007/978-3-032-16635-7_29

In developing countries where higher education institutions often face distinct and pressing challenges, the issue of predicting undergraduate degree completion is particularly significant [5]. High dropout rates not only undermine institutional performance but also represent a significant loss of human potential and financial investment for both students and governments [6]. Similarly, resource constraints such as limited access to academic support services, inadequate infrastructure, and overburdened faculty make it more difficult for institutions to proactively support struggling students [5]. Moreover, educational equity is a major concern in many developing countries, where students from disadvantaged backgrounds often face systemic barriers to degree completion [5].

To support struggling students, higher institutions are implementing academic intervention plans. These plans, based on student performance predictions, also benefit school administrators and stakeholders by guiding the development and improvement of educational interventions [7]. For example, the applications of the data-intensive approaches have been used to predict student examination performance [8], create learning prediction models [9], and develop feedback dashboards [10]. Those applications have significantly improved the understanding of students' learning process and performance.

However, while several systematic literature review (SLR) studies have explored various AI techniques used for academic performance predictions [1, 2, 11], there are limited studies that have comprehensively explored the dynamic nature of student behavior and circumstances over time, particularly for undergraduate students. Also, students' trajectories often change due to personal, academic, or environmental factors that are not always captured in static data snapshots used in many studies. Moreover, while academic attributes like grades and attendance are commonly used to predict student success, non-academic factors such as behavior, demographics, and financial status can also significantly impact degree completion but are overlooked by most SLR studies. This represents a gap in the literature and offers an opportunity for this study to address. Thus, this paper contributes by providing a comprehensive review of the different AI techniques used to predict undergraduate degree completion. It also highlights how researchers have successfully mapped relationships between student characteristics and their academic outcomes. The following three research questions (RQs) were posed:

RQ1. What are the various AI techniques used to predict undergraduate degree completion?

RQ2. What are the variables and datasets used to predict undergraduate degree completion?

RQ3. What are the challenges encountered in predicting undergraduate degree completion?

The paper is structured as follows. Section 1 above briefly introduced the concept of the study. Section 2 explains the research methods employed. Section 3 presents and discusses the findings of the study as they relate to the research questions posed. Section 4 presents the limitation and future research, and Sect. 5 concludes the study.

2 Method

An SLR was conducted to examine the various AI techniques used in predicting undergraduate degree completion. An SLR employs structured methods to collect, analyze, and interpret secondary data that is directly related to the research question/s [12]. This process allows for the collection of pertinent evidence on a given topic that meets pre-defined eligibility criteria, providing answers to the formulated research questions [13]. Hence, this method was chosen to gather and summarize current evidence on various AI techniques used in predicting undergraduate degree completion, which was then analyzed to inform how the educational sector can leverage its benefits.

2.1 Sample Search Strategy

This study data was obtained from the Scopus database accessed on the 23rd of August 2024. The Scopus database was selected due to its comprehensive coverage, high-quality content, and advanced analytical tools compared to other databases [14]. According to Baas, Schotten, Plume, Côté and Karimi [15], wider coverage is beneficial for mapping out smaller research areas. This extensive coverage is particularly important in the context of AI. Moreover, articles were assessed and screened for eligibility using the following basic search string applied to all searchable fields of the Scopus database.

("Higher Education" OR "Undergraduate Studies" OR "Tertiary Education" OR "University Education") AND ("Degree Completion" OR "Graduation" OR "Academic Achievement" OR "Graduation Rates" OR "Degree Attainment") AND ("Machine Learning" OR "Artificial Intelligence" OR "Deep Learning" OR "Neural Networks" OR "Natural Language Processing")

2.2 Inclusion and Exclusion Criteria

The inclusion and exclusion criteria are presented in Table 1. Using the Preferred Reporting Items for Systematic Reviews and Meta-Analyses (PRISMA) guidelines as a guide, a total of 221 articles were identified in the Scopus database. The PRISMA standard includes identification, screening, eligibility, and inclusion [16].

As presented in Fig. 1, the PRISMA framework consists of a checklist and a flow diagram to help ensure the transparent and complete reporting of research. The 221 records were screened for eligibility. Automation tools removed 119 articles, 28 were excluded based on title and keyword criteria, and 12 were excluded based on abstracts alone. In addition, 2 non-English articles were excluded, and 9 articles that did not align with the thematic area were removed. Ultimately, 51 articles were successfully retrieved and included in the final analysis.

The annual publication count is presented in Table 2. This table provides a summary of research papers published between 2013 and 2024, grouped by the year of publication, author(s), and the number of papers. Each year lists the key authors who contributed to the publications. The paper count indicates the number of papers published each year. For example, 1 paper was published in 2013, 3 papers in 2018, and so on. Also, the percentage count reflects the percentage of total papers published during that specific year. For instance, 11 papers published in 2019 constitute 22% of the total papers. It is important to note that most publications occurred between 2019 and 2022, with the highest percentage (27.45%) in 2021. The publishers include IEEE, Elsevier, Taylor & Francis and Springer Nature.

Table 1. Inclusion and Exclusion Criteria

S/No	Inclusion	Exclusion
1	The full text of the study is available	The publication includes abstracts, corrections, data papers, book reviews, lecture notes, proposals and letters
2	The study is peer-reviewed	The paper is less than 6 pages in length
3	The study is written in English	The full text of the publication is not available
4	Articles published between 2013–2024	Publication from a doctoral symposium
5	The focus of the publication is on using AI in predicting undergraduate degree completion	Research that does not employ AI, machine learning (ML) and deep learning (DL) techniques
6	Subject areas: Computer Science, Engineering, Decision Science and Multidisciplinary	Publications that do not focus on undergraduate degree programs

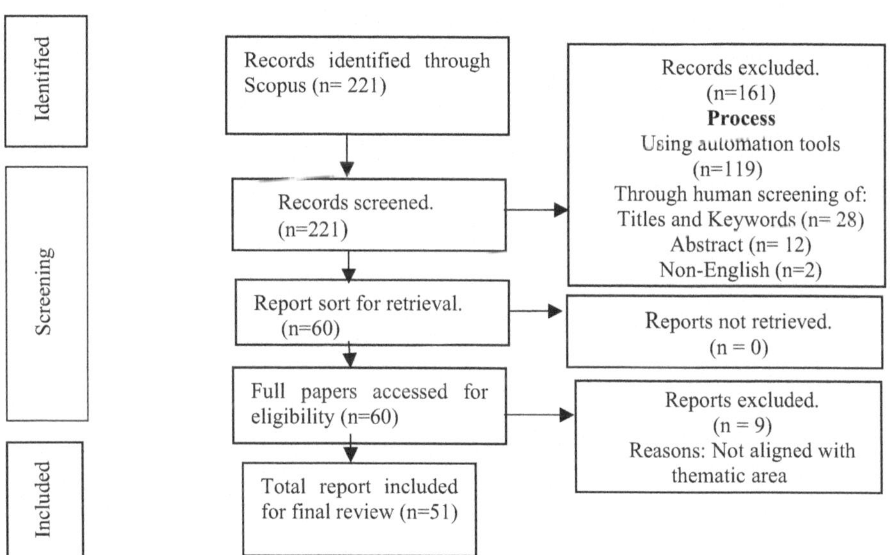

Fig. 1. PRISMA flow diagram

The 51 records obtained were subsequently classified into 3 major document types (as depicted in Table 3). The data extracted were synthesized using the core themes identified. Thematic synopsis was crucial in examining the various techniques used to predict undergraduate degree completion. In addition, two independent researchers were consulted to extract data from the selected research papers based on the study's RQs. The data extracted by the two researchers were compared, and their findings were discussed.

Table 2. Distribution of reviewed articles included in the study by year of publication

Year of publication	Authors	Paper count	
		Number of papers	Percentage count
2013	[17]	1	1.96%
2015	[18]	1	1.96%
2016	[19]	1	1.96%
2018	[20–22]	3	5.88%
2019	[23–33]	11	21.57%
2020	[34–38]	5	9.8%
2021	[39–52]	14	27.45%
2022	[7, 11, 53–60]	10	19.6%
2023	[61, 62]	3	5.88%
2024	[2, 63]	2	3.92%

Disparities in studies can be minimized by mutual agreement among the researchers involved in the study, who review their codes to ensure their consistency and relevance [64]. Table 3 presents the distribution of the reviewed research papers by document type; it shows the number of papers on AI in predicting undergraduate degree completion. Most articles (92.2%) were published in journals, followed by book chapters (3.9%), and conference proceedings (3.9%).

Table 3. Summary of the reviewed research papers by document type

Reviewed papers	Number of articles	Percentage
Journals	47	92.2%
Book chapters	2	3.9%
Conference proceedings	2	3.9%

3 Findings and Discussion

This section provides a detailed discussion of the data extracted from the reviewed research papers. The papers were mapped as they related to each research question and are presented in Tables 4, 5, and 6 respectively

3.1 AI Techniques Used to Predict Undergraduate Degree Completion

In response to RQ1, this subsection discusses the various AI algorithms used to predict undergraduate degree completion. Likewise, it highlights the data resources utilized, which are predominantly learning management systems (LMS) and student information systems (SIS). According to Pelima, Sukmana and Rosmansyah [2], AI techniques have been widely applied in predicting undergraduate degree completion, leveraging various types of data, such as academic performance, demographic information, and behavioral patterns. Techniques such as decision trees (DT), random forests (RF), support vector machines (SVM), artificial neural networks (ANN), and logistic regression (LR) have been employed to build predictive models that identify students at risk of not completing their degrees [1, 6, 65]. In this subsection, AI techniques and algorithms used by various authors are discussed and summarized in Table 4.

SVM: is widely recognized as one of the most reliable and effective techniques in various ML applications [1]. Several studies utilized SVM due to their robust classification capabilities, especially in educational contexts where distinguishing between different student outcomes is crucial [21, 34, 40–42, 53]. For example, Liao, Zingaro, Thai, Alvarado, Griswold and Porter [26] applied SVM to predict student performance and identify at-risk students. Figueroa-Cañas and Sancho-Vinuesa [35] utilized SVM for predicting student dropout rates in online learning environments. Alcaraz, Martínez-Rodrigo, Zangróniz and Rieta [43] employed SVM to predict student academic success by analyzing a range of academic and behavioral data. Singelmann and Ewert [54] used SVM to predict student retention and graduation rates. All the data sources used primarily consisted of LMS interaction data, allowing the models to make accurate predictions about student performance, retention, and dropout rates.

RF: Akçapınar, Altun and Aşkar [27] applied the RF technique to classify students into different risk categories based on their likelihood of failing or dropping out of a course. The model considered various features derived from learning analytics data, including students' online interactions, assignment completion rates, quiz scores, and other academic activities. The study further developed a reliable early-warning system for identifying students at risk of academic failure. This early-warning system aims to provide timely interventions by detecting patterns in students' online behavior that correlate with poor academic performance, enabling educators to offer support before students reach critical points of failure. Similarly, Xing, Du, Bakhshi, Chiu and Du [39] employed the RF technique in designing a transferable predictive model for online learning. In addition, Demeter, Dorodchi, Al-Hossami, Benedict, Slattery Walker, and Smail [11] developed an ML algorithm, specifically RF, to accurately predict if and when first-time-in-college undergraduates will graduate based on admissions, academic, and financial aid records two to six semesters after matriculation. The model was able to classify students' graduation outcomes with an accuracy of up to 79% overall, with up to 92% accuracy in predicting whether a student would graduate or not, and 81% accuracy in predicting whether graduation would be within 4 years or in more than 4 years.

ANN: Qu, Li, Zhang and Wang [22] utilized ANN to predict student academic performance. The ANN model was designed to process various input features related to students' academic and behavioral data, and it was trained to classify students based on their likelihood of achieving specific academic outcomes. Jiao, Ouyang, Zhang and Alavi [7] employed ANN to forecast student dropout rates in higher education institutions. The ANN technique was trained to recognize patterns in student data that indicated a higher risk of dropping out, allowing for early intervention by educators. Ghorbani and Ghousi [38] applied ANN for predicting student success in engineering courses. Their model analyzed input features, such as previous academic performance and student behavior in online courses to predict outcomes like course completion and grades. Similarly, Xing, Du, Bakhshi, Chiu and Du [39] used ANN to identify students at risk of failing in massive open online courses (MOOCs). Their model analyzed complex patterns in students' interaction data with the course content and assessments to predict who might struggle to complete the course. Also, Deeva, De Smedt and De Weerdt [55] utilized ANN to predict student retention in blended learning environments. Their model was trained to identify students who were at risk of dropping out by analyzing a wide range of data points, including both online and offline engagement metrics. The data sources ranged from LMS to SIS.

LR: Forecasts the probabilities of two or more results and permits categorical estimations [6]. Livieris, Kotsilieris, Tampakas and Pintelas [28] applied LR to predict student academic performance, focusing specifically on binary outcomes such as pass/fail in courses. Sghir, Adadi and Lahmer [61] utilized LR to predict student dropout rates in higher education. The model was designed to identify students at risk of leaving before completing their studies by analyzing key predictors such as academic performance and engagement levels. The study by Hooshyar, Yang, Pedaste and Huang [34] employed LR to forecast student success in programming courses. The LR technique was used to predict whether students would pass or fail based on features such as previous academic performance, participation in coding exercises, and interaction with course materials. Chen, Huang, Chen, Su and Yur-Austin [62] also applied LR to predict student retention and dropout rates in online learning environments. The model was trained to identify factors that contribute to students' likelihood of dropping out, using a combination of academic, behavioral, and demographic data.

K-Nearest Neighbor (KNN): Herrera, Crespo, Baena and Burgos [29] employed the KNN technique to predict student academic performance. KNN was used to classify students based on their likelihood of succeeding or failing in a course by analyzing the similarities between their performance and that of other students. The technique identifies the '*k*' nearest neighbors in the dataset and classifies the target student based on the majority class of these neighbors.

Bidirectional Long Short-Term Memory (BLSTM) and Condition Random Field (CRF): Uliyan, Aljaloud, Alkhalil, Al Amer, Mohamed and Alogali [50] used DL techniques such as the CRF and (BLSTM to study each student's label and those students whose retention was at risk. Their method and framework focused on first-year students' retention and graduation rate for the undergraduates across the analyzed period. The findings indicate that prediction of student retention is possible with an accuracy of over 0.85 in most scenarios, and with FP (false positive) rates ranging from 0.05 to 0.10 in most cases. Souai, Mihoub, Tarhouni, Zidi, Krichen and Mahfoudhi [59] also conducted a study using the BLSTM approach to model the learning behaviors of students in a virtual learning environment, predict their performance, and prevent students at risk from failure. The model shows high accuracy (96.90%) when assessment weights and scores are included in the input features. This finding demonstrates the importance of a student's learning path during the module in obtaining excellent academic results.

Fuzzy AI-Based Model: Bressane, Spalding, Zwirn, Loureiro, Bankole, Negri, de Brito Junior, Formiga, Medeiros, and Pampuch Bortolozo [58] utilized a fuzzy AI-based model to predict student performance and assess retention risk, specifically within engineering education. The model was designed to make predictions with small datasets. Historical records of students' grades and retention from the last 5 years before the COVID-19 pandemic were used. The findings show that the fuzzy AI-based model was capable of providing an accurate prediction, confirming the research hypothesis. A study by Petra and Aziz [49] proposed a fuzzy expert system to investigate and analyze students' performance at a university in Malaysia. Fuzzy logic was developed with selected attributes of student assessment performance by using MATLAB software. In this method, students' characteristics through assessment (knowledge, problem-solving skills, etc.) were the weighting factors for evaluating their academic performance and personality development. Subsequently, an expert system using fuzzy logic based on the Mamdani technique was designed and tested on students' real mark samples.

Hybrid/Ensemble Learning: Hybrid techniques refer to the combination of multiple AI algorithms [52]. Adejo and Connolly [20] investigated and compared the use of multiple data sources, different classifiers, and ensemble methods of classifiers in predicting student academic performance. The three different classification techniques used in the study were DT, ANN, and SVM. In addition, the ensemble technique used in the study was stacking (stacked generalization). The study by Pandey and Taruna [19] proposed an integrated model for predicting the academic performance of students, specifically in an engineering discipline. Three complementing classifiers, namely, KNN, Aggregating one-dependence estimators (AODE), DT, were integrated to form a single composite model (KNNAD) based on voting strategy. This composite model was tested against three students' datasets, and results reflected consistent behavior and performance accuracy. Similarly, Saleem, Ullah, Fakieh, and Kateb [51] experimented with five ML models (DT, RF, Naïve Bayes (NB), KNN, and gradient boosting trees (GBT)), using a stacking and voting approach. The dataset used was from an LMS, which provides several features predicting students' performance. Their proposed model has shown successful implementation of ML techniques to predict the students' performance. The overall F1 score of the single models was recorded as follows: DT (0.675), RF (0.777), GBT (0.714), NB (0.654), and KNN (0.664). The results of this study emphasize that the ensemble approach is feasible and can be more effective in improving prediction accuracy.

Sentiment Annotations, Entity Annotations, Text Summarization, and Topic Modeling: The study by Shaik, Tao, Li, Dann, McDonald, Redmond and Galligan [60] focused on analyzing large amounts of textual information, such as students' assignments and forum posts, using natural language processing (NLP) methodologies: sentiment annotations, entity annotations, text summarization, and topic modelling that allow for the quick identification of students at risk. The results concerning students' emotional activity suggest that this information can be considered a predictor of early school dropout.

Table 4. AI techniques widely used for degree completion prediction

S/No	AI subset	AI technique	Data source	Authors
1	Machine learning	RF	SIS	[11, 27, 39]
2		SVM	LMS	[21, 26, 34, 35, 40–43, 53, 54]
3		LR	LMS and SIS	[28, 61, 62]
4		KNN	LMS and SIS	[29]
5		Stacking (DT, ANN and SVM) KNNAD (DT, KNN and AODE) Stacking and Voting (DT, RF, NB, KNN, GBT)	LMS SIS SIS	[20] [19] [51]
6	Deep learning	ANN	LMS and SIS	[7, 22, 38, 39, 55]
7		BLSTM and CRF	SIS and LMS	[50, 59]
8	Fuzzy logic	Fuzzy AI-based model	LMS and SIS	[49, 58]
9	Natural Language Processing	Sentiment annotations, Entity annotations, Text summarization, and Topic modelling	LMS	[60]

3.2 Variables and Datasets Employed to Predict Undergraduate Degree Completion

RQ2 investigated the variables and datasets used to predict undergraduate degree completion. According to Pelima, Sukmana and Rosmansyah [2], several studies have identified various characteristics that impact prediction accuracy. While these traits may be labeled differently, many share similar meanings and can be grouped together. Examples include students' educational history, demographic information, social network data, behavioral factors, extracurricular activities, school structure, academic performance, and socioeconomic background data related to their families. In this study, three major variables were identified: academic, demographic, and behavioral. In addition, some of these variables are hybrids, combining features from both academic and behavioral variables, as well as from academic and demographic variables, as summarized in Table 5.

The academic variable comprises many features that depict students' performance in a particular course, such as assignment details, class information, attendance records and grades [28, 35–37, 56]. On the other hand, the behavioral variable captures information about students' activities and behaviors, both within the LMS and through physical interactions. This variable encompasses features such as logins, number of clicks, library interactions, learning frequency, attendance calculations, and emotional responses during online learning [23, 24, 30, 57, 66]. The demographic variable includes various socio-demographic factors such as gender, age, ethnicity, major of study, marital status, household income, grade point average (GPA), full-time or part-time student status, parents' education level, and financial reliance status [25, 33, 66, 67].

Integrating academic and behavioral features helps create more comprehensive models that capture both the cognitive and engagement aspects of student success. Ghorbani and Ghousi [38] integrated academic and behavioral data using ML techniques such as ANN, RF, and KNN, among others, to predict student success in engineering courses. Hooshyar, Yang, Pedaste and Huang [34] combined behavioral and academic data in their KNN model to predict student performance in programming courses, highlighting the importance of addressing both academic and behavioral factors. Also, integrating academic and demographic variables, e.g., grades (GPA) with demographic information (e.g., age, gender, socioeconomic status), allows for more nuanced and accurate predictions about student success. Livieris, Kotsilieris, Tampakas and Pintelas [28] combined academic data such as GPA and course grades with socio-economic variables in an LR technique to predict student success. This hybrid approach enabled the model to account for the influence of financial challenges on academic performance. Moreover, Sghir, Adadi and Lahmer [61] incorporated gender and ethnicity data into their LR model, alongside academic variables like test scores, to predict degree completion. This approach highlighted the different challenges faced by students from diverse backgrounds.

Table 5. Variables and datasets used in predicting degree completion.

Variables	Datasets/Features	Author
Academic	Grade level, grade point average (GPA), assignment details, and attendance records	[35–37, 56]
Demographic	Age, gender, place of birth, ethnicity, marital status, full-time or part-time student status, major of study, number of courses per semester, parents' household income and education level of parents	[25, 33, 66, 67]
Behavioral	Number of class logins, time spent, Wi-Fi data indicating students' movements, emotional responses during online learning interaction, visit resources, library interactions, and discussion	[23, 24, 30, 57, 66]
Academic and behavioral	GPA, time spent, attendance calculations and number of class logins	[34, 38]

(continued)

Table 5. *(continued)*

Variables	Datasets/Features	Author
Academic and demographic	GPA and course grades, gender and ethnicity	[28, 61]

3.3 Challenges Encountered in Predicting Undergraduate Degree Completion

RQ3 concerned the challenges encountered when using AI techniques in predicting undergraduate degree completion. While this study clearly demonstrates that predicting undergraduate degree completion has significant potential to benefit students, educators, and academic institutions, there are certain challenges and limitations [68], which are summarized in Table 6.

Predictive models used to predict undergraduate degree completion can inadvertently introduce or perpetuate biases, particularly if the training data reflects existing inequalities [43, 63, 69]. This can lead to unfair predictions that disproportionately affect certain demographic groups [2]. Ortigosa, Carro, Bravo-Agapito, Lizcano, Alcolea and Blanco [32] and Hussain, Zhu, Zhang, Abidi and Ali [31] highlighted some shortcomings, such as algorithmic choices and limited model interpretability, in the modeling approaches. Additionally, data quality and availability pose significant challenges. Data fragmentation across different institutional systems complicates issues such as, when student information is stored separately in academic, financial, and administrative databases with inconsistent formats, or when outdated records lead to inaccuracies in performance tracking and decision-making [47]. According to Slade and Prinsloo [17], collecting and using student data for predictive purposes raises privacy concerns. It has been found that several studies have not adequately addressed concerns related to privacy and consent [26, 46]. Moreover, there is a significant concern about the reliance of many of these studies on a single dataset, which raises questions about the broader applicability of their findings [48].

Ethical implications also arise, as labeling students as "at risk" may lead to stigmatization or unfair treatment in resource allocation prediction [44, 45]. While early identification of struggling students can enable timely support and intervention, it can also lead to unintended consequences, such as stigmatization, where students may internalize negative labels or be perceived differently by educators and peers. This can affect their academic self-concept, motivation, and engagement [45]. Moreover, resource allocation based on predictive labels may result in biased or inequitable distribution of support services, especially if the models are trained on data that reflects historical or systemic inequalities [17]. For instance, students from underrepresented or disadvantaged backgrounds may be disproportionately flagged as "at risk" due to contextual factors beyond their control, leading to discriminatory outcomes. Furthermore, the generalizability of these models is limited, as predictions based on one student group may not apply to diverse populations or different institutional contexts, making scalability difficult [18].

Table 6. Challenges encountered using AI techniques in predicting undergraduate degree completion

Authors	Model accuracy and bias	Data quality and availability	Ethical considerations	Biased or inequitable distribution of support services	Generalization
[43]	✓				
[48]		✓			
[45]			✓		
[47]		✓			
[46]		✓			
[18]					✓
[26]		✓			
[63]	✓				
[31]	✓				
[32]	✓				
[2]	✓	✓			
[17]		✓		✓	
[69]	✓				
[44]			✓		

4 Limitation and Future Research

The limitation of the study is the possibility of overlooking relevant research due to database constraints and biases in data extraction. While the Scopus database was used, other databases might contain pertinent studies, restricting the generalizability of our findings. Nevertheless, given the comprehensive nature of the initial search within the Scopus database, the study offers valuable insights into the domain's key trends.

Future research should prioritize addressing biases in AI models, particularly those related to demographic factors such as race, gender, and socio-economic status. Ensuring fairness and reducing discriminatory outcomes are crucial for the ethical application of AI in education. Additionally, future research should focus on how AI predictions can be used to design personalized interventions. Exploring how these predictions can be translated into actionable strategies to support students at risk of not completing their degrees is a critical area of study. As AI models rely heavily on student data, future research must prioritize ethical considerations and data privacy. Establishing clear guidelines for the responsible use of student data is essential for maintaining trust and compliance with regulations. Moreover, other databases such as Web of Science (WoS) and EBSCOhost can also be explored. Integrating several databases increases the depth and accuracy of literature reviews. In addition, a granular comparison of each model's performance is recommended for future research.

5 Conclusion

The use of AI in predicting undergraduate degree completion presents a promising avenue for enhancing educational outcomes. By leveraging diverse data sources and advanced techniques, AI can provide valuable insights into student performance, enabling early interventions and personalized support. However, to fully realize its potential, it is essential to address challenges related to data quality, bias, interpretability, and ethical considerations. As research in this field progresses, AI-driven models such as generative AI and explainable AI can become powerful tools for educators and institutions, ultimately contributing to improved student success and a more equitable educational landscape.

References

1. Issah, I., Appiah, O., Appiahene, P., Inusah, F.: A systematic review of the literature on machine learning application of determining the attributes influencing academic performance. Decis. Anal. J. **7**, 100204 (2023)
2. Pelima, L.R., Sukmana, Y., Rosmansyah, Y.: Predicting university student graduation using academic performance and machine learning: a systematic literature review. IEEE Access **12**, 23451–23465 (2024)
3. Mabel, Z., Britton, T.A.: Leaving late: understanding the extent and predictors of college late departure. Soc. Sci. Res. **69**, 34–51 (2018)
4. National Center for Education Statistics (NCES): Undergraduate retention and graduation rates', U.S. Department of Education, Institute of Education Sciences. https://nces.ed.gov/programs/coe/indicator/ctr/undergrad-retention-graduation. Accessed 30 Aug 2024
5. Mustafa, M.N., Chowdhury, L., Kamal, M.S.: Students dropout prediction for intelligent system from tertiary level in developing country. In: 2012 International Conference on Informatics, Electronics & Vision (ICIEV), pp. 113–118. IEEE (2012)
6. Fahd, K., Venkatraman, S., Miah, S.J., Ahmed, K.: Application of machine learning in higher education to assess student academic performance, at-risk, and attrition: a meta-analysis of literature. Educ. Inform. Technol. 1–33 (2022)
7. Jiao, P., Ouyang, F., Zhang, Q., Alavi, A.H.: Artificial intelligence-enabled prediction model of student academic performance in online engineering education. Artif. Intell. Rev. **55**(8), 6321–6344 (2022)
8. Agudo-Peregrina, Á.F., Iglesias-Pradas, S., Conde-González, M.Á., Hernández-García, Á.: Can we predict success from log data in VLEs? Classification of interactions for learning analytics and their relation with performance in VLE-supported F2F and online learning. Comput. Hum. Behav. **31**, 542–550 (2014)
9. Paquette, L., Baker, R.S., de Carvalho, A., Ocumpaugh, J.: Cross-system transfer of machine learned and knowledge engineered models of gaming the system. In: User Modeling, Adaptation and Personalization: 23rd International Conference, UMAP 2015, Dublin, Ireland, June 29--July 3, 2015. Proceedings 23, pp. 183–194. Springer International Publishing (2015)
10. Jivet, I., Scheffel, M., Specht, M., Drachsler, H.: License to evaluate: preparing learning analytics dashboards for educational practice. In: Proceedings of the 8th International Conference on Learning Analytics and Knowledge, pp. 31–40 (2018)

11. Demeter, E., Dorodchi, M., Al-Hossami, E., Benedict, A., Slattery Walker, L., Smail, J.: Predicting first-time-in-college students' degree completion outcomes. High. Educ. 1–21 (2022)
12. Mohamed Shaffril, H.A., Samsuddin, S.F., Abu Samah, A.: The ABC of systematic literature review: the basic methodological guidance for beginners. Qual. Quant. **55**, 1319–1346 (2021)
13. Sarkis-Onofre, R., Catalá-López, F., Aromataris, E., Lockwood, C.: How to properly use the PRISMA Statement. Syst. Rev. **10**, 1–3 (2021)
14. Schotten, M., Meester, W.J., Steiginga, S., Ross, C.A.: A brief history of Scopus: The world's largest abstract and citation database of scientific literature. Research Analytics (Auerbach Publications), pp. 31–58 (2017)
15. Baas, J., Schotten, M., Plume, A., Côté, G., Karimi, R.: Scopus as a curated, high-quality bibliometric data source for academic research in quantitative science studies. Quant. Sci. Stud. **1**(1), 377–386 (2020)
16. Albhirat, M.M., et al.: The PRISMA statement in enviropreneurship study: a systematic literature and a research agenda. Cleaner Eng. Technol. **18**, 100721 (2024)
17. Slade, S., Prinsloo, P.: Learning analytics: ethical issues and dilemmas. Am. Behav. Sci. **57**(10), 1510–1529 (2013)
18. Lakkaraju, H., et al.: A machine learning framework to identify students at risk of adverse academic outcomes. In: Proceedings of the 21th ACM SIGKDD International Conference on Knowledge Discovery and Data Mining, pp. 1909–1918 (2015)
19. Pandey, M., Taruna, S.: Towards the integration of multiple classifier pertaining to the Student's performance prediction. Perspect. Sci. **8**, 364–366 (2016)
20. Adejo, O.W., Connolly, T.: Predicting student academic performance using multi-model heterogeneous ensemble approach. J. Appl. Res. High. Educ. **10**(1), 61–75 (2018)
21. Kausar, S., Huahu, X., Hussain, I., Wenhao, Z., Zahid, M.: Integration of data mining clustering approach in the personalized E-learning system. IEEE Access **6**, 72724–72734 (2018)
22. Qu, S., Li, K., Zhang, S., Wang, Y.: Predicting achievement of students in smart campus. IEEE Access **6**, 60264–60273 (2018)
23. Akram, A., et al.: Predicting students' academic procrastination in blended learning course using homework submission data. IEEE Access **7**, 102487–102498 (2019)
24. Jokhan, A., Sharma, B., Singh, S.: Early warning system as a predictor for student performance in higher education blended courses. Stud. High. Educ. **44**(11), 1900–1911 (2019)
25. Fernandes, E., Holanda, M., Victorino, M., Borges, V., Carvalho, R., Van Erven, G.: Educational data mining: predictive analysis of academic performance of public school students in the capital of Brazil. J. Bus. Res. **94**, 335–343 (2019)
26. Liao, S.N., Zingaro, D., Thai, K., Alvarado, C., Griswold, W.G., Porter, L.: A robust machine learning technique to predict low-performing students. ACM Trans. Comput. Educ. (TOCE) **19**(3), 1–19 (2019)
27. Akçapınar, G., Altun, A., Aşkar, P.: Using learning analytics to develop early-warning system for at-risk students. Int. J. Educ. Technol. High. Educ. **16**(1), 1–20 (2019)
28. Livieris, I.E., Kotsilieris, T., Tampakas, V., Pintelas, P.: Improving the evaluation process of students' performance utilizing a decision support software. Neural Comput. Appl. **31**, 1683–1694 (2019)
29. Herrera, F.A.S., Crespo, R.G., Baena, L.R., Burgos, D.: A solution to manage the full life cycle of learning analytics in a learning management system: analytic. IEEE Revista Iberoamericana de Tecnologias del Aprendizaje **14**(4), 127–134 (2019)
30. Wen, Y., Tian, Y., Wen, B., Zhou, Q., Cai, G., Liu, S.: Consideration of the local correlation of learning behaviors to predict dropouts from MOOCs. Tsinghua Sci. Technol. **25**(3), 336–347 (2019)

31. Hussain, M., Zhu, W., Zhang, W., Abidi, S.M.R., Ali, S.: Using machine learning to predict student difficulties from learning session data. Artif. Intell. Rev. **52**, 381–407 (2019)
32. Ortigosa, A., Carro, R.M., Bravo-Agapito, J., Lizcano, D., Alcolea, J.J., Blanco, O.: From lab to production: lessons learnt and real-life challenges of an early student-dropout prevention system. IEEE Trans. Learn. Technol. **12**(2), 264–277 (2019)
33. Olive, D.M., Huynh, D.Q., Reynolds, M., Dougiamas, M., Wiese, D.: A quest for a one-size-fits-all neural network: early prediction of students at risk in online courses. IEEE Trans. Learn. Technol. **12**(2), 171–183 (2019)
34. Hooshyar, D., Yang, Y., Pedaste, M., Huang, Y.-M.: Clustering algorithms in an educational context: an automatic comparative approach. IEEE Access **8**, 146994–147014 (2020)
35. Figueroa-Cañas, J., Sancho-Vinuesa, T.: Early prediction of dropout and final exam performance in an online statistics course. IEEE Revista Iberoamericana de Tecnologias del Aprendizaje **15**(2), 86–94 (2020)
36. Alshanqiti, A., Namoun, A.: Predicting student performance and its influential factors using hybrid regression and multi-label classification. IEEE Access **8**, 203827–203844 (2020)
37. Moreno-Marcos, P.M., Pong, T.C., Munoz-Merino, P.J., Kloos, C.D.: Analysis of the factors influencing learners' performance prediction with learning analytics. IEEE Access **8**, 5264–5282 (2020)
38. Ghorbani, R., Ghousi, R.: Comparing different resampling methods in predicting students' performance using machine learning techniques. IEEE Access **8**, 67899–67911 (2020)
39. Xing, W., Du, D., Bakhshi, A., Chiu, K.-C., Du, H.: Designing a transferable predictive model for online learning using a Bayesian updating approach. IEEE Trans. Learn. Technol. **14**(4), 474–485 (2021)
40. Rafique, A., et al.: Integrating learning analytics and collaborative learning for improving student's academic performance. IEEE Access **9**, 167812–167826 (2021)
41. Mangaroska, K., Vesin, B., Kostakos, V., Brusilovsky, P., Giannakos, M.N.: Architecting analytics across multiple e-learning systems to enhance learning design. IEEE Trans. Learn. Technol. **14**(2), 173–188 (2021)
42. Rahman, M.M., Watanobe, Y., Kiran, R.U., Thang, T.C., Paik, I.: Impact of practical skills on academic performance: a data-driven analysis. IEEE Access **9**, 139975–139993 (2021)
43. Alcaraz, R., Martínez-Rodrigo, A., Zangróniz, R., Rieta, J.J.: Early prediction of students at risk of failing a face-to-face course in power electronic systems. IEEE Trans. Learn. Technol. **14**(5), 590–603 (2021)
44. Tzimas, D., Demetriadis, S.: Ethical issues in learning analytics: a review of the field. Educ. Tech. Res. Dev. **69**, 1101–1133 (2021)
45. Cerratto Pargman, T., McGrath, C.: Mapping the ethics of learning analytics in higher education: a systematic literature review of empirical research. J. Learn. Anal. **8**(2), 123–139 (2021)
46. Guerrero-Roldán, A.-E., Rodríguez-González, M.E., Bañeres, D., Elasri-Ejjaberi, A., Cortadas, P.: Experiences in the use of an adaptive intelligent system to enhance online learners performance: a case study in economics and business courses. Int. J. Educ. Technol. High. Educ. **18**, 1–27 (2021)
47. Holliday-Millard, P.S.: Understanding the complexities of advising transfer students in an institution-driven system. The University of North Carolina at Charlotte (2021)
48. Bertolini, R., Finch, S.J., Nehm, R.H.: Enhancing data pipelines for forecasting student performance: integrating feature selection with cross-validation. Int. J. Educ. Technol. High. Educ. **18**, 1–23 (2021)
49. Petra, T., Aziz, M.: Analysing student performance in higher education using fuzzy logic evaluation. Int. J. Sci. Technol. Res. **10**(1), 322–327 (2021)
50. Uliyan, D., et al.: Deep learning model to predict students retention using BLSTM and CRF. IEEE Access **9**, 135550–135558 (2021)

51. Saleem, F., Ullah, Z., Fakieh, B., Kateb, F.: Intelligent decision support system for predicting student's e-learning performance using ensemble machine learning. Math. **9**(17), 2078 (2021)
52. Nawang, H., Makhtar, M., Hamzah, W.: A systematic literature review on student performance predictions. Int. J. Adv. Technol. Eng. Explor. **8**(84), 1441–1453 (2021)
53. Yoo, J.E., Rho, M., Lee, Y.: Online students' learning behaviors and academic success: an analysis of LMS log data from flipped classrooms via regularization. IEEE Access **10**, 10740–10753 (2022)
54. Singelmann, L.N., Ewert, D.L.: Leveraging the innovation-based learning framework to predict and understand student success in innovation. IEEE Access **10**, 36123–36139 (2022)
55. Deeva, G., De Smedt, J., De Weerdt, J.: Educational sequence mining for dropout prediction in MOOCs: model building, evaluation, and benchmarking. IEEE Trans. Learn. Technol. **15**(6), 720–735 (2022)
56. Rahman, M.M., Watanobe, Y., Matsumoto, T., Kiran, R.U., Nakamura, K.: Educational data mining to support programming learning using problem-solving data. IEEE Access **10**, 26186–26202 (2022)
57. Krieter, P.: Are you still there? An exploratory case study on estimating students LMS online time by combining log files and screen recordings. IEEE Trans. Learn. Technol. **15**(1), 55–63 (2022)
58. Bressane, A., et al.: Fuzzy artificial intelligence-based model proposal to forecast student performance and retention risk in engineering education: an alternative for handling with small data. Sustainability **14**(21), 14071 (2022)
59. Souai, W., Mihoub, A., Tarhouni, M., Zidi, S., Krichen, M., Mahfoudhi, S.: Predicting at-risk students using the deep learning BLSTM approach. In: 2022 2nd International Conference of Smart Systems and Emerging Technologies (SMARTTECH), pp. 32–37. IEEE (2022)
60. Shaik, T., et al.: A review of the trends and challenges in adopting natural language processing methods for education feedback analysis. IEEE Access **10**, 56720–56739 (2022)
61. Sghir, N., Adadi, A., Lahmer, M.: Recent advances in predictive learning analytics: a decade systematic review (2012–2022). Educ. Inf. Technol. **28**(7), 8299–8333 (2023)
62. Chen, M., Huang, X., Chen, H., Su, X., Yur-Austin, J.: Data-driven course scheduling to ensure timely graduation. Int. J. Prod. Res. **61**(1), 336–361 (2023)
63. Lee, J., Hicke, Y., Yu, R., Brooks, C., Kizilcec, R.F.: The life cycle of large language models: A review of biases in education. arXiv preprint arXiv:2407.11203 (2024)
64. Busetto, L., Wick, W., Gumbinger, C.: How to use and assess qualitative research methods. Neurol. Res. Pract. **2**(1), 14 (2020)
65. Shafiq, D.A., Marjani, M., Habeeb, R.A.A., Asirvatham, D.: Student retention using educational data mining and predictive analytics: a systematic literature review. IEEE Access **10**, 72480–72503 (2022)
66. Popescu, E., Leon, F.: Predicting academic performance based on learner traces in a social learning environment. IEEE Access **6**, 72774–72785 (2018)
67. Riestra-González, M., del Puerto Paule-Ruíz, M., Ortin, F.: Massive LMS log data analysis for the early prediction of course-agnostic student performance. Comput. Educ. **163**, 104108 (2021)
68. Deckker, D., Sumanasekara, S.: Emotional AI for student motivation and retention: a systematic review and future directions. Int. J. Glob. Econ. Light **11**(3), 35–50 (2025)
69. Talamás-Carvajal, J.A., Ceballos, H.G.: A stacking ensemble machine learning method for early identification of students at risk of dropout. Educ. Inf. Technol. **28**(9), 12169–12189 (2023)

Evalia: Artificial Intelligence and Human Judgment for the Evaluation of Oral Presentations

Amine Marouki(✉)

Esprit School of Engineering (ESPRIT), 1, 2 rue André Ampère - 2083, Pôle Technologique - El Ghazala, Tunisia
amine.marrouki@esprit.tn

Abstract. Teachers often struggle to assess oral presentations in real time due to multitasking and cognitive load. During live assessments, the teacher must simultaneously listen to the student's discourse, observe non-verbal communication, analyze slide content, and take structured notes. This multitasking often leads to incomplete or imprecise evaluations, especially regarding the verbal, paraverbal, and non-verbal dimensions.

This paper introduces EvalIA, a hybrid evaluation method that combines artificial intelligence (AI) and human judgment. The aim is to assist teachers in analyzing specific oral performance criteria while offering students detailed and reusable feedback.

To explore its feasibility, five student presentations were recorded, transcribed, and analyzed using ChatGPT, using three criteria: originality, verbal communication, and paraverbal features. The AI-generated scores were then compared to the teacher's assessments using Cohen's Kappa coefficient to evaluate the level of agreement.

The results show strong convergence on technical criteria such as rhythm and lexical structure, while discrepancies appeared in more subjective aspects like fluency. One case highlighted the limits of automatic transcription when articulation is unclear.

EvalIA demonstrates potential as a supportive assessment tool: it helps relieve the teacher's cognitive load, increases the fairness of evaluations, and empowers students to understand better and improve their oral performance. Future work will include testing the method on a larger sample to further validate its reliability and scalability in educational settings and ultimately support the creation of an automated tool for oral performance analysis.

Keywords: emerging technologies · oral presentations · assessment · Artificial Intelligence · oral communication

1 Introduction

When evaluating students' oral presentations, the teacher must focus on many essential aspects. Among the elements to be evaluated are oral communication: verbal communication, non-verbal communication, and paraverbal communication. This "triple analysis"

F. Kamoun et al. (Eds.): AFRICATEK 2025, LNICST 676, pp. 466–474, 2026.
https://doi.org/10.1007/978-3-032-16635-7_30

is difficult to manage because the teacher must assess the clarity and fluency of speech, vocabulary, posture, gestures, tone of voice, and other elements. Not to mention the tools that students use to present (PowerPoint, Canva, etc.), they can contain errors: spelling, structure of the plan, etc. After the evaluation, the teacher assigns a grade to the students. The latter do not always have precise and exhaustive feedback on their mistakes and their areas for improvement. In some cases, they may find themselves in the dark about the score awarded, which can lead to disputes. Combining Artificial Intelligence (AI) and human skills would optimize this evaluation process during oral presentations. This method is similar to VAR (Video Assistant Referees) in professional football [1]. Indeed, the referee has the support of the VAR. In case of doubt about a foul or a penalty, for example, he can consult the video assistance, but the final decision is up to him. He then explains his choice to the two team captains to respond to their protest and provide an answer to their incomprehension.

This is where the Evalia method comes in. How can it be defined? Evalia is a portmanteau word that merges the terms "Evaluation" and "Artificial Intelligence". It is an innovative evaluation method whose main objective is to objectively measure students' oral presentations by analysing the clarity of speech, vocabulary, grammar errors, pronunciation... The teacher is free from this task thanks to his "assistant" and can focus on body language, interaction, complicity between team members, and many other criteria that the AI cannot detect. We mainly think of criteria related to sensitivity and emotions, such as enthusiasm, spontaneity, and ease. The combination of the technological performance of AI tools and the skills of the teacher will optimize the evaluation process. Also, thanks to feedback and the personalization of remarks, students will be able to progress by promoting continuous improvement of their communication skills.

2 Literature Review

Artificial Intelligence is increasingly penetrating the world of oral presentations. These are based on the judgment of the teachers who must provide precise and transparent feedback to the students. Recently, there has been growing interest in the integration of artificial intelligence (AI) in this field. We can cite the example of the oral assessment platform "The Socratic Mind"[2], which uses the Socratic method to encourage students to explain, justify, and defend their answers, thus providing a deeper assessment of their understanding. This platform is powered by AI.

As another example, the article "CHOP: Integrating ChatGPT into EFL Oral Presentation Practice"[3] features a platform called CHOP that integrates ChatGPT to provide personalized feedback to students in English as a Foreign Language (EFL).

Other initiatives have been put in place to reinvent oral assessment in the age of AI. For example, to counter issues related to AI and plagiarism, the University of South Australia has adopted the oral examination method of "viva voce" [4], a Latin term that means "voice on live". Through this approach, in-depth conversations are created to assess students' understanding.

However, questions remain about the effectiveness of AI in the evaluation of oral presentations. One study [5] found a preference among students for teacher feedback and human feedback over AI-generated feedback, highlighting the complexity of its integration. In addition, the decrease in critical thinking and reflection among students is one of the concerns related to the excessive use of AI, which can lead to a form of addiction.

Evalia is an innovative method that relies on the teacher's judgment and AI tools (audio recording, transcription, speech analysis). It allows a detailed analysis of aspects related to verbal and para-verbal communication (vocabulary, grammar, conjugation, flow, fluency of speech, etc.) thanks to AI. At the same time, the teacher focuses on more subjective criteria such as commitment, creativity, and non-verbal communication. In addition, by recording presentations, Evalia allows students and teachers to review performance and better manage challenges based on concrete evidence. This complementarity between the teacher and his "assistant" aims to improve the quality of the feedback, making the feedback more precise and personalized. Finally, this method transforms the role of the teacher, who becomes a real coach guiding students in a process of continuous improvement, via easy-to-use and inexpensive tools.

3 Methods and Procedures

3.1 Steps of the Method

The EvalIA method is used according to a multi-step protocol, combining recording of the performance, linguistic processing, and cross-analysis of the evaluation criteria. This process has been designed to be easily integrated into an existing teaching practice, while ensuring reliability and clarity of results.

3.2 Recording of the Oral Performance

The student's presentation is recorded in live conditions, using a simple audio device (phone or digital recorder). This step does not require sophisticated equipment, which ensures the reproducibility of the method.

3.3 Automatic Transcription

The audio is then transcribed using an automatic transcription tool (e.g., Whisper, TurboScribe), ensuring that the text respects the content of the speech. This transcription is the basis on which the AI analysis will be based.

3.4 Analysis with AI (with ChatGPT)

The transcription is subjected to a natural language processing model (in this case, ChatGPT), guided by a simplified evaluation grid focused on three automatically analyzable criteria: Originality of the idea, verbal communication (structure, fluency, vocabulary) and paraverbal communication (intonation perceived through punctuation, rhythm, time segments).

3.5 Teacher Evaluation

The teacher also conducts a direct evaluation of the performance, based on the same criteria as the AI. This double evaluation identifies the gaps or convergences between automated analysis and pedagogical judgment.

3.6 Comparison and Calculation of Spreads

The results are then quantitatively compared using Cohen's Kappa coefficient, which measures the level of agreement between the teacher and the AI. The discrepancies are interpreted qualitatively to identify the limitations or strengths of the AI analysis.

4 Results

The experimentation of the EvalIA method was applied during the week of April 21, 2025, as part of the final project's evaluation. The students, divided into groups, had to design a virtual museum around a theme related to the Sustainable Development Goals (SDGs). This configuration made it possible to test the EvalIA method on five individual presentations, recorded with the prior agreement of the students.

The interventions were recorded via a mobile phone and then transcribed. These transcripts were subjected to analysis by the ChatGPT AI model (version 4.0), based on an evaluation grid usually used in our teaching unit.

The initial evaluation grid used by the teachers of the "Communication, Culture and Citizenship" module includes six criteria: Originality of the idea, verbal communication, paraverbal communication, non-verbal communication, collaboration/contribution, and argumentation. For our method, only three were retained: Originality of the idea (/1), Verbal communication (/2), and Paraverbal communication (/1) for a total of 4 points.

The criteria not analyzed by the AI and entrusted to the teacher are: Non-verbal (lack of video recording - 2 points), collaboration and contribution (criterion based on teamwork and not individually measurable - 2 points), and argumentation (highly dependent on the interaction with the jury - 2 points).

The comparison was therefore made on a total of 4 points per student (Figs. 1, 2, 3 and 4):

Speech	Originality	Verbal	Paraverbal	Total
Speech 1	0.50	1.50	0.50	**2.50**
Speech 2	0.50	0.50	0.25	**1.25**
Speech 3	0.75	1.00	0.50	**2.25**
Speech 4	0.50	0.75	0.50	**1.75**
Speech 5	0.75	1.25	0.75	**2.75**

Fig. 1. Teacher evaluation

Speech	Originality	Verbal	Paraverbal	Total
Speech 1	0.50	1.25	0.50	**2.25**
Speech 2	0.50	0.50	0.25	**1.25**
Speech 3	0.75	0.50	0.50	**1,75**
Speech 4	0.75	0.50	0.50	**1.75**
Speech 5	0.75	1.00	0.75	**2.50**

Fig. 2. ChatGPT evaluation

Speech	Kappa	Interpretation
Speech 1	0.40	Low to moderate agreement
Speech 2	1.00	Perfect Match
Speech 3	0.50	Moderate agreement
Speech 4	-0.50	Clear disagreement
Speech 5	0.67	Good agreement

Fig. 3. Cohen's Kappa - Speeches

Criterion	Cohen's Kappa	Interpretation
Originality	0.62	Good agreement
Verbal communication	0.00	Weak agreement
Paraverbal (tone, rhythm...)	1.00	Excellent agreement

Fig. 4. Cohen's Kappa - Criteria

5 Discussion

The results of this exploratory experiment show that a hybrid approach, combining artificial intelligence and human judgment, is possible to strengthen the evaluation of oral presentations. The use of a natural language processing model such as ChatGPT made it possible to partially reproduce the analysis criteria usually used by the teacher, particularly those related to verbal communication, paraverbal communication, and originality.

The overall agreement between the teacher's and the AI's evaluations, as measured by the Kappa coefficient, was found to be satisfactory in several cases (Kappa $\geq$ 0.40), and even perfect for a speech (Kappa = 1.00). This confirms that AI can identify formal elements such as speech structure, rhythm, or lexical richness, which are traditionally difficult for the teacher to note live. This finding facilitates the complementary use of AI in support of human evaluation.

However, notable differences were observed in some discourses, especially the criterion of verbal communication. The analysis reveals that AI, limited to transcription, cannot capture the finesse of certain formulations or compensate for a fuzzy articulation or a particular accent. An extreme case (Kappa negative) underlines the importance of maintaining a human presence to interpret ambiguous or poorly transcribed cases. These discrepancies highlight the current limitations of AI in the evaluation of heterogeneous oral productions and the need for human supervision.

From a pedagogical point of view, EvalIA offers a double promise: to lighten the cognitive load of the evaluator by delegating the analysis of certain objective criteria, and to provide the student with detailed, contextualized, and reusable feedback. This represents a significant step forward for students in difficulty, who are often left without precise reference points after an oral evaluation.

This experiment constitutes a solid basis for extending the study to a wider number of future students, refining the automated evaluation grid, and in the long term, considering the development of a tool dedicated to the analysis of oral performance, which can be used in different educational contexts and which would allow AI to evaluate certain criteria to let the teacher focus on others.

5.1 Advantages for the Teacher

With this method, the teacher can provide detailed feedback based on both the results of the AI analysis and their human observations. He has an "assistant" who can free him from certain tasks during the evaluation. This reinforces the collaborative aspect between AI and the teacher.

5.2 Benefits for the Student

One of the biggest benefits for the student is the opportunity for them to receive both detailed and objective feedback. Indeed, AI allows a sharp analysis of several elements such as the fluidity of speech, vocabulary, grammar, etc. This method also offers a considerable advantage in terms of transparency. Students can not only get feedback on the strengths and weaknesses of their output, but also understand how each criterion was evaluated, reducing the risk of challenge.

And finally, students can listen back to their recordings, ask the AI to analyze the transcript of the recording, and compare their performance as they go. This allows them to better identify their areas of improvement and to follow the evolution of their oral skills over time. Instead of simply receiving a grade, the student understands his mistakes and progresses.

This direct interaction with the AI not only provided relevant feedback but also fulfilled one of EvalIA's key objectives: helping students become more autonomous in identifying and addressing their weaknesses in oral communication.

One student, after receiving the AI evaluation of his presentation, was invited to engage in a direct conversation with the model to obtain personalized feedback. The exchange covered multiple aspects of his performance, including clarity of articulation, speech rhythm, use of transitions, and vocal intonation. Based on the discussion, the student received detailed suggestions for improvement, such as diction exercises, use of strategic pauses, and vocal variation techniques.

Reflecting on this experience, the student wrote:

> *"I enjoyed talking to Chat to assess myself. It gave me a clear picture of my strengths and weaknesses. The advice was relevant, and I plan to apply it. I think this approach could truly help students improve their speaking skills."*

This interaction illustrates how EvalIA can be used not only as an assessment tool but also as a form of personalized oral coaching, accessible, engaging, and adapted to each student's specific needs.

5.3 Benefits for the Teacher and the Student

This method can ensure transparency during the evaluation by justifying each criterion. If a student disputes a grade, they can listen to their recording again and analyse their mistakes objectively. This will result in constructive contestation, where the student and the teacher can discuss the grading.

5.4 Evalia at the Service of Continuous Student Improvement

AI could not only detect errors but also offer personalized suggestions for each student, based on their weaknesses. This would help students improve faster and in a targeted manner. For example, after detecting a weakness in vocabulary or fluency, the AI could come up with specific practice exercises, examples of vocabulary to use, or videos on improving speaking.

Also, it could be beneficial to offer students coaching tools before their presentation so that they can practise improving their public speaking. AI could, for example, offer preparation exercises, such as diction exercises, stress management exercises, or even presentation simulations. This would help them prepare more effectively before moving on to the final assessment.

Finally, in oral presentations, time management is a key point. The student must not exceed the number of minutes set by the teacher, which will push him to structure his speech well. AI could analyze the length of the presentation, provide guidance on how to meet time limits, and improve its management (e.g., improving brevity).

5.5 Limitations

First, AI, while powerful, cannot always detect elements such as humor, irony, or emotions. In addition, the pronunciation of certain words or accents can lead to a wrong transcription. It is therefore essential to explain to students that AI is a support tool and not a definitive solution.

Second, the teacher must keep the role of "lead" interpreter and evaluator, adjusting and contextualizing the results. For example, if the AI detects slowness in speech, the teacher could specify that this slowness was justified by a relevant time for reflection.

Third, it is important to ensure the good quality of the audio recordings to avoid skewing the analysis. To do this, students must have easy access to suitable equipment (quality microphones, quiet spaces for recording, etc.).

Fourthly, this first experiment on a small sample remains limited in terms of statistical scope. Indeed, the number of candidates is low and needs to be increased.

6 Conclusion

The EvalIA method is part of a pedagogical innovation approach aimed at modernizing the assessment of oral skills using artificial intelligence tools. By comparing human ratings with automated analysis based on the transcription of the performances, this experiment shows that it is possible to delegate part of the evaluation process while maintaining the quality of educational judgment.

The results obtained highlight real potential: the AI evaluates certain technical criteria, allowing the teacher to focus on the most subjective and contextual dimensions, such as gestures, interaction, or disciplinary content. At the same time, the student benefits from more structured, documented feedback conducive to self-improvement.

It is not a question of replacing the teacher, but of offering him reliable and reproducible support, in a logic of fairer and more demanding support. EvalIA's ambition is to promote a fairer, more transparent, and more formative evaluation, while respecting the diversity of student profiles.

Future perspectives include expanding the number of students tested, adjusting the automatic analysis criteria, and co-constructing an evaluation tool integrated into pedagogical practices. This work thus paves the way for a new method of conceiving oral assessment, based on the alliance between technology, pedagogy, and human judgment.

References

1. Kim, C.H.: Evaluation of the impact of the video assistant referee technology on home advantage and referee bias in professional football (2023)
2. Orynbassarova, D., Porta, S.D.L.: Implementing the socratic method with AI: opportunities and challenges of integrating ChatGPT into teaching pedagogy. In: 2024 International Conference on Emerging eLearning Technologies and Applications (ICETA). IEEE (2024)
3. Cha, J., et al.: CHOP: integrating ChatGPT into EFL oral presentation practice. arXiv preprint arXiv:2407.07393 (2024)
4. Pearce, G., Lee, G.: Viva voce (oral examination) as an assessment method: insights from marketing students. J. Mark. Educ. **31**(2), 120–130 (2009). https://doi.org/10.1177/0273475309334050 (Original work published 2009)
5. Nazaretsky, T., Mejia-Domenzain, P., Swamy, V., et al.: AI or human? Evaluating student feedback perceptions in higher education. In: European Conference on Technology Enhanced Learning, p. 284–298. Springer Nature Switzerland, Cham (2024). https://doi.org/10.1007/978-3-031-72315-5_20

Enhancing Student-Centric Learning Approaches and Exploring AI Integration

Khadija Raissi(✉), Halima Othmani, Soumaya Argoubi, and Anis Benhajyoussef

ESPRIT School of Engineering, Ariana, Tunis, Tunisia
{khadija.raissi,halima.othmani,soumaya.argoubi, anis.hajyoussef}@esprit.tn

Abstract. The integration of Artificial Intelligence (AI) with innovative teaching strategies, such as the flipped classroom approach and the blended learning method, alongside the use of Learning Management Systems (LMS), has reshaped higher education, enhancing remote knowledge acquisition. This article highlights how adopting LMS, such as Moodle, within a flipped classroom approach for Object-Oriented Programming (OOP) in C++ has enhanced engineering students' learning experience. Through blended learning method, students can engage in self-paced learning, conduct online assessments, and receive real-time feedback. Furthermore, the integration of AI in coding C++ enhances programming efficiency and problem-solving through smart suggestions, debugging support, and personalized guidance. The main goal of this article is to highlight the added value of an e-learning platform, coupled with AI-driven coding support, successfully promotes self-regulated learning among second-year common core engineering students at Esprit School of Engineering. Precisely, it explores the integration of AI-driven assistants in programming to enhance C++ learning. It examines the feasibility of AI-powered scripting for skill acquisition, defining its pedagogical benefits and identifying key constraints. The study also proposes a structured learning methodology through a C++ programming workshop, demonstrating how AI assistance improves coding efficiency, error detection, and conceptual understanding.

Keywords: e-learning · blended learning · flipped classroom · self-regulated learning · AI assistant · standards: 8, 11

1 Introduction

Innovative teaching methods are essential to ensure that engineering training meets the needs of the job market and professional standards. These exceptional approaches aim to equip learners with engineering skills, facilitating their smooth integration into the professional world. Many engineering institutions are making significant efforts to innovate their teaching methods, using active approaches and scenarios that simulate the professional environment [1].

K.Raissi, H. Othmani, S. Argoubi and a. Benhajyoussef—contributed equally to this work

F. Kamoun et al. (Eds.): AFRICATEK 2025, LNICST 676, pp. 475–485, 2026.
https://doi.org/10.1007/978-3-032-16635-7_31

This article describes the implementation of the Conceive–Design–Implement–Operate (CDIO) standards, designed to integrate an innovative pedagogical method into the teaching of object-oriented programming. This approach is based on the use of the C++ language and is targeting engineering students at ESPRIT.

Additionally, we will showcase how the suggested approach supports both educators and students in diverse learning activities, enabling teachers to evaluate the degree of knowledge acquisition through assessments and quizzes. Furthermore, the article emphasizes the exploitation of feedback-drive assessment through the review shared with the learners after sending their attempt to enhance proficiency building.

Moreover, the article investigates the future implications of Artificial Intelligence (AI) in the context of C++ programming education. Exploring how AI can aid students in coding by providing suggestions, identifying errors, and generating more efficient and accurate code, thereby reducing the time required to complete programming assignments [2]. It specifically delves into the possibilities of advancement through AI-based Integrated Development Environment (IDE) assistants to support the enhancement of students' understanding and knowledge while also fostering the cultivation of coaching skills among students.

The structure of the article is as follows: initially, it provides context by reviewing related works. It subsequently outlines the adopted pedagogical approach. Following that, we demonstrate our alignment with the CDIO standard. The next section details the outcomes of this implementation and its effects on our students. Following that, we suggest a method for integrating AI-based tools into the described module to enhance skill acquisition among our students. Finally, we conclude the article and provide a brief overview of our future work.

2 Literature Review

Several earlier research articles have focused on the effectiveness of online learning platforms such as Moodle [3] in higher education aiming to support students in fostering their engagement and establishing a more dynamic, interactive, and scalable educational ecosystem. Recent work undertaken by Dijana [4].focuses on descriptive and predictive learning analytics to support students in achieving their academic objectives and forecasting their success. The author applied the Cubic Clustering Criterion value to create effective student clusters, a decision tree, as well as supervised and unsupervised machine learning algorithms on Moodle data to predict student behavior and success. The results suggest that test logs and choices have the greatest impact on grades for students with higher LMS activity. In contrast, student report views and assignments significantly impact the grades of students with lower LMS activity.

Moodle e-learning has become the mandatory system adopted by universities in higher education to implement their innovation policies [5]. This research article introduces a novel perspective, aiming to investigate how Moodle enhances the effectiveness of innovative education to foster knowledge in pedagogy. Additionally, it offers students the flexibility to access teaching materials without the limitations of physical attendance.

The project conducted in Australia in 2021 within a private higher education institution, demonstrated that the Moodle platform could enhance and support students in various learning activities to provide high-quality online education [6]. However, several tools like Q&A sites, chat rooms, discussion forums, self-paced quizzes, surveys, feedback boxes, and polls, not only serve to stimulate student engagement but also contribute to retaining their online learning. Additionally, the customization of diverse communication and learning tools across the platform encourages interaction between students and teachers, as well as among students.

The study of the impact of Moodle Quiz in pre-class, in-class, and post-class activities proves that it is a powerful tool to motivate students to be more attentive, curious, and passionate about subject content at different paces and in various scenarios. To cover topics that are easy to learn, students are encouraged to answer some relevant questions before class an unlimited number of times until they pass, through short clips or video courses. It is important to note that flipped learning supports reflective teaching and deep learning. Therefore, the use of quizzes in class serves as an informal formative assessment that engages students as active learners to achieve the intended learning outcomes and assists teachers in measuring understanding while identifying gaps in the content knowledge presented in class. Self-evaluation is a crucial process that can be fostered through quizzes after class to enhance student engagement, and it is also a good method to identify a more appropriate teaching strategy [7].

However, many research articles presume that the combination of a flipped classroom approach and a learning management system such as Moodle fosters online behaviour engagement and achievement by promoting self-assessment and self-reflection [8].

3 Pedagogical Approach

The blended-learning method allows students to engage in a self-paced learning experience to acquire skills targeted by the Object-Oriented Programming module which uses the LMS Moodle.

This innovative module offers a hybrid learning approach, combining captivating classroom sessions for a total of 42 h face-to-face with complementary interactive e-learning activities, totalling 58 h. It carries a credit value of 4 ECTS (European Credit Transfer and Accumulation System).

The flipped classroom approach assisted by the Moodle platform where the course material of the module is exposed motivates students to study at home and discuss their learning outcomes during classroom sessions. The teaching outcomes of this course are based on the incorporation of practical programming exercises, which are utilized to reinforce students' learning experiences through various tools. To encourage higher student participation and capture their attention in class, we use an interrogative approach.

Alongside regular classes and exercise sessions, students have three asynchronous quizzes and a final quiz conducted in the classroom. Each quiz consists of 30 single or multiple-choice questions and serves as an informal formative assessment that makes students active learners to achieve the intended learning outcomes. These quizzes are created using a set of questions derived from a question bank within the Moodle platform.

The course assessment comprised 40% for continuous assessment and 60% for the practical exam. Continuous Assessment allows the measurement of students' progress and involvement during the study period. It primarily includes a practical test, an evaluation of three quizzes, and a Final one. Continuous assessment is calculated by assigning

60% to the practical test, 20% for the average of scores for the three quizzes, and 20% for the Final quiz.

4 Alignment with Cdio Standards

In alignment with CDIO standard 8 which is related to "teaching and learning based on active and experiential learning methods", our study brings out how we gained insight into learners' conduct based on descriptive and predictive learning analytics. The obtained results suggest that, among the features provided by Moodle, such as course creation, discussion forums, quizzes, and assessments, we had the opportunity to implement a student-centric environment and develop self-directed learning skills among our students.

In accordance to CDIO standard 11 associated with "Learning Assessment" the integration of online assessments, complemented by quizzes with real-time feedback, represents a dynamic approach to exploiting feedback-driven assessments. The use of in-class quizzes not only serves as an informal formative assessment tool but also engages students as active participants in achieving intended learning objectives. This approach helps teachers' measure understanding while identifying gaps in the knowledge presented during class sessions. Beyond the classroom, self-assessment becomes a crucial element that can be fostered through post-course quizzes, reinforcing student engagement. Continuous assessment also plays a central role in measuring student progress and involvement throughout the study period. In addition, practical exams contribute to outcome-based assessment, providing a comprehensive evaluation of the application of theoretical knowledge in practical scenarios. The combined use of these assessment methods ensures a holistic approach to understanding and evaluating students' academic performance [9].

5 Methodology

This study investigates the effectiveness of flipped classroom and blended learning strategies in enhancing student engagement and knowledge acquisition in Object-Oriented Programming (OOP), with a particular focus on self-paced learning. The participants, enrolled in a C++ programming course, engaged in both conventional and AI-assisted instructional activities. The research pursues two main objectives. The first is to evaluate the pedagogical value of interactive quizzes, administered via the Moodle platform, in fostering skill development and strengthening the link between student motivation and active participation in formative assessments. The second objective aims to examine the impact of using AI-integrated IDEs in programming on student engagement, knowledge acquisition, and time efficiency during coding tasks (Table 1).

Table 1. Methodology Overview

Element	Description
Participants	Students enrolled in a C++ programming course
Learning Approach	Blended learning combining online content and in-person sessions
Technological Tools	AI-integrated IDEs, Moodle platform
Assessment Methods	Quizzes on Moodle and an AI-based programming assignment

6 Result and Discussion

In the current study, different metrics are performed to analyze the performance of the self-paced learning experience associated with flipped-classroom and blended-learning approaches for teaching C++ programming. We aim to collect data from two separate instances of Moodle across two different generations, employing two diverse assessment methods to make a further comparison of their effectiveness. This section aims to compare two distinct methods that we have implemented in the online part, to ensure formative assessment of students and improve the acquisition rate of targeted skills.

In the first method, we have chosen to propose one quiz per objective to be taken after the session. In this initial approach, the student has to answer 8 quizzes, targeting the learning outcomes of each chapter individually. Grading is binary, indicating whether or not the student has completed the quiz, with an unlimited number of attempts to encourage self-directed learning through the answers provided after each quiz. However, we have found that several students do not take the quizzes on Moodle. To lighten the workload, we decided to reduce the number of quizzes to three, each targeting the learning outcomes of two or three objectives simultaneously. We also limited the number of attempts to two and opted for non-binary marks out of 20. The research was carried out with a cohort of around 300 students. Table 2 summarizes the characteristics of both methods.

Table 2. Descriptions of assessment methods

Method 1	Method 2
8 Quizzes: One quiz per objective	3 Quizzes: one quiz per 2–3 objectives
Unlimited number of attempts	Only two attempts
Grading is binary	Grading is non-binary marks out of 20

6.1 Assessment through Quizzes

These approaches allow students to develop self-directed learning skills through multiple interactive quizzes, and continuous assessment sessions. Quizzes include several types of questions related to all the objectives of the module to assess the student's knowledge and understanding after the interactive learning process.

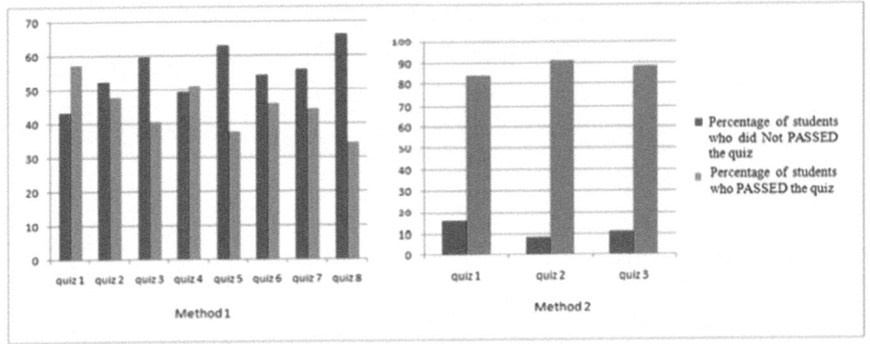

Fig. 1. Percentage of students who PASSED/ did NOT PASSED quizzes

In Fig. 1 we notice that the percentage of students who did not passed the quizzes while using method 1 is almost always higher than the percentage of students who passed the quizzes, and in this case, they will fail the online assessment and subsequently other evaluations. Whereas, most of the percentages of students who passed the quizzes are below 47% and above 34%, except for the first quiz, which has a success percentage of 57%, and the fourth quiz, which has a medium value of 50%. However, the percentage of students who passed quizzes while adopting method 2 exceeds 84% in the three quizzes while those who did not pass are less than 11%. Thus, we notice that the higher average percentage value (55%) of students who did not pass the quizzes is achieved by the first method compared to the second method (11%). These results showed that method 2 performed better than method 1 as we reduced the number of quizzes so that the student could focus more on his course material and have enough time to review the different chapters before taking the quiz. This indicates that both the performance and motivation of students increase when the number of quizzes decreases significantly from 8 quizzes to only 3 quizzes. As such, the students do not feel stressed due to the number of quizzes and the spacing between them, thus alleviating the pressure associated with managing multiple assignments concurrently. This makes them more comfortable and more productive.

6.2 Assessment through Final Quiz

This section is devoted to analyzing the impact of previous results on the realization of the final quiz to evaluate the knowledge acquisition by the target students on all course objectives using both methods. Fig. 2, shows that the success rate in the final quiz reaches (56%) completed with a score above 10 while 44% scored under 10 in method 1. However, the use of the second assessment method decreases the failure percentage to 29% and increases the success rate to 71%compared to the first assessment method.

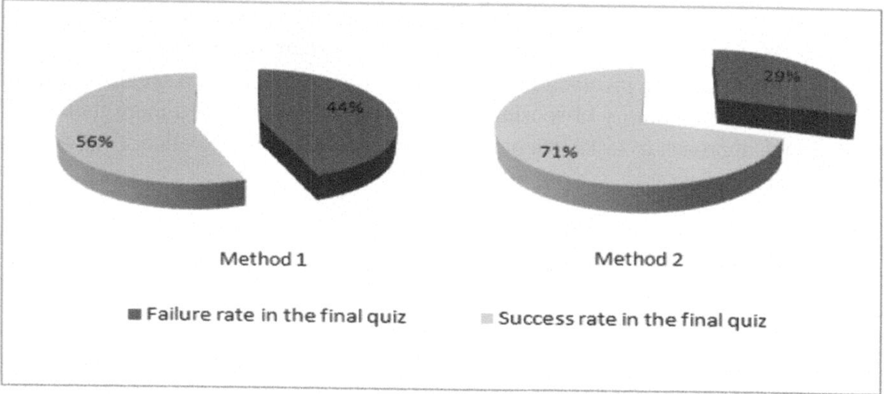

Fig. 2. Success/Failure rate in the final quiz

6.3 Assessment through Practical Exam

The quizzes aim to support students in preparing for the practical exam and enhance their examination performance. Therefore, according to Fig. 3 the success rate in the practical exam using method 2 reaches 64.52%, while in method 1, it does not exceed 47.37%.

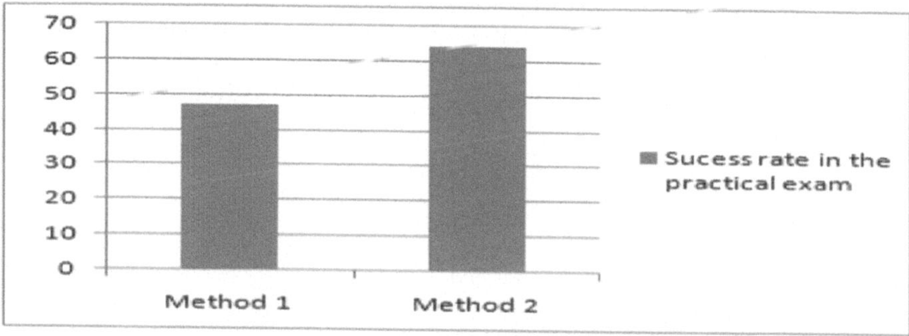

Fig. 3. Success rate in the Practical Exam

These results demonstrate that the second feedback-drive assessment method presents better performance than the first one. Nevertheless, interactive quizzes are essential for fostering students' knowledge and engagement. Thus, they highlight the impact of the adopted Self evaluation approach. The improvement in the final quiz and the practical exam results can be explained by the limited number of attempts which enhanced the feedback-drive assessment by encouraging students to give more importance to the auto-generated answers after the first tentative so that they can have a better online self-paced learning experience. Assessment graded out of 20 offered greater granularity and precision in measuring learners' performance. Unlike the binary assessment in method 1, this simply indicates whether or not a task has been accomplished. In other words, a grade out of 20 enabled a more in-depth, individualized assessment of learners' performance. Moreover, the assessment in method 2 was more detailed which motivated students to become more involved in the learning process, as they can see the results of their efforts. The granularity of scoring out of 20 can also stimulate a more thoughtful and thorough approach to tasks, encouraging students to aim for excellence rather than simply binary success.

7 AI-Based Programming

7.1 AI Assistant-Based Coding

The recent development of artificial intelligence has clearly impacted computer development with the emergence of AI assistants that became an integral part of IDEs (Integrated Development Environments) [10]. AI assistants offer now various functionalities that address the claimed AI-assistant development. For pedagogical reasons, we separate these functionalities into two categories: main and secondary ones. The latter are considered, here, as secondary because they are indirectly covered, and they don't have a significant impact in an educational and pedagogic context.

In this article, we focus on the following three main functionalities:

Code Generation: This involves describing a part or entire function with its arguments in natural language and letting the assistant generate the corresponding code. **Debugging:** In a debugging context, a candidate usually utilizes conventional debugging features, such as debugging compilation, step-by-step execution, breakpoints, and conditional breakpoints ... However, with an AI assistant, the candidate can communicate in natural language to quickly identify a bug and receive proposals for fixes. **Testing:** Here, the candidate can ask its AI assistant to generate a unit function for a given section or request the output of a function for given inputs.

7.2 Existing AI Assistant IDEs

Recently, a lot of AI assistants have emerged with rather similar features. Among these assistants, we focus here on two Major Ones; GitHub Copilot [11], a collaboration work between Github and Open AI, and JetBrains AI assistant [12]. These tools aim to enhance the programming learning experience by providing contextual code explanations, suggestions, and completions. We present in this section, an examination of the key differences between these two AI assistants in the educational context:

Performance of Code Generation: Initial practical tests suggest that JetBrains AI assistant recommendations are more finely attuned to immediate coding requirements. However, GitHub Copilot illustrates a greater proficiency in generating complete code blocks based on comments.

Language Support: Another key consideration is the languages and frameworks supported by these AI assistants. Currently, JetBrains AI is concentrating on Java and has intentions to broaden its scope to include Kotlin and Python, providing tailored recommendations for JVMbased languages. In contrast, GitHub Copilot supports dozens of languages, including Python, JavaScript, TypeScript, Ruby, and C++, providing multilingual support in a single tool. Currently, GitHub Copilot offers more flexibility to developers working in multiple languages.

Integration with Development Environments: The ease of integration into existing workflows is another key consideration when evaluating these tools. JetBrains AI is tightly integrated with JetBrains IDEs such as IntelliJ, PyCharm, and WebStorm, tailoring its suggestions specifically to these environments. GitHub Copilot, as a plugin for editors like Neovim and Visual Studio Code, can integrate into a broader range of configurations. Developers using JetBrains IDEs may find that JetBrains AI seamlessly integrates into their stacks, while those using other editors may prefer GitHub Copilot for its flexibility.

8 Proposed AI-Based Assignment

8.1 Coding Via an AI Assistant in Academic Context

To justify the rationale behind the proposed assignment, this section presents experimental observations aimed at exploring student interactions with an AI coding assistant.

The primary focus is on the time efficiency gained when coding with an AI assistant compared to the traditional non-assisted method. In Table 3, we present the coding times with and without the use of GitHub Copilot, across two experiments conducted by teachers. The first experiment involved solving a typical classroom exercise with an estimated duration of 30 min. The second involved coding a student test of 60 min duration.

As shown in Table 3, the use of GitHub Copilot resulted in a reduction in coding time of 43% and 36% for the two experiments, respectively, yielding an average time saving of 40%. The 55% efficiency gain claimed by GitHub appears to be relative. This finding is corroborated by some professionals that note more modest gains of 10–15%, particularly in contexts with established coding styles or project structures.

Table 3. Coding time profile using an AI assistant

Experiment	Coding time (min)		
	Without assistant	With assiatant	Gain
Exp1: Typical exercise of 30 min duration	30	17	43%
Exp2: Test of 60 min duration	50	32	36%
Ave.			40%

In a second investigation, we focus on the acceptance rate of suggestions provided by the AI assistant. Table 4 presents data from the second experiment shown in Table 3, specifically detailing how the assistant's suggestions were handled by users. We differentiate between fully accepted suggestions, rejected ones, and suggestions that were accepted with correction.

The presentation of the latter metric is based on practical observations: in some cases, it is faster to correct an AI-generated suggestion than to decline it and code manually or change the script. The various metrics presented were collected manually during the experiment. As shown in Table 3, 44% of the suggestions were fully accepted, while another 42% were accepted with corrections, indicating an overall acceptance rate of 86%. This strongly supports the value of AI-assisted coding. However, this metric should be interpreted with caution, as users tend to adjust their interaction over time, asking the assistant only those questions for which they anticipate receiving an acceptable response.

Table 4. Acceptance rate of GitHub Copilot.

Reactions to the assistant's proposals			Acceptance rate	
Fully accepted	Accepted but rectified	Declined	Full acceptance	Mixed Acceptance
22	21	7	44%	42%

8.2 AI Assignment Methodology Considerations

To support the integration of AI-based coding practices into the C++ course, a new learning objective has been introduced: "coding via an AI assistant." This learning outcome refers to a student's ability to accomplish a defined programming task using the capabilities of an AI assistant, with the aim of completing the task more efficiently or with reduced complexity.

The primary goal of the assignment is to engage students in working indirectly with an AI assistant. More specifically, it aims to raise awareness about the relevance and potential of AI-assisted coding, a practice that students are increasingly likely to encounter in a professional context.

The assignment is scheduled mid-period of the course to ensure that students possess a minimum level of C++ proficiency. This is a prerequisite for enabling them to critically evaluate the assistant's suggestions and decide whether to accept or revise them accordingly. Such considerations are crucial to ensuring that the assignment supports continued learning of the C++ language through the use of the assistant.

Regarding the assessment of the assignment, the focus is not being on the technical use or mastery of the AI assistant itself. From a pedagogical standpoint, evaluating proficiency with a specific version of an AI tool is not meaningful, as performance can vary considerably depending on the tool's version and the development environment.

Instead, the evaluation is guided by outcome-oriented criteria. Students are assessed indirectly based on their ability to effectively leverage the AI assistant, adapt to its suggestions, and guide its output toward achieving a measurable programming objective, ideally in less time than would be required without the assistant.

9 Conclusion

This article highlights the effectiveness of the flipped classroom and the blended learning method in fostering students' knowledge and engagement in a self-paced learning experience to understand OOP. From the obtained results, we can conclude that the second assessment method outperforms the first, improving skill acquisition through interactive quizzes, and establishing a strong correlation between student motivation and engagement in various activities such as quizzes for enhanced assessment. Furthermore, this article has investigated the integration of AI in C++ programming within educational contexts. It specifically delved into the potential of utilizing an AI assistant for programming an IDE. It explored the different needs of introducing coding via an AI assistant as a learning skill in the C++ programming module, along with defining and detailing the associated limitations of this integration. Additionally, this article expanded this investigation to propose an inclusive learning methodology through a C++ programming Assignment, offering a solution to the examined challenges associated with incorporating AI into C++ education. This proposed approach represents a forward-thinking strategy for educators and learners alike.

References

1. Abusalem, A., Bennett, L., Antonelou-Abusalem, D.: Engaging and retaining students in online learning, pp. 1–19 (2023).
2. Alkhulaifat, D., Rafful, P., Khalkhali, V., Welsh, M., Sotardi, S.T.: Implications of pediatric artificial intelligence challenges for artificial intelligence education and curriculum development. J. Am. Coll. Radiol. **20**(8), 724–729 (2023)
3. Al Sebae, A., Rihawi, Z., Azmat, F.: Moodle quiz: a method for measuring students'engagement. In: The 15th International Cdio Conference (p. 333) (2019).
4. Lungu, M.: What is moodle? What are online learning management systems? In study portals online courses (2022). Available at: https://www.distancelearningportal.com /articles/161/whatis-moodle-what-are-online-learning-managements-systems.Html.
5. Oreški, D.: Using descriptive and predictive learning analytics to understand student behavior at lms moodle. In: The Thirteenth International Conference on e-Learning, (pp. 18–24) (2022).
6. Sibgatullina, A., vanova, R., Yushchik, E.: Moodle Learning System as an Effective Tool for Implementing the Innovation Policy of the University," International Journal of Web-Based Learning and Teaching Technologies (IJWLTT), IGI global, vol. 17(1), pages 1–12, (Jan 2022)
7. Sivarajah, R.T., Curci, N.E., Johnson, E.M., Lam, D.L., Lee, J.T., Richardson, M.L.: A review of innovative teaching methods. Acad. Radiol. **26**(1), 101–113 (2019)
8. Wang, F.H.: An exploration of online behaviour engagement and achievement in flipped classroom supported by learning management system. Comput. Educ. **114**, 79–91 (2017)
9. Crawley, E.F., Malmqvist, J., Östlund, S., Brodeur, D.R., Edström, K.: Rethinking engineering education. In: The CDIO Approach, 2nd edn. Springer (2014). https://doi.org/10.1007/978-3-319-05561-9
10. Zhang, Q., Yang, L., Chen, Y., Yu, P.S.: A survey on AI copilot: from software engineering to education. ACM Comput. Surv. **54**(10), 1–36 (2021). https://doi.org/10.1145/3465415
11. Ziegler, C., Aftandilian, E., Hsu, W.: Productivity assessment of neural code completion. In: Proceedings of the 44th International Conference on Software Engineering (ICSE), pp. 1207–1218 (2022). https://doi.org/10.1145/3510003.3510075
12. Jetbrains ai assistant. Retrieved from https://www.jetbrains.com/ai. Accessed 28 Mar 2025

Gamification in STEM Education: Designing Adaptive Scoring Systems for Student Classification

Bilel Charfi(✉), Ahmed Ammar, and Mohamed Hedi Riahi

Technological Pole - El Ghazala, ESPRIT, 2083 Ariana, Tunisia
{bilel.charfi,ammar.ahmed,mohamedhediriahi}@esprit.tn

Abstract. As artificial intelligence (AI) and gamification continue to transform education, innovative frameworks are needed to create more engaging, adaptive, and effective learning experiences. This paper introduces a structured three-phase adaptive framework that leverages AI-driven techniques and gamified mechanisms to enhance machine learning (ML) education. The first phase assesses individual student performance through timed quizzes, dynamically classifying learners based on their accuracy and response time. In the second phase, AI-powered decision-tree algorithms form balanced teams, fostering collaborative problem-solving while maintaining a competitive dynamic. The final phase introduces AI-adjusted strategic challenges, such as real-time betting on question difficulty, to develop risk management skills and reinforce conceptual mastery. By integrating leaderboards, adaptive question difficulty, and gamified incentives, the framework transforms traditional ML education into a personalized, interactive, and student-centered experience. This framework provides a scalable and data-driven foundation for future empirical studies on student motivation, conceptual understanding, and learning outcomes in adaptive gamified environments.

Keywords: Gamification in Education · Adaptive Learning · Machine Learning Education · AI-Driven Assessment · Student Engagement · Game-Based Learning · Collaborative Learning in STEM

1 Introduction

In today's digital era, students have unprecedented access to sophisticated artificial intelligence (AI) tools, enabling instantaneous retrieval of extensive information and immediate assistance in complex tasks [2, 7]. This widespread availability of advanced technologies challenges the traditional educational paradigm, raising a fundamental question: What unique value does formal education provide when knowledge and solutions are readily accessible? Addressing this challenge requires a rethinking and redesigning of educational strategies toward approaches that prioritize active engagement, critical thinking, and contextualized understanding rather than mere memorization or passive theoretical absorption [13, 16].

F. Kamoun et al. (Eds.): AFRICATEK 2025, LNICST 676, pp. 486–492, 2026.
https://doi.org/10.1007/978-3-032-16635-7_32

Historically, higher education has predominantly focused on theoretical instruction, relegating the practical acquisition of applied skills to post-educational professional experiences [15]. However, today's accelerated technological evolution necessitates embedding practical competencies directly within curricula through active and participatory learning methodologies [17]. Consider, for instance, an engineer facing a complex supply-chain optimization problem. While various machine learning algorithms—such as linear regression, decision trees, or neural networks—could provide solutions, selecting the most suitable method demands a nuanced understanding of each algorithm's strengths, weaknesses, and contextual applicability [16]. This example illustrates a significant limitation in traditional instructional models, which typically emphasize algorithmic knowledge without sufficient attention to practical decision-making contexts [13].

Previous research underscores the effectiveness of gamification in enhancing student motivation and engagement [5, 7, 8, 15]. Digital platforms like Kahoot! have been widely adopted to create interactive, competitive learning environments [16]. Building upon these successful precedents, we propose an adaptive, AI-driven gamified platform that can be specifically utilized for machine learning education. Our approach emphasizes comparative analysis, strategic thinking, and real-time decision-making within a dynamically adaptive environment. This method leverages artificial intelligence to tailor difficulty and adjust challenges based on real-time performance metrics, thus ensuring an individualized yet collaborative learning experience.

This paper advocates for the integration of AI-driven gamification into higher education curricula to foster not only technical proficiency but also the nuanced decision-making skills necessary for navigating complex professional scenarios, thereby aligning educational outcomes more closely with contemporary industry requirements.

2 Adaptive Gamification Framework: Design and Strategic Implementation

The framework is structured into three interconnected phases: Individual Assessment, Dynamic Grouping, and Strategic Resource Allocation. While designed for STEM education, this paper focuses on its application in machine learning (ML). Each phase integrates AI-driven adaptability, ensuring performance in earlier stages directly shapes subsequent opportunities while fostering equity and engagement. Central to this design is a point-based progression system, where learners earn, accumulate, and strategically deploy points to advance, mirroring real-world ML workflows like resource optimization and risk-reward analysis.

2.1 Phase 1 – Rapid Assessment and Adaptive Student Classification

Phase 1 evaluates students' machine learning (ML) competencies through a time-constrained, dual-metric scoring system. Balancing speed and accuracy, this phase categorizes learners into individualized or collaborative pathways.

Timed Individual Quizzes:
Students answer a customizable number of questions (e.g., 3–5 questions) on foundational ML concepts such as dataset preprocessing or algorithm selection. Each question has a strict time limit (e.g., 10 s) to simulate real-world decision-making pressures.

Dual-Metric Scoring:
Performance is evaluated using a weighted formula that combines accuracy and response time, with customizable weightings (e.g., 70% for accuracy and 30% for response time).

Dynamic Student Classification:
Students are categorized using a threshold based on class statistics (e.g., $\mu C + k\sigma C$). High performers advance individually to Phase 2, while others form balanced teams via clustering algorithms (e.g., DBSCAN, GMM).

Design Innovations:
The phase is completed in under 2 min per student, ensuring scalability. Time limits deter reliance on external tools, emphasizing intrinsic problem-solving.

Figure 1 outlines the structured process of *Phase 1 – Evaluation Process,* the initial stage of the game.

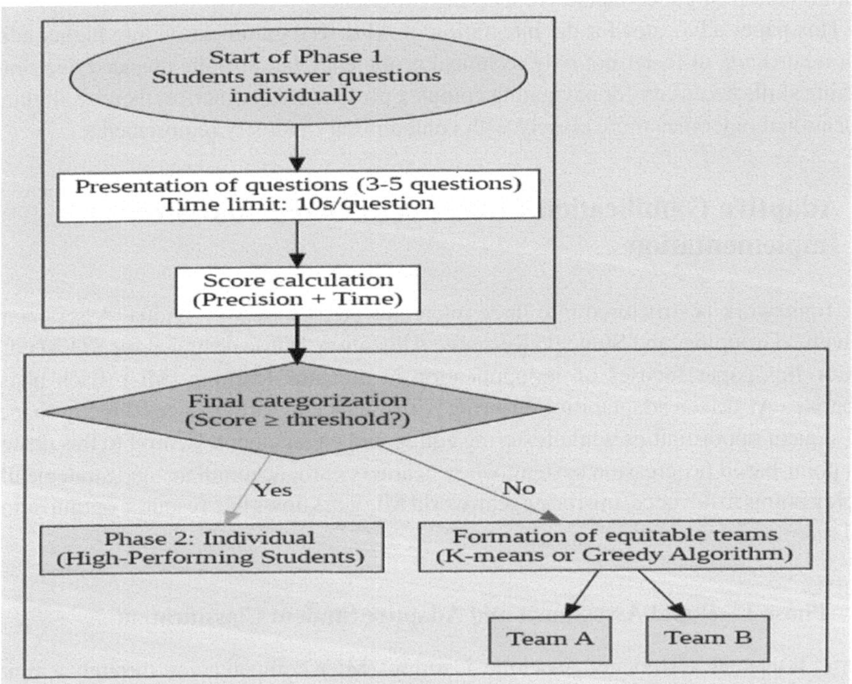

Fig. 1. Evaluation Process

2.2 Phase 2 – Dynamic Grouping

Phase 2 builds on the initial assessments from Phase 1, focusing on adaptive collaboration and competitive skill refinement. Participants are dynamically grouped into individualized or team-based pathways, fostering both personal excellence and collective problem-solving. The process unfolds through three key stages, ensuring equitable challenges and continuous engagement. Figure 2 details the structure of Phase 2 – Points Accumulation and Ranking, a pivotal stage where participants are categorized into Individuals or Initial Groups (Team A and Team B) and progress through a unified assessment process.

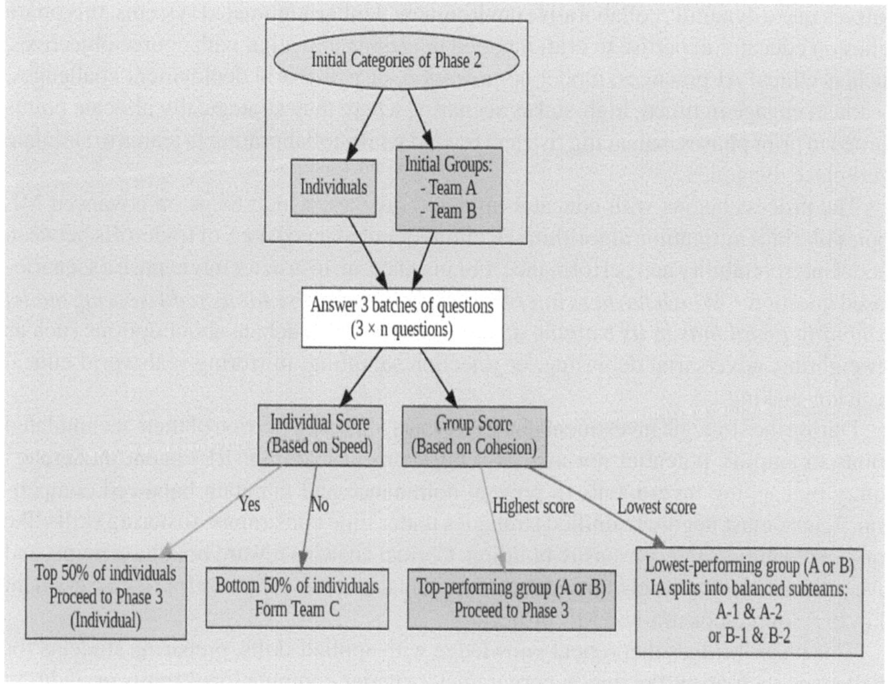

Fig. 2. Phase 2 – Points Accumulation and Ranking

The outcomes of these calculations determine transitions to subsequent stages:

The top 50% of individuals advance to Phase 3 as high performers, while the remaining 50% form Team C.

For groups, the highest-scoring team (either A or B) proceeds to Phase 3, whereas the lower-performing group is split by an AI algorithm into balanced subteams (e.g., A-1/A-2 or B-1/B-2).

The diagram highlights the dual evaluation criteria (speed vs. cohesion) and the adaptive structure of Phase 2, which dynamically redistributes participants into new teams or retains top performers for advanced competition. Visual cues like green ("Yes"/"Highest score") and red ("No"/"Lowest score") clarify decision pathways, emphasizing the phase's focus on performance-based progression and equitable redistribution of resources.

2.3 Phase 3 – Strategic Competition

Phase 3 consolidates machine learning (ML) mastery by integrating instructor-designed quizzes into a dynamic, collaborative environment. Unlike automated systems, this phase relies on educator expertise to craft targeted questions that align with course objectives, such as ethical AI practices, model optimization, or real-world deployment challenges. Learners engage in timed, high-stakes scenarios where they strategically allocate points earned in prior phases, balancing risk and reward while collaborating in teams to simulate workplace dynamics.

The process begins with educator-authored quizzes, which focus on advanced ML topics like bias mitigation, algorithm selection for imbalanced data, or trade-offs between model interpretability and performance. For instance, an instructor might pose a scenario-based question: *"Which fairness intervention is most effective for a credit-scoring model exhibiting racial bias in its training data?"* Students then debate about options such as reweighting, adversarial debiasing, or rejection sampling, mirroring real-world ethical decision-making.

During the strategic investment phase, learners allocate a portion of their accumulated points to amplify potential rewards. A reinforcement learning (RL) agent moderates' equity by capping investments to prevent dominance and maintain balanced competition. Teams must negotiate unified strategies under time constraints, fostering skills like conflict resolution and consensus-building. Correct answers reward both base points and invested amounts, while errors deduct investments, incentivizing careful risk assessment akin to resource-constrained ML projects.

This phase bridges theoretical knowledge with applied skills, preparing students for challenges such as optimizing hyperparameters under computational limits or auditing models for fairness. By emphasizing educator-curated content, the framework ensures alignment with pedagogical goals while retaining flexibility for instructors to emphasize emerging topics like generative AI ethics or sustainability in ML.

Figure 3 illustrates the game structure of phase 3, a strategic phase in which players use the points they have accumulated in phase 2 to battle it out in highly competitive round.

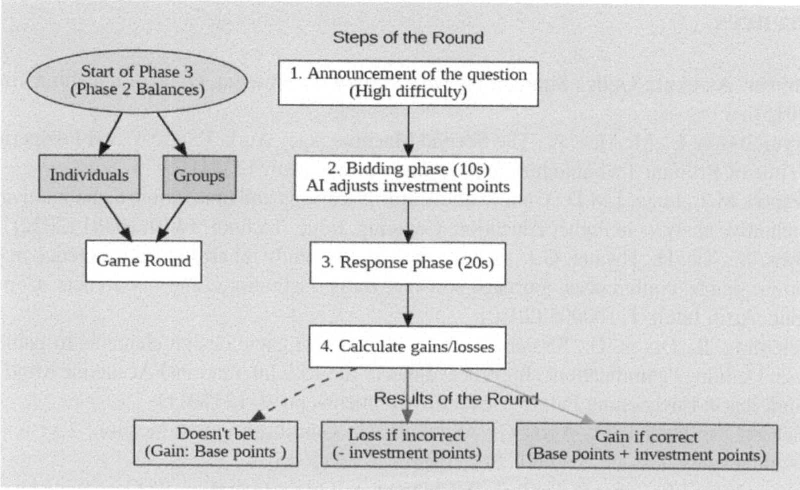

Fig. 3. Phase 3 – Strategic competition and resource allocation

2.4 Integration with Prior Phases

Each phase of the framework is designed to feed into the next, creating a cohesive learning journey. Data from Phase 1's individual assessments informs the team compositions in Phase 2. The collaborative experiences and team dynamics cultivated in Phase 2 prepare learners for the strategic negotiations of Phase 3. Finally, Phase 3 serves as a capstone experience that synthesizes students' technical mastery with ethical reasoning and teamwork. The result is a continuous progression that transforms students into agile, critically thinking practitioners who are better equipped to navigate the complexities of modern ML workflows.

3 Conclusion

This work offers educators a novel framework for integrating gamification and AI into machine learning (ML) education, building on prior successes in simulations and active learning methodologies [1, 9]. By combining theoretical principles with hands-on activities, the framework empowers educators to design interactive and adaptive learning experiences that cater to diverse student needs. The proposed three-phase system—*Individual Assessment*, *Dynamic Grouping*, and *Strategic Competition* —leverages adaptive scoring, equitable team formation via decision-tree algorithms, and gamified challenges (e.g., real-time betting) to enhance student engagement, conceptual mastery, and success in ML courses.

Future work will empirically validate the framework's impact through classroom trials and longitudinal studies, aiming to quantify improvements in motivation, learning outcomes, and equity. This study contributes to the growing field of AI-driven gamification in STEM education, providing a scalable and adaptable toolset to modernize ML pedagogy. By bridging the gap between cutting-edge AI techniques and pedagogical innovation, this framework paves the way for more inclusive, engaging, and effective ML education strategies.

References

1. Ammar, A., et al.: Optics Simulations with Python: Diffraction. Optica Publishing Group. (2015)
2. Brynjolfsson, E., McAfee, A.: The Second Machine Age: Work, Progress, and Prosperity in a Time of Brilliant Technologies. W.W. Norton & Company (2014)
3. Cespón, M.T., Lage, J.M.D.: Gamification, online learning and motivation: a quantitative and qualitative analysis in higher education. Contemp. Educ. Technol. **14**(4), ep381 (2022)
4. Chen, X., Xie, H., Hwang, G.J.: A multi-perspective study on artificial intelligence in education: grants, conferences, journals, software tools, institutions, and researchers. Comput. Educ. Artif. Intell. **1**, 100005 (2020)
5. Deterding, S., Dixon, D., Khaled, R., Nacke, L.: From game design elements to gamefulness: Defining "gamification". In: Proceedings of the 15th International Academic MindTrek Conference: Envisioning Future Media Environments, pp. 9–15 (2011)
6. Dicheva, D., Dichev, C., Agre, G., Angelova, G.: Gamification in education: a systematic mapping study. J. Educ. Technol. Soc. **18**(3), 75–88 (2015)
7. Gómez Niño, J.R., Árias Delgado, L.P., Chiappe, A., Ortega González, E.: Gamifying learning with AI: a pathway to 21st-century skills. J. Res. Childhood Educ., 1–16 (2024). https://doi.org/10.1080/02568543.2024.2421974
8. Jaramillo-Mediavilla, L., Basantes-Andrade, A., Cabezas-González, M., Casillas-Martín, S.: Impact of gamification on motivation and academic performance: a systematic review. Educ. Sci. **14**(6), 639 (2024)
9. Lakshminarayanan, V., Ghalila, H., Ammar, A., Varadharajan, S.: Role of Simulations in Optics Education. SPIE (2016)
10. Marcus, G., Davis, E.: Rebooting AI: Building Artificial Intelligence, We Can trust. Pantheon Books, New York (2019)
11. Miller, T., Durlik, I., Łobodzińska, A., Dorobczyński, L., Jasionowski, R.: AI in context: harnessing domain knowledge for smarter machine learning. Appl. Sci. **14**(24), 11612 (2024)
12. O'Brien, K., Pitera, J.: Gamifying instruction and engaging students with Breakout EDU. J. Educ. Technol. Syst. **48**(2), 192–212 (2019)
13. O'Neill, G., Short, A.: Relevant, practical and connected to the real world: what higher education students say engages them in the curriculum. Irish Educ. Stud. **42**(3), 269–286 (2023)
14. Sailer, M., Homner, L.: The gamification of learning: a meta-analysis. Educ. Psychol. Rev. **32**(1), 77–112 (2020)
15. Seaborn, K., Fels, D.I.: Gamification in theory and action: a survey. Int. J. Hum. Comput. Stud. **74**, 14–31 (2015)
16. Wang, A.I., Tahir, R.: The effect of using Kahoot! for learning – a literature review. Comput. Educ. **149**, 103818 (2020)
17. Zawacki-Richter, O., Marín, V.I., Bond, M., Gouverneur, F.: Systematic review of research on artificial intelligence applications in higher education–where are the educators? Int. J. Educ. Technol. High. Educ. **16**(1), 39 (2019)

A PPBL Pedagogy for Transforming Engineering Education at ESPRIT School of Engineering

Badia Bouhdid[1(✉)] and Akram Khémiri[1,2]

[1] ESPRIT School of Engineering, Ariana, Tunisia
{badiaa.bouhdid,khemiri.akram}@esprit.tn
[2] LaTICE, ENSIT, Université de Tunis, Tunis, Tunisia

Abstract. In an era where information is readily accessible and AI tools can generate solutions effortlessly, the modern student's challenge lies not in acquiring knowledge, but in applying it effectively within collaborative contexts. This paper presents a hybrid Project and Problem Based Learning (PPBL) approach, designed to enhance the engineering student's learning journey by fostering teamwork, practical skill application, and industry readiness. Implemented at ESPRIT School of Engineering with software engineering students, this approach leverages Blackboard as the primary Learning Management System (LMS) to deliver resources and assessments, while GitHub serves as a complementary platform for version control, task management, and peer collaboration, mirroring real-world software development workflows. An experimental study was conducted, engaging students in PPBL projects where they applied theoretical knowledge from Blackboard in practical, team-driven scenarios on GitHub. Results indicate notable improvements in student performance, engagement, and motivation compared to traditional methods, with enhanced technical proficiency and collaborative abilities evident in project deliverables and self-reported feedback. These findings highlight how integrating GitHub into PPBL bridges the divide between theoretical understanding and hands-on application, cultivating collective intelligence and preparing students for the demands of a tech-driven industry.

Keywords: Higher Education · Github · Collaborative Engineering · Project Based Learning · Software Engineering Education · Active Learning

1 Introduction

Engineering education faces significant challenges in preparing students for the dynamic demands of industry, where technical proficiency, collaboration, and innovation are paramount. Traditional pedagogical approaches, often centered on lectures, theoretical content, and individual assessments, have been criticized for their inability to promote active participation, practical skills, and teamwork,

F. Kamoun et al. (Eds.): AFRICATEK 2025, LNICST 676, pp. 493–510, 2026.
https://doi.org/10.1007/978-3-032-16635-7_33

leaving students poorly equipped for real-world challenges [7]. Existing project-based learning (PBL) approaches, while promising, frequently lack robust technological integration and do not address the collaborative and iterative nature of modern software engineering practices [9]. Moreover, many PBL implementations do not adequately leverage digital tools to support active learning, limiting their scalability and adaptability to diverse learner needs.

Active learning, characterized by student-centered activities that promote participation and critical thinking, offers a promising framework to address these gaps [8]. By integrating active learning with a Learning Management System and GitHub, we propose an innovative PPBL (Project-Problem-Based Learning) pedagogy that merges project-based and problem-based learning to create a dynamic, collaborative, and industry-aligned educational experience. LMS, such as Blackboard [10], facilitates autonomous learning by providing resources, quizzes, and feedback mechanisms, aligned with lower-order cognitive skills such as recall and understanding. GitHub [11], a widely used platform for version control and collaborative development, enhances peer and peer-assisted learning by enabling students to work in teams, manage projects using features such as forks, pull requests, and project boards, and develop higher-order skills such as analysis, creation, and innovation. By merging these tools, our approach overcomes the limitations of traditional methods -low collaboration, limited practical application, and lack of engagement - while addressing industry needs for technically proficient and teamwork-savvy graduates.

This paper presents a comprehensive study conducted at ESPRIT School of Engineering, which has a strong foundation in project-based learning. First, we collected student feedback on the classical approach to understand its perceived effectiveness and shortcomings. Next, we review existing PBL approaches in engineering education, critiquing their lack of technological integration and failure to foster active, collaborative learning. We then introduce our proposed PPBL pedagogy, detailing the tools and methods used to implement it. Finally, we present the results of our experimental evaluation, comparing the classical and PPBL approaches across two modules with 32 students each, and analyze student feedback on the proposed pedagogy. The findings demonstrate that our approach significantly enhances student competencies, engagement, and industry readiness, offering a transformative model for engineering education.

2 Case Study and Motivation

2.1 Study of the Existing at ESPRIT School of Engineering

This section is dedicated to a study conducted at Esprit among engineering students from various levels and disciplines. The objective is to address two key criteria: first, the evaluation of our students' experience with Esprit's official teaching platforms (Blackboard), and second, their attitudes toward collaborative work among students and the use of new solutions that enhance this aspect of collaboration such as GitHub.

The survey shows that Esprit students are keen to improve the use of new solutions to increase interactivity and collaboration among students. Our survey consists of 10 questions. The number of samples is a few dozen students. Table 1 presents the content of our survey and Table 2 gives the results.

Table 1. The content of our survey

Question	Content
Q1	Have you ever worked in a group to learn a concept or solve an exercise?
Q2	Do you prefer to learn a new tool on your own or with the help of your classmates?
Q3	Do you think peer learning (learning among students) is effective for understanding difficult concepts?
Q4	Have you ever used collaborative platforms for learning (such as GitHub)?
Q5	What aspects of peer learning do you enjoy the most?
Q6	Do you think Blackboard (or any other platform used) is sufficient to promote collaborative learning?
Q7	When you're stuck on a problem, what do you do first?
Q8	Would you like more collaborative activities in class (group work, discussions, peer review)?
Q9	Have you ever learned something important thanks to a classmate?
Q10	How would you rate your experience with collaborative learning so far?

The survey shows that Esprit students are familiar with GitHub and have used it in other contexts (project management, etc.) at a rate of 87%.

On the other hand, they are not opposed to improving the existing platform; the majority believes that improving the use of this platform would be a good solution, with 65.2% in favor. Furthermore, the students at Esprit enjoy collaborative work (they have often learned from their colleagues, 60.9%, and sometimes, 8.7%).

They also rate their experience in collaborative work as good (52%), which shows that the students here are open to collaboration projects and peer learning. For those who rated their experience as average (43.5%), the proposed project will aim to improve their experience.

2.2 Motivation

While students value collaborative work, with a notable proportion (60.9%) having learned from their peers and expressing an interest in working together, their

Table 2. The results of our survey

Question	Response A	Response B	Response C
Q1	Yes, often (41.7%)	Yes, sometimes (50%)	No, I prefer to learn alone (8.3%)
Q2	Independently (13.6%)	With the help of my classmates (9.1%)	A mix of both (77.3%)
Q3	Yes, it's very useful (34.8%)	It depends on the subjects (56.5%)	No, I prefer traditional learning (8.7%)
Q4	Yes (87%)	No (13%)	–
Q5	Working in a group on projects (39.2%)	Explaining concepts to other students (13%)	Exchanging tips and resources (47.8%)
Q6	Yes, it is sufficient (26.1%)	No, more interactive tools are needed (65.2%)	I don't use it enough to judge (8.7%)
Q7	I try to find the solution on my own (73.9%)	I ask a classmate (17.4%)	I ask the teacher (8.7%)
Q8	Yes, much more (47.8%)	Yes, a little more (8.7%)	No, it's fine as it is (43.5%)
Q9	Yes, several times (60.9%)	Yes, but rarely (8.7%)	No, never (30.4%)
Q10	Very positive (52.2%)	Average (43.5%)	Not very useful for me (4.3%)

experiences are often rated as 'average' by 43.5% of respondents. This highlights a lack of collaborative opportunities, suggesting that current teaching methods and tools do not provide enough interactive, real-time, or project-based learning experiences.

Furthermore, while students are aware of GitHub (87%), the platform's potential for collaborative problem-solving has yet to be fully exploited. As industry requirements evolve, with an increasing emphasis on teamwork and iterative development, Esprit students need an approach that not only reinforces technical knowledge, but also adaptive learning, collaboration, and real-world problem-solving skills.

The challenge lies in improving the current learning ecosystem by integrating tools like GitHub in ways that promote active, peer-driven collaboration while bridging the gap between individual learning (Blackboard) and collective team experiences.

3 State of the Art

3.1 Study and Description of Existing Research

The research results on active learning and the use of educational digital tools have highlighted several advantages and challenges in teaching. Active learning has been identified as one of the most effective methods for engaging students and refining their understanding of concepts. Studies such as those by [1], [2], and [3] show that when effectively implemented, active learning can improve students' academic performance, promote the development of their problem-solving skills, and encourage collaboration among students. Additionally, the use of platforms like GitHub has been widely explored to foster student engagement in collaborative projects [4] and [5].

However, several practical barriers have been identified in this research. Lack of time and resources, as well as student resistance to certain learning methods, are recurring challenges in the implementation of active learning [1] and [2]. Regarding digital tools, such as GitHub, although they promote collaboration and student engagement, adaptation difficulties have been reported, especially for less experienced teachers and students [4] and [6].

3.2 Critique of Existing Work

Existing work, while relevant, has several notable limitations. First, practical barriers such as lack of resources and time, are often only superficially addressed [1]. Proposed solutions are sometimes vague and lack specific details regarding the management of students with learning difficulties. Furthermore, student resistance to active learning is not always sufficiently considered, which can make these approaches less effective, especially for students who are less motivated or unfamiliar with these methods [2].

Regarding the use of tools like GitHub, while there is an improvement in student collaboration and engagement, widespread adoption of these technologies is hampered by the complexity of the tools and a lack of appropriate training for teachers and students. Research by [4] and [6] highlights that less experienced students sometimes have difficulty navigating these tools, and that this can limit their effectiveness as learning tools.

3.3 Our Solution and Its Improvement Over Previous Work

Our solution provides tangible improvements to the challenges identified in previous research. In response to the obstacles related to a lack of resources and time, we have implemented a mentoring system for struggling students. This system offers personalized guidance and continuous support, helping to better address the individual needs of students and sustain their motivation. Each student is assigned a mentor who accompanies them week after week, contributing to improved retention of information and greater academic success.

In conclusion, our work overcomes some of the limitations of previous research by proposing more practical solutions that are tailored to the realities of both students and teachers. Our improvements focus primarily on personalized student monitoring, the simplification of digital tools, and the adaptation of teaching methods to accommodate diverse learners, all while ensuring the motivation of our students remains a priority.

4 Proposed Approach

The GitHub-Driven PPBL Approach is a pedagogical innovation implemented at ESPRIT School of Engineering to develop collaborative, technically proficient engineers through an integration of Project Problem-Based Learning (PPBL) with GitHub. In a context where artificial intelligence (AI) tools can effortlessly produce code or solutions, this approach prioritizes the acquisition and practical application of problem-solving skills, teamwork, and adaptive learning over mere technical output. Unlike traditional Learning Management Systems (LMS) such as Blackboard, which serves as the primary platform for delivering resources and conducting formative assessments (e.g., quizzes), GitHub functions as a complementary tool. It extends the theoretical and foundational knowledge acquired via Blackboard into a practical, group-based learning environment, enabling students to operationalize their skills collaboratively on authentic engineering challenges. Infact, industry demands engineers adept in teamwork and iterative development. GitHub bridges the gap between Blackboard's individual learning resources and the group dynamics of real-world engineering, enabling students to apply theoretical skills in a synchronized, collaborative context.

The primary objective of the proposed approach is to produce "collaborative engineers" who excel in technical proficiency, teamwork, and adaptability. The proposed approach aims to:

- Enhance problem-solving through project based, iterative and team-based exploration.
- Improved technical and soft skills, evidenced by contributions tracked on GitHub.
- Improve student engagement and performance, driven by ownership of real-world challenges.
- Boost the development of a participatory mindset, preparing students to thrive in collective, industry-like settings.

4.1 Learning Situations in the Proposed Approach

This pedagogical approach leverages GitHub as a cornerstone for project-based and problem-based learning, structured across four distinct learning situations. The assisted learner benefits from teacher-led guidance, mastering foundational concepts with low collaboration and limited confidence growth. Conversely, the autonomous learner engages in self-directed study via LMS resources, building confidence through independent GitHub experimentation, albeit with minimal peer interaction. The peer learner thrives in high-collaboration settings, using GitHub's collaborative tools to solve problems collectively, fostering both technical and interpersonal confidence. Finally, the peer-assisted learner integrates instructor feedback into peer-driven projects, optimizing solutions and balancing collaboration with guided refinement. Together, these situations create a dynamic, scaffolded approach to academic learning, preparing students for both individual and team-based challenges in a digital age.

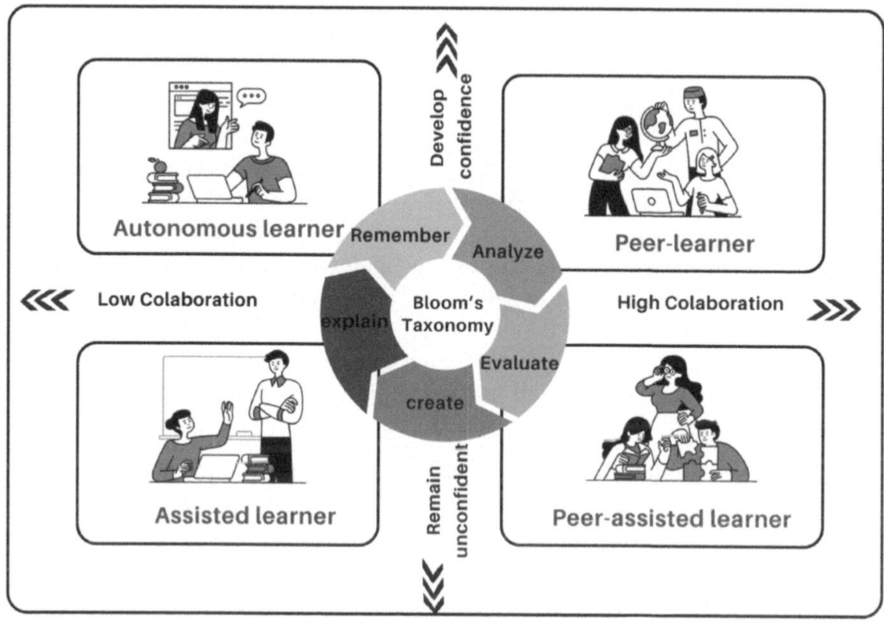

Fig. 1. Learning Situations in the GitHub-Driven Project-Based Learning Approach.

Assisted Learner: In this situation, the learner relies heavily on the teacher's orientation and guidance during synchronous sessions. The teacher introduces key concepts and demonstrates their application through live examples. The student follows step-by-step instructions, asking questions to clarify understanding.

Collaboration Level : Low. Interaction is primarily vertical (teacher-to-student), with minimal peer engagement.

Confidence Impact : Limited. Students gain foundational knowledge but remain dependent on the teacher, resulting in lower self-efficacy and confidence in independent problem-solving.

Autonomous Learner (Self-Directed Study): Here, the learner engages in asynchronous learning, using content provided via a Learning Management System (LMS) (e.g., tutorials, videos, courses...). The focus is on recalling and remembering information and practicing skills independently.

Collaboration Level : Low. The learner works alone, relying on self-motivation and preprepared resources.

Confidence Impact : High. Successfully completing tasks independently builds confidence in technical skills and decision-making, though it may lack the social reinforcement of peer feedback.

Peer Learner: Students work in small groups to analyze a project or problem state (e.g., debugging code, designing a feature, or optimizing a workflow) and develop solutions collaboratively. Interaction and exchange are central, with each student contributing ideas and expertise.

Collaboration Level : High. Peer-to-peer engagement drives collective problem-solving, simulating team-based development environments.

Confidence Impact : High. Collaborative success reinforces individual contributions, boosting confidence through mutual support and validation.

Peer Assisted Learner: Building on peer learning, students incorporate instructor feedback to create and evaluate their solutions, aiming for efficiency and optimality. After initial group work, the teacher reviews progress and provides targeted suggestions, which the group then implements.

Collaboration Level : High. Combines peer interaction with teacher guidance, creating a balanced collaborative dynamic.

Confidence Impact : Moderate to High. While instructor input may initially highlight weaknesses, successfully integrating feedback strengthens confidence in producing high-quality outcomes. Table 3 provides a comparative overview of these situations, detailing their collaboration levels, confidence outcomes, and specific applications within a GitHub-enhanced project-based learning environment.

4.2 Rationale for Integration

The combination of Blackboard and GitHub within the proposed approach addresses key educational imperatives:

Table 3. Comparison of Learning Situations in the Proposed Approach. CL: Collaboration Level, CD: Confidence Impact

Learning Situation	CL	CD	LMS Role: Blackboard	Github Role
Assisted Learner	Low	Low	Delivers introductory materials	Teacher-led demos, basic tasks
Autonomous Learner	Low	High	Provides tutorials, exercises, and reference materials for self-study	Solo experimentation, practice
Peer Learner	High	High	Hosts discussion forums, project briefs	Group projects, peer reviews
Peer-Assisted Learner	High	Moderate to High	Distributes instructor feedback, rubrics, Todos	Feedback iteration, optimization

Practical Application in Teams: Industry demands engineers adept in teamwork and iterative development. GitHub bridges the gap between Blackboard's individual learning resources and the group dynamics of real-world engineering, enabling students to apply theoretical skills in a synchronized, collaborative context.

Skill Development and Exploration: Students build on Blackboard-delivered content to acquire and refine technical skills (e.g., coding frameworks, testing methodologies) through hands-on group projects, fostering adaptability and opening new avenues for inquiry.

Project Problem-Based Learning Core: Students are presented with real-world software engineering problems (e.g., designing a scalable application, optimizing an algorithm) that lack predefined solutions, requiring research, experimentation, and teamwork. The PPBL cycle—problem identification, knowledge acquisition, solution development, and reflection—is guided by the instructor who poses questions rather than provide answers, fostering student ownership in peer assisted learning situation.

Fostering Collective Intelligence: The approach stimulates collective intelligence by requiring students to negotiate roles, integrate diverse perspectives, and synthesize individual contributions into cohesive solutions. GitHub's visibility—showing who did what and when—reinforces accountability while highlighting the group's emergent capability. Students learn not just to solve problems, but to be active parts of a solution ecosystem, a skill critical for interdisciplinary engineering projects.

4.3 Session Dynamics in a PPBL Approach: Synchronous and Asynchronous Engagement

This section delineates the operational structure of sessions within the PPBL framework, detailing how synchronous and asynchronous interactions scaffold student learning at ESPRIT School of Engineering. By leveraging the Learning Management System (LMS) and GitHub, these sessions foster a progression from individual recall to collaborative innovation, aligning with the learning situations outlined in Table 3, and the progressive framework in Fig. 2.

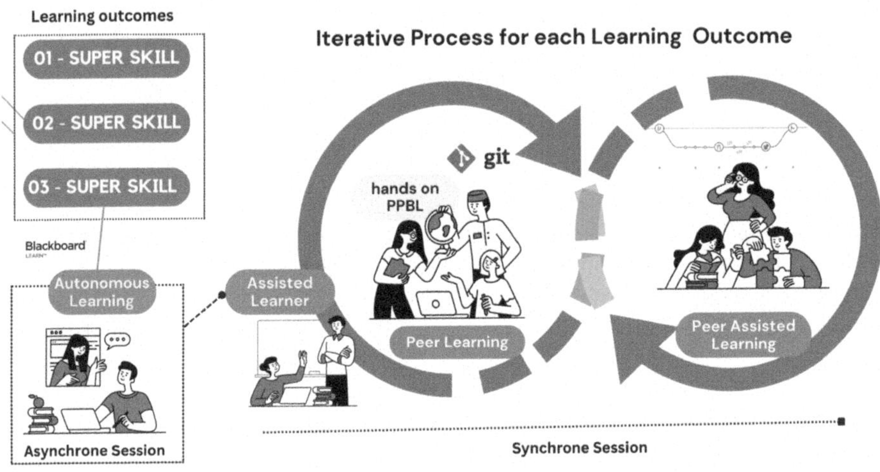

Fig. 2. Session Dynamics in a PPBL Approach: Synchronous and Asynchronous Engagement.

Synchronous Sessions: Interactive Collaboration Across Learning Situations: Synchronous sessions, conducted in real-time via video conferencing or in-person, are pivotal for fostering interaction between students and teachers, as well as among peers, across three learning situations: assisted learning, peer learning, and peer-assisted learning. These sessions are structured to address specific needs, enhance collaboration, and build higher-order cognitive skills (Analyze, Evaluate, Create, Innovate) as depicted in Fig. 1.

Assisted Learning (Teacher-Student Interaction): During initial synchronous sessions, students engage directly with the instructor to clarify foundational concepts and address gaps identified from asynchronous work. For instance, after completing LMS quizzes (Step 1), students with deficiencies in the learning outcomes and their associated skills, can ask questions. The teacher provides live demonstrations in a shared GitHub repository, walking students through processes like cloning or branching. This low-collaboration, high-guidance phase ensures personalized support, as the teacher uses LMS data (e.g., quiz scores) to tailor explanations, fostering understanding and application.

Peer Learning (Student-Student Interaction): As students gain proficiency, synchronous sessions shift to peer-driven collaboration, positioning learners as peer learners. Groups tackle PBL projects—such as designing a software feature or debugging code—using GitHub's collaborative tools, including issues, project boards, and pull requests. For example, one student might propose a solution in a pull request, while others review and comment, simulating real-world team dynamics. The LMS supports this phase by hosting discussion forums for peer brainstorming and sharing project briefs. These high-collaboration sessions build confidence through mutual validation and collective problem-solving, advancing skills like analysis and evaluation.

Peer-Assisted Learning (Student-Student with Teacher Feedback): In advanced synchronous sessions, peer groups integrate instructor feedback, transitioning to a peer-assisted learning situation. After peer collaboration, the teacher reviews group submissions (e.g., GitHub pull requests or project milestones) and provides targeted critiques via the LMS or directly in GitHub comments. Students then refine their work—such as optimizing code or improving documentation—during the session, guided by rubrics and real-time discussions. This high-collaboration phase, combining peer effort with instructor input, enhances creation and innovation, preparing learners for professional standards.

At ESPRIT School of Engineering, these synchronous sessions are scheduled regularly (e.g., weekly) to ensure continuous interaction, with each phase building on the previous to scaffold learning from guided mastery to collaborative innovation.

Asynchronous Sessions: Independent Exploration via LMS Resources: Complementing synchronous engagement, asynchronous sessions enable students to work offline as autonomous learners, focusing on recalling and remembering information through LMS-provided resources. These sessions align with the lower-order cognitive levels (Recall, Remember, Understand, Apply) in Fig. 1, laying the groundwork for synchronous collaboration.

In asynchronous mode, students access LMS materials, PBL project descriptions, and formative assessments (e.g., quizzes). The LMS tracks progress, providing feedback to guide self-directed learning and prepare students for synchronous sessions. This low-collaboration phase fosters independence and confidence, as learners engage with content at their own pace, aligning with the autonomous learner situation.

To ensure alignment with PPBL approach goals, asynchronous tasks are structured around project components (e.g., researching a problem, drafting code), which students later refine in synchronous sessions. The LMS also hosts discussion boards for optional peer interaction, though the focus remains on individual effort.

Together, synchronous and asynchronous sessions create a dynamic learning ecosystem, leveraging GitHub and LMS to transition students from autonomous exploration to collaborative innovation, transforming engineering education at ESPRIT School of Engineering.

4.4 Comparison of Traditional Pedagogy and PPBL Driven Pedagogy

To highlight the transformative potential of our PPBL pedagogy, Table 4 compares traditional pedagogy with the proposed approach at ESPRIT School of Engineering, demonstrating enhanced collaboration, technology integration, and student outcomes.

5 Experimentations, Observations and Discussion

5.1 Experimentation

Table 4. Comparison of Traditional Pedagogy and PPBL Driven Pedagogy at ESPRIT School of Engineering

Dimension	Traditional Pedagogy	PPBL Driven Pedagogy
Learning Approach	Lecture-based, teacher-centered, focusing on rote memorization and theoretical knowledge	Project-Problem Based Learning (PPBL), student-centered, emphasizing hands-on projects, problem-solving, and progressive cognitive skills
Collaboration Level	Primarily teacher-student interaction, with minimal peer engagement (e.g., individual assignments, exams).	High (peer and peer-assisted learning) to Low (autonomous and assisted learning). Uses GitHub for collaborative projects and LMS for peer forums and feedback
Confidence Development	Low to Moderate. Students may lack confidence due to dependency on teacher and limited practical experience.	High (autonomous, peer) to Moderate to High (assisted, peer-assisted). Builds self-efficacy through independence, peer validation, and iterative feedback
Session Structure	Primarily synchronous lectures; asynchronous work limited to homework or reading, with little interactivity	Combines synchronous sessions (assisted, peer, peer-assisted learning) for interaction and asynchronous sessions (autonomous learning) for self-directed LMS exploration
Assessment Methods	Exams, quizzes, and written assignments focusing on recall and understanding.	Formative quizzes (LMS), GitHub activity (commits, pull requests), peer reviews, project deliverables, and instructor feedback, assessing higher-order skills (analyze, create, innovate).
Outcomes	Theoretical knowledge, limited practical skills, and minimal preparation for teamwork or industry tools.	Enhanced technical proficiency (GitHub, coding), collaboration, problem-solving, and readiness for engineering challenges, transforming education at ESPRIT.
Scalability	Limited; relies on physical resources and teacher availability, difficult to adapt to diverse learners.	High; scalable via LMS and GitHub, supports personalized and collaborative learning across large cohorts.

To validate the transformative potential of the PPBL (Project-Problem Based Learning) pedagogy, an experimental evaluation was conducted at ESPRIT School of Engineering with 32 students, second engineering level, across two distinct modules. The study compared classical pedagogy, LMS lecture-based, teacher-centered, and focused on theoretical knowledge, with the proposed PPBL approach, which integrates GitHub and LMS tools to foster collaborative, hands-on learning. This section details the methodology, results, and implications of the experiment.

The experiment involved two engineering modules with 32 students each, conducted over a 7-week period. Module A: "Service Oriented Architecture" employed the classical pedagogy, featuring lectures, textbook and LMS-based assignments, and traditional exams. Module B: "Distributed Web Application" implemented the PPBL pedagogy, following the session dynamics (synchronous and asynchronous engagement). Students in Module B engaged in a software development project, using GitHub for version control (e.g., fork, pull request, merge), conflict management, and project boards, supported by LMS resources and formative assessments. Competencies assessed included technical skills (e.g., GitHub proficiency), collaboration (e.g., peer interaction), and confidence (e.g., self-reported efficacy), measured through pre- and post-intervention surveys, project deliverables, and GitHub activity logs.

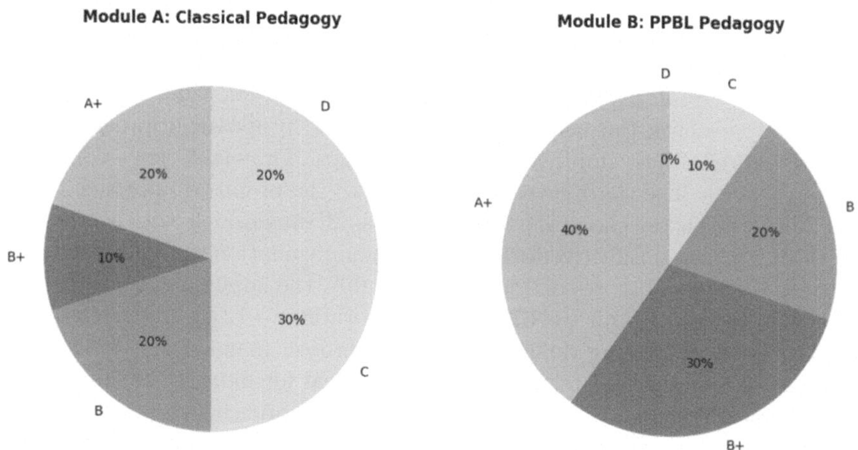

Fig. 3. Grade Distribution of Module A vs Grade Distribution of Module B.

Figure 3 illustrates the grade distributions for Module A (Classical Pedagogy) and Module B (Technology-Driven PPBL), respectively, highlighting stark differences in student performance. In Module A, the distribution is relatively balanced, with 30% of students achieving a C grade, 20% each for A+, B, and D, and only 10% for B+. This indicates a moderate success rate, with a significant portion (20%) receiving a failing D grade, reflecting the limitations of the classical approach in fostering consistent high performance. In contrast, Module B shows a marked improvement, with 40% of students achieving an A+ grade, 30% B+, 20% B, and only 10% C, with no students receiving a D grade. This skewed distribution toward higher grades (70% at A+ or B+) demonstrates the PPBL approach's effectiveness in enhancing student outcomes, likely due to its emphasis on active learning, collaboration, and practical skill development through digital tools. The absence of failing grades in Module B further underscores its success in supporting all students to achieve at least a passing level, aligning with this work's goal of preparing students for industry demands.

5.2 Student Feedback

Post-intervention, a survey was conducted with 30 students in Module B to gather feedback on the PPBL approach, using a 5-point Likert scale (1 = Strongly Disagree, 5 = Strongly Agree). Competencies assessed included understanding of concepts, collaboration, technical skills, practical skills, motivation, engagement, and overall effectiveness.

The survey results, presented in Table 5, from Module B (PPBL) indicate strong positive feedback, with average scores ranging from 3.7 to 4.6 in 14 statements (Table 5). These findings underscore the PPBL approach's effectiveness in transforming engineering education at ESPRIT, enhancing student competencies and preparing them for industry demands. The high recommendation score (4.6) suggests strong student satisfaction and potential for wider adoption.

Figure 4 presents the comparison between the proposed approach scores, classical scores, and improvement percentages for eight key competencies/perceptions. The chart reveals a clear trend: the proposed approach consistently outperforms the classical pedagogy across all dimensions, with scores ranging from 4.2 (Overall Effectiveness) to 4.6 (Recommendation to Other Students), compared to classical scores of 2.5 to 3.2. Notably, the largest improvements are observed in technical skills (+76%) and collaboration (+72%), underscoring the effectiveness of integrating version control and project management tools to foster hands-on learning and teamwork—skills critical for industry readiness. The high engagement score (4.5, +50%) highlights the approach's success in shifting students from passive to active learning. The recommendation score (4.6, +44%) indicates strong student satisfaction and advocacy for this pedagogy, suggesting its potential for wider adoption. However, the smallest improvement in motivation (+47%) suggests that while students were motivated (4.4), additional strategies (e.g., gamification, personalized feedback) might further enhance participation, an area for future exploration.

5.3 Discussion

This study represents a significant step toward sustainable learning in engineering education, by promoting active learning and collaboration through a

Table 5. The survey results from Module B

Statement	Average Score
S1 - PPBL helped me understand software engineering concepts better than lectures.	4.5
S2 - Blackboard prepared me well for PjBL projects.	3.7
S3 - GitHub made it easier to apply Blackboard learning in a project setting.	4.5
S4 - Working in a team on GitHub improved my collaboration skills.	4.3
S5 - GitHub's features (e.g., Issues, Pull Requests) helped coordinate tasks.	4.3
S6 - I felt like an active contributor to our project's success.	4.4
S7 - This method helped me learn new technical skills.	4.4
S8 - I gained practical skills for my future career.	4.5
S9 - The approach encouraged me to explore new strategies.	4.3
S10 - I felt motivated to participate in PPBL projects using GitHub.	4.4
S11 - This approach made me more engaged compared to traditional methods.	4.5
S12 - The projects were interesting and relevant to real-world software engineering.	4.5
S13 - The combination of Blackboard, PPBL, and GitHub was effective.	4.2
S14 - I would recommend this approach to other students.	4.6

technology-driven PPBL approach. By simulating collaborative intelligence mirroring the teamwork and iterative problem-solving found in industry settings this pedagogy leverages digital tools like GitHub and Blackboard to create a dynamic learning environment. The primary goal of this work is to provide a unified approach for implementing an active pedagogy, integrating LMS-supported autonomous learning with GitHub-enabled peer and peer-assisted learning. This framework ensures that students develop both lower-order (e.g., recall via Blackboard quizzes) and higher-order skills (e.g., creation through GitHub projects), as outlined in Bloom's Taxonomy, creating a sustainable model that prepares students for lifelong learning and industry demands.

Despite these advancements, implementing this pedagogy presents notable challenges. Effective student management to work as a team remains a critical hurdle, as collaborative intelligence requires students to adapt to shared responsibilities, resolve conflicts, and maintain consistent engagement—skills not all students possess initially. The absence of failing grades in Module B (Fig. 3) indicates improved outcomes, but the moderate motivation score (4.4, +47%) suggests that some students may struggle with the transition to team-based

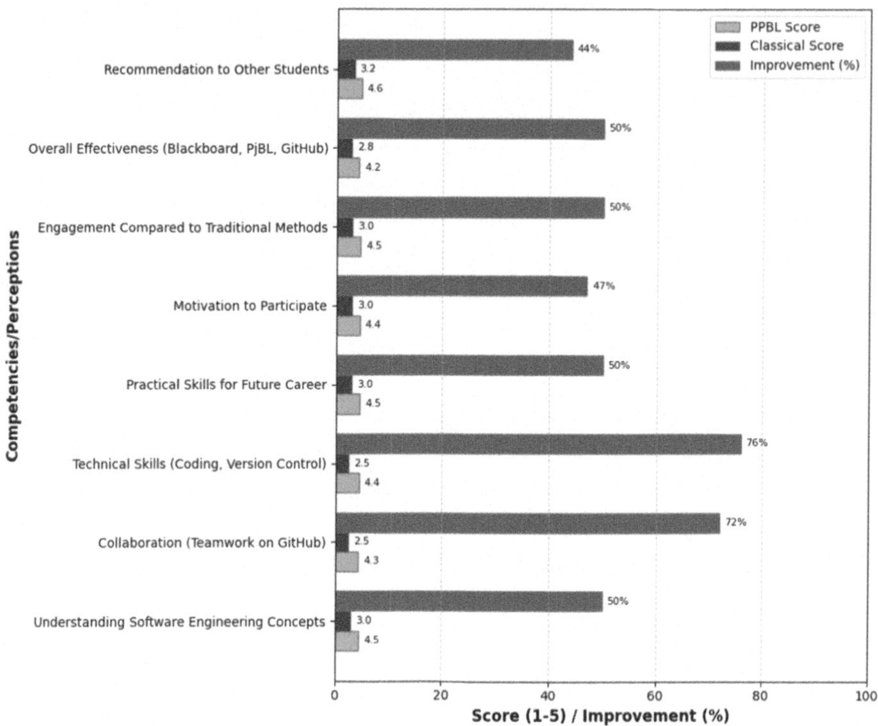

Fig. 4. Comparison of Student Feedback: Classical vs. PPBL Pedagogy (Module A vs. Module B).

learning (Fig. 4). Additionally, equipping teachers with the necessary skills to manage technologies like Blackboard and GitHub is essential for tracking student progress and delivering an optimized learning experience that fits individual needs. Teachers must master Blackboard for resource distribution and formative assessments, and GitHub for monitoring contributions (e.g., commits, pull requests) and facilitating collaborative workflows. Without adequate training, the potential for personalized feedback and tailored support diminishes, limiting the pedagogy's effectiveness. Addressing these challenges through teacher training programs and student workshops on teamwork could enhance the approach's scalability and impact, as discussed in the Conclusion.

6 Conclusion

The PPBL (Project-Problem Based Learning) pedagogy proposed in this study offers a transformative framework for engineering education at ESPRIT School of Engineering, effectively addressing the limitations of traditional and existing PBL approaches. By integrating active learning with Learning Management

System (LMS) resources and GitHub's collaborative tools, this approach fosters technical proficiency, collaboration, and innovation among students, aligning with industry demands. This study confirms that merging LMS-supported autonomous learning with GitHub-enabled peer and peer-assisted learning creates a scalable, student-centered model that overcomes the passive, theory-focused nature of traditional methods. However, adopting this innovative pedagogy faces challenges that must be addressed to ensure its sustainability. A primary obstacle is equipping teachers with the necessary skills to leverage GitHub features and integrate them with LMS platforms, requiring targeted training and technical support. Additionally, shifting student mindsets from passive learning to active, collaborative participation demands a cultural change, supported by clear guidance and incentives.

These challenges open new axes of research to enhance the PPBL approach. Investigating student motivation and mindset transformation through longitudinal studies could inform strategies to sustain engagement. Furthermore, researching the scalability of this model across diverse engineering disciplines and institutions, or integrating emerging technologies (e.g., AI-driven feedback in GitHub), could broaden its transformative potential. By addressing these challenges and research gaps, the PPBL pedagogy can evolve into a global standard for engineering education, preparing students to thrive in an industry-driven world.

Acknowledgments. The authors acknowledge the use of AI tools for assistance in editing and refining portions of the manuscript.

References

1. Hsing, P., et al.: Using GitHub in the classroom predicts student learning outcomes and classroom experiences: findings from a survey of students and teachers. In: SIGCSE '19, February 27–March 2, 2019, Minneapolis, MN, USA (2019)
2. Gunnarsson, M., et al.: Enhancing Student Engagement Using GitHub as an Educational Tool. Genombrottet (2017)
3. Heck, A.J., Cross, C.E., Tatum, V.Y., et al.: Active learning among health professions' educators: perceptions, barriers, and use. Med. Sci. Educ. **33**, 719–727 (2023)
4. Rahman, A.A., Sahid, S., Mohamad Nasri, N.: Literature review on the benefits and challenges of active learning on students' achievement. Cypriot J. Educ. Sci. **17**(12), 4856–4869 (2022). https://doi.org/10.18844/cjes.v17i12.8133
5. Feliciano, J., et al.: Student Experiences Using GitHub in Software Engineering Courses: A Case Study. In: Proceedings of the 38th International Conference on Software Engineering Companion, ICSE '16, pp. 422–431, New York, NY, USA (2016)
6. El Hajj, M., Harb, H.: Rethinking education: an in-depth examination of modern technologies and pedagogic recommendations. IAFOR J. Educ. **11**(2), 97–113 (2023)
7. Smith, J.K., Davis, R., Taylor, P.: Rethinking traditional pedagogy in higher education: a case for collaborative learning technologies. Innov. High. Educ. **44**(5), 321–338 (2019). https://doi.org/10.1007/s10755-019-9468-9

8. Bonwell, C.C., Eison, J.A.: Active Learning: Creating Excitement in the Classroom. ASHE-ERIC Higher Education Report No. 1. George Washington University, School of Education and Human Development (1991)
9. Venugopala, P.S., Ashwini, B., Shrinivasa Pai, P., Aravinda, C.V.: Issues and challenges of implementing project based learning in engineering courses: student and faculty perspective. J. Eng. Educ. Trans., 86–98 (2024)
10. Blackboard. https://esprit.blackboard.com/. Accessed 12 May 2025
11. GitHub. https://github.com/. Accessed 12 May 2025

Author Index

F. Kamoun et al. (Eds.): AFRICATEK 2025, LNICST 676, pp. 511–512, 2026.
https://doi.org/10.1007/978-3-032-16635-7

The manufacturer's authorised representative in the EU is Springer Nature Customer Service Centre GmbH, Europaplatz 3, 69115 Heidelberg, Germany. If you have any concerns regarding our products, please contact ProductSafety@springernature.com

Printed and bound by CPI Group (UK) Ltd, Croydon, CR0 4YY
07/07/2026
02160913-0016